Get the eBook FREE!

(PDF, ePub, Kindle, and liveBook all included)

We believe that once you buy a book from us, you should be able to read it in any format we have available. To get electronic versions of this book at no additional cost to you, purchase and then register this book at the Manning website.

Go to https://www.manning.com/freebook and follow the instructions to complete your pBook registration.

That's it!
Thanks from Manning!

From the 2nd edition of PostGIS in Action
by Regina O. Obe and Leo S. Hsu

"PostGIS In Action is a great book to learn how GIS servers function. Reading this book will give any reader insight into how best to provide map services for a wide audience."

—Marcus Brown, GIS Architect/Administrator, Enel Green Power

"I answered so many questions with traditional SQL that, just for curiosity, I went in to see what difference PostGIS could make; now it seems to me that not enough questions were asked, at least not as many as I could think of to resolve with this new toolbox."

—Arnaldo Ayala, Software Architect, Consultores Informáticos S.R.L.

"PostGIS in Action is a book that gets you swiftly started with PostGIS and gives you all the skills you need to get you going with GIS and helps you leverage your spatial data in new creative ways."

—Weyert de Boer

"This book is the best introduction I've seen for engineers that want to get ramped up quickly and build expert knowledge to build advanced GIS applications."

—Ikechukwu Okonkwo, Lead Data Scientist, Orum.io

"As a long time Postgres users I've always been curious how to make use of PostGIS but never knew where to start. This book provided that for me, and now I feel comfortable implementing Postgis for clients to help support their needs."

—Mike Haller, Senior Manager

"An extraordinarily great book for the technology world of GIS. Truly learned a lot!"

—DeUndre' Rushon, CEO, DigiDiscover LLC

"This book is a gem with a wealth of information and showcases how powerful PostGIS is."

—Luis Moux-Dominguez, Software Architect, EMO

PostGIS in Action, Third Edition

PostGIS in Action,
Third Edition

REGINA O. OBE
AND LEO S. HSU

MANNING
SHELTER ISLAND

For online information and ordering of this and other Manning books, please visit
www.manning.com. The publisher offers discounts on this book when ordered in quantity.
For more information, please contact

> Special Sales Department
> Manning Publications Co.
> 20 Baldwin Road
> PO Box 761
> Shelter Island, NY 11964
> Email: orders@manning.com

Manning Publications Co.
20 Baldwin Road
PO Box 761
Shelter Island, NY 11964

Development editor:	Susan Ethridge
Technical development editor:	Alain Couniot
Review editor:	Aleksandar Dragosavljević
Production editor:	Deirdre S. Hiam
Copy editor:	Andy Caroll
Proofreader:	Melody Dolab
Technical proofreader:	Jan Hartman
Typesetter:	Dennis Dalinnik
Cover designer:	Marija Tudor

ISBN: 9781617296697
Printed in the United States of America

To Dr. Joan Alice Burnett Obe (1937-2021), a trailblazer, courageous doctor, and mommy, and Dr. Ernest Olagbade Obe (1935–2012), a great professor, chief, and daddy.

brief contents

PART 1 INTRODUCTION TO POSTGIS 1

    1 ■ What is a spatial database? 3

    2 ■ Spatial data types 29

    3 ■ Spatial reference systems 66

    4 ■ Working with real data 95

    5 ■ Using PostGIS on the desktop 138

    6 ■ Geometry and geography functions 178

    7 ■ Raster functions 217

    8 ■ Spatial relationships 248

PART 2 PUTTING POSTGIS TO WORK 275

    9 ■ Proximity analysis 277

    10 ■ PostGIS TIGER geocoder 294

    11 ■ Geometry and geography processing 313

    12 ■ Raster processing 345

    13 ■ Building and using topologies 371

14 ▪ Organizing spatial data 403

15 ▪ Query performance tuning 438

PART 3   USING POSTGIS WITH OTHER TOOLS 485

16 ▪ Extending PostGIS with pgRouting and
        procedural languages 487

17 ▪ Using PostGIS in web applications 522

contents

foreword *xxi*
preface *xxiii*
acknowledgments *xxiv*
about this book *xxvi*
about the Author *xxxiii*
about the cover illustration *xxxiv*

PART 1 INTRODUCTION TO POSTGIS 1

1 ■ What is a spatial database? 3
  1.1 Thinking spatially 4
  1.2 Introducing PostGIS 6
    Why PostGIS 7 ■ *Standards conformance* 7 ■ *PostGIS is powerful* 8 ■ *Built on top of PostgreSQL* 9 ■ *Free—as in money* 10 ■ *Free—as in freedom* 10 ■ *Alternatives to PostGIS* 11
  1.3 Installing PostGIS 13
    Verifying versions of PostGIS and PostgreSQL 15
  1.4 Spatial data types 16
    Geometry type 17 ■ *Geography type* 18 ■ *Raster type* 18
    Topology type 19

1.5   Hello real world   20

Digesting the problem   20 ▪ Modeling   21 ▪ Loading data   23
Writing the query   26 ▪ Viewing spatial data with OpenJump   27

2   *Spatial data types   29*

2.1   Type modifiers   31

Subtype type modifiers   31 ▪ Spatial reference identifier   32

2.2   Geometry   32

Points   33 ▪ Linestrings   34 ▪ Polygons   35 ▪ Collection
geometries   38 ▪ The M coordinate   43 ▪ The Z coordinate   45
Polyhedral surfaces and TINs   46 ▪ Generating TINs   49
Curved geometries   49 ▪ Spatial catalog for geometry   54

2.3   Geography   58

Differences between geography and geometry   58 ▪ Spatial catalogs
for geography   59

2.4   Raster   60

Properties of rasters   60 ▪ Creating rasters   62 ▪ Spatial catalog
for rasters   64

3   *Spatial reference systems   66*

3.1   Spatial reference systems: What are they?   67

Geoids   67 ▪ Ellipsoids   69 ▪ Datum   71 ▪ Coordinate
reference system   72 ▪ Spatial reference system essentials   72
Projections   73

3.2   Selecting a spatial reference system for storing data   76

Pros and cons of using EPSG:4326   77 ▪ Geography data type for
EPSG:4326   78 ▪ Mapping just for presentation   79 ▪ Covering
the globe when distance is a concern   81

3.3   Determining the spatial reference system of
source data   85

Guessing at a spatial reference system   86 ▪ When the SRS is
missing from the spatial_ref_sys table   91

3.4   History of PROJ support in PostGIS   91

PROJ 4   91 ▪ PROJ 5   92 ▪ PROJ 6   92 ▪ PROJ 7   93
PROJ 8 and beyond   93

4   *Working with real data   95*

4.1   PostgreSQL built-in tools   96

Psql   96 ▪ pgAdmin4   97 ▪ Pg_dump and pg_restore   99
Downloading files   100

4.2 Extracting files 100

4.3 Importing and exporting shapefiles 101

Importing with shp2pgsql 102 ▪ Importing and exporting with shp2pgsql-gui 104 ▪ Exporting with pgsql2shp 107

4.4 Importing and exporting vector data with ogr2ogr 108

Environment variables in ogr2ogr 109 ▪ Ogrinfo 110 Importing with ogr2ogr 110 ▪ Exporting with ogr2ogr 114

4.5 Querying external data using PostgreSQL foreign data wrappers 117

File_fdw foreign data wrapper 119 ▪ Ogr_fdw foreign data wrapper 121 ▪ Converting hstore tags to jsonb 127

4.6 Importing raster data with raster2pgsql 128

Raster2pgsql command-line switches 128 ▪ Raster2pgsql supported formats 129 ▪ Loading a single file with raster2pgsql 130 ▪ Loading multiple files and tiling in shell script 130 ▪ Using PostgreSQL functions to output raster data 131

4.7 Exporting raster data with GDAL 132

Using gdalinfo to inspect rasters 133 ▪ Gdal_translate and gdalwarp 134

5 **Using PostGIS on the desktop 138**

5.1 Desktop viewing tools at a glance 139

OpenJUMP 140 ▪ QGIS 140 ▪ gvSIG 140 ▪ Jupyter Notebook and JupyterLab 141 ▪ Spatial database support 141 Format support 143 ▪ Web services supported 144

5.2 OpenJUMP 145

OpenJUMP feature summary 146 ▪ Installing OpenJUMP 146 Ease of use 146 ▪ OpenJUMP plug-ins 146 ▪ OpenJUMP scripting 147 ▪ OpenJUMP format support 147 ▪ PostGIS support 147 ▪ Registering data sources 147 ▪ Rendering PostGIS geometries 149 ▪ Exporting data 151

5.3 QGIS 151

Installing QGIS 152 ▪ Using QGIS with PostGIS 152

5.4 GvSIG 161

Using gvSIG with PostGIS 161 ▪ Exporting data 165

5.5 JupyterLab and Jupyter Notebook 166

Installing Jupyter 167 ▪ Launching Jupyter Notebook 167 Launching JupyterLab 168 ▪ Creating a Python notebook 168

Magic commands   169 ▪ Performing raw queries with Jupyter
Notebook   170 ▪ Using GeoPandas, Shapely, and Matplotlib
to work with spatial data   172 ▪ Viewing data on a map
with folium   175

6 ***Geometry and geography functions   178***

6.1   Output functions   179

Well-known text (WKT) and well-known binary (WKB)   180
Keyhole Markup Language (KML)   180 ▪ Geography Markup
Language (GML)   180 ▪ Geometry JavaScript Object Notation
(GeoJSON)   181 ▪ Scalable Vector Graphics (SVG)   181
Mapbox Vector Tiles (MVT) and protocol buffers   182 ▪ Tiny
WKB (TWKB)   183 ▪ Extensible 3D Graphics (X3D)   183
Examples of output functions   184 ▪ Geohash   185

6.2   Constructor functions   186

Creating geometries from text and binary formats   186 ▪ Creating
geographies from text and binary formats   190 ▪ Using text or
binary representations as function arguments   190

6.3   Accessor and setter functions   191

Spatial reference identifiers   192 ▪ Transforming geometry to
different spatial references   192 ▪ Using transformation with
the geography type   193 ▪ Geometry type functions   194
Geometry and coordinate dimensions   195 ▪ Retrieving
coordinates   196 ▪ Checking geometry validity   196
Number of points that define a geometry   197

6.4   Measurement functions   198

Geometry planar measurements   199 ▪ Geodetic
measurements   200

6.5   Decomposition functions   202

Bounding box of geometries   202 ▪ Boundaries and converting
polygons to linestrings   204 ▪ Centroid, median, and point
on surface   206 ▪ Returning points defining a geometry   208
Decomposing multi-geometries and geometry collections   208

6.6   Composition functions   210

Making points   210 ▪ Making polygons   211 ▪ Promoting single
geometries to multi-geometries   213

6.7   Simplification functions   213

Grid snapping and coordinate rounding   213 ▪ Simplification   214

CONTENTS

xv

7 Raster functions   217

7.1   Raster terminology   218

7.2   Raster constructors   220

Converting geometries to rasters with ST_AsRaster   222 ▪ Loading rasters with raster2pgsql   224 ▪ Constructing rasters from scratch: ST_MakeEmptyRaster and ST_AddBand   225 ▪ Setting pixels: ST_SetValue and ST_SetValues   225 ▪ Creating rasters from other rasters   227 ▪ Converting other raster formats with ST_FromGDALRaster   229

7.3   Raster output functions   229

ST_AsPNG, ST_AsJPEG, and ST_AsTiff   229 ▪ Output using ST_AsGDALRaster   230 ▪ Using psql to export rasters   232

7.4   Raster accessors and setters   234

Basic raster metadata properties   235 ▪ Pixel statistics   236 Pixel value accessors   238 ▪ Band metadata setters   239

7.5   Georeferencing functions   240

Metadata setters   240 ▪ Processing functions   242

7.6   Reclassing functions   244

7.7   Polygonizing functions   245

ST_ConvexHull   245 ▪ ST_Envelope   245 ▪ ST_Polygon   245 ST_MinConvexHull   246

8 Spatial relationships   248

8.1   Bounding box and geometry comparators   249

The bounding box   250 ▪ Bounding box comparators   251

8.2   Relating two geometries   252

Interior, exterior, and boundary of a geometry   252 Intersections   253 ▪ A house plan model   258 ▪ Contains and within   259 ▪ Covers and covered by   261 ▪ Contains properly   262 ▪ Overlapping geometries   263 ▪ Touching geometries   264 ▪ The faces of equality: geometry   266 Underpinnings of relationship functions   268

PART 2   PUTTING POSTGIS TO WORK 275

9 Proximity analysis   277

9.1   Nearest neighbor searches   278

Which places are within X distance?   278 ▪ Using ST_DWithin and ST_Distance for N closest results   279 ▪ Using ST_DWithin

and DISTINCT ON to find closest locations   279 ▪ *Intersects with
tolerance   280* ▪ *Items between distances   280* ▪ *Finding the N
closest places using KNN distance operators   281*

9.2   Using KNN with geography types   284

Using window functions to number the closest N places   285

9.3   Geotagging   287

Tagging data to a specific region   287 ▪ *Linear referencing:
snapping points to the closest linestring   288* ▪ *PostGIS cluster
window functions   290*

10   **PostGIS TIGER geocoder   294**

10.1   Installing the PostGIS TIGER geocoder   295

10.2   Loading TIGER data   296

Configuration tables   296 ▪ *Loading nation and state data   298*

10.3   Normalizing addresses   301

Using normalize_address   301 ▪ *Using the PAGC address
normalizer   302*

10.4   Geocoding   305

Geocoding using address text   306 ▪ *Geocoding using normalized
addresses   308* ▪ *Geocoding intersections   308* ▪ *Batch
geocoding   309*

10.5   Reverse geocoding   311

11   **Geometry and geography processing   313**

11.1   Using spatial aggregate functions   314

*Creating a multipolygon from many multipolygon records   314
Creating linestrings from points   318*

11.2   Clipping, splitting, tessellating   320

Clipping   320 ▪ *Splitting   322* ▪ *Tessellating   323*

11.3   Breaking linestrings into smaller segments   332

Segmentizing linestrings   333 ▪ *Creating two-point linestrings
from many-point linestrings   333* ▪ *Breaking linestrings at point
junctions   335*

11.4   Translating, scaling, and rotating geometries   338

Translating   338 ▪ *Scaling   339* ▪ *Rotating   341*

11.5   Using geometry functions to manipulate
and create geographies   342

Cast-safe functions   342

12 **Raster processing 345**

12.1 Loading and preparing raster data 346

12.2 Forming larger rasters using spatial aggregate functions 348

Reconstituting tiled files 348 ▪ Carving out areas of interest using clipping and unioning 349 ▪ Using specific expression types with ST_Union 349

12.3 Working with bands 350

Using ST_AddBand to form multiband rasters from single-band rasters 350 ▪ Using ST_Band to process a subset of bands 351

12.4 Tiling rasters 352

12.5 Raster and geometry intersections 354

Pixel stats 355 ▪ Adding a Z coordinate to a 2D linestring using ST_Value and ST_SetZ 356 ▪ Converting 2D polygons to 3D polygons 358

12.6 Raster statistics 360

Extruding pixel values 360 ▪ Raster statistics functions 362

12.7 Map algebra 364

Choosing between expression or callback function 365 ▪ Using a single-band map algebra expression 366 ▪ Using a single-band map algebra function 367 ▪ Map algebra with neighborhoods 368

13 **Building and using topologies 371**

13.1 What topology is 372

13.2 Using topologies 373

Installing the topology extension 374 ▪ Creating a topology 374 The topogeometry type 380 ▪ Recap of using topologies 383

13.3 Topology of Victoria, BC 384

Creating the Victoria topology 384 ▪ Adding primitives to a topology 384 ▪ Creating topogeometries 387

13.4 Fixing topogeometry issues by editing topology primitives 392

Removing faces by removing edges 393 ▪ Checking for shared faces 395 ▪ Editing topogeometries 396

13.5 Inserting and editing large data sets 396

13.6 Simplifying with topology in mind 399

13.7 Topology validation and summary functions 400

14 *Organizing spatial data 403*

  14.1   Spatial storage approaches   404

          Heterogeneous columns   404 ▪ Homogeneous columns   406
          Typmod vs. constraints   407 ▪ Table inheritance   409
          Table partitioning   413

  14.2   Modeling a real city   417

          Modeling using heterogeneous geometry columns   419 ▪ Modeling
          using homogeneous geometry columns   423 ▪ Modeling using
          partitioning   425

  14.3   Making auto-updatable views   431

  14.4   Using triggers and rules   432

          Triggers   432 ▪ Using INSTEAD OF triggers   433 ▪ Using other
          triggers   435

15 *Query performance tuning 438*

  15.1   The query planner   439

          Different kinds of spatial queries   439 ▪ Common table expressions
          and how they affect plans   442

  15.2   Planner statistics   443

  15.3   Using explain to diagnose problems   445

          Text explain vs. pgAdmin graphical explain   446 ▪ The plan with
          no index   447

  15.4   Planner and indexes   451

          The plan with a spatial index   452 ▪ Indexes   454

  15.5   Common SQL patterns and how they affect plans   459

          Subqueries in SELECT   459 ▪ FROM subqueries and basic
          CTEscommon table expressions (CTEs)   466 ▪ Window functions
          and self joins   468 ▪ Lateral joins   470

  15.6   System and function settings   473

          Key system variables that affect plan strategies   473 ▪ Function-
          specific settings   476 ▪ Encouraging parallel plans   478

  15.7   Optimizing spatial data   479

          Fixing invalid geometries   479 ▪ Reducing the number of vertices
          by simplification   480 ▪ Reducing the number of vertices by
          breaking geometries apart   480 ▪ Clustering   480

PART 3 USING POSTGIS WITH OTHER TOOLS 485

16 Extending PostGIS with pgRouting and procedural languages 487

16.1 Solving network routing problems with pgRouting 488

Installing pgRouting 488

16.2 Extending PostgreSQL with PLs 495

Basic installation of PLs 496 ▪ What you can do with PLs 496

16.3 PL/R 498

Getting started with PL/R 498 ▪ What you can do with PL/R 499 ▪ Using R packages in PL/R 503 ▪ Converting geometries into R spatial objects and plotting spatial objects 505 Outputting plots as binaries 507

16.4 PL/Python 508

Installing PL/Python 508 ▪ Writing a PL/Python function 509 ▪ Using Python packages 510 ▪ Geocoding example 512

16.5 PL/V8: JavaScript in the database 514

Installing PL/V8 514 ▪ Enabling PL/V8 in a database 514 Using other JavaScript libraries and functions in PL/V8 514 Using PL/V8 to write map algebra functions 518

17 Using PostGIS in web applications 522

17.1 Limitations of conventional web technologies 523

17.2 Mapping servers 524

Lightweight mapping servers 525 ▪ Full mapping servers 527

17.3 Mapping clients 532

Proprietary services 532

17.4 Using MapServer 534

Installing MapServer 534 ▪ Security considerations 536 Creating WMS and WFS services 536 ▪ Calling a mapping service using a reverse proxy 540

17.5 Using GeoServer 541

Installing GeoServer 541 ▪ Setting up PostGIS workspaces 541 Accessing PostGIS layers via GeoServer WMS/WFS 544

17.6 Basics of OpenLayers and Leaflet 544

OpenLayers primer 546 ▪ Leaflet primer 549 ▪ Synopsis of the OpenLayers and Leaflet APIs 551

17.7   Displaying data with PostGIS queries
        and web scripting   552
            Using PostGIS and PostgreSQL geometry output functions   552
            *Using PostGIS MVT output functionsMapbox Vector Tiles
            (MVT)   556*

appendix A   *Additional resources   561*
appendix B   *Installing, compiling, and upgrading   565*
appendix C   *SQL primer   577*

            index   601

foreword

As children, we were probably all told at one time or another that "we are what we eat," as a reminder that our diet is integral to our health and quality of life. In the modern world, with location-aware smartphones in our pockets, GPS units in our vehicles, and the internet addresses of our computers geocoded, it has also become true that "who we are is where we are"—every individual is now a mobile sensor, generating a ceaseless flow of location-encoded data as they move about the planet.

To manage and tame that flow of data, and the parallel flow of data opened up by economical satellite imaging and crowdsourced mapping, we need a tool equal to the task. A tool that can persistently store the data, efficiently access it, and powerfully analyze it. We need a spatial database, like PostGIS.

Prior to the advent of spatial databases, computer analysis of location and mapping data was done with *geographic information systems* (GISs) running on desktop workstations. When it was first released in 2001, the project name was just a simple play on words—naturally a spatial extension of the "PostgreSQL" database would be named "PostGIS."

But the name has come to have further significance as the project has matured. Each year, new functions have been added for data analysis, and each year users have pressed those functions further and further, doing the kinds of work that in earlier years would have required a specialized GIS workstation. PostGIS is actually creating a world that is post-GIS—we don't need GIS software to do GIS work anymore. A spatial database suffices.

In March of 2002, not even one year after the first release of PostGIS, I asked on the user mailing list for examples of how people were using PostGIS.

In her first post to the list, Regina Obe answered this way:

> *We use it here [city of Boston] for proximity analysis. Part of our department is in charge of distributing foreclosed property to developers, etc., to build houses, businesses, etc. We use PostGIS to list properties by proximity … so that if a developer wants to develop on a piece of land that is, say, X in size, they will be able to get a better sense of whether it can be done.*

Even at that early date in the project, Regina Obe was already testing the capabilities of PostGIS and creating clever analyses.

Since *PostGIS in Action* was first released in 2011, PostGIS has itself remained very much in action, adding new features for raster analysis, 3D, clustering, temporal data, topologies, and more. And the world has kept on moving too.

Almost two decades ago, when PostGIS was brand new, the idea that almost every person would have a GPS unit (a phone) in their pocket was pretty crazy, and now it's commonplace. The features of PostGIS for managing location are now being used widely by developers who only a few years ago had never heard of spatial data.

Over the last few years, satellite and aerial imagery have moved into the mass market, drone systems are commonplace, and location sensors are mounted on nearly any asset that moves. The amount of data to analyze—and the velocity and volume of that data—is higher than ever.

At the same time, PostGIS has never been easier to put to work for you. You can spin up a copy at any cloud provider, you can download builds for any platform, and if you're sufficiently interested you can still download the open source code and build it yourself, just as Regina did so many years ago.

Enjoy this book and the insights it provides into putting location data to work. Regina and Leo have distilled a huge body of information into a concise guide that is truly one of a kind.

PAUL RAMSEY
Chair, PostGIS Project Steering Committee

preface

PostGIS (pronounced *post-jis*) is a spatial database extender for the PostgreSQL open source relational database management system. It's the most powerful open source spatial database engine around. It adds to PostgreSQL several spatial data types and over 400 functions for working with these spatial types. PostGIS supports many of the OGC/ISO SQL/MM–compliant spatial functions you'll find in other relational databases such as Oracle, SQL Server, MySQL, and IBM DB2, as well as numerous additional spatial features that are unique to PostGIS.

Since the last edition of this book, other databases have added on spatial functionality which is often a subset of the functionality PostGIS provides. You'll see same-named functions in Google BigQuery and Snowflake. Many cloud providers also now offer PostgreSQL/PostGIS in a Database as a Service (DBaaS).

Readers coming from other ANSI/ISO–compliant spatial databases, or other relational databases, will feel right at home with PostgreSQL and PostGIS. PostgreSQL is one of the most ANSI/ISO SQL–compliant database management systems around.

The main raison d'être of this book is to provide a companion volume to the official PostGIS documentation—to serve as a guidebook for navigating through the hundreds of functions offered by PostGIS. We wanted to create a book that would catalog many of the common spatial problems we've come across and various strategies for solving them with PostGIS.

Above and beyond our primary mission, we hope to lay the foundation for thinking spatially. We hope that you'll be able to adapt our numerous examples and recipes to your own field of endeavor, and perhaps even spawn creative scions of your own.

acknowledgments

We'd like to thank first the many PostGIS package maintainers; in particular, Sebastiaan Couwenberg, Devrim Gündüz, Greg Troxel, and Christoph Berg who have provided much guidance in improving PostGIS releases and without whom many would be without PostGIS.

We'd also like to thank the PostGIS development team and Project Steering Committee, in particular Paul Ramsey, Sandro Santilli, Raúl Marín Rodríguez, Darafei Praliaskouski, Bborie Park, Dan Baston, Martin Davis, and Nicklas Avén who contributed to new features discussed in this book.

We thank everyone at Manning Publications. In particular, our development editor, Susan Ethridge, who helped us polish our chapters and provided much needed nagging; our copy editor, Andy Carroll, who caught many of our nonsensical sentences, invalid code references, and invalid links, and fact-checked many of our statements; and our technical reviewers who tested our code and caught errors in code early on. We also acknowledge publisher Marjan Bace; review editor Aleksandar Dragosavljević for organizing reviewer feedback; and our production and editorial team of Becky Whitney and Deirdre Hiam, our proofreader, Melody Dolab, as well as others who kept us focused during the whole process.

A special thanks to past contributors of PostGIS whose contributions make up the bread and butter of PostGIS: Olivier Courtin (in loving memory), Mateusz Loskot, Pierre Racine, and countless others. We thank the PostGIS community of newsgroup subscribers who answer questions as best and as quickly as they can, and PostGIS bloggers—each in their own way gives newcomers to PostGIS a warm and fuzzy feeling.

Our exposure to PostGIS would not be possible without the City of Boston Department of Neighborhood Development (DND), particularly the MIS and Policy Development and Research divisions where Regina was first exposed to GIS and PostGIS.

We would also like to thank our reviewers: Alvin Scudder, Arnaldo Ayala, Billy O'Callaghan, Biswanath Chowdhury, Carla Butler, Chris Viner, Daniel Tomás Lares, Daniele Andreis, DeUndre' Rushon, Dhivya Sivasubramanian, Evyatar Kafkafi, Hilde Van Gysel, Ikechukwu, Okonkwo, Jesus Manuel Lopez Becerra, Luis Moux-Dominguez, Marcus Brown, Mike Haller, Mike Jensen, Paulo Vieira, Philip Patterson, Richard Meinsen, Vladimir Kuptsov, and Weyert de Boer. Your suggestions helped make this a better book.

Finally, we thank our MEAP readers who provided invaluable constructive criticism and caught mistakes early in our code and explanations.

about this book

This book is focused on the PostGIS 3 and 3.1 series and PostgreSQL 11–13. This book isn't a substitute for either the official PostGIS or PostgreSQL documentation. The official PostGIS documentation does a good job of introducing you to the myriad of functions available in PostGIS and provides examples of how to use each. But it won't tell you how to combine all these functions into a recipe to solve your problems. That's the purpose of our book. Although it doesn't cover all the functions available in PostGIS, this book does cover the more commonly used and interesting ones and gives you the skills you need to combine them to solve classic and more esoteric but interesting problems in spatial analysis and modeling.

Although you can use this book as a reference source, we recommend that you also visit the official PostGIS site at https://postgis.net.

This book focuses on two- and three-dimensional non-curved Cartesian vector geometries, two-dimensional geodetic vector geometries, raster data, and network topologies.

Although the main purpose of this book is the use of PostGIS, we'd fall short of our mission if we neglected to provide some perspective on the landscape it lives in. PostGIS is not an island and rarely works alone. To complete the cycle, we also include the following:

- An extensive appendix that covers PostgreSQL in great detail from setup, to backup, to security management. The appendix also covers the fundamentals of SQL and creating functions and other objects with it.

- Several chapters dedicated to the use of PostGIS in web mapping, viewing using desktop tools, PostgreSQL PL languages commonly used with PostGIS, and extra open source add-ons such as the PostGIS-packaged TIGER geocoder and separately packaged pgRouting.

This book in no way attempts to provide a rigorous treatment of the math underlying the PostGIS libraries. We rely on intuitive understanding for concepts such as points, lines, and polygons. In the same vein, we're not able to delve into database theory. If we predict that a particular index should be more effective than another, we're making educated guesses from experience, not from having mastered relational algebra and dissecting a few computer chips along the way.

Who should read this book?

This book provides an introduction to PostGIS, and it assumes a basic comfort level with programming and working with data. The types of people we've found to be most attracted to PostGIS and are best suited for reading this book are listed here.

GIS PRACTITIONERS AND PROGRAMMERS

You know everything about data, geoids, and projections. You know where to find sources of data. You can create stunning applications with ArcGIS, MapInfo, Leaflet, OpenLayers, Google Maps, or other Ajax-enabled toolkits. You're adept at generating data sources in Esri shapefiles, using QGIS or ArcGIS, and creating cartographic masterpieces. You may even be able to add data to and extract it from a spatially enabled database, but when asked questions about the data, you're stuck. Being able to draw all the Walmarts in the United States on a map is one thing, but being able to answer the question, "How many Walmarts are east of the Mississippi," without counting individual pushpins is a whole different ball game. Sure, you may have used desktop tools and written procedural code to answer these questions, but we hope to show you a much faster way.

So what does a spatially enabled database offer that you don't already have at your fingertips?

- It provides the ability to easily intermingle spatial data with other corporate data, such as financial information, observational data, and marketing information. Yes, you can do these with Esri shapefiles, KML files, and other GIS file formats, but that requires an extra step and limits your options for joining with other relevant data. A database such as PostgreSQL has features such as a query planner that improves the speed of your joins and many commonly used statistical functions to make fairly complex questions and summary stats relatively fast to run and quick to write.
- When collecting user data, whether that user is drawing a geometry on the screen and inputting related information or clicking a point on the map, there's so much infrastructure built around databases that the task is much easier if you're using one. Take, for example, rolling your own web application in

.NET, PHP, Perl, Python, Java, or some other language. Each already has a driver for PostgreSQL to make inserting and querying data easy. Add to that mix the text-to-geometry functions, geometry-to-SVG, -KML, and -GeoJSON functions, and other processing functions that PostGIS provides, along with the geometry generation and manipulation functions that platforms like OpenLayers, MapServer, and GeoServer have, and you have a myriad of options to choose from.

- A relational database provides administrative support to easily control who has access to what, whether that be a text attribute or a geometry.

- PostgreSQL offers triggers that can allow the generation of other things like related geometries in other tables when certain database events happen.

- PostgreSQL has a multi-version concurrency control (MVCC) transactional core to ensure that when 100 users are reading or updating your data at the same time, your system doesn't come screeching to a halt.

- PostgreSQL provides the ability to write custom functions in the database that can be called from disparate applications. PostgreSQL offers several choices of languages to choose from when writing stored functions.

- If you're married to your preferred GIS desktop tools, don't worry. Choosing a spatial DBMS such as PostGIS doesn't mean you need to abandon your tools of choice. Manifold, Cadcorp, MapInfo 10+, AutoCAD, Esri ArcGIS, ArcMap, Server tools, and various commonly used desktop tools have built-in support for PostGIS. Safe FME, an extract-transform-load (ETL) favorite of GIS professionals, has supported PostGIS for a long time.

DB PRACTITIONERS

At some point in your database career, someone might have asked you a spatially oriented question about the data. Without a spatially enabled database, you're forced to limit your thinking in terms of coordinates, location names, or other geographical attributes that can be reduced to numbers and letters. This works fine for point data, but you're at a complete loss once areas and regions come into play. You may be able to find all the people named Smith within a county, but if we were to ask you to find all the Smiths living within 10 miles of the county, you'd be stuck.

We want readers coming from a standard relational database background to realize that data is more than just numbers, dates, and characters, and that amazing feats of SQL can be accomplished against non-textual data. Sure, you might have stored images, documents, and other oddities in your relational database, but we doubt you were able to do much in the way of writing SQL joins against these fields.

SCIENTISTS, RESEARCHERS, EDUCATORS, AND ENGINEERS

A lot of highly skilled scientists, researchers, educators, and engineers use spatial analysis tools to analyze their collected data, model their inventions, or train students. Although we don't consider ourselves the same as them, we admire these people the most because they create knowledge and improve our lives in fundamental ways. They may know a lot about mathematics, biology, chemistry, geology, physics, engineering, and so forth, but they aren't trained in database management, relational database use, or GIS. If you're one of these people, we hope to provide just enough of a framework to get you up to speed without too much fuss.

What does PostgreSQL/PostGIS hold for you?

- It gives you the ability to integrate with statistical packages such as R, and you can even write database procedural functions in PL/R that leverage the power of R.
- PostgreSQL also supports PL/Python and PL/JavaScript, which allows you to leverage the growing Python and JavaScript libraries for scientific research right in the database, where it can work even closer with the data than in a plain Python environment.
- While many think of PostGIS as a tool for geographic information systems, and that's implied by the name, we see it as a tool for spatial analysis. The distinction is that whereas geography focuses on the earth and the reference systems that bind the earth, spatial analysis focuses on space and the use of space. That space and coordinate reference system may be specific to an ant hill, or to a map of a nuclear plant whose location is yet to be defined, or to the different regions of the brain, or it may be used as a visualization tool to model the inherently non-visual, such as in process modeling. Although you may think of your particular area of interest as not being touched by spatial analysis, we challenge you to dig deeper.
- A database is a natural repository for large quantities of data and has a lot of built-in statistical/rollup functions and constructs for producing useful reports and analyses. If you're dealing with data of a spatial nature or using space as a visualization tool, PostGIS provides more functions to extend that analysis.
- Much of the data needed for scientific research can be easily collected by machines (GPS, alarm systems, remote sensing devices) and directly piped to the database via automated feeds or standard import formats. In fact, collection tools such as smartphones and unmanned aircraft are becoming cheaper each day and more accessible to the general population, and the hardware to store the data is also getting cheaper.
- Portions of data are easily distributed. A relational database is ideal for creating what we call "data dispensers" or "datamarts," which allow other researchers to easily grab just the subset of data they need for their research or to provide data for easy download by the public.

These profiles are the basic groups of spatial database users, but they're not the only ones. If you've ever looked at the world and thought, wouldn't it be great if I could correlate crime statistics with the locations where we've planted trees, or where's the best place and time to plant our crops given the elevation model and temperature fluctuations of an area, then PostGIS might be the easiest and most cost-effective tool for you.

How this book is organized: a roadmap

This book is divided into three major parts and has several supporting appendixes.

PART 1: LEARNING POSTGIS

Part 1 covers the fundamental concepts of spatial relational databases and PostGIS/
PostgreSQL in particular. The goal of this part is to introduce you to industry-standard
GIS database concepts and practices. By the end of this part, you should have a solid
foundation in the various geometry, geography, raster, and topology types, and what
problems each strives to solve. You'll have a basic understanding of spatial reference
systems and database storage options. Most important, you'll have the ability to load,
query, and view spatial data in a PostGIS-enabled PostgreSQL database.

PART 2: PUTTING POSTGIS TO WORK

This part focuses on using PostGIS to solve real-world spatial problems and on optimizing for speed. You'll learn how to do a variety of things:

- How to do proximity analysis using both geometry and geography
- How to use different kinds of vector operations to optimize your data
- How to perform seamless raster processing using raster and vector data
- How to create new vector data using raster processing, map algebra, histograms,
  and other raster statistics functions to compute statistics about an area of interest
- How to create big rasters from smaller rasters using raster aggregate functions
- How to use the packaged PostGIS TIGER geocoder for address normalization,
  geocoding, and reverse geocoding
- How to use topology to ensure consistency of editing
- How to simplify a whole network of geometries and still maintain connected-
  ness in your simplified dataset

PART 3: USING POSTGIS WITH OTHER TOOLS

Part 3 encompasses the tools most commonly used with PostGIS for building applications. We'll cover pgRouting, a tool you can use with PostGIS directly in the database
for creating network routing applications. In addition, we'll cover PostgreSQL stored
procedure languages: PL/Python, PL/R, and PL/V8 (a.k.a. PL/JavaScript). Finally,
we'll end with a brief study of PostGIS in web applications. We'll cover the various
mapping servers used with PostGIS as well as the OpenLayers and Leaflet mapping
JavaScript APIs. We'll also look at how to use PostGIS JSON and vector tile output
functions to build an interactive web map.

APPENDIXES

There are three appendixes.

Appendix A provides additional resources for getting help on PostGIS and the
ancillary tools discussed in the book.

Appendix B shows how to get up and running with PostgreSQL and PostGIS.

Appendix C is an SQL primer that explains the concepts of JOIN, UNION, INTERSECT,
EXCEPT, common table expressions (CTEs), and LATERAL. It discusses the fundamentals

of rolling up data with aggregate functions and aggregate constructs, as well as the more advanced topics of using window functions and frames.

About the code

The following typographical conventions are used throughout the book:

- Courier typeface is used in all code listings.
- Courier typeface is used within the text for certain code words.
- Sidebars and notes are used to highlight key points or introduce new terminology.
- Code annotations are used in place of inline comments in the code. These highlight important concepts or areas of the code. Some annotations appear with numbered bullets like this, ❶, that are referenced later in the text.

The examples and data for all chapters of this book can be downloaded via www.postgis.us/chapters_edition_3. On the book's site you'll also find descriptions of each chapter with related links for each chapter. Each chapter page has a link where you can download the full data and code for that chapter.

The code can also be downloaded from the publisher's website at www.manning.com/obe3.

liveBook discussion forum

The purchase of *PostGIS In Action, Third Edition* includes free access to a private forum run by Manning Publications where you can make comments about the book, ask technical questions, and receive help from the authors and other users. You can access and subscribe to the forum at https://livebook.manning.com/#!/book/obe3discussion. This page provides information on how to get on the forum once you're registered, what kind of help is available, and the rules of conduct in the forum.

Manning's commitment to our readers is to provide a venue where a meaningful dialogue among individual readers and between readers and authors can take place. It's not a commitment to any specific amount of participation on the part of the authors, whose contribution to the book's forum remains voluntary (and unpaid). We suggest you try asking the authors some challenging questions, lest their interest stray!

The discussion forum and the archives of previous discussions will be accessible from the publisher's website as long as the book is in print. Lastly, there will be additions to the content added to the author's online website for the book, located at www.postgis.us.

You may also visit the authors at the PostgreSQL and Open Source GIS companion sites: www.postgresonline.com and www.bostongis.com.

About the title

By combining introductions, overviews, and how-to examples, the *In Action* books are designed to help with learning and remembering. According to research in cognitive science, the things people remember are things they discover during self-motivated exploration.

Although no one at Manning is a cognitive scientist, we are convinced that for learning to become permanent, it must pass through stages of exploration, play, and, interestingly, retelling of what's being learned. People understand and remember new things, which is to say they master them, only after actively exploring them. Humans learn in action. An essential part of an *In Action* book is that it's example-driven. It encourages the reader to try things out, to play with new code, and to explore new ideas.

There's another, more mundane, reason for the title of this book: Our readers are busy. They use books to do a job or solve a problem. They need books that allow them to jump in and jump out easily and learn just what they want just when they want it. They need books that aid them in action. The books in this series are designed for such readers.

about the Author

REGINA OBE and LEO HSU are database consultants and authors. Regina is a member of the PostGIS core development team and the Project Steering Committee.

about the cover illustration

The figure on the cover of *PostGIS in Action* is captioned "A woman from Ubli, Croatia." The illustration is taken from a reproduction of an album of Croatian traditional costumes from the mid-nineteenth century by Nikola Arsenović, published by the Ethnographic Museum in Split, Croatia, in 2003. The illustrations were obtained from a helpful librarian at the Ethnographic Museum in Split, itself situated in the Roman core of the medieval center of the town: the ruins of Emperor Diocletian's retirement palace from around AD 304. The book includes finely colored illustrations of figures from different regions of Croatia, accompanied by descriptions of the costumes and of everyday life. Dress codes and lifestyles have changed over the last 200 years, and the diversity by region, so rich at the time, has faded away. It's now hard to tell apart the inhabitants of different continents, let alone of different hamlets or towns separated by only a few miles.

Perhaps we have traded cultural diversity for a more varied personal life–certainly for a more varied and fast-paced technological life. Manning celebrates the inventiveness and initiative of the computer business with book covers based on the rich diversity of regional life of two centuries ago, brought back to life by illustrations from old books and collections like this one.

Part 1

Introduction to PostGIS

Welcome to *PostGIS in Action, Third Edition*. PostGIS is a spatial database extender for the PostgreSQL database management system. This book will teach you the fundamentals of spatial databases in general, key concepts in geographic information systems (GIS), and more specifically how to configure, load, and query a PostGIS-enabled database. You'll learn how to perform actions with single lines of SQL code that you thought were possible only with a desktop GIS system. By using spatial SQL, much of the heavy lifting that would require many manual steps in desktop GIS tools can be scripted and automated.

This book is divided into three sections and four appendixes. Part 1 covers the fundamentals of spatial databases, GIS, and working with spatial data. Although part 1 is focused on PostGIS, many of the concepts you'll learn in this part are equally applicable to other spatial relational databases.

Chapter 1 covers the fundamentals of spatial databases and what you can do with a spatially enabled database that you can't do with a standard relational database. It also introduces features that are fairly unique to PostGIS. It concludes with a fast-paced example of loading fast-food restaurant longitude/latitude data and converting it to geometric points, loading road data from Esri shapefiles, and doing spatial summaries by joining these two sets of data.

Chapter 2 covers all the spatial types that PostGIS has to offer. You'll learn how to create these using various functions and learn about concepts unique to each spatial type.

Chapter 3 is an introduction to spatial reference systems, and we'll explain the concepts behind them, why they're important for working with geometry, raster, and topology, and how to work with them.

Chapter 4 covers how to load spatial data into PostGIS using packaged tools as well as additional third-party open source tools. You'll learn how to load geometry and geography data using the shp2pgsql command-line tool commonly packaged with PostGIS distributions, as well as the shp2pgsql-gui GUI loader/exporter that's packaged with some desktop distributions of PostGIS. You'll also learn how to load raster data using the PostGIS-packaged raster2pgsql command-line tool and how to import and export both raster and vector data of various formats using the GDAL/OGR suite. You'll also learn how to query data from external sources without loading them by using PostgreSQL foreign data wrappers (FDWs).

Chapter 5 covers some of the more common open source desktop tools for viewing and querying PostGIS data.

Chapter 6 starts getting into the simpler core functions that are used with geometry and geography functions. These all take single geometry or geography objects and morph them or take text representations of them and convert them to PostGIS spatial objects.

Chapter 7 is an introduction to raster functions. It covers some functions for creating rasters, interrogating rasters, and setting pixel values.

Chapter 8 concludes this first part by introducing you to spatial relationships. Spatial relationships are most important when working with sets of data. In later sections of the book, we'll use these concepts to do things like spatial joins.

What is
a spatial database?

Most folks experience their first spatially enabled application when they see push-pins tacked onto points of interest on an interactive map. This provides a glimpse into the vast and varied field of geographic information systems (GIS).

We'll begin this chapter with a pushpin model. As we demonstrate its limited usefulness, we'll introduce the need for a spatial database—not just any database, but PostGIS. PostGIS is a spatial database extender for the PostgreSQL database management system. We'll provide a brief introduction to the entire PostGIS suite and whet your appetite with an example that goes far beyond what you can accomplish with pushpins.

The data and code used in this chapter can be found at www.postgis.us/chapter_ 01_edition_3.

1.1   *Thinking spatially*

Popular mapping sites such as OpenStreetMap, Mapbox, Google Maps, Bing Maps, and MapQuest have empowered people in many walks of life to answer the question "Where is something?" by displaying teardrop shapes on a gorgeously detailed, interactive map. No longer are we restricted to textual descriptions of "where," like "Turn right at the supermarket, and it'll be the third house on the right with a mangy dog out front." Nor are we faced with the frustrating problem of not being able to figure out our current location on a paper map.

Going beyond getting directions, organizations large and small have discovered that mapping can be a great resource for analyzing patterns in data. By plotting the addresses of pizza lovers, a national pizza chain can assess where to locate the next grand opening. Political organizations planning grassroots campaigns can easily see on a map where the undecided or unregistered voters are located and target their route walks accordingly. Even though the pushpin model offers unprecedented geographical insight, the reasoning that germinates from it is entirely visual.

In the pizza example, the chain might be able to see the concentration of pizza lovers in a city by means of adding pushpins, but what if they needed to differentiate pizza lovers by income level? If the chain has a gourmet offering, it would be a good idea to locate new restaurants in the midst of mid- to high-income pizza lovers. The pizza planners could use pushpins of different colors on an interactive map to indicate various income tiers, but the heuristic visual reasoning will now be much more complicated, as shown in figure 1.1. Not only do the planners need to look at the concentration of pushpins, they must also keep the varying colors or icons of the pin in mind. Add another variable to the map, like households with lactose-intolerant adults, and the problem overwhelms our feeble minds. Spatial databases come to the rescue.

A *spatial database* is a database with column data types specifically designed to store objects in space—these data types can be added to database tables. The information stored is usually geographic in nature, such as a point location or the boundary of a lake. A spatial database also provides functions and indexes for querying and manipulating the spatial data, which can be called from a query language such as Structured Query Language (SQL). A spatial database is often just used as a storage container for spatial data, but it can do much more than that. Although a spatial database need not be relational in nature, most are. A spatial database gives you a storage tool, an analysis tool, and an organizing tool all in one.

Presenting data visually isn't a spatial database's only goal. The pizza shop planners can store an infinite number of attributes of the pizza-loving household, including income level, number of children in the household, pizza-ordering history, and even religious preferences and cultural upbringing (as they relate to topping choices on a pizza). More important, the analysis need not be limited to the number of variables that can be juggled in the brain. The planners can make very specific requests, like "Give me a list of neighborhoods ranked by the number of high-income

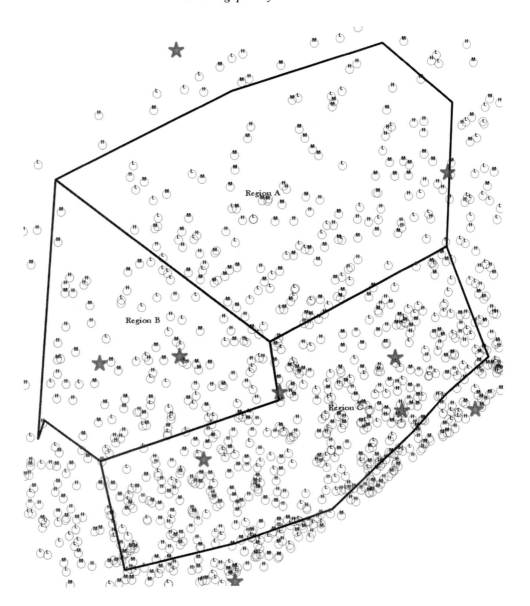

Figure 1.1 Pushpin madness!

pizza lovers who have more than two children." Furthermore, they can easily incorporate additional data from varied sources, such as the location and rating of existing pizzerias from restaurant review sites or the health-consciousness level of various neighborhoods as identified by the local health commission. Their questions of the database could be as complicated as "Show me the region with the highest number of households where the average closest distance to any pizza parlor with a star-ranking below 5 is greater than 16 kilometers (10 miles). Oh, and toss out the health-conscious neighborhoods."

Table 1.1 shows what the results of such a spatial query might look like.

Table 1.1   Result of a spatial query

Region	Households	Restaurants	Distance
Region A	194	1	17.1 km

Suppose you aren't a mapping user but are more of a data user. You work with data day in and day out, never needing to plot anything on a map. You're familiar with questions like "Give me all the employees who live in Chicago" or "Count up the number of customers in each postal code." Suppose you have the latitude and longitude of all the employees' addresses; you could ask questions like "Give me the average distance that each employee must travel to work." This is the extent of the kind of spatial queries that you can formulate with conventional databases, where data types consist mainly of text, numbers, and dates.

But suppose the question posed is "Give me the number of houses within two miles of the coastline requiring evacuation in the event of a hurricane" or "How many households would be affected by the noise of a newly proposed runway?" Without spatial support, these questions would require you to collect or derive additional values for each data point. For the coastline question, you'd need to determine the distance from the beach, house by house. This could involve algorithms to find the shortest distance to fixed intervals along the coastline or require a series of SQL queries to order all the houses by proximity to the beach and then make a cut. With spatial support, all you need to do is reformulate the question slightly as "Find all houses within a two-mile radius of the coastline." A spatially enabled database can intrinsically work with data types like coastlines (modeled as linestrings), buffer zones (modeled as polygons), and beach houses (modeled as points).

As with most things in life worth pursuing, nothing comes without some effort. You'll need to climb a gentle learning curve to tap into the power of spatial analysis. The good news is that unlike other good things in life, the database that we'll introduce you to is completely free—moneywise.

If you're able to figure out how to get data into your Google map, you'll have no problem taking the next step. If you can write queries in non-spatially enabled databases, we'll open your eyes and mind to something beyond the mundane world of numbers, dates, and strings. Let's get started.

1.2   *Introducing PostGIS*

PostGIS is a free and open source library that spatially enables the free and open source PostgreSQL object-relational database management system (ORDBMS). We want you to choose PostgreSQL as your relational database and PostGIS as your spatial database extender for PostgreSQL.

1.2.1   Why PostGIS

PostGIS started as a project of Refractions Research (http://refractions.net), a geospatial consulting company located in Victoria, Canada, and has since been adopted and improved on by governments, universities, public organizations, and other companies.

The power of PostGIS is enhanced by other supporting projects:

- *Proj*—Provides projection support, now in its seventh generation
- *Geometry Engine Open Source (GEOS)*—Advanced geometry processing support
- *Geospatial Data Abstraction Library (GDAL)*—Provides many advanced raster-processing features
- *Computational Geometry Algorithms Library (CGAL/SFCGAL)*—Enables advanced 3D analysis

Most of these projects, including PostGIS, now fall under the umbrella of the Open Source Geospatial Foundation (OSGeo).

The foundation of PostGIS is the PostgreSQL object-relational database management system (ORDBMS), which provides transactional support, gist index support for spatial objects, and a query planner out of the box. It's a great testament to the power and flexibility of PostgreSQL that Refractions Research chose to build on top of PostgreSQL rather than on any other open source database.

1.2.2   Standards conformance

PostGIS and PostgreSQL conform to industry standards more closely than most products. PostgreSQL supports many of the newer ANSI SQL features. PostGIS supports OGC standards and the SQL Multimedia spec (SQL/MM) spatial standard. This means that you aren't simply learning how to use a set of products; you're garnering knowledge about industry standards that will help you understand other commercial and open source geospatial databases and mapping tools.

> **What are OGC, OSGeo, ANSI SQL, and SQL/MM?**
>
> OGC stands for Open Geospatial Consortium, and it's the body that exists to standardize how geographic and spatial data is accessed and distributed. Toward that goal, they have numerous specifications that govern accessing geospatial data from web services, geospatial data delivery formats, and querying of geospatial data.
>
> OSGeo stands for Open Source Geospatial Foundation, and it's the body whose initiative is to fund, support, and market open source tools and free data for GIS. There's some overlap between the OSGeo and OGC. Both strive to make GIS data and tools available to everyone, which means they're both concerned about open standards.
>
> You'll also often hear the term American National Standards Institute (ANSI) or International Organization of Standardization (ISO) SQL. The ANSI/ISO SQL standards define general guidelines that SQL implementations should follow. These guidelines are often year-dated, like ANSI SQL 92 and ANSI SQL:2016, and they build upon prior

(continued)

year specs. You'll find that many relational databases support most of the ANSI SQL 92 spec but not as much of the later specs. PostgreSQL supports many of the newer guidelines, some of which we'll cover in appendix C.

The ANSI/ISO SQL Multimedia spec (SQL/MM) is a specification that, among other things, defines standard functions for spatial data used in SQL.

As spatial became not so special and almost an expected part of high-end relational databases, much of what OGC governed fell under the ANSI/ISO SQL making body. As a result, you'll often see the newer SQL/MM specs referring to spatial types with an `ST_` prefix, like `ST_Geometry` and `ST_Polygon`, instead of the unadorned `Geometry` and `Polygon` from the older OGC/SFSQL (Spatial Features for SQL) specs.

If your data and your APIs implement standards supported by many kinds of software—Cadcorp, Safe FME, AutoCAD, Manifold, MapInfo, Esri ArcGIS, ogr2ogr/GDAL, OpenJUMP, QGIS, Deegree, MapGuide, UMN MapServer, GeoServer, or even standard programming tools like SQL, JavaScript, PHP, Python, Ruby, Java, Perl, ASP.NET, SQL, or new emerging tools—then everyone can use the tools that they feel most comfortable with, or that fit their work processes, or that they can afford, and share information with one another. OSGeo tries to ensure that regardless of how small your pocketbook is, you can still afford to view and analyze GIS data. OGC and ANSI/ISO SQL try to enforce standards across all products so that regardless of how expensive your GIS platform is, you can still make your hard work available to everyone. This is especially important for government agencies whose salaries and tools are paid for with tax dollars; for students who have a lot of will and the intelligence to learn advanced technology, but have small pockets; and even for smaller vendors who have a compelling offering for specific kinds of users but who are often snubbed by larger vendors because they can't support (or lack access to) the private API standards of the big-name vendors.

PostGIS is supported by a vast number of GIS proprietary desktop and server tools. PostGIS is also the preferred spatial relational database of most open source geospatial desktop and web mapping server tools and the preferred spatial relational database platform for most government and start-ups.

We'll cover some of the more common tools that work with PostGIS in chapters 5 and 17.

1.2.3   *PostGIS is powerful*

PostGIS provides many spatial operators, spatial functions, spatial data types, and spatial indexing enhancements to PostgreSQL. If you add to the mix the complementary features that PostgreSQL and other related projects provide, you have a jam-packed powerhouse at your disposal that's well suited for sophisticated GIS analysis and that is a valuable tool for learning GIS.

You'll be hard pressed to find the following features in other spatial databases:

- Functions to work with GeoJSON, Keyhole Markup Language (KML), Mapbox Vector Tiles (MVT) allowing web applications to talk directly to PostGIS without the need for additional serializing schemes or translations
- Comprehensive geometry processing functions that go far beyond basic geometric operations, including functions for fixing invalid geometries and for simplifying and deconstructing geometries
- Built-in 3D and topology support
- Over 300 seamless operations for working with vectors and rasters in tandem, as well as for converting between the two families

---

GeoJSON, KML, and MVT data formats

Geographic JavaScript Object Notation (GeoJSON; http://geojson.org) and Keyhole Markup Language (KML; http://en.wikipedia.org/wiki/Keyhole_Markup_Language) are two of the older, more popular vector formats used by web mapping applications. Mapbox Vector Tiles (MVT) is a relatively new standard that has gained quite a bit of popularity in the last few years.

- GeoJSON is an extension of JSON that's used for representing JavaScript objects. It adds to the JSON standard support for geographic objects.
- KML is an XML format developed by Keyhole (which was purchased by Google), first used in Google's mapping products and later supported by various mapping APIs.
- Mapbox Vector Tiles (MVT) is a binary vector format popularized by Mapbox that dishes out data in tiles of binary vector data, allowing client-side styling of vector data, often lighter than standard raster tiles, and for scaling resolution.

These are only three of the many formats that PostGIS can output.

1.2.4 *Built on top of PostgreSQL*

The major reason PostGIS was built on the PostgreSQL platform was the ease of extensibility that PostgreSQL provided for building new types and operators and for controlling the index operators. PostgreSQL was designed to be extensible from the ground up.

PostgreSQL has a regal lineage that dates back almost to the dawn of relational databases. It's a cousin of the Sybase and Microsoft SQL Server databases, because the people who started Sybase came from UC Berkeley and worked on the Ingres or PostgreSQL projects with Michael Stonebraker. Michael Stonebraker is considered by many to be the father of Ingres and PostgreSQL and to be one of the founding fathers of object-relational database management systems. The source code of Sybase SQL Server was later licensed to Microsoft to produce Microsoft SQL Server.

PostgreSQL's claim to fame is that it's the most advanced open source database in existence. It has the speed and functionality to compete with the popular commercial enterprise offerings, and it's used to power databases petabytes in size. As time has moved on, new usability features have been added, making it not only the most advanced, but perhaps the most flexible and best relational database out there. For more details about the features of PostgreSQL and the key enhancements in newer versions that are lacking in most other databases (including expensive proprietary ones), please refer to appendix D.

PostgreSQL is becoming a one-size-fits-all database that doesn't sacrifice the needs and wants of any database users. Most OS distributions carry a fairly new version that provides a quick and painless install process. Since the last edition of this book, cloud offerings have come on board that provide PostgreSQL with PostGIS out of the box. Some popular cloud versions of PostgreSQL that PostGIS users use are CartoDB, Heroku PostgreSQL, Microsoft Azure database for PostgreSQL, and Amazon RDS and Aurora for PostgreSQL. Google BigQuery, a data warehouse service provided by Google, though not PostgreSQL, has adopted PostgreSQL constructs and PostGIS function names and spatial types for querying their spatial data (https://cloud.google .com/bigquery/docs/gis-data).

1.2.5   *Free—as in money*

Licenses for SQL Server Standard start at $5,000 and can easily cost you $20,000 for a modest server. The free version of SQL Server, while it has the same spatial functionality as the paid version, is crippled by its memory and processor limits.

Oracle Standard prior to Oracle 19c shipped only with Oracle Locator, which had only elementary functionality. Oracle spatial prior to Oracle 19c required Oracle Spatial purchase to get the advanced spatial features. Starting with Oracle 19c, all editions include the Oracle spatial support.

PostGIS is free. 'Nuff said.

1.2.6   *Free—as in freedom*

PostGIS and PostgreSQL are open source. PostGIS is under a GPLv2+ license; PostgreSQL is under a BSD-style license, which means you can both see and modify the source code. If you find a feature missing, you can contribute a patch or pay a developer to add the feature. Adding features to PostGIS and PostgreSQL generally costs much less than the licensing costs for proprietary counterparts. If you discover a bug in PostGIS or PostgreSQL, you'll find the PostGIS and PostgreSQL teams very responsive in addressing bugs—more so than most proprietary database vendors.

You have more freedom to control your destiny with PostGIS and PostgreSQL than you do with comparable proprietary offerings. You can install PostGIS on as many servers as you want, and you aren't limited by artificial restrictions on how many cores you can use.

The openness of PostGIS has spawned an explosion of user-contributed add-ons and community-funded features. These are the most notable ones to date: raster support, geodetic support, topology support, improved 3D support, faster spatial indexes, TIGER geocoder enhancements, and a PostGIS spatial viewer in the pgAdmin4 database management tool commonly shipped with PostgreSQL.

The release cycles for PostGIS and PostgreSQL are radically shorter than those of commercial offerings. With contributions from users, PostgreSQL evolves at a rate of one major version per year and one patch release version every two or three months, with bugs getting immediate attention. You don't have to wait years in anticipation of features promised in subsequent releases. If you choose to live on the bleeding edge, you can even download a new build every other week.

1.2.7 Alternatives to PostGIS

Admittedly, PostGIS isn't the only spatial database in use today. Early entrants were dominated by proprietary offerings, and PostGIS broke this mold. Successors to PostGIS are gravitating towards installations with lightweight footprints for use on mobile devices. We're also beginning to see spatial features in NoSQL databases like MongoDB, CouchDB, Elastic Search, and Solr.

ORACLE SPATIAL

Oracle was the one that started it all. In Oracle 7, joint development efforts with Canadian scientists gave birth to SDO (Spatial Data Option). In later releases, Oracle redubbed this lovechild as Oracle Spatial.

Oracle Spatial isn't available with lower-priced editions of Oracle. Only when you fork out the money for Oracle Enterprise Edition will you have the luxury of being able to buy the Oracle Spatial option.

Standard Oracle installations do come with something called Oracle Locator, which offers the basic geometry types, proximity functions, some spatial aggregates, and limited spatial processing. Oracle has been pressured by users to provide more spatial support in Oracle Locator, so newer versions of Oracle Locator do provide basic functions like union and intersection but leave out union aggregate options and many other functions you'll find in PostGIS, SQL Server, and Oracle Spatial.

MICROSOFT SQL SERVER

Microsoft introduced spatial support in their SQL Server 2008 offering, with its built-in Geometry and Geodetic Geography types and companion spatial functions. To Microsoft's credit, you'll get the same feature set with their Express, Standard, Enterprise, and Datacenter offerings. You may just be limited regarding database size, how many processors you can use, and what query plan features you're allowed.

Microsoft's spatial feature, except their curved and geodetic support, pales in comparison to PostGIS. Admittedly, Microsoft SQL Server has probably got the best curve and geodetic support of any database—it's the only one to support curved geometries in geodetic space. But don't expect to find numerous output/input functions, such as input/output for KML, GeoJSON, and MVT, or raster support, or the numerous processing functions that PostGIS has.

SPATIALITE AND GEOPACKAGE

Our favorite kids on the block are SpatiaLite and GeoPackage, which are both add-ons to the open source SQLite portable database. These are especially interesting because they can be used as low-end companions to PostGIS and other high-end spatially enabled databases.

GeoPackage is an OGC standard storage and transport mechanism that can store both vector and raster data. Internally, it is a relational database just like PostGIS, and it's growing in popularity with tools such as QGIS, making it a default standard for exporting data.

GeoPackage is touted more as a data storage than a querying tool, and it leaves the query functionality to tools that use it. SpatiaLite, on the other hand, includes much of the same functionality you'll find in PostGIS and builds using the same libraries that PostGIS uses: GEOS, PROJ, and GDAL. This makes it an even more fitting companion to PostGIS because many of the conventions are the same and much of the ecosystem around PostGIS also supports or is starting to support SpatiaLite/RasterLite.

What SpatiaLite lacks is a strong enterprise database behind it for writing advanced functions and spatial aggregate functions. That's why some spatial queries possible in PostGIS are harder to write or are not even possible in SpatiaLite.

SpatiaLite, SQLite, and GeoPackage store data as a single file that's easily transportable. This makes it less threatening to deploy for users new to databases or GIS and easier to deploy as a lightweight offline database companion to a server-side database like PostGIS/PostgreSQL.

MYSQL

MySQL has had elementary spatial support since version 4, but MySQL, as a database, is handicapped by its lack of a powerful SQL engine. Its primary audience is still developers who are looking for a database that will *store* something, rather than *do* something. Earlier MySQL spatial support made the fatal mistake of not providing indexing capabilities except on MyISAM tables—spatial queries rely heavily on indexing for speedy performance. In version 5.6, MySQL extended geometric operations to work beyond bounding boxes and also allowed spatial indexes on its InnoDB storage engine. Newer versions of MySQL and MariaDb offer even more functions, such as GeoJSON and other output functions.

Oracle MySQL and other MySQL forks like MariaDB have made strides in the 5.6 variants by improving the performance of subqueries, but the query planner and SQL feature set in the MySQL family is still a kid when compared to the likes of PostgreSQL, SQL Server, and Oracle, so MySQL is not suitable for doing anything as complex as most spatial analysis. The spatial support has vastly improved in MySQL 8 and MariaDb 10, but it's still no competition for PostGIS.

Although Oracle MySQL and MariaDb have mostly the same functionality, their spatial offerings are not exactly the same. For a comparison of the differences, see the MariaDB website (https://mariadb.com/kb/en/library/mysqlmariadb-spatial-support-matrix/).

ARCGIS BY ESRI

We must give a nod to Esri, which has long packaged its spatial database engine (SDE) with its ArcGIS for Server product. The SDE engine is integrated into the ArcGIS line of products and is often used to spatially enable or augment legacy or weak database products, such as Microsoft SQL Server 2005 and Oracle Locator.

Older versions of ArcGIS desktop required going through an SDE middle tier to get at the native offerings of your spatial database. Newer versions, starting around ArcGIS 10.0, allow for direct access to PostGIS and other databases. By sidestepping the middleware, you're free to use any version of PostGIS with ArcGIS desktop.

Be careful when using ArcGIS as it installs its own flavor of geometry in PostgreSQL. This often causes users of PostGIS confusion as they sometimes pick the `sde.st_geometry` database type instead of the PostGIS `geometry` type and are further locked into Esri middleware. The `sde.st_geometry` type is needed to use Esri versioning tools, but for most other uses it's a hinderance.

Although the Esri proprietary model doesn't sit well with us, we must give them credit—a lot of credit, in fact—for being one of the first major companies to introduce GIS analysis to commercial and government organizations. They paved the way for, but still stand in the way of, the rise of free and open source GIS.

1.3 *Installing PostGIS*

We encourage you to install the latest versions of PostgreSQL and PostGIS—PostgreSQL 13 and PostGIS 3.1 at the time of writing. The introduction of the extension model in PostgreSQL 9.1 greatly simplified the installation of add-ons (such as PostGIS) to two steps:

1 Locate and install the binaries for your particular OS into your PostgreSQL directories.
2 Individually enable the extensions for each database as needed. For instance, if you have 10 databases on your server, but only 2 require PostGIS, you'd only enable PostGIS for the 2.

> **PostGIS must be enabled in each database**
>
> One characteristic of PostgreSQL that confuses many people coming from other database systems is that custom extensions like PostGIS, hstore, PL/JavaScript, and PL/Python must be enabled in each database they will be used in. This isn't the case for built-in types like Full-Text, XML, JSON, JSONB, and so on, which are always present.

Many of the popular Linux/Unix distributions include PostGIS 3.1 in their repositories. Use `yum` or `apt` to install the binaries. For Mac users, there are a couple of popular distributions, all itemized on the PostGIS install page (http://postgis.net/install). For MS Windows, we recommend using the EnterpriseDB (EDB) application Stack Builder, if you are uncomfortable with command lines. We also are the package maintainers for the "Spatial Extensions" category in the EDB Windows application Stack Builder. We try to pack the "Spatial Extensions" category with all the PostGIS extensions and many related PostGIS extensions, such as pgRouting and pgPointcloud. Please refer to appendix B for more details on where to obtain binaries for your OS.

Two popular tools come packaged with PostgreSQL: *psql* and *pgAdmin*. You use these tools to create databases, users, and compose queries.

Psql is strictly a command-line tool. If you don't have a GUI, psql is your only option.

If you have the luxury of a graphical interface, we encourage you to use the more newbie-friendly pgAdmin. PgAdmin can be installed separately from PostgreSQL. You can find source code as well as precompiled binaries at the pgAdmin site (www.pgadmin.org).

Once you've successfully installed the binaries, you can create a database with a command such as this, using the psql or pgAdmin query tool:

```
CREATE DATABASE postgis_in_action;
```

After creating the database, you should connect to it. You can do this in psql with `\connect postgis_in_action` and in pgAdmin by refreshing the database tree and selecting the new database.

You should next enable PostGIS in your database by connecting to the database and running the code in the following listing. Enabling the extension rarely fails, but you may encounter dependency errors, especially if you have earlier versions of PostGIS floating around.

Listing 1.1   Enabling PostGIS in a database

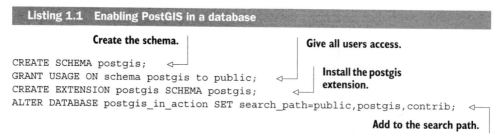

Create the schema.   **Give all users access.**

```
CREATE SCHEMA postgis;
GRANT USAGE ON schema postgis to public;              Install the postgis
CREATE EXTENSION postgis SCHEMA postgis;              extension.
ALTER DATABASE postgis_in_action SET search_path=public,postgis,contrib;
```

Add to the search path.

TIP   Although it's not required, we always install postgis in a separate schema such as `postgis` so the functions don't clutter up the default public schema.

You can also enable extensions in pgAdmin, using the Extensions install section pictured in figure 1.2.

Figure 1.2   Database with postgis extension installed

WARNING Installing postgis with the pgAdmin Extensions interface doesn't allow you to set which schema it should be installed in. It defaults to installing postgis in the public schema. As a result, we prefer running CREATE EXTENSION from the query window instead of using the Extensions interface.

If postgis isn't listed, you can install it by right-clicking the Extensions branch, choosing New Extension, and picking postgis from the menu.

You should see postgis listed in the Add Extension menu if you installed the binaries and don't have it already installed in your selected database.

PostGIS 3 raster support packages separately

Prior to PostGIS 3, the postgis raster support was included as part of the postgis extension. If you are using PostGIS 3+ and want to use raster and raster functions, you'll need to perform the following additional step:

```
CREATE EXTENSION postgis_raster SCHEMA postgis;
```

1.3.1 Verifying versions of PostGIS and PostgreSQL

After a PostGIS install, disconnect from your database and reconnect. Then quickly verify the versions to make sure the installation succeeded. Execute the following query:

```
SELECT postgis_full_version();
```

If all is well, you should see the version of PostGIS, as well as the versions of the supporting GEOS, GDAL, PROJ, LIBXML, and LIBJSON libraries, as shown here:

```
POSTGIS="3.1.1 3.1.1" [EXTENSION]
PGSQL="130" GEOS="3.9.1-CAPI-1.14.1" PROJ="7.1.1"
GDAL="GDAL 3.2.1, released 2020/12/29"
LIBXML="2.9.9" LIBJSON="0.12"
LIBPROTOBUF="1.2.1" WAGYU="0.5.0 (Internal)" TOPOLOGY RASTER
```

Installing visualization tools

Unlike conventional character-based databases, spatial databases must be experienced visually. When you view a bitmap file, you'd much rather see the rendered bitmap than the bits themselves. Similarly, you'd much rather see your spatial objects rendered rather than their textual representations.

Many visualization tools are available for free download, with OpenJump and QGIS being two of the more popular ones. pgAdmin, starting at the pgAdmin4 3.3 version, includes a lightweight PostGIS viewer for viewing the output of spatial queries. The pgAdmin4 tool, however, does not allow you to overlay multiple queries as you can with OpenJump and QGIS. It also doesn't allow the viewing of PostGIS rasters, as you can with QGIS.

> **(continued)**
> We encourage you to install multiple viewing tools for comparison. Chapter 5 offers a quick guide to installing and will get you started with these tools.

1.4 *Spatial data types*

Four key spatial types are offered by PostGIS: `geometry`, `geography`, `raster`, and `topology`. PostGIS has always supported the *geometry* type from its inception. It introduced support for *geography* in PostGIS 1.5. PostGIS 2.0 raised the bar further by incorporating *raster*, introducing areal types in the geometry type and *network topology* support. Although PostGIS 2.1 introduced many more functions, perhaps the most important feature it provided was faster speed, particularly for raster and geography operations. Newer versions of PostGIS have introduced newer spatial index types such as spgist, BRIN, and support for parallelizing queries:

- *Geometry*—The planar type. This is the very first model, and it's still the most popular type that PostGIS supports. It's the foundation of the other types. It uses the Cartesian math you learned about in high school geometry.
- *Geography*—The spheroidal geodetic type. Lines and polygons are drawn on the earth's curved surface, so they're curved rather than straight lines. PostGIS 2.2 introduced support for any geodetic spatial reference systems, which means you can use geography for other planets, such as Mars or your own made-up world.
- *Raster*—The multi-band cell type. Rasters model space as a grid of rectangular cells, each containing a numeric array of values.
- *Topology*—The relational model type. Topology models the world as a network of connected nodes, edges, and faces. Objects are composed of these elements and may share these with other objects. There are really two related concepts in topology—the *network*, which defines what elements each thing is composed of, and *routing*. PostGIS 2+ packages the *network topology* model, which is often just referred to as *topology*.

Network topology ensures that when you change the edge of an object, other objects sharing that edge will change accordingly. *Routing* is commonly used with PostGIS via a long-supported add-on called pgRouting. Routing not only cares about connectedness but also how costly that connectedness is. pgRouting is mostly used for building trip navigation applications (taking into account the cost of tolls or delays due to construction), but it can be used for any application where costs along a path are important. We'll cover pgRouting in later chapters of this book.

All these four types can coexist in the same database and even as separate columns in the same table. For example, you can have a geometry that defines the boundaries of a plant, and you can have a raster that defines the concentration of toxic waste along each part of the boundary.

1.4.1 Geometry type

In two dimensions, you can represent all geographical entities with three building blocks: points, linestrings, and polygons (see figure 1.3). For example, an interstate highway crossing the salt flats of Utah clearly jumps out as linestrings cutting through a polygon. A desolate gas station located somewhere along the interstate can be a point.

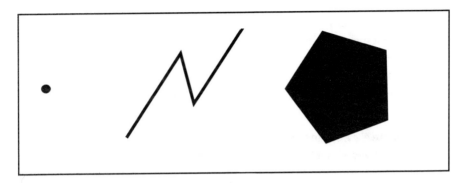

Figure 1.3 Basic geometries: a point, a linestring, and a polygon

But you need not limit yourself to the macro dimensions of road atlases. Look around your home. Use rectangular polygons to represent rooms. The wiring and the piping running behind the walls would be linestrings. You can use either a point or a polygon to stand in for the dog house, depending on its size. Just by abstracting the landscape to 2D points, linestrings, and polygons, you have enough to model everything that could crop up on a map or a blueprint.

Don't be overly concerned with the rigorous definition of the geometries. Questions such as "how many angels will fit into a point," and "what is the width of a linestring" are best left for mathematicians and philosophers. To us, points, linestrings, and polygons are simplified models of reality. As such, they'll never perfectly mimic the real thing. Also, don't worry if you feel that we're leaving out other geometries. Two good examples are beltways around a metropolis and hippodromes. The former could be well represented by circles, the latter by ellipses. You'll do fine by approximating them using linestrings with many segments and polygons with many edges.

The geometry type treats the world as a flat Cartesian grid. The mathematics behind the model requires nothing more than the analytic geometry you learned in high school. The geometry model is intuitively appealing and computationally speedy, but it suffers from one major shortcoming—the flat earth.

1.4.2   Geography type

The curvature of the earth comes into play when you're modeling anything that extends beyond the visual horizon. Although geometry works for architectural floor plans, city blocks, and runway diagrams, it comes up short when you model shipping lanes, airways, or continents, or whenever you consider two locations that are far apart. You can still perform distance computations without abandoning the Cartesian underpinnings by sprinkling a few sines and cosines into your formulas, but the minute you need to compute areas, the math becomes intractable.

A better solution is to use a family of data types based on geodetic coordinates— geography. Geography shields the complexity of the math from the PostGIS user. As a trade-off, geography offers fewer functions, and it trails geometry in speed. You'll find the same point, linestring, and polygon data types in geography; just keep in mind that the linestrings and polygons conform to the curves of a globe.

Are geometry and geography standard or not?

The geometry type is a long-accepted OGC SQL/MM type that you'll find in other relational databases. Geography, on the other hand, isn't a standard type and is only found in a few spatial databases. PostGIS, SQL Server, and Google BigQuery are the only ones we know of that have it. You'll find newer MySQL and Oracle versions repurpose their geometry type and switch to a round earth model if the coordinates of the geometry are in degrees.

The PostGIS geography type is loosely patterned after the SQL Server geography type. For general use cases, you can think of the SQL Server geography type and PostGIS geography type as the same kind of animal.

1.4.3   Raster type

Geometry and geography are vector-based data types. Loosely speaking, anything you can sketch with an ultra-fine pen without running short on ink lends itself to vector representation. Vectors are well suited to modeling designed or constructed features, but suppose you snap a colored photo of the coral-rich Coral Sea. With its motley colors and fractal patterns, you're going to have a hard time constructing lines and polygons out of the photo. Your best hope is to quantize the photo into microscopic rectangles and assign a color value to each. *Raster data* is exactly this—a mosaic of pixels.

Perhaps the best example of a raster is the television you stare into every day, for hours on end. A TV screen is nothing more than a giant raster with some two million pixels. Each pixel stores three different color values: the intensity of red, green, and blue (hence the term RGB). In raster-speak, each color is called a *band*. The pixel represents some area of geographic space, which can vary based on the dimensions of the film you are watching and the number of pixels on your TV set.

If you're buying a TV, the physical number of pixels will matter greatly to you: the larger the number of pixels, the bigger the viewing area and the more money it'll cost you. A pixel *represents* a certain unit of area in reality, and raster data is stored in those pixels.

Raster data almost always originates from instrumental data collection and often serves as the raw material for generating vector data. As such, you'll encounter a lot more sources of raster data than vector data. PostGIS will let you overlay vector data atop raster data and vice versa. The satellite view you often see in maps is a perfect example of such an overlay. You see roads (vector data) superimposed on top of the satellite imagery (raster).

Rasters appear in the following applications:

- Land coverage or land use.
- Temperature and elevation variations. This is a single-band raster where each square holds a measured temperature or elevation value.
- Color aerial and satellite photos. These have four bands—one for each of the colors of the RGB, and A for alpha intensity color space.

1.4.4 Topology type

When you gaze down at the terrain from your private jet, what you witness is not distinct geometries on a barren terrestrial plane, but an interwoven network of points, linestrings, and polygons. A cornfield abuts a wheat field, which abuts a pasture, which abuts a large expanse of prairie. Roads, rivers, fences, or other artificial boundaries divide them all. The surface of the earth (at least the parts that host humanity) resembles a completed jigsaw puzzle. Topology models take on this jigsaw perspective of the world. Topology recognizes the inherent interconnection of geographic features and exploits it to help you better manage data.

Consider a historical example where you want to model the United States and Mexico as two large polygons. Prior to the Gadsden Purchase, the northern boundary of Mexico extended well into present day Arizona and parts of New Mexico. For 33 cents per acre, the US "purchased" 30 million acres from Mexico. The US polygon grew as the Mexico polygon shrank. If you were using the geometry family to model the two polygons, you'd have to perform two operations to get your record-keeping straight: enlarge the US and shrink Mexico. Using the topology model, you only need to perform one operation—either the enlargement or the shrinkage—because topology tracks the fact that the US abuts Mexico. If the US grows on its southern border, Mexico must shrink on its northern border. One operation implies the other.

Topology isn't concerned with the exact shape and location of geographic features, but with how they're connected to each other.

Topology is useful in the following applications:

- Parcel (land lot) data, where you want to ensure that the change of one parcel boundary adjusts all other parcels that share that boundary change as well.
- Road management, water boundaries, and jurisdiction divisions. U.S. Census MAF/Topologically Integrated Geographic Encoding and Referencing system

(TIGER) data is a perfect example (www.census.gov/geographies/mapping-files/time-series/geo/tiger-line-file.html).

- Architecture.

1.5   *Hello real world*

In this section, we'll walk you through a full example from start to finish. Unfortunately, PostGIS is not a programming language where a few lines of code will print a "Hello World" message on your screen. Instead, to provide you with a true taste of PostGIS, we're going to guide you through the following steps:

1 Digesting a problem and formulating a solution
2 Modeling
3 Gathering and loading data
4 Writing a query
5 Viewing the result

If you're completely new to PostGIS, just perform the tasks we ask of you for now. You won't understand most of what you're typing, but you'll have the rest of this book for that. Right now, we want to give you an overview of the steps involved in writing a spatial query.

Before going further, you'll need to have working copies of PostGIS and Postgre-SQL, as well as ancillary tools such as pgAdmin to compose and execute your queries. Information about acquiring and installing these can be found in appendix B. As always, if you're starting from scratch, we recommend you install the latest versions.

1.5.1   *Digesting the problem*

Here's the scenario you're faced with: you need to find the number of fast-food restaurants within one mile of a highway. As for why someone might want to do this, any of the following reasons could apply:

- A fast-food chain is trying to locate a new store where supply falls short.
- A highway commissioner wants to satisfy the needs of motorists, who will be paying tolls.
- A health-conscious parent is trying to cut down the availability of fast food in the neighborhood.
- Hungry travelers are looking for their next meal.

First, you need to realize that you're not going to be able to answer this question quickly or accurately with your usual arsenal of Google Maps, Bing, or MapQuest, or even with the latest paper map you picked up from the auto association. Learning PostGIS may not be any quicker, but you'll have at your disposal the tools and skills to solve any and all problems of this kind in the future. Replace the highway with a lake, and you can determine how many homes surrounding the lake can be considered waterfront property. On a geodetic scale, replace the highway with the continent of Australia, and you can determine the number of islands within territorial waters. From there, you can even go on to a planetary scale and ask how many moons are within 10 million kilometers at perigee.

Once you have an initial understanding of the problem, we recommend that you immediately perform a feasibility study, even if it's just in your mind. You don't want to devote time toward a solution if the problem itself is impossible to solve, lacking specificity, or, worse, you have no available data source.

Before going further, you need the postgis_in_action database you set up in section 1.3.

1.5.2 Modeling

You need to translate the real world to a model that is composed of database objects. For this example, you'll represent the highway as a geometric linestring and the locations of fast-food restaurants as points. You'll then create two tables: highways and restaurants.

USING SCHEMAS

First you need to create a schema to hold your data for this chapter. A *schema* is a container, similar to a directory, that you'll find in most high-end databases. It logically segments objects (tables, views, functions, and so on) for easier management:

```
CREATE SCHEMA ch01;
```

In PostgreSQL it's very easy to back up selected schemas and also to set up permissions based on schemas. You could, for example, have a big schema of fairly static data that you exclude from your daily backups, and you could divide schemas along user groups so that you can allow each group to manage their own schema set of data. The postgis_in_action database schemas are chapter-themed so that it's easy to download just the set of data you need for a specific chapter. Refer to appendix D for more details about schemas and security management.

RESTAURANTS TABLE

Next you need to create a lookup table to map franchise codes to meaningful names, as in the following listing. You can then add all the franchises you'll be dealing with.

> **Listing 1.2   Create a franchise lookup table**

```
CREATE TABLE ch01.lu_franchises (id char(3) PRIMARY KEY
  , franchise varchar(30));                          ◁─┐  Create a table.

INSERT INTO ch01.lu_franchises(id, franchise)        ◁─┐  Populate
VALUES                                                  │  the table.
    ('BKG', 'Burger King'), ('CJR', 'Carl''s Jr'),
    ('HDE', 'Hardee'), ('INO', 'In-N-Out'),
    ('JIB', 'Jack in the Box'), ('KFC', 'Kentucky Fried Chicken'),
    ('MCD', 'McDonald'), ('PZH', 'Pizza Hut'),
    ('TCB', 'Taco Bell'), ('WDY', 'Wendys');
```

Finally, you need to create a table to hold the data you'll be loading as follows.

Listing 1.3   Create a restaurants table

```
CREATE TABLE ch01.restaurants                    ❶ Create a
(                                                    primary key.
  id serial primary key,
  franchise char(3) NOT NULL,
  geom geometry(point,2163)                         Create a spatial
);                                                   geometry column.
```

For your later analysis, you'll need to uniquely identify restaurants so that you don't double-count them. Also, certain mapping servers and viewers, such as MapServer and QGIS, balk at tables without integer primary keys or unique indexes. The restaurant data has no primary key, and nothing in the data file lends itself to a good natural primary key, so you create an autonumber primary key ❶.

Next, you need to place a spatial index on your geometry column. This step can be done before or after the data load.

```
CREATE INDEX ix_code_restaurants_geom
  ON ch01.restaurants USING gist(geom);
```

If you are planning to load a lot of data into the table, it is more efficient to create the spatial index and any other indexes after the data load is complete so the indexing of each record doesn't impact the load performance.

As part of the definition of an index in PostgreSQL, you must specify the type of index, as we did in the preceding CREATE INDEX. PostGIS spatial indexes are of the gist, spgist, or brin index types. For most use cases, you'll want to stick with gist. We'll go over when to use each index type later in this book.

Although it's not necessary for this particular data set, because it won't be updated, you'll create a foreign key relationship between the franchise column in the restaurants table and the lookup table. This helps prevent people from mistyping franchises in the restaurants table. Adding CASCADE UPDATE DELETE rules when you add foreign key relationships will allow you to change the franchise ID for your franchises if you want, and to have those changes update the restaurants table automatically:

```
ALTER TABLE ch01.restaurants
  ADD CONSTRAINT fk_restaurants_lu_franchises
  FOREIGN KEY (franchise)
  REFERENCES ch01.lu_franchises (id)
  ON UPDATE CASCADE ON DELETE RESTRICT;
```

By restricting deletes, you prevent inadvertent removal of franchises with extant records in the restaurants table. (One added benefit of foreign keys is that relational designers, such as those you'll find in OpenOffice Base and other ERD tools, will automatically draw lines between the two tables to visually alert you to the relationships.)

You can then create an index to make the join between the two tables more efficient:

```
CREATE INDEX fi_restaurants_franchises
 ON ch01.restaurants (franchise);
```

Next you need to create a highways table to contain the road segments that are highways.

Listing 1.4 Create a highways table

```
CREATE TABLE ch01.highways          ◁─┐  Create the
(                                      └  highways table.
  gid integer NOT NULL,
  feature character varying(80),
  name character varying(120),
  state character varying(2),          ┌  Multilinestring
  geom geometry(multilinestring,2163), ◁─┘  equal area
  CONSTRAINT pk_highways PRIMARY KEY (gid)
);

CREATE INDEX ix_highways             ┌  Add a spatial
 ON ch01.highways USING gist(geom);  ◁─┘  index.
```

In this case, you're creating the spatial index before loading the data, but for large tables that are loaded only once, it's more efficient to create the indexes after you have loaded the data.

1.5.3 Loading data

To give this example some real-world flavor, we'll scope out real data sources.

In this chapter, you first created the data tables and are now chasing after data to populate them. Ideally, these are the steps you'd want to take. In reality, though, you'll sometimes find yourself subservient to the available data and begrudgingly have to alter your ideal table structure to fit what's available.

But don't surrender to the availability of real data too easily. You can often create SQL scripts that will translate the less-than-perfect data from your source into your perfected data structure. Always give primacy to your model. A well-thought-out model can often ride out the vagaries of a data source. We'll follow this mantra as we continue.

IMPORTING A CSV FILE

Fastfoodmaps.com graciously provided us with a comma-delimited file of all fast-food restaurants circa 2005. To import a CSV file, you need to create a table beforehand. After quickly studying the CSV file, you can create a staging table:

```
CREATE TABLE ch01.restaurants_staging (
  franchise text, lat double precision, lon double precision);
```

Use the psql \copy command to import the CSV file into your staging table:

```
\copy ch01.restaurants_staging FROM '/data/restaurants.csv' DELIMITER as ',';
```

NOTE If your file is on the database server and you have superuser postgres access, you have the additional option of using the SQL `COPY` command: `COPY ch01.restaurants_staging FROM '/data/restaurants.csv' DELIMITER as ',';`

Your purpose here is to get the CSV data into a table so you can scrutinize it more carefully and write any additional queries to sanitize the data before you insert it into the production table. In this case, the data passes the quality check, so you can proceed with the insert:

```
INSERT INTO ch01.restaurants (franchise, geom)
SELECT franchise
, ST_Transform(
  ST_SetSRID(ST_Point(lon , lat), 4326)
  , 2163) As geom
FROM ch01.restaurants_staging;
```

Next, you use a point geometry column to store your restaurant locations. The second argument to the geometry function indicates the spatial reference ID (SRID) that you've selected for the restaurant data. The SRID denotes the coordinate range and how the spherical space is projected on a flat surface. In this example we use SRID 4326 (which corresponds to WGS 84 lon/lat), but then transform all the data to our desired planar projection for faster analysis. We'll get into more detail about spatial reference systems in chapter 3.

If you're coming from a GIS background, you'll know that you must have common projections before you can compare two data sets. This example uses EPSG:2163, which is an equal-area projection covering the continental United States.

Spatial reference IDs (SRIDs) and spatial reference systems

You'll often find number identifiers such as `4326` and `2163` in PostGIS and other spatial database code. These refer to records in the spatial_ref_sys table, where `srid` is the column that uniquely identifies the record. The ID 4326 is the most popular and refers to a spatial reference system that often goes by the name WGS 84 lon/lat. We'll go into spatial reference systems in more detail in chapter 3.

IMPORTING FROM AN ESRI SHAPEFILE

You'll find Esri shapefiles to be a common storage format for spatial data, mostly due Esri's early predominance in GIS. To load data from shapefiles into a PostGIS database, use the shp2pgsql command-line utility that comes with all PostGIS installations. If you're on Windows or Linux/Unix with a graphical desktop, you can also use the DbManager tool within a desktop tool called QGIS, which we'll cover later in this book. Both shp2pgsql and QGIS can load DBF files in addition to the Esri shapefile format.

We know our projection to be NAD 83 lon/lat, so we indicate this by changing the SRID to 4269, but be careful here! You're simply telling the importer what the SRID is for the data coming in. You're not transforming it! In this example, we also changed the name of the imported table to highways_staging. Click the Import button once you're ready.

Once the import finishes, you should see the new highways_staging table in your database. You may have to refresh the browse tree in pgAdmin. Both shp2pgsql-gui and its command-line sibling automatically add a column named geom during the import and set its data type by reading information contained in the shapefile. If you're unfamiliar with the raw data, this is the time to study it. Perform general sanity checks, such as checking the total record count, inspecting columns that came in without data, and so on.

To load the highway data into a staging table using the shp2pgsql command-line, you would do the following:

```
shp2pgsql -D -s 4269 -g geom -I /data/roadtrl020.shp ch01.highways_staging
| psql -h localhost -U postgres -p 5432 -d postgis_in_action
```

After you're satisfied that the importer did its job without dropping any information, you can write an INSERT query to move the data from your staging table to the production table. In the query, you want to transform the SRID from 4269 to 2163 and only select columns that you defined in your production table. You can also filter the data to only the needed rows. The highway data has approximately 47,000 rows and includes every major and state highway in the U.S., and you're only going to be looking at major highways, so you can add a filter that will bring the row count down to about 14,000.

Listing 1.5 Populating the highways table

```
INSERT INTO ch01.highways (gid, feature, name, state, geom)
SELECT gid, feature, name, state, ST_Transform(geom, 2163)
FROM ch01.highways_staging
WHERE feature LIKE 'Principal Highway%';
```

The shp2pgsql command line lets you transform the SRID with an additional :<to_srid>, so you could skip the ST_Transform step in your code by replacing the 4269 with -s 4269:2163 as follows:

```
shp2pgsql -s 4269:2163 -g geom
➥ -I /data/roadtrl020.shp ch01.highways_staging
➥ | psql -h localhost -U postgres -p 5432 -d postgis_in_action
```

After you've finished loading the data, it's good to follow up with a vacuum analyze so the statistics are up to date:

```
vacuum analyze ch01.highways;
```

shp2pgsql transform improved in PostGIS 3.0
Prior to PostGIS 3.0, the shp2pgsql transform process was much slower. If you are running PostGIS 3.0 or later and have a large table, the speed is faster when loading as is and then transforming in the database. The shp2pgsql transform logic was improved in PostGIS 3.0 so you can now use the -D (faster dump format) switch. Prior versions did not support -D with constructs such as -s 4269:2163.

1.5.4   Writing the query

It's now time to write the query. Remember the question we set out to answer: "How many fast-food restaurants are within one mile of a highway?" The query that will answer this question is shown in the following listing.

Listing 1.6   Restaurants within one mile of a highway

```
SELECT f.franchise
  , COUNT(DISTINCT r.id) As total          ◄── Remove
FROM ch01.restaurants As r                     duplicates.
  INNER JOIN ch01.lu_franchises As f ON r.franchise = f.id
    INNER JOIN ch01.highways As h
      ON ST_DWithin(r.geom, h.geom, 1609)   ◄── Spatial
GROUP BY f.franchise                            join
ORDER BY total DESC;
```

The crux of this example is where you join the restaurants table with the highways table using the ST_DWithin function. This commonly used function accepts two geometries and returns TRUE if the minimum distance between the two geometries is within the specified distance. In this case, you pass in a point for the restaurant, a multi-linestring for the highway, and 1609 meters as the distance. All restaurant-highway pairs matching the join condition will filter through.

The join condition does allow for duplicate restaurants. For example, a McDonald's located at the intersection of two major highways would show up twice. To only count each restaurant once, you use the COUNT(DISTINCT) construct.

The rest of the code is elementary SQL. If you're a little rusty on SQL, please see appendix C for a refresher. As fair warning, the SQL we use in this book will get harder.

Finally, here's the fruit of your labor:

```
franchise_name         | total
-----------------------+------
  McDonald's           | 5343
  Burger King          | 3049
  Pizza Hut            | 2920
  Wendy's              | 2446
  Taco Bell            | 2428
  Kentucky Fried Chicken | 2371
  :
```

1.5.5 *Viewing spatial data with OpenJump*

What's more gratifying than to see your query output displayed on a map? You don't want to display some 20,000 dots on a map of the US—you can find that on each chain's restaurant locator. Instead, you're going to draw a buffer zone around highway segments and see how many dots fall within them.

For this you'll use the ST_Buffer function. This function will take any geometry and radially expand it by a specified number of units. The post-expansion polygonal geometry is called a *buffer zone* or *corridor*.

> **NOTE** If you haven't installed OpenJump, do so now before continuing. Chapter 5 discusses the installation and use of OpenJump, among other tools.

For this example, we'll locate Hardee's restaurants within a 20-mile buffer of US Route 1 in the state of Maryland. Here's the query to get the count:

```
SELECT COUNT(DISTINCT r.id) As total
FROM ch01.restaurants As r
     INNER JOIN ch01.highways As h
     ON ST_DWithin(r.geom, h.geom, 1609*20)
WHERE r.franchise = 'HDE'
 AND h.name  = 'US Route 1' AND h.state = 'MD';
```

Let's see where the three Hardee's restaurants are located. Fire up OpenJump and connect to your PostgreSQL database. You can first draw US Route 1 using the following query:

```
SELECT gid, name, geom
FROM ch01.highways
WHERE name = 'US Route 1' AND state = 'MD';
```

Next, overlay the 20-mile corridor:

```
SELECT ST_Union(ST_Buffer(geom, 1609*20))
FROM ch01.highways
WHERE name = 'US Route 1' AND state = 'MD';
```

Finally, position the Hardee's restaurants in the buffer zone routes.

```
SELECT r.geom
FROM ch01.restaurants r
WHERE EXISTS
 (SELECT gid FROM ch01.highways
  WHERE ST_DWithin(r.geom, geom, 1609*20) AND
  name = 'US Route 1'
   AND state = 'MD' AND r.franchise = 'HDE');
```

The results are shown in figure 1.4.

Play around with this example. Use your home state and your favorite chain to see how far you have to go to grab your next nutritious meal.

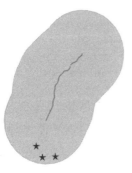

Figure 1.4   US Route 1 in Maryland, with three Hardee's restaurants in the 20-mile buffer, and the 20-mile buffer around the route

Some of the SQL examples we demonstrated were at an intermediate level. If you're new to SQL or spatial databases, these examples may have seemed daunting. In the chapters that follow, we'll explain the functions we used here and the SQL constructs in greater detail. For now, we hope that you focused on the general steps we followed and the strategies that we chose.

Although spatial modeling is an integral part of any spatial analysis, there's no right or wrong answer in modeling. Modeling is inherently a balance between simplicity and adequacy. You want to make your model as simple as possible so you can focus on the problem you're trying to solve, but you must retain enough complexity to simulate the world you're trying to model. Therein lies the challenge.

Summary

- PostGIS spatially enables PostgreSQL, allowing you to model real-world objects in a database and answer questions of where and how far.
- PostGIS and PostgreSQL provide tools to load data from common data sources.
- There are freely available tools such as OpenJump, QGIS, and pgAdmin that allow you to experience your spatial data visually.
- PostGIS adds functions that can be used in SQL to answer questions about where and how far quickly and succinctly.
- Sometimes a table of statistics is more digestible than a figure of dots, colors, and shapes.

Spatial data types 2

This chapter covers

- `geometry`, `geography`, and `raster` spatial types and subtypes
- `geometry` and `geography` type modifiers
- Spatial catalog tables
- How to create spatial columns and populate them

In the first chapter we teased you with the potential that you can unlock with Post-GIS. This chapter will start to show you how by delving deeper into the core spatial data types bundled with PostGIS. We'll discuss each spatial type in detail. Once you've completed this chapter, you should know how to create table columns of these various types and how to populate them with spatial data.

Do keep in the back of your mind that PostgreSQL has its own built-in geometric types. These are `point`, `polygon`, `lseg`, `box`, `circle`, and `path`. PostgreSQL geometry types have almost no functional support, are not adapted for GIS work, and are incompatible with the PostGIS `geometry` type. These geometry types have existed since the dawn of PostgreSQL and don't follow the SQL/MM standards, nor do they support spatial coordinate systems. We advise staying away from them for GIS.

If you've already started using them, PostGIS rescues you with functions and casts to convert the PostgreSQL types to PostGIS geometry. For example, the following code converts a PostgreSQL polygon, path, box, and circle to an equivalent PostGIS geometry. PostGIS doesn't have conversions for all PostgreSQL geometry types. As a work-around, we cast box and circle to PostgreSQL polygons before casting to PostGIS geometry:

```
SELECT polygon('((10,20),(25,30),(30, 30),(10,20))')::geometry
UNION ALL
SELECT path('(1,21),  (5,15),  (9,20),  (12,5)')::geometry
UNION ALL
SELECT box('(10, 21)'::point, '(16,10)'::point)::polygon::geometry
UNION ALL
SELECT circle('(20,10)'::point, 3)::polygon::geometry;
```

Even if you choose to remain with PostgreSQL geometry types, casting to PostGIS geometry will let you take advantage of visualization tools for PostGIS, such as the pgAdmin4 PostGIS viewer. Run the preceding code in pgAdmin4. An eye icon will appear in the header of the geometry column. Click on the eye and you'll see your geometries rendered as in figure 2.1.

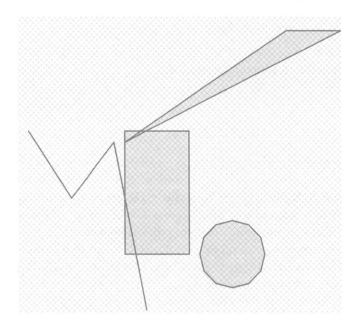

Figure 2.1   PostgreSQL native geometric types cast to geometry, shown in pgAdmin4

NOTE   geometry, geography, and raster columns are often referred to as *layers* or *feature classes* when displayed in mapping applications.

Before we begin, you'll need to create a schema to house the data for this chapter:

```
CREATE SCHEMA ch02;
```

The data and code used in this chapter can be found at www.postgis.us/chapter_02_edition_3.

The most basic statement to create a spatial table with a `geometry` column is as follows:

```
CREATE TABLE ch02.my_geometries(id serial PRIMARY KEY,name text, geom geometry);
```

Such a table would welcome any kind of `geometry` in the `geom` column.

2.1 *Type modifiers*

Before we get into data types themselves, we must explain the role of type modifiers (sometimes known simply as *typmods*). You have been using type modifiers all the time in PostgreSQL, perhaps without knowing. When you declare a column as `character(8)`, the number 8 is a type modifier of the type `character`, specifically, the length modifier. When you write `numeric(8,2)`, you're declaring the data type to be `numeric`, the length (precision) type modifier to be 8, and the scale type modifier to be 2.

Generally, you specify type modifiers when you declare the data type of a column. Alternatively, you can use check constraints to achieve the same effect as type modifiers after column creation. For example, you can declare a column as `character` and then add a check constraint that limits the length to be 8. You can add constraints to any attributes of a column, but keep in mind that not all constraints are type modifiers—only the most frequently used attributes are promoted to be type modifiers. In the `character` example, the length qualifies as a type modifier, but a lesser attribute, such as the number of vowels in the `char`, does not.

2.1.1 *Subtype type modifiers*

In PostGIS, `geometry` and `geography` data types have subtype type modifiers. Although `geometry` and `geography` are types in their own right, you should avoid declaring columns as these parental types without subtype modifiers. Examples of `geometry` subtypes are `POINTZ`, `POINT`, `LINESTRING`, `LINESTRINGM`, `POLYGON`, `POLYGONZ`, `POLYHEDRAL-SURFACE`, `POLYHEDRALSURFACEZ`, `TIN`, and `TINZ`. A typical type declaration in PostGIS is `geometry(POINT,4326)`, where `geometry` is the data type, `POINT` is the subtype type modifier, and `4326` is the SRID type modifier. To make the subtype stand out from other type modifiers, we often capitalize subtypes, even though PostgreSQL is case-insensitive for types and type modifiers.

You may also use `GEOMETRY`, `GEOMETRYZ`, `GEOMETRYZM` as type modifiers. These type modifiers constrain the `coordinate dimension` of a geometry.

If you declare a column as `geometry(GEOMETRY)`, the geometry column is constrained to allow only two-dimensional geometries.

Only `geometry` and `geography` data types support type modifiers. The PostGIS `raster` data type doesn't, nor does the `topogeometry` data type.

NOTE We use the term *typmod* both as an abbreviation for *type modifier* and also to refer to the practice of adding type modifiers in parentheses during column creation.

2.1.2 *Spatial reference identifier*

All PostGIS spatial data types have a spatial reference identifier (SRID). We'll cover SRIDs and spatial reference systems in chapter 3. For now, know that two PostGIS data types must share a common SRID if you wish to "overlay" the pair. Use the PostGIS function `ST_Transform()` to transform data types from one SRID to another. If the SRID is unspecified, but known, you can set the SRID using `ST_SetSRID()`.

PostGIS relies on the spatial_ref_sys table to figure out if an SRID is valid and how to perform the reprojection to transform between SRIDs. The spatial_ref_sys table is the only table created and populated during the installation of PostGIS. Most SRIDs that you'll ever need are already included in spatial_ref_sys. You can add missing SRIDS to the table; you'll need to be sure to include reprojection information.

You can leave the SRID as unknown—an unknown SRID takes the value of 0 for `geometry`, `raster`, and `topogeometry` types. The SRID for `geography` is never unknown; if not specified, `geography` is assumed to be 4326 (WGS 84 lon/lat). An unknown SRID still means that the data resides in Cartesian coordinate space, even though it has no geographical placement meaning. For example, if you're trying to plan out your dream home on a blueprint, the SRID is unimportant but the geometries representing walls are still necessary, and placing them on a coordinate system won't hurt. Go one step further and mentally assign a unit of measure. (One unit equals one foot, for instance.) The architect will be grateful that you handed over more than a sketch from your imagination. Until you buy the land for your dream home, SRID doesn't come into play.

2.2 *Geometry*

At the dawn of PostGIS, `geometry` was the only data type available. The `geometry` data type was so named because its basis is analytical geometry. All `geometry` subtypes assume a Cartesian coordinate system: parallel lines never meet, the Pythagorean theorem applies, the distances between coordinates are uniform throughout, and so on.

Often you'll find people using latitude and longitude to specify a point geometry, but don't let this mislead you into thinking that they've abandoned the Cartesian plane. The use of lon/lat coordinates in `geometry` means that the area under consideration is small enough that you can consider degrees of longitude and latitude as uniform, and that the curvature of the earth doesn't come into play. When dealing with distances on a global scale, however, the `geometry` data type is grossly inadequate, leading to the advent of the `geography` data type.

2.2.1 Points

Subtypes of points differentiate themselves by the dimension of the Cartesian space (X,Y,Z) they occupy. In addition, they can have a measured (M) coordinate value, which can represent any kind of measure you want. We'll discuss this later.

Here's a complete listing of POINT subtype modifiers for geometry and geography:

- POINT—A point in 2D space specified by its X and Y coordinates
- POINTZ—A point in 3D space specified by its X, Y, and Z coordinates
- POINTM—A point in 2D space with a measured value specified by its spatial X and Y coordinates plus an M value
- POINTZM—A point in 3D space with a measured value specified by its X, Y, and Z coordinates plus an M value

The code in the following listing creates a table with one column for each of the point subtypes and appends one record.

> **Listing 2.1 Points**

```
CREATE TABLE ch02.my_points (
    id serial PRIMARY KEY,
    p geometry(POINT),
    pz geometry(POINTZ),
    pm geometry(POINTM),
    pzm geometry(POINTZM),
    p_srid geometry(POINT,4269)
);
INSERT INTO ch02.my_points (p, pz, pm, pzm, p_srid)
VALUES (
    ST_GeomFromText('POINT(1 -1)'),
    ST_GeomFromText('POINT Z(1 -1 1)'),
    ST_GeomFromText('POINT M(1 -1 1)'),
    ST_GeomFromText('POINT ZM(1 -1 1 1)'),
    ST_GeomFromText('POINT(1 -1)',4269)
);
```

In the preceding listing, we didn't specify the SRID of any point except for the last one. When unspecified, SRIDs take on the value of 0. SRID 4269 is North America Datum 1983 Lon/Lat (NAD 83).

> **POINTZ versus POINT Z**
>
> In listing 2.1, the ST_GeomFromText function used the SQL/MM format ST_Geom-FromText('POINT Z(1 -1 1)'). PostGIS will also allow ST_GeomFromText ('POINTZ (1 -1 1)') or even ST_GeomFromText ('POINT(1 -1 1)'). However, for cross-compatibility with other spatial relational databases, you should keep with the more conventional form of ST_GeomFromText ('POINT Z(1 -1 1)'), which includes the space. The same goes for POINT ZM, LINESTRING ZM, and so on.

> **(continued)**
> When defining columns, you should omit the spaces. For instance, `geometry (PointZM)` is equivalent to `geometry(POINTZM)`, but `geometry(POINT ZM)` won't work. Casing is not enforced, but for consistency we like to use fully uppercase subtypes.

2.2.2 *Linestrings*

Connected straight lines between two or more distinct points form *linestrings*. Individual lines between points are called *segments*. Segments aren't data types or subtypes in PostGIS, but it is possible for a linestring to have just one segment.

Although a linestring is defined using a finite set of points, in reality it's composed of an infinite number of points, and each line segment defines a straight line. This distinction becomes clear when you need to determine something like the closest point on a linestring to a polygon or other geometric form. The closest point rarely coincides with any point used to define the linestring but is somewhere between two of the points.

Like points, linestrings have four dimensional variants:

- `LINESTRING`—A linestring in 2D specified by two or more distinct `POINT`s
- `LINESTRINGZ`—A linestring in 3D space specified by two or more distinct `POINTZ`s
- `LINESTRINGM`—A linestring in 2D space with measure values specified by two or more distinct `POINTM`s
- `LINESTRINGZM`—A linestring in 3D space with measure values specified by two or more distinct `POINTZM`s

The following listing adds some 2D linestrings.

Listing 2.2 Add linestrings

```
CREATE TABLE ch02.my_linestrings (
    id serial PRIMARY KEY,
    name varchar(20),
    my_linestrings geometry(LINESTRING)        ❶ Create
);                                                a table.

INSERT INTO ch02.my_linestrings (name, my_linestrings)     ❷ Insert
VALUES                                                        an open
    ('Open', ST_GeomFromText('LINESTRING(0 0, 1 1, 1 -1)')),   linestring.
    ('Closed', ST_GeomFromText('LINESTRING(0 0, 1 1, 1 -1, 0 0)'))
;        Insert a closed
         ❸ linestring.
```

In this listing, you create a new table to hold 2D linestrings of an unknown spatial reference system ❶ and formulate a set of values to insert into the table. The first `VALUES` entry adds a linestring starting at the origin, going to (1,1) and terminating at (1,–1) ❷. This is an example of an open linestring. The second VALUES entry adds a closed linestring ❸.

Figure 2.2 illustrates the linestrings created in listing 2.2.

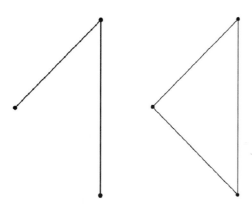

Figure 2.2 Open and closed linestrings created using the code in listing 2.2. The points that make up the lines are shown as well.

Listing 2.2 introduces the concept of open and closed linestrings. In open linestrings, the starting and ending points aren't the same, whereas in closed linestrings, they are the same, forming a loop. In modeling real-world geographic features, open line-strings predominate over closed linestrings. Rivers, trails, fault lines, and roads do not start where they end. However, as you'll soon see, closed linestrings play an indispens-able part in constructing polygons.

The concept of simple and non-simple geometries also comes into play when describing linestrings. A simple linestring can't have self-intersections (can't cross itself) except at the start and end points. All points in the linestring being unique enforces this restriction. Conversely, a linestring with self-intersection is non-simple.

PostGIS provides a geometry function, ST_IsSimple, to test for simpleness. The following query returns false:

```
SELECT ST_IsSimple(ST_GeomFromText('LINESTRING(2 0,0 0,1 1,1 -1)'));
```

Figure 2.3 displays the non-simple linestring.

2.2.3 *Polygons*

Closed linestrings are the building blocks of polygons. Let's start by creating a triangle. Any closed linestring with three distinct, noncollinear points will build a triangle. By definition, a polygon contains all the enclosed area and its boundary—the linestring that forms the perimeter. The closed linestring outlining the boundary of the polygon is called the *ring of the polygon* when used in this context; more specifically, it's the *exterior ring*.

Figure 2.3 A non-simple linestring

The following listing demonstrates forming a solid polygon whose boundary is the closed linestring from listing 2.2.

Listing 2.3 Triangular polygon with no holes

```
ALTER TABLE ch02.my_geometries ADD COLUMN my_polygons geometry(POLYGON);
INSERT INTO ch02.my_geometries (name, my_polygons)
VALUES (
    'Triangle',
    ST_GeomFromText('POLYGON((0 0, 1 1, 1 -1, 0 0))')
);
```

Figure 2.4 illustrates the solid triangular polygon formed with listing 2.3.

A single ring surrounds most polygons used in geographical modeling, but polygons can have multiple rings, carving out holes. To be precise, a polygon must have exactly one exterior ring and can have one or more inner rings. Each interior ring creates a hole in the overall polygon. You can see such a hole generated in listing 2.4. This is why you need the seemingly redundant set of parentheses in the text representations of polygons. The well-known text representation (WKT) of a polygon is a set of closed linestrings. The first one designates the exterior ring, and all subsequent ones designate inner rings. Always include the extra set of parentheses in the WKT, even if your polygon has just a single ring. Some tools may tolerate single-ringed polygons with only one pair of parentheses, but not PostGIS.

Figure 2.4
Triangular polygon

Listing 2.4 Polygon with two holes

```
INSERT INTO ch02.my_geometries (name,my_polygons)
VALUES (
    'Square with two holes',
    ST_GeomFromText(
        'POLYGON(
            (-0.25 -1.25,-0.25 1.25,2.5 1.25,2.5 -1.25,-0.25 -1.25),
            (2.25 0,1.25 1,1.25 -1,2.25 0),(1 -1,1 1,0 0,1 -1)
        )'
    )
);
SELECT my_polygons
FROM ch02.my_geometries
WHERE name = 'Square with two holes';
```

The output of listing 2.4 is shown in figure 2.5.

In the real world, multi-ringed polygons play an important part in excluding bodies of water within geographical boundaries. For example, if you were planning a surface transit system

Figure 2.5 Polygon with interior rings (holes)

in the greater Seattle area, you could start by outlining a big polygon bounded by Interstate 5 on the west and Interstate 405 on the east, as shown in figure 2.6. You could then start to place terminals of popular bus lines and let a routing program, such as pgRouting, choose the shortest path within the polygon. Soon enough, you'd realize that most of those popular routes are over water—Lake Washington to be specific. To have the program avoid drownings, your polygon of greater Seattle needs an inner ring outlining the shape of Lake Washington. This way, if you run a query seeking the shortest path between two points on the polygon and completely within the polygon, you won't end up with underwater buses.

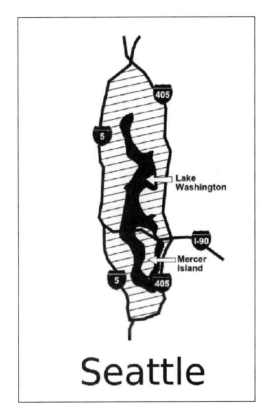

Figure 2.6 The Seattle area modeled as a polygon with two rings. (Lake Washington fills up the hole.)

NOTE Our model of Seattle is a polygon with a hole (ring) with Lake Washington filling up the hole. If we were to also consider the existence of Mercer Island in Lake Washington, pictured as part of Seattle, then this would be called a *multipolygon*. We'll cover multipolygons in the next section.

Polygons have the concept of *validity*. The rings of a valid polygon may only intersect at distinct points—rings can't overlap, and they can't share a common boundary. A polygon whose inner rings partly lie outside its exterior ring is also invalid.

Figure 2.7 shows an example of a single polygon with self-intersections. Visually, you can't discern that it's an invalid `geometry` because such a visual can also be created with two valid polygons or with one valid multipolygon that happens to be touching at a point. We'll cover multipolygons in the next section.

Figure 2.7   A self-intersecting polygon. This is an invalid polygon, but just by looking, it's impossible to see that it's not one valid multipolygon or two valid polygons.

Not every invalid polygon lends itself to a pictorial representation. Degenerate polygons, such as polygons that don't have enough points and polygons with non-closed rings, are difficult to illustrate. Fortunately these polygons are difficult to generate in PostGIS and don't serve any purpose in real-world modeling. Unless you're mathematically minded, stick to your common sense when it comes to thinking about validity. The construction of a polygon representative of real-world features should not be mindboggling!

PostGIS does have functions for dealing with invalid geometries. You can use the `ST_IsValid` function, which returns `true` or `false` if a geometry is valid (https://postgis .net/docs/ST_IsValid.html). `ST_IsValidReason` gives a detailed description of what makes a geometry invalid, and says `Valid Geometry` if valid (https://postgis.net/docs/ ST_IsValidReason.html). For geometries with many kinds of invalidity, you can use `ST_IsValidDetail`, which details why your geometry is invalid and itemizes each kind of invalidity on separate rows (https://postgis.net/docs/ST_IsValidDetail.html). It will return `true` with no extra details if the geometry is valid. Finally the `ST_MakeValid` function can be used to convert an invalid geometry to a valid one (https://post-gis.net/docs/ST_MakeValid.html). In doing so, it may change the type of the geometry such as from a polygon to a multipolygon or geometry collection. It strives to keep as many points from the original geometry as possible. In the case of our bow tie in figure 2.7, `ST_MakeValid` would turn that into a valid multipolygon.

2.2.4   *Collection geometries*

To demonstrate the concept of collection geometries, try mentally picturing the 50 states of the United States as polygons. Interior rings allow you to handle states with large bodies of water within their boundaries, such as Utah (the Great Salt Lake), Florida (Lake Okeechobee), and Minnesota with its 10,000-plus lakes. There's at least one state that you'll have trouble handling: Hawaii. Hawaii has at least five big pieces. You could conceivably model Hawaii as five separate polygons, but this would complicate your storage. For example, if you wanted to create a table of states, you'd expect to have 50 rows. Breaking states into different polygons would call for storing a state using a state-polygon table, where each state could have up to hundreds of geometries depending on how fragmented the state is. You'd lose the simplicity associated with one geometry per state.

To overcome this problem, PostGIS and the OGC standard offer collections of geometries as data types in their own right. A collection of geometries groups distinct geometries that logically belong together. With the use of collections, each of the fifty states becomes a collection of polygons—a multipolygon.

US states as multipolygons

To give you a taste of real-world GIS, consider the state polygon data set you can download from the US Census Bureau's TIGER (Topologically Integrated Geographic Encoding and Referencing) data set: https://www2.census.gov/geo/tiger/TIGER2018/ STATE. In this data set, only the following states are modeled as multipolygons: Alaska, California, Hawaii, Florida, Kentucky, New York, and Rhode Island.

In reality, more states are multipolygons based on `geography` alone. Almost all states border large bodies of water and have detached islands. Because the census is more concerned with people living in the states rather than their physical outlines, it uses the political boundaries for its table of states. Political boundaries extend to adjacent bodies of water and stretch for a few miles into oceans. These encompassing boundaries eliminate most states as multipolygons.

In PostGIS, all single `geometry` subtypes have a collection counterpart: multipoints, multilinestrings, and multipolygons. In addition, PostGIS includes a data type called `geometrycollection`. This data type can contain any kind of `geometry` as long as all geometries in the set have the same spatial reference system and the same coordinate dimensions.

MULTIPOINTS

We'll start with multipoints, which are nothing more than collections of points. Figure 2.8 shows an example of a multipoint.

Let's look at the WKT syntax for multipoints. If you have only X and Y coordinates for a multipoint, each comma-delimited value would have two coordinates. The following example is pictured in figure 2.8:

```
SELECT ST_GeomFromText('MULTIPOINT(-1 1, 0 0, 2 3)');
```

If you have an additional coordinate, such as a coordinate to measure elevation, then you'd have a Z coordinate. If you needed to track another kind of coordinate that is not

Figure 2.8 A single multipoint `geometry` (not three distinct points!)

necessarily spatial in nature, you'd use the M coordinate. The M coordinate is known as the measure coordinate and is often used to measure time or some other kind of measurement like a mile marker position.

For a multipoint, having X, Y, Z, M, you'd have four coordinates:

```
SELECT ST_GeomFromText('MULTIPOINT ZM(-1 1 3 4, 0 0 1 2, 2 3 1 2)');
```

For a regular 3D multipoint composed of X, Y, Z, you'd have the following:

```
SELECT ST_GeomFromText('MULTIPOINT Z(-1 1 3, 0 0 1, 2 3 1)');
```

For a multipoint where each point is composed of X, Y, M, you must write out `MULTI-POINT M` to distinguish it from an X, Y, Z multipoint:

```
SELECT ST_GeomFromText('MULTIPOINT M(-1 1 4, 0 0 2, 2 3 2)');
```

> **NOTE** When we use the term 3D, we're almost always referring to coordinate dimensions, not geometry dimensions. A flag fluttering in the wind is a 2D geometry living in 3D space. The same goes for most hollow chocolate bunnies. If you're rich enough to own a solid chocolate bunny, that bunny would be a 3D geometry living in 3D space.

An alternate and acceptable WKT representation for multipoints uses parentheses to separate each point as follows: `MULTIPOINT ( (-1 1), (0 0), (2 3) )`. PostGIS accepts this multi-parenthetical format as well as the simpler `MULTIPOINT (-1 1, 0 0, 2 3)` format. Output functions, such as `ST_AsText` and `ST_AsEWKT`, return the non-parenthetical format.

MULTILINESTRINGS

Unsurprisingly, a multilinestring is a collection of linestrings. Be mindful of the extra sets of parentheses in the WKT representation of a multilinestring that surround each individual linestring in the set. The following examples of multilinestrings are shown in figure 2.9:

```
SELECT ST_GeomFromText('MULTILINESTRING((0 0,0 1,1 1), (-1 1,-1 -1))');
SELECT ST_GeomFromText('MULTILINESTRING ZM ((0 0 1 1,0 1 1 2,1 1 1 3),
    (-1 1 1 1,-1 -1 1 2))');
SELECT ST_GeomFromText('MULTILINESTRING M((0 0 1,0 1 2,1 1 3), (-1 1 1,-1
    -1 2))');
```

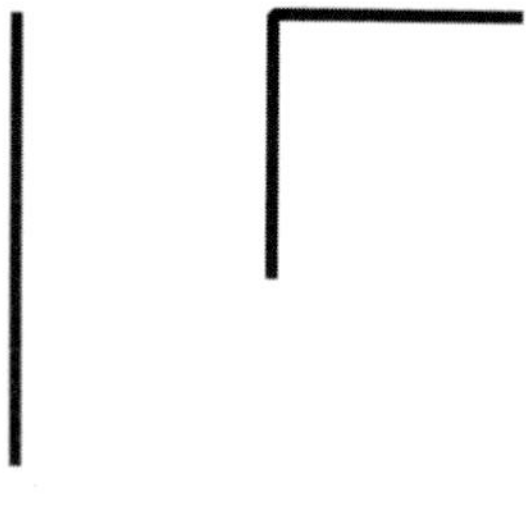

Figure 2.9 Multilinestrings

Note that because the M coordinate can't be visually displayed, the `MULTILINESTRING` and `MULTILINESTRING M` code examples have the same visual representation.

Before moving on to multipolygons, let's return to the concept of simplicity. In section 2.2.2 we tested a linestring for simplicity. Simplicity is relevant for all linestring type geometries. Multilinestrings are considered *simple* if all constituent linestrings are simple and the collective set of linestrings doesn't intersect each other at any point except boundary points. For example, if you create a multiline-string with two intersecting simple linestrings, the resultant multilinestring isn't simple.

MULTIPOLYGONS

The WKT of multipolygons has even more parentheses than its singular counterpart. Because you use parentheses to represent each ring of a polygon, you'll need another set of outer parentheses to represent multipolygons. With multipolygons, we highly recommend that you follow the PostGIS conventions and not omit any inner parentheses for single-ringed polygons.

Following are some examples of multipolygons, the first of which is shown in figure 2.10:

```
SELECT 'MULTIPOLYGON(
    ((2.25 0,1.25 1,1.25 -1,2.25 0)),
    ((1 -1,1 1,0 0,1 -1))
)'::geometry;
SELECT 'MULTIPOLYGON Z(
    ((2.25 0 1,1.25 1 1,1.25 -1 1,2.25 0 1)),
    ((1 -1 2,1 1 2,0 0 2,1 -1 2))
)'::geometry;
SELECT 'MULTIPOLYGON ZM(
    ((2.25 0 1 1,1.25 1 1 2,1.25 -1 1 1,2.25 0 1 1)),
    ((1 -1 2 1,1 1 2 2,0 0 2 3,1 -1 1 4))
)'::geometry;
SELECT 'MULTIPOLYGON M(
    ((2.25 0 1,1.25 1 2,1.25 -1 1,2.25 0 1)),
    ((1 -1 1,1 1 2,0 0 3,1 -1 4))
)'::geometry;
```

Figure 2.10 `MULTIPOLYGON (2.25 0,1.25 1,1.25 -1, 2.25 0,1 -1,1 1,0 0,1 -1)`

NOTE You can use `ST_GeomFromText` or `'somewktwkb'::geometry` to convert well-known text to a `geometry`. Both approaches are more or less equivalent, except `::geometry` is a bit shorter to write and works with other geometry string representations such as well-known binary. Since PostGIS 3.1, ::geometry will also work for converting the geoJSON string format to PostGIS geometry.

Recall from our discussion of single polygons that a polygon is valid if its rings don't intersect or they intersect only at distinct points. For a multipolygon to qualify as valid, it must pass two tests:

- Each constituent polygon must be valid in its own right.
- Constituent polygons can't overlap. Once you lay down a polygon, subsequent polygons can't be laid on top.

GEOMETRYCOLLECTION

The GEOMETRYCOLLECTION is a PostGIS geometry subtype that can contain heterogeneous geometries. Unlike multi-geometries, where the constituent geometries must be of the same subtype, GEOMETRYCOLLECTION can include points, linestrings, polygons, and their collection counterparts. It can even contain other geometry collections. In short, you can stuff every geometry subtype known to PostGIS into a GEOMETRYCOLLECTION.

The following listing presents the WKT for geometry collections, but instead of building the geometries using ST_GeomFromText and the WKT representation, we'll build them by collecting simpler geometries using the ST_Collect function.

> **Listing 2.5 Forming geometry collections by collecting constituent geometries**

```
SELECT ST_AsText(ST_Collect(g))
FROM (
    SELECT ST_GeomFromText('MULTIPOINT(-1 1, 0 0, 2 3)') As g
    UNION ALL
    SELECT ST_GeomFromText(
        'MULTILINESTRING((0 0, 0 1, 1 1), (-1 1, -1 -1))'
    ) As g
    UNION ALL
    SELECT ST_GeomFromText(
        'POLYGON(
            (-0.25 -1.25, -0.25 1.25, 2.5 1.25, 2.5 -1.25, -0.25 -1.25),
            (2.25 0, 1.25 1, 1.25 -1, 2.25 0),
            (1 -1, 1 1, 0 0, 1 -1)
        )'
    ) As g
) x;
```

The output of the preceding listing is as follows:

```
GEOMETRYCOLLECTION(
    MULTIPOINT(-1 1, 0 0, 2 3),
    MULTILINESTRING((0 0, 0 1, 1 1), (-1 1, -1 -1)),
    POLYGON(
        (-0.25 -1.25, -0.25 1.25, 2.5 1.25, 2.5 -1.25, -0.25 -1.25),
        (2.25 0,1.25 1,1.25 -1,2.25 0),
        (1 -1, 1 1, 0 0, 1 -1)
    )
)
```

The visual representation of the `geometrycollection` is shown in figure 2.11.

In real-world applications, you should rarely define a data column as `geometrycollection`. Although having a collection is perfectly reasonable for storage purposes, using it within a function rarely makes any sense. For example, you can ask what the area of a multipolygon is, but you can't ask for the area of a geometrycollection that has linestrings and points in addition to polygons. Geometry collections almost always originate as the result of queries rather than as predefined geometries. You should be prepared to work with them, but avoid using them in your table design.

Figure 2.11 Geometrycollection formed from listing 2.5

Finally, a `geometrycollection` is considered valid if all the geometries in the collection are valid. It's invalid if any of the geometries in the collection are invalid.

2.2.5 *The M coordinate*

The M coordinate is an additional coordinate added for the convenience of recording measured values taken at various points along spatial coordinates. The benefit of using M to store additional information becomes clear as soon as you move beyond points. Suppose that you have a linestring made up of many points, each with its own measure. Without the M coordinate, you'd always need an additional table to store the measurement data.

The M coordinate need not have any spatial interpretation and is therefore impervious to the reference system of the other spatial X, Y, Z coordinates. It can be negative or positive, and its units have no relationship to the units of the other spatial coordinates. The M coordinates of a `geometry` are unchanged when you transform a `geometry` to another spatial reference system. All functions of PostGIS that work with M treat the coordinate as linear, allowing you to interpolate along the M dimension.

The M coordinate is a full-fledged coordinate, and as such we offer the following recommendations:

- Support for M has grown over the years, but it is still fairly limited.
- M is often used to represent time, and as such you'll find functions such as `ST_IsValidTrajectory` that will tell you if M is increasing along the vector or `ST_ClosestPointOfApproach` and `ST_LocateAlong` that identify when two trajectories (with M representing linear time) come closest to each other and at what points this happens.
- Don't use M for sparsely populated data. Once you introduce the M dimension, all your geometries must live in this space. If most of your data points don't have an M value, you'll have to resort to some convention to tag the missing data. A coordinate can't have `null` values.

- You should be consistent in your use of the M value. For instance, if you're using M to measure temperature or ocean depth, keep the units consistent.

- Try to use M for linear measures, as opposed to logarithmic ones, even though you're free to populate the coordinate with any numeric value. All PostGIS functions that take M coordinates into consideration assume that the M dimension is linear, like its spatial counterparts. For instance, if you take a pH measure for a linestring with points spaced far apart, and you try to estimate the pH at the midpoint, PostGIS only has linear interpolation functions, which will be woefully inadequate for your logarithmic measurements. In this case, you're better off storing the pH as an additional attribute of each point or writing your own functions to do the correct interpolation.

- Once you introduce M, avoid using interrogative functions and applying spatial concepts. For instance, you probably can't trust the answer if you ask if a LINE-STRINGM is closed or open. Did the function consider the M coordinate? If so, what is closure for an M coordinate? Spare yourself the headache; don't ask and PostGIS won't tell.

The M coordinate can also exist in a GEOMETRYCOLLECTION. The following listing is a GEOMETRYCOLLECTIONM example similar to listing 2.5 but with an M component.

Listing 2.6 Forming a GEOMETRYCOLLECTIONM from constituent geometries

```
SELECT ST_AsText(ST_Collect(g))
FROM (
    SELECT ST_GeomFromEWKT('MULTIPOINTM(-1 1 4, 0 0 2, 2 3 2)') As g
    UNION ALL
    SELECT ST_GeomFromEWKT(
        'MULTILINESTRINGM((0 0 1, 0 1 2, 1 1 3), (-1 1 1,-1 -1 2))'
    ) As g
    UNION ALL
    SELECT ST_GeomFromEWKT(
        'POLYGONM(
            (-0.25 -1.25 1, -0.25 1.25 2, 2.5 1.25 3, 2.5 -1.25 1, -0.25
    -1.25 1),
            (2.25 0 2, 1.25 1 1, 1.25 -1 1, 2.25 0 2),
            (1 -1 2,1 1 2,0 0 2,1 -1 2)
        )'
    ) As g
) x;
```

The output of the preceding listing is as follows:

```
GEOMETRYCOLLECTION M (
    MULTIPOINT M (-1 1 4, 0 0 2, 2 3 2),
    MULTILINESTRING M ((0 0 1, 0 1 2, 1 1 3), (-1 1 1, -1 -1 2)),
    POLYGON M (
        (-0.25 -1.25 1, -0.25 1.25 2, 2.5 1.25 3, 2.5 -1.25 1, -0.25 -1.25 1),
        (2.25 0 2, 1.25 1 1, 1.25 -1 1, 2.25 0 2),
```

```
      (1 -1 2, 1 1 2, 0 0 2,1 -1 2)
   )
 )
```

PostGIS does offer `POLYGON M`, `POLYHEDRAL ZM`, `TIN ZM`, and so on, but we have yet to see any real-world need for these more abstruse dimensional types.

2.2.6 *The Z coordinate*

First, to clear up any misconceptions, just because a `geometry` has a Z coordinate doesn't make it a volumetric geometry. A polygon in three-coordinate dimensional space is still a planar 2D geometry. It has an area but no volume. The story will get a little more interesting when we get to polyhedral surfaces in the next section.

PostGIS 2 introduced new relationship and measurement functions prefixed with `ST_3D`, specifically designed to work with subtypes in X, Y, Z coordinate space. Common ones are `ST_3DIntersects`, `ST_3DDistance`, `ST_3DDWithin` for 3D radius searches, `ST_3DMaxDistance`, and `ST_3DClosestPoint`. PostGIS 2 also introduced the n-D spatial index (the index class is suffixed with `_nd`), which considers the Z coordinate and M coordinate. The default spatial index ignores the Z and M coordinate. We'll cover spatial indexes in chapter 15.

PostGIS 2.1 introduced additional 3D functions based on the SFCGAL library, which is a 3D enhancement built atop the Computational Geometry Algorithms Library (CGAL); the SF stands for *spatial features*. SFCGAL added functions such as `ST_3DIntersection` and `ST_3DArea`. It also brought its own implementation of some existing `ST_3D` functions such as `ST_3DIntersects`. For more details about the PostGIS SFCGAL, visit www.sfcgal.org. As of PostGIS 3, the `ST_3DIntersects` built into PostGIS now supports volumetric geometries as well. As such, SFCGAL's `ST_3DIntersects` has been removed.

In order to take advantage of these additional 3D functions and 3D enhanced functions, you need to compile PostGIS with SFCGAL support or find a distribution of PostGIS already compiled with it. As of PostGIS 2.5, Windows, Ubuntu/Debian, and yum.postgresql.org include SFCGAL.

Regardless of how you get a SFCGAL-fortified version of PostGIS, be sure to run this command:

```
CREATE EXTENSION postgis_sfcgal SCHEMA postgis;
```

The `postgis_sfcgal` extension must be installed in the same schema as `postgis` for PostGIS 2.3 and later.

Prior to PostGIS 3.0, some functions provided by SFCGAL, such as `ST_Intersects` and `ST_3DIntersects`, are named the same as the functions packaged with PostGIS but behave differently or support more `geometry` types than those packaged with the postgis extension. By default, the PostGIS ones are used. If you instead want the SFCGAL ones to be used where they have the same names, and you are using a version of

PostGIS before version 3, you'll want to set postgis .backend=sfcgal. This is covered in more detail in the PostGIS manual.

SFCGAL backend removed in PostGIS 3.0

For PostGIS 3.0, ST_3DIntersects and ST_Intersects, as well as other functions that were same-named, were augmented to support geometry types such as TIN and TRIANGLE. As such, the backend switch was removed, and those same-named functions were removed from SFCGAL.

Prior to PostGIS 2.0, support for the Z coordinate was sketchy. PostGIS relied on a library called GEOS, which is not well known for 3D support. When using PostGIS functions against your 3D geometry, the functions won't error out if they can't handle the Z coordinate; they'll either pretend the Z isn't there or do some interpolation to give you some semblance of processing the Z dimension. For example, when you use ST_Intersection and ST_Union with geometries having Z coordinates, both functions will handle the X and the Y perfectly but only approximate the Z coordinate. This may be acceptable when you don't need precision, such as when mapping a mountainous hiking trail. But the outcome could be deadly if you used it to program a flight GPS to navigate around mountainous terrain. The PostGIS reference guide will tell you how each function behaves when the Z coordinate is present. If you're doing serious modeling in 3D, consult the manual to make sure Z behaves within your specifications.

For PostGIS prior to version 3, there is no support in ST_Transform for geometries with a Z coordinate. If you are using PostGIS 3+ and Proj 6+, some spatial reference systems that have a Z component will also transform the Z coordinate. Refer to chapter 3 for details of this change. Most commonly used spatial reference systems are 2D and as such will leave the Z coordinate alone. This should be fine, because reprojections rarely affect Z anyway. Mount Everest stays the same height regardless of how you draw your map.

2.2.7   *Polyhedral surfaces and TINs*

Float a bunch of polygons in 3D space and glue them together at their edges, and you'll form a patchwork referred to as a *polyhedral surface*. Although polygons make up both multipolygons and polyhedral surfaces, there is one fundamental difference between them: polygons in multipolygons can't share edges; polygons in a polyhedral surface almost always do. There are two other notable restrictions in the construction of polyhedral surfaces: polygons can't overlap, and each edge can be mated with at most one other edge.

NOTE You can read the more rigorous definition of polyhedral surfaces in the OGC and SQL/MM specifications at www.opengeospatial.org/standards/sfa.

Some real-world examples of polyhedral surfaces that come to mind are geodetic domes, a jigsaw puzzle that you pieced together but later spilled drinks on so now it's warped, a honeycomb, or the checkered flag at a car race as it flaps in the wind.

Polyhedral surfaces allow you to create closed surfaces in three dimensions. The simplest example is the triangular pyramid formed by four equilateral triangular polygons. Prior to PostGIS 2.2 there was no way to denote if a surface was a solid (having volume) or just area. A polyhedral surface that is closed can be treated as a solid, with a geometry dimension of three, or as a surface, with a geometry dimension of two. A solid would mean that all points inside the surface would count as part of the geometry, and the intersection of two solids could generate another solid. Solid or planar?

In PostGIS 2.2 and above there is an ST_MakeSolid function that will mark a closed polyhedral surface as solid, and there is a companion ST_IsSolid function that will return true or false to denote whether a 3D geometry is solid. Some functions, such as ST_Dimension, will return 3 for closed polyhedral surfaces. Prior to PostGIS 3, if you applied the native ST_3DIntersects built into PostGIS for two closed polyhedral surfaces, the result just considered the surface. However, if you have the SFCGAL engine enabled, ST_3DIntersects and the SFCGAL ST_3DIntersection treat the surfaces as solids if they were created via SFCGAL functions. The native ST_3DIntersects in PostGIS 3 can now work with solids and TINs, and as such the SFCGAL ST_3DIntersects was removed in version 3.0, since it was redundant.

TINs stands for *triangular irregular networks*. They're a subset of polyhedral surfaces where all the constituent polygons must be triangles. TINs are widely used to describe terrain surfaces. Recall from basic geometry (or common sense) the minimum number of points needed to form an area: three—a triangle. The mathematical underpinning of TINs is based on triangulating key peak and valley point locations of a surface to form non-overlapping connected area pockets. The most common form of triangulation used in GIS is Delaunay triangulation (explained on Wikipedia: http://en .wikipedia.org/wiki/Delaunay_triangulation).

PostGIS over the years has added more support for surface and volumetric geometries. The powerful ST_DelaunayTriangles function converts a "well-behaved" polygon collection into a TIN, but it can't convert polyhedral surfaces to TINs. For that conversion, you need to use ST_Tesselate, which is packaged with SFCGAL and will convert polygon collections as well.

PostGIS 2.0 added many new functions specifically for use with polyhedral surfaces and TINs; section 9.11 of the *PostGIS Special Functions Index* provides the full list (http://mng.bz/rmnx). Many existing functions, such as ST_Dump and ST_DumpPoints, were augmented to accept these two subtypes as well.

To fully appreciate geometries in 3D space, you'll need rendering software. The PostGIS ST_AsX3D function will output geometry in X3D XML format, which you can view with various X3D viewers. The JavaScript x3dom.js library (www.x3dom.org) has logic for rendering X3D in HTML5-compatible browsers.

We've created a PostGIS X3D web viewer for PHP and ASP.NET built on the x3dom.js library to demonstrate the process. You can download the code for that at https://github.com/robe2/postgis_x3d_viewer. We used our minimalist X3D viewer to render the images of polyhedral surfaces and TINs you'll see in this chapter.

In addition, the latest version of the QGIS Open Source Desktop (3.18 as of this writing) supports viewing of polyhedral surfaces and TINs. By default in QGIS, 3D geometries are rendered in 2D mode, but there is a 3D Map panel you can add to your canvas that will show your data in its full 3D glory. We'll cover this in greater detail in chapter 5.

GENERATING POLYHEDRAL SURFACES

The following listing demonstrates two ways of generating a three-faced polyhedral surface.

> **Listing 2.7 A three-faced polyhedral surface**

```
SELECT ST_GeomFromText(
    'POLYHEDRALSURFACE Z (
        ((12 0 10, 8 8 10, 8 10 20, 12 2 20, 12 0 10)),
        ((8 8 10, 0 12 10, 0 14 20, 8 10 20, 8 8 10)),
        ((0 12 10, -8 8 10, -8 10 20, 0 14 20, 0 12 10))
    )'
);

  -- Which can be generated using --
SELECT ST_Extrude(ST_GeomFromText(
    'LINESTRING(12 0 10, 8 8 10, 0 12 10,-8 8 10)'),
    0, 2, 10
);
```

Both examples in the preceding listing generate the same polyhedral surface. The second example uses the SFCGAL ST_Extrude function, whereas the first uses the WKT representation of the resulting geometry when extruding the linestring. A rendering of listing 2.7 is shown in figure 2.12. If you were to extrude a polygon, you'd end up with a closed polyhedral surface (a volume).

Note that like the MULTIPOLYGON, the POLYHEDRALSURFACE has double-braced rings with the coordinates of each POLYGON Z that makes up the element.

Figure 2.12 A three-faced polyhedral surface generated from the code in listing 2.7

2.2.8 Generating TINs

A TIN is a collection subtype formed from a `geometry` subtype called `TRIANGLE`. You'll rarely see the `TRIANGLE` subtype in use, especially not in its column data type form of `geometry(TRIANGLE)`. But you may come across it if you use the `ST_Dump` function to dump out all the triangles in a TIN.

In the next example, we'll demonstrate a four-triangled TIN and we'll color-code each triangle so it's clear where the delineations are. Many rendering packages won't delineate the triangles by design, so that the result ends up looking like a regular polyhedral surface.

Listing 2.8   A `TIN` made up of four triangles

```
SELECT ST_GeomFromText(
    'TIN Z (
        ((12 2 20, 8 8 10, 8 10 20, 12 2 20)),
        ((12 2 20, 12 0 10, 8 8 10, 12 2 20)),
        ((8 10 20, 0 12 10, 0 14 20, 8 10 20)),
        ((8 10 20, 8 8 10, 0 12 10, 8 10 20))
    )'
);
```

The visual output of listing 2.8 is shown in figure 2.13.

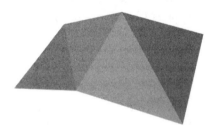

Figure 2.13   A four-triangle `TIN` surface generated from listing 2.8

2.2.9 Curved geometries

Curved geometries came into existence with the OGC SQL/MM Part 3 specs, and PostGIS has almost complete support for what's defined in the specs, but tools for rendering PostGIS curved geometries still lag behind and are somewhat spotty as to what they support.

Curved geometries aren't as mature as other geometries and aren't widely used. Natural terrestrial features rarely manifest themselves as curved geometries. Architectural structures and artificial boundaries do have curves, but linestrings will adequately serve as approximations for many modeling cases. Aeronautical charts are full of curves because the sweep of radar is circular. Dams, dikes, breakwaters, stadiums, hippodromes, coliseums, Greek and Shakespearean theaters, and crop circles (both those made by humans and by aliens) are other curved structures that come to mind.

Some highway segments come close to being curves, but linestrings are often more appropriate for modeling them when processing speed is more important than accuracy.

Because of the lack of support, consider the following points before you decide to go down the path of using curved geometries:

- Few third-party tools, either open source or commercial, currently support curved geometries.
- The advanced spatial library called GEOS that PostGIS uses for much of its functionality, such as performing intersections, containment checks, and other spatial-relation checks, doesn't support curved geometries. As a work-around, you can convert curved geometries to linestrings and regular polygons using the ST_CurveToLine function, and then convert back with ST_LineToCurve. The downside of this method is the loss of speed and the inaccuracies introduced when interpolating arcs using linestrings. ST_LineToCurve is also useful for rendering curved geometries in tools that don't support curved geometries.
- Many native PostGIS functions don't support curved geometries. You can find a full list of functions that do support curved geometries in the PostGIS reference manual. Again, for cases where you need to use functions that don't support curved geometries, you can apply the ST_CurveToLine function and then apply ST_LineToCurve to convert back if needed.
- PostGIS hasn't supported curved geometries for as long as the other geometries, so you're more likely to run into bugs when working with them. More recent releases of PostGIS have cleaned up many of the bugs and have expanded the number of functions that support curved geometries.

Given all the drawbacks of curved geometries, you might be wondering why you'd ever want to use them. Here are a few reasons:

- You can represent a truly curved geometry with less data. A perfect circle is defined by a centroid and a radius. A perfect circle described using linestrings would require an infinite number of points.
- More tools are planning to add support for curved geometries. Safe FME and QGIS are two tools we know of that already support PostGIS curved geometries.
- Even if you don't ultimately store your data as curved geometry types, it's often easier to use such types as intermediaries. For example, if you have a closed linestring that comes close to a circle, you can create a curved geometry and then convert it to a linestring using ST_CurveToLine, rather than typing out all the points to form the linestring. ST_ForceCurve does the reverse, allowing you change, say, a buffer of a point to a CURVEPOLYGON as follows: ST_ForceCurve(ST_Buffer(ST_Point(1,1),10)).

Let's now take a closer look at the wide variety of curved geometries. For simplicity, you can think of curved geometries in PostGIS as geometries with arcs. To build an arc, you must have exactly three distinct points. The first and last points denote the starting and ending points of the arc. The point in the middle is called the control point because this point controls the degree of curvature of the arc.

CIRCULARSTRINGS

A series of one or more arcs where the endpoint of one is the starting point of another makes up a geometry called a *circularstring*. Figure 2.14 illustrates a five-point circularstring.

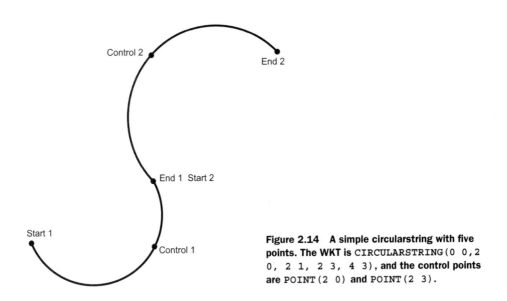

Figure 2.14 A simple circularstring with five points. The WKT is `CIRCULARSTRING(0 0,2 0, 2 1, 2 3, 4 3)`**, and the control points are** `POINT(2 0)` **and** `POINT(2 3)`**.**

The circularstring is the simplest of all curved geometries and contains only arcs. The following listing contains more examples of circularstrings and how you'd register them in the database.

Listing 2.9 Building circularstrings

```
ALTER TABLE ch02.my_geometries
ADD COLUMN my_circular_strings geometry(CIRCULARSTRING);

INSERT INTO ch02.my_geometries(name, my_circular_strings)
VALUES
    ('Circle',
    ST_GeomFromText('CIRCULARSTRING(0 0, 2 0, 2 2, 0 2, 0 0)')),
    ('Half circle',
    ST_GeomFromText('CIRCULARSTRING(2.5 2.5, 4.5 2.5, 4.5 4.5)')),
    ('Several arcs',
    ST_GeomFromText('CIRCULARSTRING(5 5, 6 6, 4 8, 7 9, 9.5 9.5, 11 12, 12 12
    )'));
```

The output is shown in figure 2.15.

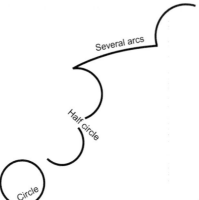

Figure 2.15   Three circularstrings generated

As you can see from these examples, a circularstring must have an odd number of points. If you were to number them starting with one, all odd-numbered points would be starting or ending points and all even-numbered points would be control points.

You'll discover that not all rendering tools can handle curved geometries. When faced with this situation, don't ditch the tool. Use the ST_CurveToLine function to fit a linestring atop your curve.

COMPOUND CURVES

Circularstrings and linestrings in series make up a collection geometry subtype called a COMPOUNDCURVE. A polygon constructed using a compound curve is called a CURVEPOLYGON.

A closed compound curve is a geometry composed of both circularstring and regular linestring segments, where the last point in the prior segment is the first point of the next segment. A square with rounded corners is a nice representation of a closed compound curve (with four circular strings and four straight linestrings).

Following is an example of a compound curve composed of an arc sandwiched between two linestrings. The output is shown in figure 2.16.

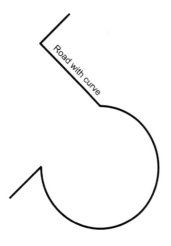

Figure 2.16   A compound curve generated from listing 2.10

Listing 2.10 Creating a compound curve

```
ALTER TABLE ch02.my_geometries
ADD COLUMN my_compound_curves geometry(COMPOUNDCURVE);
INSERT INTO ch02.my_geometries (name, my_compound_curves)
VALUES (
    'Road with curve',
    ST_GeomFromText(
        'COMPOUNDCURVE(
            (2 2, 2.5 2.5),
            CIRCULARSTRING(2.5 2.5, 4.5 2.5, 3.5 3.5),
            (3.5 3.5, 2.5 4.5, 3 5)
        )'
    )
);
```

As you can see in the WKT, the circularstring portion of the curve is identified as such, and the rest of the components are linestrings. You might be tempted to make everything clearer by adding the word LINESTRING, but refrain from doing so because you'll get an error.

CURVEPOLYGONS

A curvepolygon is a polygon that has exterior or inner rings of circularstrings. Listing 2.11 and figure 2.17 show some examples of curvepolygons.

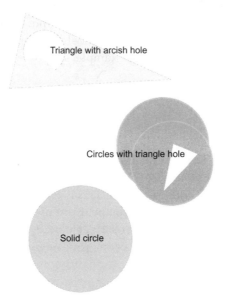

Triangle with arcish hole

Circles with triangle hole

Solid circle

Figure 2.17 Curvepolygons created in listing 2.11

Listing 2.11 Creating curvepolygons

```
ALTER TABLE ch02.my_geometries
ADD COLUMN my_curve_polygons geometry(CURVEPOLYGON);
```

```
INSERT INTO ch02.my_geometries (name, my_curve_polygons)
VALUES
    ('Solid circle',
    ST_GeomFromText('CURVEPOLYGON(
        CIRCULARSTRING(0 0, 2 0, 2 2, 0 2, 0 0)
    )')),
    ('Circles with triangle hole',
    ST_GeomFromText('CURVEPOLYGON(
        CIRCULARSTRING(2.5 2.5, 4.5 2.5, 4.5 3.5, 2.5 4.5, 2.5 2.5),
        (3.5 3.5, 3.25 2.25, 4.25 3.25, 3.5 3.5)
    )')),
    ('Triangle with arcish hole',
    ST_GeomFromText('CURVEPOLYGON(
        (-0.5 7, -1 5, 3.5 5.25, -0.5 7),
        CIRCULARSTRING(0.25 5.5, -0.25 6.5, -0.5 5.75, 0 5.75, 0.25 5.5)
    )'));
```

2.2.10 *Spatial catalog for geometry*

PostGIS comes packaged with a read-only view named geometry_columns that lists all geometry columns within the database. The geometry_columns view reads from the PostgreSQL system catalogs, so the information in it will stay in sync with any definition changes or addition of geometry columns you make to tables.

PostGIS will also automatically register views, materialized views, and foreign tables that contain columns of the geometry data type. You can retrieve this registration information from the geometry_columns view just as you do with tables.

To ensure registration with all the relevant metadata, such as subtype, dimension, and SRID, you may need to take the extra step of casting the geometry column in your view definition if the column is based on a function. For example, suppose you create a view as follows:

```
CREATE VIEW my_view AS
 SELECT gid, ST_Transform(geom,4326) geom
  FROM some_table;
```

PostGIS is not smart enough to infer the SRID from your view definition or to know that ST_Transform will always result in the same geometry type as the input. It'll lazily record the column as just geometry without additional info. This is especially likely to happen if you use check constraints to restrict the subtype or if you use any PostGIS function to morph the geometry, such as ST_Transform or ST_Centroid, in your view definition. If any of these apply to your view, you should create your view with an extra cast, like this:

```
CREATE VIEW my_view AS
 SELECT gid, ST_Transform(geom,2163)::geometry(POINT,2163) geom
  FROM some_table;
```

If you have no functions applied to a column, PostGIS geometry_columns will show the column information from the underlying table column. As such, if you are using type modifiers on your `geometry` column and using the column directly, the following definition is sufficient:

```
CREATE VIEW my_view AS
 SELECT gid, geom
 FROM some_table;
```

The structure of the `geometry_columns` view is shown in table 2.1.

Table 2.1   The structure of the `geometry_columns` view

Column	Description
`f_table_catalog`	Name of the database (catalog in computer-science parlance)
`f_table_schema`	Name of the schema
`f_table_name`	Name of the table
`f_geometry_column`	Name of the column holding the geometry
`type`	Subtype of the geometry column. If this isn't specified or is specified with `geometry(GEOMETRY)`, then it will just show GEOMETRY.
`coord_dimension`	Coordinate dimensions
`SRID`	Spatial reference identifier

The last two rows merit more discussion: `coord_dimension` and `SRID`.

COORD_DIMENSION

`Coord_dimension` is the coordinate dimension of the `geometry` column; permissible values are 2, 3, and 4. Yes, PostGIS supports up to four dimensions: X, Y, Z, M. Don't forget M.

In spatial speak, there are two kinds of dimensions—the coordinate dimension and the geometry dimension:

- The *coordinate dimension* defines the number of linearly independent axes in your space. Mathematically speaking, the coordinate dimension is the number of vectors forming the basis. For example, geometries that occupy X, Y, Z or X, Y, M have a coordinate dimension of 3. Those that have X, Y, Z, M have a coordinate dimension of 4.
- The *geometry dimension* describes the size and shape of a geometry. A flat polygon is a two-dimensional geometry because you can speak in terms of length and width. A linestring is a one-dimensional geometry because only the length is a relevant measure. A point, by definition, has zero dimensions.

Most people expect you to know which kind of dimension, coordinate, or geometry is being referred to from the context alone, but this becomes confusing when you use both simultaneously. For example, a cobra emerging out of a snake charmer's basket is a one-dimensional geometry (the serpentine linestring has a geometry dimension of one) living in three-dimensional space (the wicker basket has three coordinate dimensions). A cobra slithering around your checkered kitchen floor is a one-dimensional geometry linestring in a two-dimensional coordinate space (your kitchen floor). PostGIS 2.0 introduced polyhedral surfaces and triangulated irregular network (TIN) geometries. Think of the former as a flying carpet and the latter as the shell of Spaceship Earth (the famous dome at Epcot). Points and linestrings always have zero and one geometry dimensions respectively, but be careful when people start talking about polygons in 3D or 4D space. Polygons are still two-dimensional. One rule that you can always count on is this: a geometry dimension can never exceed the coordinate dimension that it's living in.

SRID

SRID stands for *spatial reference identifier* and it's an integer that relates back to the primary key of the spatial_ref_sys table. PostGIS uses this table to catalog all the spatial reference systems available to the database. The spatial_ref_sys table contains the name of the spatial reference system (SRS), the parameters needed to reproject from one SRID to another, and the organization that gave rise to the particular SRID. Even though the spatial_ref_sys table has close to 6,000 entries, you'll encounter plenty of instances where you have to add SRIDs not already in the table. You can also be adventurous and define your own custom SRS and add it to the spatial_ref_sys table in any PostGIS database.

Be aware of a similar term in GIS lingo called *SRS ID* (spatial reference system identifier). This identifier adds the authority that created the SRID. For example, the common WGS 84 lon/lat has an SRID of 4326 but an SRS ID of EPSG:4326, where EPSG stands for European Petroleum Survey Group (www.epsg.org). Most of the SRIDs in PostGIS came from EPSG, so the SRID used in the table is by PostGIS convention the same as the EPSG identifier. Keep in mind that the SRID column in spatial_ref_sys is just a user-input (or in this case, PostGIS-distributed) primary key in the spatial_ref_sys table. This isn't the case with all spatial databases, so from database vendor to database vendor you can't guarantee that SRID 4326 corresponds to the global SRS EPSG:4326.

The default value of a `geometry` SRID is 0 to conform to the SQL/MM standard. Should you use the unknown SRID? The answer is no if you're working with geographic data. If you know the SRS of your data, and presumably you should if you have real geographic data, then you should explicitly specify it. If you're using PostGIS for non-geographical purposes, such as modeling a localized architecture plan or demonstrating analytic geometry principles, it's perfectly fine to keep your spatial reference as unknown. For most functions that require an SRID, you can leave out the SRID and it'll default to the unknown value. The `ST_Transform` function is an obvious exception.

Finally, keep in mind that switching SRIDs doesn't alter the fact that the coordinate system underlying the `geometry` data type is always Cartesian.

MANAGING GEOMETRY COLUMNS

A big pre-PostGIS 2.0 headache when adding new columns was the need to manage your geometry columns. For instance, if you manually added a geometry column with an ALTER TABLE statement, you had the additional task of adding check constraints to restrict the column to a particular subtype and SRID, and of recording this information in geometry_columns. PostGIS 2.0 introduced the type-modifier syntax that allows you to add new columns using the SQL data definition language (DDL) and not have to worry about adding constraints for subtype and SRID. PostGIS will now also automatically list the column in the geometry_columns view for you.

To ease all the additional management tasks before version 2.0, PostGIS made available a few helper functions. These are AddGeometryColumns, DropGeometryColumn, UpdateGeometrySRID, and DropGeometryTable. They're still around for backward compatibility, but we strongly discourage you from using them. In fact, should you run into them, replace them with equivalent DDLs. Let's look at two DDL examples that you'll probably come across often.

CHANGING THE SRID OF AN EXISTING GEOMETRY COLUMN

Should you stamp the wrong SRID on your geometry column, you'll want to change it to the right SRID. Use the ALTER TABLE syntax as follows:

```
ALTER TABLE us_states
ALTER COLUMN geom TYPE geometry(MULTIPOLYGON,4326)
USING ST_SetSRID(geom,4326);
```

CONVERTING A GEOMETRY COLUMN TO A GEOGRAPHY COLUMN

This example will convert a geometry column called way in osm_roads from its current spatial reference geometry to geography by first transforming and then casting to geography:

```
ALTER TABLE osm_roads
ALTER COLUMN way TYPE geography(MULTIPOLYGON,4326)
USING ST_Transform(way,4326)::geography;
```

THE POPULATE_GEOMETRY_COLUMNS FUNCTION

Although most alterations are easier to do with SQL, we find that the old Populate_Geometry_Columns management function is still handy at times. This powerful function will scan all unregistered geometry columns in your database or in a table that you specify. If the column is a generic geometry column or has an unknown SRID, it will examine the data to try to pinpoint the subtype and SRID. If it can identify a uniform subtype, it will add the subtype to your column definition using typmod syntax or check constraints. Similarly, if it can determine the SRID, it will add the SRID to your column definition using typmod syntax or check constraints. Populate_Geometry_Columns will obviously be unable to arrive at a subtype and SRID for columns with no data or for tables with mixed subtypes.

2.3   Geography

PostGIS hit the scene with only the geometry data type. As devotees grew in number, a common need arose to perform calculations taking the spherical nature of Mother Earth into consideration.

Remember that the geometry data type is based on a Cartesian grid? As people began to plot cities using geometry points and calculating distances where the curvature of the earth came into play, they had to constantly resort to the rather hairy formula for finding distances on a sphere. Soon all this became a nuisance, and PostGIS introduced a new data type—geography.

2.3.1   Differences between geography and geometry

Unlike its geometry forebears, geography starts by assuming that all your data is based on a geodetic coordinate system, specifically the WGS 84 lon/lat SRID of 4326. No exceptions. This greatly simplified matters for people using PostGIS on a global scale because lon/lat is a coordinate system familiar to everyone.

Prior to PostGIS 2.2, geography only supported SRID 4326. In PostGIS 2.2, geography changed to support any lon/lat-based spatial reference system. This means even other planets such as Mars can now be explored with PostGIS. 4326 is still the default, and if no SRID is specified, 4326 is assumed.

Because the geography data type is specialized for geodetic applications, you're going to find yourself missing support for all but the basic subtypes of points, linestrings, and polygons. Furthermore, don't expect much support for anything above 2D space. PostGIS has yet to completely embrace the space age.

Because the structure of the geography data subtypes mimic those of geometry, everything you already know about geometry applies to geography with no changes, except for swapping out the term *geometry* for *geography* in both data type and function names. For example, ST_GeomFromText becomes ST_GeogFromText. Let's look at a few examples in the next listing, which we will use in later examples.

> **Listing 2.12   Using the geography data type**

```
CREATE TABLE ch02.my_geogs (
    id serial PRIMARY KEY,
    name varchar(20),
    my_point geography(POINT)
);
INSERT INTO ch02.my_geogs (name, my_point)
VALUES
    ('Home',ST_GeogFromText('POINT(0 0)')),
    ('Pizza 1',ST_GeogFromText('POINT(1 1)')),
    ('Pizza 2',ST_GeogFromText('POINT(1 -1)'));
```

The difference between geometry and geography becomes apparent when you ask the question, How far is my house from each pizza restaurant?, as shown in the following listing.

Listing 2.13 How far am I from pizza? (spheroid distance)

```
SELECT
    h.name As house, p.name As pizza,
    ST_Distance(h.my_point, p.my_point) As dist
FROM
    (SELECT name, my_point FROM ch02.my_geogs WHERE name = 'Home') As h
    CROSS JOIN
    (SELECT name, my_point FROM ch02.my_geogs WHERE name LIKE 'Pizza%') As p;
```

The output of listing 2.13 follows:

```
house | pizza   |      dist
-------+---------+-----------------
 Home  | Pizza 1 | 156899.56829134
 Home  | Pizza 2 | 156899.56829134
```

In the preceding listing, the distance is 156899.568... meters for both pizza parlors. Points in geography correspond to longitude and latitude, and distances are always computed in meters. This example puts your home on the Republic of Null Island (https://en.wikipedia.org/wiki/Null_Island), and the pizza stores are on islands to the northeast and the southeast.

If you performed the same distance computation using geometry, you'd end up with 1.414... (the square root of 2)—a straightforward Pythagorean calculation. At the equator, one degree is approximately 110.944 kilometers, so the previous geometry answers tell us that we're about 156,874 meters from pizza.

Here's another example to drive home the difference.

For geography it returns 0:

```
SELECT ST_Distance(ST_Point(0,180)::geography, ST_Point(0,-180)::geography);
```

For geometry it returns 360:

```
SELECT ST_Distance(ST_Point(0,180)::geometry, ST_Point(0,-180)::geometry);
```

geography is smart enough to know that you're measuring the distance between the same point on the globe and returns a result of 0. geometry continues to assume that you're on a flat earth and returns 360 *degree* units, close to 40,000 kilometers!

2.3.2 *Spatial catalogs for geography*

The geography_columns view is very similar to the geometry_columns view, except it lists columns in your database that are of type geography. Most of the columns in geography_columns are the same as those in geometry_columns except for one. In the geography_columns view, f_geometry_column is replaced with f_geography_column.

2.4   *Raster*

Rasters are all around us. You're probably staring at one now. Rasters organize information using pixels; pixels, sometimes called cells, form the basis of rasters. Unlike when you're shopping for a color TV, the actual shape and size of the pixels don't matter for database applications. Each pixel is really a space holder for data, nothing more.

Pixels are organized in rows and columns to form tiles. To make life easier, all tiles should be rectangular. When we speak of the size of a raster tile, we're referring to the number of horizontal pixels and vertical pixels. For example, your 1080p HDTV can be said to have 1920 columns and 1080 rows of pixels, a 1920×1080 raster tile, giving you a total count of 2.1 megapixels.

Remember that pixels are positional designations, not data. The actual data elements rest in *bands* (sometimes known as *channels* or *dimensions*). On your RGB TV raster, you can have three bands of data—one for each of the primary colors. PostGIS rasters can have as many as 255 bands in PostGIS 2.0, and even more in later versions.

Let's consider an example of raster modeling. Many city districts are laid out in grids: midtown Manhattan, the Chicago Loop, and the French Quarter of New Orleans, just to name a few. You can model each city block as a pixel, and you can then add bands to store data about each block. You could have a band that records the height of the tallest building in the block, another band to record the number of inhabitants, another to record the average property value, and another to record the number of pizzerias in the block. Rasters are more than pretty JPEGs and LCD displays—they're a powerful way to organize data.

GIS makes frequent use of georeferenced rasters. Pixels in a georeferenced raster correspond to actual geographical locations, and the physical size of the pixels takes on a real unit of measure. You can even assign an SRID to a georeferenced raster. For example, when flattened out, the globe can be modeled as a raster with 360 vertical columns and 180 horizontal rows, for a total of 64,800 pixels. Each pixel is one degree high and one degree wide. This example has conveniently created a raster data structure that has geographic meaning. Remember that for data modeling, the actual shape and size of the pixels don't matter. The physical size of the globe raster goes from tiny triangles near the poles to big squares at the equator.

2.4.1   *Properties of rasters*

Rasters have more common properties than other data types, and more than PostgreSQL allows to be stored as type modifiers, so you should use check constraints whenever possible to enforce property values.

PostGIS raster data is stored in a table with a column of type `raster`. Data is usually evenly tiled so that one row holds the same rectangular size of pixels as other rows. We recommend that you keep each row between 50 and 500 pixels for both width and height. You'll experience faster processing if you break large rasters into tiles for storage in multiple rows rather than keeping them in a single row.

Unlike other PostGIS spatial data types, raster data can be stored in the database or outside of the database. When stored outside of the database, the raster field only contains the metadata defining the width, height, and geometric bounding box as well as a reference to the file and the file region the raster tile references.

The raster2pgsql loader packaged with PostGIS is capable of taking larger rasters and chunking them into smaller tiles for database storage. We'll talk more about selecting suitable tile sizes in later chapters.

RASTER WIDTH AND HEIGHT

Each raster tile (a row in the raster column) has a width and height that's measured in pixels.

BANDS

Each raster can have multiple bands, but you must have at least one. You can have as many as 65,535 bands in an in-database raster tile and 255 bands in an out-of-database raster tile.

BAND PIXEL TYPES

Rasters can only store numeric values in their pixels. The number of bands determines the number of values that each pixel can store. For example, a 100-band raster can store 100 values in each pixel; an RGB raster can store 3.

Pixel types describe the type of numbers that a given band in a pixel can accommodate. There are several possible choices:

- 1-bit Boolean, abbreviated as 1BB
- Unsigned integer of 2, 8, 16, or 32 bits, abbreviated as 2BUI, 8BUI, 16BUI, 32BUI
- Signed integers of 8, 16, or 32 bits, abbreviated as 8BSI, 16BSI, 32BSI
- Two float types of 32 bits and 64 bits, abbreviated as 32BF and 64BF

The most common pixel type by far is 8BUI. Each band has a single pixel type defined for all pixels. You can't vary the pixel type except across bands. Use the ST_Band-PixelType function to obtain the pixel type of a specific band. We'll cover its use in chapter 7.

RASTERS AND SRIDs

Georeferenced rasters have spatial coordinates defined within a spatial reference system and therefore have an SRID. Transformation functions are available to convert rasters from one spatial reference system to another.

PIXEL WIDTH AND HEIGHT

For georeferenced rasters, pixels do have heights and widths that reflect units of measurement. For example, if you're using a raster to represent downtown Manhattan's grid of streets and avenues, the width of your cell would be 274 meters and the height would be 80 meters (the typical area of a city block).

Two functions are useful for reading off a pixel's width and height: ST_PixelWidth and ST_PixelHeight.

PIXEL SCALE

In order to reference a particular pixel on a raster, you must have some pixel-numbering convention relative to spatial coordinates. This convention is generally positive in the X direction and negative in the Y direction of coordinate space, though it need not be. A raster's pixel cell numbering always starts at the top-left corner of the tile rectangle, whereas when we talk about coordinate space we generally start numbering from the bottom-left corner. A negative Y pixel scale means that increasing pixel row cell numbers correspond to decreasing Y spatial coordinates, and a positive X pixel scale means increasing column cell numbers correspond to increasing X coordinates.

If you assign a unit grid to your rasters, you can speak in terms of scale for georeferenced rasters. For the Manhattan raster example, the width of each pixel represents 274 meters, so it would be said to have an X scale of 1:274. Similarly, the Y scale is 1:80. You often encounter scales on a printed map. If you use a unit grid of 1 mm to map Manhattan, then each block would occupy 274 by 80 mm on paper, and the map could be said to have a 1:1000 scale.

SKEW X AND Y

The skew values are generally 0. Most rasters are aligned with the spatial reference coordinate axis, but on occasion they may be rotated, and the skew angle would define the rotation from the geocoordinate axis.

2.4.2   *Creating rasters*

Starting with PostGIS 3.0, the raster type and companion functions are no longer in the postgis extension. To use the raster type for PostGIS 3+, you will need to perform an additional step, as follows.

Listing 2.14   Install postgis_raster extension

```
CREATE EXTENSION postgis_raster SCHEMA postgis;
```

People generally use a loader such as raster2pgsql to import or register external rasters in the database. We'll demonstrate this technique in chapter 4. For now, we want to show you how to create raster data from scratch and how to insert the data using SQL. Remember that you can't add type modifiers during column creation for rasters, so the common practice is to first get data into a raster table and then apply constraints using the AddRasterConstraints function.

The AddRasterConstraints function has some intelligence built into it. You don't need to specify the particular constraint you're adding. The function will scan the data and try to apply as many check constraints as possible, namely SRID, width, height of each tile, alignment, bands, and so on, but it will skip over any constraints where the data is already in violation. It can also take additional arguments specifying the constraint types to enforce, if you only want certain constraints enforced.

In listing 2.15 you'll generate a raster table consisting of tiles that cover the world. To do so, you'll project the earth out in a simple way: one degree of longitude and one degree of latitude corresponds to one pixel. Each raster tile will be 90 pixels wide and 45 pixels high. There will be one band to hold temperature readings in each pixel.

Listing 2.15 Creating a raster table of the world

```
CREATE TABLE ch02.my_rasters (
    rid SERIAL PRIMARY KEY,
    name varchar(150),
    rast raster
);

INSERT INTO ch02.my_rasters (name, rast)
SELECT
    'quad ' || x::text || ' ' || y::text,
    ST_AddBand(                              ◁——  ❶ Add temperature band.
        ST_MakeEmptyRaster(
            90, 45,
            (x-2) * 90,
            (2-y) * 45,
            1, -1, 0, 0,
            4326                             ❷ Add 90×45 pixel
        ),                     ◁——              raster rows, WGS
        '16BUI'::text,                          84 lon/lat.
        0
    )
FROM generate_series(0,3) As x CROSS JOIN generate_series(0,3) As y;
```

In the preceding listing, you first create a table to hold your raster tiles. You then add 16 raster tiles (rows) to the table ❷. Each tile is 90 pixels wide by 45 pixels high. Given that you're using WGS 84 lon/lat, each pixel represents 1 square degree. Then, as part of the creation process, you add a single band to hold temperature fluctuations around the world and initialize the temperature to 0 ❶. For this example, the temperature is recorded in Kelvin. Just like when you're using the M coordinate, you should consistently use a given band to store the same type of measurement using the same unit of measurement.

ADDING BANDS

You might later decide to add more bands to your rasters, and you can do so with an UPDATE statement. Generally, though, it's best to add all the bands when you create the raster.

The next example creates an 8BUI band to store some measure of vegetation between 0 and 255. Note that 8BUI has a maximum value of 255 ($2^8 - 1$). You can ascribe any meaning to the values. For example, we can record really bad or non-existent as a 0, really good as 255, and the range from bad to good as the values in between:

```
UPDATE ch02.my_rasters SET rast = ST_AddBand(rast, '8BUI'::text,0);
```

APPLYING CONSTRAINTS

Once you're done adding bands, you'll want to add constraints to get the raster table column to register properly in the raster_columns view:

```
SELECT AddRasterConstraints('ch02', 'my_rasters'::name, 'rast'::name);
```

2.4.3   *Spatial catalog for rasters*

The raster_columns view is a catalog of all the columns in your database that are of type raster.

When you create a table with a raster column data type or import rasters with the raster2pgsql utility, you'll see entries in the raster_columns view. As you add additional constraints using the AddRasterConstraints function, this view will show the relevant constraint information. The raster_columns view utilizes the constraints applied on the raster columns to infer key properties.

You can query raster_columns much like any other table or view with a query like this:

```
SELECT
    r_table_name As tname,r_raster_column As cname,
    srid,
    scale_x As sx, scale_y As sy,
    blocksize_x As bx, blocksize_y As by,
    same_alignment As sa,
    num_bands As nb,
    pixel_types As ptypes
FROM raster_columns
WHERE r_table_schema = 'ch02';
```

This is the output of the preceding query:

```
tname    | cname | srid | sx | sy | bx | by | sa | nb |    ptypes
---------+-------+------+----+----+----+----+----+----+------------
my_rast..| rast  | 4326 | 1  | -1 | 90 | 45 | t  | 2  | {16BUI,8BUI}
```

The raster2pgsql raster loader is capable of creating overview tables. These are tables that have the same data as the main table, but at lower resolutions. They're particularly useful for running fast calculations for showing raster data zoomed out on a map. We'll cover overview tables in more detail when we discuss loading raster data. For now, just keep in mind that the raster_overviews view lists these tables, their resolutions, and their parent tables. The raster_columns view will list columns from the overview tables. At times, you may need to join raster_columns with raster_overviews to obtain all the columnar details you need.

Summary

- The PostGIS extensions postgis and postgis_raster include the spatial column data types `geometry`, `geography`, and `raster` as well as supporting functions for these.

- PostGIS provides the `geometry_columns`, `geography_columns`, and `raster_columns` views, which list what tables and columns these types are used in.

- `geometry` allows you to model objects, including 3D, as if they are on a localized flat playing field. This is the flat-world model.

- `geography` allows you to model 2D objects on a spheroidal surface and uses degrees for defining objects, but measurements in meters. This is the round-world model.

- `geometry` computations are simpler and faster than `geography`, and it is capable of handling 3D, but its assumptions about a flat world fall apart when dealing with large distances.

- `raster` models the world as a tapestry of cells on a flat world with each cell having one or more values.

- `raster` data can be created directly in the database or loaded in using the raster2pgsql command-line tool that is packaged with PostGIS.

- `raster` is useful for recording key attributes along spaces that are derived from statistics or generated by machines.

- PostGIS provides a spatial_ref_sys table that defines many known spatial reference systems.

- Two objects that have the same spatial reference system can be drawn on the same grid.

- `Raster` and `geometry` objects can be related together if they share the same spatial reference system.

Spatial reference systems 3

This chapter covers

- What spatial reference systems are
- How to determine the spatial reference system of a dataset
- How to choose appropriate spatial reference systems

Up to this point, we've been working mostly with fictitious data. Using sample data to learn the basics of PostGIS is an excellent first step: you're immediately rewarded with results without facing the messiness of real-world data. But reality is messy. From this chapter forward, you'll confront the fact that the earth is not the nice beachball that you thought it was. The same exact point on the face of the earth could be described differently by different groups. With time, the point shifts and the accuracy of our instrumentation gets better.

One big conundrum facing geographers is that an absolute frame of reference is missing. Your frame of reference is the earth itself, on which you're trying to establish absolute positions. The earth spins, tilts, and sometimes even wobbles. The measurements you take of the earth are not durable. The best you can do is to make known how and when you made your measurements.

This chapter begins by discussing different types of spatial reference systems (SRSs). It then follows up with sections on choosing suitable SRSs and uncovering the SRS of the source data when it is not apparent.

The art and science of modeling this bulbous earth and getting a 2D representation on paper have been around since antiquity. *Geodetics* is the science of measuring and modeling the earth. *Cartography* is the science of representing the earth on flat maps. The intricacies of these two venerated sciences are far beyond the scope of this book, but together with a lot of math they produce something that's of utmost importance to GIS: spatial reference systems.

In this chapter, we're not going to take the easy way out by accepting spatial reference systems without understanding them. We'll also avoid the path of arcane mathematics necessary to study the science in all its glory. We will take a middle road so that you can at least have more than a one-sentence explanation of SRSs when your kids finally get around to asking you about them. Your journey into the real world begins.

The data and code used in this chapter can be found at www.postgis.us/chapter _03_edition_3.

3.1 Spatial reference systems: What are they?

The topic of spatial reference systems is one of the more abstruse in GIS, attributable to the loose way in which people use the term *spatial reference system*. Also, SRS is not glamorous. If GIS is Disneyland, then SRS is the bookkeeping necessary to keep the theme park operation afloat.

Take any two paper maps having one point in common; overlay one atop the other using the common point as a reference. Both maps represent sections of the earth, but unless you're extremely lucky, the two maps will have no geographical relation to each other. Travel five centimeters on one map, and you end up on another street. Travel five centimeters on the other, and you're on another continent. Your two maps don't overlay well because they don't share a common spatial reference system.

The GIS practitioner must be acquainted with SRSs in order to combine data from disparate sources. Several universally accepted systems make this task easy without you having to delve into the nuances. The most common SRS authority is the European Petroleum Survey Group (EPSG) numbering system. Take any two sources of data with the same EPSG number, and you'll be guaranteed a perfect overlay. But EPSG is a recent SRS numbering system; if you uncover data from a few decades ago, you won't find an EPSG number. You'll have no choice but to delve into the constituent pieces that form an SRS: ellipsoid, datum, and projection.

3.1.1 Geoids

From outer space, our good earth appears spherical, often described as a blue marble. To anyone living on its surface, though, nothing could be further from the truth. The slick glossy surface seen from outer space devolves into mountain ranges, canyons, fissures, and ocean trenches with mind-boggling depths. The surface of the earth with all its nooks and crannies resembles a slightly charred English muffin much more than a lustrous marble. Even the idea of the earth being spherical isn't accurate, because the equator bulges out—a trip around the equator is 42.72 km longer than a trip around one of the meridians.

In light of the fact that you have a deeply pitted and somewhat squashed orange-like ball under your feet, what can you do when it comes to identifying a point on its surface? With new GPS toys, you could conceivably represent every square meter on earth on a satellite map, assigning it a spherical 3D-coordinate, and be done with it. This is the approach taken by many digital elevation models. You may even be able to pin your reference on a celestial object (constructed or otherwise), removing the annoyance of having to use a reference point on this shifty planet. Though these measuring methodologies could certainly become the norm one day soon, you'll still need a simpler, more computationally cost-effective model for most use cases. Just because you can locate a point on, above, or within earth to twenty decimal places doesn't mean you should.

A *model*, by definition, is a simplified representation of reality. All models are inherently flawed in one way or another, but in exchange for their shortcomings, each provides you with a more expedient way of solving your problems. The model must match the mission. A cartoonish map of New York City would be fine for a tourist but disastrous for a helicopter pilot navigating the Hudson skyway.

A starting point for any geodesic model is deciding what constitutes the surface of the earth. Perhaps it's something you haven't given much thought to, but do you use the mean sea level? Do you flatten the peaks and the valleys? What about the ocean? Do you consider the ocean surface or the ocean depth? And what about plate tectonics? Should our surface be the plates or the surface of the molten goo underneath? Once you start thinking about the earth's surface, a bewildering number of possibilities jump out at you, but they all suffer from a common problem—you can't establish a standard of measurement that will work for all portions of the planet. Take the notion of sea level. Someone in Cardiff, Wales, can say that her house is 50 meters above the sea during low tide and use this as a reference against her neighbor's house. Suppose a fellow in Pago Pago has a small house and measures his house also to be 50 meters above sea level. What can we say about the elevation of the two houses relative to each other? Not much. Sea level varies from place to place relative to the center of the earth. And even the notion of *center of the earth* is ambiguous.

Along comes Gauss, who, with the help of a crude pendulum, determined in the early nineteenth century that the surface of the earth can be defined, with some consistency, using gravitational measurements. Though he lacked a digital gravity meter, he envisioned the idea of going around the surface of the globe with such a device, like a simple pendulum, and mapping out a surface where gravity was constant—an equipotential surface. This is the basic idea of what we call *the geoid*. We take gravity readings at various sea levels to come up with a consensus and then use this constant gravitational force to map out an equigravitational surface around the globe. Many consider the geoid to be the true figure of the earth.

Surprisingly, the geoid is far from spherical—see figure 3.1. You must not forget that the core of the earth isn't homogeneous. Mass is distributed unevenly, giving rise to bulges and craters that rival those found on the lunar surface. The advent of the geoid didn't simplify matters. On the contrary, it created even more headaches. The true surface of the earth is now even less marble-like, and even a slightly squashed orange is no longer a reasonable approximation.

Figure 3.1 The geoid representing the earth seen from different angles

Although the geoid is rarely mentioned in GIS, it's the foundation of both planar and geodetic models. In the next section we'll discuss the more commonly used ellipsoids, which are simplifications of the geoid and are generally good enough for most geographic modeling needs.

3.1.2 Ellipsoids

The ancient Greeks were the first recorded as having used ellipsoids to model the earth. Geometrically, an ellipsoid is nothing but a 3D ellipse, an ellipse with an added Z-axis. Like a sphere, an ellipsoid has three radii. Unlike a sphere, the length of the radii can vary. When two radii are the same length, the ellipsoid is also called a spheroid. Notation-wise, a and b generally refer to the equatorial radii (along the X and Y axes), and c is the polar radius (along the Z axis). A perfect sphere is defined by $a = b = c$; an oblate spheroid is where $a = b$, but $c > a$. Our earth closely approximates an oblate spheroid; think clementines.

By varying the equatorial and polar radii on the ellipsoid, you can model the equatorial bulge. At some point in the history of geodesy, it was accepted that one ellipsoid could be used all around the world as a reference ellipsoid. Everyone could locate each other by finding their placement on this reference ellipsoid.

The appearance of Gauss's geoid shattered the idea of a single standard ellipsoid. One look at the geoid will show why: the curvature of the geoid varies wildly from place to place. An ellipsoid that fits the curvature for one spot may be woefully inaccurate for another, as shown in figure 3.2. Instead of one ellipsoid to rule us all, people

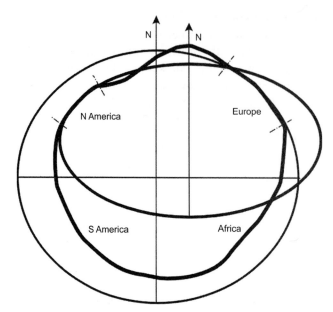

Figure 3.2   The geoid and the ellipsoid seen together

on different continents wanted their own ellipsoids to better reflect the regional curvature of the earth. This gave rise to the multitude of ellipsoids in use today.

This was all well and good when people on different continents communicated little with each other, and ships only steered in the direction of whales and galleons. This use of different ellipsoids became an obstacle as geologists from different countries collaborated to mine precious minerals (oil, really). Ships outgrew their sails and were overtaken by airplanes. Having to toggle between different ellipsoids became an annoyance. Fortunately, today the world has settled on two ellipsoids: the World Geodetic System (WGS 84) and the Geodetic Reference System (GRS 80), with WGS 84 becoming the standard of choice. WGS 84 is the basis of all GPS navigation systems.

> **NOTE**   The 80 and 84 in GRS 80 and WGS 84 stand for 1980 and 1984, when the standards came out. The ellipsoids are very similar.

To call WGS 84 an ellipsoid isn't quite accurate. The WGS 84 GPS system in use has a geoid component as well. To be precise, the present WGS 84 system uses the 1996 Earth Gravitational Model (EGM96) geoid and is the ellipsoid that best fits the geoid model for the selected survey points in the set. Many ellipsoids have been used over the years, and some continue to be used because of their better fit for particular regions. All historical data is still referenced against other ellipsoids. Table 3.1 lists some common ellipsoids and their ellipsoidal parameters.

One common old ellipsoid is Clarke 1866, and it's so close to the NAD 27 ellipsoid that they're interchangeable for most applications.

Table 3.1 Ellipsoids used over time

Ellipsoid	Equatorial radius (m)	Polar radius (m)	Inverse flattening	Where used
Clarke 1866	6,378,206.4	6,356,583.8	294.9786982	North America
NAD 27	6,378,206.4	6,356,583.8	294.978698208	North America
Australian 1966	6,378,160	6,356,774.719	298.25	Australia
GRS 80	6,378,137	6,356,752.3141	298.257222101	North America
WGS 84	6,378,137	6,356,752.3142	298.257223563	GPS (World)
IERS 1989	6,378,136	6,356,751.302	298.257	Time (World)

In the next section we'll discuss the concept of datums and how they fit into the overall picture of the spatial reference system.

Lon/lat, but which ellipsoid?

Even though humanity has used longitude and latitude for centuries, the same longitude and latitude coordinates are probably not the ones we use today. Mariners in the Renaissance didn't have the sophisticated electronics we have now, and their guesses at the locations of the poles would be specious at best. Also, the earth changes it's shape over time. This is why it's important to not just pinpoint a location by lon/lat only. You can have NAD 27 lon/lat, NAD 80 lon/lat, and WGS 84 lon/lat, and each will be subtly different. A pirate during the golden age of pirates probably recorded his buried treasures using lon/lat significant to one-tenth of a degree. He probably didn't mention ellipsoids. Good luck trying to find his treasure.

Nowadays, when referring to lon/lat, the WGS 84 datum and WGS 84 ellipsoid in lon/lat units are implied when not specified. However, WGS 84 has undergone changes over the years, mostly with the geoid component (https://en.wikipedia.org/wiki/World_Geodetic_System#Updates_and_new_standards). Since it does still use the same ellipsoid, we can treat the older WGS 84 and the newer WGS 84 as equivalent for our use cases.

3.1.3 Datum

The ellipsoid only models the overall shape of the earth. After picking out an ellipsoid, you need to anchor it to use it for real-world navigation. Every ellipsoid that's not a perfect sphere has two poles. This is where the axis arrives at the surface. These ellipsoid poles must be tagged permanently to actual points on the earth. This is where the datum comes into play. Even if two reference systems use the same ellipsoid, they could still have different anchors, or datum, on earth.

The simplest example of different datums is the difference between the geographic pole and the magnetic pole. In both models, the earth has the same spherical shape, but one is anchored at the North Pole, and the other is anchored somewhere near northern Canada.

To anchor an ellipsoid to a point on earth, you need two types of datum: a horizontal datum to specify where on the plane of the earth to pin down the ellipsoid, and a vertical datum to specify the height. For example, the North American Datum of 1927 (NAD 27) is anchored at Meades Ranch in Kansas because it's close to the geographical centroid of the United States. NAD 27 is both a horizontal and a vertical datum.

Here are some commonly used datums:

- NAD 83—North American Datum 1983, which is often accompanied by the GRS 80 ellipsoid
- NAD 27—North American Datum 1927, which is generally accompanied by the Clarke 1866/NAD 27 ellipsoid
- European Datum 1950
- Australian Geodetic System 1984

3.1.4 *Coordinate reference system*

Many people confuse coordinate reference systems with spatial reference systems. A coordinate reference system is only one necessary ingredient that goes into the making of an SRS and isn't the SRS itself. To identify a point on your reference ellipsoid, you need a coordinate system.

The most popular coordinate reference system for use on a reference ellipsoid is the geographical coordinate system (also known as *geodetic coordinate system* or simply as *lon/lat*). You're already intimately familiar with this coordinate system. You find the two poles on an ellipsoid and draw longitude (meridian) lines from pole to pole. You then find the equator of your ellipsoid and start drawing latitude lines.

Keep in mind that even though you may only have seen geographical coordinate systems used on a globe, the concept applies to any reference ellipsoid. For that matter, it applies to anything resembling an ellipsoid. For instance, a watermelon has nice longitudinal bands on its surface.

3.1.5 *Spatial reference system essentials*

Let's summarize what we've discussed thus far about spatial reference systems:

- You start by modeling the earth using some variant of a reference ellipsoid, which should be the ellipsoid that deviates least from the geoid for the regions on earth you care about.
- You use a datum to pin the ellipsoid to an actual place on earth, and you assign a coordinate reference system to the ellipsoid so you can identify every point on the surface. For example, the zero milestone in Washington, D.C., is W –77.03655 and N 38.8951 (in spatial, x: –77.03655, y: 38.8951) on a WGS 84 ellipsoid using the WGS 84 datum. On the NAD 27 datum and Clarke 1866 ellipsoid, this would be W –77.03685, N 38.8950.

We can quit at this point, because we have all the elements necessary to tag every spot on earth. We can even develop transformation algorithms to convert coordinates based on one ellipsoid to another. Many sources of geographic data do stop at this point and don't go on to the next step of projecting the data onto a flat surface. We term this data *unprojected data*. All data served up in the form of latitude and longitude is unprojected.

You can do quite a bit with unprojected data. By using the great circle distance formula, you can get distances between any two points. You can also use it to navigate to and from any point on earth.

3.1.6 *Projections*

The concept of *projection* generally refers to taking an ellipsoidal earth and squashing it onto a flat surface. Projection has distortion built in. Because geodetic and 3D globes are ellipsoidal, they by definition don't refer to a flat surface. So why do we have 2D projections of our ellipsoid or geoid? The obvious reason is eminently practical: you can't carry a huge globe everywhere you go. Less obvious but more relevant is the mathematical and visual simplicity that comes with planar (Euclidean) geometry.

As we've repeated many times, PostGIS works for the most part on a Cartesian plane, and most of the powerful functions assume a Cartesian model. Your brain and the quite different brain of PostGIS can perform area and distance calculations quickly on a Cartesian plane. On a plane, the area of a square is its side squared. Distance is calculated simply by applying the Pythagorean theorem. A planar model fits nicely on a piece of paper. In contrast, calculating the area of a square directly on the surface of an ellipsoid is quite a challenge, not the least aspect of which is deciding what constitutes a square on an ellipsoid in the first place.

> **PostGIS supports modeling other planets besides earth**
> Since PostGIS 2.3 the spheroidal model (geography) expanded support to any spheroid, meaning you can model other planets besides earth using geography. Also keep in mind that although PostGIS mostly focuses on earth, the spatial reference support can handle any registered spatial reference systems, including non-earthly ones.

How exactly you squash an ellipsoidal earth on a flat surface depends on what you're trying to optimize for. There are several classes of Cartesian coordinate systems, which we call kinds of projections, that are named for how they flatten the earth. Each class tries to optimize for a set of features. Each specific instance of a coordinate system is bounded by a particular region on earth and uses a particular unit (usually meters or feet) for units of Cartesian space.

In creating a projection, you try to balance four conflicting features. The importance you place on each will dictate your choice of coordinate system and eventually the spatial reference system:

- Measurement
- Shape—how accurately does it represent angles?
- Direction—is north really north?
- Range of area supported

The general tradeoff is that if you want to span a large area, you have to either give up measurement accuracy or deal with the pain of maintaining multiple SRSs and some mechanism to shift among them. The larger your area, the less accurate and potentially unusable your measurements will be. If you try to optimize for shape and to cover a large range, your measurements may be off, perhaps way off.

There are many flavors of projections that you can use to optimize for different things. Here are the most common ones:

- *Cylindrical projections*—Imagine a piece of paper rolled around the globe, imprinting the globe on its surface. Then you unroll it to make it flat. The most common of these is the Mercator projection, which has the bottom of the rolled cylinder parallel to the equator. This results in great distortion at the polar regions, with measurement accuracy better the closer you are to the equator, because there the approximation of flat is most accurate.
- *Conic projections*—These are sort of like cylindrical projections, except you wrap a cone around the globe, take the imprint of the globe on the cone, and then roll it out.
- *Azimuthal projections*—You project a spherical surface onto a plane tangential to the spheroid.

Within these three kinds of projections, you must also consider the orientation of the paper you roll around the globe. These are the possibilities:

- *Oblique*—Neither parallel nor perpendicular to the equator; some other angle
- *Equatorial*—Perpendicular to the plane of the equator
- *Transverse*—Parallel along the equator

Combinations of these categories form the main classes of planar coordinate systems:

- *Lambert Azimuthal Equal Area (LAEA)*—These are reasonably good for measurement and can cover some large areas, but are not great for shape. The one we like most when dealing with United States data and when we're concerned with somewhat decent measurement is US National Atlas (EPSG:2163). This is a meter-based spatial reference system. LAEAs are generally not good at maintaining direction or angle.
- *Lambert Conformal Conic (LCC)*—These preserve shape more than they preserve area and are generally good for measurement for the regions they serve. They distort poles. The projection commonly uses two lines of latitude for its bounds of a portion of a cone. The closer the two lines of latitude, the better the measurement accuracy. LCCs are best used for middle latitudes with east-west orientation.

They are often used for aeronautical charts, US state plane coordinate systems, and national and regional mapping.

- *Universal Trans Mercator (UTM)*—These are generally good for maintaining measurement and shape and direction, but they only span six-degree longitudinal strips. If you need to cover the whole globe and you use one of these, you'll have to maintain about 60 SRS IDs. You can't use them for the polar regions.

- *Mercator*—These are good for maintaining shape and direction and spanning the globe, but they're not good for measurement, and they make the regions near the poles look huge. The measurements you get from them are nothing less than cartoonish, depending on where you are. The most common Mercator projections in use are variants of World Mercator (SRID 3395) or Spherical Mercator (a.k.a. Google Mercator (SRID 900913)), which is now an EPSG standard with EPSG:3857 (ellipsoidal) (but for a time was EPSG:3785, which was spherical instead of ellipsoidal-based). Mercator systems are common favorites for web map display because you only have to maintain one SRID, and they look good to most people.

- *National grid systems*—These are generally a variant of UTM or LAEA but are used to define a restricted region, such as a country. As mentioned, US National Atlas (SRID 2163, US National Atlas Equal Area) is common for the United States. These are generally decent for measurement (but not super-accurate; they don't always maintain good shape), and they cover a fair amount of area, which is in many cases the national area you care about.

- *State plane*—These are US spatial reference systems. They're usually designed for a specific state, and most are derived from UTM. Generally there are two for a state—one measured in meters and one measured in feet—although some larger states have four or more. Optimal for measurement, these are commonly used by state and city land surveyors, but, as we said, they can deal with only a single state.

- *Geodetic*—PostGIS can store WGS 84 lon/lat (4326) as a geometry data type, but more often than not you'll want to transform it to another SRS or store it in the geography data type so it's usable. You can sometimes get away with using it as a geometry data type for small distances along the same longitude and when two things intersect, but keep in mind that when you use it, PostGIS is really projecting it. PostGIS squashes it on a flat surface, treating longitude as X and latitude as Y, so even though it looks unprojected, in reality it's projected and in a mostly unusable way. The colloquial name for this kind of projection is *plate carrée*.

Given all these different options for SRSs, determining which one your source data is in and choosing one for storage is often a tricky undertaking. In the next section we'll show you how to select a spatial reference system, and we'll look at some simple exercises for determining which SRS your source data is in.

3.2   *Selecting a spatial reference system for storing data*

One of the most common questions people ask is what spatial reference system is appropriate for their data. The answer is, "It depends."

Table 3.2 lists the most commonly used SRSs and their PostGIS/EPSG SRIDs. Post-GIS SRIDs follow the EPSG numberings, so you can assume for the sake of argument that they're the same. This isn't necessarily true for other spatial databases, so keep in mind that a spatial reference system can have several different IDs. Although EPSG is the most common authority on SRSs, it isn't the only one. Many people, for example, load up their tables with Esri definitions, which are sometimes identical to EPSG definitions, but under SRID codes that are more ArcGIS-friendly.

Table 3.2   Common spatial reference systems and their fitness for particular purposes

EPSG/PostGIS SRID	Colloquial name	Range	Measurement	Shape
4326	WGS 84 lon/lat	Excellent	Bad	Bad
3785/900913 (old number)	Spherical Mercator	Good	Bad	Good
900913 (deprecated)	Google Mercator	Good	Bad	Good
32601-32760	UTM WGS 84 zones	Medium	Good	Good
2163	US National Atlas EA	Good	Medium	Medium
State planes	US state planes	Medium	Good	Good

> **NOTE**   In table 3.2, the range, measurement, and shape values are relative. For range, *excellent* means it covers the globe, *good* means it covers a largish country like the U.S., and *medium* covers several degrees or a large state. For measurement, *good* means the measurements for the area served are usually within a meter for length, area, and distance calculations; *medium* means the measurements are accurate within meters, but distances can be as much as 10 meters off if two things are far from each other; and *bad* means the measurements don't have useful units, or they exaggerate areas as you get closer to the poles. Shape refers to how distorted shapes are and how well angles are preserved.

If you deal with mostly regional data, such as for a country or state, then it's generally best to stick with one of the national grid or state plane systems. You'll get fairly good measurement accuracy, and it will also look good on a map.

> **NOTE**   Cartesian coordinate systems that are measure-preserving only support a limited region. If you use the `geometry` type, you may have to use several spatial reference systems to span large areas and maintain measurement accuracy.

3.2.1 Pros and cons of using EPSG:4326

The most common SRS people use is WGS 84 lon/lat (EPSG:4326). It's used by many people who don't know anything about SRSs, but knowledgeable people use this system for a couple of main reasons:

- It covers the whole globe and is the most common SRS for sharing data. For example, all GPS data is stored in this SRS. If you need to cover the world, dish out data to lots of people, and deal with lots of GPS data, this isn't a bad choice.

- Most commercial mapping toolkit APIs accept data mapped only in WGS 84 lon/lat (although they use some variant of Mercator for display). ST_Transform also introduces some rounding errors as you retransform data, so it's best to transform only once from the source format. ST_Transform is a fairly cheap process, so it's okay to run it for each geometry if you keep functional indexes on the transformations of the form CREATE INDEX idx _geomt ON sometable USING gist(ST_Transform(geom,some_srid) and then use ST_DWithin(a.geom, ST_Transform(sometable.geom,some_srid), some_distance) for distance checking. With a functional index in place, when ST_DWithin is used with the ST_Transform geometry, the functional spatial index will be used to speed up the query.

There are also reasons not to use EPSG:4326:

- It's bad for measurement. If measurement is something you do often, and especially if you're concerned about small regions such as a country or state, you are better off using a measure-preserving localized spatial reference system such as a UTM SRS. There are hacks for getting precise measurements with EPSG:4326 by using a combination of ST_DistanceSpheroid, ST_DistanceSphere, and ST_DWithin. You can also use the geography data type instead, in exchange for fewer functions and much slower performance with most operations (on order of 10 times slower).

- Things like intersects, intersections, and unions generally work fine for small geometries but fall apart for large geometries, such as continents or long fault lines.

- It's bad for shape and it doesn't look good on a map. It's squashed because you're showing longitude and latitude, which are meant to be measured around an ellipsoid, and you're showing them on planar axes (X and Y).

> **Why is web map data in EPSG:4326?**
> Despite what we said about EPSG being bad for viewing on maps, most web mapping tools, such as Leaflet, Google Maps, Mapbox, and the pgAdmin4 Geometry viewer (built using Leaflet), expect your data to be in EPSG:4326 to be overlaid on the world base layers. However, when you overlay it, they are projecting the data to Web Mercator and only use EPSG:4326 as input, since lon/lat is the extent to which most people understand geographic data.

> **(continued)**
> You can check this out by taking your EPSG:4326 data, setting `ST_SetSRID(geom,0)`, and trying to view it in pgAdmin4. You will see the base layer is gone, and your geometry looks completely different in shape. That is really what 4326 data looks like when x = longitude and y = latitude plotted on a flat grid.

3.2.2 *Geography data type for EPSG:4326*

If you'll be storing your data in a WGS 84 spatial reference system, you should consider using the `geography` data type. The key benefit it provides over the `geometry` EPSG:4326 data type is that it's ideal for measurement because it's not projected, and measurements are always in meters. The pros are as follows:

- It will more or less work out of the box for you.
- Distance and area measurements are as good as or better than UTM, so if your data covers the globe and you just need distance, area, and length measurements, geography may be the best option.
- Intersects calculations are more correct with geography, especially for large geometries like earthquake fault lines and airline routes. These may intersect in flat EPSG:4326 geometry space when they do not intersect in true spheroidal space.
- Most web-mapping layers, such as Google, Virtual Earth (Bing), and the like, expect data to be fed to them in WGS 84 coordinates, so geography will work fine out of the box.

If geography is great, why should you use `geometry` instead?

- `geography`, except for point-to-point distance and intersect checks, is much slower than geometry. How much slower depends on the complexity of your shapes and the area of the shapes.
- Processing functions for `geography` are limited. For example, you can do an `ST_Intersection` and an `ST_Buffer`, but many processing functions are missing, such as the `ST_Union` aggregate function and `ST_Simplify`.
- Although you can piggyback on the `geometry` processing functions by casting and transforming to `geometry` and casting back, the `ST_Transform` operation isn't a lossless operation. `ST_Transform` introduces some floating-point errors that can quickly accumulate if you do a fair amount of geometry processing.
- If you're dealing with regional data, WGS 84 is generally not quite as accurate for measurements as regional SRSs.
- If you're building your own mapping app, you'll still need to learn how to transform your data to other SRSs if you want them to look good on a map. Although the transformation process is fairly cheap, it can quickly become taxing the

more data you pull, the more users hit your database, or the greater number of points you have in a geometry.

- Not as many tools support geography.

3.2.3 *Mapping just for presentation*

Although the basic Mercator projections are horrible for measurement calculations, especially far from the equator, they're a favorite for web mappers because they look good on a map. The advantage of Google Mercator, for example, is that the whole globe is covered with just one spatial reference system.

If your primary concern is looking good on a map and overlaying Google Maps with something like OpenLayers, Leaflet, or some other JavaScript API, Mercator isn't a bad option for native data storage. If you're concerned with distances and areas, however, your choice depends on the accuracy you need.

To compare distances across the globe and how they fare with Mercator, you can use the query shown in the next listing. Don't worry about understanding the full details in the listing just yet; we'll cover those topics in chapter 8 and later parts of this book.

> **Listing 3.1 Distance calculation in kilometers of city pairs**

```
WITH g1 AS (SELECT city, geog FROM ch03.city_airports          Spherical
        WHERE city IN('Beijing', 'Cairo','Sydney') ),          distance
     g2 AS  (SELECT city, geog FROM ch03.city_airports
        WHERE city IN('Melbourne', 'Philadelphia', 'São Paulo', 'Shanghai', 'T
    el Aviv') )
SELECT g1.city AS city1, g2.city AS city2,
    (ST_Distance(g1.geog,g2.geog, use_spheroid=>false)/1000)::integer AS sp,
    (ST_Distance(g1.geog,g2.geog, use_spheroid=>true)/1000)::integer AS spwgs84,
    (ST_Distance(ST_Transform(g1.geog::geometry,3857 ),
              ST_Transform(g2.geog::geometry,3857 ) )
              / 1000)::integer AS wm                      Spheroidal
FROM g1 CROSS JOIN g2                      Web Mercator   distance
WHERE g1.city <> g2.city                   distance
ORDER BY g1.city, g2.city;
```

Table 3.3 is generated using listing 3.1 and lists the distances between city airport pairs measured using various SRSs: WGS 84 sphere (sp), WGS 84spheroid (spwgs84), and Web Mercator (wm). The WGS 84 spheroid or sphere calculations are generally what most applications use for long-distance measurement. The sphere is a little less accurate because it treats the earth as a sphere rather than the more accurate ellipsoid model. The WGS 84 spheroid is as accurate as you can get for long-distance measurement. As you can see, the Web Mercator distance precision is very different from the WGS 84 spheroid, and therefore much worse for measurement, and it gets worse the farther away two cities are from each other or for regions farther from the equator. The computed distance between Beijing and Philadelphia, for example, is really poor with Mercator. The sphere calculations are pretty good for long-range/short-range rule-of-thumb calculations.

Table 3.3   Results of distance calculations in kilometers

city1	city2	sp	spwgs84	wm
Beijing	Melbourne	9113	9080	9923
Beijing	Philadelphia	11044	11070	21354
Beijing	São Paulo	17576	17577	19664
Beijing	Shanghai	1100	1098	1357
Beijing	Tel Aviv	7141	7156	9162
Cairo	Melbourne	13942	13938	14977
Cairo	Philadelphia	9167	9186	11946
Cairo	São Paulo	10218	10210	10661
Cairo	Shanghai	8369	8385	10064
Cairo	Tel Aviv	392	393	459
Sydney	Melbourne	705	706	871
Sydney	Philadelphia	15883	15882	26720
Sydney	São Paulo	13367	13386	22043
Sydney	Shanghai	7865	7837	8341
Sydney	Tel Aviv	14168	14166	15107

Table 3.3 covers distance, but what about the areas of geometries? How bad is the story there? Again, this depends on where you are on the globe, but in general the situation is bad. You can test it using the next listing, which uses the function in listing 3.3.

Listing 3.2   Ten-meter buffer at various points

```
WITH g1 AS (SELECT city,
      ST_Area( ST_Buffer(
          ST_Transform(geog::geometry, upgis_utmzone_wgs84(geog::geometry) ), 10
          )
      )::numeric(10,2) AS utm,
      ST_Area( ST_Transform(ST_Buffer(
          ST_Transform(geog::geometry, upgis_utmzone_wgs84(geog::geometry) ), 10
          ),4326)::geography )::numeric(10,2) AS geog,
      ST_Area( ST_Transform(ST_Buffer(
          ST_Transform(geog::geometry, upgis_utmzone_wgs84(geog::geometry) ), 10
          ),3857) )::numeric(10,2) AS wm
      FROM ch03.city_airports
          WHERE city IN( 'Arlhangelsk', 'Bergen', 'Boston', 'Helsinki', 'Honolulu',
                  'Murmansk', 'Oslo', 'Paris','San Francisco', 'St.
          Petersburg') )
SELECT g1.*, geog - utm AS diff_geog_utm, wm - utm AS diff_wm_utm
FROM g1
ORDER BY diff_wm_utm ASC;
```

- **UTM buffer** → `)::numeric(10,2) AS utm,`
- **UTM buffer measured in spheroidal** → `),4326)::geography )::numeric(10,2) AS geog,`
- **UTM buffer measured in Web Mercator** → `),3857) )::numeric(10,2) AS wm`

Table 3.4 shows the areas of 10-meter buffers around the globe produced by listing 3.2. The table shows the area of the buffers in the UTM (utm), geography (geog), and Web Mercator (wm) spatial reference systems. The two columns on the right show the differences between UTM and the other two buffer sizes. The buffer is created by picking a specific point and drawing a circle polygon around it with a 10-meter radius centered at the point using a UTM projection and then taking the area of the buffer after transformation to another spatial reference system (this will be covered in chapter 8).

Table 3.4   Ten-meter buffer areas in different regions of the world

city	utm	geog	wm	diff_geog_utm	diff_wm_utm
Honolulu	312.14	312.30	361.66	0.16	49.52
San Francisco	312.14	312.37	498.74	0.23	186.60
Boston	312.14	312.18	572.19	0.04	260.05
Paris	312.14	312.39	725.48	0.25	413.34
St. Petersburg	312.14	312.21	1229.85	0.07	917.71
Oslo	312.14	312.29	1259.67	0.15	947.53
Bergen	312.14	312.28	1267.28	0.14	955.14
Helsinki	312.14	312.30	1269.19	0.16	957.05
Arkhangelsk	312.14	312.34	1663.95	0.20	1351.81
Arkhangelsk	312.14	312.34	1690.51	0.20	1378.37
Murmansk	312.14	312.39	2373.13	0.25	2060.99

Why is a PostGIS 10-meter buffer of a point 312 and not 314 sq m?

If you do the calculation, a 10-meter buffer around a point should be a perfect circle with an area of $10*10*pi()$, which is around 314 square meters. The default buffer around a point in PostGIS is instead a 32-sided polygon (eight points approximate a quarter segment of a circle). You can make this more accurate by using the overloaded version of the ST_Buffer function that allows you to pass in the number of points used to approximate a quarter segment.

3.2.4   Covering the globe when distance is a concern

If you're in the unfortunate predicament of needing to cover the whole globe with good measurement and shape accuracy, then a single spatial reference system isn't likely to cut it. A common favorite for measurement accuracy that also preserves shape is the UTM family of SRSs. The UTM family has coordinates in meters, so it's easy to use for measurement. There are about 60 UTM SRIDs in the spatial_ref_sys table covering the globe that are based on the WGS 84 ellipsoid. Each UTM SRS covers six-degree longitudinal strips. There are also a series of UTMs for the NAD 83 ellipsoid, but the WGS 84 series is more common.

You'll need to figure out the WGS 84 UTM SRID for your particular data set, and there's a function for that in the PostGIS wiki at http://trac.osgeo.org/postgis. The following listing shows a slight variant of that function that takes any geometry and returns the WGS 84 UTM SRID of the centroid of that geometry.

Listing 3.3   Determining the WGS 84 UTM SRID of a geometry

```
CREATE OR REPLACE FUNCTION postgis.upgis_utmzone_wgs84(geometry) RETURNS
    integer AS
$$
DECLARE
    geomgeog geometry;
    zone int;
    pref int;
BEGIN
geomgeog:=ST_Transform(ST_Centroid($1),4326);        ❶ Convert to a
                                                         lon/lat point.

IF (ST_Y(geomgeog))>0 THEN
    pref:=32600;                                       ❷ Determine UTM
ELSE                                                     start and number
    pref:=32700;                                         of zones to add to
END IF;                                                  get the SRID
zone:=floor((ST_X(geomgeog)+180)/6)+1;

RETURN zone+pref;
END;
$$ LANGUAGE plpgsql immutable PARALLEL SAFE;
```

You convert your geometry to a point ❶ and then transform it to WGS 84 lon/lat. This function assumes the SRIDs are named the same as the EPSG for UTMs, which is the case with the default spatial_ref_sys table that comes packaged with PostGIS. WGS 84 UTM North Zones range from EPSG:32601 through EPSG:32660 and from EPSG:32701 through EPSG:32760 in the south. For example, the SRID of WGS 84 UTM Zone 1N is 32601, and the corresponding EPSG code is EPSG:32601; for WGS 84 UTM Zone 1S the SRID is 32701, and the corresponding EPSG code is EPSG:32701.

You determine whether latitude is positive or negative ❷. UTM EPSG numbers start with 32600 and increment every six degrees. Negative latitude, or 0, starts at 32700. The final SRID will be between these numbers.

If you need to maintain multiple SRIDs, you have three approaches:

- Store one SRID (usually 4326) and transform on the fly as needed.
- Maintain one SRID for each region and possibly partition your data by region using table inheritance or table partitions.
- Maintain multiple geometries—one field for each you commonly use.

There are many philosophies about the correct way to go, and none are right or wrong. For our cases, we've found that keeping one SRID (usually 4326) and transforming as needed works best, provided we maintain functional indexes on transforms used for distance calculations. We also like using views as an abstraction layer where the view contains the calculated transform. For PostgreSQL 12 and above, you can use PostgreSQL computed columns, which allow you to store the computed ST_Transform column right in the same table. Using computed columns will, however, impact insert and update speed. If things become too slow with views or computed columns, you could opt for using materialized views. The downside of materialized views for large tables is that they might take a while to rebuild, but they can be queried concurrently during building. You also need to set up a scheduling system to refresh them.

PostgreSQL supports not only functional indexes but also partial ones. A partial index allows you to index only part of your data. In general, you should only apply an ST_Transform function for the region defined for a given UTM; otherwise you'll run into coordinate bounds issues. It's also generally best to partition your data using table inheritance, and to use different transform indexes for each table.

The next listing shows an example of a functional ST_Transform index and of a possible view you might create to take advantage of it.

Listing 3.4 Using functional indexes

```
CREATE INDEX ix_feature_data_geom_utm_gist        Functional
  ON feature_data                                 index
  USING gist
  (st_transform(geom, 32611));
                                                  View to take advantage
CREATE VIEW vwfeature_data AS                     of the function
    SELECT gid, f_name, geom,
        ST_Transform(geom,32611) AS geom_utm
    FROM feature_data;
```

In this view, you're transforming your native data to SRID 32611, which is one of the UTM SRIDs for a region of California in the United States.

Functional indexes on ST_Transform

Putting functional indexes on ST_Transform is something we do when building a view on our data with the transformed version of the data. It's a gray zone, in the sense that we're exploiting a small violation by treating ST_Transform as an immutable function, when technically it isn't.

In PostGIS, ST_Transform is marked as immutable mostly for performance reasons, which means that when you calculate it for a given geometry, it can be assumed to never change. PostgreSQL kindly believes PostGIS and often caches the answer to ST_Transform and allows ST_Transform to be used in what are called functional indexes. A functional index is an index that involves the use of functions. Only functions marked as immutable can be used in functional indexes. An immutable function

(continued)

is a function that, given the same input, always returns the same output; in theory, a function that relies on a table (except possibly for a static system table in pg_catalog) is at best considered stable (meaning it won't change within a query given the same inputs).

In actuality, it's a bit of a lie that ST_Transform is immutable because it relies on entries in the spatial_ref_sys table. If you change the entry for your transform in the table, you'll need to re-index your data; otherwise it will be wrong. Computed columns in PostgreSQL, like indexes, can only use immutable functions for the same reason. So similarly, any other stored computation such as a computed column on ST_Transform would have stale data if you changed the definition of the records in the spatial_ref_sys table that the computation depends on (the native srid of the geometry or the target srid). We tend to think a bit liberally and consider the spatial_ref_sys table to be immutable in practice, because existing entries in the table rarely change. You might add entries to the table, but it's rare that you'd change the definitions of entries distributed with PostGIS or that you'd update an entry after you add it, so the immutability argument is valid.

The other issue with functional indexes is that they're dropped when you restore your data, unless you set the search_path of the ST_Transform function to include the schema that the spatial_ref_sys table resides in. Read our "Restore of functional indexes gotcha" diatribe on the Postgres OnLine Journal for more details: http://mng.bz/qedN.

So why do we use functional indexes on ST_Transform, even though it's a bit of a no-no? The alternative is to keep a geometry field for your alternative spatial references. This is annoying for two reasons:

- You have to ensure the second geometry field is updated when your main geometry field is, which means putting in a trigger. Someone may get confused and update the secondary geometry field instead of the primary geometry field.
- If you have big geometries, having a second big geometry in your table slows down updates considerably, because PostgreSQL creates a copy of the original record during updates and marks the original as deleted. It slows down selects too, because you have a fatter row to contend with.

Using ST_Transform on the fly is cheap, but doing an index search on this calculated call isn't possible without a gist index on this transformed data.

If you are running PostgreSQL 12 or above you can take advantage of generated columns. This has the benefit of not requiring you to use ST_Transform in your query and to have the transformation computed only once. The computed column will get recomputed for any update to dependent columns. This is covered in greater detail in appendix D.

The next listing achieves the same goal as listing 3.4, but using generated columns instead of a view.

Listing 3.5 Using functional indexes

```
ALTER TABLE feature_data                                    ⎤  Create a
  ADD COLUMN geom_utm geometry(POLYGON,32611)           ◁─┘  generated column.
  GENERATED ALWAYS AS ( ST_Transform(geom, 32611) )  STORED;

CREATE INDEX ix_feature_data_geom_utm_gist       ◁─┐  Create an index on the
  ON feature_data                                   │  generated column.
  USING gist(geom_utm);                             ┘
```

Although generated columns improve the speed of querying, they are not without their problems:

- They take up space, as opposed to a view that is always computed on the fly.
- They will slow down inserts and updates, especially for big geometries because extra data needs to be stored.
- If you change the definition of a function used by the column, you need to force a recomputation.

Often you'll have to load spatial data that you didn't create into your database. Before you worry about what spatial reference system you should use to transform your source data for storage, you'll first have to figure out what SRS your source data is in. If you guess wrong about that, all your spatial transformations will be wrong. In the next section we'll look at how you can determine the SRS of your source data.

3.3 *Determining the spatial reference system of source data*

In this section, we'll go through some exercises that will help you determine the spatial reference system of source data. This will prepare you for the next chapter, where we'll finally start loading real data.

Determining the SRS of your source data is sometimes a fairly easy task and sometimes not. Sometimes a site will tell you the EPSG code for its data, and your work is done. Often, it will give you a text representation of the SRS either in WKT SRS notation or some sort of free text. In these cases you'll need to match up the description with a record in the spatial_ref_sys table.

With newer ESRI shapefiles, there is often a file with a .prj extension giving the SRS information in WKT SRS notation. This file is often used by third-party tools to derive the projection in cases where different layers need to be transformed to the same SRS to be overlaid on a map. In the following exercises, we'll present some SRS text descriptions and demonstrate how you can match these to an SRID in the spatial_ref_sys table. In some cases, your task may be difficult, especially if the record you're looking for doesn't exist and you need to add it. We'll go over that too.

More shockingly, some data comes with no SRS or (even worse) the wrong information. The easiest way to determine if you have the wrong information is to overlay a map where you suspect this to be the case on top of a layer for the same region with a known SRS, and reproject to the suspected projection. Common errors include using NAD 27 data in a NAD 83 spatial reference system. In cases like this, you'll see a shift when you overlay the two because the same degree is not in the same spot between NAD 27 and NAD 83 spatial reference systems. If things are way off, one of your layers won't even show when you transform it to the same SRS as your known layer. This is the cause for a well-known beginner's FAQ: "Why don't I see anything?"

3.3.1   Guessing at a spatial reference system

Let's go over some simple but common exercises for determining the SRS of source data. In these examples, we'll pick out key elements in spatial reference system text representations.

EXERCISE 1: THE US STATES DATA

We downloaded a states data file that includes a states020.txt file, which gives spatial reference information as well as lots of details about how the data set was made and its licensing.

The spatial reference information at the bottom of the file reads as follows:

```
Spatial_Reference_Information:
    Horizontal_Coordinate_System_Definition:
    Geographic:
    Latitude_Resolution: 0.000278
    Longitude_Resolution: 0.000278
    Geographic_Coordinate_Units: Decimal degrees
    Geodetic_Model:
    Horizontal_Datum_Name: North American Datum of 1983
    Ellipsoid_Name: GRS1980
    Semi-major_Axis: 6378137
    Denominator_of_Flattening_Ratio: 298.257222
```

This is an important piece of information. It tells us that the data is in decimal degrees and that it uses ellipsoid GRS1980 and the North American Datum of 1983. These are the three ingredients you need to know about every data source you have:

- Unit: degrees
- Ellipsoid: GRS 80
- Datum: NAD 83

If you're dealing with projected data (non-degree data), there are some other fuzzy pieces you'll need to know. One is the projection, and each type of projection has additional parameters you'll want to look for. These are the common projections you'll find in spatial reference system text files:

- Degree (longlat)
- Lambert Azimuthal Equal Area (laea)
- Universal Trans Mercator (utm)
- Trans Mercator (tmerc)

- Lambert Conformal Conic (`lcc`)
- Stereographic (`stere`)

The short corresponding lowercase acronym is how you'll see these referred to in the `spatial_ref_sys.proj4text` field. For example, you'll see a `proj4text` entry start with `proj=utm` to denote a Universal Trans Mercator projection.

Once you've figured out these pieces, the next thing to do is match your source to an SRS defined in the spatial_ref_sys table and then record the SRID number for it. Sometimes the record you're seeking isn't in the table, and you'll need to add it, or there may be multiple matches.

Living without an SRID is only an option if you know that your data is planar, you know the units, and you know that all the data you'll be getting is from the same source and was made using the same SRS. In this case, you'll be using the unknown SRID, which is `-1` in pre-PostGIS 2.0 and `0` in the OGC standard and PostGIS 2+ series.

Two fields of information in the spatial_ref_sys table can help you guess at the projection. For the previous data, you can do a simple `SELECT` query to determine the SRID and use the PostgreSQL `ILIKE` predicate to do a case-insensitive search:

```
SELECT srid, srtext, proj4text, auth_srid, auth_name
FROM spatial_ref_sys
WHERE srtext ILIKE '%nad83%'
    AND proj4text ILIKE '%grs80%'
    AND proj4text ILIKE '%longlat%';
```

Some spatial reference systems consider the Z axis

Some spatial reference systems have a vertical datum component or are Compound CRS or Geographic 3D CRS. These consider the Z axis as well. The behavior of these SRSs is also different depending on which version of `PROJ` your PostGIS is compiled with; PROJ 6 and PROJ 7 have more functionality for these, whereas older `PROJ` versions can't handle many of these at all. Just know that vertical transformations exist, and if you have Z coordinates, and you use these, your Z will be transformed as well. People often assume the Z axis is untouched and may, for example, store their coordinates in degrees but their Z in feet. If you apply a transform that also changes the Z, and both your source and target SRS have a vertical component, you may get unpleasant results. For example, this query

```
SELECT ST_AsText(ST_Transform(ST_GeomFromText('SRID=4326;POINTZ(-100 400
    5)'), 5500) )
```

will output

```
POINT Z (-100 400 5)
```

In contrast,

```
SELECT ST_AsText(ST_Transform(ST_GeomFromText('SRID=7406;POINTZ(-100 400
    5)'), 5500) )
```

(continued)

will output

```
POINT Z (-100 400 1.524003048006096)
```

Also keep in mind that the vertical datum units may not be the same as the horizontal datum. For example, you may have a spatial reference system where the vertical datum is in meters but the horizontal (x,y) is in degrees longitude/latitude. If you look up the records in spatial_ref_sys, you will find that both srid 5500 and 7406 have a vertical component, with 7406 being NAD27 with vertical units measured in feet and 5500 being GRS 80 based with vertical units in meters.

The SELECT query will return several records; among them are SRIDs 4140, 4152, 4269, 4617, and 4759, which all have the same proj4text. The srtext is useful for matching up textual representations with SRSs in the table. Any records that have the same proj4text are most likely equivalent, so it doesn't matter which one of the set you use, as long as you consistently use the same one for the same projected data.

Also note that our states020.txt file has a Horizontal_Datum_Name filled in but no Vertical_Datum_Name. Some spatial reference systems also consider the Z axis (or height). In these cases you'll often find a Vertical_Datum_Name or VERT_DATUM or similar to denote that the SRS considers Z as well. If you have a geometry that has x, y, and z, the z coordinate will be transformed as well when you transform if you are moving to an SRS that has a vertical datum component. An example of this is a Compound CRS (http://mng.bz/7j1V)—one like auth_srid=5500, auth_name = EPSG that has a proj4text that looks like the following. The vunits tells you that the vertical units (z axis) are measured in meters:

```
+proj=longlat +ellps=GRS80 +towgs84=0,0,0,0,0,0,0 +geoidgrids=g2012a_conus.gt
    x,g2012a_alaska.gtx,g2012a_guam.gtx,g2012a_hawaii.gtx
,g2012a_puertorico.gtx,g2012a_samoa.gtx
+vunits=m +no_defs `
```

It has the following corresponding srtext:

```
COMPD_CS["NAD83(NSRS2007) + NAVD88 height",GEOGCS["NAD83(NSRS2007)",
DATUM["NAD83_National_Spatial_Reference_System_2007",
SPHEROID["GRS1980",6378137,298.257222101,AUTHORITY["EPSG","7019"]],
TOWGS84[0,0,0,0,0,0,0],AUTHORITY["EPSG","6759"]],PRIMEM["Greenwich",0,AUTHORI
    TY["EPSG","8901"]],UNIT["degree",0.0174532925199433,AUTHORITY["EPSG","91
    22"]],AUTHORITY["EPSG","4759"]],
VERT_CS["NAVD88 height",VERT_DATUM["North American Vertical Datum 1988",2005,
EXTENSION["PROJ4_GRIDS","g2012a_conus.gtx,g2012a_alaska.gtx,
 g2012a_guam.gtx,g2012a_hawaii.gtx,g2012a_puertorico.gtx,g2012a_samoa.gtx"],
AUTHORITY["EPSG","5103"]],
UNIT["metre",1,AUTHORITY["EPSG","9001"]],
AXIS["Up",UP],AUTHORITY["EPSG","5703"]],
AUTHORITY["EPSG","5500"]]
```

Changes in PROJ use between PostGIS 2 and 3

Starting with PostGIS 3, PostGIS is capable of using the PROJ 6 library and above, which is the next generation of PROJ.4 for coordinate reference transformations, which you'll learn a bit about at the end of this chapter. If you are running PROJ 6 or above, PostGIS will opt first to use `auth_srid` and `auth_name` if available. If there is no match, it then uses the `srtext` field, and as a last resort uses `proj4text` and passes that off to PROJ to consume. As such, the `proj4text` is not as important as it used to be, and the `auth_srid`, `auth_name` and `srtext` fields are no longer just informational. Much of this is explained in Paul Ramsey's "Proj 6 in PostGIS" blog post (http://mng.bz/myJy).

EXERCISE 2: SAN FRANCISCO DATA (READING FROM .PRJ FILES)

For this second exercise, we grabbed a zip file of San Francisco data that included a .prj file. The .prj contents look like this:

```
PROJCS["NAD_1983_StatePlane_California_III_FIPS_0403_Feet",
    GEOGCS["GCS_North_American_1983",
    DATUM["D_North_American_1983",
      SPHEROID["GRS_1980",6378137.0,298.257222101]],
      PRIMEM["Greenwich",0.0],
    UNIT["Degree",0.0174532925199433]],
    PROJECTION["Lambert_Conformal_Conic"],
     PARAMETER["False_Easting",6561666.666666666],
    PARAMETER["False_Northing",1640416.666666667],
    PARAMETER["Central_Meridian",-120.5],
    PARAMETER["Standard_Parallel_1",37.06666666666667],
    PARAMETER["Standard_Parallel_2",38.43333333333333],
    PARAMETER["Latitude_Of_Origin",36.5],
    UNIT["Foot_US",0.3048006096012192]]
```

You can surmise from this that the units are feet, it uses the NAD 83 datum, and the projection is some California state plane. Now you can guess by doing a query:

```
SELECT srid, srtext, proj4text, auth_srid, auth_name
FROM spatial_ref_sys
WHERE srtext ILIKE '%california%'
    AND proj4text ILIKE '%nad83%'
    AND proj4text ILIKE '%ft%';
```

This query yields several records. When you look at the `srtext` fields, each has something of the form "NAD83/California zone 1 (ftUS)," where the number ranges from 1 to 6. You may recall that III (which shows up in the .prj file) is the Roman numeral for 3. Also, depending on your spatial_ref_sys dataset, you might find a mix of `auth_name` = EPSG and `auth_name` = ESRI. Most of the ESRI ones can be found in the EPSG set, and EPSG is a more official body for spatial reference systems. When in doubt, choose the EPSG equivalent. So the answer must be SRID 2227, 2872, or 3494, each of which has an `srtext` field with all those elements. SRID 2227 seems closest in the srtext representation to what's in the file and is shown next. Keep in mind that all three SRIDs returned have essentially the same proj4text definition and so are equivalent:

```
"PROJCS["NAD83 / California zone 3 (ftUS)",
    GEOGCS["NAD83",DATUM["North_American_Datum_1983",
    SPHEROID["GRS 1980",6378137,298.257222101,AUTHORITY["EPSG","7019"]],
    AUTHORITY["EPSG","6269"]],
    PRIMEM["Greenwich",0,AUTHORITY["EPSG","8901"]],
    UNIT["degree",0.01745329251994328,AUTHORITY["EPSG","9122"]],
    AUTHORITY["EPSG","4269"]],
    UNIT["US survey foot",0.3048006096012192,AUTHORITY["EPSG","9003"]],
    PROJECTION["Lambert_Conformal_Conic_2SP"],
    PARAMETER["standard_parallel_1",38.43333333333333],
    PARAMETER["standard_parallel_2",37.06666666666667],
    PARAMETER["latitude_of_origin",36.5],
    PARAMETER["central_meridian",120.5],
    PARAMETER["false_easting",6561666.667],
    PARAMETER["false_northing",1640416.667],
    AUTHORITY["EPSG","2227"],
    AXIS["X",EAST],AXIS["Y",NORTH]]"
```

Now that you have some idea of how to match a spatial reference system to one in your table, what can you do if you guess wrong?

EXERCISE 3: IF YOU GUESS WRONG

Let's imagine you guessed the wrong SRID, and you've already loaded in all your data. What do you do now?

There are two ways to solve this problem. First, you can use the longstanding maintenance function in PostGIS called UpdateGeometrySRID, which will correct the mistake:

```
SELECT UpdateGeometrySRID('ch03', 'bayarea_bridges', 'geom', 2227);
```

The newer way is to use a typmod conversion:

```
ALTER TABLE ch03.bayarea_bridges
 ALTER COLUMN geom TYPE geometry(LINESTRING,2227)
  USING ST_SetSRID(geom,2227);
```

If we brought our San Francisco data in as unknown with a 0 SRID or with the wrong SRID, this would become quite apparent if we tried to transform our data. We'd get errors such as NaN when doing distance checks on the transformed data, or a transform error when doing the transformation.

In the next section we'll talk a bit about what to do when you've concluded that your spatial_ref_sys table doesn't have the spatial reference you're looking for.

3.3.2 When the SRS is missing from the spatial_ref_sys table

Sometimes you may come up short, and no record in the SRS matches what you're looking at. The best place to go at that point is EPSG: https://epsg.org. The older site, http://spatialreference.org, was useful in the past but is now largely defunct. The https://epsg.org site contains thousands of EPSG standard codes. The older site has many user-contributed ones.

> **NOTE** The older Spatial Reference site by default assigns an SRID starting with 9 to indicate that it was grabbed from the spatialreference.org site. For the sake of consistency, we replace this SRID with what's listed in the auth_srid field. By following this convention, you won't accidentally insert a record into spatial_ref_sys that's already in the table.

Although it's possible to create your own custom spatial reference system to suit your specific needs, this topic is beyond the scope of this book. PostGIS uses the PROJ library to underpin its projection support. If you're interested in how to do this, appendix A has links to articles on SRSs and PROJ syntax that may be of use.

3.4 History of PROJ support in PostGIS

PostGIS uses the PROJ library (https://proj.org/) to underpin its spatial reference and projection support. For a good chunk of PostGIS's existence, PROJ was known as PROJ.4 because it was largely the same for the past 15 years, except for additions of spatial reference systems, datum shifts, and bug corrections. Around 2018 this all changed, and an initiative was started to fund PROJ development (https://gdalbarn.com). The initiative funded both direct PROJ work and enhancements needed in GDAL to use the new features. This resulted in major changes in both PROJ and GDAL, and, to a smaller extent, other projects that rely on PROJ such as PostGIS. There were so many changes that the most recent version of PROJ is PROJ.7. Since the major leap from PROJ.4 to PROJ.7, the major version number is generally not included in the name; it is now more commonly referred to as PROJ.

So why is this such a huge deal? What happened between PROJ version 4 and PROJ version 7? Much of it is detailed on the PROJ "Known differences between versions" page: https://proj.org/usage/differences.html.

3.4.1 PROJ 4

PROJ 4.9, the last minor version of PROJ 4, provided better geodetic support, which mostly helped the geography data type and geodetic measurement functions like ST_DistanceSpheroid, and it allowed for the use of another library called geographiclib.

PostGIS 2.5 and 3.0 use these benefits but fall back on old ways, which really confused people comparing answers from PostGIS 2.5 compiled with different versions of PROJ. If you compile with a lower version of PROJ, you will be missing out on these enhancements in PostGIS.

3.4.2 *PROJ 5*

PROJ 5 provided better geodetic support with some longitudinal wrapping issue fixes. It still remains largely compatible with PROJ 4.

3.4.3 *PROJ 6*

PROJ 6 was a major turning point of PROJ. Proj 6 defines a new API, but it can support the older PROJ 4 APIs (if you enable a backward-compatible switch). PROJ 6 added support for vertical gridshifts (z axis), and it introduced pipelines, which are sequences of spatial projection paths.

PROJ 6 was also a major turning point for PostGIS. PostGIS 3 and beyond can take advantage of the new features in PROJ; for example, PROJ can now understand more than the short proj4text we have grown to love. How does this impact PostGIS? In the past, we've said that what was really important in the spatial_ref_sys table is proj4text, and all other columns in the table were informational. But if you are using PROJ 6+ with PostGIS 3+, this is no longer true. The new PROJ API, in addition to understanding proj4text, can also understand the srtext and auth_srid/auth_name columns in the spatial_ref_sys table.

This is the new order of relevance:

1 authname + authsrid—If these are filled in and found in the proj.db database file (the SQLite databases (caches) that the proj library provides), they are used to find the right coordinate reference system (CRS) transformation.
2 srtext—If this is filled in and can be found in the proj database, use this to formulate a CRS transformation.
3 proj4text—This is now only used if the preceding options fail.

PROJ 6 leads the way for better handling of time-based coordinate systems and transformations between them (such as NAD27/NAD83).

Also, in the past all reference system transformations as defined by proj4text were expressed in relation to WGS 84. This meant that datum shifts going from one coordinate system to another that was not WGS 84 still required going through WGS 84 first. This added a few errors to the computation. Now when the transformation is defined in the proj.db database, you can go straight from one reference system to another. This results in more accurate answers.

The aforementioned changes came not without a bit of pain. One of the new quirks of PROJ 6 and later is that for many EPSG systems, instead of the long-understood database longitude/latitude ordering, the default order of many coordinates is now latitude/longitude (which is more how mappers think). PostGIS, however, maintains the longitude/latitude (X/Y) standard for backward-compatibility.

Another major change that caused packaging issues was the introduced dependency on SQLite to store the projections and coordinate shift information. In the past, PROJ data files were provided in plain text CSV format. From PROJ 6 on, this information is stored in SQLite. For some OSs, particularly RedHat and Centos, the stable release carried an older version of SQLite, which made PROJ operations super slow, as discussed in the PROJ issue 1718 on GitHub: "proj 6.2.1 is very slow with sqlite 3.7.17-8 on RHEL 7" (https://github.com/OSGeo/PROJ/issues/1718).

In addition, GDAL 3+ now directly links to PROJ, and PROJ is making milestones every 6 months. In the past, PROJ could be dynamically loaded as needed, and it didn't change much, so it was unlikely you'd be using two versions of PROJ that were incompatible. This caused a few issues with packaging, because PostGIS and GDAL now directly rely on PROJ but may be compiled with different versions of PROJ. In the past, GDAL would load whatever PROJ was available; now it relies on a specific major version. The SQLite proj.db databases shipped with PROJ also often change from major release to major release. Packagers that package PostgreSQL and PostGIS are often different than the packagers packaging PROJ and GDAL. It is now possible to build GDAL with a different version of PROJ than PostGIS is built with. This causes all sorts of runtime issues, particularly with PostGIS rasters that depend on both GDAL and PostGIS core, as detailed in a thread on postgis-users ("Problem raster2pgsql on Centos 8 - postgres 12 / postgis 2.5," http://mng.bz/pJdw).

3.4.4 *PROJ 7*

The new APIs in PROJ 7 offer newer kinds of projections and support for more coordinate transformation data, a.k.a. *datumgrids*. The proj.db SQLite database could get huge very quickly if you were to store every available datumgrid, and for much of your use you probably only need a very small subset. PROJ 7 introduced the ability to pull datumgrids from online resources and cache them locally for future use. If you were to store the whole thing, it would take up about 500 MB of space, which is not a trivial size for a piece of dependency software.

3.4.5 *PROJ 8 and beyond*

The old PROJ API support (defined in proj_api.h) is dropped, and proj.h, which has the new API, will remain.

In addition to the direct transformation capabilities added to PROJ 6 and PROJ 7, new projections are being added (https://proj.org/operations/projections/index .html). In fact, you can see from the release notes that adding projections to PROJ will be a much more common occurrence.

Summary

- The world is not flat, but a flat model is sufficient for many kinds of analysis, and it makes calculations faster and easier.
- Spatial reference systems are used to reference our world on a flat surface.
- There are thousands of spatial reference systems, each differing by their ellipsoid, datum, projection, and coordinate system.
- The ellipsoid models the overall shape of a planet (the earth in most cases).
- The datum anchors the ellipsoid.

- The projection flattens all or a portion of the ellipsoid on a flat grid.
- The coordinate system defines the flat grid and its units. Units can be in meters, feet, degrees, or other units.
- The PROJ library is what PostGIS uses for coordinate transformations, and it has undergone a lot of enhancements recently.

Working with real data

4

This chapter covers

- PostGIS backup and restore utilities
- Utilities for downloading and uncompressing files
- Importing and exporting Esri shapefile data
- Importing and exporting vector data using ogr2ogr
- Querying external data using foreign data wrappers
- Importing and exporting raster data
- PostGIS raster output functions

In this chapter we'll look at how you can load real-world data into PostGIS and export it. We'll point you to specific data sources for the examples in this chapter, but if you're interested in other sources, see the list we've compiled in appendix A. We encourage you to explore on your own and report back on any discoveries of interesting data sources at our Manning author forum: www.manning.com/obe3.

> **NOTE** Geographic data that covers a swath of areas on our spheroidal earth needs special attention. You need to understand, at least on a rudimentary level, ellipsoids, datums, and projections in order to understand the pros and cons of different spatial reference systems so that you can

determine which ones suit your use. The fundamentals we provided in the previous chapter should guide you in the right direction.

Before we get started, we recommend that you create a separate schema to house the raw data you import. We generally name this schema *staging*, but call it whatever you like. Group your database assets into schemas instead of stuffing everything into the default *public* schema, which gets unwieldy after it grows to about 30 tables. We find the use of staging schemas especially helpful when importing data. They act as staging areas in which we inspect and cleanse preparatory tables. In a production environment, be sure to remove access for the general users.

The data and code used in this chapter can be found at www.postgis.us/chapter_04_edition_3.

In this chapter's code samples, the data we load will reside in the ch04 schema. You can create the same schema with the following SQL command:

```
CREATE SCHEMA IF NOT EXISTS ch04;
```

Also make sure your search_path includes the contrib schema in addition to the postgis schema:

```
ALTER DATABASE postgis_in_action SET search_path=public,contrib,postgis,topol
    ogy,tiger;
```

We'll start by introducing utilities not packaged with PostGIS that you can use to load data into PostGIS-enabled databases. These include packaged PostgreSQL command-line tools as well as OS-specific tools for downloading and extracting files.

4.1 PostgreSQL built-in tools

PostgreSQL server installations come with command-line tools for importing and exporting data. We'll be reviewing these tools in this section.

You'll also find these command-line tools packaged in the pgAdmin4 client tool. The backup and restore GUI options in pgAdmin4 use these tools, though you can directly access them from the pgAdmin4 install folder. If you're already adept at psql, pg_dump, pg_restore, and pgAdmin4, feel free to skip ahead.

4.1.1 Psql

Psql is a standard PostgreSQL command-line tool. If you're working in a non-GUI environment, you should already be intimately familiar with it.

Psql has both interactive and non-interactive modes:

- *Interactive mode*—Psql executes commands as you type them. You can use the \copy command to load comma- and tab-delimited data, as you read in chapter 1. The \copy command copies to and from the client machine—this is the machine from which psql was launched and it need not be the PostgreSQL server. The \copy command got a boost in PostgreSQL 9.3 and can now support copying from the output of other programs. This allows you to load the outputs from wget and curl in a single command line.

- *Non-interactive mode*—You prepare script files and pass them to psql for execution. This mode lets you load data in batches. The popular PostGIS shp2pgsql tool relies on psql to silently process its generated SQL.

When you invoke psql, you can add switches to indicate the host name (--host or -h), user (--user or -u), and database (--database or -d). If you're authenticating via trust, peer, or ident, these settings will be sufficient. Authentication requiring a password is tricky because you can't specify a password. Psql will either prompt or read the password from the pgpass.conf file (or ~/.pgpass), should you have one defined in your home directory. Psql will also honor passwords set using environment variables.

If you intend to use psql as your main workhorse, you should set the following variables or use the pgpass file so you can call psql without always having to string together a chain of switches:

- PGPORT—The port that the PostgreSQL service is running on
- PGHOST—The IP address or host name of the PostgreSQL server
- PGUSER—The PostgreSQL role to connect as
- PGPASSWORD—The password for the role
- PGDATABASE—The database to connect to

To set these environment variables on Windows, create a .bat file, and on each line add a set command such as the following:

```
set PGPORT=5432
```

For many Windows users, the psql file may not be in your execution PATH, so you may need to add a line such as this:

```
set PATH="%PATH%;C:\Program Files\PostgreSQL\13\bin"
```

For Linux/Unix users, use export in a shell (.sh) script.

For a full list of PostgreSQL environment variables, refer to the PostgreSQL documentation at www.postgresql.org/docs/current/static/libpq-envars.html.

4.1.2 pgAdmin4

pgAdmin4 is a graphical interface tool packaged with many versions of PostgreSQL. It's also available as a separate install via the pgAdmin site (www.pgadmin.org). You can run it on any machine with a graphical interface, or as a hosted Python WSGI web app on non-GUI based systems (www.pgadmin.org/download/pgadmin-4-python/). Its functionality rivals that of psql, and you can use it in place of psql. Many users will find using GUI-based administration tools to be more productive than using command-line tools.

One shortcoming of pgAdmin4 is that it doesn't support a client-side \copy command. For delimited files, pgAdmin4 offers a GUI interface, and you can always resort to the SQL COPY command. You can access the import/export GUI through the context menu of each table as shown in figure 4.1.

Figure 4.1   pgAdmin table Import/Export menu

The options tab, shown in figure 4.2, allows you to choose between import and export as well as which file and encoding to use.

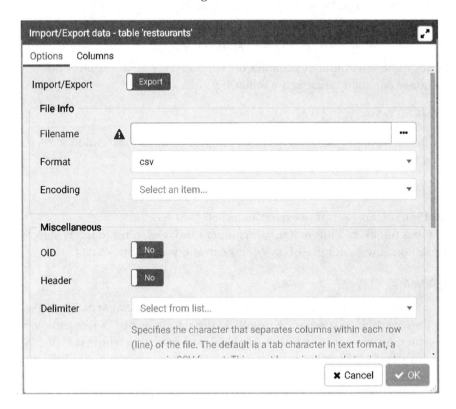

Figure 4.2   pgAdmin table Import/Export Options Tab

The Columns tab, shown in figure 4.3, allows you to choose which columns to import or export.

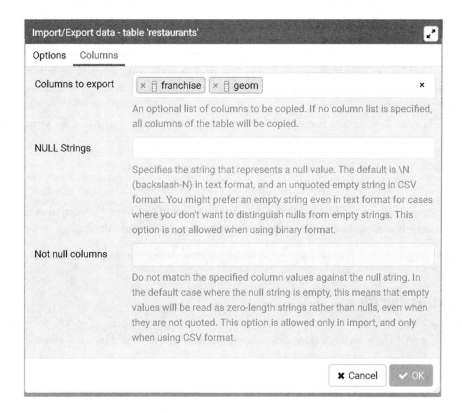

Figure 4.3   pgAdmin table Import/Export Columns tab

For importing, you'll need to make sure you have the same number of columns in your file as the number of columns you have specified, and ensure that they are of compatible data types.

4.1.3   Pg_dump and pg_restore

If you need to distribute large amounts of data, or to back up data for restoring to other databases, pg_dump and pg_restore are the tools. Pg_dump can back up data in a compressed format to save space. You can then use pg_restore to restore these tables, functions, and the like to another PostgreSQL database.

When you restore using pg_restore, avail yourself of the -j switch to enable multiple processes. This can speed the restore up to the number of processes you have running. You should limit -j to no more than the number of processing cores that you have.

4.2   *Downloading files*

Wget is a command-line tool for grabbing files from the internet, generally prepackaged with Linux and Unix systems or installable via package managers such as yum or apt. For Windows, download it using the Scoop package manager (https://scoop.sh) or the Chocolatey package manager (https://chocolatey.org/packages/Wget). Standalone binaries can be found at https://eternallybored.org/misc/wget.

If you're on Windows or any OS with a GUI, wget is not essential, as you can download files using your browser, but you may still find wget handy for automating the download of many files.

The following command will download the specified zip file to your current directory:

```
wget https://www2.census.gov/geo/tiger/TIGER2020/ZCTA5/
 tl_2020_us_zcta510.zip
```

If the site supports FTP and exposes a directory listing of files, you can also use a wildcard as follows to download multiple files in a single command:

```
wget ftp://rockyftp.cr.usgs.gov/vdelivery/Datasets/Staged/Tran/Shape/
 *Connecticut*.zip
```

4.3   *Extracting files*

Most files you'll download will be compressed in tar.bz, tar.gz, or zip format. Most Linux and Unix systems have programs to extract these files. Here are some examples:

- Unzip a single zip file:

  ```
  unzip somefile.zip
  ```

- Unzip all zip files in folders, recurse down, and put them in the same folder:

  ```
  for z in */*.zip; do unzip -o $z; done
  ```

- Unzip a single .tar gzipped file and extract its contents (two equivalent commands)

  ```
  tar xvfz somefile.tar.gz
  ```

  or

  ```
  gzip -d -c somefile.tar.gz | tar xvf
  ```

- Unzip tar.bz2 files:

  ```
  tar -jxvf filename.tar.bz2
  ```

For Windows, we recommend the 7-Zip extraction and compression utility. 7-Zip is free for both personal and commercial use, and it can extract all the aforementioned formats and more. For zip files, you can also use the built-in uncompress in Windows. We've found 7-Zip to be better than the built-in Windows tool because it can handle compressing and extracting files over 4 GB in size, and it gives you many more compression options, such as password protection and level of compression. You can download 7-Zip from www.7-zip.org. Installation automatically adds it to the Windows Explorer context menu so that you can right-click on a zip file and unzip with ease.

After you install, 7-Zip may not be in your PATH. You can add it to your PATH by doing the following:

```
set PATH="%PATH%;C:\Program Files\7-zip\"
```

Although most people think of 7-Zip as a nice GUI tool for extracting various compression formats, it also has a handy command-line interface (the 7z.exe file) that's useful for automating zip and unzip processes. To make this portable, you can copy the 7z.exe and 7z.dll files to a USB flash drive or a folder, and use them from anywhere without an install.

Following are some simple tips for using the 7-Zip command-line interface:

- Extract a single file (tar.gz) in the same directory. The first example decompresses the .gz into a .tar file and the second extracts the .tar:

  ```
  7z e somefile.tar.gz

  7z x somefile.tar -oC:\gisdata\states
  ```

- Extract all zip files in the current folder to a new folder called extracteddata using a flat folder structure:

  ```
  7z e C:\gisdata\*.zip -oC:\gisdata\extracteddata
  ```

- Extract all zip files in the current folder to a new folder called extracteddata, and keep the same folder structure as in the archive:

  ```
  7z x *.zip -y -oC:\gisdata\extracteddata
  ```

- Extract all zip files in the current folder to a new folder called extracteddata, and recursively search for .zip files:

  ```
  for /r %%z in (*.zip ) do 7z e %%z -oC:\gisdata\extracteddata
  ```

4.4 Importing and exporting shapefiles

PostGIS comes packaged with a pair of command-line tools, shp2pgsql and pgsql2shp, for importing and exporting Esri shapefiles respectively. A GUI version of both exists: shp2pgsql-gui. Despite its name, the GUI version both imports and exports.

What is an Esri shapefile? Esri produces some of the most widely used commercial GIS software; Esri's preponderance during the early days of GIS allowed it to popularize its proprietary file format—*Esri shapefiles*. Shapefiles continue to be the most widely used format for distributing GIS data.

The term *shapefile* actually refers to an entire entourage of files:

- *.shp*—The main file containing the geographical data ends in a .shp extension. Against expectations, including a .shp file is optional.
- *.dbf*—This is a dBase formatted file. Including a .dbf file for storing non-GIS data is mandatory.
- *.prj*—The .prj file is optional and describes the projection of the main shapefile.
- *.shx*—These are one or more index files.
- *.cpg, .ldif*—These files denote the encoding of the .dbf file data. When present, shp2pgsql will read the encoding from the file.

4.4.1   Importing with shp2pgsql

If you launch shp2pgsql from the command line without any arguments, the help will come up with a plethora of switches. The most important ones are as follows:

- -D—Uses the postgresql dump format. This makes loading much faster than the default SQL INSERT mode. However, it cannot be manually edited easily to fix minor issues like bad geometries or to allow the skipping of bad records.
- -s—Specifies the spatial reference system (SRS) of the source data; you should always include this switch. Even if a projection is present, PostGIS still can't make an accurate determination of the SRID. For example -s 4269 means the source data is in 4269 and the destination table should be 4269. You can also indicate the SRID of the destination, effectively letting you transform during the loading. The format of the switch is -s srid_from:srid_to. For example, -s 26986:4326 means that the source data is in Massachusetts State Plane Meters but should be reprojected to WGS 84 lon/lat during the load. Unfortunately, the -s 26986:4326 transform feature can't be used in conjunction with the -D switch for versions of PostGIS earlier than 3.0. If you are using PostGIS 2.5 or below and loading a large table, the transform syntax will be much slower than loading the data first and transforming after the load.
- -W—Specifies the encoding of the source dBase file. As of PostGIS 2.2, shp2pgsql will read the encoding from a .cpg or .ldid file if present. Omit this switch and shp2pgsql will assume the dBase file to be in UTF-8. Should shp2pgsql find characters outside of those expected, it will write a line to the console for each encounter, but you'll probably miss these messages as they fly by, and you'll unknowingly end up with incomplete data.
- -I—Creates a spatial index on the geometry column after loading. You may wish to hold off adding indexes to a table until you're done loading, because indexes slow down insertions. This switch is useful if you don't plan to append more data to this table in the near future.

- -g—Sets the name of the geometry or geography column in the table created by shp2pgsql. The default is geom for geometry and geog for geography.
- -G—Loads to the geography data type instead of the default geometry data type. Shp2pgsql will only honor this switch if your data is in WGS 84 lon/lat (SRID 4326). You can, however, transform during the load to WGS 84 with the -s switch, as in -G -s 26986:4326.

Additional switches let you take advantage of other useful shp2pgsql features, such as saving a file with an SQL INSERT command for later use, converting column names to PostgreSQL standards, and loading just the non-geographical data from the dBase file.

Since PostGIS 2.2, you can also specify a mapping file with -m; this allows you to specify a file that contains name mappings between the dBase file and the PostgreSQL table column names. Any columns with a match in the dBase file will be renamed, while others will retain their original name.

Let's go through a step-by-step example of loading data with shp2pgsql. For this exercise, we'll load state boundaries from the 2020 United States Census. You can find the data file at https://www2.census.gov/geo/tiger/TIGER2020/STATE/tl_2020_us_state.zip.

First, download and extract the file using your tool of choice. You should end up with seven files. The three used by shp2pgsql are tl_2020_us_state.shp, tl_2020_us_state.dbf, and tl_2020_us_state.shx. Shp2pgsql will also try to use the .cpg file to make sense of the encoding, but this file is not required.

Next, figure out the spatial reference system. For this dataset, we know the SRS to be NAD 83 lon/lat, which has an SRID number of 4269. (In chapter 3, we showed you how to arrive at this SRID.)

Finally, open up a console and execute shp2pgsql using this command:

```
shp2pgsql -s 4269 -g geom_4269 -I -W "latin1"
➥ "tl_2020_us_state" staging.tl_2020_us_state |
➥ psql -h localhost -p 5432 -d postgis_in_action -U postgres
```

For Linux, if you have the GUI installed, shp2pgsql is part of your default path. If you are on Windows, you may need to set the path with a command such as this:

```
set PATH="%PATH%;C:\Program Files\PostgreSQL\13\bin\"
```

Shp2pgsql outputs SQL. In the preceding example, we immediately execute the SQL by piping it to psql. Loading the data should take just a few seconds. After it's done, you should see a new table in your staging schema with a geometry column named geom_4269. Shp2pgsql also loads the textual information, creating additional columns with data culled from the attending dBase file.

If you don't want the data loaded immediately but wish to save the SQL file, execute the following command instead:

```
shp2pgsql -s 4269 -g geom_4269 -I -W "latin1"
➥ "tl_2020_us_state" staging.tl_2020_us_state > tl_2020_us_state.sql
```

The SQL output is then dumped to a .sql file named tl_2020_us_state.sql. You can edit this file, fixing any misbehaving data points or text. If the file is so large that it can't fit into memory for loading, you can break it apart so that you can load it piecemeal. When you're ready to perform the loading, run the psql command.

If you don't specify a user with the -u switch, the user defaults to what psql defaults to, which is usually the logged-in OS username:

```
psql -h localhost -p 5432 -d postgis_in_action -f tl_2020_us_state.sql
```

You can also load the data from the file interactively within psql by doing the following from the psql console:

```
\connect postgis_in_action
\i tl_2020_us_state.sql
```

4.4.2 *Importing and exporting with shp2pgsql-gui*

Shp2pgsql-gui is the graphical counterpart of shp2pgsql. It isn't available in all Post-GIS installs, as it can only run on platforms with a graphical user interface.

For Windows, shp2pgsql-gui is part of the StackBuilder PostGIS Bundle installer, which installs to bin/postgis-gui in your PostgreSQL folder. On other platforms, shp2pgsql-gui is often available as a separate package. The name of the package varies depending on the distribution. For example, on apt-based packaging, it's called postgis-gui but it ends up installing all of PostGIS and shp2pgsql-gui.

Although postgis-gui is not packaged with pgAdmin, it is often used in conjunction with it. pgAdmin3 had an option to allow you to call shp2pgsql-gui from the Plugins menu, and it would read your connection settings from your currently connected database if you had shp2pgsql-gui installed. The new incarnation of pgAdmin, pgAdmin4, doesn't have the ability to invoke shp2pgsql-gui.

> **StackBuilder**
>
> PostgreSQL StackBuilder is distributed as part of EnterpriseDb desktop installations. The StackBuilder simplifies upgrading PostgreSQL and the installation of extensions and utilities. The EnterpriseDb installer is currently the most widely used installer for PostgreSQL/PostGIS on Windows.

Shp2pgsql-gui is user-friendly and obviates the need to memorize and look up command-line syntax and switches. The main deficiencies of shp2pgsql-gui are that you can't create an SQL file to save for later, and it's generally slower than shp2pgsql for loading large files. shp2pgsql-gui takes you straight from Esri shapefiles to Post-GIS tables.

We're not going to show you how to use shp2pgsql-gui in detail, because the GUI is intuitive enough. Figure 4.4 shows what shp2pgsql-gui looks like after you've filled in

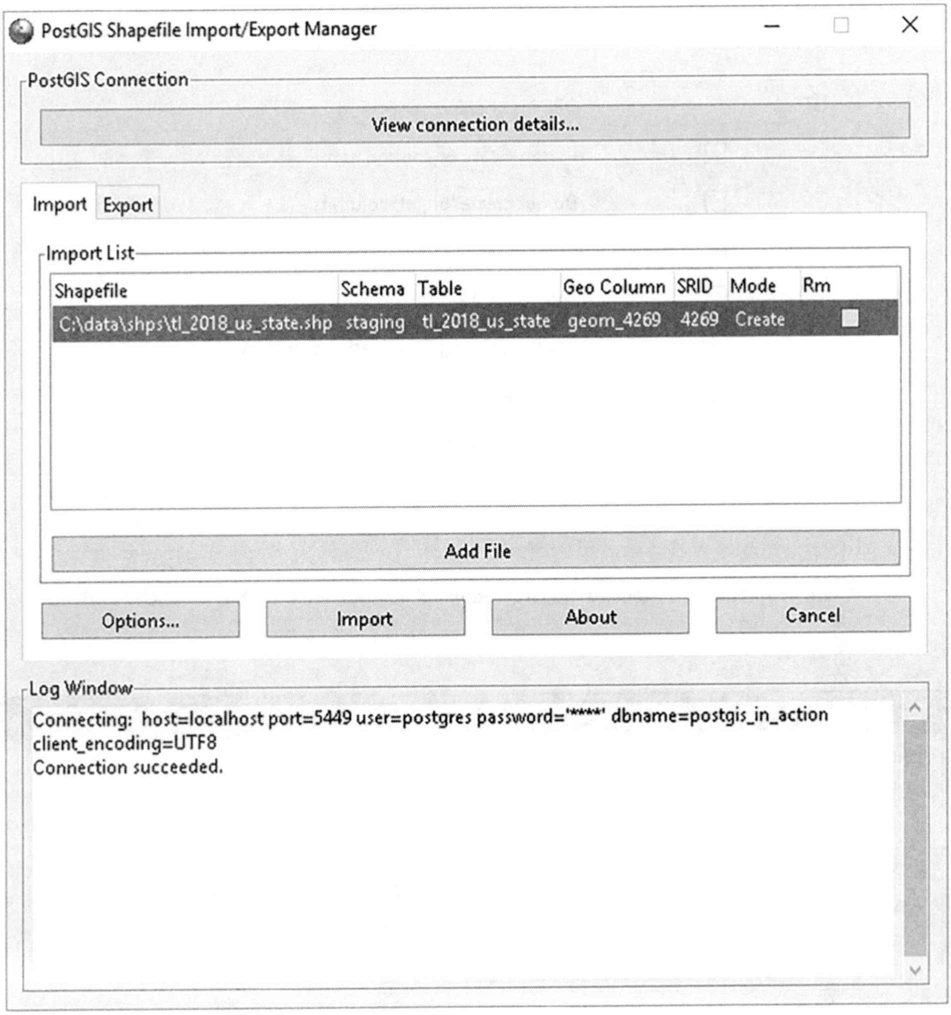

Figure 4.4   Using shp2pgsql-gui

the connection info using the View Connection Details button, specified an import path by browsing to the states table using the browser icon, and filled in the relevant information for geometry column and srid.

Next you need to click Options, as shown in figure 4.5, to choose or verify additional settings.

The shp2pgsql-gui name has become somewhat of a misnomer because you can now use it to export PostGIS data to shapefiles. To export, switch to the Export tab, click Add Tables, and select all the tables you'd like to export. For tables with more than one geometry or geography column, a drop-down lets you pick which column to export (see figure 4.6).

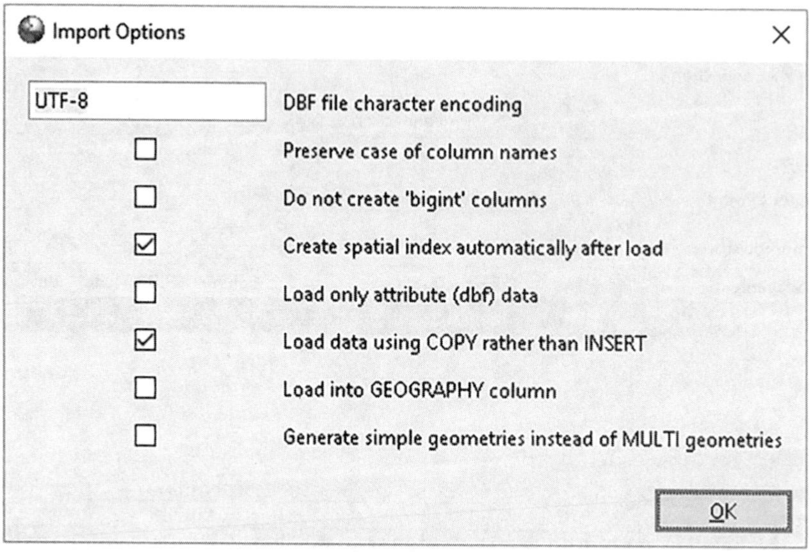

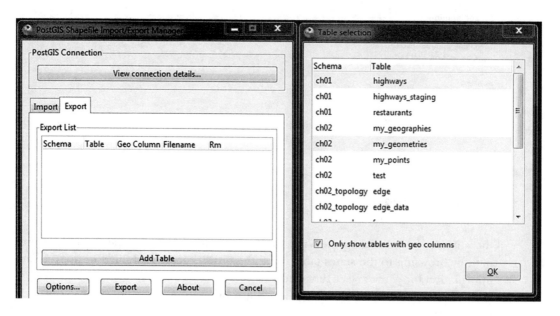

Figure 4.5   The shp2pgsql-gui Import Options dialog box showing the advanced options

Figure 4.6   Adding tables for export in shp2pgsql-gui

When you're ready, click the Export button and you'll be prompted about where to save the generated shapefile.

4.4.3 *Exporting with pgsql2shp*

You can use pgsql2shp to export PostgreSQL tables, views, and queries to Esri shapefiles and the dBase file format. Keep in mind that a shapefile isn't a single file but a set of files. In most cases, pgsql2shp outputs .dbf, .shp, .shx, and .prj files. It will omit the projection file (.prj) if it can't determine the SRID of the geometry or geography column. If you export a table without a geometry or geography column, pgsql2shp will create a dBase file (.dbf) and nothing else. This means you can use pgsql2shp as a dBase export utility for PostgreSQL.

> **NOTE** Some packages install command-line programs in a separate location from the server install; refer to appendix B if you have trouble locating pgsql2shp or shp2pgsql.

You'll often find pgsql2shp in the bin folder of your PostgreSQL install. Launch it without any arguments to see the help. There are two caveats to keep in mind:

- Column names longer than ten characters will be truncated. If this creates duplicate column names, pgsql2shp will add a sequence number. You can create a mapping file to exercise more control over column names.
- Esri shapefiles can't handle textual columns with more than 255 characters and will silently drop anything over the limit.

Let's look at two examples of pgsql2shp: one to export a table, and one to export a query.

USING PGSQL2SHP TO EXPORT A TABLE

This example exports a table called zips in the ca schema of the database named gisdb (California zip codes). Once finished, you should end up with four new files—cazips.shp, cazips.dbf, cazips.shx, and cazips.prj:

```
pgsql2shp -f /gisdata/cazips gisdb ca.zips
```

The next example accomplishes the same task, but includes switches to indicate the hostname and credentials:

```
pgsql2shp -f /gisdata/cazips -h localhost -u pguser -P qwerty -p 5432 gisdb
    ca.zips
```

USING PGSQL2SHP TO EXPORT A QUERY

Although exporting whole tables is common, you may want to export only a subset of rows from a large table, filtered using a query. The following query outputs filtered rows:

```
pgsql2shp -f boszips -h localhost -u postgres gisdb
    "SELECT * FROM ca.zips WHERE city = 'Napa'"
```

The next query transforms the SRID to 4326 (WGS 84 lon/lat) during export:

```
pgsql2shp -f boszips -h localhost -u postgres gisdb
➡ "SELECT zip5, ST_Transform(the_geom, 4326) AS geom
➡ FROM ca.zips
➡ WHERE city = 'Napa'"
```

4.5   *Importing and exporting vector data with ogr2ogr*

For working with spatial data, nothing rivals the GDAL toolkit. Ogr2ogr (https://gdal
.org/programs/ogr2ogr.html#ogr2ogr) is a command-line tool included in the toolkit, and you can use it to import an ever-growing list of spatial and non-spatial formats
into PostgreSQL and PostGIS. You can see the complete list at https://gdal.org/
drivers/vector. Shp2pgsql does a great job of importing Esri shapefiles, but if your
source data is not a shapefile, you'll need ogr2ogr.

GDAL is available for Linux, Unix, Windows, and macOS. You can download the
appropriate version here: https://trac.osgeo.org/gdal/wiki/DownloadingGdalBinaries.
You can also compile your own version, if you can't find a ready-made version for
your OS.

Ogr2ogr and other GDAL utilities also come packaged with QGIS desktop (https://
qgis.org/en/site/) and are accessible via the QGIS shell console. The latest stable version of QGIS always includes the latest stable GDAL.

Many formats that ogr2ogr can work with are optionally compiled. To determine
which formats your ogr2ogr can handle, run this command:

```
ogr2ogr --formats
```

That should output a list similar to this one:

```
Supported Formats:
  netCDF -raster,vector- (rw+s): Network Common Data Format
  AmigoCloud -vector- (rw+): AmigoCloud
  PCIDSK -raster,vector- (rw+v): PCIDSK Database File
  PDS4 -raster,vector- (rw+vs): NASA Planetary Data System 4
  JP2OpenJPEG -raster,vector- (rwv): JPEG-2000 driver based on OpenJPEG library
  PDF -raster,vector- (rw+vs): Geospatial PDF
  MBTiles -raster,vector- (rw+v): MBTiles
  :
  ESRI Shapefile -vector- (rw+v): ESRI Shapefile
  MapInfo File -vector- (rw+v): MapInfo File
  :
  :
  GPKG -raster,vector- (rw+vs): GeoPackage
  SQLite -vector- (rw+v): SQLite / Spatialite
  ODBC -vector- (rw+): ODBC
  WAsP -vector- (rw+v): WAsP .map format
  PGeo -vector- (ro): ESRI Personal GeoDatabase
  MSSQLSpatial -vector- (rw+): Microsoft SQL Server Spatial Database
  PostgreSQL -vector- (rw+): PostgreSQL/PostGIS
```

Next to each format, you will see in parentheses one or more of these letters:

```
rw - read/write
 rw+ - read/write create
 ro - read only
 v - reference in a virtual table
```

The GDAL toolkit is a big toolkit, deserving a book of its own. We'll cover the most common import and export features in this chapter, but for other uses, check out these sites:

- Examples of non-spatial data loading are included in our article, "GDAL ogr2ogr for data loading," at www.postgresonline.com/journal/archives/31-GDAL.html.
- Additional information about spatial data loading and installation for Windows is available on the Boston GIS site: www.bostongis.com/PrinterFriendly.aspx?content_name=ogr_cheatsheet.

4.5.1   *Environment variables in ogr2ogr*

Unlike shp2pgsql, ogr2ogr ignores encoding. Whatever encoding goes in, also comes out. To ensure that PostgreSQL will convert when necessary, you need to set the client encoding environment variable to the encoding of the incoming data.

The client encoding is the encoding that PostgreSQL honors for each connection session. This is different from database encoding, which varies by database and is set when you first create the database. If PostgreSQL sees a difference between the client encoding and the database encoding, it will automatically convert for you both ways, but you must tell PostgreSQL what the client encoding is. It can't look at the incoming data and make a guess, and it certainly can't read your mind as to how you want to encode the data coming back to you.

The name of the environment variable is PGCLIENTENCODING. To set it, use export in Linux/Unix/macOS:

```
export PGCLIENTENCODING=LATIN1
```

Use set in Windows:

```
set PGCLIENTENCODING=LATIN1
```

Another environment variable worth setting is PG_USE_COPY. This should be set to YES if you want to use the faster PostgreSQL copy command for appending data, instead of the slower SQL inserts. Newer ogr2ogr versions (GDAL 2.0 and above) automatically use copy, but older versions may still heed this variable.

Additional PostgreSQL-specific settings and environment variables can be found in the GDAL documentation (https://gdal.org/drivers/vector/pg.html). Ogr2ogr can also use PostgreSQL libpq environment variables.

NOTE Although we specify port, host, and password for PostgreSQL in these examples, keep in mind that if your port is 5432 or the host is localhost, these setting are optional and can be left out. Ogr2ogr is also capable of using the libpq environment variables PGHOST, PGPASSWORD, PGUSER, and PGDATABASE as detailed in the PostgreSQL docs (www.postgresql.org/docs/11/libpq-envars.html) or pgpass files. You can set the environment variables in lieu of passing them in the connection string.

4.5.2   *Ogrinfo*

Ogrinfo is a tool that analyzes the source data and extracts what metadata it can, such as the spatial reference system, bounding box, layers (for multilayer formats), and attributes.

What ogrinfo uncovers depends on the format of the data source. For GPX, ogrinfo provides little more than the field names and geometry type, but for Esri personal geodatabase, ogrinfo will thoroughly inundate you with information. We suggest that you always run a quick ogrinfo prior to every import, especially for large files; you don't want to expend the effort of importing a large file only to find that a field you need is not part of the import.

To get more information on ogrinfo and see the variety of switches available, see the GDAL documentation (www.gdal.org/ogrinfo.html).

4.5.3   *Importing with ogr2ogr*

Ogr2ogr can be used to import numerous vector data formats and non-spatial data such as spreadsheets. In this section we'll cover the more common vector formats you need to load.

OGR2OGR IMPORT SWITCHES

Ogr2ogr lets you add a -lco switch to control various aspects of the tables that it creates during import. These are some common arguments for the switch:

- GEOM_TYPE—Options are geometry, BYTEA, or OID to force the type of geometry used for a table. In general, there's no need to set this.
- GEOMETRY_NAME—Names the new geometry column. If omitted, the default is wkb_geometry.
- LAUNDER—Set this to YES, the default, and column names will be rechristened to be more PostgreSQL-friendly; specifically, LAUNDER will lowercase the column names and replace any characters not allowed in PostgreSQL identifiers.
- PRECISION—Set this to YES, the default, and ogr2ogr will choose numeric data types over floats and integers, and character over character varying.

To specify more than one option, repeat the -lco switch.

Another often-used switch is -nln. This allows you to name the table that ogr2ogr creates.

You can find the full details of the ogr2ogr PostgreSQL switches in the GDAL/OGR PostgreSQL documentation (https://gdal.org/ogr/drv_pg.html). When you read the vector documentation, keep in mind that *layers* in GIS translate to tables in databases.

LOADING GPS EXCHANGE FILES (GPX)

GPX files are the standard transport format for GPS-generated data. GPX textual data is in XML, so you can take advantage of all the XML functionality built into PostgreSQL. GPX data is always in the WGS 84 lon/lat spatial reference system (SRID 4326). Ogr2ogr is smart enough to put in the correct SRID for you. For more details about command-line switches specific to the OGR GPX driver, see the GDAL documentation (www.gdal.org/ogr/drv_gpx.html).

OpenStreetMap is full of user-contributed GPX files uploaded by users worldwide. You can find these at www.openstreetmap.org/traces. We randomly selected one from Australia titled "A bike trip around Narangba" by going to www.openstreetmap .org/traces/tag/australia and downloading the file www.openstreetmap.org/user/ Ash%20Kyd/traces/468761.

You can find out more about the data you're about to load by using ogrinfo:

```
ogrinfo 468761.gpx                    ←⎤ Command
INFO: Open of '468761.gpx' using driver 'GPX' successful.    ←⎤ Output
1: waypoints (Point)
2: routes (Line String)
3: tracks (Multi Line String)
4: route_points (Point)
5: track_points (Point)
```

Next, you can load this up into a staging schema with the following simple ogr2ogr command:

```
ogr2ogr -f "PostgreSQL"
➥ PG:"host=localhost user=postgres port=5432
➥ dbname=postgis_in_action password=mypassword"
➥ 468761.gpx -overwrite -lco GEOMETRY_NAME=geom
➥ -nln "staging.aus_biketrip_narangba" track_points
```

The preceding code loads the track_points layer into a new table called aus_biketrip _narangba in a schema called staging.

The following command loads all the layers, creating new tables for each layer. The command specifies the schema in which the tables should be created, but it does not specify which layers to import. When unspecified, ogr2ogr will import all the layers:

```
ogr2ogr -f "PostgreSQL" PG:"host=localhost user=postgres
➥ port=5432 dbname=postgis_in_action password=>mypassword"
➥ 468761.gpx -overwrite -lco GEOMETRY_NAME=geom -lco SCHEMA=staging
```

LOADING A GEOPACKAGE

The GeoPackage format (www.geopackage.org/) is an OGC standard format that is an SQLite database with a standard way of storing vector and raster data. The format is convenient for sharing data. You can use it to export both PostGIS vector and raster data as well as to load in data provided by other groups.

Ogr2ogr version 2 and later supports reading, updating, and creating GeoPackages. More details for using GeoPackages can be found in the GDAL documentation (https://gdal.org/drivers/vector/gpkg.html).

In the next example, you'll download a GeoPackage of global political boundaries from www.gadm.org/download_world.html. You can download either the whole world or go country by country. Whichever you choose, make sure to select the GeoPackage database format for this exercise. Once it's extracted, you'll get an MDB file.

To learn more about your data, you can use ogrinfo as follows:

```
ogrinfo gadm36_levels.gpkg
```

Specifying only the file name will give you just the list of layers in the file as shown in the following output

```
INFO: Open of `gadm36_levels.gpkg'
      using driver `GPKG' successful.
1: level0 (Multi Polygon)
2: level1 (Multi Polygon)
3: level2 (Multi Polygon)
4: level3 (Multi Polygon)
5: level4 (Multi Polygon)
6: level5 (Multi Polygon)
```

If you want to know more about a specific layer, you can specify the layer of interest. If this is a large database, ogrinfo will take a bit of time to churn through it. The following command applies the -so switch to let ogrinfo know that we only want summary data. The last set of arguments in the command are the layers we are interested in:

```
ogrinfo gadm36_levels.gpkg -so -geom=YES level0 level5
```

In the preceding command we ask for summary information for level0 and level5 layers. This is the output we get when we run the preceding command:

```
INFO: Open of `gadm36_levels.gpkg'
      using driver `GPKG' successful.

Layer name: level0
Geometry: Multi Polygon
Feature Count: 256
Extent: (-180.000000, -90.000000) - (180.000000, 83.658300)
Layer SRS WKT:
GEOGCS["WGS 84",
    DATUM["WGS_1984",
        SPHEROID["WGS 84",6378137,298.257223563,
```

```
                AUTHORITY["EPSG","7030"]],
            AUTHORITY["EPSG","6326"]],
        PRIMEM["Greenwich",0,
            AUTHORITY["EPSG","8901"]],
        UNIT["degree",0.0174532925199433,
            AUTHORITY["EPSG","9122"]],
        AUTHORITY["EPSG","4326"]]
FID Column = fid
Geometry Column = geom
GID_0: String (0.0)
NAME_0: String (0.0)


Layer name: level5
Geometry: Multi Polygon
Feature Count: 51427
Extent: (-5.143750, -2.839970) - (30.899100, 51.089400)
Layer SRS WKT:
:
FID Column = fid
Geometry Column = geom
GID_0: String (0.0)
NAME_0: String (0.0)
GID_1: String (0.0)
NAME_1: String (0.0)
GID_2: String (0.0)
NAME_2: String (0.0)
GID_3: String (0.0)
NAME_3: String (0.0)
GID_4: String (0.0)
NAME_4: String (0.0)
GID_5: String (0.0)
NAME_5: String (0.0)
TYPE_5: String (0.0)
ENGTYPE_5: String (0.0)
CC_5: String (0.0)
```

The output lists the names of the fields, their sizes, and also the spatial reference system of the data—WGS 84 lon/lat (**SRID 4326**). The output also tells us the geometry type of each layer and the number of records.

We can filter down to the United States, bring it into the database, and transform it to US National Atlas Equal Area:

```
ogr2ogr -f "PostgreSQL"
➥ PG:"host=localhost user=postgres port=5432
➥ dbname=postgis_in_action password=mypassword" gadm36_levels.gpkg
➥ -lco GEOMETRY_NAME=geom
➥ -where "ISO='USA'"
➥ -t_srs "EPSG:2163"
➥ -nln "us.admin_boundaries" gadm1
```

In this example, we limit ourselves to within the US boundaries using the ISO= 'USA' where predicate and we transform it from the original 4326 SRID to the 2163

SRID. If you look in the PostGIS spatial_ref_sys table, you'll see that 2163 corresponds to US National Atlas. We also load the data into a new table called admin_boundaries that resides in the us schema. In this particular case, ogr2ogr has enough information to guess at the source SRID, so we didn't proffer it. If you have to tell ogr2ogr what the source SRID is, use the -s_srs switch.

If you try to load the full data set, you might run into errors because of the multitude of languages that might be in a file containing global data. To accommodate this, you'll need to set the client encoding of the data to LATIN1. Unfortunately, you can't set the client encoding with a switch in ogr2ogr, so you'll have to resort to setting environment variables.

LOADING A MAPINFO TAB FILE

Another popular format is the MapInfo TAB file format. MapInfo files encode the spatial reference information, obviating the need for a separate projection file. Field names can be upper, lower, or mixed case without any character-size limitations. Because we use MapInfo files for mapping, they are usually chock full of cartographic formatting instructions that ogr2ogr conveniently ignores.

The next example uses a file from Statistics Canada, which you can download from www12.statcan.gc.ca/census-recensement/2011/geo/bound-limit/files-fichiers/gecu 000e11m_e.zip. The zip file you download will include several TAB files.

The following code shows how you can load the entire folder in one swoop, which is a handy feature of ogr2ogr, especially if you have hundreds of files:

```
ogr2ogr -f "PostgreSQL" PG:"host=localhost user=postgres port=5432    Folder of
  dbname=postgis_in_action password=mypassword" "/gisdata/canada"   ◄──  input files
  -lco GEOMETRY_NAME=geom -lco SCHEMA=canada   ◄──┐  Name of the geometry column in
  -a_srs "EPSG:4269"   ◄──┐                           the new table and the schema
                          │ SRS of the                that will house new table
                          │ source
```

In the preceding code, you tell ogr2ogr which folder to look in for the files; it will pull all the files it recognizes and create separate tables named after the files. You also explicitly specify the source SRID. If you don't, ogr2ogr would create an arbitrary SRID and add this to the spatial_ref_sys table to ensure you end up with the correct projection. This is highly undesirable, but we have yet to figure out why ogr2ogr can't discern the correct SRID, even though it has no problem reading the projection information.

Now that you've learned how to import data with ogr2ogr, you'll want to know how to export data as well. In the next section, we'll cover exporting PostGIS data into various spatial vector formats with ogr2ogr.

4.5.4 *Exporting with ogr2ogr*

Ogr2ogr allows you to output tables, views, and queries. With ogr2ogr, you can export multiple tables at once.

OGR2OGR EXPORT SWITCHES

The most important switches for outputting data with ogr2ogr are the following:

- `-select`—Specifies the fields you want to output.
- `-where`—Sets the filter condition. The syntax is the same as a SQL WHERE clause.
- `-sql`—Use this if you want to output a more complex query than what `-select` and `-where` offer. The output column data types may not reflect the data types of your query columns.
- `-t_srs`—Specifies the SRID that you want ogr2ogr to output to. Ogr2ogr will ignore this if it can't figure out the SRID of the source, or if the source SRID is not in the list of projections included with your particular installation of ogr2ogr.
- `-s_srs`—Specifies the SRID of the data you're exporting. You can usually get away with leaving this out because ogr2ogr does a good job of determining the SRID.
- `-dsco overwrite=YES`—Instructs ogr2ogr to delete the old files first, if they exist. It's useful if you have a nightly scheduled dump where you're constantly overwriting the same files.

Now that you know the fundamental switches used when exporting data from PostgreSQL with ogr2ogr, we'll demonstrate exporting PostgreSQL data to popular geospatial file formats.

EXPORTING TO GEOJSON USING OGR2OGR

JavaScript Object Notation (JSON) and its extended sibling, Geography JavaScript Object Notation (GeoJSON), are the most widely used transport formats for web services. GeoJSON data is most always output using SRID 4326. (To learn more about the KML driver used by ogr2ogr, see the GDAL documentation: https://gdal.org/drivers/vector/geojson.html.)

The next example requires gdal 2.3 or higher. If you are using a lower version, leave out the `-dsco ID_FIELD=<some field>`:

```
ogr2ogr -f "GeoJSON" /gisdata/us_adminbd.json            ◁──┐ Simple export of the
➥ PG:"host=localhost user=postgres port=5432 dbname=postgis_in_action       whole table to KML
➥ password=mypassword" -dsco ID_FIELD=name_2 us.admin_boundaries
```

```
                                                         ◁──┐ Exports a subset of records
ogr2ogr -f "GeoJSON"                                        based on a filter to KML
➥ /gisdata/biketrip.json PG:"host=localhost user=postgres port=5432
➥ dbname=postgis_in_action password=mypassword"
    -dsco ID_FIELD=track_seg_point_id
➥ -select "SELECT track_seg_point_id, ele, time"
➥ -where "time BETWEEN '2009-07-18 04:33-04' AND '2009-07-18 04:34-04'"
➥   staging.aus_biketrip_narangba
                                        ◁──┐ Exports multiple tables
ogr2ogr -f "GeoJSON"                       to a single KML file
➥ /gisdata/biketrail.json PG:"host=localhost user=postgres port=5432
```

```
➥ dbname=postgis_in_action password=mypassword"
➥ staging.track_points staging.tracks
```

EXPORTING TO KML USING OGR2OGR

Keyhole Markup Language (KML) is a format popularized by Google Earth and Google Maps. It is used much less frequently today and has been largely replaced by GeoJSON. The following code demonstrates how you can output a single table, a query, and multiple tables. KML data is always in WGS 84 lon/lat (SRID 4326). If your data is in a known projection, ogr2ogr will transform it to 4326 without you having to specify either the source or the output SRID. If you want finer control, PostGIS offers a ST_AsKML function that you can use in lieu of ogr2ogr (to learn more about the KML driver used by ogr2ogr, see the GDAL documentation at https://gdal.org/drivers/vector/kml.html):

```
ogr2ogr -f "KML" /gisdata/us_adminbd.kml        ◁──┐ Simple export of the
➥ PG:"host=localhost user=postgres port=5432 dbname=postgis_in_action    whole table to KML
➥ password=mypassword" us.admin_boundaries -dsco NameField=name_2
```

```
                                                    ┌── Exports a subset of records
ogr2ogr -f "KML"                                 ◁──┘ based on a filter to KML
➥ /gisdata/biketrip.kml PG:"host=localhost user=postgres port=5432
➥ dbname=postgis_in_action password=mypassword" -dsco NameField=time
➥ -select "SELECT track_seg_point_id, ele, time"
➥ -where "time BETWEEN '2009-07-18 04:33-04' AND '2009-07-18 04:34-04'"
➥ staging.aus_biketrip_narangba
                          ┌── Exports multiple tables
ogr2ogr -f "KML"       ◁──┘ to a single KML file
➥ /gisdata/biketrail.kml PG:"host=localhost user=postgres port=5432
➥ dbname=postgis_in_action password=mypassword" -dsco NameField=time
➥ staging.track_points staging.tracks
```

These examples include a NameField argument, which tells ogr2ogr which field to use as the KML title.

When exporting multiple tables, ogr2ogr places them all into the same KML file. Take a look at the KML generated by the preceding multi-table export in Google Earth, and you'll see two layers in the biketrail.kml file: one for track_point and one for tracks.

EXPORTING TO MAPINFO TAB FILE FORMAT USING OGR2OGR

The next example outputs to MapInfo TAB format. Unlike KML, which is always in WGS 84 lon/lat (SRID 4326), MapInfo data can be in any SRID. In many cases, the SRID of the data in PostGIS is not the one you want to end up with in the output.

In the first example in the following listing, you use the -f_srs switch to transform the SRID.

Listing 4.1   Export PostGIS tables and queries to MapInfo TAB format

```
ogr2ogr -f "MapInfo file"          ◁──┐     Exports PostGIS data to an EPSG
➥ /gisdata/us_boundaries.tab         ❶     4326 projected MapInfo file
```

```
➡ PG:"host=localhost user=postgres
➡ port=5432 dbname=postgis_in_action password=mypassword"
➡ -t_srs "EPSG:4326" us.admin_boundaries
ogr2ogr -f "MapInfo file"          ◄──────────┐    Exports a subset of
➡ /gisdata/biketrip.tab                       │    the PostGIS data
➡ PG:"host=localhost user=postgres port=5432  │    (no transformation,
➡ dbname=postgis_in_action password=mypassword"  ❷  native projections)
➡ -select "SELECT track_seg_point_id, ele, time"
➡ -where "time BETWEEN '2009-07-18 04:33-04' AND '2009-07-18 04:34-04'"
➡ staging.aus_biketrip_narangba
ogr2ogr -f "MapInfo file"          ◄──────────┐    Exports multiple
➡/gisdata/tab_files                           │    PostGIS tables to the
➡ PG:"host=localhost user=postgres port=5432  ❸  same MapInfo file
➡ dbname=postgis_in_action password=mypassword"
➡ staging.track_points staging.tracks
```

In the first example, you transform the data from the National Atlas projection to WGS 84 lon/lat ❶. In the second example, you keep the data in the original PostGIS SRID (National Atlas projection), but only output a subset of the data using a -where switch ❷. In the third example, you export two tables and ogr2ogr creates a set of four files (.tab, .map, .dat, .id) for each table ❸. It also creates a containing folder called tab_files. If the containing folder already exists, you must include the -dsco overwrite=YES switch, or ogr2ogr will balk.

EXPORTING TO A GEOPACKAGE

GeoPackages are a great way to share a portion of your database with other users. They can be used in a number of desktop and mobile tools. QGIS, which we'll cover in a later chapter, makes heavy use of them.

In this next example, we'll export a whole database into GeoPackage format:

```
ogr2ogr -f GPKG postgis_in_action.gpkg
➡ PG:"host=localhost user=postgres port=5432 dbname=postgis_in_action
     password=mypassword"
```

4.6 Querying external data using PostgreSQL foreign data wrappers

Foreign data wrapper (FDW) technology was introduced in PostgreSQL 9.3 as a uniform and seamless method for querying data in different formats external to the database. FDW hides the complexity of interfacing and translating an external data source and allows you to query external data as if it was in tables residing in your PostgreSQL database. To connect to a foreign data source, you must use the appropriate foreign data wrapper. FDWs are packaged as PostgreSQL extensions.

Many individuals have contributed FDWs to handle countless varieties of data formats. You'll find wrappers for connecting to other relational databases, NoSQL databases, column stores, and even web services. Many FDWs are well maintained, but some have fallen into disrepair.

Unfortunately there is no single listing that covers all of FDWs available for PostgreSQL. Searching GitHub for "postgresql+fdw" will give you the largest array of FDWs, since most FDWs have a presence on GitHub (https://github.com/search?p =2&q=postgresql+fdw). Many of these FDWs are not carried by packagers, so they will require compilation.

Most FDW extensions, if not all, follow the convention of ending their extension name in "_fdw". To find out which ones are available through your packager, you can search for "fdw" in the extension name in the package list:

- For Debian/Ubuntu users: `apt list | grep fdw`
- For Yum users: `yum list | grep fdw`

The preceding commands won't list `postgres_fdw` or `file_fdw`, since these are part of the PostgreSQL package. They can be enabled without additional installs by using CREATE EXTENSION **postgres_fdw**.

To get a listing of all the FDWs you already have binaries installed for and can therefore enable with CREATE EXTENSION, run this SQL query:

```
SELECT *
FROM pg_available_extensions
WHERE name LIKE '%fdw';
```

As with all extensions, the FDW extension binaries must be installed for your version of PostgreSQL and then be enabled in each database you want to use them in.

There are four elements to establishing a data connection using FDW:

- *Foreign data wrapper*—This is the piece of code that handles the actual data exchange between PostgreSQL and a foreign source. It is packaged as a Postgre-SQL extension. Install it first by installing the binaries via your package manager, and then use CREATE EXTENSION **name-of-fdw** to enable it in your database of choice. Different data formats have different wrappers. For example, the following three wrappers handle PostgreSQL, MySQL, and ODBC-compliant databases: postgres_fdw, mysql_fdw, and odbc_fdw. Yes, you can and should use FDW to connect to other PostgreSQL servers.
- *Foreign server*—This represents the data source. Although the word *server* is in the name, the source need not be a server. It could be another database on the same server, a folder, or even a web service. Each foreign data wrapper can have one or more foreign servers.
- *User mapping*—This establishes the mapping from a local PostgreSQL role to a user on a foreign server. The Postgre role can be a user or group role. Not all wrappers support user mapping.
- *Foreign table*—A foreign server can have one or more foreign tables. You can then query the foreign table like any other PostgreSQL table. You can even join foreign tables to other tables in your database. Again, the name *table* doesn't

mean that it's a table. A foreign table could be a sheet in an Excel or Libre-Office workbook, a file in a directory, and so on.

Figure 4.7 shows a view in pgAdmin4 of the Foreign Data Wrappers section. In this view we have two FDWs installed, and you can see that each has a node for servers and user mappings.

Figure 4.7 List of foreign servers in pgAdmin4

If you don't see the node for Foreign Data Wrappers in pgAdmin, you need to go into File > Preferences > Browser-Nodes and set Foreign Data Wrappers, Foreign Servers, and Foreign Tables to Show.

> **NOTE** Postgres_fdw is an FDW commonly packaged with PostgreSQL that allows you to connect to other PostgreSQL databases. Naturally, you'll find it to have the most extensive support and best performance because it is the reference implementation for new FDW features added in each PostgreSQL release. If you need to query or update data on another PostGIS-enabled database on the same server, on a different server, or even on a different server with a different version of PostgreSQL and PostGIS, postgres_fdw is the way to go.

4.6.1 *File_fdw foreign data wrapper*

File_fdw is a read-only foreign data wrapper that connects to any delimited text file. Most PostgreSQL distributions include file_fdw. Like all PostgreSQL extensions, you install it on a database-by-database basis. Further, you can specify a schema to install into. We don't recommend installing extensions in the default public schema, or any schema where you store data tables.

Use the following commands to create a contrib schema, if it doesn't exist, and install the file_fdw extension.

```
CREATE SCHEMA IF NOT EXISTS contrib;
CREATE EXTENSION file_fdw SCHEMA contrib;
```

Once file_fdw is installed, you next need to create a foreign server. In the case of file_fdw, a foreign server is more of a formality. The concept of a server, when it comes to a file, is nonexistent. In fact, you can create a single foreign server as the container for all the files you intend to connect to:

```
CREATE SERVER fiserver FOREIGN DATA WRAPPER file_fdw;
```

Next you can link in any delimited text files as long as they're accessible by the PostgreSQL service (postgres) account. In this next example, we'll link in the restaurants.csv file we loaded in chapter 1:

```
CREATE FOREIGN TABLE ch04.ft_restaurants (
    franchise text,
    lat double precision,
    lon double precision
)
SERVER fiserver
OPTIONS (
    format 'csv',
    header 'false',
    filename '/data/restaurants.csv',
    delimiter ',',
    null '',
    encoding 'latin1'
);
```

If you want non-superusers to be able to create foreign tables in file_fdw, you need to add them or a role they are already a member of to the pg_read_server_files built-in role.

> **NOTE** If you are on Windows, you should include the drive letter in the path, like C:/data/ch01/restaurants.csv.

Once you have everything set up, you should be able to query ch04.ft_restaurants using code like this:

```
CREATE TABLE ch04.restaurants_bkg AS        ◁──┐  Creates a new
SELECT                                           │  table from the
    franchise,                                    │  query
    ST_Transform(
        ST_SetSRID(
            ST_Point(lon,lat),
            4326
        ),                                          Uses typmod
        2163                                        to constrain
    )::geometry(POINT,2163) AS geom    ◁──┘        the data
FROM ch04.ft_restaurants
WHERE franchise = 'BKG';    ◁──┐  Limits the query to
                                │  just one franchise
```

Even though this code is querying a file, not a database table, the querying speed is fast. On our low-end experimental server, the preceding query took 300 ms and created a table with 7,435 rows. Removing the filter, we loaded a table of over 50,000

rows in about 450 ms. These speeds are comparable to using the SQL COPY or psql
\copy commands.

Here are some key points to keep in mind when using file_fdw:

- A FDW connection is reusable. The data you are querying is in the file, and not
physically in your database. If you swap the restaurants.csv file with a newer data
set, you gain access to the refreshed data immediately.

- You can apply functions to the data, use any clause available with the SQL
SELECT command, and join with other tables. In the preceding example we
used lon,lat to make a point column and then transformed the SRID. We
added the typmod to ensure that the final table has the geometry column registered correctly in the geometry_columns table.

- The file must be accessible by the server, which generally means it needs to
reside on the server itself; the postgres system account needs to have read rights
to it.

- Although you can query the data in the file much like a table, you can't modify
the foreign table in any way. This means no indexes to speed up your query.
Some FDWs, such as postgres_fdw, can take advantage of indexes on the remote
database, but not file_fdw.

Starting with PostgreSQL 9.4, file_fdw can also link to outputs of programs. This
means that you could query a file you pull via wget or curl. You can query the output
of any of your programs. To tap into this feature, the postgres process must have execute rights to the program.

4.6.2   Ogr_fdw foreign data wrapper

The ogr_fdw foreign data wrapper piggybacks on GDAL/OGR for linking to both vector and non-spatial data sources. Think of ogr_fdw as being a bit like ogr2ogr. Any format that ogr2ogr can import, ogr_fdw can link to. Ogr_fdw is also capable of updating
data on the data source if writing is supported for that format and the postgres service
account has the needed permissions. The ogr_fdw extension is available via yum.post-
gresql.org or apt.postgresql.org. For Windows users, the Application Stack Builder
PostGIS bundle installs it by default. If your distribution doesn't have ogr_fdw, or you
feel adventurous, the source code is located on GitHub (https://github.com/pram-
sey/pgsql-ogr-fdw). You'll also find helpful examples of how to use all the features on
that page.

The ogr_fdw extension also includes a command-line tool, ogr_fdw_info, that is
usually installed in the PostgreSQL bin. It can list layers in an ogr data source or show
you the CREATE FOREIGN TABLE statement that will be generated for a specific layer.
For PostgreSQL versions before 9.5, this tool was needed to determine the CREATE
FOREIGN TABLE ... statement. In PostgreSQL 9.5, the IMPORT FOREIGN SCHEMA SQL
command was introduced, which allowed for the autocreation of foreign tables.
Ogr_fdw_info also list the formats supported, which should give you mostly the same

answer as your ogr2ogr command. Although ogr_fdw_info is not needed as much any-more, it is still useful for determining what formats your ogr_fdw extension supports or for doing a quick inspection of your data source.

Ogr_fdw version 1.1.0 introduced the utility SQL functions `ogr_fdw_drivers()` and `ogr_fdw_version()`. This further reduces the need for the ogr_fdw_info command-line tool. Also new in ogr_fdw version 1.1.0 is support for `character_encoding`. Prior to that, non-UTF-8 data sources would often cause encoding error notices in Postgre-SQL. Now you can specify `character_encoding` as an extra FDW argument in the `CREATE FOREIGN SERVER` statement.

If you are using an older version of ogr_fdw, you can determine what data sources are supported by using the ogr_fdw_info command-line tool:

```
ogr_fdw_info -f
```

To install the ogr_fdw extension in your database after you have the necessary binaries in place, execute the usual `CREATE` extension command:

```
CREATE EXTENSION ogr_fdw SCHEMA postgis;
```

Although you don't need to install it in the `postgis` schema, we prefer to do so because ogr_fdw exposes spatial ogr columns as PostGIS `geometry` columns. PostGIS-ish things belong together.

You can use ogr_fdw to read delimited files as well, and you might prefer it over using file_fdw. Ogr_fdw can infer column names from CSV header columns. It can also link many files in a folder as individual foreign tables in one step, whereas file_fdw requires that you define each foreign table one-by-one.

The downside of using ogr_fdw to read delimited files over file_fdw is that it tends to be slower. You pay a penalty for the extra amenities. But for a file size of less than a million rows, you probably won't notice much of a speed difference. Once you get to a million rows with ten or more columns, you could be looking at 5 minutes instead of 1 minute.

QUERYING ESRI SHAPEFILES

As mentioned earlier, ogr2ogr and ogr_fdw can treat a whole folder of files as a data source, and elements in the folder will be individual layers. Ogr_fdw exposes ogr lay-ers as PostgreSQL foreign tables. In this next example, you will copy all your Esri shapefiles into a folder, and you will reference that folder as a foreign server. For this example you'll need to create a /data/shps folder and dump all the Esri extracted shapefiles into it.

Ensure the following:

- The folder you put the files in should be accessible to the PostgreSQL service account.
- If you want to be able to update files, make sure the PostgreSQL service account has write rights to the folder.

- The folder should only contain Esri shapefiles (such as .shp, .dbf, .shx, .cpg, .ldif).
- Make sure you don't have any tables in the schema with the same names as your files. Foreign tables and regular tables share the same namespace and must be uniquely named in a given schema.

Run the following code, making sure you replace the path with the location where you put your files. Unlike ogr2ogr, which is a client-side tool, ogr_fdw is server-side, so the path to the files is relative to how the server accesses them and how you access them locally. If your PostgreSQL server is on Windows, make sure you specify the drive path, such as `c:/data/shps`:

```
CREATE SERVER svr_shp FOREIGN DATA WRAPPER ogr_fdw        ◁───┐  Creates a foreign
OPTIONS (                                                      server from the ogr
    datasource '/data/shps',        ┌── The ogr driver        folder data source
    format 'ESRI Shapefile'    ◁────┘   to use
);

                                 ┌── ogr_all means it applies
                                 │   no filters to table names.
IMPORT FOREIGN SCHEMA ogr_all    ◁─┘
FROM SERVER svr_shp INTO ch04;    ◁───┐  Links all the Esri shapefiles as foreign
                                       tables into the ch04 schema
```

The preceding code uses the `IMPORT FOREIGN SCHEMA` command, which requires the name of a schema to import. In the case of ogr_fdw, since many data sources don't have schemas, this is used as a prefix filter. If you don't want to apply a filter, you should set this to `ogr_all`. If, for example, we only wanted to import tables that start with `tl_`, we would replace `ogr_all` with `"tl_"`.

The main caveat when using `IMPORT FOREIGN SCHEMA` is that you can't define the names of the tables as you can with ogr2ogr. However, once they are linked, you can rename the table and column names. You should see the list of your shapefiles linked in as tables, in addition to any foreign tables you already created in the `ch04` schema (see figure 4.8).

Esri shapefiles are one of many formats that ogr supports updating, so ogr_fdw can update them. You will notice that ogr_fdw adds an additional column named `fid`.

Figure 4.8 Foreign tables after importing the foreign schema

This is to denote the feature ID, and it is usually the primary key of the table or an autogenerated key when there is no key that can be inferred. This is used internally for referencing the external data. By default, ogr_fdw will mark all tables that can be updated as updatable, but you can turn this setting off at the foreign server or individual foreign table level.

We'll delete Guam from the ch04.tl_2020_us_state foreign table:

```
DELETE FROM ch04.tl_2020_us_state
WHERE name = 'Guam';
```

If you inspect the file tl_2020_us_state.dbf, you will notice that Guam is now gone. Ogr_fdw edited the files.

When updating or deleting entries from ogr_fdw foreign tables, remember that GDAL's support for various formats varies a lot. For example, you can, in theory, update a CSV file, but if you do so, ogr_fdw ends up rewriting the file, which may not be what you want. In the case of dBase and Esri shapefiles, it does an in-place edit, so it is fairly safe to run update, delete, and insert operations on those sources.

QUERYING OPENSTREETMAP DATA

OpenStreetMap (OSM) is an exciting project that makes spatial data freely available to all via mapping web services, similar to Google Maps and MS Virtual Earth. Most of the data provided through OSM is licensed under the Open Database License or Creative Commons Attribution-ShareAlike 2.0. This means that you can use the data for both personal pleasure and commercial ventures.

You can import OSM data into PostGIS. Having the data in your own PostGIS database is useful for advanced querying, managing your own services, or building your own custom tiles. The only downside to having your own set of OSM data is that you'll miss any updates that come after your download.

OSM data is exported in XML format with the resultant file having an .osm or .osm.bz extension or in Protobuf format with a .pbf extension.

In the next sections we'll discuss how you can carve out specific areas of OpenStreetMap data and download them in OSM XML format, and then import the resulting file into your PostGIS-enabled database using ogr2ogr or link to the data using ogr_fdw.

Imposm (https://imposm.org) and osm2pgsql (https://github.com/openstreetmap/osm2pgsql) are two other free, open source command-line tools that are commonly used for importing OSM data. If you need data in a routable format for pgRouting, you can use the osm2pgrouting tool (https://github.com/pgRouting/osm2pgrouting), which we'll cover later in this book.

GETTING OSM DATA

You can choose to download the entire OSM database (about 16 GB), or you can download extracts of population centers, such as those available at http://download.geofabrik.de/.

To export a section from the OSM world map, follow these steps:

1 Go to www.openstreetmap.org/export and type in the corner longitudes and latitudes of the block you want, or just draw a box on the map.

2 If you manually drew a region, the bounding box (BBOX) should be automatically filled in. For example, if you sectioned off the Arc de Triomphe, something like `2.28568,48.87957,2.30371,48.8676` will appear in the bounding coordinates text boxes.

3 Select OpenStreetMap XML Data as the export format, and name your file. We selected a region encompassing the Arc de Triomphe in Paris, so we called ours arctriomphe.osm.

You can also use one of the REST APIs provided by OpenStreetMap to achieve the same result. The following listing demonstrates carving out a similar section using a `wget` call. Note that the bbox argument corresponds to the minimum longitude/latitude and maximum longitude/latitude of the area you're interested in.

Listing 4.2   Download a bounding box area covering the Arc de Triomphe

```
wget -O arc.osm
➥ http://www.overpass-api.de/api/xapi?*[bbox=2.29,48.87,2.30,48.88]
```

Be sure to execute the preceding listing as a single line.

A wizard for using the REST XAPI services for OpenStreetMap can be found at http://harrywood.co.uk/maps/uixapi/xapi.html: the XAPI Query Builder. Not only does the XAPI service allow you to carve out specific areas of OSM data, but you can also filter out attributes such as hospitals or features such as roads.

QUERYING OSM DATA WITH OGR_FDW

Before querying your OSM data, you need to install the hstore extension. The hstore extension provides a key/value datatype, and OSM makes liberal use of key/value pairs to describe attributes associated with features, such as `oneway:yes`, `speed_limit:55`, and `cuisine:Nouveau French`. Some of these pairs get their own dedicated column and the remaining ones are put in a column called `other_tags`, which can be cast to an `hstore` data type.

Install the hstore extension using the following SQL command:

```
CREATE EXTENSION hstore SCHEMA contrib;
```

Now you're ready to load your OSM data into PostgreSQL with the following statement.

Listing 4.3   Link to OSM XML file with ogr_fdw

```
CREATE EXTENSION IF NOT EXISTS hstore SCHEMA contrib;
CREATE SERVER svr_osm FOREIGN DATA WRAPPER ogr_fdw
OPTIONS (
```

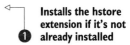

Installs the hstore extension if it's not ❶ already installed

```
        datasource '/data/arc.osm',
        format 'OSM'
);
```

Creates a link
to the OSM
❷ data file

```
IMPORT FOREIGN SCHEMA ogr_all
FROM SERVER svr_osm
INTO staging;
```

❸ Links in all layers
as tables

We first install hstore ❶ so that we can make sense of the key/value store data in OSM. Next, the first step to using ogr_fdw is to create a foreign server ❷, which establishes the link to the foreign data. This definition must include the ogr driver, OSM in this case, and a path to the data. You can link to all the layers at once using the command IMPORT FOREIGN SCHEMA ❸.

For OSM, XML, and PBF files, you will see five foreign tables appear in your staging schema as shown here:

READING HSTORE TAGS

Each OSM foreign table has a column called other_tags that is of the type hstore. The hstore data type is based on schemaless design. Tags do not need to be homogeneous for the same table. In some rows you may have a speed_limit tag; in other rows, speed_limit can be missing. If you query for a tag that's not present, PostgreSQL returns a NULL. Most of the key OSM tags are already included as database columns in the OSM PostgreSQL output, but querying the other_tags column is useful for getting at less common attributes.

> **TIP** If you are using ogr2ogr to import OSM data, you can add -lco COLUMN_TYPES "other_tags=hstore" to your load command to automatically bring in other_tags as an hstore column. This assumes you have the hstore extension already installed.

Unfortunately, even in the latest version of ogr_fdw, the tags columns is treated as text instead of hstore, so you need to cast the column to hstore using ::hstore to take advantage of the hstore functions offered by the hstore extension.

To demonstrate querying, suppose you wanted to pull out all the cycleways from the lines table. You could write a query such as the following:

```
SELECT name, tags->'cycleway' AS cycleway
FROM (SELECT name, other_tags::hstore AS tags FROM staging.lines) X
WHERE tags ? 'cycleway';
```

If you wanted to pull out each tag as a separate row, which is more suitable for storing tags in other relational databases, you could write a query like the following one, which would create a new table called osm_key_values consisting of a row with three columns: `osm_id`, `key`, and `value`. You'd get a record for each key/value pair, so if you had 10 entries in each tags column, you'd get 10 rows for each row:

```
CREATE TABLE ch04.osm_key_values AS
SELECT osm_id, (x.e).key, (x.e).value
FROM (
    SELECT osm_id, each(other_tags::hstore) AS e
    FROM staging.lines
) AS x;
```

4.6.3 Converting hstore tags to jsonb

The `hstore` data type was the very first schemaless design data type that PostgreSQL offered. Since its inception, JavaScript Object Notation (JSON) and PostgreSQL's built-in `json` (plain text) and `jsonb` (binary JSON) have warmed the hearts of many. JSON is everywhere, including the ANSI-SQL boardrooms. It's now a standard, with its own ANSI-SQL query pathways for navigating it, which many databases are jumping on, to prove they are the JSON leader.

Wouldn't it be nice if you could convert the minimalistic `hstore` type to the currently more loved and grander `jsonb` type? Well, luckily the hstore extension in the newer versions of PostgreSQL includes a cast to convert itself to `json` and `jsonb` for those folks who'd rather work with JSON.

In the following example, we'll create a new physical table by querying all our highways and cast our tags to `jsonb` by hopping through `hstore` casting first:

```
CREATE TABLE ch04.osm_roads AS
SELECT
    osm_id, name, highway, geom,
    other_tags::hstore::jsonb AS tags
FROM staging.lines
WHERE highway > '';
```

> **NOTE** Although PostgreSQL has had perhaps the richest support for JSON of any database since PostgreSQL 9.4, it got even richer in PostgreSQL 12 with the introduction of the ANSI-SQL/JSON standard path language, which is well suited for more complex JSON documents with many nestings. (See the "JSON Path support in Postgres 12" article on the Thoughts About SQL blog for more info: https://blog.sql-workbench.eu/post/json-path/.)

As you can see, there are numerous open source tools freely available for getting vector data into and out of your PostgreSQL/PostGIS database. Many of these tools grew up alongside PostGIS, so the free PostGIS import tools are often more tested and functional than those you'll find for other spatial databases. You can similarly import and export PostGIS raster data, as you'll see in the next section.

4.7   *Importing raster data with raster2pgsql*

Raster-enabled PostGIS distributions includes a command-line tool called raster2pgsql. You'll find it in the bin folder of your PostgreSQL install. Raster2pgsql is built atop the GDAL library, so it's capable of loading raster formats supported by your particular version of the GDAL library. (The GDAL library—not the toolkit—is part of every raster-enabled PostGIS install.)

One powerful feature of raster2pgsql is that it allows the use of wildcard names in some switches. With this, you can load an entire folder of files into a single table. Raster2pgsql also lets you break up large raster files into smaller chunks and store each chunk as a separate table row, suitable for magnification. It can also create overview tables for zooming out when displaying raster maps or for reducing the size of high-resolution images.

4.7.1   *Raster2pgsql command-line switches*

To see the available command-line switches, type `raster2pgsql` on the command line by itself. The most frequently used switches are listed here:

- `-s SRID`—Specifies the SRID of the source raster. Raster2pgsql will check the metadata of the incoming raster to determine an appropriate SRID, if one is not specified. If it can't discern the SRID, the raster will be imported with an SRID of 0.

- `-t tile size`—Sets the size of the tiles. This divides the raster into tiles (*chunking* in raster lingo), to be inserted one per table row. You express the tile size as width by height in pixels. In PostGIS 2.1 you can set the tile size to `auto`, and raster2pgsql will compute the appropriate tile size, which is usually between 32 and 100 pixels and as close as possible to evenly dividing the original dimension. Raster2pgsql will never create a raster row from more than one original file, so regardless of tiling, the number of rows created during import will always be the same as or more than the number of files.

- `-R`—Registers the raster as an out-of-database raster, meaning the data is not stored in the database but instead on the filesystem or accessed via a web service.

- `-F`—Adds a column with the filename of the raster. The default column name is the filename. This is especially useful if you're tiling the files during import—keeping the original filename allows you to easily reconstitute the original file should that ever become necessary.

- `-n column name`—Specifies the name of the filename column. This implies `-F`.

- `-l overview factor`—Creates overview tables of the raster. If you have more than one factor, separate them with commas. The overview table name follows the pattern `o_overviewFactor_tableName` (for example, `o_2_srtm`). The overview table is always stored in the database, unaffected by the `-R switch`. The overview factor must be an integer value greater than 0.

- -I—Creates a gist spatial index on the raster column. The PostgreSQL ANALYZE command will automatically be issued for the created index to update column statistics information.
- -C—Sets the standard set of constraints on the raster column after loading. Some constraints may fail if one or more rasters violate the constraint.
- -e—Executes each statement individually and doesn't use a transaction.
- -G—Prints the supported GDAL raster formats.

The next four switches take a table name as an argument and are mutually exclusive:

- -d table name—Drops the table, re-creates it, and populates it with current raster data.
- -a table name—Appends the raster into an existing table denoted by table name.
- -c table name—Creates a new table and populates it. This is the default if you don't specify any options.
- -p table name—Creates the table and does nothing else (prepare mode).

Raster2pgsql can't perform transformations and therefore doesn't have a switch where you can specify the destination SRID. Your imported raster will always use the SRID of the source.

4.7.2 *Raster2pgsql supported formats*

Raster2pgsql has a -G switch that lists all the raster formats it supports. This is an abridged version of the output:

```
raster2pgsql -G                          ◁─────── Command
Supported GDAL raster formats:           ◁──┐ Output
  Virtual Raster
  Derived datasets using VRT pixel functions
  GeoTIFF
  National Imagery Transmission Format
  Ground-based SAR Applications Testbed File Format (.gff)
  ELAS
  Arc/Info Binary Grid
  Arc/Info ASCII Grid
  GRASS ASCII Grid
  SDTS Raster
  DTED Elevation Raster
  Portable Network Graphics
  JPEG JFIF
  MS Windows Device Independent Bitmap
  JPEG-2000 driver based on OpenJPEG library
  NOAA Polar Orbiter Level 1b Data Set
  NOAA Vertical Datum .GTX
  NTv1 Datum Grid Shift
  :
```

As you can see, you can import numerous raster formats with raster2pgsql. You'll get even more formats if you compile with additional extensions.

4.7.3   *Loading a single file with raster2pgsql*

Let's use raster2pgsql to load the elevation data from N48E086.hgt included in the data folder for this chapter. This particular elevation data is derived from Shuttle Radar Topography Mission (SRTM; https://en.wikipedia.org/wiki/Shuttle_Radar_Topography_Mission) and is the standard format of SRTM data. Later we'll demonstrate how you can load entire folders into multiple rows, chunked for easier analysis:

```
raster2pgsql -s 4326 -C N48E086.hgt staging.n48e086 |
    psql -h localhost -U postgres -p 5432 -d postgis_in_action
```

This example loads the single file into a table called staging.n48e086. The `-C` switch tells raster2pgsql to add all necessary spatial constraints, thereby ensuring that the properties of the raster are correctly shown in the `raster_columns` view. We also specified the SRID of the raster files using the `-s` switch. If you omit the SRID, `raster2pgsql` will try to guess based on the metadata of the file.

4.7.4   *Loading multiple files and tiling in shell script*

In this example, we'll load multiple elevation files in one step. This time the data comes from https://earthexplorer.usgs.gov/. Download and extract the data using your choice of utility. Then place the files into a folder called usgs_srtm (to match the name used in the following code). Finally, create a plain-text script file by copying the following:

```
export PGPORT=5432              ◁──┐  Sets environment
export PGHOST=localhost            │  variables
export PGUSER=postgres
export PGPASSWORD=xyz                            Executes raster2pgsql
export PGDATABASE=postgis_in_action             with copy mode, srid, file,
raster2pgsql -Y -s 4326 -C -F -t 100x100  ◁──┘  and constraint switches
    usgs_srtm/*.hgt       ◁──┐  Pulls many files
    staging.usgs_srtm     ◁──  Loads to the table
    | psql      ◁──┐
                   │  Pipes it to psql
```

The preceding code is an example of a raster-loading shell script. We took the extra step of setting environment variables so that we can simplify the call to psql. If you're on Windows, replace the word `export` with `set`.

Raster2pgsql will vertically and horizontally slice each file into 100x100 pixel tiles. Each tile enters the table as one row. If the file cannot be evenly divided into 100x100 pixels, some tiles will have fewer than 10,000 pixels, but you can expect that no tile will exceed 100 pixels in width or height. The wildcard lets you import only files fitting a specified pattern.

After loading the table, it's a good idea to check the `raster_columns` view to verify that all the constraints were added properly. You can also save the script for use at a later time.

Although you can pipe the output of raster2pgsql directly to a database, sometimes it's convenient to just store the data as SQL `INSERT` statements in a file for later use. The next example does that and also uses the `auto` command for tile size, so raster2pgsql will come up with a suitable tiling solution instead of explicitly specifying one:

```
raster2pgsql -C Ella.png ch04.ella_chunked -t auto > ella_chunked.sql
```

You can also use raster2pgsql to load just the metadata for rasters, and reference the physical location in the database. Such a use is called *out-db*. Check out Paul Ramsey's "PostGIS Raster and Crunchy Bridge" article for an example: https://info.crunchy-data.com/blog/postgis-raster-and-crunchy-bridge.

4.7.5   *Using PostgreSQL functions to output raster data*

PostGIS has a number of output functions for raster data. `ST_AsPNG`, `ST_AsJPEG`, and `ST_AsTiff` are functions for outputting to popular raster formats. To have more granular control of the output, you may want to use `ST_AsGDALRaster`.

`ST_AsGDALRaster` is an all-purpose function that outputs to all formats supported by GDAL including PNG, JPEG, and TIFF.

`ST_FromGDALRaster` is a function for converting other raster formats into PostGIS raster format. It will accept any raster supported by GDAL, provided that the entire raster fits into a single row of a table in a `bytea` data type column. With the combination of `ST_AsGDALRaster` and `ST_FromGDALRaster`, you can easily perform powerful image processing using PostGIS. Take your old black and white photos, digitize them into JPEGs, copy them into a PostgreSQL table, store the JPEG in a `bytea` column, convert to PostGIS raster so you can apply colorization and other PostGIS raster operations, and then dump them out back as JPEGs using `ST_AsJPEG` or `ST_AsGDALRaster`.

To get a listing of supported formats for your particular GDAL version, execute this query:

```
SELECT short_name, long_name
FROM ST_GdalDrivers()
ORDER BY short_name;
```

Due to security concerns with some formats being capable of accessing network resources, you must enable two environment variables before using any raster export and import functions. To enable all raster formats, set the environment variables `POSTGIS_GDAL_ENABLED_DRIVERS` and `POSTGIS_ENABLE_OUTDB_RASTERS` to `ENABLE_ALL`. To be more selective, you can set PostgreSQL variables as discussed in the postgis.gdal_enabled_drivers documentation: https://postgis.net/docs/postgis_gdal_enabled_drivers.html.

If you set the configuration via OS environment variables, it applies for all databases and requires a PostgreSQL restart. Setting the configuration via PostgreSQL

GUC variables for system or database level requires running `SELECT pg_reload_conf();` for the settings to take effect, and they will be in effect after you reconnect.

The specialized `ST_AsRaster` function converts any 2D geometry into a PostGIS raster format, and from there you can convert it into countless other raster formats. The following SQL statement outputs an image of the geometries stored in ch04.osm _roads as a PNG file.

Listing 4.4   Output OSM roads as a PNG file

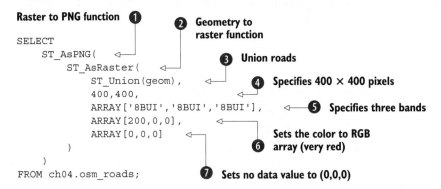

In listing 4.4 you first take all the roads in ch04.osm_roads and spatially union them into a collection of multilinestrings ❸. Then you rasterize that geometry ❷ into a 400 × 400 pixel raster ❹ composed of three 8BUI bands ❺ and set the band value of the multilinestrings to a reddish color during output ❻. You then initialize non-geometry pixels to 0,0,0 ❼ and finally convert the PostGIS raster to a PNG raster ❶.

The output of listing 4.14 is the bytes that make up the PNG image as a Post-greSQL `bytea` data type. You can then use a standard query connection like JDBC, PHP pgsql, ODBC, ADO.NET, or Python psychopg to retrieve the image for rendering in a web application. We have a demonstration of rendering for web applications on the BostonGIS site: "Minimalist Web-based PHP PostGIS 2.0 Spatial Geometry/Raster Viewer" (http://mng.bz/0ryv).

LibreOffice/OpenOffice can also read images stored in a field. With them you can easily incorporate your image in spreadsheets and presentations. We demonstrate the use of OpenOffice and LibreOffice on the Postgres OnLine Journal: "Rendering Post-GIS Raster Graphics with LibreOffice Base Reports" (http://mng.bz/K4lO).

4.8   *Exporting raster data with GDAL*

GDAL also includes three utilities for raster data. You can use them for exporting to different raster types, transforming rasters from one SRID to another, and converting rasters to vectors. Although GDAL can export to other raster types and can inspect PostGIS rasters, you can't use it to import rasters into a PostGIS database. To import raster data into PostGIS, use raster2pgsql.

The command-line GDAL packaged tools commonly used when working with Post-GIS rasters are as follows:

- *gdalinfo*—To inspect a raster, both PostGIS and non-PostGIS
- *gdal_translate*—To export PostGIS rasters
- *gdalwarp*—To transform SRIDs and to export PostGIS rasters

Gdal_translate accepts both spatially referenced and non-spatially referenced rasters alike, never translating between SRIDs, whereas the main purpose of gdalwarp is to transform or add spatial references. Gdal_translate has more capabilities than gdalwarp, such as resizing during the output.

What you can accomplish using the GDAL toolkit is virtually unlimited. After all, it is a tool, like a Swiss Army knife. We've compiled some common tasks for which gdalinfo, gdal_translate, and gdalwarp have proved indispensable.

4.8.1 *Using gdalinfo to inspect rasters*

When you encounter raster data, it's worth taking a closer look before you take the trouble of importing it. Gdalinfo provides detailed information about specific raster sources.

Depending on your installation, gdalinfo may only be able to inspect certain raster formats. To see which ones, use the `--formats` switch as follows:

```
gdalinfo --formats
```

Besides providing information about the raster, gdalinfo also gives you information that will help you troubleshoot when an import goes awry. To read the metadata of a raster, run gdalinfo as shown in the following listing.

Listing 4.5   Using gdalinfo

```
gdalinfo N48E086.hgt
```

The output of listing 4.5 follows.

```
Driver: SRTMHGT/SRTMHGT File Format
Files: N48E086.hgt
Size is 1201, 1201
Coordinate System is:
GEOGCS["WGS 84",
    DATUM[
        "WGS_1984",
        SPHEROID[
            "WGS 84",
            6378137,
            298.257223563,
            AUTHORITY["EPSG","7030"]
        ],
        AUTHORITY["EPSG","6326"]
    ],
```

```
    PRIMEM["Greenwich",0,AUTHORITY["EPSG","8901"]],
    UNIT["degree",0.0174532925199433,AUTHORITY["EPSG","9122"]],
    AUTHORITY["EPSG","4326"]
]
Origin = (85.999583333333334,49.000416666666666)
Pixel Size = (0.000833333333333,-0.000833333333333)
Metadata: AREA_OR_POINT=Point
Corner Coordinates:
Upper Left  (85.9995833, 49.0004167) (85d59'58.50"E, 49d 0' 1.50"N)
Lower Left  (85.9995833, 47.9995833) (85d59'58.50"E, 47d59'58.50"N)
Upper Right (87.0004167, 49.0004167) (87d 0' 1.50"E, 49d 0' 1.50"N)
Lower Right (87.0004167, 47.9995833) (87d 0' 1.50"E, 47d59'58.50"N)
Center      (86.5000000, 48.5000000) (86d30' 0.00"E, 48d30' 0.00"N)
Band 1 Block=1201x1 Type=Int16, ColorInterp=Undefined
NoData Value=-32768
Unit Type: m
```

The output will always contain size, bands and type of each band, and corner coordinates of the raster. The corner coordinates correspond to geospatial coordinates (degrees in the preceding example). If a raster isn't georeferenced, these coordinates will range from 0 to the number of columns or rows of the raster, whichever is larger. Only georeferenced rasters will output the section with coordinate system information.

4.8.2   *Gdal_translate and gdalwarp*

Gdal_translate and gdalwarp are command-line tools packaged with GDAL to export rasters to another format. Gdal_translate has the ability to change the resolution of the output and can export both georeferenced and non-georeferenced rasters, but it can't transform spatial reference systems. For this, you'll need gdalwarp.

When you work through the following examples and create output files, it's a really good idea to look at what you export to make sure that the elephant image is still an elephant and the Arc de Triomphe is not sitting in Atlantis, and so on. Viewers built using GDAL, such as the popular QGIS and MapServer, are guaranteed to render every format that gdal_translate exports. We will discuss installing GDAL-based viewers in chapter 5.

USING GDAL_TRANSLATE TO SHRINK OR ENLARGE RASTERS

Let's start by shrinking a raster to 10% of its original size and outputting it as a Geo-TIFF file:

```
gdal_translate -of GTiff -outsize 10% 10%
⇒ PG:'host=localhost port=5432 dbname=postgis_in_action
⇒ user=postgres password=xyz
⇒ schema=staging table=usgs_srtm mode=2'
⇒ elev_small.tif
```

In this example, we set the mode argument to 2. As of GDAL 1.8, you must include this mode value when you export a raster spanning multiple rows in a table to a file format that supports only a single raster. Also, width comes before height when specifying the output size.

USING GDAL_TRANSLATE TO EXPORT A SINGLE BAND

Let's now export only the first band of a multiband raster to a JPEG file. For this next example, you'll need to load in the file ch04_data_ella.sql:

```
gdal_translate -of JPEG -b 1
  PG:"host=localhost port=5432 dbname=postgis_in_action
  user=postgres password='xyz'
  schema=ch04 table=ella_chunked
  column=rast mode=2"
  ella_grey.png
```

Our raster (Ella the elephant) is RGB: three bands of red, green, and blue. We export the first band only, outputting a monochromatic elephant. We also explicitly named the raster column to export. For tables with multiple raster columns, you must name the column you wish to export. Gdal_translate will resort to arbitrary picking if you don't.

USING GDAL_TRANSLATE WITH A WHERE CLAUSE

Gdal_translate accepts an SQL-like where clause that allows you to filter the rows you wish to export. In the next example, we limit our export to the first two hundred rows of the usgs_srtm table:

```
gdal_translate -of GTiff
  PG:"host=localhost port=5432 dbname=postgis_in_action
  user=postgres password=xyz
  schema=staging table=usgs_srtm
  where='rid BETWEEN 1 and 200'
  mode=2"
  subset.tif
```

USING GDAL_TRANSLATE TO EXPORT A REGION

Nothing stops you from building fancy where clauses that take advantage of PostGIS functions. In this example, we only output a rectangular portion of the raster centered on the Arc de Triomphe:

```
gdal_translate -of GTiff
  PG:"host=localhost port=5432 dbname=postgis_in_action
  user=postgres password=xyz
  schema=staging table=usgs_srtm
  where=
    'ST_Intersects(
        rast,
        ST_MakeEnvelope(2.28568,48.8676,2.30371,48.87957,4326)
    )'
  mode=2"
  arctriomphe.tif
```

This where clause gives you a glimpse of how raster and geometry data types can interact in PostGIS.

USING GDAL_TRANSLATE TO RECONSTITUTE AN IMPORTED FILE

If you imported your rasters with the -F option, the name of the original file should be in the database. By filtering for the filename, you can rebuild the original file, even if you tiled it across many rows:

```
gdal_translate -of USGSDEM
  PG:"host=localhost port=5432 dbname=postgis_in_action
  user=postgres password=xyz
  schema=staging table=usgs_srtm
  where='filename=\'N48E086.hgt\''
  mode=2"
  N48E086.dem
```

USING GDALWARP TO TRANSFORM SPATIAL REFERENCES

One deficiency of gdal_translate is that it can't transform as part of the export. You need to use gdalwarp, which accepts arguments for the source and target spatial references. For this example, you'll need GDAL 1.8 (or, even better, GDAL 1.9) compiled with PostGIS raster support.

Gdalwarp has two switches that distinguish it from gdal_translate:

- -s_srs—This switch specifies the spatial reference system of the source raster. Even though gdalwarp can determine the spatial reference system of the source, gdalwarp will gladly skip this step if you specify the SRS, and you should if you know it.
- -t_srs—This switch is required and states the SRS of the output.

These two switches will accept both proj4 and EPSG codes, but to use EPSG the GDAL _DATA path environment variable must point to a file that translates EPSG codes to proj4. So even though the EPSG code is infinitely easier to type than the monstrous proj4 string, you have to do some prep work.

This next example transforms data in the PostgreSQL staging.usdem table, which is in SRID 4326 (WGS 84 Lon/Lat), to SRID 2163 (US National Atlas):

```
gdalwarp -s_srs EPSG:4326 -t_srs EPSG:2163
  PG:"host=localhost port=5432 dbname=postgis_in_action
  user=postgres password=xyz
  schema=staging table=usdem
  where='ST_Intersects(
    rast,
    ST_MakeEnvelope(-115.60,32.54,-112.96,26.03,4326)
  )'
  mode=2"
  usdem_sub.tif
```

Visualize your data

Our last bit of advice is this: look at what you've imported and exported with a visualization tool. Just because your routine ran successfully doesn't mean you ended up with what you wanted. What you thought was Portland, OR, could actually be Portland, ME. Too many times we've seen people go on to subsequent steps, assuming the data to be flawless, only to find their later efforts wasted due to bad data.

Be extra careful when using data from quasi-authoritative sources. For instance, just because you found a source for downloading the borders of all continents doesn't mean it wasn't drawn by some toddler for a kindergarten thesis (and posted online by an overly proud mommy or daddy). Equally bad, the continents could be from 300 million years ago—Pangaea. Unfortunately, no import or export utility can guard against human error. Save yourself time and embarrassment down the road. Make it a habit to check your data the minute you import or export.

Summary

- Shp2pgsql is a PostGIS packaged tool for loading Esri shapefiles into PostgreSQL.
- Pgsql2shp is a tool for exporting PostgreSQL data as Esri shapefiles and dBase files.
- Shp2pgsql-gui is a graphical interface that combines both shp2pgsql and pgsql2shp in a single interface.
- GDAL is a suite of tools for working with vector and raster data.
- Ogr2ogr is a command-line tool packaged with GDAL that can load spatial vector data and non-spatial formatted data into your PostgreSQL database.
- Ogrinfo is a command-line tool packaged with GDAL to inspect vector and non-spatial data formats.
- Gdal_translate and gdalwarp are command-line tools packaged with GDAL that can be used for exporting PostGIS raster data.
- Gdalinfo is a command-line tool packaged with GDAL to inspect raster data.
- Foreign data wrappers and their foreign tables allow you to query external data as if the tables were in your database.
- File_fdw is a foreign data wrapper extension that allows you to reference delimited text files like PostgreSQL tables.
- Ogr_fdw is a spatial foreign data wrapper extension that allows you to reference many external data sources and query them like tables, with spatial vector fields exposed as a PostGIS `geometry` column.
- Raster2pgsql is a PostGIS packaged tool for loading rasters into PostGIS raster format.

Using PostGIS
on the desktop

5

This chapter covers

- OpenJUMP
- QGIS
- gvSIG
- Jupyter (JupyterLab and Notebook)

In this chapter we'll cover some popular open source GIS desktop viewing and loading tools that are often paired with PostGIS. We'll also cover Jupyter Notebook and JupyterLab, which are not GIS desktop tools, but are very popular among GIS and data science folks for ad hoc analysis. You'll find that each of these tools has its own strengths and weaknesses and each caters to a certain niche of users or tasks. We'll cover these tools, look at differences between them, and walk you through getting them installed and configured so you can try them out. For more in-depth coverage, you should refer to the websites and manuals provided for these tools.

We'll start off by providing a brief summary of these tools, liberally ladling out our personal opinions. Then we'll go into a little more detail about each tool. We'll focus mostly on the use of these tools to view and query data, but we'll also highlight the features each offers for building custom desktop applications, and the availability of plug-ins and scripting to extend the built-in features. We hope that once you've read this chapter, you'll have a better understanding of which tools will be best for what you're doing and for your particular style of working.

The data and code used in this chapter can be found at www.postgis.us/chapter _05_edition_3.

5.1 Desktop viewing tools at a glance

We'll start with a quick summary of the various tools' features. After reading this section, you may be able to rule out some of the tools altogether for your purposes, and you can skip the sections that pertain to them. If you've already invested in one of the tools, we recommend that you go through this section to at least see what you might have missed. New features are being added to these tools all the time. If you've dismissed a tool due to the lack of some critical feature a year ago, you may find it now incorporated.

Table 5.1 provides a quick overview of the four tools covered in this chapter.

Table 5.1 Features of tools discussed in this chapter

Feature	OpenJUMP[a]	QGIS	gvSIG	Jupyter
Current version	1.15	3.12	2.5	6.0.2 (Notebook), 1.2.5 (JupyterLab)
Plug-ins	JARs, Jython, beans	Python/Qt	JARs	Python
Scripting	Jython, BeanShell	Python	Jython[b]	Julia, Python, R, and other languages[c]
Download size	30–50 MB	150–250 MB	270 MB	500+ MB
Extract and go	Yes	No	No	No
Ease of use[d]	Moderate	Easy	Moderate	Moderate
Mobile version[e]	No	Yes	Yes	No[f]

a. The JUMP unified mapping platform is the platform for OpenJUMP, but some other applications use it as a framework, including the namesake desktop application JUMP.

b. Jython is the Java framework that allows you to run Python code in a JVM.

c. Jupyter always allows scripting with Python, and additional languages can be enabled with additional installs.

d. Indicates how easy the tool is to get up and running after performing basic configurations.

e. Indicates whether the tool has, or claims to have, a mobile companion version.

f. The Jupyter project doesn't have a mobile version, but there is a proprietary mobile app called Juno for Android and iPhone for developing Jupyter notebooks.

We've used all these tools in various capacities and have solicited input from other users. In this section, we'll offer our opinion of each. This is subjective, so your mileage may vary. We'll go into more detail about each tool later in the chapter.

5.1.1   OpenJUMP

OpenJUMP is our favorite tool because it's lightweight and it lets us write spatial SQL and immediately view the visual results (www.openjump.org). OpenJUMP also has nice features for fixing and analyzing geometries and has tools to fix up faulty shapefiles. It's probably best suited for people who aren't afraid of querying directly against the database and who appreciate tidy workspaces. For Java and Python/Jython programmers, OpenJUMP automates common tasks.

On the downside, we wish that OpenJUMP would provide support for the PostGIS raster type. In addition, the fact that it is written in Java and doesn't ship a JRE might make it tricky to get it working on desktops with no Java runtime installed.

5.1.2   QGIS

New GIS users tend to gravitate toward QGIS for its user-friendly interface, GPS and raster support, Python scriptability, and overall polish (https://qgis.org). QGIS also often bundles another open source application called Geographic Resources Analysis Support System (GRASS), used for raster analysis (both 2D pixel and 3D voxels) and geospatial modeling. Many GRASS users get their GRASS via a QGIS install. GIS crowdsourcers and Python programmers also tend to choose QGIS. Its speed and spatial SQL capabilities are fairly decent. It's also the only tool we're discussing that has native support for PostGIS topology via additional plug-ins, and it has the best PostGIS raster support. QGIS also supports Oracle and SQL Server spatial types. This ability to connect to disparate database products appeals to folks who need to use various spatial databases.

Much of QGIS's support of data sources is provided via GDAL, which is covered in chapter 4. Newer versions of QGIS desktop include GDAL command-line tools.

QGIS provides a user-friendly query interface. If you're strictly an SQL writer, the extension called DB Manager is one click away on the menu and is installed by default. QGIS has a huge developer base and following, so new features arrive at a lightning pace, and bugs are quickly worked out.

QGIS uses the C++ Qt framework (http://qt-project.org), which is similar to the pgAdmin4 PostgreSQL administration tool. QGIS has both 32-bit and 64-bit versions. For mobile users, there is a companion Android application called QField (https://qfield.org), intended for in-the-field editing of spatial data.

5.1.3   gvSIG

GvSIG (www.gvsig.com) has basic support for various databases, OGC services, and non-OGC Esri products. It's also extensible via Java.

As far as PostGIS goes, we found gvSIG to be somewhat clunky. Older versions of gvSIG supported PostGIS rasters natively, but the latest version seems to have dropped support for that PostGIS raster feature.

If you've invested in Esri and are looking for something to tap into your legacy Esri stack, gvSIG may be your best choice. As a bonus, gvSIG has a mobile edition.

5.1.4 Jupyter Notebook and JupyterLab

Jupyter is a development tool suite (https://jupyter.org). It is born from another project called IPython (Interactive Python). The Notebook and JupyterLab apps are two of its tools that we'll cover.

Notebooks (.ipynb files) are files that define cells. Each cell has a set of script lines and can be run cell by cell. Each cell can use variables defined in earlier-run cells. Once a cell is run, the output by default is included as part of the notebook.

These script lines are most popularly written in Python, Julia, or R (where it gets its name: *Julia Python R*). Markdown script lines are also supported for easy documentation of notebooks. Jupyter can support other scripting languages via plug-ins.

Both JupyterLab and Jupyter Notebook are most commonly used to edit and view .ipynb files. JupyterLab is the next generation product, with the intent to completely replace Jupyter Notebook. Although Jupyter Notebook and JupyterLab are generally used on the desktop, the application is hosted on a self-contained web server in the background, and you interact with it using a web browser, similar to the way pgAdmin4 works.

When referring to Jupyter in this chapter, if not otherwise specified, we're referring to the functionality of both the Notebook and JupyterLab applications.

The main beauty of Jupyter notebooks is that they allow people to share steps for research analysis, allow for quick reporting with add-ons that output to PDFs, slides, and so on, and allow these to be reproduced by other users. They are also a great learning tool for teaching data analysis. The power of Jupyter is mostly in the plug-ins. You'll find many GIS-specific libraries that you can use within a notebook to include maps, and load and analyze data. You will also find many database drivers available that allow you to connect to PostgreSQL and other databases.

For teaching and other non-local needs, where you need many users to share the same notebook, you can use JupyterHub (https://jupyter.org/hub) or Google's Colab (https://colab.research.google.com/). Both provide server-side Jupyter Notebook hosted environments. Google's Colab allows you to launch notebooks you have saved on a Google Drive.

5.1.5 Spatial database support

All four of the desktop tools we're discussing support PostGIS. The first three do so without additional plug-ins. The last, Jupyter, requires you to install database driver plug-ins and GIS plug-ins.

In this section we'll catalog various features we find important when using these tools to connect to spatial data stores. We reviewed each tool against the following list of features:

- *Support for other databases (SpatiaLite, Oracle, SQL Server, DB2, MySQL)*—Can the tool render geometries stored in these other databases?
- *Multiple geometry columns*—Can the tool read PostGIS tables with more than one geometry or geography column? Does it randomly pick one or fail?

- *PostGIS geography*—Can it read the PostGIS `geography` data type?
- *PostGIS raster*—Can the tool read PostGIS raster columns?
- *Save PostGIS*—Can the tool save tables to PostGIS? For instance, if you opened a shapefile, would you be able to save it to PostGIS?
- *Edit PostGIS*—Can the tool load PostGIS data and permit editing using drawing tools and form fields?
- *Curve support*—Can the tool render curved geometries?
- *3D geometry*—Can the tool render 3D geometries?
- *Heterogeneous column*—Is the tool capable of rendering a `geometry` column that stores multiple subtypes?
- *SQL queries*—Are you able to compose PostGIS queries in SQL and see their output visually?
- *Integer unique key required*—Does the tool expect an integer to uniquely identify the rows?
- *Views*—Can the tool read PostgreSQL views with PostGIS geometry/geography columns?

Table 5.2 summarizes the results of our review. In the table, if we marked a tool as supporting a particular feature, we might not have tested it ourselves but instead have culled the information from the documentation or by exploring the menu options. If we marked a "Yes" entry with an asterisk, the tool claims to support the feature via additional extensions. If we marked a "No" entry with an asterisk, the tool has workarounds to adequately emulate the feature.

Table 5.2   Spatial database support

Feature	OpenJUMP	QGIS	gvSIG	Jupyter
SpatiaLite	Yes*	Yes	No	Yes*
Oracle Spatial	Yes*	Yes*	Yes*	Yes*
SQL Server	No	Yes	No*	Yes*
DB2	No	No	No	Yes*
MySQL	Yes*	Yes	Yes	Yes*
Multiple geometry columns	Yes	Yes	Yes	Yes*
PostGIS geography	No*	Yes	No	Yes*
PostGIS raster	No*	Yes*	Yes*	Yes*
Read PostGIS	Yes	Yes	Yes	Yes*
Save PostGIS	Yes*	Yes*	Yes	Yes*
Edit PostGIS	Yes	Yes	Yes	Yes*

Table 5.2   Spatial database support *(continued)*

Feature	OpenJUMP	QGIS	gvSIG	Jupyter
Curve support	No	No	No	No
3D geometry	No	Yes	Yes*	No
Heterogeneous column	Yes	Yes	Yes*	No
SQL queries	Yes	Yes	No	Yes*
Integer unique key required	No	No	No	No
Views	Yes	Yes	Yes*	Yes*

5.1.6   *Format support*

Table 5.3 identifies the various vector, raster, and web service formats supported by each tool. This list isn't comprehensive but tries to cover the more common formats that people expect in a desktop tool. A "Yes" entry means the tool supports the format either as an import, export, edit, or all of these. A "Yes*" entry means it supports the format via an additional extension not installed by default.

Table 5.3   Vector file data formats

Format	OpenJUMP	QGIS	gvSIG	Jupyter
Esri shapefile	Yes	Yes	Yes	Yes*
SpatiaLite	Yes*	Yes	No	Yes*
GeoPackage (GPKG)	Yes	Yes	Yes	Yes*
GPX	Yes	Yes	No	Yes*
GML	Yes	Yes	Yes	Yes*
KML	Yes*	Yes	Yes	Yes*
GeoJSON	Yes*	Yes	Yes	Yes*
DXF	Yes	Yes	No	Yes*
DWG	No	Yes	Yes	Yes*
MIF/MID	Yes	Yes	No	Yes*
TAB	No*	Yes	No	Yes*
Excel	Yes	Yes	Yes	Yes*
CSV	Yes	Yes	Yes	Yes*
SVG	Yes	No	No	Yes*

Here are a few notes about some of the formats:

- *TAB*—This is the default MapInfo format.
- *MIF/MID*—These are MapInfo interchange formats that MapInfo can export to while maintaining most of the functionality of the default TAB format.
- *SpatiaLite*—This is the spatial database extender for SQLite. It builds on GEOS and PROJ and extends SQLite similar to the way PostGIS builds on GEOS and PROJ and extends PostgreSQL. Think of SpatiaLite as a lightweight single-file PostGIS.
- *GeoPackage*—This is an OGC standard for distributing data in SQLite format. It supports both vector and raster data.
- *Esri File Geodatabase (gdb)*—This storage format has support via the OGR/GDAL library. To our knowledge, only QGIS (if compiled with OGR/GDAL 1.10+) and the commercial tools Esri ArcGIS and Safe FME support this file-storage format.

Table 5.4 lists the various raster formats supported by these tools. We didn't investigate their editing and exporting capabilities, so a "Yes" here means that it can render or export the format. A "Yes*" means it can render or export that format with an extra downloadable plug-in.

Table 5.4   Raster file data formats

Format	OpenJUMP	QGIS	gvSIG	Jupyter
JPG	Yes	Yes	Yes	Yes
TIFF	Yes	Yes	Yes	Yes
ECW	Yes*	Yes	No	Yes*
PNG	Yes	Yes	Yes	Yes
MrSID	Yes*	Yes	No	Yes*

5.1.7   Web services supported

Table 5.5 lists the common OGC web services and the support each tool has for them. We didn't test any of these, so this is based purely on literature or menu items. "Yes" means there is built-in support, and "Yes*" means the support requires an additional downloadable plug-in.

Table 5.5   Web services support

Format	OpenJUMP	QGIS	gvSIG	Jupyter
WMS	Yes*	Yes	Yes	Yes*
WFS	Yes*	Yes	Yes	Yes*
WFS-T	Yes*	No	Yes	Yes*

Table 5.5 Web services support *(continued)*

Format	OpenJUMP	QGIS	gvSIG	Jupyter
WPS	Yes*	No	Yes	Yes*
WCS	No	No	No	Yes*

Following is a brief description of what these different web services are designed for:

- *WMS (Web Mapping Service)*—This is the oldest and most common of these services. It allows you to make requests for image data based on layer names and bounding regions using the `GetMap` method. It also has a simple `GetFeature-Info` call that can retrieve already-formatted text information.
- *WFS (Web Feature Service)*—This web service generally returns vector-formatted data based on a web query. The standard format is Geography Markup Language (GML). There are also WFS service providers that return other formats, such as KML and GeoJSON.
- *WFS-T (Web Feature Service Transactional)*—This is an extension of the standard WFS protocol that allows for editing geometries across the web via vector formats such as GML or WKT.
- *WPS (Web Processing Service)*—This is the OGC GIS web service protocol for exposing generic work processes. Key parts are `DescribeProcess`, `GetCapabilities`, and `Execute` (`Execute` takes a named process with arguments and executes it).
- *WCS (Web Coverage Service)*—This is the OGC GIS web service protocol for raster coverage and the like.

5.2 OpenJUMP

OpenJUMP is a Java-based, cross-platform, open source GIS analysis and query tool. It's rich in functions for statistical analysis and geometry processing. It works well with Esri shapefiles, PostGIS data stores, and numerous other data formats. We've found it to be an excellent option for composing ad hoc spatial queries overlaying ad hoc queries and viewing the rendered results immediately. Its cartography offering is adequate, but not as extensive as some other desktop tools. OpenJUMP is speedy when it comes to editing geometries, but it lags somewhat when it comes to cartography tasks such as printing.

Under the hood, OpenJUMP is powered by the Java Topology Suite (JTS) engine. JTS is the Javanese parent of the Geometry Engine Open Source (GEOS) library, the very library that serves as the foundation of PostGIS. Because JTS leads GEOS in the timing of new releases, you'll find that many new features will appear in OpenJUMP before they become available in PostGIS.

In the sections that follow, we'll continue to expound on the prowess of Open-JUMP, go through setup procedures, detail useful plug-ins, and demonstrate some sample uses.

5.2.1   OpenJUMP feature summary

OpenJUMP is our tool of choice for rendering PostGIS geometries. In fact, we used OpenJUMP to generate many of the geometry figures you see in this book. It has a small download size, provided you have a Java Virtual Machine (JVM) already running. Its analytical tools for processing geometries are easy to use, letting you speed through tasks such as performing unions, fixing faulty geometries, and getting stats. For Python aficionados, OpenJUMP sports a Jython scripting and plug-in framework.

You can use OpenJUMP's ad hoc query tool to write any PostGIS geometry SQL query and see the geometry output without fuss. However, it lacks the ability to display PostGIS rasters, which QGIS offers. But although it cannot output PostGIS raster geometries, you can still use it to query PostGIS raster data, provided you use one of the geometry output functions such as ST_DumpAsPolygons, which the postgis_raster extension provides.

5.2.2   Installing OpenJUMP

Installing OpenJUMP is a cinch: extract the zip file and launch the executable. Open-JUMP doesn't package its own JVM like gvSIG does, so the download is small, but you must have a JVM ready.

You can get a copy of OpenJUMP at the website: www.OpenJUMP.org.

5.2.3   Ease of use

We ranked OpenJUMP behind QGIS in terms of ease of use. Although OpenJUMP has facilities to create new tables, we found it to be a bit quirky. You can't transform between SRIDs without additional plug-ins.

Perhaps the biggest disappointment is that our beloved ad hoc query tool can't handle geography, raster, or topology data types. As a workaround, you can first cast to geometry (PostGIS allows direct casting from geography and topology to geometry), but not being able to display rasters is a big drawback. For output in rasters, we turn to QGIS.

5.2.4   OpenJUMP plug-ins

OpenJUMP supports plug-ins, extensions, and registries:

- A *plug-in* is a Java archive file (JAR) that you drop into the lib or lib/ext directory of your OpenJUMP install. The plug-ins could be additional database drivers, geometry functions, and so on.
- An *extension* manages a set of plug-ins to accomplish a particular workflow, and it manages the installation and configuration of plug-ins. Extensions come as JAR files or Python or BeanShell scripts. You would also place these in the lib/ext directory.
- A *registry* is nothing more than a dictionary of what's available in an extension.

5.2.5 *OpenJUMP scripting*

In addition to adding new JARs, you can enhance OpenJUMP by using BeanShell and Jython scripting. Place your own scripts and Python classes in either the BeanTools or Jython subdirectory under the lib/ext directory in the OpenJUMP install.

5.2.6 *OpenJUMP format support*

To load a supported vector file, right-click the workspace and select the Load Dataset option or use the File > Open menu option. To load a raster file, use the File > Open File menu option. To load a spatial database layer, use the Load Data Store or Ad Hoc Query tools.

OpenJUMP can open the following vector formats: GML, JML, Esri shapefile, WKT, and PostGIS. You can save your work to the following vector formats: Scalable Vector Graphics (SVG), Esri shapefile, and GML. You can save to the following raster formats: GIF, TIFF, JPG, and PNG.

With additional plug-ins, you'll find support for MrSID, MIF, ArcSDE, Oracle, GPX, and Excel. Be sure to visit SourceForge and search for "Plugins_for_Open-JUMP" for all the latest and greatest OpenJUMP plug-ins (http://mng.bz/rmWy).

5.2.7 *PostGIS support*

OpenJUMP has good support for PostGIS. It has two key features:

- *Heterogeneous columns*—OpenJUMP is capable of rendering a heterogeneous column of geometries in Add Data Store mode as well as Ad Hoc Query mode, and it treats the column like a single layer.
- *SQL queries*—OpenJUMP, via its Layer > Run Datastore Query menu option, allows you to type in freehand SQL statements and view them. The only restriction is that the ad hoc query must have at least one geometry column. If more than one geometry column is output, the first geometry column is rendered.

5.2.8 *Registering data sources*

OpenJUMP maintains a list of data sources you can connect to, but you must register these prior to using them. You register a data source by using the OpenJUMP Connection Manager.

Drivers used by data sources

Behind the scenes, OpenJUMP uses JDBC drivers to connect to databases. If you live on the bleeding edge and want the newest PostgreSQL drivers, swap out the packaged drivers using these simple steps:

1 Download the latest PostgreSQL JDBC3 driver from http://jdbc.postgresql.org/download.html.
2 Copy the PostgreSQL JDBC driver into your OpenJUMP lib directory and delete the version that's there. The driver filename usually begins with the word "postgresql."

There are several ways to get to the Connection Manager. Here's one:

1   Select File > Run Data Store Query from the menu.
2   Click the database icon next to the connection drop-down list (see figure 5.1) to open the Connection Manager (figure 5.2) and click Add.

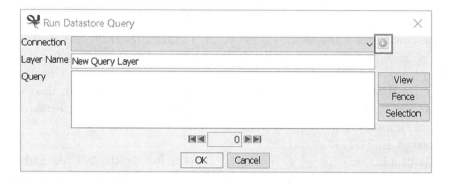

Figure 5.1   OpenJUMP drop-down list for database connections

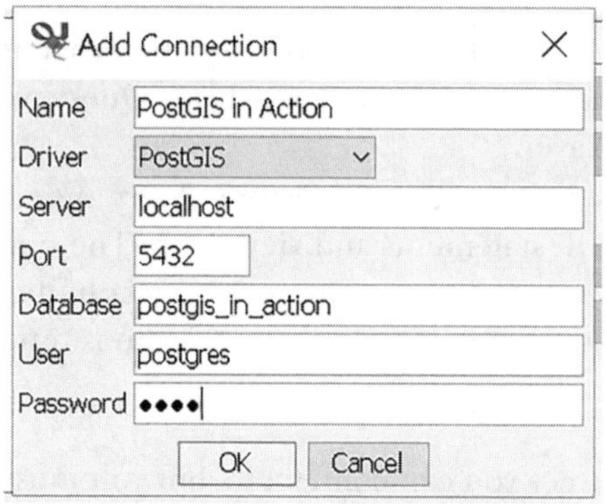

Figure 5.2   Adding a new PostGIS database connection

In the Add Connection dialog box, enter the name you want for the connection, the database name (in the Instance field), and all other relevant information. Then click OK.

Once you've successfully added the connection, you should see it in your Connection Manager list, as shown in figure 5.3. Should you end up with a connection error (often shown with a red dot), delete the connection and try again.

One annoyance with OpenJUMP is that you can't edit connections. You can, however, copy an existing connection, which gives you a screen to edit the values, and you can then save that edited connection under a new name.

Figure 5.3 OpenJUMP Connection Manager with a new connection

5.2.9 *Rendering PostGIS geometries*

The Add DataStore Layer dialog box is the quickest way to render data that's stored in an existing geometry column. To get to this dialog box, right-click Working and choose Open > Data Store Layer as shown in figure 5.4.

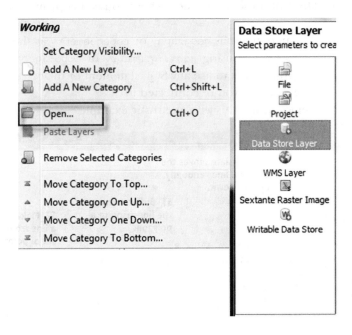

Figure 5.4 Adding a PostGIS table in OpenJUMP using the Data Store Layer

Next, select a connection and then a table and the geometry column you want to display. You can filter the data with an optional WHERE clause (see figure 5.5). Then click Finish.

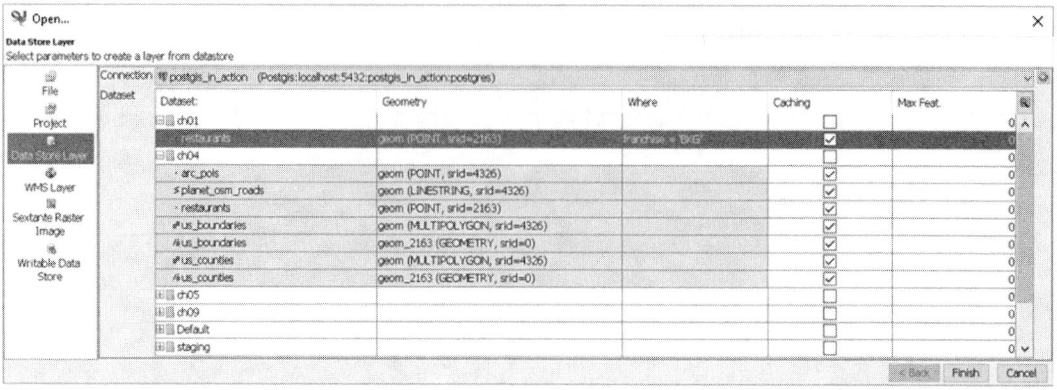

Figure 5.5   Datastore layer setup in OpenJUMP

If nothing appears on the main display window after you click Finish, select the layer from the Working group, right-click, and choose Zoom to Layer. OpenJUMP is finicky in that it considers the extent (the area that fully contains all the data) to always be the extent of all records in the table, even when a WHERE clause has shrunk the extent.

To display the result of an ad hoc query, select File > (SQL) Run Data Source Query from the menu. This will present a window where you can copy in a full SQL statement.

If you want to display a query that has geography or topogeometry as the spatial type, you'll need to cast to geometry using geog::geometry or topo::geometry as part of your SQL statement. You're free to use any SQL statement or to access custom objects you've created in the database you're connected to.

The following listing demonstrates this with an artistic example.

Listing 5.1   Abstract SQL art

```
SELECT art.n, art.geom         ST_Translate moves the
FROM (                          buffered line randomly
    SELECT                      up and down.
        n,
        ST_Translate(  ◁──────────────────┐   ST_Buffer converts
            ST_Buffer(  ◁───────────────────┐  the linestring to a     ST_Makeline creates
                ST_MakeLine(pt), mod(n,6) + 2,   polygon.              a line from random
                'endcap=' || endcaps[mod(n,3) + 1] || ' join=' ||       set of points.
                joins[mod(n,array_upper(joins,1)) + 1] ||
                ' quad_segs=' || n
            ),
        n*10,n*random()*pi()
    ) As geom
FROM (
    SELECT ceiling(random()*100)::integer As n,
        ARRAY['square', 'round', 'flat'] As endcaps,
        ARRAY['round','mitre','bevel'] As joins,
```

```
        ST_Point(x*random(),y*random()) As pt
   FROM generate_series(1,200, 7) As x
       CROSS JOIN generate_series(1,500,20) As y
) As foo
GROUP BY foo.n, foo.endcaps, foo.joins
HAVING count(foo.n) > 10) As art;
```

The result of the query changes each time you run it.

To apply styles in OpenJUMP, right-click a layer and choose Style > Change Styles > Enable Color Theming. Figure 5.6 shows the output of one run of the query after applying styles.

Figure 5.6   SQL art after applying custom styles

5.2.10 *Exporting data*

OpenJUMP comes with basic import and export capabilities to save files in Esri, GML, WKT, raster, and SVG formats. By installing additional plug-ins, you can export to AutoCAD DXF and print to PDF. Visit SourceForge for the plug-ins (http://source-forge.net/projects/jump-pilot/files). To export a layer, right-click the layer and choose Save Dataset As. To save the current view to PNG or JPG, select File > Save View as Raster from the menu.

We've given you a taste of what OpenJUMP offers. OpenJUMP also has a Jython scripting environment that allows you to write custom plug-ins in Python. We encourage you to explore all these features.

In the next section, we'll take a look at QGIS.

5.3   *QGIS*

QGIS, formerly Quantum GIS, is a free and open source desktop GIS viewing, editing, and analysis tool. Its polished and intuitive interface makes it well suited for GIS novices. QGIS also has a devoted Python and Geographic Resources Analysis Support System (GRASS) following. QGIS is built on the Qt framework, a C/C++ cross-platform windowing framework.

What makes QGIS stand out is its high level of integration with GRASS, its extensive support for rasters, its rich integration with the OGR/GDAL suite, and its native Python scripting framework. Finally, perhaps the most appealing aspect of QGIS is the user-friendly interface. With the other tools, we often have to second-guess the UI; with QGIS, everything is nicely organized and we find ourselves not having to question whether we're missing a key feature simply because we're unfamiliar with its navigation.

We ranked QGIS as "easy" in "ease of use" because of its tight integration with data tables. With the QGIS interface, you can add tables, edit rows, and filter rows. We particularly like the feature where you can highlight a data row and QGIS will automatically zoom to the corresponding area of the viewing window.

Because QGIS is so intuitively organized, you probably won't need to peruse the 1,000-plus-page manual, but if you do, you'll find that it comes in many languages and is quite helpful.

5.3.1   Installing QGIS

Installing QGIS is straightforward. QGIS sometimes prompts for a reboot after install, but because QGIS doesn't rely on Java, you avoid the nuisance of installing and updating the Java runtime. You can download QGIS from www.qgis.org. Both 32-bit and 64-bit flavors are available for most operating systems.

QGIS is also part of the OSGeo4W suite, so you can choose instead to install OSGeo4W, which will give you QGIS along with a bevy of GIS-related tools. You can find OSGeo4W here: http://trac.osgeo.org/osgeo4w. It is also linked to from the QGIS page.

5.3.2   Using QGIS with PostGIS

QGIS matured alongside PostGIS, so QGIS's spatial database support for PostGIS has been time-tested more than any of the other spatial databases it supports. The PostGIS `geometry` type support in QGIS is stronger than its support for other PostGIS spatial types. QGIS has always been first to jump on board to support new PostGIS spatial features, and as such its PostGIS raster, 3D geometry, geography, and topogeometry support is stronger than you'll find in most other desktop products. Check out Kartoza's "Introduction to PostgreSQL and PostGIS" video for a visual walk-through of interacting with PostGIS using QGIS (http://mng.bz/VG1G).

The Database > DB Manager menu option is our favorite. Within DB Manager you will find DB Manager_TopoViewer, which allows you to view PostGIS topologies (which we cover in chapter 13). That option shows under the Schema menu after you launch DB Manager, and only if you have a PostGIS schema selected. PostGIS raster viewing is available via the DB Manager plug-in. Both the TopoViewer and selecting a table with a raster column will load the respective items in the main map view.

For pgRouting, look for the pgRouting Layer plug-in, which is an additional extension. You can install most extensions with a single click from the extensions menu option.

ADDING A POSTGIS CONNECTION

Adding a PostGIS geometry connection in QGIS is easy. There are two common ways of doing it. Start by going to the Layer menu shown in figure 5.7 and select Add Layer > Add PostGIS Layer > New.

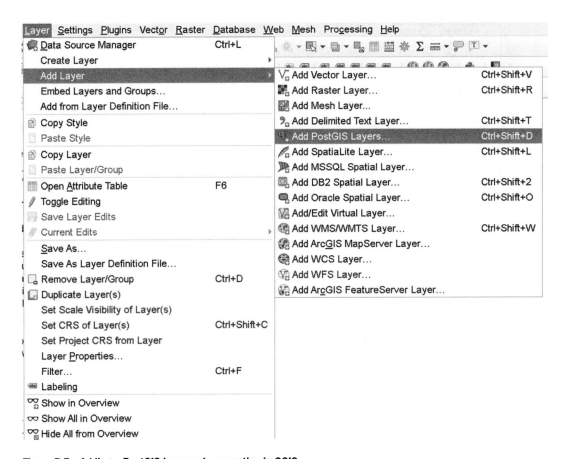

Figure 5.7 Adding a PostGIS layer and connection in QGIS

Alternatively you can create a connection from the Browser pane by right-clicking PostGIS and choosing the New Connection option, as shown in figure 5.8. If you don't see the Browser pane, you can enable it from the menu: View > Panels > Browser.

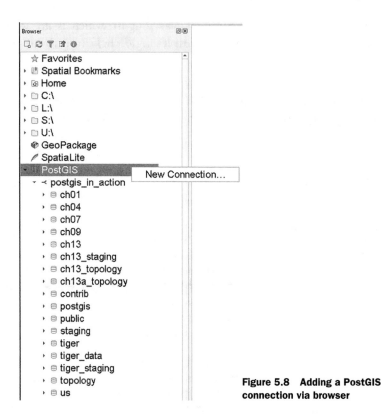

Figure 5.8   Adding a PostGIS connection via browser

Figure 5.9 shows the QGIS PostGIS connection dialog box you get after clicking New in the Layer menu or New Connection from the Browser pane. You'll get better load speeds for large tables if you check the Use Estimated Table Metadata check box. The drawback is that if your table stats are out of date, you may end up with weird results, like the QGIS viewport not fully containing the extent of your data. The other drawback is that the metadata may be incomplete. For example, if you have a mixed geometry type column that contains both points and linestrings, it may arbitrarily assume the table consists of all one or the other.

If you have lots of tables or tables with many rows that have unconstrained geometry columns (those not constrained by typmod), you'll want to check the box Don't Resolve Type of Unrestricted Columns (GEOMETRY). If this is not checked, QGIS will try to inspect the data in these tables to infer the geometry type. This will slow down the listing of layers.

A new feature added in QGIS 3.2 is the ability to save QGIS projects in a Postgre-SQL database. This feature is particularly handy if you need to share project database layers, custom forms, and styling with other users. This is set in the Connection Information dialog box with the Allow Saving/Loading QGIS Projects in the Database check box. By default this setting is unchecked, but figure 5.9 shows it checked. We

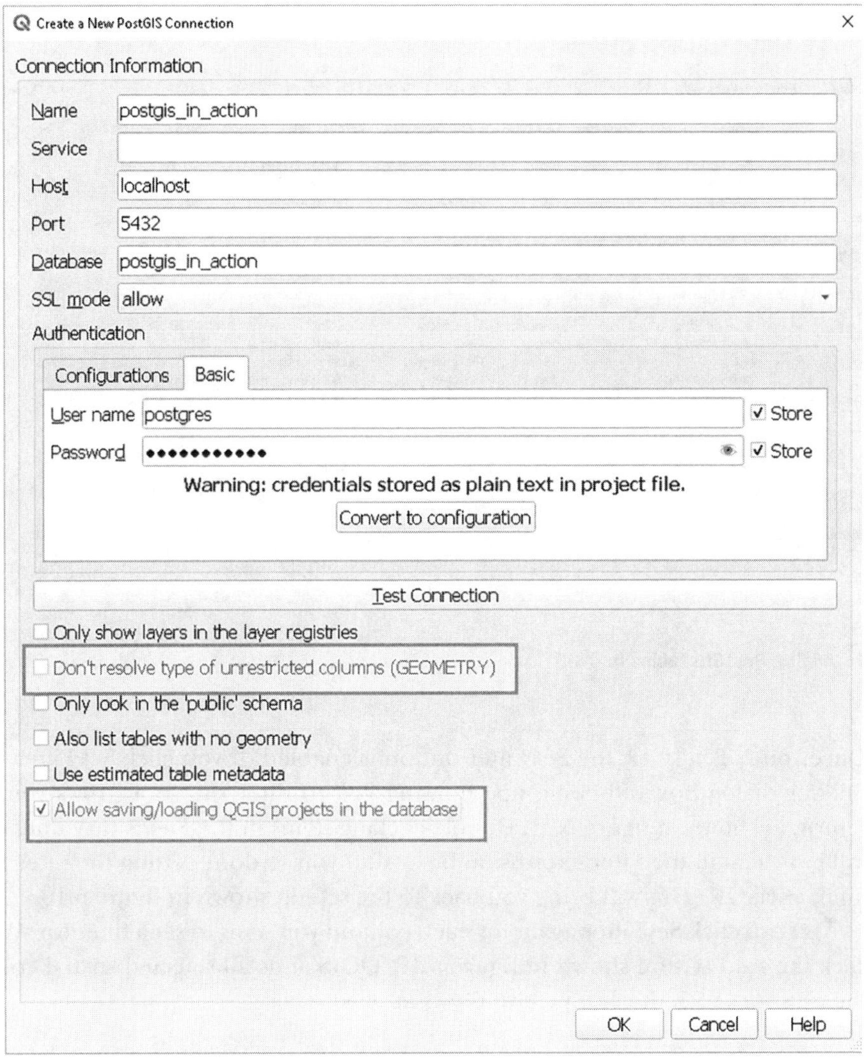

Figure 5.9 Adding a PostGIS connection in QGIS

cover this in our "New in QGIS 3.2 Save Project to PostgreSQL" blog post (http://mng
.bz/xG4X).

VIEWING AND FILTERING POSTGIS DATA

When using the Layer > Add PostGIS Layer menu option, you get the QGIS dialog
box for adding new tables. This dialog box displays each spatial column with a stylized
icon. If a table has more than one spatial column or a particular column contains
mixed geometry, QGIS lists each type as a separate layer, as shown in figure 5.10.

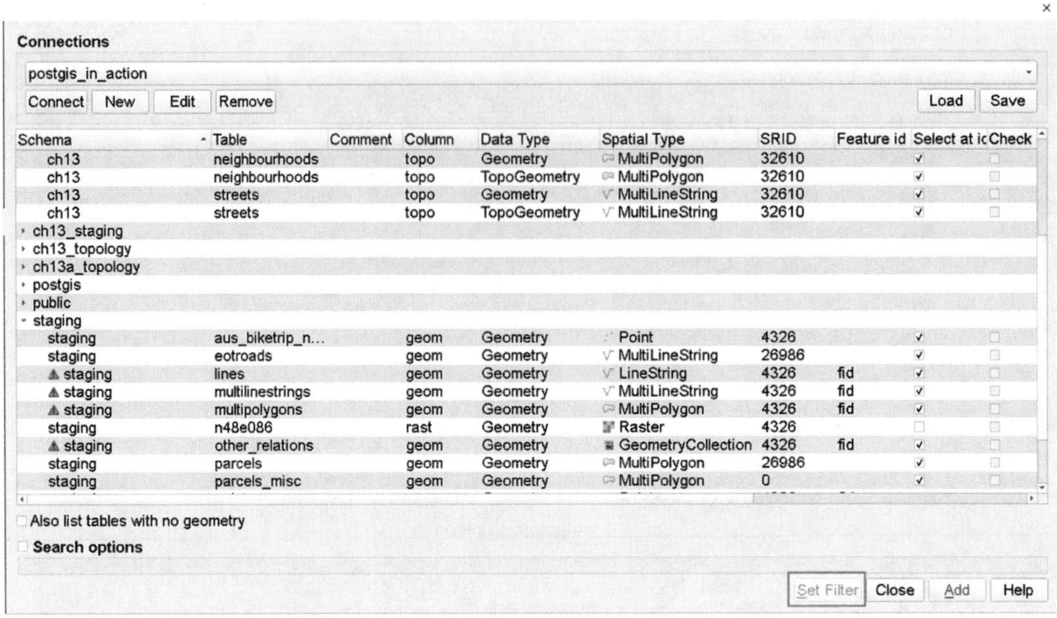

Figure 5.10   Adding PostGIS tables in QGIS

Once you pick a layer, the Set Filter button is enabled. If you click Set Filter, a Query Builder dialog box will come up, allowing you to filter the set of rows you want to return, as shown in figure 5.11. Double-clicking items in the Fields or Values columns will put them in the filter expression box. After you're done setting the filter for a column, click OK. This will bring you back to the screen shown in figure 5.10.

You can click Set Filter again for each column you want to set a filter for. When you click the Add button shown in figure 5.10, QGIS adds all selected spatial columns to the viewport, with their respective filters applied.

> **WARNING**   There is a bug in QGIS 3.12.0 that prevents PostGIS `raster` layers from being displayed. This is fixed in later versions of QGIS and is not an issue with earlier versions.

USING THE DB MANAGER

More advanced PostGIS users may find the QGIS query building limiting. Luckily, QGIS's DB Manager plug-in lets you write ad hoc queries. In newer versions of QGIS, DB Manager appears to be installed by default, but if you don't see it in your install, go to the Plugins > Manage And Install Plugins menu option to install it. Once it's in place, you can launch DB Manager from the Database > DB Manager menu option.

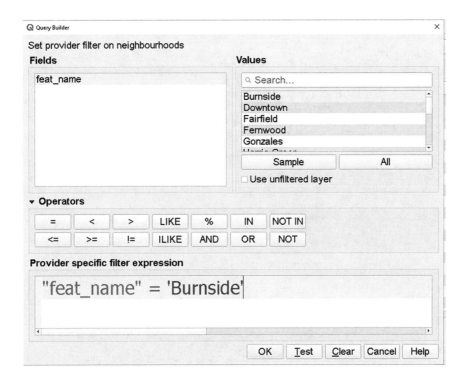

Figure 5.11 Filtering table data in QGIS

You can launch DB Manager's SQL window by selecting Database > SQL Window in the main DB Manager window. Figure 5.12 shows the DB Manager window with the SQL window open. In this window you can write any query for QGIS to render, as long as you abide by some rules:

- Don't end your SQL with a semicolon. This is because DB Manager sometimes changes your query to add a dummy integer key and can't wrap your query in a larger one.
- If you want to render `raster`, `geography`, or `topogeometry` data types, you'll have to cast to `geometry`.
- Your `geometry` column must be a single type of geometry. For example, a column with some rows that have points and others with polygons won't work.

If you'd like to see an entire table rendered, you can skip the SQL window and drag and drop tables with a `geometry` or `raster` column directly from the DB Manager to the main QGIS map window. Although dragging `topogeometry` tables doesn't work from DB Manager, `topogeometry` columns work fine from the PostGIS data layer tool. There is also a dedicated PostGIS topology viewer tool you can use to see the topology network.

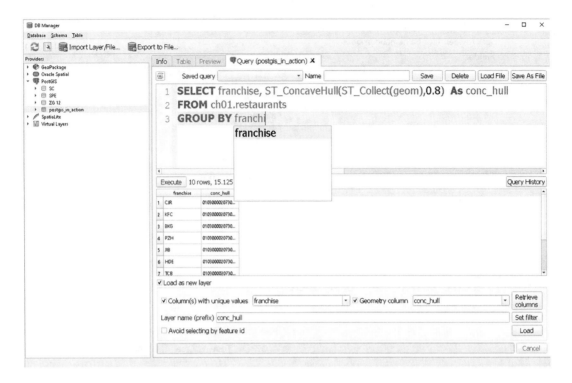

Figure 5.12   QGIS DB Manager

Surprisingly, the drag-and-drop approach also works for tables with a `raster` column, but if your raster is large, we suggest that you use accompanying overview tables, which you learned how to load in chapter 4 with raster2pgsql—QGIS is smart enough to take advantage of them and speed up loading. Another approach is to create a view to isolate the area of interest. All in all, we find that `raster` support in QGIS improves with each successive release.

Besides the SQL and the drag-and-drop rendering, DB Manager has a few more talents:

- It allows you to see a tree-view listing of all your tables, with the ability to browse the attribute data and preview a map rendering of your table. This feature is also available for `raster` tables.
- It has a PostGIS topology viewer, accessible from the DB Manager > Schema > TopoViewer menu option.
- You can use DB Manager to import and export data into and out of PostGIS. Access this via the Table menu option, or use the import and export icon.
- You can perform database administration tasks like deleting tables, creating new schemas, and so on.

- The SQL window has syntax coloring and type-ahead, where table names will drop down for you to pick.
- It has a versioning feature that will add triggers to tables you specify for tracking changes.

IMPORTING AND EXPORTING LAYERS

QGIS can import files in an incredible number of formats, and the list is ever-growing. Many of these imports are made possible by the GDAL/OGR library.

To import a vector file, choose Layer > Add Vector Layer > File or Directory; you'll be amazed at the number of file types available, as shown in figure 5.13.

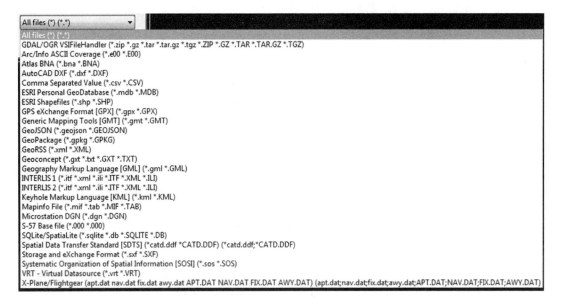

Figure 5.13   QGIS vector file sampling

QGIS can also import a number of raster formats; we last counted 15. Installing additional plug-ins will encompass even more raster formats.

Exporting layers to other file formats is just as easy. Right-click a layer and select Save Vector Layer As. You'll have a choice of over 10 different formats.

Our preferred way of importing data into PostGIS within QGIS is to use the DB Manager Import menu, as shown in figure 5.14. You access the import menu from the DB Manager > Import Layer/File menu option. The importer can import both spatial data and generic delimited data such as .csv files and spreadsheets.

In this section, we've only touched the surface of all that QGIS has to offer. We encourage you to visit the QGIS website or peruse the well-prepared user manual to

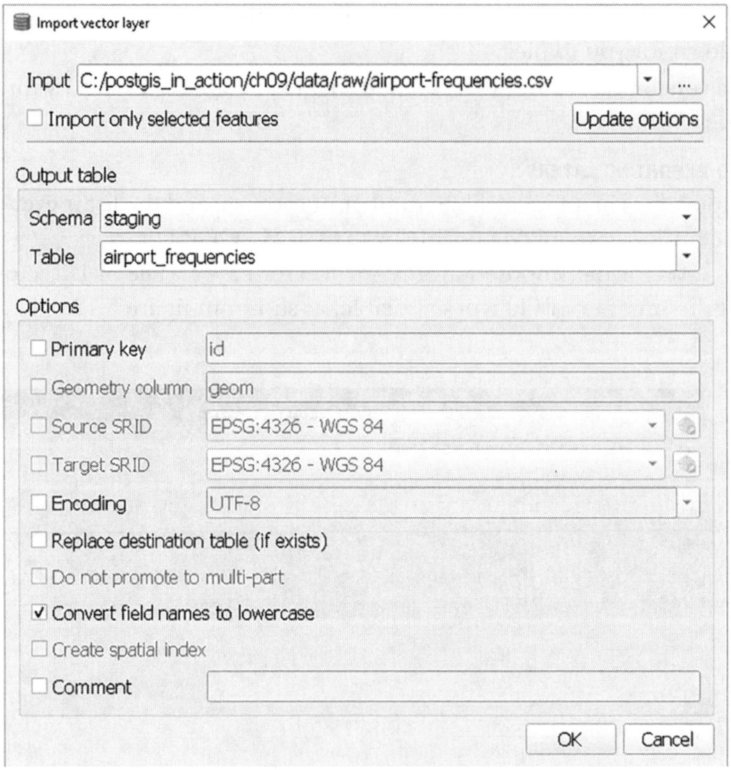

Figure 5.14   QGIS DB Manager Import Vector Layer dialog box

learn more. Also keep in mind the growing number of plug-ins, especially for working with PostGIS rasters, PostGIS topology, and PostGIS 3D data types.

Finally, QGIS also sports a server component called QGIS Server. You can convert your workspace to a web service suitable for use in QGIS Server. OSGeoLive includes QGIS server along with PostGIS and many other OSGeo projects. Its use is detailed on the OSGeoLive "QGIS Server Quickstart" page (http://mng.bz/A1ox).

QGIS also comes with a Python development tool called QT Designer with QGIS custom widgets, which allows you to develop your frontends for your QGIS plug-ins. Discussion of the QGIS plug-in development is beyond the scope of this book but you can explore it in the PyQGIS Developer Cookbook (https://docs.qgis.org/3.16/en/docs/pyqgis_developer_cookbook/).

In the next section we'll cover gvSIG, another popular GIS desktop tool.

5.4 *GvSIG*

GvSIG has three products under its umbrella:

- *gvSIG desktop*—A GIS tool licensed under the GNU/GPL license for accessing various data sources from a desktop.
- *gvSIG Online*—A tool licensed under AGPL (Affero) for sharing data across organizations, and it can be used as Software as a Service (SaaS) or on premises. As a result, you may find that much of the layout, workflow, and idioms in ArcGIS have carried over to gvSIG.
- *gvSIG Mobile*—An application for Android devices with a focus on field work.

This section will only cover the gvSIG desktop.

GvSIG is built on top of Java and uses the Java Advanced Imaging (JAI) framework for image processing. Like other tools, gvSIG is both a desktop tool and an extensible mapping platform that will let you code your own extensions in Java. All extensions reside in the gvSIG/extensions directory. Each extension gets its own subdirectory and consists of one or more JAR files, various language configuration files, an XML configuration file, and a .def file that defines the field columns that will be displayed in the extension dialog. In addition to supporting extensions via Java programming, you can also script in Jython.

You can download gvSIG from the gvSIG page (www.gvsig.com/en/products/gvsig-desktop/downloads). There are 32-bit and 64-bit installers for Linux and Windows. A 64-bit installer for macOS is forthcoming as of this writing. The installers are all-inclusive and contain the JRE. As such, the download size is a bit hefty, ranging from 500 to 800 MB. In addition to the installers, there are portable versions, which you can extract and run without installation.

5.4.1 *Using gvSIG with PostGIS*

GvSIG is organized around documents. To add PostGIS data, you must first create a view document. Once you've established a view document, you're free to add as many layers as you like. Follow these steps:

1 Create a new view document from the Project Manager window and give it a name. We used PostGIS Test for this example, as shown in figure 5.15.

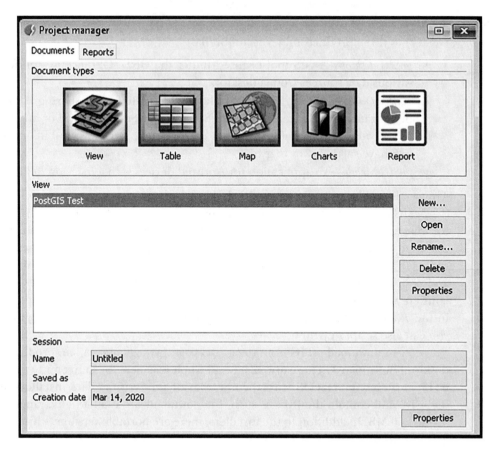

Figure 5.15   Project Manager window in gvSIG

2 Select the View you created, click the Open button, and then in the view right-click and select Add Layer. Switch to the Database tab and click Connect to create a new PostGIS connection, as shown in figure 5.16.

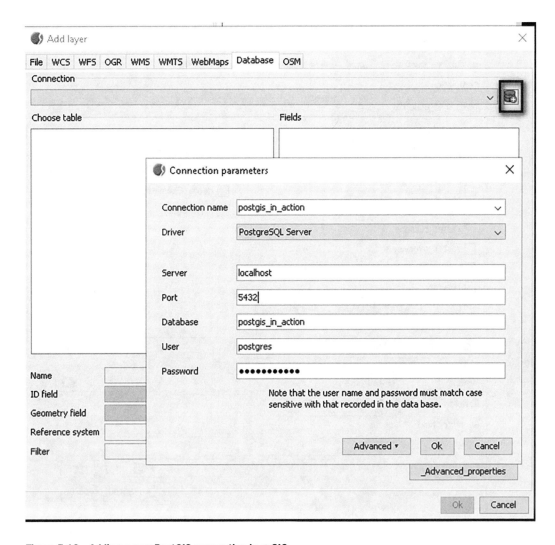

Figure 5.16 Adding a new PostGIS connection in gvSIG

3 Fill in the connection information and click OK. Then select the connection and the tables you want to add, and fill in the parameters for each, as shown in figure 5.17.

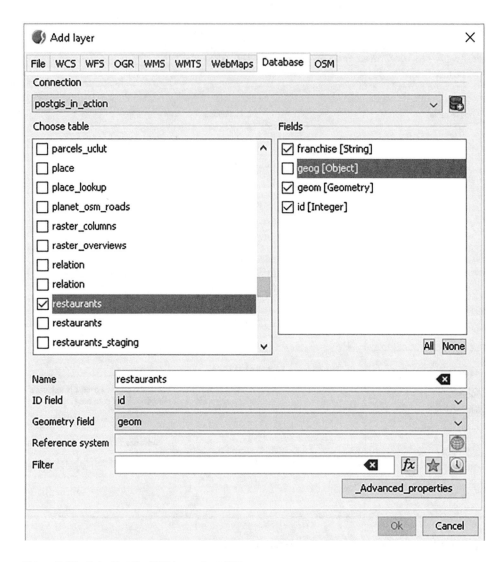

Figure 5.17   Selecting PostGIS layers in gvSIG

You can filter rows by typing in a SQL WHERE clause in the filter text box, but that's the extent of the SQL at your disposal.

GvSIG can handle heterogeneous geometry columns, but not geography, raster, or topogeometry columns.

5.4.2   Exporting data

Exporting data to other formats is straightforward in gvSIG. Follow these steps:

- Select the layer.
- Select the Layer > Export To menu option.
- Choose the format to export to, as shown in figure 5.18.

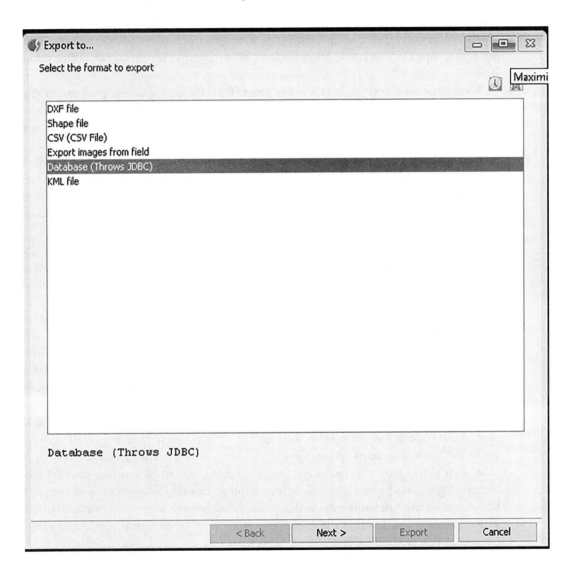

Figure 5.18   GvSIG export options

The Database (Throws JDBC) option allows you to export to other databases that have JDBC drivers installed, such as MySQL and PostgreSQL.

5.5   *JupyterLab and Jupyter Notebook*

Jupyter is an open source project released under a BSD-styled license (https://jupyter
.org/). It includes a suite of tools primarily designed for data analysis and teaching.
We'll cover its flagship Notebook and next-generation JupyterLab, which run on most
every operating system. Both the Notebook and JupyterLab interfaces allow you to
edit, run, and view notebook files, which by convention end with .ipynb extensions.
The Notebook interface sports a browser, allowing you to browse through a folder of
notebook files and view one at a time. The JupyterLab interface, in addition to allowing you to open a notebook, allows you to have multiple windows, including other
IDEs.

Both Notebook and JupyterLab offer many formats for exporting your notebook.
Our favorites are the revealjs format output (https://revealjs.com/), which allows you
to output the notebook as slides for use in presentations, and the AsciiDoc format for
easy inclusion into publications such as this book (http://asciidoc.org/).

Although Jupyter Notebook and JupyterLab are the most common tools for viewing and editing Jupyter notebooks, you'll find that many hosted code repositories can
also render Jupyter notebooks. There are also hosted tools, such as JupyterHub and
Google Colab, that allow you to run a notebook on a hosted server instead of on your
desktop.

Although the Jupyter project itself does not offer a mobile edition, you can get
Jupyter Notebook to install on Android devices using the Pydroid app (http://mng
.bz/ZYqA). There is also a proprietary tool called Juno that offers iOS and iPad plug-
ins for running Jupyter Notebook.

Hosted solutions, such as JupyterHub (https://jupyter.org/hub) or Google Colab
(https://colab.research.google.com/), should work just fine on a phone without any
installation, since the Jupyter interface is exposed as a web application. Even on a
desktop, Jupyter Notebook and JupyterLab run in their own self-contained web server.

Jupyter is built on top of Python. While it still works with Python 2, Python 3 is preferred and Python 2 support will be short-lived. Jupyter notebooks contain both procedural code and narrative describing what is being done in the workbook. Most
procedural code in Jupyter notebook is done in Python and narrative is generally written in the Markdown markup language. You can use other scripting languages such as
Julia or R if you have the necessary environments installed. There are over 30 language plug-ins for Jupyter that allow for scripting in other languages. You can also
launch command-line tools from within a notebook by prefixing the command with !.
The command-line feature allows you to interact easily with psql, gdal, and other
command-line loading tools we covered in chapter 4.

The easiest way to install Jupyter on a desktop is to use the Anaconda distribution
(www.anaconda.com/distribution/). Anaconda provides installers for Linux, Windows, and macOS. Another popular way of running Jupyter is on a Docker container,
which you can find several of here: https://hub.docker.com/u/jupyter. We will cover
installing Jupyter via the Anaconda Python distribution next.

5.5.1 Installing Jupyter

To install Jupyter, download the Anaconda Python distribution for your desktop from www.anaconda.com/distribution/ and then install. Accepting the default options in the installer is generally sufficient. Anaconda is a hefty installer, weighing in at around 500 MB. It comes prepackaged with quite a few Python libraries, including Jupyter applications.

Once you have Anaconda installed, you'll want to update your install and download a couple more extensions to make your life in Notebook comfy.

Find the Anaconda Prompt in your Apps menu and launch it. You'll want to launch this in Admin mode or with elevated privileges.

Anaconda uses a package manager called conda to install and update libraries that will live in the Anaconda install folder. The first thing you'll want to do is update your Anaconda to ensure you have the latest libs:

```
conda update --all --yes
```

Next, install the database libraries you'll need for connecting to PostgreSQL server:

```
conda install -y sqlalchemy psycopg2
```

For additional packages, there is a repository of libs called conda-forge. This is where you'll get less common or more bleeding-edge libraries.

Next, install the following packages from conda-forge:

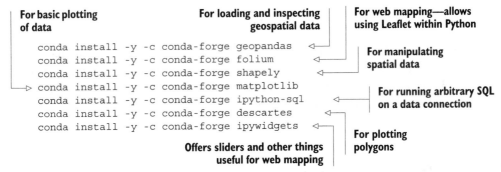

You'll notice that GeoPandas and Shapely also pull down libraries you may recognize, such as GEOS, Proj, and GDAL, which PostGIS also uses for its heavy lifting.

5.5.2 Launching Jupyter Notebook

You can either launch the Notebook app from your operating system, or you can use the Anaconda console to launch it. If you do so via the console, it's easy to designate the path that contains the notebooks.

While still in the console, do the following, replacing the notebook-dir path with the location where you have the postgis_in_action chapter 5 download:

```
jupyter notebook --notebook-dir=/postgis_in_action/ch05/
```

When you run the preceding command, your web browser should open up to the Notebook interface, listing all the files in the notebook-dir folder you designated, as shown in figure 5.19.

Figure 5.19 Jupyter Notebook app

5.5.3 *Launching JupyterLab*

You can open the JupyterLab app in a similar fashion to the Notebook app, replacing the word notebook with lab:

```
jupyter lab --notebook-dir=/postgis_in_action/ch05/
```

The main distinction between the Notebook and JupyterLab apps is that the Notebook app is a single document interface. When you are using the Notebook app, you are either looking at the folder of files or a particular notebook. In contrast, the JupyterLab app, as shown in figure 5.20, has a multi-document interface that allows you to open up a shell window and other windows of your choosing, all neatly docked as tabs within the JupyterLab interface.

5.5.4 *Creating a Python notebook*

You can create a Python notebook from either the Notebook or JupyterLab interface.

In Notebook, use the New button on the Files tab, as shown in figure 5.19, and choose Python3. In JupyterLab use the File > New > Notebook menu options, as shown in figure 5.20, and choose Python3 from the drop-down list. Next, open the notebook you created by selecting it from Files. You can rename the notebook using the File > Rename menu option from the Notebook screen or by clicking on the name of the notebook.

A notebook is composed of cells, and each cell has a bit of executable content. When you click the Run icon on a cell, the output is shown below in an output cell.

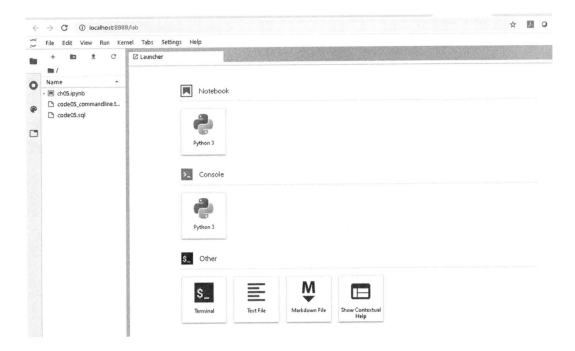

Figure 5.20   JupyterLab app

5.5.5   *Magic commands*

Jupyter has special commands that are prefixed with %. These are called *magic* commands. When a cell is prefixed with %%, that means that what follows in the whole cell should be read by the specified magic command interpreter. If a line is prefixed with just one %, that means that particular line should be read by the specified magic interpreter.

To get a list of magic commands available, add a cell with the following content:

```
%lsmagic
```

Then run it. You'll see something similar to figure 5.21.

There are two kinds of magic commands. There is a cell magic command, which is prefixed with %%, making the whole cell magical. There is also a line magic keyword that is prefixed with %, making only the line it appears on magical. You'll see that many magic commands are both line and cell magical.

Some magic commands don't become readily available until you load the associated extension that contains them. One such magic command is the sql magic command, which you'll learn about next.

```
[1]: ▼ root:
        ► line:
        ▼ cell:
            js: "DisplayMagics"
            javascript: "DisplayMagics"
            latex: "DisplayMagics"
            svg: "DisplayMagics"
            html: "DisplayMagics"
            markdown: "DisplayMagics"
            prun: "ExecutionMagics"
            debug: "ExecutionMagics"
            timeit: "ExecutionMagics"
            time: "ExecutionMagics"
            capture: "ExecutionMagics"
            sx: "OSMagics"
            system: "OSMagics"
            !: "OSMagics"
            writefile: "OSMagics"
            script: "ScriptMagics"
            sh: "Other"
            bash: "Other"
            perl: "Other"
            ruby: "Other"
            python: "Other"
            python2: "Other"
            python3: "Other"
            pypy: "Other"
            cmd: "Other"
            SVG: "Other"
            HTML: "Other"
            file: "Other"
```

Figure 5.21   Jupyter magic commands

5.5.6   *Performing raw queries with Jupyter Notebook*

There are a number of ways to query a database from within a notebook. One is to use the ipython-sql library you installed earlier, which introduces SQL magic. To be able to use this SQL, you need to add a cell in your notebook with the following content:

```
%load_ext sql
```

Then click the Run icon. If you rerun the cell with `%lsmagic`, you will see that you now have an additional magic `sql` in both the `line` and `cell` sections.

Now every time you start a line in a cell with `%%sql`, the notebook knows that the rest of the lines in the cell will be SQL or a connection string to an SQL-enabled database. You can have several lines in a cell with each SQL command followed by a semicolon (`;`). When you run the cell, all those SQL commands will be executed.

To connect to a database using the magic `%%sql` command, you specify the database connection string as in the next cell, which connects to the postgis_in_action database:

```
%%sql
postgresql://postgres:mypassword@localhost:5432/postgis_in_action
```

Any commands in subsequent cells will use this database.

Let's start by copying a table you created in chapter 4. Create a cell that has the following contents:

```
%%sql
CREATE SCHEMA IF NOT EXISTS ch05;          ⟵  Create chapter 5 schema
CREATE TABLE ch05.arc_test AS              ⟵  if it doesn't exist.
SELECT * FROM ch04.arc_pois;                   Create a new table in chapter 5
                                               from a table in chapter 4.
```

The output of the preceding command should show something like the following:

```
* postgresql://postgres:***@localhost:5432/postgis_in_action
Done.
508 rows affected.
```

You can load the contents of the table to a memory variable called `arc_pois` with the following code in a cell:

```
%%sql arc_pois << SELECT osm_id, name, geom
    FROM ch05.arc_test
    ORDER BY name
```

The `<<` command allows you to have a single statement continue on multiple lines. To see the first five rows of the memory variable, you would add the following code to a new cell and run it. Note that the `DataFrame()` function converts the output to a pandas dataframe, so that you can then apply standard pandas functions to it:

```
df = arc_pois.DataFrame()
df.head(5)
```

The output you get should look something like table 5.6.

Note that table 5.6 shows the `geometry` column in hexewkb format, which is the canonical format for PostGIS `geometry`. Since pandas itself has no mechanism for handling spatial data, it has no mechanism to display it in a useful format.

Table 5.6   Jupyter Notebook outputs to a Python variable, and then outputs the variable to cell

	osm_id	name	geom
0	4885347732	1.2.3	0101000020E610000096AC2FB7206002408384CDA55D70...
1	4418418790	20 rue Lauriston, Paris	0101000020E61000009EC59CB17956024077AC08ED8B6F...
2	4971661021	À l'Étoile d'Or	0101000020E6100000101DA78D8F5B02408CFA7F304B70...
3	2733570086	Acuitis	0101000020E61000007F24366964610240918CE6125870...
4	1549564356	airbnb - Philip	0101000020E610000046ABFF18DF5C0240114CDAF92370...

5.5.7   *Using GeoPandas, Shapely, and Matplotlib to work with spatial data*

To make sense of spatial data, you'll want to use a library called GeoPandas (https://geopandas.org/), which is an extension of pandas (the Python Data Analysis Library; https://pandas.pydata.org). As you saw earlier, ipython_sql has a `DataFrame()` method to output to a pandas dataframe if you have the pandas library installed.

The pandas Python library is popular for working with basic tabular data. GeoPandas adds on support for things like PostGIS spatial columns, and it employs GDAL and Shapely for reading and manipulating other spatial formats such as shapefiles.

The cell example in the following listing will convert the dataframe `df` to a geodataframe called `gdf` by using the Shapely library to convert the PostGIS hexewkb format to a Shapely geometry format (which is what GeoPandas uses for geometry).

Listing 5.2   Convert pandas dataframe to GeoPandas dataframe

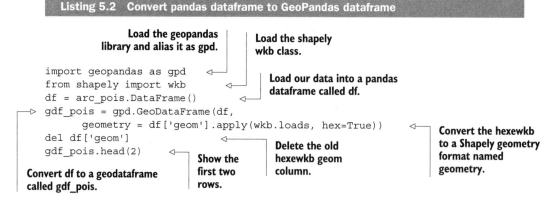

The output of listing 5.2 is shown in table 5.7.

> **NOTE**   You can also use `gpd.read_postgis(sql, con)`, where `con` is a psychopg2 connection to read data directly from PostGIS to create a GeoPandas dataframe, and where `sql` is the `SELECT` statement.

Table 5.7   Jupyter Notebook output converted from panda to GeoPandas dataframe

	osm_id	name	geometry
0	4885347732	1.2.3	POINT (2.29694 48.87786)
1	4418418790	20 rue Lauriston, Paris	POINT (2.29222 48.87146)

Paste the following in the next cell of your notebook and run it. You should see a simple plot of the points, as shown in figure 5.22:

```
gdf_pois.plot()
```

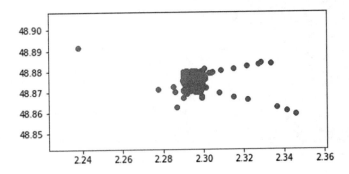

Figure 5.22   Plotting a GeoPandas frame with Matplotlib

Internally, GeoPandas uses Matplotlib to handle the plotting when you call the `plot` method on the geodataframe.

You can then output the data to a file in GeoPandas' supported format. The next cell code outputs to shapefile format in the notebook directory:

```
gdf_pois.to_file("pois.shp")
```

To output to a subfolder in your notebook, you can replace the name with a relative path, such as `data/pois.shp`. To output to another folder on your computer, use the full path, such as `/postgis_in_action/data/pois.shp`. These folders should exist first.

LOADING DATA WITH GEOPANDAS

One popular use of the geopandas library is to load spatial data from external sources such as websites. Internally, GeoPandas uses a library called fiona, which itself wraps the functionality of GDAL.

The next example pulls the timezones polygons dataset from the Natural Earth website and then loads it into a GeoPandas dataframe called timezones:

```
import geopandas as gpd
timezones = gpd.read_file('https://www.naturalearthdata.com/http//
    www.naturalearthdata.com/download/10m/cultural/ne_10m_time_zones.zip')
```

You can view the data with Matplotlib as follows. The output will look like figure 5.23:

```
timezones.plot(figsize=(20,8),
        edgecolor='white', column='zone', legend=True,
        linewidth=2)
```

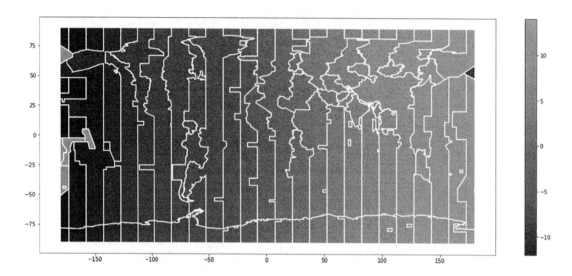

Figure 5.23 Jupyter Matplotlib plotting polygons

NOTE If you get an error, make sure you have the descartes library installed. It is required to plot polygons and linestrings.

If you wanted to store this dataset in your database, you could do so as follows, with the help of sqlachemy and geoalchemy2 Python libraries.

Listing 5.3 Loading a GeoPandas dataframe into PostGIS

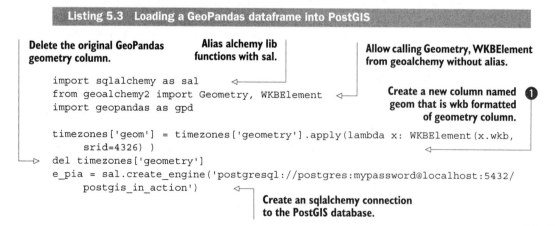

Delete the original GeoPandas geometry column.

Alias alchemy lib functions with sal.

Allow calling Geometry, WKBElement from geoalchemy without alias.

Create a new column named geom that is wkb formatted of geometry column. ❶

```
import sqlalchemy as sal
from geoalchemy2 import Geometry, WKBElement
import geopandas as gpd

timezones['geom'] = timezones['geometry'].apply(lambda x: WKBElement(x.wkb,
        srid=4326) )
del timezones['geometry']
e_pia = sal.create_engine('postgresql://postgres:mypassword@localhost:5432/
        postgis_in_action')
```

Create an sqlalchemy connection to the PostGIS database.

```
timezones.to_sql('timezones', engine, schema='ch05', if_exists='replace',
                        dtype={'geom': Geometry(srid= 4326)})

pgtimezones = gpd.read_postgis("SELECT zone, places, geom FROM ch05.timezones
    ", con = e_pia)
pgtimezones.head(2)
```

Read some columns from the new table into a new geodataframe.

Display the first two rows.

❷ **Use the to_sql pandas method to load the geodataframe into PostGIS.**

The to_sql function ❷ is a function of geodataframe that is borrowed from sqlalchemy. As such, it doesn't know how to deal with the GeoPandas geometry type to convert it to a PostGIS type. You can employ geoalchemy2's Geometry and WKBElement types to convert the GeoPandas type to the well-known binary (WKB) geometry format ❶ and use the Geometry data type provided by geoalchemy2 to convert this to a PostGIS geometry type. For the Geometry type, we only passed in the SRID because our geodataframe geometry is a mix of polygons and multipolygons. If your data was all of the same type, say, all polygons, you could replace Geometry(srid= 4326) with Geometry('POLYGON', srid= 4326). Doing that in this case would cause the to_sql call to error out.

5.5.8 Viewing data on a map with folium

You saw in the previous sections that you can use Matplotlib to view mapping geometries. More useful for viewing spatial data is viewing it on a map overlaid with other geographic data. Python has a number of libraries for doing this, and many of these can be used within a Jupyter notebook.

In the next example, you'll see how you can employ Folium, a common Python web mapping library that wraps the Leaflet JavaScript Mapping API. This allows you to use Leaflet with Python classes right in your notebook. You'll learn more about the use of Leaflet in web applications in chapter 17. Two of the most common ways to use Leaflet within Jupyter are to use the ipyLeaflet or folium libraries. We found folium much easier to use than ipyleaflet, but your mileage may vary. You can read more about ipyLeaflet (https://ipyleaflet.readthedocs.io) and folium (https://python-visualization .github.io/folium/) on their websites.

Listing 5.4 Creating a Folium Leaflet map and overlaying PostGIS data

```
import folium
import geopandas as gpd
import sqlalchemy as sal

e_pgia = sal.create_engine('postgresql://postgres:mypassword@localhost:5432/post
    gis_in_action')
pgtimezone_et = gpd.read_postgis("SELECT concat('#',right(to_hex(
➥ (random()*255*255)::integer ),6) ) AS color, zone, places, geom FROM
➥ ch05.timezones WHERE zone BETWEEN '-8' AND '-3' ORDER BY zone", con = e_pgia)

m = folium.Map([42.359283, -71.058831], zoom_start=5)        ◁── Create the map.
```

```
folium.GeoJson(                                              ◁──────────────
    pgtimezone_et,
    style_function=lambda feature: {
        'fillColor': feature['properties']['color'],    ◁──
        'color': 'black',
        'weight': 2,
        'dashArray': '5, 5'
    }
).add_to(m)                              ◁──────────────
```

Convert the GeoPandas pgtimezone_et data set to GeoJSON and overlay it.

Apply a styling function based on column color in the geodataframe.

Add a layer to the map.

```
m.fit_bounds(m.get_bounds())            ◁──
```
Zoom out to the bounds of the layers.

```
folium.LayerControl().add_to(m)         ◁──
display(m)                ◁──
```
Display the map.

Add a layer control.

The output of listing 5.4 is shown in figure 5.24.

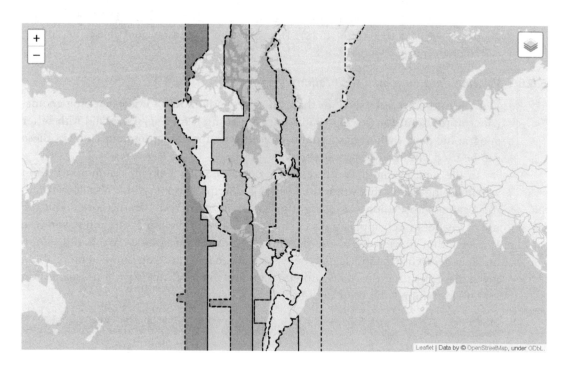

Figure 5.24   Jupyter Folium Leaflet map

If you are using jupyter lab, you'll want to install the following plug-ins at your Anaconda prompt because the map does not render otherwise. jupyter notebook does not need installation of these:

```
jupyter labextension install @jupyter-widgets/jupyterlab-manager
jupyter labextension install @jupyter-widgets/jupyterlab-sidecar
jupyter labextension install jupyter-leaflet
pip install sidecar
```

Then, to show the map in a side panel in JupyterLab instead of the cell output field, you can do this:

```
from sidecar import Sidecar
sc = Sidecar(title='Timezones from -8 to -3')
with sc:
    display(m)
```

Summary

- OpenJUMP, QGIS, and gvSIG are open source tools for viewing and editing geospatial data.
- GRASS is another GIS tool primarily for analyzing raster data, and it's often packaged with QGIS.
- Jupyter Notebook and JupyterLab are all-purpose tools for analyzing data, including spatial.
- All these tools can be used to view, load, and edit PostGIS data.

Geometry and geography functions

This chapter covers

- Output functions
- Constructor functions
- Accessor and setter functions
- Measurement functions
- Composition and decomposition functions
- Simplification functions

In previous chapters we've discussed PostGIS spatial types—how to create them and how to add them to your database. In this chapter we'll introduce the core set of functions that work with the geometry and geography spatial types. This chapter concentrates on functions that work with single geometries and geographies.

PostGIS offers lots of functions and operators, and in this chapter we've grouped them by intent of use. This is by no means a rigorous classification, nor one that will neatly sort each function into a unique group without ambiguity, but grouping functions by the type of tasks you're trying to accomplish is the handiest approach, in our experience. We'll refer to geometries and geographies as *spatial objects* when discussing both. This is the classification scheme we'll use:

- *Output functions*—These functions output spatial object representations in various standard formats (WKT, WKB, GML, SVG, KML, GeoJSON, MVT, PBF).
- *Constructor functions*—These functions create PostGIS spatial objects from a well-known format, such as a well-known text (WKT) format, a well-known binary (WKB) format, or Geography JavaScript Object Notation (GeoJSON).
- *Accessor and setter functions*—These functions work against a single spatial object and return or set attributes of the object.
- *Measurement functions*—These functions return scalar measurements of a spatial object.
- *Decomposition functions*—These functions extract other spatial objects from an input spatial object.
- *Composition functions*—These functions stitch, splice, or group together spatial objects.
- *Simplification functions*—Sometimes you don't need the full resolution of a spatial object. These functions, in the case of geometry and geography, return simplified representations by removing points or linestrings or by rounding the coordinates. The resultant spatial objects still have the basic look and feel of the originals but contain fewer points or elements of lower precision.

In this chapter we'll introduce a dozen or so commonly used functions. You can find an exhaustive listing of all functions and their usage in the official PostGIS manuals (http://postgis.net/documentation).

6.1 Output functions

We'll start by looking at the various functions PostGIS provides for outputting geometries and geographies in standard formats. These functions allow PostGIS to be used with tools not designed specifically for PostGIS. Output functions return spatial objects in another standard format, allowing third-party rendering tools with no knowledge of PostGIS to be used as display tools for PostGIS.

In this section, we'll summarize the output formats available, give some general usage scenarios, and discuss the PostGIS functions that output them. We'll cover some of the more popular output formats, but you should check the official PostGIS site for the ever-growing list. To learn more about the various output formats themselves, be sure to visit their own sites. We won't go into detail about the various formats.

Finally, we advise that you use good judgement when it comes to determining whether the output format makes sense for your particular geometry types. For example, if you have only known a particular function to support 2D with SRID 4326, check the PostGIS manual before trying on other types. The PostGIS manual often dictates when functions change and what geometry types they support. In cases where the manual is unclear, do some experiments to verify that the output is what you are expecting.

Many of the functions we'll describe support both geometry and geography. In cases where only geometry is supported, you can usually cast geography to geometry and use them.

6.1.1   *Well-known text (WKT) and well-known binary (WKB)*

Well-known text and well-known binary are the most common OGC text and binary formats for spatial objects. In fact, many spatial databases, PostGIS included, store their geometry data in a format based on the WKB standard. We've already used the WKT format quite extensively in the book to show the output of queries, because it provides a clear text representation of the underlying geometry.

Two functions that output geometries in WKT format are ST_AsText and ST_AsEWKT. Recall from earlier discussions that the ST_AsEWKT function is a PostGIS-specific extension loosely based on the SQL/MM and OGC SFSQL WKT standards, but it isn't considered OGC-compliant. The OGC-compliant function is ST_AsText, but this function won't output the SRID. In PostGIS versions prior to 2.0, it didn't output the M or Z coordinates either. Textual representations will always lack the precision of binary representations and will preserve only about 15 significant digits.

Two functions that output geometries in WKB format are ST_AsBinary and ST_AsEWKB. ST_AsBinary is the OGC- and SQL/MM-compliant version, whereas ST_AsEWKB is a PostGIS-specific version that includes the SRID.

6.1.2   *Keyhole Markup Language (KML)*

Keyhole Markup Language is an XML-based format created by Keyhole, Inc. to render geospatial data in its applications. KML gained enormous popularity after Google acquired it and integrated it into Google Maps and Google Earth. OGC accepted KML as a standard transport format in its own right.

The PostGIS geometry and geography function for exporting to KML is called ST_AsKML. The default output is KML version 2 with 15-digit precision. ST_AsKML isn't one function, but several with the same name that take different arguments. Other variants of the function allow you to change the target KML version and level of precision.

The spatial reference system for KML is always WGS 84 lon/lat (SRID 4326). As long as your geometry is in a known SRID (present in the spatial_ref_sys table), ST_AsKML will automatically convert it to SRID 4326 for you.

ST_AsKML supports both 2D and 3D basic geometries but will throw an error when exporting curved geometries, geometry collections, polyhedral surfaces, or TINs (triangular irregular networks). Also keep in mind that although ST_AsKML will accept geometries containing an M coordinate, it won't output the M coordinate.

Although KML is a format that can contain other data besides spatial, ST_AsKML will only work with the spatial part.

6.1.3   *Geography Markup Language (GML)*

Geography Markup Language is an XML-based format and an OGC-defined transport format for both geometry and geography types. It's commonly used in Web Feature Service (WFS) to output the columns of a query. It's also a building block of the budding CityGML standard (http://en.wikipedia.org/wiki/CityGML), used for modeling cityscapes, including buildings and bridges.

The PostGIS function for exporting to GML is ST_AsGML, and it's supported for both geometry and geography spatial types. There are many variants of ST_AsGML, giving you control over GML version and precision. Supported GML versions are 2.1.2 (pass in 2 for the version number) and 3.1.1 (pass in 3 for the version number). If no version parameter is passed in, GML version 2.1.2 is assumed. Two additional parameters control the number of significant digits and whether to use short CRS (Coordinate Reference Systems).

ST_AsGML supports 2D and 3D for both geometries and geometry collections. If a geometry has an M coordinate, the M is dropped. Passing in curved geometries will throw an error in PostGIS versions 1.4 and above and will return NULL in older versions. ST_AsGML version 3 does support the advanced 3D geometries of TIN and PolyhedralSurface. The version 2 variant only supports basic 3D geometries like 3D linestrings, points, and polygons.

6.1.4 *Geometry JavaScript Object Notation (GeoJSON)*

Geometry JavaScript Object Notation is a format based on JavaScript Object Notation (JSON). GeoJSON is geared toward consumption by Ajax-oriented applications such as OpenLayers and Leaflet because its output notation is in JavaScript format. JSON is the standard object representation in JavaScript data structures, and GeoJSON extends JSON by adding specifications for storing geographic objects. You can read more about GeoJSON here: http://geojson.org.

The PostGIS function for exporting geography and geometry data types to Geo-JSON is ST_AsGeoJSON (first introduced in PostGIS 1.3.5). There are seven variants of this function as of PostGIS 3. The arguments are similar to those for ST_AsGML, with overloads for different targeted versions, numbers of decimal places, short or long CRS, an encoded flag denoting whether to include the bounding box, and various other options. ST_AsGeoJSON supports 2D, basic 3D, and geometry collections. It will drop the M coordinate and throw an error for TINs, polyhedral surfaces, and curved geometries.

Prior to PostGIS 3, the ST_AsGeoJSON function in PostGIS only handled the spatial component. Introduced in PostGIS 3 is a variant that takes a PostgreSQL record as input and returns a GeoJSON feature. A GeoJSON feature includes both the geometry and non-spatial attributes of an item.

6.1.5 *Scalable Vector Graphics (SVG)*

The Scalable Vector Graphics format has been around for a while and is popular among high-end rendering tools as well as drawing tools such as Inkscape. Toolkits such as ImageMagick can easily convert SVG to many other image formats. Most web browsers support SVG, either natively or via an installable plug-in.

The PostGIS function for exporting to SVG is ST_AsSVG . This function outputs only 2D geometries without SRIDs or Z or M coordinates, and it doesn't output curved geometries. Three variants of the function allow you to specify whether the output points are relative to an origin or to the coordinate system and to indicate the level of precision desired.

6.1.6   *Mapbox Vector Tiles (MVT) and protocol buffers*

Mapbox Vector Tiles is a newer format popularized by the company Mapbox (https:// docs.mapbox.com/vector-tiles/specification/). Support for this format was introduced in PostGIS 2.4 and has been enhanced in later versions to support more properties and have better performance. MVTs are nuggets of vector and attribute data packaged as tiles encoded using the Google protocol buffers (PBF) standard (https:// developers.google.com/protocol-buffers). They are similar to raster tiles in that the tiles are usually in the Web Mercator spatial reference system, and for each z-x-y are often optimized for viewing at 256 x 256 pixel resolution. That allows them to be used easily in conjunction with raster tiles.

Since MVTs are vector rather than raster in nature and contain other attribute data, they allow for client-side styling of features using specialized style languages, such as CartoCSS (https://cartocss.readthedocs.io). MVT tiles are often much lighter in weight than an equivalent raster tile. The fact that they are vector allows them to be viewed at higher resolutions than they were designed for, without looking pixelated as raster tiles do. The ability to view the feature at a higher resolution without jagged pixelation is often referred to as *graceful degradation of resolution*. MVT is very similar in function to GeoJSON, but it's much lighter because it uses the PBF binary compression format and the geometries are simplified to the target zoom level.

You'll find many tools already designed to work with this format, including many projects that support converting your PostGIS data into a fast and simple MVT tile dispenser. Search GitHub for "postgis+mvt" for numerous examples (https://github .com/search?q=postgis+mvt).

Although MVT is lighter than GeoJSON, you may still want to pair it with JSON if you have a lot of attribute data. This is because the attribute data for a feature will be repeated for each tile the geometry intersects. This is not desirable for large geometries that often intersect many tiles.

PostGIS offers several related format functions:

- ST_AsGeobuf is an aggregate function that encodes a set of PostgreSQL rows of data into PBF format but doesn't concern itself with tiling.
- ST_TileEnvelope was introduced in PostGIS 3. It takes as input tileZoom, tileX, tileY (the XYZ tile system, used commonly by raster tiles) and returns a square geometry with those bounds. The default spatial reference system it returns in is Web Mercator unless you overwrite it with optional arguments.
- ST_AsMVTGeom is a function that clips a geometry to the specified bounds and simplifies it to 256 x 256, though the size can be changed using the buffer argument. You will often find this function paired with ST_TileEnvelope, which computes the bounds to feed to this function.

- ST_AsMVT is an aggregate function that takes a set of rows, clips it to the specified extent, and returns a binary blob encoded in MVT format. You will often find this function paired with ST_AsMVTGeom, which returns a geometry clipped and simplified to the input tile dimensions.

Although ST_TileEnvelope was designed as a helper function for making MVT tiles, you could just as easily use it to create raster tiles by combining it with the PostGIS raster ST_Clip and ST_Transform functions. In addition to this function being added in PostGIS 3, major enhancements to the MVT functions were added to PostGIS 3 using the Mapbox Wagyu library. Wagyu is currently used for the simplification and unioning work needed to make MVT tiles.

For an example of how you could take advantage of MVT, check out Paul Ramsey's "Serving Dynamic Vector Tiles" video on YouTube (http://mng.bz/JvgZ).

6.1.7 Tiny WKB (TWKB)

Tiny WKB is another format used for web mapping that was introduced in PostGIS 2.2. Similar to the MVT format, it is a compressed binary format, but it's based on WKB format. It deals with whole geometries, similar to GeoJSON/GML/KML, instead of chopping vectors into tiles like MVT does. TWKB packages both a geometry and an ID to reference the geometry. It does not support storing other attribute information as MVT or GeoJSON does. As such, it's common to combine TWKB with a plain JSON dataset that has IDs referencing the TWKB record.

PostGIS provides the following functions for working with TWKB format:

- ST_AsTWKB is a function that converts a PostGIS geometry to TWKB binary format.
- ST_GeomFromTWKB is a function that takes as input a TWKB binary format and returns the geometry part of it as a PostGIS geometry.

6.1.8 Extensible 3D Graphics (X3D)

Extensible 3D Graphics is an ISO XML format for defining objects in 3D space (http://en.wikipedia.org/wiki/X3D). It was born out of the older Virtual Reality Modeling Language (VRML). PostGIS 3D objects such as TINs and polyhedral surfaces translate to IndexedTriangleSet and IndexedFaceSet elements, respectively, in X3D. You can get the latest news on this format at the Web3D consortium standards page: www.web3d.org/standards/.

The most popular JavaScript library for X3D is X3DOM (www.x3dom.org/), which is an MIT-licensed open source library for rendering X3D in browsers (including smartphone web browsers) without any plug-ins. We've demonstrated its use in our ASP.NET/PHP postgis_x3d_viewer (https://github.com/robe2/postgis_x3d_viewer) and NodeJS-based node_postgis_express (https://github.com/robe2/node_postgis_express) PostGIS query viewers.

The ST_AsX3D function was introduced in PostGIS 2.0 and enhanced in PostGIS 2.2 to support coordinate flipping. ST_AsX3D only supports geometries, not geographies—it's primarily focused on 3D geometries. It's the only format function, aside from ST_AsGML, that supports TIN and polyhedral surface geometries.

6.1.9   *Examples of output functions*

Let's now look at an example that brings all the aforementioned output functions together. The next listing uses the functions to output a 3D linestring in SRID 4326 to a precision of five significant digits. The linestring originates in northern France and terminates in southern England at an altitude of 1 unit (generally assumed to be meters).

Listing 6.1   Outputting geometry in various standard formats

```
SELECT
    ST_AsGML(X.geom,5) as GML,
    ST_AsKML(X.geom,5) As KML,
    ST_AsGeoJSON(X,'geom', 5) As GeoJSON,
    ST_AsSVG(X.geom,0,5) As SVG_Absolute,
    ST_AsSVG(X.geom,1,5) As SVG_Relative,
    ST_AsX3D(X.geom,6) As X3D,
    ST_AsTWKB(X.geom,5) AS TWKB,
    ST_AsGeobuf(X, 'geom') OVER() AS PBF
FROM
    (SELECT
        'My street' As label, ST_GeomFromText('LINESTRING(2 48 1,0 51
    1)',4326) As geom
    ) X;
```

The preceding listing utilizes the GeoJSON variant introduced in PostGIS 3, which can output the whole record and requires you to specify the geometry column to use. We are utilizing the ANSI-SQL window OVER() clause with ST_GeoBuf because ST_Geo-Buf is an aggregate function that would otherwise need a GROUP BY clause to aggregate data. Using OVER() treats it like an ANSI-SQL window aggregate, which prevents the collapsing of rows. The ANSI-SQL window OVER() and related window clauses are covered in appendix C.

The output of the preceding listing is shown here:

```
---
gml          | <gml:LineString srsName="EPSG:4326"><gml:coordinates>2,48,1 0,51,
    1</gml:coordinates></gml:LineString>
kml          | <LineString><coordinates>2,48,1 0,51,1</coordinates></LineString>
geojson      | {"type": "Feature", "geometry": {"type":"LineString","coordinates
    ":[[2,48,1],[0,51,1]]},
                "properties": {"label": "My street"}}
svg_absolute | M 2 -48 L 0 -51
svg_relative | M 2 -48 l -2 -3
x3d          | <LineSet  vertexCount='2'><Coordinate point='2 48 1 0 51 1'
    /></LineSet>
```

```
twkb          | \xa208010280b51880f8c90402ffb418c0cf2400
pbf           | \x0a056c6162656c10031800221f0a1d0a0a08021a060460020306006a0b0a094
    d79207374726565747472020000
---
```

All of the functions in listing 6.1 output the Z coordinate except for the SVG functions, which are strictly 2D.

6.1.10 *Geohash*

Geohash is a lossy geocoding system for longitudes and latitudes. It's meant more as a tool for the easy exchange of coordinates or as a poor man's indexing strategy than for visual presentation. Geohash is a darling of lightweight spatial apps that don't need precise proximity checks. You'll find many such apps in the NoSQL camp. You can explore more at http://en.wikipedia.org/wiki/Geohash.

PostGIS outputs to Geohash using ST_GeoHash. ST_GeoHash always outputs WGS 84 lon/lat coordinates, and your data must have a known SRID so that ST_GeoHash can automatically transform it for you during output. ST_GeoHash supports curved geometries but not M or Z coordinates.

Keep in mind that Geohash is most accurate for points. If you output anything other than points, ST_GeoHash will output a hash corresponding to the bounding box of the geometry. The larger the bounding box, the shorter the hash will be. In fact, for some large areas, Geohash will just give up and output nothing. The following listing demonstrates this behavior as you take a point and expand it to ever-larger circles.

Listing 6.2 Computing a Geohash of a buffer as the radius is expanded from 0.02 meters

```
SELECT i As rad_meters, ST_GeoHash(geog::geometry) as ghash
FROM (
    SELECT i, ST_Buffer(ST_GeogFromText('POINT(2 48)'), i) As geog
    FROM unnest(ARRAY[0.02,1,1000,10000,50000,150000]) AS i
) As X;
```

The output follows.

```
rad_meters |    ghash
-----------+------------
      0.02 | u093jd0k72
         1 | u093jd0k
      1000 | u093j
     10000 | u09
     50000 | u0
    150000 |
(6 rows)
```

The reason why the hash decreases in size as your box gets larger is that Geohash is designed as a simple strategy for filtering geometries by a bounding box that can be employed even by databases that only support indexes on text. In the preceding example, to find anything within a 1000 × 1000 meter box, you'd look for all geometries that have a hash that starts with u093j. In this way you can create a simple mapping application that filters by the hashed box to grab lots of things in the window.

Before we move on to the next section, you need to keep in mind that many of the output functions we covered here export only geometry and geography components. The newer functions for ST_AsGeoJSON, ST_AsMVT, and ST_AsGeoBuf do support outputting non-spatial data as well.

Many formats also carry non-spatial data. For example, KML and GML data formats often include data such as name, date, and category within KMLed and GMLed data. In chapter 17 we'll demonstrate how you can export attendant data with scripting tools.

PostGIS not only has functions for outputting data in standard formats—it also has functions to do the reverse, constructing geometries and geographies from various representational formats. In the next section we'll cover these constructor functions.

6.2   *Constructor functions*

As the name implies, constructor functions create new spatial objects. There are two common ways to do this:

- Build them from scratch using raw data in various formats
- Utilize existing spatial objects and decompose, splice, slice, dice, or morph them to form new ones

In this section we'll start with the first approach. We'll go through the list of common representations and the functions used to transform them into bona fide PostGIS geometries and geographies. We'll then cover functions that create new geometries and geographies from existing ones.

6.2.1   *Creating geometries from text and binary formats*

In this section we'll look at functions that return geometries when you feed them various text or binary representations. They're especially useful for quickly viewing geometries in various desktop tools. In tools that accept only geometries, and not their textual representations, the use of these functions is necessary.

ST_GeomFromText

Well-known text (WKT) representations are a common way to express geometries, and the ST_GeomFromText function builds geometries from WKT. Prior to PostGIS 2.0, this function only accepted 2D geometries; since version 2.0, it accepts geometries of all dimensions. ST_GeomFromText is an SQL/MM function that can be found in other SQL/MM-compliant spatial database products.

The following listing demonstrates its use.

Listing 6.3 Using `ST_GeomFromText`

```
SELECT * INTO ch06.unconstrained_geoms
FROM (
    VALUES
        (ST_GeomFromText('POINT(-100 28 1)',4326)),
        (ST_GeomFromText('LINESTRING(-80 28 1,-90 29 1)',4326)),
        (ST_GeomFromText('POLYGONZ((10 28 1,9 29 1,7 30 1,10 28 1))')),
        (ST_GeomFromText(
            'POLYHEDRALSURFACE(
                ((0 0 0,0 0 1,0 1 1,0 1 0,0 0 0)),
                ((0 0 0,0 1 0,1 1 0,1 0 0,0 0 0)),
                ((0 0 0,1 0 0,1 0 1,0 0 1,0 0 0)),
                ((1 1 0,1 1 1,1 0 1,1 0 0,1 1 0)),
                ((0 1 0,0 1 1,1 1 1,1 1 0,0 1 0)),
                ((0 0 1,1 0 1,1 1 1,0 1 1,0 0 1))
            )'
        ))
) As z(geom);
```

The preceding listing creates a table called unconstrained_geoms with a generic geo-metric column that has no meaningful constraints. Generally, this isn't a good idea, because you can easily run into data integrity issues.

The next listing demonstrates how you can enforce constraints by casting to a typ-mod, `::geometry(type,srid)`. In order for the cast to work, your geometries must be of that type and SRID. You can ensure the SRID by passing it as the second argument to ST_GeomFromText.

Listing 6.4 Using `ST_GeomFromText` **with the SRID specified**

```
SELECT geom::geometry(LineString,4326) INTO ch06.constrained_geoms
FROM (
    VALUES
        (ST_GeomFromText('LINESTRING(-80 28, -90 29)', 4326)),
        (ST_GeomFromText('LINESTRING(10 28, 9 29, 7 30)', 4326 ))
) As x(geom);
```

In the preceding listing, you only add linestrings, and all items have an SRID of 4326. Also, you explicitly cast the output: `geom::geometry(LineString,4326)`. This forces the created table to be geometry type- and SRID-constrained. If you left out the cast-ing step, the resulting table's geometry column would still be unconstrained.

If you forget to cast to a constrained type and specify the SRID when you do a bulk insert, you can always fix the issue by altering the table as follows:

```
ALTER TABLE ch06.constrained_geoms
ALTER COLUMN geom TYPE geometry(LineString,4326);
```

If you only want to constrain the spatial reference system for future inserts, and not the geometry type, you can do this:

```
ALTER TABLE constrained_geoms
ALTER COLUMN geom TYPE geometry(Geometry,4326);
```

ST_GEOMFROMWKB AND ST_GEOMFROMEWKBTEXT FORMATCREATING GEOMETRIES FROM ST_GEOMFROMEWKB

Often you'll find yourself needing to import data from a client application where geometries are already stored in binary representations. This is where the functions ST_GeomFromWKB and ST_GeomFromEWKB come into play. ST_GeomFromWKB is an SQL/MM-defined function, and ST_GeomFromEWKB is a PostGIS extension offering SRID encoding.

These two functions accept byte arrays instead of text strings, and PostGIS geometry types derive from byte arrays. In this sense, using byte arrays as input or output formats results in no loss of data.

Any textual representation will only carry about 15 significant digits. Thus, the following operation would result in a loss for geometries having many significant digits:

```
SELECT ST_GeomFromText(ST_AsText(geom));
```

In contrast, the following operation results in no loss:

```
SELECT ST_WKBFromText(ST_AsWKB(geom));
```

The following example uses ST_GeomFromWKB:

```
SELECT ST_GeomFromWKB(
    E'\\001\\001\\000\\000\\000\\321\\256B\\312O
    \\304Q\\300\\347\\030\\220\\275\\336%E@',
    4326
);
```

The WKB representation uses a backslash as an internal separator. Because the backslash is a token in SQL, you must escape it with yet another backslash.

To avoid the nuisance of the extra slash, you can set the PostgreSQL standard_conforming_strings variable to on as follows:

```
SET standard_conforming_strings = on;
SELECT ST_GeomFromWKB(
    '\001\001\000\000\000\321\256B\312O\304Q\300\347\030\220\275\336%E@'
);
```

A similar PostgreSQL variable, bytea_output, controls the format of the output. The default is generally hex, as you'll see by running the following:

```
SET bytea_output = hex;
SELECT ST_AsBinary(
```

```
ST_GeomFromWKB(
    E'\\001\\001\\000\\000\\000\\321\\256B\\
    312O\\304Q\\300\\347\\030\\220\\275\\336%E@',
    4326
  )
);
```

The output looks like this:

```
\x0101000000d1ae42ca4fc451c0e71890bdde254540
```

Another option for `bytea_output` is escape, which will render the output with single slashes, as in the following:

```
\001\001\000\000\000\321\256B\312O\304Q\300\347\030\220\275\336%E@
```

Canonical representation

If you peek at the data stored in a `geometry` column, you'll see something that looks like a long string of alphanumeric characters. This is the hexadecimal representation of the Enhanced Well-Known Binary (EWKB) notation, which is what you'd get by using the `ST_AsEWKB` function. You can cast it to a geometry without using any functions and not lose anything:

```
SELECT '0101000020E61000008048BF7D1D20...'::geometry;
```

To conform with OGC-MM, PostGIS offers other functions such as `ST_PointFrom-Text`, `ST_LineFromText`, `ST_PolyFromText`, `ST_GeometryFromText`, and other plain text or binary input functions that require specific geometry subtypes. Our advice, as far as using PostGIS is concerned, is to stay away from them and stick with `ST_Geom-FromText` and `ST_GeomFromWKB`. Functions such as `ST_PointFromText` are wrappers for `ST_GeomFromText` and `ST_GeomFromWKB`, and they perform an additional check to make sure you're feeding in the correct subtype (returning NULL if not), adding additional overhead for the check and also potentially resulting in data loss if you're not aware of this side effect. In the course of setting up your tables, you should have already added the necessary subtype constraints. If you want to filter out rows that don't fit your type constraints and prevent pollution of your table with NULLs, you should filter using the `ST_GeometryType` or `GeometryType` functions.

ST_GEOMFROMGML, ST_GEOMFROMGEOJSON, ST_GEOMFROMKML, ST_GEOMFROMTWKB, ST_GEOMFROMGEOHASH

In addition to WKT and WKB functions, PostGIS also offers input functions for various other formats:

- *Geography Markup Language (GML)*—`ST_GeomFromGML`
- *GeoJSON*—`ST_GeomFromGeoJSON`
- *Keyhole Markup Format (KML)*—`ST_GeomFromKML`

- *Tiny WKB*—ST_GeomFromTWKB
- *GeoHash*—ST_GeomFromGeoHash

KML is the format used by Google Maps and Google Earth. It differs from other formats in that the spatial reference system is always assumed to be WGS 84 lon/lat (SRID 4326). As such, the ST_GeomFromKML function will always output a geometry that's in SRID 4326. You'll need to use ST_Transform to convert to another SRID.

6.2.2 *Creating geographies from text and binary formats*

The geography type has functions, similar to the geometry type, for converting from various formats to geography: ST_GeogFromText, ST_GeogFromWKB, ST_GeogFromKML, ST_GeogFromGML, and ST_GeogFromGeoJSON.

These functions have some notable limitations compared to their geometry siblings:

- They don't support types such as TINs, polyhedral surfaces, or curved geometries because geography itself does not support these.
- Unless you specify otherwise, these functions will always assume the input format to be in SRID 4326.

6.2.3 *Using text or binary representations as function arguments*

You'll encounter instances where someone might take a text or binary representation of a geometry or geography and use it as a parameter to a function. Although this is convenient, you should avoid doing so. The following example demonstrates what can go wrong:

```
SELECT ST_Perimeter('POLYGON((
    145.007 13.581,144.765 13.21,
    144.602 13.2,144.589 13.494,
    144.845 13.705,145.007 13.581
))');
```

The preceding example throws an "ST_Perimeter(unknown) is not unique" error. PostGIS has no idea what type the WKT representation should be because the ST_Perimeter function exists for both geometry and geography types in PostGIS 2.1+.

You can sometimes get away with text/binary representation input and allowing PostgreSQL to autocast it to the right spatial data type when the function you use has no overloading. For example, the following will work in PostGIS 2.1 and even PostGIS 3.0:

```
SELECT (ST_Centroid('LINESTRING(1 2,3 4)'));
```

But just because something works doesn't mean it's a good idea. The preceding example will break as soon as PostGIS overloads the ST_Centroid function to accept geographies. We recommend that you always use a constructor function, as in the next example:

```
SELECT ST_Centroid(ST_GeomFromText('LINESTRING(1 2,3 4)'));
```

Or you can explicitly cast your textual or binary representation to a type:

```
SELECT ST_Centroid('LINESTRING(1 2, 3 4)'::geometry);
```

Geometry and geography objects have various properties that you can read or set to change the object that can be accessed using accessor and setter functions. In the next section we'll cover some of the more common accessor and setter functions.

6.3 *Accessor and setter functions*

If you're experienced with any object-oriented language, accessor and setter functions will be nothing new. The terms come from object-oriented programming and refer to any function that accesses or sets the intrinsic properties of an object.

Because quite a large number of functions fall under this classification, we'll use the terms *accessor* and *setter* only for functions that return or set textual values or scalars. For example, if you have a square polygon, only functions that return or set the type, the SRID, and dimensions will be considered *accessors* and *setters*. Functions that return the centroid (a point), the diagonal (a linestring), or the boundary (a linestring collection) we'll call *decomposition* functions and save for discussion in a later section. We also don't consider measurement functions, such as those for computing length, area, and perimeter, to be accessors.

It's important to know a few defining characteristics of spatial objects when you're using spatial accessor functions:

- The *spatial reference identifier (SRID)* defines the projection, ellipsoid or spheroid, and datum of the coordinates of a geometry or geography.
- The *subtype* is the finer categorization of geometry and geography types, such as points, linestrings, polygons, multipolygons, multicurves, and so on.
- The *coordinate dimension* is the dimension of the vector space in which your geometry lives. In PostGIS, this can be 2, 3, or 4.
- The *geometric dimension* is the minimal dimension of the vector space necessary to fully contain the geometry. (There are many more rigorous definitions, but we'll stick with something intuitive.) In PostGIS, geometry dimensions can be 0 (points), 1 (linestrings), 2 (polygons), 3 (TINs and polyhedral surfaces).

In this section we'll go into detail about these intrinsic properties of geometries and the various functions you can use to retrieve and set them.

6.3.1 *Spatial reference identifiers*

In PostGIS, the `ST_SRID` function retrieves the SRID of geometries. This function doesn't exist for geographies because the SRID is usually 4326. You'll find this OGC SQL/MM standard function in most spatial databases. As of PostGIS 2.2, geographies can use any degree-based spatial reference system. As such, knowing the SRID may be important if you don't use the default. You can cast your `geography` to `geometry` to get the SRID as follows:

```
SELECT ST_SRID(geog::geometry);
```

The companion setter function is `ST_SetSRID`, which is also an SQL/MM standard. Again, `ST_SetSRID` doesn't exist for `geography`. This setter function will replace the spatial reference metadata embedded within a `geometry`. Remember that all geometries must have an SRID, even if it's the unknown SRID (0 for PostGIS 2 or higher).

Let's take a look at the uses of this accessor and setter.

Listing 6.5 Example uses of `ST_SRID` and `ST_SetSRID`

```
SELECT ST_SRID(ST_GeomFromText('POLYGON((1 1,2 2,2 0,1 1))',4326));    ◁─┐ Simple use
                                                                          │ of ST_SRID

SELECT ST_SRID(geom) As srid, COUNT(*) As number_of_geoms   ◁──┐
FROM sometable                                                 │
GROUP BY ST_SRID(geom);                                        Counts number
                                                               of distinct SRIDs

SELECT
    ST_SRID(geom) As srid,                          Uses ST_SetSRID
    ST_SRID(ST_SetSRID(geom,4326)) as srid_new  ◁──┘ to change the SRID
FROM (
    VALUES
        (ST_GeomFromText('POLYGON((70 20,71 21,71 19,70 20))',4269)),
        (ST_Point(1,2))
) As X (geom);
```

If you set up your production tables properly, your geometries should contain only SRIDs found in the spatial_ref_sys table. Although nothing in the OGC specification requires SRIDs to have real-world significance, PostGIS prepopulates the spatial_ref_sys table with only EPSG-approved SRIDs.

You're free to invent your own SRIDs and add them to the table. Esri product users often add spatial reference systems defined by Esri to ease the sharing of data between PostGIS and Esri products.

6.3.2 *Transforming geometry to different spatial references*

The `ST_Transform` function converts all the points of a given `geometry` to coordinates in a different spatial reference system. Common applications of this function are to take a `geometry` in longitude and latitude and transform it to a planar SRS so that you can take meaningful measurements or transform a non-WGS 84 `geometry` to WGS 84 so you can then cast it to `geography`.

The following example converts a road somewhere in New York state expressed in WGS 84 lon/lat to WGS 84 UTM Zone 18N meters:

```
SELECT ST_AsEWKT(
    ST_Transform('SRID=4326;LINESTRING(-73 41,-72 42)'::geometry,32618)
);
```

The output of this code snippet is as follows:

```
SRID=32618;
LINESTRING(
    668207.88519421 4540683.52927698,
    748464.920715711 4654130.89132385
)
```

Now that you've transformed from longitude and latitude to planar coordinates, you can obtain the length with a simple application of the Pythagorean theorem.

People often confuse `ST_SetSRID` with `ST_Transform`. Just remember that `ST_SetSRID` doesn't change the coordinates of a geometry; it only sets an attribute called SRID—there's nothing in PostGIS that says the true SRID of the geometry must match its manifested SRID.

`ST_SetSRID` comes in handy when you realize that you made a mistake during data import. For example, if you import your geometries as WGS 84 lon/lat (SRID 4326), and you later realize they were defined using NAD 27 lon/lat coordinates (SRID 4267), `ST_SetSRID` will quickly correct the mistake.

If your table was constrained to the wrong SRID, updating the data to the right SRID will yield a data type validation error. To get around that, you need to change the data type typmod at the same time as you correct the SRID of the data as follows:

```
ALTER TABLE my_table
    ALTER COLUMN geom TYPE geometry(POINT,4267)
    USING ST_SetSRID(geom,4267);
```

6.3.3 *Using transformation with the geography type*

The geography type doesn't have `ST_Transform`, `ST_SetSRID`, or `ST_SRID` functions because it almost always uses WGS 84 lon/lat. Nevertheless, the `ST_Transform` function is crucial when working with the geography type. At times you may need to take advantage of geometry functions that aren't available for geography. The use of geometry functions for geography shouldn't pose a problem as long as you're working with a small area and don't need pinpoint accuracy.

The following code shows how you can cast to geometry to find the closest point on a line to a geometry and then cast back to geography:

```
SELECT
    ST_Transform(
        ST_ClosestPoint(
            ST_Transform(geog::geometry,32618),
```

```
            ST_Transform(
                'SRID=4326;LINESTRING(-73 41,-72 42)'::geometry,32618
            )
        ),
        4326
    )::geography
FROM ( VALUES
        (
            'SRID=4326;LINESTRING(-73.5 41,-72.456 41.34)'::geography
        ) ,
        (
            'SRID=4326;POINT(-73.2 41.123)'::geography
        )

)AS f(geog);
```

The preceding code operates on a set of geographies, ones in or close to New York State. For each, it finds the closest point on the geography to a specific road. It does so by first casting the geography to a geometry and then transforming to a New York state plane (SRID 32618). The ST_ClosestPoint function only accepts geometries. Like other functions we'll discuss that take two or more geometries, all input geometries must have the same SRID. Once you have the answer in planar coordinates, you transform back to 4326, because only geometries in 4326 can be cast to geography.

A number of geography functions, such as ST_Buffer, piggyback on geometry via a transformation under the hood. These functions are denoted with a *(T)* in the Post-GIS manual. You should be cautious when using these functions, especially for large areas where the curvature of the earth becomes a concern, and in regions of longitude and latitude singularities, such as the poles.

6.3.4 *Geometry type functions*

In most situations, you're keenly aware of the geometry types you're working with, but when importing data containing heterogeneous geometry columns, you may not be. PostGIS offers two functions to help you identify geometry types: GeometryType and ST_GeometryType. We've mentioned that functions in PostGIS without the ST prefix are deprecated functions, but in the case of GeometryType versus ST_GeometryType, not only are they different from each other, but both are very much in use.

The GeometryType function is the older of the two. It's part of the OGC simple features for SQL. It returns the geometry types that you're familiar with in all uppercase. Its younger counterpart, ST_GeometryType, is part of the OpenGIS SQL/MM standard. It outputs the familiar geometry names but prepends ST_ to comply with the MM geometry class-hierarchy naming standards. The following listing demonstrates the differences between the two.

> Listing 6.6   Differences between ST_GeometryType and GeometryType

```
SELECT ST_GeometryType(geom) As new_name, GeometryType(geom) As old_name
FROM (VALUES
```

```
    (ST_GeomFromText('POLYGON((0 0,1 1,0 1,0 0))')),
    (ST_Point(1,2)),
    (ST_MakeLine(ST_Point(1,2), ST_Point(1,2))),
    (ST_Collect(ST_Point(1,2), ST_Buffer(ST_Point(1,2),3))),
    (ST_LineToCurve(ST_Buffer(ST_Point(1,2),3))),
    (ST_LineToCurve(ST_Boundary(ST_Buffer(ST_Point(1,2),3)))),
    (ST_Multi(ST_LineToCurve(ST_Boundary(ST_Buffer(ST_Point(1,2),3)))))))
) As x(geom);
```

Table 6.1 shows the results of listing 6.6.

Table 6.1 Using `ST_GeometryType` and `GeometryType`

new_name	old_name
ST_Polygon	POLYGON
ST_Point	POINT
ST_LineString	LINESTRING
ST_Geometry	GEOMETRYCOLLECTION
ST_CurvePolygon	CURVEPOLYGON
ST_CircularString	CIRCULARSTRING
ST_MultiCurve	MULTICURVE

Determining the geometry type is particularly useful when various functions have to be applied to a heterogeneous geometry column. Remember that some functions accept only certain geometry types or may behave differently for different geometry types. For example, asking for the area of a line is pointless, as is asking for the length of a polygon.

Using an SQL CASE statement is a compact way to selectively apply functions against a heterogeneous geometry column. Here's an example:

```
SELECT
    CASE
        WHEN GeometryType(geom) = 'POLYGON' THEN ST_Area(geom)
        WHEN GeometryType(geom) = 'LINESTRING' THEN ST_Length(geom)
        ELSE NULL
    END As measure
FROM sometable;
```

6.3.5 *Geometry and coordinate dimensions*

Two kinds of dimensions are relevant when talking about geometries:

- *Coordinate dimension*—The dimension of the space that the geometry lives in
- *Geometry dimension*—The smallest dimensional space that will fully contain the geometry

The coordinate dimension is always greater than or equal to the geometry dimension.

PostGIS provides the `ST_CoordDim` and `ST_Dimension` functions to return the coordinate and geometry dimensions respectively. In the following example, these two functions are applied to the mixed bag of 3D geometries created earlier:

```
SELECT
    ST_GeometryType(geom) As type,
    ST_Dimension(geom) As gdim,
    ST_CoordDim(geom) as cdim
FROM unconstrained_geoms;
```

Table 6.2 shows the output.

Table 6.2   **Differences between geometry dimension and coordinate dimension**

type	gdim	cdim
ST_Point	0	3
ST_LineString	1	3
ST_Polygon	2	3
ST_PolyhedralSurface	3	3

In table 6.2, all geometries have a coordinate dimension (cdim) of 3 because all have X, Y, Z components for coordinates. Only the polyhedral surface also has a geometric dimension (gdim) of 3 because it's the only true 3D type.

6.3.6 *Retrieving coordinates*

`ST_X`, `ST_Y`, and `ST_Z` are functions that you can use to return the underlying coordinates of point geometries. Although `geography` points don't have this function, you can access it by casting your `geography` point to `geometry`. These functions are generally combined with `ST_Centroid` to get the X and Y coordinates of a centroid for non-point geometries.

`ST_Xmin`, `ST_Xmax`, `ST_Ymin`, `ST_Ymax`, `ST_Zmin`, and `ST_Zmax` are functions meant to take bounding boxes as input, but feel free to use these functions against geometries too, because PostGIS autocasts a geometry to its bounding box when needed. These functions are used to return the minimum or maximum coordinates of each geometry. They're rarely used alone but are generally combined with each other to obtain approximate widths and heights for mapping the extent of geometries. We'll demonstrate their use when we talk about translation.

6.3.7 *Checking geometry validity*

We introduced the concept of validity in chapter 2. As you'll recall, pathological geometries such as polygons with self-intersections and polygons with holes outside the exterior ring are invalid. Generally speaking, the higher the geometry dimension of a geometry, the more prone it is to invalidity. Unfortunately, functions for checking validity only work for geometries, not geographies.

The ST_IsValid function tests for validity, and ST_IsValidReason provides a brief description as to why a geometry isn't valid. ST_IsValidReason will offer up a description only for the first offense encountered, so if your geometry is invalid for multiple reasons, you'll see only the first reason. If a geometry is valid, it will return the string "Valid Geometry."

ST_IsValidDetail is a function available since PostGIS 2.0. This function returns a set of valid_detail objects, each containing a reason and location for a particular violation, allowing you to review all the violations, not just the first. Also introduced in version 2.0 is the ST_MakeValid function, which will try to fix the invalid geometry for you. Both of these functions require PostGIS compiled with GEOS 3.3.0 or above.

All validity-checking functions only check X and Y, not Z. They will automatically reject polyhedral surfaces and TINs.

We remind you again that it's important to make sure your geometries are valid. Don't even try to work with geometries unless they're valid. Many of the GEOS-based functions in PostGIS will behave unpredictably upon encountering invalid geometries.

6.3.8 *Number of points that define a geometry*

The ST_NPoints function returns the number of points defining a geometry. It won't work for geography, but you can cast your geography to geometry and then use the function without any loss of information. ST_NPoints is a PostGIS creation; you may not find it in other OGC-compliant spatial databases.

Many people make the mistake of using the function ST_NumPoints instead of ST_NPoints. ST_NumPoints only works when applied to linestrings, as dictated by the OGC specification.

You may be wondering why there are two functions when one completely performs the duties of another. This has to do with the fact that most spatial databases, PostGIS included, offer functions that adhere strictly to the OGC specification. After meeting the OGC specifications to the letter, spatial databases continue on to extend OGC functions where they find deficiencies.

In versions prior to PostGIS 2.0, when used with multilinestrings, ST_NumPoints exhibited the undocumented behavior of only using the first linestring. To avoid this problem, PostGIS 2.0 and higher removed support for multilinestrings altogether. If you pass in a multilinestring or a collection containing a multilinestring, ST_Num-Points will return NULL, to better conform to OGC requirements. Other functions with similar behavior changes are ST_StartPoint and ST_EndPoint. Our advice is to avoid using all three functions with multilinestrings, even if the multilinestring is made up of only a single linestring.

The following listing demonstrates the difference in results between ST_NPoints and ST_NumPoints.

Listing 6.7   Example of using `ST_NPoints` and `ST_NumPoints`

```
SELECT
    type,
    ST_NPoints(geom) As npoints,
    ST_NumPoints(geom) As numpoints
FROM (VALUES
    ('LinestringM',
        ST_GeomFromEWKT('LINESTRINGM(1 2 3,3 4 5,5 8 7,6 10 11)')
    ),
    ('Circularstring',
        ST_GeomFromText('CIRCULARSTRING(2.5 2.5,4.5 2.5,4.5 4.5)')
    ),
    ('Polygon (Triangle)',
        ST_GeomFromText('POLYGON((0 1,1 -1,-1 -1,0 1))')
    ),
    ('Multilinestring',
        ST_GeomFromText('MULTILINESTRING((1 2,3 4,5 6),(10 20,30 40))')
    ),
    ('Collection',
        ST_Collect(
            ST_GeomFromText('POLYGON((0 1,1 -1,-1 -1,0 1))'),
            ST_Point(1,3)
        )
    )
) As x(type, geom);
```

Table 6.3 shows the output of the preceding listing.

Table 6.3   Output of `ST_NPoints` and `ST_NumPoints`

type	npoints	numpoints
LinestringM	4	4
Circularstring	3	3
Polygon (Triangle)	4	NULL
Multilinestring	5	NULL
Collection	5	NULL

The table demonstrates that `ST_NPoints` works for all geometry subtypes, whereas `ST_NumPoints` works only for linestrings and circularstrings. For multilinestrings, `ST_NumPoints` will return `NULL` for version 2 or higher, but in prior versions would count the vertices in the first linestring only.

6.4   *Measurement functions*

Before taking any measurements in GIS, you must concern yourself with the scale of what you're measuring. This goes back to the fact that we live on a spheroid called Earth and that you're measuring something on its surface. When your measurements cover a small area where the curvature of the earth doesn't come into play, it's perfectly fine to assume a planar model that treats the earth as essentially flat.

What distances should be considered *small* depends on the accuracy of the measure you're trying to achieve. We've found that planar measurements are often people's first choice, even across very long measures. People prefer the simplicity and intuitiveness that comes with planar measurements even at the expense of accuracy. Planar measurements are generally in units of meters or feet, and planar models are better supported by GIS tools and are faster to process.

Once measures start to cross continents and oceans, as is the case with areas and perimeters of entire continents, or long air travel routes, planar measures deteriorate rapidly. You'll have to use geodetic measurements in these cases, where you must consider the spherical nature of the earth. A geodetic measurement models the world as a sphere or spheroid. Coordinates are expressed using degrees or radians. The classic SRID 4326 (WGS 84 lon/lat) is the most common geodetic spatial reference system in use today.

In this section we'll cover both kinds of measurements, but we'll only focus on internal measurements like length, perimeter, and area. We'll leave measurements between objects, such as distance measures, as a topic for a later chapter. PostGIS does have dedicated functions that work only on spheroids and can be used with the `geometry` type. These are used when your application requires you to keep your data in the `geometry` type, but once in a while you need to measure using a geodetic model.

One last point to keep in mind: measurement functions are always used as getters. Setting the measurement of a geometry doesn't make sense. To change a measurement, you must change the geometry itself.

6.4.1 Geometry planar measurements

All the planar measurement functions we're about to discuss are in the same units as the spatial reference system that's defined for the geometry. For example, if your spatial reference system is in feet, the lengths and the areas are in feet and square feet. Common measurement functions are `ST_Length`, `ST_3DLength`, `ST_Area`, `ST_Perimeter`, and `ST_3DPerimeter`. If your spatial reference system is in degrees of longitude and latitude (spherical coordinates), then your units of measure will be in degrees after PostGIS naively maps longitude to X coordinate values and latitude to Y coordinate values. This may only be acceptable for small areas far from the poles, where the longitude and latitude grid still has some semblance of being uniform squares.

Since PostGIS 2.0, you can pass in 3D geometries, but be warned: only the 2D projection of the geometry will be measured. To get true 3D measures, use one of the newer functions: `ST_3DClosestPoint`, `ST_3DDistance`, `ST_3DIntersects`, `ST_3DMaxDistance`, or `ST_3DPerimeter`. `ST_Length3D` was renamed in PostGIS 2.0 to `ST_3DLength` to better conform to SQL/MM standards. These newer 3D functions support points, polygons, linestrings, and their multi- counterparts. The functions

`ST_3DIntersects`, `ST_3DDistance`, `ST_3DMaxDistance`, and `ST_3DClosestPoint` also work with polyhedral surfaces and TINs. The TIN support was introduced in Post-GIS 3.0.

The following example demonstrates the 2D and 3D lengths of a 3D linestring:

```
SELECT ST_Length(geom) As length_2d, ST_3DLength(geom) As length_3d
FROM (
    VALUES
        (ST_GeomFromText('LINESTRING(1 2 3,4 5 6)')),
        (ST_GeomFromText('LINESTRING(1 2,4 5)')))
As x(geom);
```

The lengths returned by `ST_Length` and `ST_Length3D` are the same for a linestring in 2D coordinate space (the first row in table 6.4) and different for the linestring in 3D coordinate space (the second row).

Table 6.4   Comparing 2D and 3D lengths

length_2D	length_3D
4.24264068711928	5.19615242270663
4.24264068711928	4.24264068711928

The two other common measurement functions for area and perimeter are fairly intuitive. Obviously, you should use them only with valid polygons and multipolygons. For multi-ringed polygons, `ST_Perimeter` calculates the length of all the rings. You should also keep in mind that `ST_Area` and `ST_Perimeter` only consider the X and Y coordinates; to consider Z as well, you should use the companion `ST_3DArea` and `ST_3DPerimeter` functions.

6.4.2   *Geodetic measurements*

All the measurements we've discussed thus far apply to geometries in Cartesian coordinate systems. Because the earth isn't flat, a more appropriate coordinate system to use when looking at large swaths of the planet is a spherical coordinate system. *Geodetic* is a fancier-sounding term for *spherical* as it relates to the earth.

Spherical coordinates literally throw a curve into our commonsense grasp of lengths, areas, and perimeters. Take the simple question of what the length is of the shortest line that connects Houston and Mumbai. The only straight line would pass through the center of the earth. Along the surface of the earth, an infinite number of curved lines connect the two cities. Even if you should always take the shortest curve, there's no guarantee that it will be unique. Try drawing the shortest line between the two geographic poles. You'll end up with not one but infinitely many.

PostGIS created the `geography` type to deal with coordinates in degrees of longitude and latitude, specifically WGS 84 lon/lat (SRID 4326). You should consider using geography when your data covers an area wide enough for the curvature of the earth to come into play. But even if you choose not to use the geography type, you can still take advantage of spheroidal computations by using the spherical family of functions in geometry. These functions piggyback on geography geodetic functions, saving you the trouble of converting back and forth.

Let's look at three examples of length measurements between Houston and Mumbai:

```
SELECT ST_Length(
    ST_GeomFromText('LINESTRING(-95.40 29.77,72.82 19.07)')
);
```

This first measure yields an answer of 168.56, and the units would be degrees. Even if you were to convert the degrees to kilometers, assuming that each degree is about 111 km, your answer would still be disastrously wrong, given that at Houston, one degree of longitude is already down to 96 km.

Next we'll use geography, whose units are always in meters and all distances compute against a spheroid:

```
SELECT ST_Length(
    ST_GeogFromText('LINESTRING(-95.40 29.77,72.82 19.07)')
);
```

The answer in this case is 14,456 km or just shy of 9,000 miles. This is the correct distance between the two cities, also known as the great circle distance. You can arrive at this distance using a spheroid calculation in geometry:

```
SELECT ST_LengthSpheroid(
    ST_GeomFromText('LINESTRING(-95.40 29.77,72.82 19.07)'),
    'SPHEROID["GRS_1980",6378137,298.257222101]'
);
```

Again, the answer is 14,456 km, the same as for geography. Notice that in this spheroid example, you need to specify the spheroid that you'd like to use. GRS 80 and WGS 84 are virtually identical. But because you're able to dictate the spheroid, you can also use geometry spheroid measures to calculate distances on Mars, the moon, or even Pluto.

When choosing between the geometry and geography types for data storage, you should consider what you'll be using the data for. If all you do are simple measurements and relationship checks on your data, and your data covers a fairly large area, you'll likely be better off storing your data using the geography type.

Although the geography data type can cover the globe, the geometry type is far from obsolete. The geometry type has a much richer set of functions than geography, relationship checks are much faster, and it currently has wider support across desktop and web mapping tools. If you need support for only a limited area, such as a state, a town, or a small country, you're better off with the geometry type. If you do a lot of geometric processing, such as unioning geometries, simplifying, performing line interpolations, and the like, geometry will provide that out of the box, whereas geography has to be cast to geometry, transformed, processed, and cast back to geography.

We've now completed our basic study of scalar properties, and we'll move on to the more exciting topic of properties that are themselves spatial objects. First on our journey are decomposition functions, which are functions that explode a spatial object into subelements or return a caricature of a spatial object.

6.5   *Decomposition functions*

You'll often find yourself needing to extract parts of an existing geometry. You may need to find the closed linestring that encloses a polygon or the multipoint that constitutes a linestring, or to expand a multipolygon into individual polygons. We call functions that extract and return one or more geometries *decomposition* functions. In this section, we'll demonstrate some of the more common PostGIS decomposition functions.

6.5.1   *Bounding box of geometries*

Boxes are the unsung heroes of geometries. Though rarely useful for modeling terrestrial features, they play an important role in spatial queries. Often, when comparing the relative spatial relationships of two or more geometries, the question can be sufficiently answered much more quickly by comparing the bounding boxes of the geometries. By encasing disparate and complicated geometries in bounding boxes, you only need to work with rectangles and can ignore the details of the geometries within. Borrowing from an engineering concept, bounding boxes are the black boxes of spatial analysis.

By definition, the bounding box of a 2D geometry is a box2D object, and it's the smallest axis-aligned, two-dimensional box that fully encloses the geometry. PostGIS also has another kind of box called box3D, which is less commonly used but is useful for working with 3D objects and is internally used by 3D indexes introduced in PostGIS 2. The box3D is also axis-aligned.

All geometries have boxes, even points. Boxes aren't geometries, but you can cast boxes into geometries. Naturally, casting a 2D box to geometry will yield a rectangular polygon, but you have to watch out for degenerate cases such as points, vertical lines, horizontal lines, or multipoints along a horizontal or vertical. The syntax and text representation for a 2D box is BOX(p1,p2) where p1 and p2 are points of any two opposite vertices.

> **box2D and box3D are axis-aligned**
>
> box2D and box3D are never rotated, meaning that the edges of the boxes are parallel to the coordinate axes. A true minimum bounding box, in contrast, may not necessarily be axis-aligned.

> PostGIS has a function introduced in PostGIS 2.5 called `ST_OrientedEnvelope` that provides a true minimum bounding box for 2D geometries. If you are running an earlier version of PostGIS, you can consider the convex hull and the minimum bounding circle as proxies for a minimum bounding box. Use the `ST_ConvexHull` and `ST_MinimumBoundingCircle` functions to get at them.

Although geographies can be thought of as having bounding boxes, these are only internal constructs used by PostGIS for spatial relationship queries and have no physical manifestation.

The following listing demonstrates how to compute box2D and box3D for various geometries.

Listing 6.8 box2D and box3D for various geometries

```
SELECT name, Box2D(geom) As box2d, Box3D(geom) As box3d
FROM (VALUES
    ('2D Line',
        ST_GeomFromText(
            'LINESTRING(121.63 25.03,3.03 6.58,-71.06 42.36)',4326
        )
    ),
    ('3D Line', ST_GeomFromText('LINESTRING(1 2 3,3 4 1000.34567)')),
    ('Vert 2D Line', ST_GeomFromText('LINESTRING(1 2,1 4)')),
    ('Point', ST_GeomFromText('POINT(1 2)')),
    ('Polygon', ST_GeomFromText('POLYGON((1 2,3 4,5 6,1 2))')),
    ('Cube',
        ST_GeomFromText(
            'POLYHEDRALSURFACE(
                ((0 0 0,0 0 1,0 1 1,0 1 0,0 0 0)),
                ((0 0 0,0 1 0,1 1 0,1 0 0,0 0 0)),
                ((0 0 0,1 0 0,1 0 1,0 0 1,0 0 0)),
                ((1 1 0,1 1 1,1 0 1,1 0 0,1 1 0)),
                ((0 1 0,0 1 1,1 1 1,1 1 0,0 1 0)),
                ((0 0 1,1 0 1,1 1 1,0 1 1,0 0 1))
            )'
        )
    )
)
AS x(name,geom);
```

Listing 6.8 produces the following output:

```
name         | box2d                | box3d
-------------+----------------------+------------------------------------
2D line      | BOX(-71.06 6.58,...) | BOX3D(-71.06 ..,121.63 42.36 0)
3D line      | BOX(1 2,3 4)         | BOX3D(1 2 3,3 4 1000.34567)
Vert 2D line | BOX(1 2,1 4)         | BOX3D(1 2 0,1 4 0)
Point        | BOX(1 2,1 2)         | BOX3D(1 2 0,1 2 0)
Polygon      | BOX(1 2,5 6)         | BOX3D(1 2 0,5 6 0)
Cube         | BOX(0 0,1 1)         | BOX3D(0 0 0,1 1 1)
```

6.5.2 *Boundaries and converting polygons to linestrings*

ST_Boundary works with all geometries, but not geographies, and it returns the geometry that determines the separation between the points in the geometry and the rest of the coordinate space. This particular way of defining boundaries will make matters easy when we discuss interactions between two geometries in chapter 9. Also note that the boundary of a geometry is at least one dimension lower than that of the geometry itself.

ST_Boundary is used to return both the interior and exterior rings of polygons and multipolygons as linestrings or the start and end points of linestrings. This is often a step when constructing new geometries. ST_Boundary does work on curved geometries, but it applies a curve-to-line operation on curved geometries before returning the boundary, as you can see in the solid circle output in table 6.5.

The following listing shows some examples of ST_Boundary in action.

> **Listing 6.9 Examples of using ST_Boundary**

```
SELECT object_name,ST_AsText(ST_Boundary(geom)) As WKT
FROM (VALUES
    ('Simple linestring',
        ST_GeomFromText('LINESTRING(-14 21,0 0,35 26)')
    ),
    ('Non-simple linestring',
        ST_GeomFromText('LINESTRING(2 0,0 0,1 1,1 -1)')
    ),
    ('Closed linestring',
        ST_GeomFromText('
            LINESTRING(
                52 218,139 82,262 207,245 261,207 267,153 207,
                125 235,90 270,55 244,51 219,52 218)'
        )
    ),
    ('Polygon',
        ST_GeomFromText('
            POLYGON((
                52 218 1,139 82 1,262 207 1,245 261 1,207 267 1,153 207 1,
                125 235 1,90 270 1,55 244 1,51 219 1,52 218 1))'
        )
    ),
    ('Polygon with holes',
        ST_GeomFromText('
            POLYGON(
                (-0.25 -1.25,-0.25 1.25,2.5 1.25,2.5 -1.25,-0.25 -1.25),
                (2.25 0,1.25 1,1.25 -1,2.25 0),
                (1 -1,1 1,0 0,1 -1))'
        )
    ),
    ('Solid circle',
    ST_GeomFromText('CURVEPOLYGON(
        CIRCULARSTRING(0 0, 2 0, 2 2, 0 2, 0 0)
    )'))

)
AS x(object_name,geom);
```

The output in table 6.5 shows the object names and WKT representations.

Table 6.5 Output of `ST_Boundary`

object_name	wkt
Simple linestring	MULTIPOINT(-14 21,35 26)
Non-simple linestring	MULTIPOINT(2 0,1 -1)
Closed linestring	MULTIPOINT EMPTY
Polygon	LINESTRING Z (52 218 1,139 82 1,262 207 1,245 261 1,207 267 1,153 207 1,125 235 1,90 270 1,55 244 1,51 219 1,52 218 1)
Polygon with holes	MULTILINESTRING-0.25 -1.25,-0.25 1.25,2.5 1.25,2.5 -1.25,-0.25 -1.25),(2.25 0,1.25 1,1.25 -1,2.25 0),(1-1,1 1,0 0,1 -1
Solid circle	LINESTRING(0 0,0.050272218122245 -0.04786313053259,0.102832413657364 -0.093201867001758,0.157553964490581 -0.135906984420143,0.214305041612898 -0.175875602419359 ..

The visual representation of some geometries in listing 6.1 is shown in figure 6.1.

Figure 6.1 Simple linestring, polygon, and polygon with holes, overlaid with their boundaries from `ST_Boundary`

Looking at the query and its output, you can surmise the following behavior of `ST_Boundary`:

- An open linestring, either simple or non-simple, will return a multipoint made up of exactly two points, one for each of the endpoints.
- A closed linestring has no boundary points.
- A polygon without holes will return a linestring of the exterior ring.
- A polygon with holes will return a multilinestring made up of closed linestrings for each of its rings. The first element of the multilinestring will always be the exterior ring.
- A multipolygon will always return a multilinestring.

A more specialized cousin of ST_Boundary is ST_ExteriorRing. This function accepts only polygons and returns the exterior ring. If you're trying to find the outer boundary of a polygon, ST_ExteriorRing will perform faster than ST_Boundary, but as its name suggests, it won't return the inner rings. You can use ST_InteriorRingN to grab individual interior rings or ST_DumpRings to get both the exterior ring and all interior rings.

6.5.3   *Centroid, median, and point on surface*

We've all seen maps where small geometries are reduced to a single point to declutter the visual representation. Most maps use a star to indicate capital cities rather than the city boundaries. Should you zoom in enough on any online map, such as to the street level, you may find a labeled dot where you expect to see a huge polygon. Try this on a top-secret military installation. If you zoom in enough, you won't see any of the details you expect but just a dot telling you that it's a place the government doesn't want you to ever visit.

In PostGIS, ST_Centroid and, to a lesser extent, ST_PointOnSurface are often used to act as point markers for polygons. These functions only work as advertised for 2D geometries. Although you can use them for 3D polygons, they will ignore the Z and M coordinates. You should think of the centroid of a geometry as the center of gravity, as if every point in the geometry had equal mass. The only caveat is that the centroid may not lie within the geometry itself (think of donuts or bagels). The ST_Centroid function doesn't work for curved geometries.

ST_Centroid sometimes produces undesirable visual results when the point isn't on the geometry itself. Take the island nation of FSM (Federated States of Micronesia); its ST_Centroid is most likely somewhere in the Pacific Ocean. If you provide a mapping service, you probably don't want people sailing to FSM and failing to end up on dry land. For this situation, ST_PointOnSurface comes to the rescue. It always returns an arbitrary point on the boundary geometry. ST_PointOnSurface works for all 2D geometries except curves. For points, linestrings, multipoints, and multilinestrings, it considers the M and Z coordinates and returns a point that's usually one used to define the geometry. For polygons, it cuts out the M and Z coordinates.

ST_GeometricMedian is a function introduced in PostGIS 2.3 for multipoints. It comes in handy when analyzing observation points and returns the point that sits medially between all the points. Since the median is not as affected by outliers as ST_Centroid, it is a better alternative than ST_Centroid when dealing with multipoints.

The following listing compares the output of ST_Centroid with that of ST_PointOnSurface for various geometries.

Listing 6.10   **Centroid and point on surface of various geometries**

```
SELECT
    name,
    ST_AsEWKT(ST_Centroid(geom)) As centroid,
    ST_AsEWKT(ST_PointOnSurface(geom)) As point_on_surface,
```

```
        CASE WHEN ST_GeometryType(geom) ILIKE '%Point%'
          THEN ST_AsEWKT(ST_GeometricMedian(geom))
          ELSE NULL END As geom_median
FROM (VALUES
     ('Multipoint',ST_GeomFromText('MULTIPOINT(-1 1,0 0,2 3)')),
     ('Multipoint 3D',ST_GeomFromText('MULTIPOINT(-1 1 1,0 0 2,2 3 1)')),
     ('Multilinestring',
         ST_GeomFromText('MULTILINESTRING((0 0,0 1,1 1),(-1 1,-1 -1))')
     ),
     ('Polygon',ST_GeomFromEWKT('
         POLYGON(
             (-0.25 -1.25,-0.25 1.25,2.5 1.25,2.5 -1.25,-0.25 -1.25),
             (2.25 0,1.25 1,1.25 -1,2.25 0),
             (1 -1,1 1,0 0,1 -1)
         )')
     )
)
)
As x(name,geom);
```

The code in listing 6.10 outputs the centroid, the point on the surface, and the geometric median of various geometries. We only apply ST_GeometricMedian to multipoints because for other geometries it will return a "Geometry type not supported"
error. Although the centroid may not always be part of the geometry, the point on the
surface is. Figure 6.2 uses the code in listing 6.10 to show the centroid overlaid with
the original geometry.

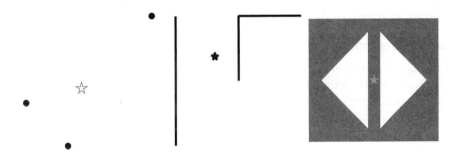

**Figure 6.2 Simple linestring, polygon, and polygon with holes, overlaid with their centroids
from listing 6.10**

The textual output follows. Note that ST_GeometricMedian preserves the Z coordinates and preserves M as well if present, whereas ST_Centroid drops the Z:

```
name           |      centroid           | point_on_surface | geom_median
---------------+-------------------------------------------------+------------
               |
 Multipoint    | POINT(0.333... 1.3333...) | POINT(-1 1)      | POINT(
     -0.210... 0.789...)
 Multipoint 3D | POINT(0.333... 1.333...)  | POINT(-1 1 1)    | POINT(
     -0.19... 0.88... 1.38...)
```

```
Multilinestring | POINT(-0.375 0.375)   | POINT(0 1)      |
Polygon         | POINT(1.125 0)        | POINT(0.125 0.5) |
(4 rows)
```

As demonstrated in figure 6.2, the centroid may not be part of the geometry. In our example, the centroids of the multipoint and multilinestring are outside.

6.5.4   *Returning points defining a geometry*

A convenient little function that works only with linestrings and circularstrings is ST_PointN. It returns the *n*th point on the linestring, with indexing starting at 1. Here's a quick example that returns POINT(3 4):

```
SELECT ST_AsText(
    ST_PointN(ST_GeomFromText('LINESTRING(1 2,3 4,5 8)'),2)
);
```

If you wanted to extract all or a good number of the points of a geometry, regardless of what geometry it is, you'd use ST_DumpPoints. ST_DumpPoints returns a set of geometry_dump objects. geometry_dump has two components: a one-dimensional path array and a geometry. In the case of ST_DumpPoints, the geometry is always a point, and the path array lists the sequence in which the points were dumped.

ST_DumpPoints is particularly useful for deconstructing a geometry and passing it to a tool such as R, which can't work directly with PostGIS types. It's also useful for breaking up large geometries into smaller pieces, such as breaking a long linestring into smaller segments.

6.5.5   *Decomposing multi-geometries and geometry collections*

Both ST_GeometryN and ST_Dump are useful for exploding multi-geometries and collection geometries into their component geometries, but they don't always return the same answers. ST_Dump recursively dumps all contained geometries, whereas ST_GeometryN drills down only a single level. ST_Dump, like its ST_DumpPoints sibling, returns a set of geometry_dump objects. The geometry returned will always be a singleton geometry, never a multi-geometry.

The following listing demonstrates ST_Dump.

Listing 6.11   ST_Dump in action

```
WITH foo(gid,geom) As (        ◄────────┐   Common table
    VALUES (                      ❶     expression (CTE)
        1,
        ST_GeomFromText('
            POLYHEDRALSURFACE(
                ((0 0 0,0 0 1,0 1 1,0 1 0,0 0 0)),
                ((0 0 0,0 1 0,1 1 0,1 0 0,0 0 0)),
                ((0 0 0,1 0 0,1 0 1,0 0 1,0 0 0)),
                ((1 1 0,1 1 1,1 0 1,1 0 0,1 1 0)),
                ((0 1 0,0 1 1,1 1 1,1 1 0,0 1 0)),
```

```
                    ((0 0 1,1 0 1,1 1 1,0 1 1,0 0 1))
              )'
          )
      ),
      (
          2,
          ST_GeomFromText('
              GEOMETRYCOLLECTION(
                  MULTIPOLYGON(
                      ((2.25 0,1.25 1,1.25 -1,2.25 0)),
                      ((1 -1,1 1,0 0,1 -1))
                  ),
                  MULTIPOINT(1 2,3 4),
                  LINESTRING(5 6,7 8),
                  MULTICURVE(CIRCULARSTRING(1 2,0 4,2 8),(1 2,5 6)))'))
      )
```

```
SELECT
    gid,
    (gdump).path As pos,
    ST_AsText((gdump).geom) As exploded_geometry
FROM (SELECT gid, ST_Dump(geom) As gdump FROM foo) As foofoo;
```

2 Expand using **ST_Dump**

3 Output path and geometry elements

In listing 6.11, you use a common table expression (CTE) named foo to create a set of geometries **1**. (Refer to appendix C to learn more about CTEs.) You then convert each geometry to a set of geometry_dump objects **3** and then break out the path and geometry properties of each dump object as separate columns **2** to get an idea of what a geometry_dump object looks like. The output of this query is shown next:

```
gid | pos    | exploded_geometry
----+--------+---------------------------------------------------
  1 | {1}    | POLYGON((0 0 0,0 0 1,0 1 1,0 1 0,0 0 0))
  1 | {2}    | POLYGON((0 0 0,0 1 0,1 1 0,1 0 0,0 0 0))
  1 | {3}    | POLYGON((0 0 0,1 0 0,1 0 1,0 0 1,0 0 0))
  1 | {4}    | POLYGON((1 1 0,1 1 1,1 0 1,1 0 0,1 1 0))
  1 | {5}    | POLYGON((0 1 0,0 1 1,1 1 1,1 1 0,0 1 0))
  1 | {6}    | POLYGON((0 0 1,1 0 1,1 1 1,0 1 1,0 0 1))
  2 | {1,1}  | POLYGON((2.25 0,1.25 1,1.25 -1,2.25 0))
  2 | {1,2}  | POLYGON((1 -1,1 1,0 0,1 -1))
  2 | {2,1}  | POINT(1 2)
  2 | {2,2}  | POINT(3 4)
  2 | {3}    | LINESTRING(5 6,7 8)
  2 | {4,1}  | CIRCULARSTRING(1 2,0 4,2 8)
  2 | {4,2}  | LINESTRING(1 2,5 6)
```

Note that the pos column in the output is an *n*-dimensional integer array that denotes the position of the subgeometry within the collection. For single-level geometries like the polyhedral surface, the integer array is one-dimensional and contains the index position within the parent. For nested collections, such as a mixed collection of geometries, the first element is the outermost geometry, and each subsequent integer is the index position in inner geometries.

ST_GeometryN extracts the *n*th geometry from a multi-geometry or collection geometry. It returns the single extracted geometry, doesn't recurse, and therefore doesn't report depth. Use ST_GeometryN when you have just one geometry to extract. If you find yourself needing to repeatedly call ST_GeometryN to explode all constituent geometries, switch to ST_Dump; otherwise you'll suffer severe performance penalties. ST_GeometryN is often used in conjunction with the PostgreSQL generate_series function, which provides an iteration index.

Now that we've looked at functions that allow you to decompose a geometry, let's take a look at composition functions that allow you to combine multiple geometries together to form bigger geometries.

6.6   Composition functions

We've already covered creating geometries from non-geometry data, either text or binary. In this section, we'll show you how to put together geometries from other geometries.

6.6.1   Making points

Points are the most elementary geometries. Two functions let you create points from raw coordinates: ST_Point and ST_MakePoint. Coordinates aren't geometries, but we feel they're more related to geometries than text representations, so we classify ST_Point and ST_MakePoint as composition functions.

ST_Point works only for 2D coordinates and can be found in other database products. ST_MakePoint and a variant, ST_MakePointM, can accept 2DM, 3D, and 4D coordinates in addition to 2D, but these two functions are PostGIS-specific. The syntax is the same for all three—just a single argument of coordinates separated by commas. Because these functions don't take an SRID as an argument, you need to combine them with ST_SetSRID to include an SRID.

You may ask yourself what these additional point-making functions offer beyond ST_GeomFromText. To put it concisely: speed and precision. Creating a handful of points or even a few hundred points doesn't take much time, but loading files with millions of points with many significant digits (a common task when working with data collected via instrumentation) is a different matter, and you'll certainly come to prefer ST_Point or ST_MakePoint over ST_GeomFromText in that context.

To illustrate these functions, listing 6.12 simulates reading data points from tracking devices attached to gray whales as they make their annual migration from Baja California to the Bering Sea. Depending on the interval of reads and the number of whales tracked, the number of data points coming into the database could be quite overwhelming, making speed an important consideration for importing.

> **Listing 6.12   Point constructor functions: Where is my whale?**

```
SELECT whale, ST_AsEWKT(spot) As spot
FROM (VALUES
    ('Mr. Whale', ST_SetSRID(ST_Point(-100.499, 28.7015), 4326)),
```

```
('Mr. Whale with M as time',
    ST_SetSRID(ST_MakePointM(-100.499,28.7015,5), 4326)
),                                                          ◄—— ❶ Whale with time
('Mr. Whale with Z as depth',
    ST_SetSRID(ST_MakePoint(-100.499,28.7015,0.5), 4326)
),                                                          ◄—┐ Whale with depth
('Mr. Whale with M and Z',
    ST_SetSRID(ST_MakePoint(-100.499,28.7015,0.5,5), 4326)
)
) As x(whale, spot);            ◄—┐  Whale with
                               ❷  time and depth
```

Listing 6.12 demonstrates various overloads to the ST_Point and ST_MakePoint functions. In the first case, you use an extra M unit to store time as a serial ❶. For example, if you take readings every 5 hours, then M = 1 would mean this reading was taken 5 hours from the start time, M = 2 means 10 hours, and so on. If you're keeping data as individual points, this isn't terribly useful, but if you later decide to stitch them together into a LINESTRINGM, the time slots could be encoded in the line. You may also be interested in knowing how far Mr. Whale dove before coming to the surface for air, so the second variant uses the Z coordinate to store the depth. SRID 4326 is unprojected data, and ST_Transform currently returns the Z coordinate unchanged. The third case includes both Z and M ❷. M is an additional measurement that you're free to use any way you like. In this example, it's used to store time.

The output of listing 6.12 follows:

```
whale                       | spot
----------------------------+------------------------------------------
Mr. Whale                   | SRID=4326;POINT(-100.499 28.7015)
Mr. Whale with M as time    | SRID=4326;POINTM(-100.499 28.7015 5)
Mr. Whale with Z as depth   | SRID=4326;POINT(-100.499 28.7015 0.5)
Mr. Whale with M and Z      | SRID=4326;POINT(-100.499 28.7015 0.5 5)
-
```

6.6.2 Making polygons

ST_MakeEnvelope, ST_MakePolygon, ST_BuildArea, and ST_Polygonize all build polygons. In addition, the ST_Buffer function, which we demonstrated in chapter 1, is capable of making polygons from linestrings and points. These functions are only supported for geometry.

ST_MAKEENVELOPE

Boxes play an important role in mapping, in that they're often used to query for geometries that fit into the viewing area of a map. A common function drafted for this purpose is the ST_MakeEnvelope function, which takes four or five arguments. The first four are the xmin, ymin, xmax, and ymax of the box. The final argument is optional and indicates the SRID of the geometry. If unused, ST_MakeEnvelope assumes the unknown SRID of 0.

ST_MAKEPOLYGON

ST_MakePolygon builds a polygon from a closed linestring representing the exterior ring. Optionally, it can accept as a second argument an array of closed linestrings for interior rings. ST_MakePolygon doesn't validate the input linestrings in any way. This means that if you aren't careful, and you pass in open linestrings or linestrings that can't form polygons, you could end up with an error or a fairly goofy polygon, such as a polygon with holes outside the exterior ring, or interior rings not completely contained by the exterior ring.

The complete absence of validation does provide an advantage in speed. ST_Make-Polygon runs much more quickly than other functions for creating polygons, and it's the only one that won't ignore Z and M coordinates. ST_MakePolygon accepts only closed linestrings as input—no multilinestrings and no collections of linestrings.

ST_BUILDAREA

You can think of ST_BuildArea as the neater roommate of ST_MakePolygon. Unlike its more reckless counterpart, you can toss it wherever you like, and it will organize what you've offered into valid polygons.

ST_BuildArea will accept linestrings, multilinestrings, polygons, multipolygons, and geometrycollections. You don't have to worry about the order or the validity of the geometries that you feed into ST_BuildArea. It will check the validity of each input geometry, determine which geometries should be interior rings and which one should be the exterior ring, and finally reshuffle them to output polygons or multipolygons. ST_BuildArea won't work with arrays, but this shortcoming is mitigated by the fact that it will accept multilinestrings and geometrycollection geometries. If you intend to feed the function an assortment of linestrings and polygons, perform an ST_Collect first to gather all the loose pieces into a single geometry.

All this neatness comes at a price: you sacrifice performance and you can't use it to build 3DM polygons. If you've already sanitized your input geometries using another procedure, and speed is of utmost importance, use ST_MakePolygon. If your input geometry came from suspect sources and you just want to see what area comes out, the sanitizing feature of ST_BuildArea will be worth the wait.

ST_POLYGONIZE

ST_Polygonize comes in two forms: an aggregate function and a function that takes an array of linestring geometries. As a database aggregate, its use makes sense only against an existing table with geometry columns. This function takes rows of linestrings and returns a geometry collection consisting of the possible polygons you can form from such linestrings. The array input form of ST_Polygonize takes an array of linestrings and returns a geometrycollection of polygons. It's often used when trying to form polygons from a potpourri of open and closed linestrings, which are then passed to ST_Dump to dump out the individual polygons as separate rows.

6.6.3 *Promoting single geometries to multi-geometries*

The ST_Multi function is used often in PostGIS, mostly to promote points, linestrings, and polygons to their multi counterparts, even if they have only a single geometry. If a geometry is already of a multi variety, it remains unchanged.

The main use case of ST_Multi is to ensure that all geometries in a table column are of the same geometry type for consistency. For instance, suppose you obtained polygons for all nations. The Kingdom of Lesotho could come in as a single polygon because it's a tiny, landlocked enclave, whereas Indonesia will come in as a multipolygon with anywhere from 17,508 to 18,306 islands and atolls. To keep your column consistent, you'd promote Lesotho to be a multipolygon.

6.7 *Simplification functions*

This section covers the four functions ST_SnapToGrid, ST_QuantizeCoordinates, ST_Simplify, and ST_SimplifyPreserveTopology and the newest addition in PostGIS 3.1, ST_ReducePrecision. These functions behave differently from one another, but they all try to achieve the same goal: reducing the bytes necessary to describe a geometry.

Simplification functions become important when passing geometries across the internet. Despite recent advances, bandwidth is still a precious commodity, especially with wearable wireless devices. With a tiny, black-and-white, 200 × 300 resolution screen on a GPS watch, transmitting geometries with thousands of vertices or coordinates with a monstrous number of significant digits is certainly overkill.

6.7.1 *Grid snapping and coordinate rounding*

ST_SnapToGrid reduces the weight of a geometry by rounding the coordinates (https://postgis.net/docs/ST_SnapToGrid.html). If, after rounding, two or more adjacent coordinates become indistinguishable, it will automatically keep only one of them, thus reducing the number of vertices.

There are four variants of this function. The most common one takes one argument for tolerance and rounds the X and Y coordinates while leaving Z and M intact. Other variants can round all four coordinates or allow you to specify tolerance. For example, a tolerance of 50 means that only coordinates within 50 units of each other can be rounded to the same value.

One common use of ST_SnapToGrid is to trim those extra floating-point decimals introduced by ST_Transform. Those extra digits can degrade performance and are generally noise, as they don't reflect the true precision of the data. Another use of ST_SnapToGrid is to group distinct nearby points into a single representational point. For example, if you obtained point data for every school in the country, but you only care about the location of school districts, then clustering schools down to points would be the way to go.

ST_QuantizeCoordinates, available since PostGIS 2.5, is another function that reduces coordinate size (https://postgis.net/docs/ST_QuantizeCoordinates.html). It works a little differently than ST_SnapToGrid. Instead of rounding the digit, it zeros out the bits that define the coordinate to a given precision. It often yields better results than ST_SnapToGrid.

As with most simplifying operations, you should exercise restraint. Too-ambitious rounding can inadvertently turn a valid polygon into an invalid one or, worse yet, into a single point.

ST_ReducePrecision, introduced in PostGIS 3.1 and only enabled if running with GEOS 3.9, also reduces coordinates but by overlaying the geometry on a precise grid (https://postgis.net/docs/ST_ReducePrecision.html). It promises to reduce the number of points and significant digits in the coordinates without ever resulting in an invalid geometry. The output is similar to ST_SnapToGrid. As such, it is often a better choice than ST_SnapToGrid and the simplification functions discussed next.

All these functions take some sort of tolerance or precision, and these tolerances are always expressed in the spatial reference system units of the geometry.

6.7.2   *Simplification*

ST_Simplify and ST_SimplifyPreserveTopology both reduce the weight of a geometry by reducing the number of vertices of the geometry, using some variant of the Douglas-Peucker algorithm. The ST_SimplifyPreserveTopology function is newer than ST_Simplify and has safeguards against oversimplification, which means it's generally preferred over the older version, even though it's a bit slower.

Both ST_Simplify and ST_SimplifyPreserveTopology take a second argument, which we'll term *tolerance*. This can be roughly treated as the maximum distance between two vertices that can be collapsed into one. For example, if you set the argument to 100, the two functions will try to collapse any vertices spaced up to 100 units apart. As you increase the tolerance, you'll experience more simplification. Putting it another way, the more tolerant you are of losing vertices, the more simplification you can achieve.

These two simplifying functions, unlike ST_SnapToGrid, don't preserve M and Z coordinates and will remove them if present. They also only work for linestrings, multilinestrings, polygons, multipolygons, and geometry collections containing these geometries. For multipoints, they return the same input geometry without any simplification. The reason for this is that ST_Simplify and ST_SimplifyPreserveTopology require edges (lines between vertices) to achieve simplification. Multipoints don't have edges.

Don't use the ST_Simplify function with data in longitude and latitude; ST_Simplify and ST_SimplifyPreserveTopology assume planar coordinates. Should you use these functions with, say, SRID 4326, the resultant geometry could range from slightly askew to completely goofy. First transform to a preferably measure-preserving spatial reference system, then apply ST_Simplify, and then transform back to your lon/lat SRID.

The following listing compares ST_Simplify and ST_SimplifyPreserveTopology.

Listing 6.13 Comparing `ST_Simplify` and `ST_SimplifyPreserveTopology`

```
SELECT
    pow(2,n) as tolerance,
    ST_AsText(ST_Simplify(geom, pow(2,n))) As simp1,
    ST_AsText(ST_SimplifyPreserveTopology(geom, pow(2,n))) As simp2
FROM
    (SELECT ST_GeomFromText(
        'POLYGON Z(
            (10 0 1,20 0 1,30 10 1,30 20 1,20 30 1,10 30 1,0 20 1,0 10 1,10 0 1)
        )') As geom) As x
    CROSS JOIN
    generate_series(1,5) As n;
```

You can see the results of listing 6.13 in table 6.6.

Table 6.6 `ST_Simplify` versus `ST_SimplifyPreserveTopology`

Tolerance	ST_Simplify	ST_SimplifyPreserveTopology
2	POLYGON Z ((10 0 1,20 0 1,30 10 1,30 20 1,20 30 1,10 30 1,0 20 1,0 10 1,10 0 1))	POLYGON Z ((10 0 1,20 0 1,30 10 1,30 20 1,20 30 1,10 30 1,0 20 1,0 10 1,10 0 1))
4	POLYGON Z ((10 0 1,20 0 1,30 10 1,30 20 1,20 30 1,10 30 1,0 20 1,0 10 1,10 0 1))	POLYGON Z ((10 0 1,20 0 1,30 10 1,30 20 1,20 30 1,10 30 1,0 20 1,0 10 1,10 0 1))
8	POLYGON Z ((10 0 1,30 10 1,20 30 1,0 20 1,10 0 1))	POLYGON Z ((10 0 1,30 10 1,20 30 1,0 20 1,10 0 1))
16		POLYGON Z ((10 0 1,30 10 1,20 30 1,0 20 1,10 0 1))
32		POLYGON Z ((10 0 1,30 10 1,20 30 1,0 20 1,10 0 1))

Notice that once you reach a tolerance of 16 with `ST_Simplify`, the geometry reduces to NULL. `ST_Simplify_PreserveTopology` reduces the eight-sided polygon to a four-sided polygon and stops there, regardless of the tolerance.

`ST_SimplifyVW` is a function introduced in PostGIS 2.2 that uses the Visvalingam-Whyatt algorithm, which is area-based rather than edge-based. The `ST_SimplifyVW` function only works with linestrings, multilinestrings, polygons, and multipolygons. We'll repeat the prior exercise in the next listing, but square our tolerance, since the `ST_SimplifyVW` tolerance is expressed in area units rather than length units.

Listing 6.14 Using `ST_SimplifyVw`

```
SELECT
    pow(2,n)*pow(2,n) as tolerance,
    ST_AsText(ST_SimplifyVW(geom, pow(2,n)*pow(2,n))) As simpvw
FROM
    (SELECT ST_GeomFromText(
        'POLYGON Z(
```

```
        (10 0 1,20 0 1,30 10 1,30 20 1,20 30 1,10 30 1,0 20 1,0 10 1,10 0 1)
    )') As geom) As x
CROSS JOIN
generate_series(1,5) As n;
```

Note that like ST_PreserveTopology, ST_SimplifyVW stops before the geometry vanishes, regardless how high a tolerance you give it:

```
tolerance |     simpvw
----------+-----------------------------------------------
     4 | POLYGON Z ((10 0 1,20 0 1,30 10 1,...))
    16 | POLYGON Z ((10 0 1,20 0 1,30 10 1,...))
    64 | POLYGON Z ((10 0 1,30 10 1,30 20 1,...))
   256 | POLYGON Z ((10 0 1,30 20 1,10 30 1,10 0 1))
  1024 | POLYGON Z ((10 0 1,30 20 1,10 30 1,10 0 1))
```

Summary

- PostGIS has many functions that output geometry and geography in various formats that are useful for web applications and desktop applications.
- PostGIS popular web-format functions for GeoBuf, MVT, GeoJSON can also output other attribute data besides the spatial part.
- PostGIS has functions for outputting internal measurements such as length, perimeter, and area of a geometry or geography.
- PostGIS has functions that allow you to set the properties of a geometry or geography and access the current values of these properties.
- PostGIS has functions that can be used to extract subelements of a geometry.
- PostGIS has functions that can combine one or more geometries into bigger geometries.
- PostGIS has functions that can output lighter versions of a geometry.

Raster functions 7

This chapter covers

- Constructor functions
- Output functions
- Raster band and pixel accessors and setters
- Georeferencing functions
- Reclassing functions
- Polygonizing functions

The raster type is different in makeup from the geometry type covered in chapter 6. Geometries model an object as a set of linear equations, whereas rasters model an object as a tapestry of cells. In PostGIS, you'll find the two types working together, leveraging each other's strengths. For example, you can output a geometry in a raster file format such as PNG. You can also clip raster images with vector boundaries. We'll touch on raster processing in this chapter, but we'll leave the more-thorough treatment for chapter 12, where we'll demonstrate advanced raster-processing functions, such as raster aggregate functions, map algebra functions, and set-returning functions.

The PostGIS raster type only supports pixels, which are 2D cells on an X-Y grid. It can't yet support voxels, which are pixels with more than two dimensions, but you can compensate by storing higher-dimensional data as a band or using multiple rasters with the same coverage area. For example, if you have a raster with elevations and measurements, you can add two more bands: one to hold the Z value, and one to hold the M value. A companion project to PostGIS is the pgpointcloud extension (https://github.com/pgpointcloud/pointcloud), which is used to store and analyze point cloud data. Point clouds are beyond the scope of this book, but they are a precursor to rasters and often come from lidar (light detection and ranging) imagery as a BLOB of *n*-dimensional points that contain metrics like color intensity and so forth.

As always, for the full breadth of raster functions, refer to the official PostGIS raster reference: http://postgis.net/docs/RT_reference.html.

Before we get started, if you are running PostGIS 3.0 or higher, make sure you have the postgis_raster extension installed by doing the following:

```
CREATE EXTENSION IF NOT EXISTS postgis_raster SCHEMA postgis;
```

If your extension install is successful, run the following command:

```
SELECT postgis_full_version();
```

You should see output like this, containing RASTER and GDAL:

```
POSTGIS="3.1.1 3.1.1" [EXTENSION] PGSQL="130" GEOS="3.9.1-CAPI-
    1.14.1" PROJ="7.1.1" GDAL="GDAL 3.2.1,
released 2020/12/29" LIBXML="2.9.9" LIBJSON="0.12" LIBPROTOBUF="1.2.1" WAGYU=
    "0.5.0 (Internal)" TOPOLOGY RASTER
```

We'll start with raster constructor functions so that you can create rasters for the examples in this chapter.

7.1   Raster terminology

Before we begin, let's define some raster terminology:

- *Georeferencing*—A georeferenced raster is one whose pixels are pinned to a geographic reference system defined in the spatial_ref_sys table. You'll generally note the spatial reference system with the spatial reference identifier recorded in the srid column in the spatial_ref_sys table. Only if you specify the SRID can you transform to other SRSs. The term *georeference* is a bit of a misnomer, in that the SRID doesn't have to be earth-based but could very well be for another planet or an artificial coordinate system such as for building a floor plan, or for a virtual gaming world. Each pixel represents *x* units of the reference system (the pixel width) and *y* units of the reference system (pixel height). Conversely, a non-georeferenced raster means that the pixels have no correlation to any coordinate system. The most common examples of non-georeferenced rasters are family pictures you snap with your camera. In contrast, if you boarded a high-altitude spy plane intending to snap pictures of enemy targets, you'd be negligent if you didn't include georeferencing.

- *Out-of-database or out-of-db*—You're free to store rasters as files outside of the database. If you choose out-of-database storage, PostGIS records a pointer to the file in the database, and you can then reference the out-of-db raster as if it were any other in-db raster. PostGIS will handle all the behind-the-scenes reading and conversion from the file—PostGIS never modifies out-of-db rasters, treating them as read-only. Out-of-db storage makes sense when you have massive amounts of reference data that must be accessible to other programs. When you're using out-of-db rasters, ensure that the postgres service account can access the path and that it has read rights to the files. Should some aspect of the out-of-db raster change, such as paths, dimensions, georeferences, number of bands, or band types, you'll need to re-register the out-of-db data.

- *Raster tile*—A raster tile is a raster like any other raster. The main reason we differentiate a raster tile from a raster is to denote that the raster tile was created by chopping a bigger raster into a set of smaller rasters that can be reconstituted together via various raster operations. The main reasons people tile rasters are speed and manageability.

- *Coverage*—Coverage is only relevant for georeferenced data, and it represents a non-overlapping expanse of space where each nth band represents the same reading in each raster tile of a raster column. In the context of a PostGIS raster, the coverage is often stored as a table of rasters where each raster in a particular table column represents a tile of space. When taken as a whole, all the rasters in the table column form a contiguous geographic space. In addition, each tile has the same number of bands, with each nth band storing the same kind of information. For example, you could define a grid covering Europe, chopped into tiles with each tile being stored as a raster that has two bands: one representing temperature and another elevation. When considered together, the set of rasters forms one huge raster covering Europe, without any tiles overlapping. Although it is possible to store rasters of variable pixel sizes in the same table column, some operations such as ST_Union may fail if pixel sizes are different for each row. A given band does share pixel metadata with other bands in the raster tile, so all bands in the same raster column/row have the same dimensions and pixel sizes as its band siblings.

- *Same alignment*—Two rasters have the same alignment if they have the same skew, the same pixel scale ratio (the size one pixel represents in spatial coordinates), and if the rasters' upper-left spatial coordinates are set such that the pixels of both can be put on the same grid. If the two rasters are georeferenced, they must also share the same spatial reference system. Many operations, such as unioning, require rasters to have the same alignment. If you're creating coverage tables, the tiles constituting the coverage must all be of the same alignment.

If you're defining a coverage table for rasters, all the tiles must similarly have the same alignment.

- *Map algebra*—Map algebra is a fancy term for mathematical operations on a set of pixels over one or more bands. You can use map algebra against as many bands as you wish, but the result of any ST_MapAlgebra operation is a single-band raster. Map algebra can use all the PostgreSQL mathematical operations. In addition, PostGIS lets you define your own map algebra functions using any procedural language (PL) supported by PostgreSQL. Map algebra forms the foundation of many functions in PostGIS rasters such as ST_Union, ST_Slope, and ST_HillShade.

- *Neighborhood*—In the context of map algebra, a neighborhood is a contiguous, rectangular grid of pixels centered around a particular pixel. The neighborhood extends both n pixels to the right and left and m pixels up and down from the central pixel. The neighborhood therefore contains $(2n + 1) \times (2m + 1)$ pixels (note that the width and length will always be odd numbers). There are several functions overloaded with the same ST_MapAlgebra name. From an API standpoint, because they all have the same name, they can be treated as a single function with many optional arguments. The neighborhood is an optional argument that is either 0 (the default if not specified, meaning the map algebra operation works on a single cell) or n pixels left/right, and m pixels up/down from the center pixel.

- *Reclass*—Reclassing is an operation that changes the range value of a raster. For example, you can reclassify all positive pixel values to be +1 and all negative values to be –1. If your pixel values represented sea-level elevations, instead of storing the actual heights, your raster would now take on the meaning of a location either above water or underwater. Reclassing is often used to remove noise introduced by instrumentation, to simplify a raster, or to convert a raster's floating-point values into integer values. Although it's similar to map algebra and can even be considered a subset of map algebra, reclassing often performs much more quickly than map algebra—in many cases, orders of magnitude faster.

7.2   *Raster constructors*

There are several ways of creating PostGIS rasters:

- Convert PostGIS geometries to rasters with ST_AsRaster. In PostGIS 3.2, ST_InterpolateRaster will convert a set of 3D points into a surface elevation grid (http://postgis.net/docs/manual-dev/RT_ST_InterpolateRaster.html).

- Load rasters with the raster2pgsql loader. If you want to maintain the rasters outside of your database, you can use the -R switch of the loader to register them instead of importing them into the database.

- Create rasters from scratch using ST_MakeEmptyRaster and ST_AddBand, and then set pixel values using various other raster functions or set the band path to an external raster file.

- Build rasters from existing rasters using processing functions such as unioning, tiling, map algebra, reclassifying, resizing, reprojecting, resampling, and so forth.
- Use the ST_FromGDALRaster function, which converts rasters in various other raster formats to PostGIS raster format. All you need to have is the binary BLOB (byte array) of the input raster. This function is especially handy if you need to keep raster data in its source form, but you occasionally want to leverage the PostGIS raster functions.

In this section, you'll see some of these approaches for creating rasters.

> **NOTE** All GDAL drivers and out-of-db rasters are disabled by default for security reasons. Many GDAL drivers (and out-of-db rasters by nature) can interact with the network, making them more vulnerable to network exploits. As such, it was decided that it was best to disable them and have the database admin decide what is needed. Refer to the documentation for details on how to reenable selected drivers (https://postgis.net/docs/postgis_gdal_enabled_drivers.html) and out-of-db support (https://postgis.net/docs/postgis_enable_outdb_rasters .html). This default means your ST_AsPNG and other GDAL-based input/output functions may not work, and ST_GDALDrivers, which we'll discuss in this chapter, will list no drivers if you haven't enabled any.

In order to utilize out-of-db rasters and all the raster import/output functions, we will make the following changes in our database. These can alternatively be set at the server, session, or user level:

```
ALTER DATABASE postgis_in_action SET postgis.enable_outdb_rasters = true;
ALTER DATABASE postgis_in_action SET postgis.gdal_enabled_drivers =
    'ENABLE_ALL';
```

If you want to set these at the database or system level, you will need to disconnect and reconnect to the database for the changes to take effect.

For the purposes of this section, we'll create a table called bag_o_rasters to house the rasters we create:

```
CREATE SCHEMA ch07;
CREATE TABLE ch07.bag_o_rasters(
    rid serial primary key, rast_name text, rast raster
);
```

Keep in mind that creating a table of rasters with no constraints is useful for demonstrations, as a transit table before pushing to other tables, or if you want to use PostGIS to manage your photo gallery. For GIS work, you'll almost always want to have georeferenced rasters with well-defined tiles, bands, SRIDs, and other constraints on the table to ensure that each raster row is a tile of a contiguous coverage.

7.2.1   *Converting geometries to rasters with ST_AsRaster*

You can convert rasters from geometries using the ST_AsRaster function. This is useful if you need to do any of the following:

- Output a geometry to an image format for viewing.
- Overlay a geometry on a raster to highlight specific areas or to incorporate boundaries, roads, or points of interest.
- Store numerical statistics about a region that you can then query with the raster analytic family of functions.

In the following subsections, you'll learn how to use ST_AsRaster to build rasters from geometries and how to use various optional arguments. Although ST_AsRaster can be used by itself, you'll often want to use it in conjunction with other raster functions, such as ST_Union, ST_MapAlgebra, and ST_SetValues.

Unfortunately, ST_AsRaster doesn't support curved or 3D geometries.

CREATE SINGLE BAND RASTERS FROM GEOMETRY

Listing 7.1 creates two single-band rasters from one geometry. Because you don't specify a band type or band value, ST_AsRaster creates bands with the 8BUI band type, which is the default when a band type is not specified (band types were discussed in chapter 2). A pixel value of 1 represents the geometry, and a pixel value of 0 represents empty space.

Listing 7.1   Disproportional and proportional fixed-width rasters

```
INSERT INTO ch07.bag_o_rasters(rast_name, rast)
WITH a1 AS (
    SELECT ST_Buffer(
        ST_GeomFromText(
            'LINESTRING(
                448252 5414206,448289 5414317,448293 5414330,
                448324 5414417,448351 5414495
            )',
            32631),
        10
    ) As geom                          ❶  Road in Paris
)
SELECT 'disprop road', ST_AsRaster(geom,50,500) FROM a1          ❷  50 × 500 pixel disproportional raster
UNION ALL
SELECT 'disprop road', ST_AsRaster(geom,50,500) FROM a1
    UNION ALL
    SELECT 'proport fixed w road',
        ST_AsRaster( geom, 200,
            ( ST_YMax(geom) - ST_YMin(geom) ) * 200 /
            ( ST_XMax(geom) - ST_XMin(geom)  )::integer)      ❸  Proportional raster
    FROM a1;
```

In listing 7.1 a common table expression (CTE) ❶ defines a road in Paris with a UTM Zone 31 N SRID (32631), which means that each unit represents a meter. From the

Paris road geometry ❷ a raster of 50 × 500 pixels is created. Because the ratio of the road is not 50/500, the raster is disproportional. The UNION ALL ❸ creates another raster with the same proportionality as the Paris road geometry, but with a fixed width of 200 pixels by using the Paris geometry bounding-box width and height for the ratio factor to compute the pixel height.

The rasters generated by the code in listing 7.1 are shown in figure 7.1.

Figure 7.1 ST_AsRaster: **the left line is fixed 50 × 500, and the second is proportional to the road but 200 px wide**

Figure 7.1 shows the Paris road drawn by squashing it in a fixed 50 × 500 box. Because the road's dimensional proportions are not 50 × 500, the first image doesn't correctly reflect the slant of the road. In the second image, the width is fixed at 200 pixels, and the height is computed based on the geometric dimensions. As a result, the image at right correctly displays the slanting of the road and the relative road thickness.

ALIGN ST_ASRASTER

If you plan to union many geometries together into a single raster or to overlay geometries on an existing raster, you'll want to make sure that your geometries and rasters are in alignment. Perfect alignment requires all geometries and rasters to share the same SRID, grid, and pixel size.

You can think of the reference raster as the grid the geometry lives on. If the coordinate region covered by the reference raster doesn't cover your geometry, part of the geometry will be cut off. If the reference raster covers more area than your geometry, the resulting raster will be a subset of the reference. You can build that reference raster from scratch using ST_MakeEmptyRaster or use an existing raster.

The following listing is similar to listing 7.1, but instead of allowing the geometry to occupy the 50 × 500 area, this listing positions it relative to an existing grid, and the final raster will be a subset of that grid.

Listing 7.2 Geometry positioned by coordinates

```
WITH
    r AS
        (SELECT
            ST_MakeEmptyRaster(
                500,500,445000,5415000,2,-2,0,0,32631
            ) As rast
        ),
```

❶ Create a 500 × 500 reference raster starting at 445000, 5415000.

```
    g AS
        (SELECT ST_Buffer(
            ST_GeomFromText(
                'LINESTRING(
                    448252 5414206,448289 5414317,448293 5414330,
                    448324 5414417,448351 5414495)',
                32631),
            10) As geom
        )
INSERT INTO ch07.bag_o_rasters(rast_name, rast)
SELECT 'canvas aligned road', ST_AsRaster(geom,rast,'8BUI'::text)
FROM r CROSS JOIN g;
```

② Road in Paris

③ 8BUI raster of geometry aligned with the reference raster

Listing 7.2 uses a CTE to define a reference raster that's 500 × 500 pixels with a spatial reference system of 32631, where each pixel represents 2 meters width/height ❶. Next, a CTE called g is created that holds a road in Paris as a geometry ❷. The final step creates a raster from the geometry road that's aligned with the reference raster ❸. The resulting raster that's inserted into bag_o_rasters will have dimensions 60 pixels wide by 155 pixels high and be labeled *canvas aligned road*.

7.2.2   *Loading rasters with raster2pgsql*

You can use raster2pgsql to both create a raster table and then populate it with a set of related raster files. If your raster encompasses a great many pixels, raster2pgsql will create tiles for you with one tile occupying one row.

We covered loading rasters in chapter 4, so we'll only show one example here. We'll load the elephant called *Reo* into the bag_o_rasters table using a command-line command. We're going to keep Reo as an out-of-db elephant.

The following example dispenses with all the niceties of constraint and index switches that you'd normally add because you're adding to an existing table that's a mixed bag of rasters. The -a switch indicates that you're loading into an existing table, so a new one won't be created. The -R switch is what makes it out-of-db. It only registers the file path in the database. If you are loading as out-of-db, you should include the full path and ensure that the path is accessible from the postgres process:

```
raster2pgsql -e -R -a C:/pics/adbadge_tall.png ch07.bag_o_rasters
  | psql -U postgres -d postgis_in_action -h localhost -p 5432
```

After this command runs, there should be one unnamed raster in the table corresponding to the elephant image you just loaded. You can then set the rast_name field to Reo for the raster that has no name:

```
UPDATE ch07.bag_o_rasters SET rast_name = 'Reo'
WHERE rast_name IS NULL;
```

7.2.3 Constructing rasters from scratch: ST_MakeEmptyRaster and ST_AddBand

The following listing creates an empty raster using `ST_MakeEmptyRaster`, adds a single `8BUI` band to the raster using `ST_AddBand`, and sets all the pixel values to `255` by passing `255` in as a default value for new pixels.

Listing 7.3   Building a raster from scratch

```
INSERT INTO ch07.bag_o_rasters(rast_name, rast)
SELECT
    'Raster 1 band scratch',          Add the band.
    ST_AddBand(                                      Create an
        ST_MakeEmptyRaster(                          empty raster.
            500,500,445000,5415000,2,-2,0,0,32631
        ),
        '8BUI'::text,255,0          Initialize the new 8BUI
) As rast;                          band with a value of 255.
```

All the pixels in listing 7.3 have the same value. It's not that interesting now, but we'll liven it up in our next example.

7.2.4 Setting pixels: ST_SetValue and ST_SetValues

Rasters store numeric values in their bands, and PostGIS has two functions for updating a raster band's pixel values with numeric values: `ST_SetValues` and `ST_SetValue`. Yes, one is singular, and one is plural.

Listing 7.4   `ST_SetValue` by column number and row number position

```
UPDATE ch07.bag_o_rasters AS b
SET rast = ST_SetValue(rast,1,10,20,146)
WHERE b.rast_name = 'Raster 1 band scratch';
```

To use `ST_SetValue` to set the value of a pixel, indicate the column and row of the pixel (or a geometry) and the new value, as shown in listing 7.4. The order of the input parameters are as follows: raster, band number, column number, row number, new value.

PostGIS rasters are capable of generating heat and bubble maps, which show metrics like population, temperature, and vegetation using different colors (where, for example, color becomes redder as temperature increases) or bubble sizes (where the size of the bubble increases by the metric). In order to accomplish this task, you'll want set pixels that intersect the raster to a specific pixel value on an existing raster.

`ST_SetValues` allows you to set all the pixel values that intersect with a set of geomvals. A geomval is a composite PostgreSQL data type consisting of a geometry and a floating-point value—all pixels that intersect the geometry can be set to the value designated by the value in the geomval.

Listing 7.5 will create a copy of the updated Raster 1 band scratch (from listing 7.4) and then use ST_SetValues to burn a set of bubbles into this new raster. ST_SetValues is particularly useful for creating thematic maps where you need to set a particular geographic region in the raster with a particular value.

Listing 7.5   ST_SetValues: building a heatmap

```
WITH heatmap As (                    ◁──────────────── ❶ CTE heatmap
    SELECT array_agg(               ◁────────┐
        (ST_Buffer(                          │     Aggregate
            ST_Translate(            ❷  geomvals
                ST_SetSRID(
                    ST_Point(445500,5414500), 32631
                ),
                -500 + i * 150,
                -200 + 160 * i
            ),
            i * 50),
            50 + i * 15.0
        )::geomval
    ) As gvals
    FROM generate_series(-3,4) As i
)
INSERT INTO ch07.bag_o_rasters(rast_name, rast)
SELECT                                                  ❸  Burn in
    'Raster 1 band heatmap',                                gvals
    ST_SetValues(rast,1, heatmap.gvals) As rast  ◁──┘
FROM ch07.bag_o_rasters As b CROSS JOIN heatmap
WHERE b.rast_name = 'Raster 1 band scratch';
```

In listing 7.5 you create a CTE called heatmap ❶ composed of a single value called gvals, which is an array of geomvals accumulated with the PostgreSQL array aggregator function array_agg ❷. You buffer and translate the geometries to create ever larger circles, and then burn the array of geomvals onto band 1 of the raster ❸. In order for this operation to be successful, you need to make sure your geometries have the same spatial reference as the reference raster.

Figure 7.2   ST_SetValues: a heatmap

Figure 7.2 shows the raster image generated from listing 7.5.

As shown in figure 7.2, the different bubbles vary in shades of gray. Both the size of the bubble and the shading intensity depends on the value of i. The top bubble is cut off because its area exceeded the borders of the canvas.

7.2.5 *Creating rasters from other rasters*

PostGIS provides many functions for creating rasters from other rasters. We'll cover the following functions in this section:

- ST_ColorMap—Converts a one-band raster to a three-band RGB or four-band RGBA raster.
- ST_Clip—Clips a raster to the bounds of an input geometry. This is an intersection operation with a geometry that returns a raster.
- ST_Band—Constructs a new raster consisting of one or more bands from an existing raster.
- ST_Intersection—Intersects two raster bands to yield a new raster.

COLORING GRAYSCALE RASTERS

The ST_ColorMap function converts a single-band raster to one with RGB bands. We can convert the grayscale heatmap we created in listing 7.5 to a colored one with intensity ranging from blue to red, by applying the ST_ColorMap function as follows:

```
INSERT INTO ch07.bag_o_rasters(rast_name, rast)
SELECT 'Raster 1 band heatmap color' AS rast_name,
  ST_ColorMap(b.rast, 1, 'bluered') AS heatmap_color
FROM ch07.bag_o_rasters As b
WHERE b.rast_name =  'Raster 1 band heatmap';
```

PostGIS comes packaged with several predefined color maps. We are using the bluered colormap, which colors low values blue and scales to red for higher pixel values. If you are not satisfied with any of the predefined color maps, you can define your own (https://postgis.net/docs/RT_ST_ColorMap.html).

ST_CLIP: CROPPING RASTERS

The ST_Clip function allows you to cut out a portion of a raster using a geometry as your cutter. Imagine petits fours here. The function can take a band number or array of band numbers as arguments. If you omit a band specification, the geometry will clip all bands. Remember, the geometry cutter you use must have the same SRID as the raster.

The following example creates a single-band Reo using ST_Clip.

Listing 7.6 Using ST_Clip

```
INSERT INTO ch07.bag_o_rasters(rast_name, rast)
SELECT
    'Reo 1 band crop',
    ST_Clip(
        rast,
        1,
        ST_Buffer(ST_Centroid(rast::geometry), 75),
        255
    )
FROM ch07.bag_o_rasters
WHERE rast_name = 'Reo';
```

The code in listing 7.6 selects the first band and clips it with a 75 radius circle centered on the middle of the image (a piece of Reo's earlobe, as shown in figure 7.3). The last argument of 255 is an optional no-data value argument—if the clipped region contains pixels without any values, ST_Clip fills the clipped raster with the no-data value.

Figure 7.3   Reo's ear

ST_Clip has many optional arguments. One worth mentioning is crop, which defaults to true. With the default setting, the extent of the new raster is the extent of the intersection of the raster and the clipping geometry. If you pass in false, the dimensions of the new raster will be the same as those of the original.

Always keep ST_Clip in the back of your mind if you're given a giant raster with tens of thousands of pixels and you only need an isolated area. Your life will be easier if you crop out the region of interest into a new raster before starting your scrutiny.

ST_BAND: SELECTING SPECIFIC BANDS

The ST_Band function allows you to select one or more bands of a raster to form a new raster with the same dimensions, coordinates, SRID, and pixel values. The number of bands in the new raster will be equal to the number of bands you selected. You can also use this function to reorder bands, and you'll find it used in conjunction with ST_AddBand to combine single-band rasters into multiband rasters.

The first argument is always the raster, and the second is either an integer to indicate the band number or an array of integers to indicate more than one band or to indicate a shuffled order. The following example creates a new raster by shuffling the bands of the original Reo:

```
INSERT INTO ch07.bag_o_rasters (rast_name,rast)
SELECT 'Reo band shuffle', ST_Band(rast,ARRAY[3,1,2])
FROM ch07.bag_o_rasters
WHERE rast_name = 'Reo';
```

Reo takes on a purplish hue in the output, which is shown in figure 7.4.

ST_Band doesn't pay attention to whether the raster is in-db or out-of-db. You shouldn't have to worry unless you're going to be saving the output of ST_Band back to the database. If you also use ST_AddBand, your source raster can be both in-db and out-of-db. This is perfectly fine.

Creating and manipulating rasters means little if you have no way to share them with the rest of the world. In the next section we'll show you some raster output functions.

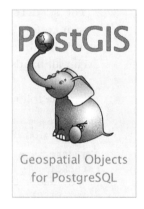

Figure 7.4   Reo shuffled

7.2.6 *Converting other raster formats with ST_FromGDALRaster*

The PostGIS raster type is a format specific to PostGIS. When you use raster2pgsql to load rasters and opt for in-db storage, the loader converts the foreign raster format into the PostGIS raster format. But sometimes, you already have bytea data (byte arrays) in your database that store the bytes of the original image, and you want to manipulate these right in the database, perhaps to resize them. In order to use the PostGIS raster functions, you'll need to convert these rasters into the Post-GIS raster format.

ST_FromGDALRaster converts another raster type, such as PNG or JPEG images, to the PostGIS raster format. It's also smart enough to figure out what raster format you're starting with.

Suppose you had a table of pictures of various formats like bitmap (BMP), PNG, and JPEG, which stored the bytea (binary BLOB) of each picture. Your table structure would look something like this:

```
CREATE TABLE ch07.pics(pic_name varchar(255), pic bytea);
```

If you wanted to convert them to PostGIS raster format so you could keep them with the rest of your growing bag of rasters, you'd run a query such as this:

```
INSERT INTO ch07.bag_o_rasters(rast_name, rast)
SELECT pic_name, ST_FromGDALRaster(pic) As rast
FROM ch07.pics;
```

This would convert all your pictures (as long as they're in a format supported by your PostGIS GDAL driver) to PostGIS raster format and insert them into the bag_o_rasters table. If you wanted to keep your images in a more common format, such as PNG or JPEG, then you'd convert back using one of the PostGIS raster companion output functions (ST_AsGDALRaster, ST_AsPNG, or ST_AsJPEG) which we'll cover in the next section.

7.3 *Raster output functions*

For distribution and interoperability, you'll want to be able to convert the PostGIS rasters to other raster formats. PostGIS offers several output functions to accomplish this conversion.

PostGIS raster output functions return byte arrays (bytea), which are the bytes that make up an image. Many rendering applications easily consume byte arrays. You'll even find that popular report writers, such as LibreOffice/OpenOffice Base and Pentaho can read byte arrays from a database.

7.3.1 *ST_AsPNG, ST_AsJPEG, and ST_AsTiff*

The ST_AsPNG, ST_AsJPEG, and ST_AsTiff functions output PostGIS rasters to the popular PNG, JPEG, and TIFF graphics formats. In order to use these functions, the raster must have binary unsigned integer (BUI) values as pixels.

You may have to perform a reclass, which we'll cover later in this chapter, or color-map if your raster contains values outside of BUI. Rasters with three or four bands tend to output without problems, but you're not precluded from outputting rasters with fewer bands. To output more than four bands, you'll need to apply some sort of raster operation such as ST_Band that will extract at most four bands from your existing raster.

> ### Ad hoc raster querying
> We used ST_AsPNG and ST_AsJPEG to generate the figures for this chapter. Using these functions, we've also built a simple ad hoc PHP/ASP.NET web application with JQuery and HTML for the frontend interface. You are welcome to download this tool for ASP.NET or PHP from the book's website at www.postgis.us/page_web_tools and customize it to suit your needs.

ST_AsPNG, ST_AsJPEG, and ST_AsTiff take optional arguments, such as compression and which band numbers to output, but the only required argument is the raster itself. To output the heatmap generated in figure 7.2 as a PNG, you'd run this query:

```
SELECT ST_AsPNG(rast) As png
FROM ch07.bag_o_rasters
WHERE rast_name = 'Raster 1 band heatmap';
```

7.3.2   *Output using ST_AsGDALRaster*

In addition to the aforementioned PNG, JPEG, and TIFF formats, PostGIS allows you to output rasters to any formats supported by your GDAL library. Keep in mind that GDAL supports many formats, and that GDAL is usually only compiled with a subset of the formats possible. You can use ST_GDALDrivers to determine your output options and ST_AsGDALRaster to output in one of those formats.

USING ST_GDALDRIVERS TO LIST RASTER TYPES AVAILABLE FOR OUTPUT

If the version of GDAL installed with PostGIS didn't compile with any additional libraries, you should still have over 20 formats available. To see a listing, use the ST_GDALDrivers function as follows:

```
SELECT short_name, long_name
FROM ST_GDALDrivers()
ORDER BY short_name;
```

The output of the query follows. Your output may vary depending on the drivers your GDAL library is compiled with and also the drivers you decide to allow:

```
short_name        | long_name
------------------+------------------------------------
AAIGrid           | Arc/Info ASCII Grid
DTED              | DTED Elevation Raster
EHdr              | ESRI .hdr Labelled
```

```
FIT                 | FIT Image
GIF                 | Graphics Interchange Format (.gif)
GSAG                | Golden Software ASCII Grid (.grd)
GSBG                | Golden Software Binary Grid (.grd)
GTiff               | GeoTIFF
:
PNG                 | Portable Network Graphics
R                   | R Object Data Store
:
USGSDEM             | USGS Optional ASCII DEM (and CDED)
:
(25 rows)
```

This list of output formats is a subset of what you'd get with raster2pgsql -G, which outputs the list of readable formats using raster2pgsql. GDAL can read more formats than it can output to.

If you find your list is much smaller than what we've listed, this may be because GDAL drivers are disabled by default, as we noted earlier in the chapter. See our previous note on security in section 7.2 for the details.

You may need to meet additional requirements in order to export. ST_GDALDrivers outputs a third column, create_options, that we didn't list in the previous output. This is an XML column detailing information that must be or can be included with your output to a certain format. The raw XML isn't all that easy to digest, but PostgreSQL has functions that will expand the tags to make the column easier to read. We demonstrate in the following code how to use the PostgreSQL built-in xpath function to extract subelements of an XML field, and how to use the PostgreSQL unnest function to expand an array of XML elements into separate rows. This is applied to the create_options column of the USGS Digital Elevation Model (USGSDEM) ST_GDALDrivers row:

```
SELECT
    (xpath('@name', g.opt))[1]::text As oname,
    (xpath('@type', g.opt))[1]::text As otype,
    (xpath('@description', g.opt))[1]::varchar(30) As descrip
FROM (
    SELECT
        unnest(
            xpath('/CreationOptionList/Option',create_options::xml)
        ) As opt
    FROM ST_GDALDrivers()
    WHERE short_name = 'USGSDEM'
) As g;
```

The preceding code truncates the description column to 30 characters with ::varchar(30) so that it can be easily displayed on the page. The output follows:

```
oname       |    otype      |        descrip
------------------+---------------+-------------------------------
 PRODUCT          | string-select | Specific Product Type
```

TOPLEFT	string	Top left product corner (ie. 1
RESAMPLE	string-select	Resampling kernel to use if re
TEMPLATE	string	File to default metadata from.
DEMLevelCode	int	DEM Level (1, 2 or 3 if set)
DataSpecVersion	int	Data and Specification version
PRODUCER	string	Producer Agency (up to 60 char
OriginCode	string	Origin code (up to 4 character
ProcessCode	string	Processing Code (8=ANUDEM, 9=F
ZRESOLUTION	float	Scaling factor for elevation v
NTS	string	NTS Mapsheet name, used to der
INTERNALNAME	string	Dataset name written into file

USING ST_AsGDALRASTER TO EXPORT RASTERS

Once you've decided on an output format and met its requirements, use ST_AsGDAL-Raster to perform the output, as demonstrated in the following listing.

> **Listing 7.7   Output a raster tile as a USGSDEM file**

```
SELECT
    ST_AsGDALRaster(ST_Band(rast,1), 'USGSDEM',
    ARRAY[
        'PRODUCER=' || quote_literal('postgis_in_action'),
        'INTERNALNAME=' || quote_literal(rast_name)
    ]) As dem
FROM ch07.bag_o_rasters
WHERE rast_name='Raster 1 band heatmap';
```

ST_AsGDALRaster takes three arguments: the band to output, the output raster format, and an array of optional or required information that GDAL needs to perform the output.

> **TIP**   PostgreSQL lets you include a query as an input to a function, so long as a single value is returned (a scalar query)—you must surround the scalar query with parentheses. If you needed to do something more complex in listing 7.7, such as building a raster from a set of rows from another table, you could replace the ST_Band(rast,1) with a correlated subquery, such as (SELECT ST_Union(ST_Band(rast,1)) FROM some_table WHERE ST_Intersects (some_table.rast, ch07.bag_o_rasters.rast)). This would return a single raster consisting of the union of raster tiles from another table for each row in ch07.bag_o_raster. This kind of query is referred to as a correlated subquery because what is returned is a function of the input values from ch07.bag_o _rasters. ST_Union is an aggregate function we'll cover in chapter 12; it takes a set of rasters and combines them into one raster.

7.3.3   *Using psql to export rasters*

In all the output discussion thus far, we've only shown you functions. Usually you have client applications or database connectors that will call these functions and perform the rendering or save the output to a file, as we've demonstrated in a couple of ad hoc web-based query tools:

- *Postgis_webviewer (PHP and ASP.NET)*—https://github.com/robe2/postgis_ webviewer
- *Node_postgis_express (NodeJS)*—https://github.com/robe2/node_postgis_express

These tools both output PostGIS-generated images when passed a spatial query from the web browser.

But what if you want to export to a raster file without using another application? Both PostgreSQL and its command-line tool psql have mechanisms for doing that. The easiest approach that works on even older versions of PostgreSQL is to use the "large object storage" mechanism and companion SQL functions and psql commands. The SQL functions are prefixed with lo_, while the psql commands are prefixed with \lo_. SQL functions run in the context of the server process, while psql commands run in the context of the system user who is using psql.

The idea is that you use one of the output functions to create a binary BLOB, store this BLOB temporarily in the large objects systems table, and then use psql or PostgreSQL to export the BLOB to a file. You would use PostgreSQL SQL functions for outputting if you wanted to export the file to a folder that the postgres service has access to (usually on the server) and if you have superuser rights. You would use psql if you wanted to export the images locally. By locally, we mean where you have psql running. If you are running psql from your server, the file can be output on the server or wherever the user account you are running psql from has access to. Using psql to output does not require superuser rights.

The following listing demonstrates how you can output the query from listing 7.7 to a file using psql.

Listing 7.8 Exporting a raster as a DEM file using psql

```
SELECT lo_from_bytea(0,                           ◁——————  Create the
       ST_AsGDALRaster(ST_Band(rast,1),                    large object.
          'USGSDEM',
          ARRAY[
              'PRODUCER=' || quote_literal('postgis_in_action'),
              'INTERNALNAME=' || quote_literal(rast_name)]
          ) -- <2>
       ) AS oid                                    ❶  Wrap the
    FROM ch07.bag_o_rasters                            raster query
       WHERE rast_name = 'Raster 1 band heatmap';       output.

\lo_export 79906 'C:/temp/heatmap.dem'    ◁——————  Use oid reference
                                                   returned from the raster
SELECT lo_unlink(79906);    ◁——  Delete the        query to output the file
                                large object
                                after export.
```

In listing 7.8 run each query one by one, and make sure you replace the 79906 number with what your query returns (❶). Run listing 7.8 in a psql client while connected to your database.

Psql creates a USGSDEM-formatted file on your local computer. To view the USGS-DEM file, fire up QGIS and choose Layer > Add Raster Layer from the menu.

If you are a superuser (or a user that is a member of the `pg_write_server_files` role), you can export all the rasters in the table to the server's filesystem with just SQL as follows.

Listing 7.9 Exporting all rasters as PNGs using server-side SQL

```
CREATE TEMP TABLE tmp_bag_oids AS
SELECT rid::text || '.png' AS file_name,              Create the
            lo_from_bytea(0,                           large object.
                ST_AsPNG(rast)     --                 Wrap the raster
            ) AS oid                                   query output.
    FROM ch07.bag_o_rasters;

SELECT lo_export(oid, '/tmp/' ||file_name)            Use oid to
    FROM tmp_bag_oids;                                output the file.

SELECT lo_unlink(oid)           Delete the large
FROM tmp_bag_oids;              object after export.

DROP TABLE tmp_bag_oids;        Drop the
                                temp table.
```

Listing 7.9 exports the whole table of rasters as PNG images to the server's filesystem. Note that the steps in listing 7.9 are very similar to those in listing 7.8, except we are using the SQL function `lo_export`, which allows us to run within a single SQL query. Within an SQL query, it executes for each row of the query. The comparable `\lo_export` command of psql is a command and not a function, so you have to create an SQL statement for each row of your table.

You'll find additional documentation for using psql, as well as information on interfacing with various programming languages, such as PL/Python, PHP, Java, and .NET, in the PostGIS documentation: "Outputting Rasters with PSQL" (http://postgis.net/docs/using_raster_dataman.html#RasterOutput_PSQL).

Even though raster output functions only accept rasters as input, you don't need to have rasters to take advantage of them. All you need is an expression that resolves to a PostGIS raster. For example, if you created geometries that you would like to output to JPEG, use `ST_AsRaster` to convert the geometry to a raster, and then use the `ST_AsJPEG` function. There's no need to create `raster` type columns.

7.4 *Raster accessors and setters*

Rasters have many intrinsic attributes, such as width, height, scale, skew, and SRID, which you can read using raster accessor functions. You'll often constrain these attributes using table constraints, and the table constraints are built using the raster accessor functions. For example, if you're using a table to store high-resolution pictures tiled to rasters of 100 × 100 per row, you'd add check constraints to the table specifying that the width and height must be 100 and use the `ST_Width` and `ST_Height` raster functions to get the values of these attributes for each raster.

7.4.1   *Basic raster metadata properties*

The bag_o_rasters table defies constraints for the most part because it's a hodgepodge of unrelated rasters. But you can still retrieve attributes by calling the relevant raster accessor functions. We'll first cover accessor functions that return measurement and positional properties.

RASTER ACCESSOR FUNCTIONS: ST_WIDTH, ST_HEIGHT, ST_PIXELWIDTH, AND ST_PIXELHEIGHT

The next listing shows some raster metadata and band metadata functions.

Listing 7.10   Show raster meta data

```
SELECT
    rid As r, rast_name,
    ST_Width(rast) As w,
    ST_Height(rast) As h,
    round(ST_PixelWidth(rast)::numeric,4) AS pw,
    round(ST_PixelHeight(rast)::numeric,4) As ph,
    ST_SRID(rast) AS srid,
    ST_BandPixelType(rast,1) AS bt
FROM ch07.bag_o_rasters;
```

The preceding query outputs the width, height, pixel width, pixel height, SRID, and band type of the first band for each raster in the bag_o_rasters table. The output follows:

```
r |       rast_name       |  w  |  h  |   pw   |   ph   |  srid  |  bt
--+----------------------+-----+-----+--------+--------+-------+-----
1 | disprop road         |  50 | 500 | 2.3791 | 0.6179 | 32631 | 8BUI
2 | proport fixed w road | 200 | 519 | 0.5948 | 0.5953 | 32631 | 8BUI
3 | Reo                  | 600 | 878 | 1.0000 | 1.0000 |     0 | 8BUI
4 | canvas aligned road  |  60 | 155 | 2.0000 | 2.0000 | 32631 | 8BUI
5 | Raster 1 band scratch | 500 | 500 | 2.0000 | 2.0000 | 32631 | 8BUI
6 | Raster 1 band heatmap | 500 | 500 | 2.0000 | 2.0000 | 32631 | 8BUI
7 | Reo  1 band crop     | 150 | 150 | 1.0000 | 1.0000 |     0 | 8BUI
8 | Reo band shuffle     | 600 | 878 | 1.0000 | 1.0000 |     0 | 8BUI
```

ST_METADATA AND ST_BANDMETADATA

If you'd like to retrieve multiple properties all at once, make a call to the ST_MetaData or ST_BandMetaData function. These two functions spit out all the properties as a composite object. The ST_MetaData function outputs properties of the raster, such as the width and height, whereas ST_BandMetaData outputs properties for a raster band, such as the band pixel type and nodata value.

The following query demonstrates the use of these functions.

Listing 7.11   Show raster band metadata

```
SELECT rid As r, (rm).upperleftx As ux, (rm).numbands As nb, (rbm).*
FROM (
    SELECT
        rid,
```

```
        ST_MetaData(rast) As rm,
        ST_BandMetaData(rast,1) As rbm
FROM ch07.bag_o_rasters) As r;
```

The output is shown next:

```
r|        ux    | nb | pixeltype |nodatavalue|isoutdb|     path
--+-------------+----+-----------+-----------+-------+-------------
1 | 448242.02.. |  1 | 8BUI      |          0| f     |
2 | 448242.02.. |  1 | 8BUI      |          0| f     |
3 |           0 |  4 | 8BUI      |           | t     | ..ge_tall.png
4 |      448242 |  1 | 8BUI      |          0| f     |
5 |      445000 |  1 | 8BUI      |          0| f     |
6 |      445000 |  1 | 8BUI      |          0| f     |
7 |         225 |  1 | 8BUI      |        255| f     |
8 |           0 |  3 | 8BUI      |           | t     | ..ge_tall.png
```

In the preceding query you output only select properties returned by the ST_Meta-
Data function. All properties of the first band of each raster are returned by ST_Band-
MetaData.

7.4.2   *Pixel statistics*

In addition to supplying functions for obtaining metadata at the raster and band levels, PostGIS provides several functions for getting stats about the composition of the
pixels and pixel values within a band. These functions return descriptive statistics that
can aid you in making decisions about how to crop or reclass rasters.

   The functions in this category are ST_Count, ST_CountAgg, ST_Histogram,
ST_Quantile, ST_SummaryStats, ST_SummaryStats, ST_SummaryStatsAgg, and
ST_ValueCount. By default, all these functions will ignore pixel values with no data.
The versions that end in Agg are exactly like their non-Agg siblings, except they
work with a set of raster rows. Use these versions if you want to do stats across a set of
rows using GROUP BY. Since all aggregates in PostgreSQL serve a secondary function
as window aggregates, you can use them in WINDOW constructs as well, which we cover
in appendix C.

   In this section we'll demonstrate the use of ST_Histogram and ST_SummaryStats.
The other functions work in the same way as these two but return a table with different columns. Examples of these functions are in the "Raster Band Statistics and Ana-
lytics" section of the PostGIS Manual (http://postgis.net/docs/RT_reference.html#
RasterBand_Stats).

ST_HISTOGRAM

ST_Histogram provides summary statistics across the pixel values in a given band. You
can ask the function to partition the values into buckets by specifying the number of
total buckets or by providing the percentage of pixels you'd like to consider for each
bucket. Keep in mind that the locations of the pixels don't factor into the histogram;
only their values do.

In the following query, you ask `ST_Histogram` to partition the pixel data into six buckets. The second argument is the band number. Although it's not demonstrated in this example, you can vary the size of the buckets by passing in a numeric array:

```
SELECT (stats).*
FROM (
    SELECT ST_Histogram(rast,2,6) As stats
    FROM ch07.bag_o_rasters
    WHERE rast_name = 'Reo'
) As foo;
```

The output follows:

```
min              |      max          | count  |     percent
-----------------+-------------------+--------+--------------------
              29 | 66.6666666666667  |   9433 | 0.0179062262718299
66.6666666666667 | 104.333333333333  |  10126 | 0.0192217160212604
104.333333333333 |              142  |  15964 | 0.0303037205770691
             142 | 179.666666666667  |  43079 | 0.0817748671222475
179.666666666667 | 217.333333333333  |  19205 | 0.036455960516325
217.333333333333 |              255  | 428993 | 0.814337509491268
(6 rows)
```

The query returned a histogram for band 2 of the Reo raster, broken into six buckets. As a result, the preceding output returns six rows corresponding to each bucket of a specific band in a raster, and each row gives the minimum, maximum, count of pixels that have values in this range, and percentage count for that bucket, with respect to the count of all pixels in that band.

ST_SUMMARYSTATS

`ST_SummaryStats` provides summary statistics for a single band or for the entire raster. In the following query, you ask for summary statistics from the second band. If you omit the band number, `ST_SummaryStats` will cover only pixel values in the first band:

```
SELECT (stats).*
FROM (
    SELECT ST_SummaryStats(rast,2) As stats
    FROM ch07.bag_o_rasters
    WHERE rast_name = 'Reo'
) As foo;
```

The summary statistics follow:

```
count  |    sum    |      mean         |       stddev       | min | max
-------+-----------+------------------+-------------------+-----+----
526800 | 119211159 | 226.293012528474 | 43.0372444228884  |  29 | 255
```

Summary statistics do just what it sounds like—they summarize—but at a certain point you may need to drill down to the pixel level. PostGIS has several accessors for pixels.

Some will pinpoint specific pixels, and some will consider a particular region sectioned off using a geometry. We'll look at these next.

7.4.3 *Pixel value accessors*

There are several functions that return pixel values. Some of the more popular ones are ST_Value, ST_DumpValues, and ST_DumpAsPolygons.

ST_VALUE

ST_Value returns a single pixel value at a geometric point or raster row/column location. It's often used with elevation data to return the elevation at a particular location of interest.

ST_DUMPVALUES

ST_DumpValues returns a band as a 2D array, where the location in the array corresponds to the raster column/row and the values are the pixel values. The function can also handle multiple bands by returning a set of composites, where each record consists of the band number and the 2D array of pixel values. Some computational environments, such as R, work best with arrays.

ST_DUMPASPOLYGONS

The functions that return geometry pixel-value combos use a special type called a geomval. You saw this type in use in listing 7.5, where you created an array of geomvals that was used to set pixels in a raster.

The ST_DumpAsPolygons function takes as input a raster and outputs a set of geomvals. The geom part of each geomval is a polygon geometry formed when you union all the pixels of a given pixel value.

ST_DumpAsPolygons is often used to render a raster in GIS software that can only handle geometry data, such as OpenJUMP. The corresponding value field of the geomval is then used for coloring the polygon.

This next query dumps the raster created in listing 7.5 along with the accompanying area of the corresponding polygons as a set of geomvals:

```
WITH X AS (
    SELECT ST_DumpAsPolygons(rast) As gv
    FROM ch07.bag_o_rasters
    WHERE rast_name = 'Raster 1 band heatmap'
)
SELECT
    ST_AsText((gv).geom)::varchar(30) AS wkt,
    ST_Area((gv).geom) As area,
    (gv).val
FROM X;
```

The textual output of the query follows:

```
wkt                             |  area  | val
--------------------------------+--------+-----
 POLYGON((445018 5414962,445018 |      4 | 146
```

```
POLYGON((445410 5415000,445410 |  85992 | 110
POLYGON((445400 5414922,445400 |  46208 |  95
POLYGON((445290 5414720,445290 |  28884 |  80
POLYGON((445140 5414510,445140 |   7840 |  65
POLYGON((445000 5415000,445000 | 831072 | 255
```

Note how most of the dump consists of a large area with a value of 255, corresponding to the large white space of the raster.

We'll demonstrate another function that returns a geomval set, ST_Intersection, in chapter 12. ST_Intersection works much like ST_DumpAsPolygons except that it first filters the raster by a geometry before dumping the results. ST_Intersection, unlike ST_DumpAsPolygons, can return any kind of geometry for the geom portion of the geomvals.

In this section you learned how to access the properties of a raster. In the next section you'll learn how to set raster properties directly or change them indirectly via raster processing functions.

7.4.4 *Band metadata setters*

You can set raster bands with a value that indicates they have no data value. We'll look at two related functions in this section: ST_SetBandNoDataValue and ST_SetBandIsNoData.

ST_SetBandNoDataValue

For a given band, ST_SetBandNoDataValue sets the value that represents no data (http://postgis.net/docs/RT_ST_SetBandNoDataValue.html). Remember that all pixels in a raster must have a non-NULL value, so you need to specify a non-NULL value to represent "no data." If you want to remove the ability to specify a no-data value, set the no-data value to NULL. This means that no value can be the no-data value, and your raster will never have a no-data value. Again, the no-data value is not NULL—all pixels must have a numeric value.

In the following example, you set the pixel value of 255 to represent no data. This means that for most operations, the 255 values will be ignored:

```
UPDATE ch07.bag_o_rasters
SET rast = ST_SetBandNoDataValue(rast,1,255)
WHERE rast_name = 'Raster 1 band heatmap';
```

This function is often used in conjunction with ST_Reclass when you need to map more than one value as no data. Using ST_Reclass allows you to set a range of values to the same values. Following that with ST_SetBandNoDataValue will mark them as no data.

ST_SetBandIsNoData

ST_SetBandIsNoData stamps the entire band as containing no useful data. You may find this function useful when working with raster coverages. Suppose that you imported a single-band raster of elevation on a Pacific atoll, which you tiled into 100 rows (100 rasters in their own right). Some 50 rows are ocean and have no analytical interest, but much third-party software expects your coverage to be rectangular. No tiles can be missing. To prevent PostGIS from considering the oceanic tiles when using processing functions, set their band to no data.

A similar situation exists when you import a multi-band raster but have no need for the data in some of the bands. You can set entire bands to "no data."

This function is also useful when you're creating a template raster to accept data. The template may not have all bands populated at once. For example, if you have a ten-year study of the height of glaciers, you may start with one raster for each glacier that you'll be tracking, and prepopulate them with ten bands of no-data value. As your decade-long measurement progresses, you can still write queries that encompass the entire ten bands, but PostGIS will automatically gloss over the bands with no data.

7.5 *Georeferencing functions*

You can't change all the properties of a raster once it's created. For example, you can reset the upper-left coordinate of a raster, or which pixel value of a band should be considered as representing no data, but you can't outright change the width and height of a raster.

In the following sections we'll cover some of the properties that you can update using setters. Then we'll look at processing functions that drill down to the pixel level, allowing you to make more fundamental changes to rasters, such as raster width and height.

7.5.1 *Metadata setters*

Raster data has an origin that starts at the upper-left, so pixels have positive X and negative Y values. Spatial coordinates, on the other hand, usually have an origin starting at the lower-left, making for both positive X and Y values.

> **World file**
>
> A world file is a metadata sister file that lists the six numbers necessary to locate a rotated (or unrotated) raster in its reference system: four numbers for the size and shape of the pixels, and two numbers to specify the upper-left corner of the raster.
>
> For some kinds of raster formats, this metadata is embedded directly in the file rather than as a separate text file. If no information is provided, raster2pgsql guesses at the X and Y pixel scale sizes and direction.

In this section we'll explore the georeferencing functions used to set the orientation and sizing of the pixels relative to spatial coordinates. You'll find a complete listing of these functions in the "Raster Editors" section of the PostGIS official reference manual (http://postgis.net/docs/RT_reference.html#Raster_Editors).

ST_SETGEOREFERENCE

ST_SetGeoReference sets the basic six georeferencing numbers in one statement. This includes scale X, skew Y, skew X, scale Y, and upper-left corner X and Y coordinates, in that order. For example, ST_SetGeoReference(rast, '10 0 0 -10 446139 2440440') would set the rast PostGIS raster object to have 1 pixel width represent 10 spatial units, 1 pixel height represent –10 spatial units, and no skew, and it would set the upper-left corner to be X 446139 and Y 2440440. If your spatial units are meters, then 1 pixel would be 10 meters wide.

ST_SETSRID

ST_SetSRID sets the spatial coordinate system that the raster uses. The upper-left corner coordinates and pixel sizes should be expressed in coordinates and units of this system.

This function is used either when you didn't set the SRID during loading, or you discovered the SRIDs of the rasters were mislabeled. Don't confuse this with ST_Transform, which also changes the SRID but reprojects all the pixels from one known spatial reference system to another known spatial reference system. ST_SetSRID does not reproject!

ST_SETUPPERLEFT

ST_SetUpperLeft sets the X and Y coordinates of the upper-left corner of the raster to coordinates in the SRID.

ST_SETSCALE

ST_SetScale sets the pixel width and height in units of the coordinate reference system. It specifies the number of units of spatial coordinate width and height that are represented by each pixel. There are two versions of this function. One takes separate X and Y values to set the ratios differently, and one takes a single XY value to set the ratios the same.

This function just changes the metadata and doesn't actually make changes to the pixels. A related function, ST_Rescale, is a processing function that changes the underlying pixels of a raster from one known scale ratio to another algorithmically.

ST_SETSKEW

ST_SetSkew sets the georeference X and Y skew (the rotation parameter). If only one coordinate is passed in, the X and Y skew will both take on the same value. The skew of 0 generally works fine for most rasters, but you may need to change this if your raster coordinate axis deviates from your spatial reference coordinate axes. Needing to account for magnetic deviation comes to mind.

This function just changes the metadata and doesn't touch the pixels. A related function, ST_ReSkew, is a processing function that changes the underlying pixels of a raster from one known skew ratio to another algorithmically.

GEOREFERENCING EXAMPLE

The next example demonstrates georeferencing a non-georeferenced raster by setting upper-left, upper-right, skew, scale, and SRID values in a single statement:

```
UPDATE ch07.bag_o_rasters
SET rast = ST_SetSRID(
    ST_SetGeoReference(rast, '1 0 0 -1 445139 5415000'),32631
)
WHERE rast_name = 'Reo 1 band crop';
```

> **TIP** Although the system will let you, do not attempt to set georeferencing properties of out-of-db rasters, aside from the SRID. This causes positioning issues with functions like ST_Transform and ST_Rescale.

7.5.2 *Processing functions*

Sometimes, changing only the metadata of a raster is insufficient, and the underlying pixels must be visited. We'll describe the most common of these functions in this section.

All these functions employ a resampling algorithm that dictates how pixels will be transformed to arrive at the new georeferenced state. The default algorithm used by all of these functions is called *nearest neighbor* (NN). NN is fast, but it often leads to less faithful transformations compared to other algorithms, such as bilinear, cubic, cubic spline, or Lanczos. The resampling algorithm is passed in as an optional argument in each of the functions. For example, ST_Transform(rast, 4326, 'Cubic') would change the algorithm to Cubic.

ST_TRANSFORM

ST_Transform changes the spatial coordinate system by projecting all the pixels from one known spatial reference system to another. It does for raster exactly what the geometry ST_Transform sibling does for geometry.

ST_RESCALE

ST_Rescale is the companion of ST_SetScale. It changes the pixel size of a raster, but does so by visiting every pixel and either reduces or increases the number of pixels. As a result, this function affects both pixel scale as well as the raster width and height (the number of pixels per column and pixels per row). This function will only work with rasters that have a known SRID.

ST_RESAMPLE

ST_Resample is similar to ST_Rescale, but instead of giving it a target pixel size, you supply the overall target raster width and height.

ST_RESIZE

ST_Resize allows you to set the width and height to a fixed number or a percentage of the original. It doesn't need a raster with a known SRID. Like the ST_Rescale function, it changes not only the width and height but also the pixel scaling to ensure that the new raster occupies the same geometric space as the old raster.

RASTER PROCESSING EXAMPLE

The following listing demonstrates all the aforementioned functions.

Listing 7.12   Effects of various georeference processing operations

```
WITH
    r As (
    SELECT rast
    FROM ch07.bag_o_rasters
    WHERE rast_name = 'canvas aligned road'
),
    r2 AS (
    SELECT 'orig' As op, ST_MetaData(rast) As rm FROM r
    UNION ALL
    SELECT 'resamp' AS op,
        ST_MetaData(ST_Resample(rast,300,300)) As rm FROM r
    UNION ALL
    SELECT 'tform' AS op,
        ST_MetaData(ST_Transform(rast,4326)) As rm FROM r
    UNION ALL
    SELECT 'resize' AS op,
        ST_MetaData(ST_Resize(rast,0.5,0.5)) As rm FROM r
    UNION ALL
    SELECT 'rescale' AS op,
        ST_MetaData(ST_Rescale(rast,0.5,-0.5)) As rm FROM r
)
SELECT
    op,
    (rm).srid,
    (rm).width::text || 'x' || (rm).height::Text as wh,
    (rm).scalex::numeric(7,5)::text || ',' ||
    (rm).scaley::numeric(7,5)::text as sxy,
    (rm).upperleftx::numeric(11,2)::text || ',' ||
    (rm).upperlefty::numeric(12,2)::text As uplxy
FROM r2;
```

❶ Resample to 300 × 300 pixels.

❷ Transform to lon/lat.

❸ Resize to 50%.

❹ Rescale to 0.5 and –0.5 meters per pixel.

The output of listing 7.12 follows:

```
op      | srid  |   wh    |      sxy          |        uplxy
--------+-------+---------+-------------------+---------------------
orig    | 32631 | 60x155  | 2.00000,-2.00000  | 448242.00,5414506.00
resamp  | 32631 | 300x300 | 0.40000,-1.03333  | 448242.00,5414506.00
tform   |  4326 | 86x143  | 0.00002,-0.00002  | 2.29,48.88
resize  | 32631 | 30x78   | 4.00000,-3.97436  | 448242.00,5414506.00
rescale | 32631 | 240x620 | 0.50000,-0.50000  | 448242.00,5414506.00
```

In listing 7.12 you pass the raster you created in listing 7.2 through various processing functions.

First, you resample, forcing the raster width and height to be 300 × 300 **❶**. To compensate, pixel scaling goes from 2 meters to 0.40000 meters in the X direction, and 2 meters to –1.03333 meters in the Y direction.

Then you transform the raster to lon/lat projection, which causes the upper-left corner to show longitude and latitude ❷. Both the scaling and the width and height change as well.

Then you resize to 50% of the original for both width and height ❸. Because scaling doesn't change, each pixel takes up twice the coordinate space—approximately 4 meters instead of the original 2.

Finally, you rescale the raster so that each pixel represents 0.5 meters by –0.5 meters of coordinate space ❹. Because each pixel now represents less space, the overall dimensions of the raster enlarge four times in both X and Y directions to compensate.

7.6   *Reclassing functions*

ST_Reclass and its more general cousin ST_MapAlgebra are powerful functions that work at the pixel level. You can use these functions for the following purposes:

- Changing a band type by mapping a band of floating-point numbers to integer values, or vice versa.
- Identifying and classifying pixel values as having no data.
- Remapping numerically close pixel values or neighboring pixels to a single value for easier vectorization. For example, you may want all pixel values from 0 to 10 to be treated as 0 and all values from 50 to 60 to be treated as 1. To smooth out spotty areas where values change because of instrumentation noise, you may want all pixels to take on the value of the average of all neighboring pixels.
- Interlacing your raster by reducing the number of overall pixels.

Although the ST_Reclass functionality is a subset of what you can do using ST_MapAlgebra, the ST_Reclass syntax is generally easier syntax-wise and faster than map algebra functions.

In the following listing, you use the histogram statistics from section 7.4.2 to isolate the boundary of Reo. The result is shown in figure 7.5.

Listing 7.13   Creating a simplified raster using reclassification

```
INSERT INTO ch07.bag_o_rasters(rast_name, rast)      Form a new
SELECT                                                raster with just
    'Reo 1 banded band 2 reclass',                    the second band.
    ST_Reclass(
        ST_Band(rast,2),          ◁                   Reclass band 1 of
        1,                        ◁                    the new raster.
        '[0-66]:0, (66-255]:255'::text , '8BUI'::text,   ◁   Values > 66 and
        255            ◁                                     <= 255 are set to
)                      Define 255                           255, and others
FROM ch07.bag_o_rasters    as no data.                      are set to 0.
WHERE rast_name = 'Reo';
```

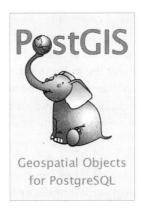

Figure 7.5 `ST_Reclass`: **band 2 before and after reclassification**

`ST_Reclass` will always return the full raster with the specified bands reclassified. You may want to use `ST_Band` to limit the input raster, as in the preceding example, if you don't want the full raster back.

We'll leave the thorough treatment of `ST_MapAlgebra` for chapter 12.

7.7 Polygonizing functions

Polygonizing is the conversion of rasters to polygons. The simplest polygonizing functions take an entire raster, a band, or a set of bands as input and then return a single polygon.

In this section we'll go over the functions that take a raster as input or a raster and raster band(s) and return a single geometry. In chapter 12 we'll explore more advanced polygonizing functions that will return multiple polygons or `geomvals`.

7.7.1 ST_ConvexHull

`ST_ConvexHull` returns the convex hull of a raster, including pixels with no data. `ST_ConvexHull` is fast—only `ST_Envelope` is faster. PostGIS internally uses this function to cast from `raster` to `geometry` and to build spatial indexes.

`ST_ConvexHull` observes the skew of the raster. For non-skewed rasters, the hull will always be a rectangle. For skewed rasters, the hull will be a parallelogram.

7.7.2 ST_Envelope

`ST_Envelope` is similar to `ST_ConvexHull`, but it always returns the minimum bounding rectangle and therefore is slightly faster. If your raster has a skew, `ST_Envelope` returns the rectangle that bounds the parallelogram.

7.7.3 ST_Polygon

`ST_Polygon` will create a polygon or multipolygon by unioning all the geometric representations of the pixels.

`ST_Polygon`, when used in conjunction with `ST_Reclass`, is indispensable for image recognition. Consider the following scenario: A volcano erupts in Iceland, sending a plume of ash into the stratosphere. A satellite produces a raster image of the dust against the backdrop of the earth below. With this raster, you first use reclassing to pick out the ash-colored pixels, setting all others to no data. You then use ST_Polygon to cast the smoke plume to a polygon. Then you can intersect the polygon with the line-strings of the North Atlantic tracks to figure out which airline routes will be affected.

To be more precise, you could use multiple satellites to create multiband rasters—one band for each 5,000 feet. You can pass specific bands or entire rasters to ST_Polygon.

7.7.4   *ST_MinConvexHull*

ST_MinConvexHull returns the same answer as ST_ConvexHull but removes nodata pixels from the edge inward. nodata pixels completely surrounded by data pixels have no chance of being excluded.

You'll find this function useful for removing pesky padding added to a raster to make it fill a given pixel width or height requirement. Think of old Polaroid photos with their uneven white frame that served no purpose.

The following query shows the difference between ST_ConvexHull and ST_Min-ConvexHull:

```
SELECT
    rast_name::varchar(10),
    ST_AsText(ST_ConvexHull(rast)) As hull,
    ST_AsText(ST_MinConvexHull(rast)) As minhull
FROM ch07.bag_o_rasters
WHERE rast_name IN('Reo','Reo 1 banded band 2 reclass');
```

The output of this listing follows:

```
rast_name | hull                  | minhull
----------+-----------------------+--------------------------
Reo       | POLYGON((0 0,600 0,   | POLYGON((0 0,600 0,
          | 600 -878,0 -878,0 0)) | 600 -878,0 -878,0 0))
Reo 1 ban | POLYGON((0 0,600 0,   | POLYGON((75 -104,490 -104,
          | 600 -878,0 -878,0 0)) | 490 -626,75 -626,75 -104))
```

Notice that although both rasters have the same convex hull, the minimum convex hull of the raster occupies a smaller area because pixels with no data on the edges were removed.

When ST_MinConvexHull is used without a band number, it will consider all bands, only considering a pixel as having no data if all of the band values in that pixel have the nodata value. When applied to a specific band, ST_MinConvexHull will only inspect that specific band and consider that pixel as having no data if the pixel value of the band is the nodata value. ST_ConvexHull always applies to all bands because it never checks pixel values.

Summary

- PostGIS has many functions that output rasters in various formats useful for data interoperability.
- PostGIS has many functions for analyzing rasters at the pixel level and georeference location.
- PostGIS has functions that allow you to convert between raster and geometry.
- You can load raster data from various formats using built-in raster functions and the packaged raster2pgsql command-line tool.

Spatial relationships

This chapter covers

- Bounding boxes
- Intersections
- Relationships
- The meaning of equality
- The Dimensionally Extended 9-Intersection Matrix (DE-9IM)

As the old saying goes, "No man is an island," and the same holds true for spatial objects. In prior chapters we described geometries and rasters in isolation. Going forward, we'll no longer entertain ourselves with one geometry at a time or one raster at a time. The richness and power of spatial queries come to light when you start working with more than a singleton.

If we liken spatial objects to tables, an SQL query that queries a single table can only go so far. It's when you have join operations at your disposal that things become interesting. Mastering join operations is what separates the casual database user from the serious database analyst. Spatial databases have a similar jumping-off point: the casual consumer of a spatial database may use PostGIS to store geometry data or to filter geometries befitting certain conditions. The serious spatial database analyst will be able to write queries that join and morph multiple geometries and rasters to solve seemingly intractable problems with brisk elegance.

But as another old saying goes, "No pain, no gain." Working with more than one geometry or raster introduces a new level of conceptual challenges. In non-spatial databases, disparate data interacts through mathematical or string operations. When one number meets another number, you can add, subtract, divide, multiply, or some combination thereof. When one string meets another, you can splice them together or use one to substring the other. In spatial databases, however, when one geometry meets another or one raster meets another, things heat up quite a bit. Things heat up even more when one raster meets a geometry. PostGIS offers many ways to consummate their mutual courting, and this chapter explores the most common choices. We'll describe each type of relationship separately, but you should keep in mind that the full analytical power of spatial SQL usually entails disparate relationship functions, operators, and processing functions being applied in unison.

We'll start our discussion with the soul of every geometry, geography, and raster—the bounding box.

8.1 Bounding box and geometry comparators

Every geometry and raster has a *bounding box*, the smallest rectangular box with edges parallel to the axes of the coordinate plane that completely encloses the object. Every geography has a bounding box as well, but its bounding box is in 3D space, so a bit beyond the scope of this discussion. Just know that a geography bounding box exists, and it too is the soul of the geography, but it's a different kind of soul than the simple rectangular type that geometry and raster share. What makes PostGIS relationship queries really fast are the box-based comparisons embedded in most of them. Instead of having to compare object to object, comparing bounding boxes often suffices and produces an answer much more quickly.

Rasters and geographies have bounding boxes? Really?

Although most of our discussion in this chapter will be focused on 2D geometries, keep in mind that rasters have an outer shell that is a 2D geometry, and that outer shell has a bounding box as well. The fact that both rasters and geometries have the same kind of bounding boxes allows them to be compared to each other using spatial relationship functions. 3D geometries have both a 2D bounding box and a 3D bounding box.

Geographies also have bounding boxes, but they have a kind of 3D bounding box. You should never relate a geometry to a geography type using a spatial relationship function without first casting one to geometry or the other to geography.

8.1.1   The bounding box

Let's demonstrate bounding boxes with a quick example. Suppose you have two multi-polygons, one representing the state of Washington and one representing the state of Florida, and you wish to know if Washington is strictly northwest of Florida. If the bounding box of Washington is strictly above and to the left of Florida, then you'll know with certainty that the geometries must share the same relationship as well. The bounding box methodology shortcuts the point-by-point checking by first drawing rectangular boxes around each state and then asking if the box enclosing Washington is above and to the left of the box enclosing Florida. You'll obtain the answer almost instantly.

Furthermore, because a rectangular box is completely specified by the coordinates of the two opposing corners, you can precalculate all of the bounding boxes for geometries in your table and store their coordinates in indexes. Once you have the bounding box of every geometry indexed, comparing any two geometries becomes a simple task of comparing two pairs of numbers.

Bounding boxes are so fundamental to spatial queries that PostGIS always computes them when a geometry changes and stores the bounding box as part of the geometry. But to make full use of bounding boxes, you'll still need to define spatial indexes.

As useful as bounding boxes are, there will be many instances when they won't do you much good. Suppose you want to know if the centroid of Washington state is to the left of the centroid of Oregon; you can't shortcut yourself to an answer by simply looking at the bounding boxes of the two states. In short, bounding boxes are useful as prechecks for more expensive spatial relationship checks and also as general rule-of-thumb tests.

The following listing contains examples of geometries with their bounding boxes.

Listing 8.1   Generating various geometries and their bounding boxes

```
SELECT ex_name, Box2D(geom) As bbox2d , geom
FROM (
VALUES
    ('A line', ST_GeomFromEWKT('LINESTRING (0 0, 1 1)')),
    ('A multipoint', ST_GeomFromText('MULTIPOINT (4.4 4.75, 5 5)')),
    ('A square', ST_GeomFromText('POLYGON ((0 0, 0 1, 1 1, 1 0, 0 0))'))
)
AS x(ex_name, geom);
```

Figure 8.1 illustrates the output of listing 8.1, showing the geometries encased in their bounding boxes.

In the next section we'll cover operators that work on the bounding boxes of geometries.

 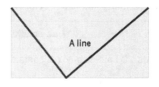

Figure 8.1   Various geometries and their bounding boxes

8.1.2   *Bounding box comparators*

PostGIS has always offered geometry bounding-box comparators for 2D geometries, and PostGIS 2.0 added comparators for 3D geometries. Some, but not all, of these comparators have counterparts that examine the entire geometry.

PostGIS uses symbols for comparators. For example, A && B returns true if the 2D bounding box of A intersects the 2D bounding box of B, or vice versa. The double ampersand symbol (&&) is the *intersects* comparator. Behind the scenes, PostGIS first checks for a bounding box intersection for many relationship functions such as ST_Intersects and ST_DWithin. If the bounding boxes fail to intersect, PostGIS can return an answer immediately.

For 3D geometries, the && comparator will compare the 2D footprints. For true 3D bounding-box intersection, you can use the &&& operator.

Table 8.1 lists the comparators for geometry and raster and the kinds of indexes they use, if available. A "(g)" in the Comparator column means the operator only exists for geometry and not raster. Geometry, raster, and geography columns almost always use a gist index. If a geometry doesn't have many points (for example, a single point, short linestring, or small polygon), you could use a B-tree. Keep in mind that you can have both a gist and a B-tree index on the same geometry column.

Table 8.1   PostGIS geometry and raster comparators

Comparator	True condition	Index
&&	If A's 2D bounding box intersects B's 2D bounding box	gist, spgist, BRIN
&&& (g)	If A's 3D bounding box intersects B's 3D bounding box	gist (geometry_ops_nd)
&<	If A's 2D bounding box overlaps or is to the left of B's	gist, spgist
&<|	If A's 2D bounding box overlaps or is below B's	gist, spgist
&>	If A's 2D bounding box overlaps or is to the right of B's	gist, spgist
<<	If A's 2D bounding box is strictly to the left of B's	gist, spgist
<<|	If A's 2D bounding box is strictly below B's	gist, spgist
=	**Pre-PostGIS 2.4** A's 2D bounding box is the same as B's; **PostGIS 2.4+** True geometry equality	B-tree
>>	If A's 2D bounding box is strictly to the right of B's	gist

Table 8.1   PostGIS geometry and raster comparators *(continued)*

Comparator	True condition	Index
@	If A's 2D bounding box is contained by B's	gist, BRIN
|&>	If A's 2D bounding box overlaps or is above B's	gist
|>>	If A's 2D bounding box is strictly above B's	gist, spgist
~-	If A's 2D bounding box contains B's	gist
~=	If A's 2D bounding box is the same as B's	gist, spgist
~	If A's 2D bounding box completely contains B's	gist, spgist

Since PostGIS 2.2, `geometry` also supports the space-partitioned generalized search tree (`spgist`) type of index. PostGIS 2.3 introduced block range indexes (BRIN) and companion operators. BRIN indexes are mostly used for large point data sets. We'll go over those in a later chapter on performance.

8.2   Relating two geometries

Two geometries intersect when they have points in common, but sometimes you need to know more than just whether they intersect. Sometimes you need more detail about the points in common, the points not in common, and the points on the boundary. PostGIS has a bevy of functions that describe how two geometries intersect or don't intersect. These functions count on both geometries having the same SRID and assume both are valid. Never trust the output if your inputs contain invalid geometries.

8.2.1   Interior, exterior, and boundary of a geometry

2D intersection functions rely on the geometry concepts of interior, exterior, and boundary:

- *Interior*—The space inside a geometry and not on the boundary
- *Exterior*—The space outside a geometry and not on the boundary
- *Boundary*—The space that's neither interior nor exterior

Any point on a plane with a geometry must be interior, on the boundary, or exterior. It can't be in two places at once. This should be intuitive for polygons. For open linestrings, the boundary is the endpoints. For closed linestrings and points, the boundary is nonexistent and in PostGIS is represented as some form of an empty geometry. For points it's a GEOMETRYCOLLECTION EMPTY and for closed linestrings it's a MULTIPOINT EMPTY. When in doubt, use the ST_Boundary function to check the boundary geometry.

What's an empty geometry?

An empty geometry is a geometry with no points within it. It's not the same as a database NULL!

You can create an empty geometry with this command: SELECT ST_GeomFromText ('GEOMETRY EMPTY');.

If you're not completely satisfied with the idea of an empty geometry, and you wish to engage in deep philosophical discussions, you can entertain yourself with POLYGON EMPTY, POINT EMPTY, MULTIPOINT EMPTY and other kinds of emptiness. Since Post-GIS 2, PostGIS has embraced the world of emptiness, and you'll find that all kinds of different empty geometries appear when you try to ask for the intersection of non-intersecting geometries.

Here's a Zen-like question for you: If a point and a polygon fail to intersect, is the intersection an empty point, an empty polygon, or Mysterion?

During an intersection operation, PostGIS creates a pairing between interior, boundary, and exterior between the two geometries and examines each pairing separately. For example, it'll check to see if the interior of one intersects the interior of the other, then if the interior intersects the boundary, then if the interior intersects the exterior, and so on, for a total of nine pair-wise checks. The result of an intersection of these nine pairs can be non-dimensional (no intersection), zero-dimensional (punctal), one-dimensional (lineal), two-dimensional (areal), or a combination thereof in the case of collection geometries.

Again, be sure that your input geometries are valid. The concepts of interior, exterior, and boundary completely fall apart otherwise.

8.2.2 *Intersections*

The idea of *intersection* encompasses a wide range of ways in which geometries can have points in common. We'll delve into the nuances in this chapter, but let's start with the basic definition of intersection: two geometries intersect when they have interior or boundary points in common. The set of all shared points is called the *intersection*.

PostGIS has two functions for 2D intersections. The first is ST_Intersects, which returns true or false. The other is ST_Intersection, which returns the geometry of the intersected region.

Geometries also have other functions called ST_3DIntersects and ST_3DIntersection to handle 3D geometries. The inner workings of these are entirely different from ST_Intersects and ST_Intersection, but ST_3DIntersects does rely on a 2D bounding-box check to ensure that the footprints of both geometries intersect in 2D before performing a more exhaustive 3D check, if necessary.

We'll demonstrate the ST_Intersects and ST_Intersection functions in action with two crafty examples.

SEGMENTING LINESTRINGS WITH POLYGONS

We'll start with a polygon and a linestring and see if they intersect with ST_Intersects, and what the resultant intersection geometry looks like with ST_Intersection.

This example is quite common in real-world scenarios. The linestring can represent the planned route for a new roadway, and the polygon can represent private property. The ST_Intersects function will quickly tell you whether the new road will cut through the private property. If so, you can determine which part of the road falls within the boundaries by using ST_Intersection to determine the cost associated with an eminent domain takeover. We'll only look at a simple example, but you can imagine how useful this could be if you have records for all the private properties in a city and you want to determine which properties the road will cut through. The route planner can virtually trace any path through the city and obtain an immediate calculation for the eminent domain purchase.

Figure 8.2 shows a planned roadway (a linestring), the private land (a polygon), and the resulting intersection geometry.

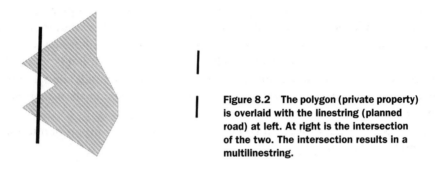

Figure 8.2   The polygon (private property) is overlaid with the linestring (planned road) at left. At right is the intersection of the two. The intersection results in a multilinestring.

The code that generates figure 8.2 is shown in the following listing.

Listing 8.2   Intersection of a polygon and a linestring

```
SELECT
    ST_Intersects(g.geom1,g.geom2) As intersect,
    GeometryType(ST_Intersection(g.geom1,g.geom2)) As intersection
FROM (
    SELECT
        ST_GeomFromText('
            POLYGON((
                2 4.5,3 2.6,3 1.8,2 0,
                -1.5 2.2,0.056 3.222,
                -1.5 4.2,2 6.5,2 4.5
            ))'
        ) As geom1,
        ST_GeomFromText('LINESTRING(-0.62 5.84,-0.8 0.59)') As geom2
) AS g;
```

Raster also has an ST_Intersection function, as well as the ST_Clip function you learned about in chapter 7. Both ST_Intersection and ST_Clip involve intersections between rasters and geometries are both kinds of intersections. ST_Clip is always between a raster and a geometry and the resulting intersection is the portion of the raster that intersects the geometry. ST_Intersection can be between two rasters or a raster and a geometry. When between two rasters, the result is a raster that is some function of the pixels and values that intersect. ST_Intersection between a raster and geometry returns a set of geomvals.

A classic example where you'll use them is if you are interested in the elevation footprint of your plot of land. You'll use ST_Clip to cut out the section of a digital elevation model that intersects your plot of land. So it's the portion of the digital elevation model raster that covers your plot of land. Then you might use one of the ST_Intersection(raster,geometry) raster functions to return the polygons that define each level of elevation on your plot of land, and you might do things like create a 3D geometry model of your plot of land and inject the altitude into the polygons returned by the intersection. We'll demonstrate this in chapter 12.

Should you be unimpressed by the previous example, the next one ought to change your mind.

CLIPPING POLYGONS WITH POLYGONS

A common use of the ST_Intersection function is to break up polygons by providing the portion that intersects with another polygon of interest, such as a grid of squares or rectangles. This process is often referred to as *clipping*.

For instance, if you were in charge of sales for a city and had a dozen sales representatives on your staff, you could break the polygon of the city into 12 sales regions, one for each representative, by clipping the city using the sales regions.

Another common use of clipping is to make your spatial database queries faster by breaking up your geometries beforehand. If you have data covering more area than you generally need to work with, you can clip the original geometry so you can query against a smaller geometry. For example, if you're working with data covering the entire island of Hispaniola but you only need to report on Haiti, you could clip the data using the geometry of Haiti to isolate only the data for the Haitian half.

We'll start with an example where we break up an arbitrarily shaped polygon (the one used in listing 8.2) into square regions, as shown in figure 8.3.

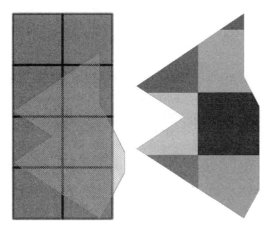

Figure 8.3 The polygon overlaid against square tiles is shown at left. At right is the result of an intersection of square tiles with the region.

To perform this cut-up, you start with a rectangle, break it into eight square cells, and then intersect it with the polygon, as shown in the following listing.

Listing 8.3   Clipping one polygon using another

```
SELECT
    x || ' ' || y As grid_x_y,                    Squares to
    CAST(                                     ❶  use for dicing
        ST_MakeBox2d(
            ST_Point(-1.5 + x, 0 + y),
            ST_Point(-1.5 + x + 2, 0 + y + 2)
        ) As geometry
    ) As geom2
FROM generate_series(0,3,2) As x CROSS JOIN generate_series(0,6,2) As y;
SELECT
    ST_GeomFromText(
        'POLYGON((
            2 4.5,3 2.6,3 1.8,2 0,-1.5 2.2,0.056 3.222,-1.5 4.2,2 6.5,
            2 4.5
        ))'
    ) As geom1;          ❷  Region to split              ❸ Dicing yields
SELECT                                                      multiple
    CAST(x AS text) || ' ' || CAST(y As text) As grid_xy,   records.
    ST_AsText(ST_Intersection(g1.geom1, g2.geom2)) As intersect_geom
FROM (
    SELECT
        ST_GeomFromText(
            'POLYGON((
                2 4.5,3 2.6,3 1.8,2 0,
                -1.5 2.2,0.056 3.222,
                -1.5 4.2,2 6.5,2 4.5
            ))'
        ) As geom1
    ) As g1
    INNER JOIN (
    SELECT x, y, ST_MakeEnvelope(-1.5+x,0+y,-1.5+x+2,0+y+2) As geom2
    FROM
        generate_series(0,3,2) As x
        CROSS JOIN
        generate_series(0,6,2) As y
    ) As g2
ON ST_Intersects(g1.geom1,g2.geom2);
```

In this code, you first use `generate_series` to create two series from the minimum X coordinate of the polygon to the maximum X coordinate, skipping two units ❶. You do the same for Y, resulting in eight 2 × 2 squares. The city is the polygon you wish to cut ❷. Then you cross-join the city polygon and the squares and take the intersection ❸, which results in your city polygon being diced.

Table 8.2 lists the WKT for each slice of our Sicilian pizza created from listing 8.3.

Table 8.2 WKT of sales regions

grid_xy	intersect_geom
0 0	POLYGON((0.5 0.942857142857143...))
2 0	POLYGON((2.5 0.9,2 0,0.5 0.942857142857143,0.5 2,2.5 2,2.5 0.9))
0 2	POLYGON((-1.18181818181818 2,-1.5 2.2...))
2 2	POLYGON((2.26315789473684 4,2.5 3.55...))
0 4	POLYGON((-1.18179959100204 4,-1.5 4.2,0.5 5...))
2 4	POLYGON((2 4.5,2.26315789473684 4,0.5 4,0.5 5.51428571428571...))
2 6	POLYGON((1.23913043478261 6,2 6.5,2 6,1.23913043478261 6))

Listing 8.3 shows how intersections can be useful for partitioning a single geometry into separate records. Notice that the cutting squares didn't need to completely cover the polygon. In this example we left out a few slivers.

Keep in mind that the `geometry` type returned by `ST_Intersection` may look rather different than the input geometries, but it's guaranteed to be of equal or lower dimension (both geometry and coordinate dimensions) than the geometry with the lowest dimension. For example, if you have two polygons that share an edge, the intersection of the two will be the linestring representing the shared edge. The polygons are two-dimensional, but the resultant linestring is one-dimensional.

> **NOTE** PostGIS 2.2 introduced the geometry functions `ST_Subdivide` and `ST_ClipByBox2D`, which chop a geometry into smaller bits. These work with any kind of geometry. Internally they use an intersection similar to the previous example, but of course they're much quicker to use. We'll cover `ST_Subdivide` in a later chapter. PostGIS 3.1 introduced the `ST_HexagonGrid` and `ST_Square-Grid` functions, which will automatically generate a grid for you based on the bounding box of the input geometry and size value, which you can then use to intersect with. The idea of hexagon grids has been made popular by Uber's Hierarchical Geospatial Indexing System (H3; https://github.com/uber/h3). The H3 system is strictly based on Dymaxion projection, whereas the `ST_HexagonGrid` function is designed to work with any planar spatial reference system.

Your output may also result in geometry collections, even if neither geometry is a geometry collection. For example, you may have two geometries of type `POLYGON` that intersect. If the two polygons share a portion of an edge (as is the case with land parcels), and one portion of the parcel crosses the border of the other parcel (because of a land dispute), then the intersection of the two geometries would be of type `GEOMETRYCOLLECTION`. This geometry collection would consist of a linestring for the agreed-upon border and a polygon for the disputed area.

To summarize, if A and B are input geometries to ST_Intersection, the following points hold true:

- ST_Intersection returns the portion shared by A and B, inclusive of boundaries.
- ST_Intersection and ST_Intersects are both commutative, meaning that ST_Intersection(A,B) = ST_Intersection(B,A) and ST_Intersects(A,B) = ST_Intersects(B,A).
- A and B need not be of the same geometry subtype.
- The geometry returned by ST_Intersection can't have dimensions higher than the lowest dimension between A and B, Least(ST_Dim(A),ST_Dim(B)).
- If A and B don't intersect, the intersection is an empty geometry.

Now that we've covered the basic concepts of intersections, we'll delve into the finer details of intersecting relationships.

8.2.3 *A house plan model*

We'll use a house plan example, shown in figure 8.4, to demonstrate more specific and less intuitive intersection relationships. Listing 8.4 generates the house plan, which uses a polygon with a hole to represent the house with a center courtyard. The linestring will be our walkway, and the multipoint will represent guards. The single triangular point represents the front door. These are laid out separately in figure 8.4, but when you combine them together as in figure 8.5, you'll see they intersect in various places.

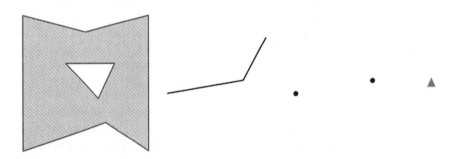

Figure 8.4 Components of the house plan

Listing 8.4 Piecing together the house plan

```
CREATE TABLE example_set(ex_name varchar(150) PRIMARY KEY,
    geom geometry);
INSERT INTO example_set(ex_name, geom)
VALUES
    (
        'A polygon with hole',
        ST_GeomFromText(
```

```
            'POLYGON(
                (110 180, 110 335,184 316,260 335,260 180,209 212.51,
                110 180), (160 280,200 240, 220 280,160 280)
            )'
        )
    ),
    ('A point', ST_GeomFromText('POINT(110 245)')),
    (
        'A linestring',
        ST_GeomFromText('LINESTRING(110 245,200 260, 227 309)')
    ),
    ('A multipoint', ST_GeomFromText('MULTIPOINT(110 245,200 260)'));
```

When you view the components in place, the house plan looks like figure 8.5.

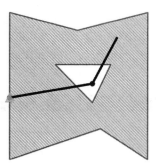

**Figure 8.5   House plan with
all components in place**

In the house, you have four geometries representing different aspects of the house:

- A polygon with a triangular hole represents the building part of the house—the covered structure. The house has a quaint courtyard, which is a part of the house's exterior.
- A linestring represents a red carpet that leads guests through the courtyard to the inner sanctum.
- A point represented by a triangle icon is the front entrance to the house.
- A multipoint represented by two dots marks the two guards stationed at the front entrance and the courtyard to screen guests.

In the next section we'll explore the different spatial relationships that the house, carpet, entrance, and guards have with each other.

8.2.4   Contains and within

When geometry A contains geometry B, no points of B can lie in the exterior of A, and at least one point of B must lie in the interior of A. So if B lies only on the boundary of A, A doesn't contain B. If B lies on the boundary and in the interior of A, A contains B.

One surprising quirk of this definition is that a geometry never contains its own boundary points. For example, a point that is the starting point of an open linestring is not contained by the linestring because it has no points in the interior of the linestring. However, if you have a multipoint that contains the starting point and a point somewhere in the middle of the line, that multipoint is contained by the linestring.

Contains and *within* are inverse relationships. If geometry A is within geometry B, then geometry B contains geometry A. To check contains and within, use the functions ST_Contains and ST_Within. Both of these functions are OGC SQL/MM functions, so you may encounter them in other spatial database products without much difference in meaning.

One of the confusing but necessary conditions for geometry A to contain geometry B is that the intersection of the boundary of A with B can't be B. In other words, B can't sit entirely on the boundary of A. A geometry doesn't contain its boundary, but a geometry always contains itself.

Let's write a query that lists all pair-wise comparisons of the house from the preceding section using ST_Contains and ST_Within. The answers from the comparison will allow you to deduce answers to questions such as "Are both guards inside the house and not in the courtyard? Are they both on the red carpet? Is one still at the front entrance?"

Listing 8.5 Compare contains and within

```
SELECT
    A.ex_name As a_name, B.ex_name As b_name,
    ST_Contains(A.geom,B.geom) As a_co_b,
    ST_Intersects(A.geom,B.geom) As a_in_b
FROM example_set As A CROSS JOIN example_set As B;
```

The result of listing 8.5 is shown in table 8.3.

Table 8.3 Where all intersect but not all contain

a_name	b_name	a_co_b	a_in_b
A polygon with hole	A polygon with hole	t	t
A polygon with hole	A point	f	t
A polygon with hole	A linestring	f	t
A polygon with hole	A multipoint	f	t
A point	A polygon with hole	f	t
A point	A point	t	t
A point	A linestring	f	t
A point	A multipoint	f	t
A linestring	A polygon with hole	f	t
A linestring	A point	f	t

Table 8.3 Where all intersect but not all contain (*continued*)

a_name	b_name	a_co_b	a_in_b
A linestring	A linestring	t	t
A linestring	A multipoint	t	t
A multipoint	A polygon with hole	f	t
A multipoint	A point	t	t
A multipoint	A linestring	f	t
A multipoint	A multipoint	t	t

This example confirms the following:

- All objects intersect. This tells us that at least one guard is at the front entrance, at least one is on the red carpet, and at least one is wholly within the confines or on the boundary of the building. They can't both be in the courtyard because if they were, they as a whole would not intersect the building. Don't forget that both guards together form the multipoint geometry.
- Because the building doesn't contain the guards, but the guards intersect the building, we know that one guard must be in the courtyard or outside the outer boundary of the building.
- We know that the red carpet isn't completely in the building but intersects it, meaning that the carpet must have some piece in the courtyard or extending beyond the building.
- If geometry B sits wholly on the boundary of geometry A, geometry A doesn't contain geometry B. Because the front entrance intersects the building but the building doesn't contain the entrance, we know that the entrance must be on the boundary of the building. The front entrance intersects the red carpet but the carpet doesn't contain the front entrance; therefore the front entrance must be on the boundary of the red carpet (the beginning or end of the carpet).
- The carpet contains both guards, so at most one guard can be at the start or end of the red carpet, but not both.
- All geometries contain themselves.

If you were to use ST_Within, you'd get the inverse of ST_Contains. The column a_co_b would have the opposite values.

8.2.5 *Covers and covered by*

As you saw in the contains example, containment at the boundaries abides by convention rather than intuition. Most people assert that a geometry should contain its boundary, but instead of changing the OGC SQL/MM meaning of containment, Post-GIS introduced the concepts of *covers* and *covered by* to mean *contain with boundary*. The related PostGIS functions are ST_Covers and ST_CoveredBy; they aren't OGC SQL/MM defined functions.

ST_Covers behaves exactly like ST_Contains except that it will also return true in the case where one geometry lies completely within the boundary of the other. ST_CoveredBy is the inverse function of ST_Covers and therefore behaves like ST_Within, but excludes the boundary.

The next listing and table 8.4 demonstrate situations where ST_Covers covers a geometry, but doesn't contain it.

Listing 8.6 How ST_Covers differs from ST_Contains

```
SELECT
    A.ex_name As a_name, B.ex_name As b_name,
    ST_Covers(A.geom,B.geom) As a_cov_b,
    ST_Contains(A.geom,B.geom) As a_con_b
FROM example_set As A CROSS JOIN example_set As B
WHERE NOT (ST_Covers(A.geom,B.geom) = ST_Contains(A.geom,B.geom));
```

The code only outputs those geometries where the ST_Covers answer is different from the ST_Contains answer. Table 8.4 shows the results.

Table 8.4 Where ST_Covers differs from ST_Contains

a_name	b_name	a_cov_b	a_con_b
A polygon with hole	A point	t	f
A linestring	A point	t	f

Because we limited the results to cases where the answer produced by ST_Covers is different from that of ST_Contains, we only get the list of cases where A covers B and B sits wholly on the boundary of A. Both the red carpet and the building cover the door, but they don't contain the door.

Next we'll look at the ST_ContainsProperly function, which provides a more stringent containment check than the ST_Contains function.

8.2.6 *Contains properly*

Contains properly is a concept that's more stringent than the contains or covers relationships. Geometry A contains properly B if all points of B are within the interior of A. Contains properly is faster to compute than other relationship functions because boundaries don't come into play. If you want to be absolutely certain that one geometry is entirely within another, use contains properly. For example, you may want to make sure your new McMansion is properly contained within one municipality to make sure you're not going to be taxed twice.

Contains properly will give you the same result as contains except in the case where any part of geometry B sits on the boundary of A. ST_ContainsProperly is a PostGIS-specific function and is not defined in the SQL/MM or OGC specs.

The next listing repeats the previous comparison exercise, except that it lists only the contains properly options where `ST_ContainsProperly` gives a different answer from `ST_Contains`.

Listing 8.7 How `ST_ContainsProperly` differs from `ST_Contains`

```
SELECT
    A.ex_name As a_name, B.ex_name As b_name,
    ST_ContainsProperly(A.geom,B.geom) As a_cop_b,
    ST_Contains(A.geom,B.geom) As a_con_b
FROM example_set As A CROSS JOIN example_set As B
WHERE NOT ( ST_ContainsProperly(A.geom,B.geom) =
    ST_Contains(A.geom,B.geom) );
```

Table 8.5 shows the results of listing 8.7. Observe that `ST_ContainsProperly` gives answers identical to `ST_Contains` except in the case of an areal geometry, a line geometry compared to itself, or a geometry sitting partly on the boundary of another. A geometry never properly contains itself except in the case of points and multipoints. The reason points and multipoints properly contain themselves is that they consist of a finite number of points and therefore have no boundary to speak of. A point can never be sitting partly on its nonexistent boundary.

Table 8.5 Where contains and contains properly are different

a_name	b_name	a_cop_b	a_con_b
A polygon with hole	A polygon with hole	f	t
A linestring	A linestring	f	t
A linestring	A multipoint	f	t

You can see from this table that the only cases where the `ST_ContainsProperly` answer is different from that of `ST_Contains` are the cases of a polygon against itself, a linestring against itself, and a point or multipoint that partly sits on the boundary of another. This tells us that in the house, one person must be on the start or end of the red carpet because the red carpet doesn't properly contain both people, but it does contain both people.

8.2.7 *Overlapping geometries*

Two geometries *overlap* when they have the same geometry dimension, they intersect, and one is not completely contained in the other. The PostGIS overlap function is `ST_Overlaps`, an OGC SQL/MM function.

If you were to check the house to see if anything overlaps, you'd find that nothing does. Here are the reasons:

- The red carpet is not of the same dimension as the building. One is lineal and the other is areal, so they can't overlap. The same mismatch in dimension holds true between the front entrance and the building and between the front entrance and the red carpet.

- The guards can't overlap with the front entrance because the entrance is contained and covered by one of the guards.
- No self-to-self comparisons overlap because a geometry always contains itself.

8.2.8   *Touching geometries*

Two geometries *touch* if they have at least one point in common and none of the common points lie in the interior of both geometries. The PostGIS function at play is ST_Touches, an OGC SQL/MM function.

The following listing contrasts ST_Touches with ST_Contains.

> **Listing 8.8   How** ST_Touches **differs from** ST_Contains

```
SELECT
    A.ex_name As a_name,B.ex_name As b_name,
    ST_Touches(A.geom,B.geom) As a_tou_b,
    ST_Contains(A.geom,B.geom) As a_co_b
FROM example_set As A CROSS JOIN example_set As B
WHERE ST_Touches(A.geom,B.geom) ;
```

The output of listing 8.8 is shown in table 8.6.

Table 8.6   Geometries that touch each other

a_name	b_name	a_tou_b	a_co_b
A polygon with hole	A point	t	f
A polygon with hole	A multipoint	t	f
A point	A polygon with hole	t	f
A point	A linestring	t	f
A linestring	A point	t	f
A multipoint	A polygon with hole	t	f

Let's examine the results in table 8.6:

- The touch relationship is commutative. If A touches B, then B touches A.
- We can also infer from the results that if two geometries touch, one can't contain the other.
- The building touches the front entrance because the front entrance sits on the boundary of the building. The front entrance itself is the common point. It lies only within one geometry's interior—its own. The same applies to the touching of the front entrance and the red carpet.

- The multipoint and front entrance are missing from the list as expected. The multipoint pair of guards doesn't touch the front entrance because the guards contain the front entrance, and the shared point is interior to both geometries. As a general rule, a point can never touch another point or another multipoint because the shared points would always be interior to both.

- The multipoint pair of guards and the polygon building touch because one guard is on the boundary of the building and the other is in the courtyard. The courtyard is part of the exterior of the building and not the interior, so even though one guard is sunning in the courtyard and the other is at the door, as a pair they're touching the building.

CROSSING GEOMETRIES

Two geometries *cross* each other if they have some interior points in common but not all. Think of two perpendicular runways here. The function that implements crossing is ST_Crosses, an OGC SQL/MM function.

The following listing contrasts ST_Crosses with ST_Contains.

Listing 8.9   How ST_Crosses differs from ST_Contains

```
SELECT
    A.ex_name As a_name,B.ex_name As b_name,
    ST_Crosses(A.geom,B.geom) As a_cr_b,
    ST_Contains(A.geom,B.geom) As a_co_b
FROM example_set As A CROSS JOIN example_set As B
WHERE ST_Crosses(A.geom,B.geom) ;
```

Table 8.7 lists the query output of listing 8.9.

Table 8.7   Geometries that cross each other

a_name	b_name	a_cr_b	a_co_b
A polygon with hole	A linestring	t	f
A linestring	A polygon with hole	t	f

We can glean a couple of things from this example:

- Only one pair of geometries crosses: the red carpet and the building. They don't touch or contain each other, but they do intersect, so they must cross. The shared region contains points interior to both, but one is not completely contained by the other. Note that this cross is made possible by the existence of the courtyard. The red carpet has a strip within the courtyard, so its interior isn't completely contained by the building's interior.

- Geometries that touch can't cross. Compare the crossing output with the touching output.

Now that we've analyzed the various intersects relationships, our last stop will be the only non-intersecting relationship—the disjoint relationship.

DISJOINT GEOMETRIES

The *disjoint* relationship is the antithesis of the *intersects* relationship. Two geometries are disjointed if they have no shared interiors or boundaries. In the case of invalid geometries, it's possible for the ST_Intersects and ST_Disjoint functions to both return false or both return true. If you encounter such illogical results, your input geometries must be invalid.

PostGIS uses ST_Disjoint, an OGC SQL/MM function, to check for disjoint relationships. Although it might appear that ST_Disjoint would be used frequently, this isn't the case. The problem with ST_Disjoint is that it can't use an index. To check if a set of geometries intersects with another, you're better off performing an unequal join using ST_Intersects and filtering for NULLs, as follows:

```
A LEFT JOIN B ON ST_Intersects(A.geom,B.geom) WHERE B.gid IS NULL
```

Because ST_Intersect can use indexes, this query will run much faster than using ST_Disjoint. Given this superior alternative, we can't say that we find much use for ST_Disjoint. Feel free to remove this function from your mind and save room for a more useful function.

Now that we've covered the various ways geometries can intersect, it's time to zoom in on the topic of equality. You'll find that in the spatial realm, equality takes on many forms.

8.2.9   *The faces of equality: geometry*

In conventional databases, you probably never gave the equal sign (=) a second thought before using it, but this clarity of purpose doesn't carry over to spatial databases. When you compare two spatial objects, equality is a multifaceted notion. You can ask whether geometries occupy the same space. You can ask whether they are represented by the same points. You can even ask if they are enclosed by the same bounding box.

Three basic kinds of equality are specific to 2D geometries in PostGIS:

- *Spatial equality* means that two geometries occupy the same space.
- *Geometric equality* is stronger than spatial equality and means that two geometries occupy the same space and have the same underlying representation.
- *Bounding-box equality* means that the bounding boxes of the two geometries share the same space. This last kind of equality is what the = operator meant prior to PostGIS 2.4.

We'll explore these facets of equality next.

SPATIAL EQUALITY VERSUS GEOMETRIC EQUALITY

Two geometries are considered spatially equal if they occupy the same underlying space. PostGIS uses ST_Equals to test for spatial equality; it's an OGC SQL/MM function that you'll find in many spatial database products.

Use ST_Equals when the directionality difference of two geometries is unimportant to you. For example, a linestring that starts at point A and runs to point B and a linestring that starts at point B and runs to point A are spatially equal. Similarly, ST_Equals will disregard the distinction between collection geometries and multi-geometries. For instance, the following three geometries are spatially equal:

- Point A
- A multipoint with only point A
- A geometry collection with only point A

Geometric equality is more strict than spatial equality. Not only must the two geometries share the same space, they must also share the same underlying representation. So although an A-to-B linestring is spatially equal to a B-to-A linestring, they aren't geometrically equal.

Geometric equality is important for routing. For example, take any interstate highway in the United States. Depending on which side of the road you're traveling on, the interstate is signed as north versus south or east versus west. Although it's the same interstate highway, the direction of travel matters. It matters greatly when you get lost.

For geometric equality comparisons, PostGIS uses ST_OrderingEquals, which is not an OGC SQL/MM–compliant function. The next listing demonstrates the difference between ST_OrderingEquals and ST_Equals.

Listing 8.10 ST_OrderingEquals versus ST_Equals

```
SELECT
    ex_name,
    ST_OrderingEquals(geom,geom) As g_oeq_g,
    ST_OrderingEquals(geom, ST_Reverse(geom)) As g_oeq_rev,
    ST_OrderingEquals(geom, ST_Multi(geom)) AS g_oeq_m,
    ST_Equals(geom, geom) As g_seq_g,
    ST_Equals(geom, ST_Multi(geom)) As g_seq_m
FROM (
VALUES
    ('A 2D linestring', ST_GeomFromText('LINESTRING(3 5,2 4,2 5)')),
    ('A point', ST_GeomFromText('POINT(2 5)')),
    ('A triangle', ST_GeomFromText('POLYGON((3 5,2.5 4.5,2 5,3 5))')),
    (
        'An invalid polygon',
        ST_GeomFromText('POLYGON((2 0,0 0,1 1,1 -1,2 0))')
    )
)
AS foo(ex_name, geom);
```

Table 8.8 shows the results of listing 8.10.

Table 8.8   Compare `ST_OrderingEquals` **and** `ST_Equals`

ex_name	g_oeq_g	g_oeq_rev	g_oeq_m	g_seq_g	g_seq_m
A 2D linestring	t	f	f	t	t
A point	t	t	f	t	t
A triangle	t	f	f	t	t
An invalid polygon	t	f	f	t	f

As demonstrated in table 8.8, even an invalid polygon is `ST_OrderingEqual` to itself in PostGIS. Observe also that the multi-geometry variant is not geometrically equal to the singular version, but they are spatially equal.

In the case of invalid geometries, `ST_Equals` may be false when two invalid geometries occupy the same space (this is the case with older versions of PostGIS). In PostGIS 2.5 and beyond, this may or may not be the case. Only in this case will you run across the paradox of geometries being geometrically equal (`ST_OrderingEquals` returns `true`) but not necessarily spatially equal (`ST_Equals`). Although PostGIS has no problem comparing the binary bytes that form the geometries to assert that they're geometrically equal, it's unable to apply the intersection matrix principles to the geometries to see if they overlap. Once again, stay clear of invalid geometries.

If you wish to ignore differences in SRIDs, you can use `ST_AsBinary(A) = ST_AsBinary(B)`.

THE = OPERATOR

Prior to PostGIS 2.4, the universally recognized equal sign (=) was reserved for bounding-box equality. This caused great confusion for over a decade, as users were confused by the answers they got when doing `GROUP BY`, `DISTINCT`, and = on geometries. After answering the same question over and over again about how = doesn't mean what you think it means, PostGIS 2.4 redefined = to really mean binary equality, which is what most people thought it meant in the first place.

If you need bounding-box equality, you should use `~=`. The PostGIS 2.4+ version of = is very similar to `ST_OrderingEquals`, but it uses a B-tree index instead of a gist index.

The = operation is internally used by operations such as `UNION`, `DISTINCT`, or `GROUP BY` against geometry columns.

> **NOTE**   2D bounding-box operators work for curved geometries and for 3D geometries, but the Z coordinate is ignored.

Next we'll look at the underpinnings of relationship functions.

8.2.10   *Underpinnings of relationship functions*

The intersects relationship function we covered earlier might have given you the impression that `ST_Intersects` is the most generic relationship between two geometries. In actuality, we can generalize one step further. The underpinning of most 2D geometry relationship functions in PostGIS and most other spatial database products is the Dimensionally Extended 9-Intersection Model (DE-9IM), which we'll loosely refer to as the intersection matrix. The PostGIS function that can work directly with an intersection matrix is the ST_Relate function.

The intersection matrix is the foundation of most geometric relationships supported by the OGC SQL/MM standard, and it's an outgrowth from the work of M.J. Egenhofer and J.R. Herring. To learn more about the intersection matrix, see their article, "Categorizing Binary Topological Relations Between Regions, Lines, and Points in Geographic Databases" (www.spatial.maine.edu/~max/9intReport.pdf).

THE INTERSECTION MATRIX

The intersection matrix is a 3 × 3 matrix that defines all possible pair-wise combinations of exterior, boundary, and interior when two geometries interact. You can use the matrix in two ways: to state the requirement that must be satisfied by a named relationship, or to describe the relationship that exists between two geometries.

When used to define a named relationship, the matrix cells can take on the following values: T, F, *, 0, 1, or 2. When used to describe two interacting geometries, the matrix cells can take on the following values: F, 0, 1, or 2. Table 8.9 explains what each value represents.

Table 8.9   Possible cell values of an intersection matrix

Value	Description
T	An intersection must exist; the resultant geometry can be 0, 1, or 2 dimensions (point, line, area).
F	An intersection must not exist.
*	It doesn't matter if an intersection exists or not.
0	An intersection must exist, and the intersection must be at finite points (dim = 0).
1	An intersection must exist, and the intersection's dimension must be 1 (finite lines).
2	An intersection must exist, and the intersection's dimension must be 2 (areal).

Figures 8.6–8.8 represent ST_Disjoint, ST_Equals, and ST_Within with intersection matrices.

		Interior	Boundary	Exterior
			B	
	Interior	F	F	*
A	Boundary	F	F	*
	Exterior	*	*	*

Figure 8.6   Intersection matrix of ST_Disjoint

	B		
	Interior	Boundary	Exterior
Interior	T	*	F
Boundary	*	*	F
Exterior	F	F	*

Figure 8.7   Intersection matrix of ST_Equals

	B		
	Interior	Boundary	Exterior
Interior	T	*	F
Boundary	*	*	F
Exterior	*	*	*

Figure 8.8   Intersection matrix of ST_Within

From the ST_Within example, you can see that for a geometry to be within another, the interiors of both must intersect, the interior of A can't fall outside B (it can't intersect with the exterior of B), and the boundary can't fall outside B (the boundary can't intersect with the exterior of B). The boundaries, however, are free to intersect or not intersect.

To avoid having to draw tic-tac-toe boxes for intersection matrices, you can use the shorthand of nine characters. ST_Disjoint would be FF*FF****, ST_Equals would be T*F**FFF*, and ST_Within would be T*F**F***. Go across and then down the matrix to fill in the slots of the shorthand notation.

For a given named relationship or an existing relationship, the intersection may not be unique. Furthermore, when defining a named relationship, you can chain intersection matrices together with Boolean operators to obtain the exact requirements you need.

Incidentally, the intersects relationship requires either a minimum of three matrices joined by Boolean ORs or negating the ST_Disjoint matrix. You can use ST_Relate to determine if two geometries satisfy a relationship. We'll cover that next.

USING ST_RELATE

PostGIS has two variants of the ST_Relate function. The first variant returns a Boolean true or false that states whether geometries A and B satisfy the specified relationship matrix. The second variant returns the most constraining relationship matrix satisfied by the two geometries.

In theory, PostGIS could replace all the relationship functions we've described with one or more generic ST_Relate calls. In practice, PostGIS never internally uses ST_Relate for a couple of reasons. For one, ST_Relate doesn't automatically use indexes. Second, having separate relationship functions lets PostGIS embed shortcuts that can bypass needing to check all the cells of the intersection matrix.

The next listing exercises both variants of the ST_Relate function. The geometries used in this example are illustrated in figure 8.9.

Listing 8.11 ST_Relate variants

```sql
WITH example_set_2 (ex_name,geom) AS (
    SELECT ex_name, geom
    FROM (
        VALUES
            ('A 2D line',
            ST_GeomFromText('LINESTRING(3 5, 2.5 4.25, 1.6 5)')),
            ('A point',
            ST_GeomFromText('POINT(1.6 5)')),
            ('A triangle',
            ST_GeomFromText('POLYGON((3 5, 2.5 4.25, 1.9 4.9, 3 5))')))
    ) AS x(ex_name, geom)
)
SELECT
    A.ex_name As a_name, B.ex_name As b_name,
    ST_Relate(A.geom, B.geom) As relates,
    ST_Intersects(A.geom, B.geom) As intersects,
    ST_Relate(A.geom, B.geom, 'FF*FF****') As relate_disjoint,
    NOT ST_Relate(A.geom, B.geom, 'FF*FF****') As relate_intersects
FROM example_set_2 As A CROSS JOIN example_set_2 As B;
```

Figure 8.9 Geometries in the ST_Relate example

Table 8.10 lists the SQL output.

Remember that we mentioned that the intersects relationship requires three intersection matrices. We cheated in our example by taking NOT ST_Disjoint instead of computing ST_Intersects. This is because intersects implies not disjoint, and not disjoint requires only one intersection matrix to compute.

Table 8.10   Results from the `ST_Relate` query

a_name	b_name	Relates	Intersects	Disjoint	Not disjoint
A 2D line	A 2D line	1FFF0FFF2	t	f	t
A 2D line	A point	FF1FF00F2	t	f	t
A 2D line	A triangle	F11F00212	t	f	t
A point	A 2D line	FF0FFF102	t	f	t
A point	A point	0FFFFFFF2	t	f	t
A point	A triangle	FF0FFF212	f	t	f
A triangle	A 2D line	FF2101102	t	f	t
A triangle	A point	FF2FF10F2	f	t	f
A triangle	A triangle	2FFF1FFF2	t	f	t

Let's look at the linestring and the triangle in more detail: figure 8.10 shows the tic-tac-toe notation of this pair of relationships.

Triangle		2D line		
		Interior	Boundary	Exterior
	Interior	F	F	2
	Boundary	1	0	1
	Exterior	1	0	2

2D line		Triangle		
		Interior	Boundary	Exterior
	Interior	F	1	1
	Boundary	F	0	0
	Exterior	2	1	2

Figure 8.10 `ST_Relate(triangle,2dline)` **and** `ST_Relate(2dline,triangle)`

In figure 8.10, notice that if you take FF2101102 and flip the rows and columns, you end up with F11F00212. The intersection matrix is symmetrical. Here are some other observations:

- The interior of the triangle and the interior of the linestring fail to intersect. You can verify this from the image of the geometries in figure 8.9.
- The interior of the triangle doesn't intersect with the boundary of the linestring (recall that the boundary of a line is the start and end points), but the interior of the linestring does intersect with the boundary of the triangle. The dimension of intersection is lineal (dimension of 1).
- You'll find areal intersections at the exteriors of the linestring with both the interior and the exterior of the triangle. This is because the exterior of the linestring encompasses all points not on the linestring, which is an area.

Summary

- The foundation of spatial relationships is the bounding-box relation.
- Raster, geometry, and geography have bounding boxes.
- Raster and geometry can have direct relationships because they share the same kind of bounding box.
- Geography bounding boxes are three-dimensional.
- PostGIS offers many operators and functions for determining and using spatial relationships.

Part 2

Putting PostGIS to work

In part 1 of *PostGIS in Action, Third Edition*, you learned about the building blocks you'll need to solve spatial problems. By now you should be able to set up a PostGIS database, populate it with data, and transform data between disparate spatial reference systems. You should also be comfortable using the most common functions in PostGIS and be able to take advantage of their prowess when writing SQL.

In part 2 you'll put the pieces together to solve real problems. The important lessons we want you to take away from part 2 entail how to tackle each problem, starting with building a correct formulation, setting up an appropriate structure to support the analysis, choosing the most appropriate PostGIS functions, and putting it all together using SQL.

Chapter 9 covers the most basic use of PostGIS: finding things and finding them fast.

Chapter 10 covers geocoding with the packaged PostGIS TIGER geocoder. You'll learn how to load US Census TIGER data using functions packaged with the TIGER geocoder. Once the data is loaded, you'll learn how to use the packaged functions to normalize, geocode, and reverse-geocode data.

Chapters 11 and 12 cover various common problems found in vector and raster spatial analyses that you'll come across in building spatial queries for applications. You'll learn how to solve these problems with PostGIS spatial functions and ANSI SQL constructs, as well as PostgreSQL–specific enhancements to SQL.

In chapter 13, you'll learn about PostGIS topology and how to use it to manage and fix your spatial data.

Chapter 14 will guide you through various database storage techniques and will take a dive into the topics of triggers and views for maintaining consistency in data.

Chapter 15 focuses on database performance. In this chapter you'll learn how to speed up queries and how to avoid common SQL pitfalls. You'll learn about the finer points of employing both spatial and non-spatial indexes and fine-tuning PostgreSQL settings. In addition, you'll learn about the often-neglected tactic of simplifying geometries to arrive at *good enough* answers to problems quickly, rather than overly precise answers slowly.

Proximity analysis

9

This chapter covers

- Nearest neighbor searches
- K-nearest neighbor (KNN) distance operators
- Using KNN with `geography` and `geometry`
- Geotagging
- PostGIS clustering window functions

Once you've located places with a set of coordinates, questions such as the following arise: How far is my house from the nearest expressway? How many burger joints are within a mile drive? What's the average distance that people have to commute to work? Which three hospitals closest to me offer emergency vasectomies? If I need to get at least this much exercise but don't want to overdo it, how many kale shake joints are between 1K and 2K away from my home? How do I assign visits to my field reps to balance the work? We'll file all these questions under the heading of *proximity analysis,* or loosely, the study of how far something is located from something else.

We'll cover both the traditional methods of finding closest neighbors as well as newer methods using k-nearest neighbor (KNN) indexes and PostGIS clustering window functions. Speed is often a concern when performing proximity analyses, and we'll offer techniques and advice on how to speed up slow queries.

You'll learn what you should consider when choosing between a geography type and geometry. You'll learn about trade-offs such as performance, features, and ease of use.

You'll learn about labeling of spatial features (a.k.a. geotagging), using data from another spatial feature, such as grouping locations into sales regions, finding all houses located along a street, and so on. Geotagging allows you to aggregate statistics more quickly and to export in formats that are friendly to spreadsheets and charts.

Finally, you'll learn about PostGIS clustering window functions, which are used to group a set of geometries by proximity to each other.

Before we dig in, we want to make clear that the distances we refer to in this chapter are most often minimum distances ("as the crow flies"), and are not subject to any path constraints. There is a function called ST_MaxDistance for geometry, which gives you the length of the longest straight line you can draw between two geometries. We'll leave pgRouting, which handles path constraints, to chapter 16.

This is a data-intensive chapter, and we gathered the data we'll use from a variety of sources. You can download the data from www.postgis.us/chapter_09_edition_3. The readme.txt file in the data folder details how we groomed the data.

Load the data into your database using this command:

```
psql -d postgis_in_action -f code09_data.sql
```

9.1   Nearest neighbor searches

In this section we'll answer the two most common questions: *Which places are within X distance* and *What are the N closest places?* These kinds of problems are often referred to as *nearest neighbor* searches.

9.1.1   Which places are within X distance?

You first learned about the versatile ST_DWithin function in chapter 1. Here you'll see some more examples of its use.

You can use ST_DWithin to find places that are close to one another or to determine if a place is within *X* units of another. You can pass both geometry and geography types to the function, but you can't use geometry and geography in the same function call. When using geography, units are always measured in meters, whereas units for geometry are specific to the spatial reference system of the geometries.

The following query finds airports within 100 kilometers of a location using the geography variant of ST_DWithin:

```
SELECT name, iso_country, iso_region
FROM ch09.airports
WHERE ST_DWithin(geog, ST_Point(-75.0664, 40.2003)::geography, 100000);
```

Although this query uses the geography data type, it runs fairly quickly on a dataset of 55,636 airports, returning 649 rows in under 70 milliseconds on our Windows Postgre-SQL 13, 64-bit PostGIS 3.1, Intel 6-core machine.

9.1.2 Using ST_DWithin and ST_Distance for N closest results

You can alter the previous query to return the *N* closest airports by adding an order-by-distance clause followed by a LIMIT *N*, as follows:

```
SELECT ident, name
FROM
    ch09.airports
    CROSS JOIN
    (SELECT ST_Point(-75.0664, 40.2003)::geography AS ref_geog) As r
WHERE ST_DWithin(geog, ref_geog, 100000)
ORDER BY ST_Distance(geog, ref_geog)
LIMIT 5;
```

With this query, you'll need to make sure that your search radius is large enough to return at least five results.

9.1.3 Using ST_DWithin and DISTINCT ON to find closest locations

In many cases, you'll begin with a set of places and need to find the closest place to another set of places. For example, how many emergency medical centers are within 10 miles of all nursing homes in a major city. You can accomplish this by combining ST_DWithin and the PostgreSQL DISTINCT ON construct. DISTINCT ON performs an implicit GROUP BY, but it's not limited to returning just the fields that you grouped on.

The following query finds the closest navaid (navigational aid) to each airport:

```
                              Distinct fields
                              (in parentheses)
SELECT DISTINCT ON (a.ident)  ⟵──┘
    a.ident, a.name As airport, n.name As closest_navaid,
    (ST_Distance(a.geog,n.geog)/1000)::integer As dist_km
FROM ch09.airports As a LEFT JOIN ch09.navaids As n
ON ST_DWithin(a.geog, n.geog,100000)   ⟵──────── Radius
ORDER BY a.ident, dist_km;   ⟵──┐ Sort by distance.
```

In the preceding code, a comma-separated list of distinct fields in parentheses must follow DISTINCT ON. This same list must appear first in the ORDER BY clause. Then you specify the maximum radius to scan for matches. The wider your radius, the slower the query, but you're more likely to be guaranteed matches.

This query uses a left join instead of an inner join to ensure that even if you find no navaids, the airport will still be in the results. You sort the navaids by dist_km to ensure that the navaid selected for output for each airport is the closest to that airport.

Partial output returned by the code follows:

```
ident | airport                      | closest_navaid      | dist_km
------+------------------------------+---------------------+---------
 00A  | Total RF Heliport            | North Philadelphia  |       7
 00AK | Lowell Field                 | Homer               |      30
 00AL | Epps Airpark                 | Capshaw             |      10
 00AR | Newport Hospital             | Newport             |       8
```

ST_DWithin can also substitute for the ST_Intersects function. When used this way, you call the approach *intersects with tolerance.*

The output of this query returned 55,636 rows and took a little over 14 seconds on our Windows PostgreSQL 13, 64-bit PostGIS 3.1, Intel 6-core machine.

9.1.4 *Intersects with tolerance*

Use ST_DWithin to check for intersections when you have two geometries that fail to intersect because of differences caused by the number of significant digits. Consider this example:

```
SELECT ST_DWithin(
    ST_GeomFromText(
        'LINESTRING(1 2, 3 4)'
    ),
    ST_Point(3.00001, 4.000001),
    0.0001
);
```

The point and the linestring are close enough that you'll want to ignore the fact that they're only .0001 units apart. You'll find that you often end up using intersects with tolerance when working with real data, where not everything lines up perfectly.

Using ST_DWithin in place of ST_Intersects has one more advantage: ST_DWithin won't choke on invalid geometries as ST_Intersects often does, especially if a geometry has self-intersecting regions. ST_DWithin doesn't care about validity because it doesn't rely on an intersection matrix. Having said this, you should always carefully inspect the output when you have invalid geometries.

> **NOTE** Prior to PostGIS 3.0, ST_3DDWithin and ST_3DIntersects did not work with triangular irregular networks (TINs) and also only returned surface distances (not considering volumes), unless you had the PostGIS sfcgal extension installed. In PostGIS 3.0, the native versions of these functions now work with TINs and volumetric geometries. So if ST_IsSolid returns true, it will consider the volume as well. ST_Intersects now also works against 2D TINs.

9.1.5 *Items between distances*

On occasion you might be interested in things that are less than some distance away and more than some distance away. An example might be finding the best joint to visit for kale shakes that is far enough from you so you feel you've got a bit of a workout, but not so far away that you feel you will not have enough energy to make the trip. Since we don't have kale shop data, let's switch the topic to finding an airport close enough that you can still make your flight, but far enough to feel like you've got your scenic fill before you jump on the plane.

How would we perform this kind of range query? Why, with two ST_DWithin calls. The main observation is that anything that is within your lower range distance is already in your higher range distance, but you only want things in the higher range that fail the lower range distance:

```
SELECT name, iso_country, iso_region
FROM ch09.airports
WHERE ST_DWithin(geog,
        ST_Point(-75.0664, 40.2003)::geography, 100000)
  AND NOT ST_DWithin(geog,
            ST_Point(-75.0664, 40.2003)::geography, 90000);
```

The answer returns in about the same amount of time as our single ST_DWithin example earlier, but it returns only 64 rows because it filters out the airports that are too close to you.

Next we'll look at finding the *N* closest objects using distance operators.

9.1.6 *Finding the N closest places using KNN distance operators*

A classic nearest-neighbor question is finding the *N* nearest points of interest to a fixed location. PostGIS includes two operators for 2D distances:

- <->—This is the KNN distance operator for both geometry and geography. A <-> B returns the distance between two geometries A and B.
- <#>—This is the KNN bounding-box distance operator for geometry. A <#> B returns the minimum distance between the bounding boxes of A and B. For a refresher on what a bounding box of a geometry is, refer to chapter 6.

NOTE Prior to PostGIS 2.2/PostgreSQL 9.5, <-> returned the distance between the bounding-box centroids. In PostGIS 2.2, this became a true distance operator. The answer it now returns is much the same as ST_Distance, so you can use it as shorthand for ST_Distance. The minor exception is that when applied to the geography type, the geography meter distance it returns is a sphere distance rather than the spheriod distance. For most purposes the sphere distance is sufficiently close enough to spheroid.

As of PostGIS 2.2 you can use <-> with both geometry and geography types. Prior PostGIS versions only supported the geometry type.

Even though you can pass in 3D geometries, the 2D operators will only consider the 2D XY-plane. There are nD KNN distance operators, <<->> and <<#>>, but the nD operators only handle bounding boxes, so they are of little use except for 3D and 4D geometry points.

The distance returned should also only be trusted if you're using a measure-preserving planar SRID or you are using the geography type.

WARNING   When using `<->`, the objects must both be geometries or both geographies. Geometries in a lon/lat spatial reference system, however, will be autocast to geography if compared against a geography; if the geometry uses a non-lon/lat spatial reference system, you will get an error. We encourage you to explicitly cast to minimize confusion and to future-proof your code.

For `LINESTRINGM` geometries, there is another distance operator called the *KNN trajectory distance operator*. A trajectory is a `LINESTRINGM` where the M is used to denote time. As such, the M must be increasing in the direction of the line in order for it to represent a realistic trajectory. A trajectory where M could decrease would imply a trajectory that can go backwards in time. Backwards time travel is something PostGIS does not yet support!

The KNN trajectory distance operator is `|=|`. A `|=|` B returns the distance between two trajectories, A and B. You can use the `ST_IsValidTrajectory` function to determine whether a `LINESTRINGM` represents a valid trajectory.

NOTE   The KNN operators behave very differently from the commonly used overlap operator (`&&`), `ST_Intersects`, and other relationship functions. KNN operators can only use a spatial index in the `ORDER BY` clause and when one side of the operator remains constant through the life of the query or subquery. A common mistake people make is trying to use KNN operators in the `WHERE` clause and wondering why they are not getting any index speed gain. KNN operators also always return numerical values. This is different from `&&`, `ST_Intersects`, and other relationship functions, which utilize spatial indexes only in `WHERE` and `JOIN` clauses and which return Boolean true/false.

Because KNN operators output distances, which you often want in your output, it's useful to define them in the `SELECT` clause with an alias name. You still get the same index boost when you use the defined alias in the `ORDER BY` clause instead of repeating the whole `<->` again in the `ORDER BY` clause.

The following listing shows the most basic of KNN examples that utilizes a spatial index and an alias.

Listing 9.1   Closest ten geometries to a point

```
SELECT
    pid,
    geom
    <->
    ST_Transform(
        ST_SetSRID(ST_Point(-71.09368, 42.35857),4326)
        ,26986) AS dist          ⟵┐ Define the constant geometry
                                   │ and alias distance as dist.
FROM ch09.land
WHERE land_type = 'apartment'       ┐ Reference the distance operator
ORDER BY dist              ⟵───────  │ call by its alias dist in the
LIMIT 10;                            │ ORDER BY clause.
```

Using an alias allows you to have shorter, easier to understand code, without compromising speed.

As with other relationship operators and functions, the spatial reference systems of both geometries need to be the same. In listing 9.1 you pass in a constant point geometry on the right side of the operator. Because both sides must always share the same SRID, you need to transform from 4326 to 26986 (Massachusetts state plane).

You can also draw values from tables for use in the operator, but one side must return exactly one value. The following query finds the ten closest parcels to another parcel (a subselect returning one geometry):

```
SELECT pid,
   geom <-> (SELECT geom FROM ch09.land WHERE pid = '58-162') AS dist
FROM ch09.land
WHERE land_type = 'apartment'
ORDER BY dist
LIMIT 10;
```

We mentioned that you must place the operator in the ORDER BY clause in order for the index on the geometry to kick in. This doesn't preclude you from using it elsewhere in the SQL—just know that you won't have the benefit of an index. If you're drawing from a small table, use of the index is immaterial, since it's often faster or of comparable speed to scan the table rather than use a spatial index.

Indexes also don't come into play in the SELECT statement and WHERE clause. So if you were to replace this

```
ORDER BY geom <`-`> ST_Transform(ST_SetSRID(ST_Point(-71.09368,
    42.35857),4326),26986) LIMIT 10
```

in listing 9.1 with this

```
AND geom <`-`> ST_Transform(ST_SetSRID(ST_Point(-71.09368,
    42.35857),4326),26986) < 700
```

the spatial index couldn't be used.

To work around the requirement that one side of the operator must be a constant geometry, you can use a correlated subquery in the SELECT clause, as shown in the following listing.

Listing 9.2   Find closest shopping to each parcel using a correlated subquery

```
SELECT
    l.pid, (
        SELECT s.pid
        FROM ch09.land As s
        WHERE s.land_type = 'church'
        ORDER BY s.geom <-> l.geom LIMIT 1
    ) As n_closest
FROM ch09.land AS l
WHERE land_type = 'apartment';
```

Listing 9.2 uses the distance operator to find the closest shopping center to each parcel of land.

Unfortunately, because subselects must return a single row when used in SELECT, you can't use them to answer the more generic *N* closest where *N* != 1. In the following listing, the LATERAL join allows you to use a correlated subquery in the FROM.

> **Listing 9.3 Find three closest shopping malls using a LATERAL join**

```
SELECT l.pid, r.pid As n_closest
FROM
    ch09.land As l
    CROSS JOIN LATERAL
    (
        SELECT s.pid
        FROM ch09.land AS s
        WHERE s.land_type = 'church'
        ORDER BY s.geom <-> l.geom
        LIMIT 3
    ) As r
WHERE land_type = 'apartment';
```

With lateral joins, you're able to access elements across the join. In listing 9.3 the right side of the join (r) draws values from the geom column on the left side (l), so that for each row of l you get a new query r where the l.geom is treated as a constant geometry.

Although we won't touch on it in this chapter, lateral joins are particularly useful when used with set-returning functions, which return a set of values rather than a single value. PostGIS, and particularly the postgis_raster extension, has many set-returning functions. Set-returning functions are also heavily used with JSON to unravel deeply nested data. You'll often see outputs of set-returning functions passed into other set-returning functions in an SQL gymnastic feat only achievable in PostgreSQL. You'll see some examples of set-returning function lateral joins in chapter 12. In the case of set-returning functions, the LATERAL keyword is optional, so it may be harder to recognize its use in that context.

Correlated subqueries and LATERAL joins are heavily used in database work and, in particular, PostGIS work. You can go a long way by mastering these two concepts. If you need a more detailed explanation of correlated subqueries and lateral joins, refer to appendix C.

9.2   *Using KNN with geography types*

Using KNN operators with geography works much as it does with geometry.

We'll look at a KNN example using airports in this section. We want to find the 10 closest airports to Boston Logan:

```
SELECT ident, name,
    geog <-> (SELECT geog
            FROM  ch09.airports WHERE ident = 'KBOS') AS dist
FROM ch09.airports
```

```
WHERE ident != 'KBOS' AND type = 'large_airport'
ORDER BY dist LIMIT 10;
```

As before, we create a subquery that returns the geography for Boston (KBOS). Further, we only want large airports that don't include Boston, so we add additional filters. Finally, we close off by using our aliased `dist`, which encapsulates our `<->` call with a constant KBOS point. We get an answer in under 70 ms.

9.2.1 *Using window functions to number the closest N places*

In the previous examples, we only output the *N* closest places, but we did not number them. Sometimes it's useful to number these instead of just listing the distance. The `ROW_NUMBER`, `RANK`, and `DENSE_RANK` window functions come in handy for outputting some ordinal ordering of a row.

A *window function* is a function that can look across the whole dataset of a query and provide information relative to its position in the data. It works similarly to an `AGGREGATE`, except it returns all rows instead of aggregating them in a single row. In fact, all `AGGREGATE`s can be used as `WINDOW` aggregates. All window function calls must have an `OVER` clause that dictates how the records can be partitioned and ordered in the window. The `OVER` clause may be empty or contain `PARTITION BY` or `ORDER BY` subclauses or a named `WINDOW` clause. An `OVER` clause can also contain other kinds of subclauses, which are detailed in appendix C.

The most popular window functions are those that number the values of a set. In this section we'll demonstrate how to use the `ROW_NUMBER`, `RANK`, and `DENSE_RANK` functions.

ROW_NUMBER, RANK, and DENSE_RANK

The difference between RANK and ROW_NUMBER is in how they handle ties. RANK will mark ties with the same number and skip the subsequent numbers (for example, 1,2,3,3,3,6,7). ROW_NUMBER will arbitrarily break ties so you always have a distinct sequence (1,2,3,4,5,6,7). By PostgreSQL convention, any operation involving ORDER BY will sort NULL values at the end unless the ordering column is followed by NULLS FIRST.

DENSE_RANK will ascribe the same number to the same ORDER BY values just like RANK, but it won't skip numbers. Instead of a sequence of 1,2,3,3,3,6,7, DENSE_RANK would return a sequence of 1,2,3,3,3,4,5.

In this next example we'll list roads within 100 meters of each school and number these based on proximity to the school.

Listing 9.4   Find two closest roads to each school within 100 meter radius

```
SELECT
    pid, rnum,
    rank, drank,
```

```
    road_name,
    round(CAST(dist_km As numeric),2) As dist_km
FROM (
    SELECT
        ROW_NUMBER() OVER w_dist As rnum,
        RANK() OVER w_dist AS rank,
        DENSE_RANK() OVER w_dist AS drank,        ⟵  Window function
        E.pid, E.road_name,                           outputs by using the
        E.dist_km                                     named w_dist window
    FROM
        (SELECT l.pid,
          round((r.geom <-> l.geom)::numeric/1000,2) As dist_km
        FROM ch09.land As l
    LEFT JOIN              ⟵                     Output land even if
        ch09.road As r                           no road is within
    ON ST_DWithin(r.geom,l.geom,100)             100 meters.
    WHERE l.land_type = 'education'
        AND l.pid LIKE '143-1%') AS E                         Define WINDOW
    WINDOW w_dist AS (PARTITION BY E.pid ORDER BY e.dist_km)  ⟵  clause to be
) As X                                                        used in OVER.
WHERE X.drank < 3        ⟵    Only return roads that are
ORDER BY pid, rnum;           within 2 ranks with ties.
```

Listing 9.4 narrows the set of roads to only those that are within a tenth of a kilometer, but the LEFT JOIN ensures that even if there are no roads within the desired distance of a school, each school will still be represented at least once. This means that you could run into situations where a school has just one road or even no roads. So be it.

The schools are partitioned by unique identifiers, PARTITION BY E.pid, which means the window functions will act over each school independently. Since we are using DENSE_RANK < 2 for our filter, we will get roads even if they are tied in distance.

The ORDER BY dist_km forces the sequential numbering to be ordered by distance to the school (rounded to 2 decimal points in km). Any additional decimal points will be ignored.

Because we are using the same partitioning and ordering clause for each of our window function calls, we create a named WINDOW clause to reuse it. If you had only one WINDOW function call or you had different clauses for each function, you could put the WINDOW clause directly in the OVER as follows: OVER(PARTITION BY E.pid ORDER BY e.dist_km).

The output follows:

```
 pid    | rnum | rank | drank |   road_name      | dist_km
--------+------+------+-------+------------------+---------
143-10 |    1 |    1 |     1 | CAMBRIDGE STREET |    0.01
143-11 |    1 |    1 |     1 | CAMBRIDGE STREET |    0.01
143-11 |    2 |    2 |     2 | QUINCY STREET    |    0.06
143-11 |    3 |    2 |     2 | CAMBRIDGE STREET |    0.06
143-11 |    4 |    2 |     2 | CAMBRIDGE STREET |    0.06
143-13 |    1 |    1 |     1 | KIRKLAND STREET  |    0.01
143-13 |    2 |    2 |     2 | QUINCY STREET    |    0.07
143-15 |    1 |    1 |     1 | CAMBRIDGE STREET |    0.06
```

```
143-15 |    2 |    2 |    2 | KIRKLAND STREET  |   0.09
143-17 |    1 |    1 |    1 | CAMBRIDGE STREET |   0.01
143-17 |    2 |    1 |    1 | QUINCY STREET    |   0.01
143-17 |    3 |    3 |    2 | BROADWAY         |   0.02
143-17 |    4 |    3 |    2 | KIRKLAND STREET  |   0.02
143-17 |    5 |    3 |    2 | CAMBRIDGE STREET |   0.02
(14 rows)
```

Note that in the preceding output you get five records back for 143-17 but each has a dense rank < 3. The row number sequentially numbers first by distance and then arbitrarily, since we have no other ordering clause. In the case of rank, we get 1 and 3 with a gap for 2 because the first roads are tied for first place, and the remainder are tied for third. For dense rank, we get 1 and 2, because the first 2 are tied for first place, and since no gaps allowed, the next 3 are tied for second place.

Although this example demonstrated the use of ST_DWithin and <-> in conjunction with various WINDOW ranking functions using geometry types, keep in mind that you can just as easily use this approach with the geography type because geography has the same functions available.

9.3   Geotagging

Geotagging refers to a class of spatial techniques where you try to situate points located within the context of another geometry. There are two forms this generally takes:

- *Region tagging*—This is a process where you tag a geometry, such as a point of interest, with the name of a region it's in, such as a state, city, or province.
- *Linear referencing*—This is another kind of tagging, particular to linestrings, whereby you refer to a point of interest by its closest point along a linestring. The tag can be the closest point on the linestring, or a measure such as a mile marker or fractional percent measured from the start of the linestring to the point on the linestring closest to your point of interest. Linear referencing is used heavily in geocoding and reverse geocoding, which we'll discuss in detail in chapter 10.

Geotagging and linear referencing are two common tasks for GIS practitioners because they're preparatory steps for many statistical analyses. For example, suppose you have a list of all McDonald's in California, and you have a table of all counties as geometries. Regional geotagging could involve trying to figure out which counties contain which McDonald's so that you can then easily get a count of McDonald's in each county. If instead you have a list of all major highways in California, linear referencing could involve trying to figure out which highways have which McDonald's on the roadside.

9.3.1   Tagging data to a specific region

One of the more common uses of spatial databases is to tag regions. Often you'll have named regions of space divided into polygons or multipolygons. These could be political districts, sales territories, states, or whatever. You'll also have points with coordinates, and you'll need to figure out which region each point lies within. Ultimately, you'll want to add a column to your points table identifying the matched regions.

Let's look at an example based on the airports table. Suppose that for each airport, you need to find and store its time zone. Your time zone regions will come from a table of multipolygons (ch09.tz_world), and for each airport you'll find what time zone multipolygon it falls in and set its time zone to the time zone value for that region. The following example updates the time zone field of the airport with the time zone value in the corresponding time zone multipolygon:

```
ALTER TABLE ch09.airports ADD COLUMN IF NOT EXISTS tz varchar(30);
UPDATE ch09.airports
SET tz = t.tzid
FROM ch09.tz_world As t
WHERE ST_Intersects(ch09.airports.geog, t.geog);
```

After this update is done, most of your airports will have a time zone. This particular update took about 1.5 minutes on a 6-core (dual core) Intel computer with Postgre-SQL 13 and PostGIS 3.1 and it updated 54,345 rows.

To display the current local time at each of these airports, you can use the built-in PostgreSQL time zone functions as follows and specify displaying the time based on the tz column you computed:

```
SELECT ident, name, CURRENT_TIMESTAMP AT TIME ZONE tz AS ts_at_airport
FROM ch09.airports
WHERE ident IN('KBOS','KSAN','LIRF','OMDB','ZLXY');
```

9.3.2   *Linear referencing: snapping points to the closest linestring*

One common form of linear referencing returns the closest point on the closest line-string to a reference point. This kind of linear referencing is often referred to as *snapping* points to the closest linestring. You begin with a set of points and a set of linestrings. You then try to associate each point with its closest linestring, and then with the closest point on that linestring. Unlike the region tagging we demonstrated, the point of interest (in the previous case, airports) is almost never on the closest geometry.

For example, say you're driving along erratically, taking GPS readings. Over the course of your journey, you've collected points with lots of curves veering both right and left of the street's centerline. You don't want to expose your bad driving habits by simply overlaying your connected GPS points over a map of street centerlines, so you perform linear referencing, where each point is snapped to a street centerline.

Paul Ramsey, the founding father of PostGIS, inspired the next example with his "Snapping Points in PostGIS" blog post (http://mng.bz/EV9R). At the time, Paul only had two functions to work with: ST_Line_Interpolate_Point and ST_Line_Locate _Point (both renamed to ST_LineInterpolatePoint and ST_LineLocationPoint in PostGIS 2.1).

For this example, we've chosen to use the `ST_ClosestPoint` function instead. Introduced in PostGIS 1.5, `ST_ClosestPoint` is faster than the older linear referencing functions, and the inputs are not limited to points. For this example, you'll be snapping land parcels (polygons) to the closest point on the centerline of the nearest road.

> **NOTE** PostGIS 2.0 unveiled `ST_3DDWithin`, `ST_3DDistance`, and `ST_3DClosest-Point`, thanks to the efforts of Nicklas Avén. PostGIS 3.0 improved on `ST_3DDWithin` and `ST_3DDistance` to handle TINs and better handle polyhedral surfaces, thanks to the efforts of Darafei Praliaskouski. These functions work with 3D points, linestrings, polygons, and polyhedral surfaces. 2D proximity functions will ignore the Z coordinate even if it's included in the input.

The basic approach to the solution is as follows:

1 Use `ST_DWithin` to narrow your choices. If a parcel has no road within 30 meters, eliminate it from consideration.

2 For every pairing of parcel and road, use `ST_ClosestPoint` to pinpoint the closest point on the road to the parcel.

3 Use a combination of `DISTINCT ON` and the `ST_Distance` function to only keep the pair of parcel and road that are closest.

When finding closest geometries for anything with a geometry dimension higher than a point, you may not end up with unique answers. For instance, there's an infinite number of points that are closest to each other when you consider two parallel linestrings. `ST_ClosestPoint` will return just one of these. The point selected will always be one of the vertices of the two-point segment returned by `ST_ShortestLine`. `ST_ShortestLine`, like `ST_ClosestPoint`, only returns one answer, even if there are multiple answers.

Listing 9.5   Finding the closest point on a road to a parcel of land

```
SELECT DISTINCT ON (p.pid)
    p.addr_num || ' ' || full_str AS parcel,
    r.road_name AS road,
    ST_ClosestPoint(p.geom,r.geom) As snapped_point
FROM ch09.land AS p INNER JOIN ch09.road AS r
ON ST_DWithin(p.geom,r.geom,20.0)
ORDER BY p.pid, ST_Distance(p.geom,r.geom);
```

Figure 9.1 illustrates the original parcels and the snapped points produced by listing 9.5.

For visualizing the original point on the parcel that's closest to the snapped point, we used the companion function `ST_ShortestLine`.

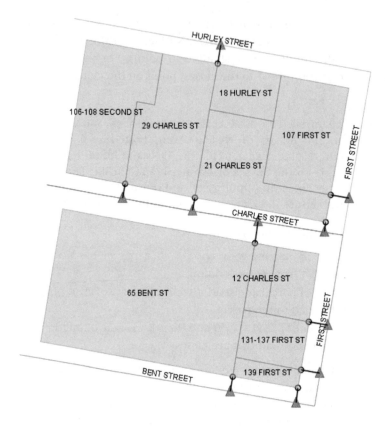

Figure 9.1   Snapping location to a line. The triangles are the snapped points, and the circles are the points on the land closest to the snapped points.

9.3.3 *PostGIS cluster window functions*

PostGIS 2.3 unveiled the very first window functions specific to PostGIS: ST_Cluster-DBSCAN and ST_ClusterKMeans.

> **NOTE**   PostGIS 2.3 unveiled ST_ClusterDBSCAN and ST_ClusterKMeans for 2D geometries, thanks to the work of Daniel Baston and Paul Ramsey. ST_Cluster-KMeans was further improved in PostGIS 3.1 by Darafei Praliaskouski to support 3D geometries and weights. Further enhancements are expected in PostGIS 3.2.

These fabulous functions allow you to clump things together based on proximity to each other. Recall that earlier in this chapter we talked about ROW_NUMBER(), RANK(), and DENSE_RANK() and demonstrated how you can use them with PostGIS distance functions. The problem with that is that they won't help you with distances relative to other rows in your data without resorting to some ugly self-joins.

Imagine you have an army of healthcare staff waiting to be dispatched to homes to provide COVID-19 vaccine shots. Now you want to make sure no staff feels overwhelmed with the number of people they need to visit, and also that no staff are underutilized. You also don't want more than one staff member assigned to an address. You have no boundaries or anything, but you do have parcels of land with addresses of people that need to be inoculated.

How would you divide up your territory? One way is to use PostGIS cluster window functions, which can divide your dataset into clumps where each clump represents a set of things that are close together. The window functions return what we'll call a *cluster number*. Records that have the same cluster number would represent a batch of addresses that should be assigned to a particular staff person.

Before getting started, you need to understand the different approaches that ST_ClusterDBSCAN and ST_ClusterKMeans use so you can decide which is best for your purposes.

ST_ClusterKMeans requires you to decide on the number of clusters you want to break your data into, and it will use this number to assign clusters to the records based on proximity to other rows in the set. You will have no more than the designated number of clusters, but you could have less. ST_ClusterDBSCAN does not require a number of clusters to be specified. ST_ClusterDBSCAN wants to know how close an object needs to be to an object in the cluster to gain membership in the cluster. In addition, there is a minpoints number, which is the minimum number of members you want in a cluster.

Now if you have, say, a fixed number of staff, and your area of interest is fairly evenly distributed by population, using ST_ClusterKMeans probably makes the most sense. However, if you want to know how many staff you need to hire to cover an area, given that each should only span a specific area and a specific number of homes, then ST_ClusterDBSCAN might suit your needs better. Keep in mind, it's possible for ST_ClusterDBSCAN to not find a suitable cluster for some geometries. In this case, it will return NULL for the cluster number.

Let's exercise these window functions using our table of parcels.

Listing 9.6   Cluster locations by window functions

```
SELECT p.pid, p.geom,
    COALESCE(p.addr_num || ' ','') || full_str AS address,
    ST_ClusterKMeans(p.geom, 4) OVER() AS kcluster,
    ST_ClusterDBSCAN(p.geom, 15, 2) OVER() AS dcluster
FROM ch09.land AS p
WHERE ST_DWithin(p.geom,
    ST_GeomFromText('POINT(233110 900676)',
    26986),
    500);
```

Cluster rows with KMeans into at most 4 clusters.

Cluster rows using DBSCAN with a max distance of 15 meters and at least 2 members in each cluster.

Listing 9.6 demonstrates the use of both ST_ClusterKMeans and ST_ClusterDBSCAN in one query. The metrics chosen result in approximately four clusters in both cases. The

ST_ClusterDBSCAN distance is always measured in the spatial reference system of your data. In this case, we have Massachusetts State Plane meters, but if your data is in another unit such as lon/lat, you'll want something like 0.001 for your distance.

Note that the number of parcels in each cluster in the ST_ClusterKMeans case, shown in figure 9.2, is fairly evenly distributed.

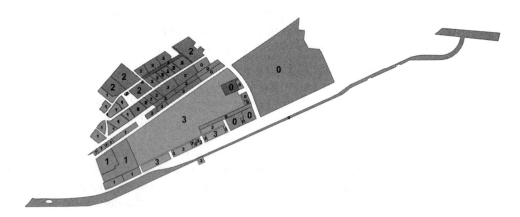

Figure 9.2   Clustering using ST_ClusterKMeans

In the case of ST_ClusterDBSCAN, shown in figure 9.3 and generated from the dcluster column of listing 9.6, the clustering is less evenly distributed, with distance playing a greater role. If you make your distances small enough, clusters are less likely to cross large streets than they are in the ST_ClusterKMeans case.

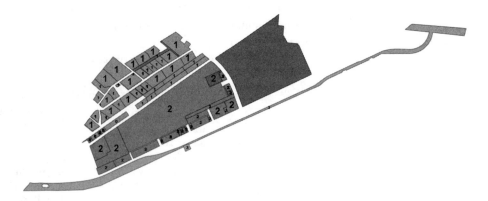

Figure 9.3   Clustering using ST_ClusterDBSCAN

Not having to cross a large street saves time, so this approach might enable staff to visit more people even if there is more travel.

These exercises did not use any of the other window features like PARTITION BY, but you can further group clusters by other factors, such as the skill set of a staff member versus what is needed for a patient by using the PARTITION BY clause. PARTITION BY will restart cluster numbering for each partition.

Summary

- KNN distance operators allow you to return *N* closest items to another item very quickly.
- PostGIS has many KNN distance operators for 2D and 3D geometries, geography, and trajectory distances, and these can use a spatial index if they are used in ORDER BY.
- ST_DWithin is available for both geometry and geography for finding all items within a 2D distance of another.
- ST_3DWithin handles 3D distances but is only available for geometry.
- ST_Distance will return distances for geometry and geography.
- For PostGIS 2.2+ and PostgreSQL 9.5+, <-> can be used as a shorthand substitute for the geometry ST_Distance and as an approximate substitute for the geography ST_Distance.
- ST_3Distance handles 3D distances for geometry only.
- DISTINCT ON is a useful construct unique to PostgreSQL allowing you to pick out distinct rows without using a GROUP BY and rejoining non-grouped columns.
- The SQL window functions ROW_NUMBER(), RANK(), and DENSE_RANK() are useful for numbering results.
- PostGIS has window functions of its own: ST_ClusterDBSCAN and ST_ClusterKMeans.

PostGIS TIGER geocoder

This chapter covers

- Geocoding
- Address standardization
- Reverse geocoding

What is a geocoder? It's a utility that takes a textual representation of a street address and finds its geographic position using data such as street centerline geometries. The textual representation of an address often goes through a standardization process called *address normalization* or *address standardization* that takes the textual representation and breaks it into its component parts, such as street number, street name, suffix, and so on, and ensures that the same type of pieces are always represented in the same way. It is this standardized address that geocoders work with. Geocoders generally return the longitude and latitude.

In this chapter, we're going to focus on the PostGIS geocoder specifically designed for TIGER. The TIGER acronym stands for *Topologically Integrated Geographic Encoding and Referencing*, and it's a geospatial database maintained by the US Census Bureau. The structure is topologically defined with edges, nodes, and faces very similar in structure to how the postgis_topology extension structures data. The database encompasses key features of geographic interest in the entire United

States, including political boundaries, lakes, reservations, major and minor roads, rivers, and so on.

> **NOTE** The postgis_tiger_geocoder extension is generally distributed with PostGIS. Prior to PostGIS 3.0, it required superuser rights to install. In PostGIS 3.0, this restriction was lifted so that non-superusers could install it in their database, provided that someone had already installed the postgis and fuzzystrmatch extensions in that database. From PostgreSQL 13 on, the fuzzystrmatch extension is also installable by non-superusers.

We'll lead you through the following steps in this chapter so that you'll have a fully functioning geocoder at the end:

1. Installing the PostGIS TIGER geocoder
2. Downloading the data from the U.S. Census Bureau for your region of interest
3. Using an address normalizer to prepare your addresses
4. Geocoding and interpreting the results
5. Reverse geocoding

Instructions for setting up the PostGIS TIGER geocoder can also be found in the PostGIS installation documentation (http://mng.bz/N8Vd).

The US Census Bureau annually updates the TIGER data to reflect new constructions. Also, in many years, the data structure itself might be slightly amended. PostGIS tries to keep up with the latest structural changes to TIGER: PostGIS 3.0 handles the 2019 data structure, and PostGIS 3.1.2+ will handle the 2020 data. The 2020 data had a much larger differential change than prior years. This is because every 10 years the census does a major update to the reference data, in parallel with their decennial census survey.

10.1 Installing the PostGIS TIGER geocoder

Installing the geocoder involves nothing more than running two SQL commands or making a few clicks in pgAdmin.

In psql or the pgAdmin query window, run the following two commands:

```
CREATE EXTENSION fuzzystrmatch;
CREATE EXTENSION postgis_tiger_geocoder;
```

You can reduce the preceding to one step with the following:

```
CREATE EXTENSION postgis_tiger_geocoder CASCADE;
```

The CASCADE clause for CREATE EXTENSION was introduced in PostgreSQL 9.5. It installs all extensions that an extension requires that aren't already installed. In this case, that would be postgis, if you didn't have it already installed, and fuzzystrmatch.

The geocoder relies on string matching to find streets with similar spellings, which is why you need to install the fuzzy-string-match extension.

Because TIGER data is public, you should grant other users unfettered access to read from it, as shown in the following listing:

```
GRANT USAGE ON SCHEMA tiger TO PUBLIC;          ◁──┐  Grant existing
GRANT USAGE ON SCHEMA tiger_data TO PUBLIC;        │  permissions.
GRANT SELECT, REFERENCES, TRIGGER
    ON ALL TABLES IN SCHEMA tiger TO PUBLIC;
GRANT SELECT, REFERENCES, TRIGGER
    ON ALL TABLES IN SCHEMA tiger_data TO PUBLIC;
GRANT EXECUTE
    ON ALL FUNCTIONS IN SCHEMA tiger TO PUBLIC;
ALTER DEFAULT PRIVILEGES IN SCHEMA tiger_data
GRANT SELECT, REFERENCES                            ┐  Grant future
    ON TABLES TO PUBLIC;            ◁───────────────┘  permissions.
```

Note that, by convention, we use uppercase for the PUBLIC role to distinguish it from the public schema.

The CREATE EXTENSION postgis_tiger_geocoder; code line, in addition to installing all the necessary skeleton tables and functions, adds the tiger schema to your database search path, but this may not happen if you have your own custom search_path. Before continuing, verify that tiger is in your search_path by first disconnecting from your database, reconnecting, and running SHOW search_path; in psql or pgAdmin.

Installing the geocoder doesn't load the TIGER data that you'll need to geocode. That comes next.

10.2 Loading TIGER data

To populate the tables created during geocoder installation, you'll have to visit the US Census FTP site, download the compressed shapefiles, decompress them, and use the shp2pgsql utility to load the files into the appropriate tables. Sound like many hours of frustration? Fortunately, the geocoder has several functions that will generate scripts to cover all these steps. We'll look at how you can generate and use these scripts for PostGIS 2.4 and above.

The scripts will vary depending on your OS, and they rely on two free additional utilities that must be on your server: Wget and 7-Zip (or unzip). For Linux, Unix, and macOS users, Wget and unzip should already be present. Windows users can install Wget for Windows and 7-Zip. See chapter 4 for the details on installing these tools.

10.2.1 Configuration tables

The postgis_tiger_geocoder extension creates a schema called tiger and several tables in that schema. You'll want to edit two or three tables that control the loader script outputs. These tables are tiger.loader_platform, tiger.loader_variables, and tiger.loader_lookuptables.

The tiger.loader_variables table is a one-record table containing various paths. You may need to edit the staging_fold field, which specifies the path where you'll download the data and create the temp folder. Less frequently, you may need to edit the other fields. For example, since the census data structure doesn't change that frequently, if you are running an older version of PostGIS pointing at an older TIGER year, it's often sufficient to edit the year and URL of the data. You may also want to use a census mirror of the data that you host for speedier access, and in that case you'd want to change the URL.

The tiger.loader_platform table contains the profiles used to generate the loader scripts. There are two records, each uniquely identified by the os field value: windows generates a DOS batch script, and sh generates a Unix sh/bash-compatible script.

In order to prevent your settings from being overwritten during TIGER geocoder upgrades, we advise you to create a copy of the record most appropriate for your operating system. So, for example, if you are on Linux/Unix/macOS, you would copy the sh record as follows:

```
INSERT INTO tiger.loader_platform(os, declare_sect, pgbin, wget, unzip_command,
          psql, path_sep, loader, environ_set_command, county_process_command)
SELECT 'postgis_in_action', declare_sect, pgbin, wget, unzip_command,
     psql, path_sep, loader, environ_set_command, county_process_command
  FROM tiger.loader_platform
  WHERE os = 'sh';
```

If you are on Windows, replace sh with windows in the preceding code.

We called our settings postgis_in_action. You can edit the declare_sect field using pgAdmin to change the database connection strings or paths to the PostgreSQL bin or to shp2pgsql, unzip, and Wget.

The tiger.loader_lookuptables table contains basic download and load scripts for each kind of census table used by the geocoder, as well as for some additional ones users find handy. In this table you will find a Boolean field called load, which is set to true for most tables, but is set to false for tabblock, bg (blockgroup), addrfeat, zcta5_raw. These tables are not used by the geocoder, but users have found them useful for other needs, such as census statistics tabulation by tabulation blocks and block groups.

The reverse_geocoder function can use the zcta5 table if it is loaded, but it only comes in handy in cases where there is no ZIP code on a street, such as highways. The addrfeat table is fairly useless and takes up a ton of space, as it's really a denormalized join between edges and feature names.

To turn on the load of other tables defined in tiger.loader_lookuptable you can run a statement such as this:

```
UPDATE tiger.loader_lookuptables SET load = true
  WHERE lookup_name IN('tabblock', 'bg', 'zcta5_raw');
```

> **WARNING** The zcta load does some additional work, breaking up the single zcta table provided by the census into state subtables. As such, it alone can take anywhere from 15 minutes to 2 hours, depending on your processing power and disk.

New versions of PostGIS often update the version of the TIGER geocoder and accommodates changes in each year. For example, PostGIS 3.1.2 includes configuration for loading Tiger 2020 data, whereas the previous version had configuration for 2019. After you install the latest PostGIS binaries, you can update to the latest version as follows

```
ALTER EXTENSION postgis_tiger_geocoder;
```

or

```
SELECT postgis_extensions_upgrade();
```

When upgrading the TIGER geocoder extension, the tiger.loader_lookuptables table gets reloaded and `load` settings are reset to their initial state. As such, you are advised to back this table up if you make changes to it.

10.2.2 Loading nation and state data

Before you can start to load in the data, you'll need to create a folder to house the downloaded TIGER zip files and a temporary folder to extract and process them. Create a directory called *gisdata* and a subdirectory within it called *temp* in the location you specified in the tiger.load_variables table's `staging_fold` field. Where you create the directories doesn't matter; just make sure the directories are writeable. For the examples that follow, replace the path `/gisdata` with what you set the `staging_fold` field to.

All the loader script functions used in the following examples use the settings designated in tiger.loader_platform. The location of executables is defined in the `tiger.loader_platform.declare_sect` field.

Now connect to your database from the interactive psql console, and make sure you are connected to the postgis_in_action database.

If you're on Linux, Unix, or macOS, run the code in the following listing. If you're on Windows, run listing 10.2.

Listing 10.1   Generate `nationscript` (for Linux/Unix/macOS)

Turn off table column name output.   Connect to the database.   Output format unaligned, so there's no padding of data

```
\c postgis_in_action
\t
\a
\o /gisdata/nationscript.sh
SELECT loader_generate_nation_script('postgis_in_action');
\o
```

Open the file for output.

Output contents to the opened file.

Close the file.

For Windows users, the psql is generally not in the default path. You should have a menu option in Start Menu > PostgreSQL 13 (or whatever version) > psql. The psql steps are much the same as those for Linux, except that you'll replace the .sh extension with .bat.

> **Listing 10.2   Generate `nationscript` (for Windows)**

```
\c postgis_in_action
\t
\a
\o /gisdata/nationscript.bat
SELECT loader_generate_nation_script('postgis_in_action');
\o
```

You can use pgAdmin4 to generate the scripts as well. If you are using pgAdmin, you only need to run the SELECT … parts of the preceding steps and then copy and paste the output into the file.

> **NOTE**   PgAdmin by default quotes text fields when you copy and paste. To prevent this, go to the File > Preferences > Query Tool > Results Grid menu option, and change the Result Copy Quoting setting to None. This sets text field output to unquoted. In older versions of pgAdmin, only the first 255 characters would show, cutting off part of the script. To prevent this truncation, in the Query Tool > Results preferences, increase the maximum number of characters by a lot.

Psql will place the script file in the gisdata directory. Open up the file in an editor, and make any additional changes you want. Once you've made the changes and double-checked your typing, go ahead and execute the `nationscript` script file from your OS command line.

After you've executed the script, you should see a couple of new tables in your `tiger_data` database schema. The two most important are states_all and county _all. Confirm those have data in them by running the following commands:

```
SELECT count(*) FROM tiger_data.county_all;
SELECT count(*) FROM tiger_data.state_all;
```

If you run into problems, or the count is 0, you can drop the tables and restart the processing as follows:

```
DO language plpgsql
$$
DECLARE var_sql text;
BEGIN
var_sql = tiger.drop_nation_tables_generate_script();
EXECUTE var_sql;
END;
$$
```

Loading the nation tables takes quite a bit of time—usually between half an hour and an hour and a half. Much of the time is spent splitting the zcta (ZIP code tabulation table) across state boundaries.

Now that you've had some practice at loading data, let's generate a script to load individual state data. To make your database a bit lighter, you can delete all the counties and states you don't need from the tiger_data.county_all and tiger_data.state_all tables. Each county record has a `statefp` field that corresponds to a state in the state_all table.

The state data load scripts covered next will only pull down county files for a given state that is specified in the county_all table. If you are only interested in a particular county of a state, you can delete all the other counties.

WARNING Do not move on to the state data load if your county_all and state_all tables are empty because these are used by the state data load scripts.

If you're on Linux, Unix, or macOS, run listing 10.3. If you're on Windows, make sure you change `statescript.sh` to `statescript.bat` before running the listing. Also, be sure to substitute in your favorite states. If you want to run the examples in this chapter, you will need to load at least DC. Even if you want data for all states, you still have to add them to the array one by one.

Listing 10.3   Generate `statescript`

```
\c postgis_in_action
\t
\a
\o /gisdata/statescript.sh
SELECT loader_generate_script(ARRAY['DC','CO'],'postgis_in_action');
```

WARNING As of this writing, the census site tends to block servers pulling down too much data at once. As such, it's not practical to try to pull all states at once. Such attempts will get you blacklisted for days. Each state takes anywhere from 10 minutes to 2 hours to load, depending on the size of the state and your network connection. DC and RI are the fastest to load.

Once you've edited the `statescript` script (if necessary), you can execute it. The script will load in data for all the states you chose. You should see new tables in the `tiger_data` schema, all prefixed with the state abbreviation. If many of the examples that follow result in no output for you, you are most likely missing the dc data. Should you wish to load additional states later, just regenerate `statescript` with different states.

After you are done loading data, run this SQL statement:

```
SELECT install_missing_indexes();
```

It is also a good idea to vacuum all the tables, as explained in the PostGIS Installation documentation (http://mng.bz/N8Vd). That will ensure that all the indexes needed by the geocoder functions are in place and the planner stats are up to date.

10.3 *Normalizing addresses*

A preparatory step before geocoding is to parse the address into components such as street numbers, directional prefixes, street names, suffixes, and so on. This step is often referred to as *address standardization* or *address normalization.*

Although address normalization is often done as part of geocoding, you should consider it a separate step. Once you've standardized the addresses, you can pass them to many different geocoders, not just the PostGIS TIGER geocoder. You can even use the standardized addresses to meet postal addressing standards or to remove duplicate addresses. And there's nothing to stop you from performing the quicker standardization step on weekdays and leaving the slower geocoding step to run over the weekend.

10.3.1 *Using normalize_address*

Standardizing the input addresses to match TIGER conventions greatly improves the accuracy of geocoding. The PostGIS TIGER geocoder includes a function called normalize_address for standardizing addresses in accordance with TIGER conventions. You pass in an address as a string, and the output is a composite object of a norm_addy data type. A norm_addy data type is a composite data type packaged with the postgis_tiger_geocoder extension that exposes the subelements of an address in separate columns.

Let's look at an example of standardizing five addresses:

```
SELECT normalize_address(a) As addy
FROM (
    VALUES
        ('ONE E PIMA ST STE 999, TUCSON, AZ'),
        ('4758 Reno Road, DC 20017'),
        ('1021 New Hampshare Avenue, Washington, DC 20010'),
        ('1731 New Hampshire Ave Northwest, Washington, DC 20010'),
        ('1 Palisades, Denver, CO')
) X(a);
```

The query selects five elements of the norm_addy object in column addy, aliased to shorter names. The output follows:

```
addy
----------------------------------------------------------
 (,,"ONE E PIMA ST",St,,"STE 999",TUCSON,AZ,,t)
 (4758,,Reno,Rd,,,,DC,20017,t)
 (1021,,"New Hampshare",Ave,,,Washington,DC,20010,t)
 (1731,,"New Hampshire",Ave,NW,,Washington,DC,20010,t)
 (1,,Palisades,,,,Denver,CO,,t)
```

To see some of the constituent parts of the addy composite column, you can use the following SQL statement:

```
WITH A AS (
    SELECT normalize_address(a) As addy
    FROM (
```

```
        VALUES
            ('ONE E PIMA ST STE 999, TUCSON, AZ'),
            ('4758 Reno Road, DC 20017'),
            ('1021 New Hampshare Avenue, Washington, DC 20010'),
            ('1731 New Hampshire Ave Northwest, Washington, DC 20010'),
            ('1 Palisades, Denver, CO')
    ) X(a)
)
SELECT
    (addy).address As num,
    (addy).predirabbrev As pre,
    (addy).streetname || ' ' || (addy).streettypeabbrev As street,
    (addy).location As city,
    (addy).stateabbrev As st
FROM A;
```

You can clearly see the distinct fields making up norm_addy in the following code:

```
num  | pre |       street       |    city    | st
-----+-----+--------------------+------------+----
     |     | ONE E PIMA ST St   | TUCSON     | AZ
4758 |     | Reno Rd            |            | DC
1021 |     | New Hampshare Ave  | Washington | DC
1731 |     | New Hampshire Ave  | Washington | DC
   1 |     |                    | Denver     | CO
```

If you wanted to see all the constituent parts of addy as separate columns, you could replace the selected fields with (addy).*. The downside of using .* is that you have no control over the column names. The use of parentheses as done with (addy) is a PostgreSQL specific way of referencing sub-columns in a composite column.

10.3.2 *Using the PAGC address normalizer*

The normalize_address function isn't without its shortcomings. We've seen cases where it fails to parse correctly when addresses have directional prefixes, such as North or South, or when there are additional elements not relevant to geocoding, such as floor numbers.

PostGIS includes another extension called address_standardizer, which you will find in most distributions of PostGIS and which is discussed in the documentation: http:// postgis.net/docs/postgis_usage.html#Address_Standardizer. This extension is a fork of the address standardizing component of a project called Public Address Geocoder (PAGC), and it was wrapped into a PostgreSQL extension by Stephen Woodbridge. There is a newer, completely rewritten address standardizer that better handles non-US addresses and other irregularities. You can find the code for this next-generation version on GitHub: https://github.com/woodbri/address-standardizer.

We'll refer to the packaged address_standardizer extension in PostGIS as the PAGC address_standardizer or simply PAGC to distinguish it from the other address standardizers, such as the one built into the postgis_tiger_geocoder. Also keep in mind that the postgis_tiger_geocoder refers to the process of address standardization as *address normalization* and such functions are suffixed with normalize_address.

Before you can use the PAGC address standardizer, you need to install the extension as follows:

```
CREATE EXTENSION address_standardizer SCHEMA postgis;
```

The pagc_normalize_address function is packaged with postgis_tiger_geocoder and wraps the more generic standardize_address function of the address_standardizer extension to do the standardization work. In order to be swappable with the regular normalize_address function, the pagc_normalize_address function returns a norm _addy custom object, just like the normalize_address function does, and it takes the same inputs.

Let's try the same set of addresses with the pagc_normalize_address function:

```
WITH A AS (
    SELECT pagc_normalize_address(a) As addy
    FROM (
        VALUES
            ('ONE E PIMA ST STE 999, TUCSON, AZ'),
            ('4758 Reno Road, DC 20017'),
            ('1021 New Hampshare Avenue, Washington, DC 20010'),
            ('1731 New Hampshire Ave Northwest, Washington, DC 20010'),
            ('1 Palisades, Denver, CO')
    ) X(a)
)
SELECT
    (addy).address As num,
    (addy).predirabbrev As pre,
    (addy).streetname || ' ' || (addy).streettypeabbrev As street,
    (addy).location As city,
    (addy).stateabbrev As st
FROM A;
```

The output follows:

```
num  | pre |       street        |    city    | st
-----+-----+---------------------+------------+----
   1 | E   | PIMA ST             | TUCSON     | AZ
4758 |     | RENO RD             | DC         |
1021 |     | NEW HAMPSHARE AVE   | WASHINGTON | DC
1731 |     | NEW HAMPSHIRE AVE   | WASHINGTON | DC
   1 |     |                     | DENVER     | CO
```

If you compare the output of normalize_address and pagc_normalize_address, you'll notice the better handling of the Tucson address in the latter. PAGC can decipher spelled-out street numbers. Also notice that PAGC always outputs in uppercase. Although the geocoder doesn't care about casing, the USPS really hates anything but uppercase.

Many standardizers follow a set of rules they use to parse out components of an address into the different parts. How these rules are expressed and whether they are even configurable is drastically different from standardizer to standardizer. In addition, standardizers often come with a set of dictionaries that they use to standardize common variations into the standard terms.

For example, some USPS standardizers adhere to a list of suffix abbreviations and always capitalize. But instead of having to write a new standardizer for each set of rules, the PAGC address_standardizer extension was designed with modularity in mind. PAGC lets users change standards simply by specifying a different set of tables.

In addition to the input address, the `standardize_address` function expects as input the names of a rules table, a lexicon table, and a gazetteer table.

The PostGIS TIGER geocoder includes its own set of PAGC-compatible dictionary and rule tables that are used as inputs to the `standardize_address` function: tiger.pagc _lex, tiger.pagc_gaz, and tiger.pagc_rules. These tables ensure that the output of the normalization process conforms to how TIGER data is structured.

Lexicon and gazetteer tables are dictionary tables. A *lexicon* handles generic replacements, such as changing the word *five* to the number *5*. A *gazetteer* handles geographical name replacements, such as changing *California* to *CA*. The structure of the lexicon and gazetteer tables are identical, and they must have at least the following columns: id, seq, word, stdword, and token.

The rules table is a table of rules where each row contains an ID and a rule. The ID is a unique number that identifies the rule. The rule is a sequence of numbers that denote tokens and separators. For more details about what the token numbers correspond to and how rules are set up, refer to the rules table details in the "Address Standardizer Tables" section in the PostGIS Manual (http://postgis.net/docs/rulestab.html).

You can create an alternate set of rules, gazetteer, and lexicon tables to suit your needs, and pass the table names in as inputs to the standardizer. This will allow you to switch between conventional address geocoding and oddballs like the grid-style addresses found in Utah and alphanumeric addresses found in Wisconsin.

The following listing demonstrates a call to `standardize_address`.

Listing 10.4 Breaking an address into parts with `standardize_address`

```
WITH A(a) AS (
    VALUES
        ('ONE E PIMA ST STE 999, TUCSON, AZ'),
        ('4758 Reno Road, DC 20017'),
        ('1021 New Hampshare Avenue, Washington, DC 20010'),
        ('1731 New Hampshire Ave Northwest, Washington, DC 20010'),
        ('1 Palisades, Denver, CO')
)
SELECT (s).house_num, (s).name, (s).predir, (s).suftype, (s).sufdir
FROM (
    SELECT standardize_address(
        'pagc_lex','pagc_gaz','pagc_rules', a
```

```
    ) As s FROM A
) AS X;
```

The output of listing 10.4 follows:

```
house_num |     name      | predir | suftype | sufdir
----------+---------------+--------+---------+--------
    1     | PIMA          | E      | ST      |
   4758   | RENO          |        | RD      |
   1021   | NEW HAMPSHARE |        | AVE     |
   1731   | NEW HAMPSHIRE |        | AVE     | NW
    1     | PALISADES     |        |         |
```

The output of the `standardize_address` function is a composite type object called `stdaddr`, which is similar in flavor to the `norm_addy` composite type we already covered. We're only outputting some of the fields that make up `stdaddr` in these examples. If you want to see all the fields, put in `(s).*` instead of selecting each component individually.

> **Speed of `standardize_address` vs. `pagc_normalize_address`**
>
> The output of `standardize_address` isn't a `norm_addy` object but rather a `stdaddr` object, which the PostGIS geocoder can't accept. The `pagc_normalize_address` function automatically maps `stdaddr` fields to `norm_addy` fields so that you can hand off the results to the geocoder, but `pagc_normalize_address` is an inefficient wrapper around `standardize_address`.
>
> If speed is important, we suggest that you call `standardize_address` directly instead of going through `pagc_normalize_address`. You'll need to put in the extra work of mapping `stdaddr` to `norm_addy`, but the speed you'll gain in the normalization could be up to ten-fold or greater. The PostGIS manual provides an example (http://postgis .net/docs/Pagc_Normalize_Address.html).

10.4 Geocoding

You have two options when calling the `geocode` function. You can pass it a `norm_addy` composite object, or you can pass it an address string. If you opt for the latter, `geocode` will apply the `normalize_address` function before geocoding.

This means that if you wish to use `pagc_normalize_address`, you must standardize first and then pass in a `norm_addy` object to `geocode`. Alternatively, you can run the following SQL statement:

```
SELECT set_geocode_setting('use_pagc_address_parser', 'true');
```

This code will change the default behavior of the `geocode` function permanently to use the `pagc_normalize_address` function instead of `normalize_address` when given a plain text address. Switch this back to `false` if you need to go back to using `normalize _address`.

By default, geocode returns up to ten matches with a rating. The lower the rating, the better the match, and a rating of 0 means a perfect match. If you have no additional means of adjudicating among the choices, and you only want the best match, geocode lets you pass in an additional argument indicating the number of records to be returned. If you just want the best match, pass in 1.

10.4.1 Geocoding using address text

This next example will use the geocode function to geocode a plain text address. Because a plain text address is passed in, the geocode function will first standardize the address before geocoding.

Listing 10.5 Basic geocoding

```
SELECT                              ❶ Rating
    g.rating As r,         ←┘
    ST_X(geomout) As lon,
    ST_Y(geomout) As lat,           ❷ Pretty-print
    pprint_addy(addy) As paddress        norm_addy.
FROM                                ←┘
    geocode(
        '1731 New Hampshire Avenue Northwest, Washington, DC 20010'
    ) As g;
```

The geocode function takes an address and returns a set of records that are possible matches for the address. One of the columns output by the geocode function is the rating field ❶. The higher the number, the worse the match. One of the objects is a composite type, norm_addy, and it's output as a field called addy in the returned records. You can pass the returned addy field to a pprint_addy function, ❷ which is packaged with the TIGER geocoder, and this will return a pretty-print text version of the address.

The point geometry in longitude and latitude that geocode outputs is called geomout. This point is interpolated along the street segment by its street number. The TIGER data is aware of which side of the street a street number should be on, and it will add an automatic 10-meter offset from the centerline. The 10-meter offset will be too little for an exclusive estate set off of the road, and it will be too much for a roadside lemonade stand. The offset combined with the interpolation means that you're not going to achieve surgical bombing accuracy with the geocoder, but perhaps this is a good thing.

The following listing shows the output of listing 10.5:

```
 r |   lon     |   lat    |  paddress
---+-----------------------+--------------------+-----------------------------
 2 | -77.039.. | 38.913.. | 1731 New Hampshire Ave NW, Washington, DC 20009
 8 | -77.024.. | 38.935.. | 3643 New Hampshire Ave NW, Washington, DC 20010
10 | -77.022.. | 38.938.. | 3801 New Hampshire Ave NW, Washington, DC 20011
(3 rows)
```

If you wanted individual elements of the addy object, you could write a query as shown in the following listing.

Listing 10.6 Example of `geocode` function and extracting properties of `addy` field

```
SELECT
    g.rating As r,
    ST_X(g.geomout)::numeric(10,5) As lon,          Round
    ST_Y(g.geomout)::numeric(10,5) As lat,          coordinates
    (g.addy).address As snum,
    (g.addy).streetname || ' '                      Extract elements
        || (g.addy).streettypeabbrev As street,     of addy.
    (g.addy).zip
FROM geocode('1021 New Hampshare Ave, Washington, DC 20009',1) As g; --

                                            Intentional misspelling and
                                            return single match ❶
```

In listing 10.6 the input address is intentionally misspelled to see if fuzzy string matching can remedy the mistake ❶. As you can see from the results shown in listing 10.7, the geocoder did find a match but assigned it a lower score of 21, compared to the 1 in the previous example. The code also specified that only one result (the top match) should be returned ❶.

Listing 10.7 Output of `geocode` function and extracting properties of `addy` field

```
 r |    lon    |    lat   | snum |       street       |  zip
---+-----------+----------+------+--------------------+-------
21 | -77.04142 | 38.91165 | 1601 | New Hampshire Ave  | 20009
(1 row)
```

Finally, the coordinate digits returned were rounded by casting to `numeric(10,5)`: ten digits overall, with no more than five to the right of the decimal point. If you find yourself not needing so many significant digits, you can change the `numeric(10,5)` cast setting.

A geometric method for rounding the longitude and latitude is to use the PostGIS function expression `ST_X(ST_SnapToGrid( geom ) )`, as shown next:

```
SELECT ST_X(ST_SnapToGrid(g.geomout, 0.00001)) AS lon,
    ST_Y(ST_SnapToGrid(g.geomout, 0.00001)) AS lat
    FROM geocode('1021 New Hampshare Ave, Washington, DC 20009',1) As g
```

The `ST_SnapToGrid` function will move the `geomout` point to the closest .00001 degree (both X and Y), and you'll end up with the same rounding as by casting to numeric.

You can also use the plain `round` function and keep your coordinates as double precision.

10.4.2 Geocoding using normalized addresses

You can pass a norm_addy object to the geocoder and save the geocoder from having to first call the normalize_address function. Separating the address normalization from the geocoding also lets you swap in a different normalizer. For example, the following example uses the pagc_normalize_address normalizer:

```
SELECT g.rating As r, ST_X(geomout) As lon, ST_Y(geomout) As lat
FROM geocode(
    pagc_normalize_address(
        '1731 New Hampshire Avenue Northwest, Washington, DC 20010'
    )
) As g;
```

As mentioned previously, the geocoder will only accept norm_addy objects. You can't pass in the stdaddr object returned by the address_standardize function.

10.4.3 Geocoding intersections

Often it is useful to describe an address in terms of street intersections, such as when reporting a crime. For this there is a function called geocode_intersection.

Listing 10.8 geocode_intersection

```
SELECT
    g.rating As r,
    ST_X(geomout) As lon,
    ST_Y(geomout) As lat,
    pprint_addy(addy) As paddress
FROM
    geocode_intersection(
        'New Hampshire Avenue Northwest',      ⟵—⏋  Road 1
        'R St NW',                   ⟵————  Road 2
        'DC',            ⟵—⏋  State
        'Washington',        ⟵—⏋  City (optional)
        '20010',     ⟵—⏋        ZIP code (optional)
        6    ⟵—⏋
    ) As g;
                                Max results (optional),
                                default 10
```

As shown in listing 10.8, the geocode_intersection function can take up to 6 arguments, with city and ZIP code being optional. Although city and ZIP code are optional, you get much better speed and accuracy by providing them. The output follows:

```
r |   lon    |   lat    |                  paddress
---+----------+----------+---------------------------------------------------
 3 | -77.04066 | 38.912608 | 1700 New Hampshire Ave NW, Washin.., DC 20009
 3 | -77.04066 | 38.912608 | 1701 New Hampshire Ave NW, Washin.., DC 20009
 3 | -77.04066 | 38.912608 | 1698 New Hampshire Ave NW, Washin.., DC 20009
 3 | -77.04066 | 38.912608 | 1699 New Hampshire Ave NW, Washin.., DC 20009
(4 rows)
```

If there is only one intersection, you will get the four addresses corresponding to it. The order of the roads matters. Note that the addresses in this example all fall on New Hampshire Ave. If we were to flip the order of the roads, we'd get answers with addresses on R St.

10.4.4 Batch geocoding

Geocoding is rarely done one address at a time. Often you're faced with having to geocode thousands, if not millions, of addresses, and geocoding is not exactly a speedy function. When faced with overwhelming geocoding tasks, we recommend that you start your query before going to bed, and wake up to find the job done.

When geocoding in a batch, you'll almost always want only the top result. You can easily later delete records where the rating of the top result is too low for you to have confidence in the match.

For an example, let's create a small table that's populated with addresses to be geocoded and that has output fields readied.

Listing 10.9   Create a table of addresses

```
DROP TABLE IF EXISTS addr_to_geocode;
CREATE TABLE addr_to_geocode (
    addid serial NOT NULL PRIMARY KEY,
    rating integer,
    address text,
    norm_address text,
    pt geometry
);
INSERT INTO addr_to_geocode(address)
VALUES
    ('ONE E PIMA ST STE 999, TUCSON, AZ'),
    ('4758 Reno Road, DC 20017'),
    ('1021 New Hampshare Avenue, Washington, DC 20010'),
    ('1731 New Hampshire Avenue Northwest, Washington, DC 20010'),
    ('1 Palisades, Denver, CO');
```

The code in the following listing performs the geocoding and updates the table with the results.

Listing 10.10   Batch geocoding

```
UPDATE addr_to_geocode            ❶ Multicolumn
SET                                  update syntax
    (rating, norm_address, pt) =
    (COALESCE((g).rating,-1 ), pprint_addy( (g).addy ), (g).geomout)   ←─┐
FROM                                                        Select output
    (SELECT *                                               fields from the
      FROM addr_to_geocode                                  geocoder results.
      WHERE rating IS NULL LIMIT 100   ←── Batches
      ) As a                                of 100
    LEFT JOIN LATERAL
    geocode(a.address, 1) As g
```

```
      ON ((g).rating < 22)
WHERE a.addid = addr_to_geocode.addid;
```
                                    ⟵ ⎤ **Return null for geocode**
                                        ⎦ **if rating is >= 22**

In the preceding listing you use a multicolumn update, setting one row object to another row object with the code (...) = (...) ❶. This syntax is easier to read than many SET statements, such as SET a1=v1, a2=v2, ...

To make sure that you don't keep retrying bad matches, you use the SQL COALESCE function to replace NULLs with -1.

By using small batches, you guard against unhandled errors in the geocoder that could halt your overnight processing. Furthermore, you economize on memory, and if the power goes out or the server crashes, you won't lose the work already done.

If you have millions of addresses to contend with, you can also use the psql \watch command, which allows you to run the same update statement repeatedly. If you want to take advantage of the psql \watch command as a very lightweight looping engine, remove the semicolon (;) at the end of the WHERE clause, and replace it with \watch 10. Then run the command in psql. This will make psql repeat the same update every 10 seconds.

If \watch is added to listing 10.10, psql will keep pulling the next batch of 100 addresses with no rating and then try to geocode them. The COALESCE((g),rating,-1) ensures that each address checked gets a rating, even if it can't be geocoded.

If you are running PostgreSQL 11 or higher, you can take advantage of stored procedures. Unlike stored functions, stored procedures can't return values, but you can commit transactions within the procedure, allowing you to commit partial work done. This makes stored procedures particularly suitable for batch processes such as batch geocoding.

Listing 10.11   Batch geocoding procedure for PostgreSQL 11+

```
CREATE OR REPLACE PROCEDURE batch_geocode()
LANGUAGE 'plpgsql' AS
$$
BEGIN
    WHILE EXISTS (SELECT 1 FROM addr_to_geocode WHERE rating IS NULL) LOOP
        WITH a AS ( SELECT addid, address FROM addr_to_geocode
                    WHERE rating IS NULL ORDER BY addid LIMIT 5
                    FOR UPDATE SKIP LOCKED)
        UPDATE addr_to_geocode
            SET (rating, new_address, pt)
            = (COALESCE(g.rating,-1),
               COALESCE ((g.addy).address::text, '')
               || COALESCE(' ' || (g.addy).predirabbrev, '')
               || COALESCE(' ' || (g.addy).streetname,'')
               || ' ' || COALESCE(' ' || (g.addy).streettypeabbrev, '')
               || COALESCE(' ' || (g.addy).location || ', ', '')
               || COALESCE(' ' || (g.addy).stateabbrev, '')
               || COALESCE(' ' || (g.addy).zip, '')
            ,
            ST_SetSRID(g.geomout,4326)::geography
            )
```

While you still have ungeocoded records in table

Pick the next five not already locked by another process.

```
            FROM (SELECT addid, (gc).rating, (gc).addy, (gc).geomout
                  FROM a
                  LEFT JOIN LATERAL geocode(address,1) AS gc ON (true)
                 ) AS g
              WHERE g.addid = addr_to_geocode.addid;

            COMMIT;    --    ◁──────┐  Commit the
       END LOOP;                   │  changes.
       RETURN;
END;
$$;
```

Listing 10.11 is a basic example of a PostgreSQL stored procedure that can process records for geocoding in batches.

Stored procedures are called using the CALL command instead of SELECT. You would execute the stored procedure in listing 10.11 as follows:

```
CALL  batch_geocode();
```

You now know how to geocode when you're starting with a real-world address, but often you'll be starting with longitude and latitude data, such as the locational data smartphone users might pass along. You'll often need to resolve the coordinates to addresses. This process is called *reverse geocoding*, and we'll cover that next.

10.5 Reverse geocoding

Reverse geocoding is the opposite of geocoding. You start with spatial coordinates and resolve them to addresses. The PostGIS geocoder comes with a function called reverse_geocode, which takes as input a geometric point in WGS 84 lon/lat coordinates and returns a composite object consisting of an array of norm_addy objects in a field called addy[] and a text array street[] consisting of cross-streets for that point.

Computationally, reverse geocoding is much easier than geocoding because there's no fuzzy string matching involved. The reverse_geocode, to maintain performance, first targets the state, city, and ZIP areas and then drills down to the streets, filtering your point each step of the way. Once the reverse geocoder is at the street level, the reverse geocoder takes your coordinates and interpolates the street number based on the length of the street and the address range for the respective side of the street.

The trickiest part of reverse geocoding is figuring out which side of the street your point is on, because TIGER streets only have centerlines. Without getting too much into topology, think of TIGER street centerlines as forming a network of connected nodes. In the parlance of topology, the centerlines would be called edges, and the nodes are the intersections of edges. With the US completely partitioned into areas bounded on all sides with streets, a point must lie in one of the areas, or *faces* in topo-speak. If the point falls in the right face relative to the closest edge, it must be on the right side of the street. If the point is on the left face, then it's on the left side. The reverse geocoder will be able to find a unique, closest interpolated numerical street number unless your point lacks sufficient significant digits and ends up on an intersection or is on a multilevel roadway.

In cases where the reverse geocoder can't pinpoint a single address, such as if it falls on the corner of two streets, it will return the set of all possible addresses. To help you pick from multiple possible addresses, the reverse geocoder also includes the coordinates of the addresses and the nearest cross-streets.

The following listing shows the reverse geocoding of the addr_to_geocode table created in listing 10.9.

Listing 10.12   Batch reverse geocoding

```
SELECT
    address::varchar(20) as address,
    pprint_addy((rc).addy[1])::varchar(20) As padd_1,     ⊲──┐    Output primary
    (rc).street[1]::varchar(12) As cstreet_1     ⊲───┐         address
FROM (                                                │    Output first
    SELECT address, reverse_geocode(pt) AS rc         │    cross-street
    FROM addr_to_geocode
    WHERE rating between 0 and 20
) AS x;
```

The reverse geocoder returns an array of addresses. The array will only have one member, the primary address, if the reverse geocoding was able to pick without ambiguity. The array could have multiple addresses if your point falls on an intersection or a multilevel roadway. The code in listing 10.12 outputs the primary address along with the cross-streets. The reverse geocoder will provide cross-streets as an array.

The output of listing 10.12 is shown next. We used varchar(.) casting to truncate the text so it could easily fit on the page:

```
address            |         padd_1         | cstreet_1
---------------------+----------------------+-------------
 4758 Reno Road, DC 2 | 4760 Reno Rd, Washin | Davenport St
 1731 New Hampshire A | 1733 New Hampshire A | S St NW
```

Note that the reverse geocoded addresses are pretty close to the addresses we geocoded, as you would expect of a reverse process.

Summary

- PostGIS has a postgis_tiger_geocoder extension for US geocoding.
- The postgis_tiger_geocoder extension comes with routines for loading data from the US Census.
- Postgis_tiger_geocoder has functions for standardizing addresses and parsing them into subelements.
- Postgis_tiger_geocoder has functions for geocoding, geocoding intersections, and reverse geocoding.
- Address_standardizer is an extension often packaged with PostGIS for general standardization rules that can be customized.

11

Geometry and geography processing

This chapter demonstrates techniques for manipulating geometries and geographies, and the end result is generally another geometry or geography. Unless we tell you otherwise, all functions that we demonstrate in this chapter work with both data types.

Through the years, we've amassed a catalog of problems that GIS users encounter, and in this chapter we'll share with you the most common problems we've witnessed and our solutions. Keep in mind that multiple solutions exist for a given problem. We by no means proclaim that our solutions trump all other solutions. In fact, if enough people run into a problem that can be generalized, PostGIS could very well introduce a wrapper function that will resolve the problem with a single call.

The data and code used in this chapter are located here: www.postgis.us/chapter_11_edition_3.

11.1   *Using spatial aggregate functions*

Aggregation is the process of rolling up several rows of data into one. For any table, aggregation begins by segregating the columns into those that you group by and those that you don't. SQL finds like values across your group-by columns and creates distinct groups. It must then apply an aggregate function to roll up the non-group-by columns, summing them, averaging them, and so on.

In a textual relational database, the most common aggregation functions used are COUNT, SUM, MIN, MAX, and AVG. With a spatial extender such as PostGIS, many spatial aggregates are added to the mix. The most common geometry aggregates are ST_MakeLine, ST_Union, ST_Collect, and ST_Polygonize. The ST_Union function is by far the most commonly used of the spatial aggregates. You can find the full list of PostGIS spatial aggregates in the "PostGIS Aggregate Functions" section of the Post-GIS manual (http://mng.bz/RKmv).

11.1.1   *Creating a multipolygon from many multipolygon records*

In many cases, you may have a city where records are broken out by districts, neighborhoods, boroughs, or precincts because you often need to view or report on each neighborhood separately. Sometimes, however, for reporting purposes you need to view the city as a single unit. In this case you can use the ST_Union aggregate function to amass one single multipolygon from constituent multipolygons.

For example, the largest city in the United States is New York, made up of the five storied boroughs of Manhattan, Bronx, Queens, Brooklyn, and Staten Island. To aggregate New York, you first need to create a boroughs table with five records—one multipolygon for each of the boroughs with littorals (see figure 11.1).

Figure 11.1   Five boroughs of New York City as five records

Then you can use the ST_Union spatial aggregate function to group all the boroughs into a single city, as follows.

Listing 11.1 New York City unified

```
SELECT ST_Union(geom) As city FROM ch11.boroughs;
```

Figure 11.2 shows the result of the union operation in listing 11.1.

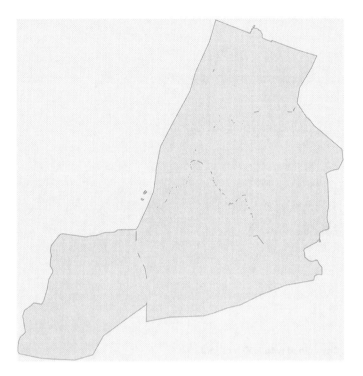

Figure 11.2   New York City unified

PostGIS 3.1 augmented the ST_Union function to allow unioning on a fixed precision grid. Unioning on a fixed precision grid can sometimes be much faster, and it also gets rid of artifacts introduced by arbitrary floating precision. Unfortunately, this feature is only enabled if you have PostGIS compiled with GEOS 3.9 or above. Many distributions carrying PostGIS 3.1 have it compiled with a GEOS lower version. If you are one of the lucky ones that have both PostGIS 3.1 compiled with GEOS 3.9 or above, listing 11.2 will not error.

Listing 11.2   New York City unified with 500-foot grid

```
SELECT ST_Union(geom, 500) As city FROM ch11.boroughs;
```

The new PostGIS 3.1 grid size feature in listing 11.2 is in units of the spatial reference system of our geometries. Our geometries are in NY State Plane Feet spatial reference, so our grid units will be in feet. Having the grid size option allows you to control the resolution of the output and discard artifacts of floating precision.

The output of listing 11.2 is shown in figure 11.3.

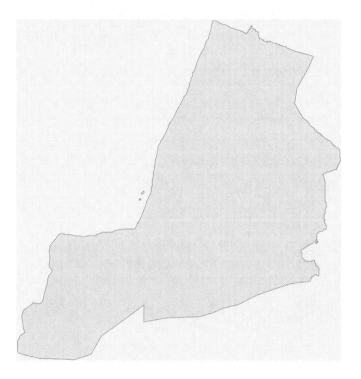

Figure 11.3   New York City unified with 500-foot grid

Note how figure 11.3 doesn't have those small gaps where the boroughs meet, which exist in figure 11.2. Compare the number of points between the two with the following query:

```
SELECT ST_Union(geom, 500) As city FROM ch11.boroughs;
```

You will find that the default union behavior results in a geometry of 1410 points, whereas the one on a 500-foot grid is only 443 points. This is because the behavior is similar to rasterizing a geometry with a fixed size of pixels, so points that collide in the same pixel are consolidated into one. If you go much further, say, to 10,000 feet, you'll notice that your image reduces to what is shown in figure 11.4.

Let's work through an example in the San Francisco area using our table of cities. This query lists which cities straddle multiple records, how many polygons each city

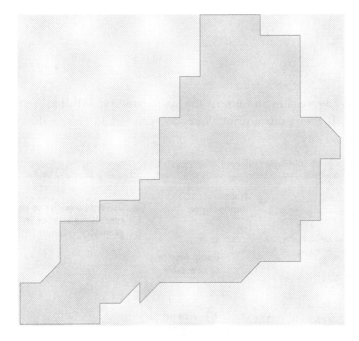

Figure 11.4 New York City unified with 10,000-foot grid

straddles, and how many polygons you'll be left with after dissolving boundaries within each city:

```
SELECT
    city,
    COUNT(city) AS num_records,
    SUM(ST_NumGeometries(geom)) AS numpoly_before,
    ST_NumGeometries(ST_Multi(ST_Union(geom))) AS num_poly_after
FROM ch11.cities
GROUP BY city
HAVING COUNT(city) > 1;
```

If you run the preceding code, you'll see that ten cities have multiple records, but you'll only be able to dissolve the boundaries of Brisbane and San Francisco, because only these two have fewer polygons per geometry than what you started out with.

The output of the preceding code follows:

```
city              | num_records | numpoly_before | num_poly_after
------------------+-------------+----------------+----------------
  ALAMEDA         |      4      |       4        |       4
  BELVEDERE TIBURON |    2      |       2        |       2
  BRISBANE        |      2      |       2        |       1
  GREENBRAE       |      2      |       2        |       2
  LARKSPUR        |      2      |       2        |       2
  REDWOOD CITY    |      2      |       2        |       2
```

```
SAN FRANCISCO       |        7 |        7 |        6
SAN MATEO           |        2 |        2 |        2
SOUTH SAN FRANCISCO |        2 |        2 |        2
SUISUN CITY         |        2 |        2 |        2
(10 rows)
```

The following listing aggregates and inserts the aggregated records into a table called ch11.distinct_cities. It then adds a primary key to each city to ensure that you have exactly one record per city.

Listing 11.3   Aggregating to one record per city

```
SELECT city, ST_Multi(           ❶ Make
    ST_Union(geom) --     ◄──┘     multipolygon        ❷ Use type modifier to ensure
    )                                                     correct registration in
    ::geometry(MULTIPOLYGON,2227) AS geom   ◄──           geometry_columns
INTO ch11.distinct_cities        ◄──
FROM ch11.cities                      Dump results
GROUP BY city, ST_SRID(geom);         to new table

ALTER TABLE ch11.distinct_cities
ADD CONSTRAINT pk_distinct_cities    ❸ Add primary
PRIMARY KEY (city);                ◄──   key to table

CREATE INDEX idx_distinct_cities_geom    ❹ Add spatial
    ON ch11.distinct_cities USING gist(geom);  ◄──┘  index to table
```

In listing 11.3 we create and populate a new table called ch11.distinct_cities ❷. We use the ST_Multi function to ensure that all the resulting geometries will be multi-polygons and not polygons. If a geometry has a single polygon, ST_Multi will upgrade it to be a multipolygon with a single polygon. Then we cast the geometry using typmod to ensure that the geometry type and spatial reference system are correctly registered in the geometry_columns view ❶. For good measure, we also put in a primary key ❸ and a spatial index ❹.

11.1.2   *Creating linestrings from points*

In the past two decades, the use of GPS devices has gone mainstream. GPS Samaritans spend their leisure time visiting points of interest (POI), taking GPS readings, and sharing their adventures via the web. Common venues have included local taverns, eateries, fishing holes, and filling stations with the lowest prices. Companies such as Foursquare and Pokémon have banked on the willingness of people to be tracked and have made a game of it with apps like Foursquare Swarm and Pokémon GO. Another use of GPS is tracking the whereabouts of animals, such as your adorable cat (https://theoatmeal.com/comics/cats_actually_kill). A common follow-up task after gathering the raw positions of the POIs is to connect them to form an unbroken course.

In this exercise, you'll use Australian track points to create linestrings. These track points consist of GPS readings taken during a span of about ten hours from afternoon to early morning on a wintry July day. We have no idea of what the readings represent. Let's say a zoologist fastened a GPS around the neck of a roo and tracked her for an evening. The readings came in every ten seconds or so, but instead of creating one linestring with more than two thousand points, you'll divide the readings into 15-minute intervals and create separate linestrings for each of the intervals.

ST_MakeLine is the spatial aggregate function that takes a set of points and forms a linestring out of them. You can add an ORDER BY clause to aggregate functions; this is particularly useful when you need to control the order in which aggregation occurs. In this example, you'll order by the input time of the readings.

Listing 11.4 Creating a linear path from point observations

```sql
SELECT
    DATE_TRUNC('minute',time) -          ❶ Define track_period as
        CAST(                               15 minute intervals.
            mod(
                CAST(DATE_PART('minute',time) AS integer),15
            ) ||' minutes' AS interval
        ) AS track_period,
    MIN(time) AS t_start,                ❷ Aggregate points
    MAX(time) AS t_end,                     by order of time.
    ST_MakeLine(geom ORDER BY time) AS geom
INTO ch11.aussie_run                     ❸ Bucket the paths into 15-minute
FROM ch11.aussie_track_points               intervals (the track_period).
GROUP BY track_period --
HAVING COUNT(time) > 1;                  ❹ Only consider tracks with
                                            more than one point.
SELECT
    CAST(track_period AS timestamp),     ❺ Calculate length,
    CAST(t_start AS timestamp) AS t_start,   time per period
    CAST(t_end AS timestamp) AS t_end,
    ST_NPoints(geom) AS np,              ❻ Cast geometry to
    CAST(ST_Length(geom::geography) AS integer) AS dist_m,   geography so you
    (t_end - t_start) AS dur                can measure in
FROM ch11.aussie_run;                       meters.
```

First you create a column called track_period specifying quarter-hour slots starting on the hour, 15 minutes past, 30 minutes past, and 45 minutes past ❶. You allocate each GPS point into the slots and create separate linestrings from each time slot via the GROUP BY clause ❸. Not all time slots need to have points, and some slots may have a single point. If a slot is devoid of points, it won't be part of the output. If a slot only has one point, it's removed ❹. For the allocation, you use the DATE_PART function and the modulo operator.

Within each slot, you create a linestring using ST_MakeLine ❷. You want the line to follow the timing of the measurements, so you add an ORDER BY clause to ST_MakeLine.

The SELECT inserts directly into a new table called aussie_run. (If you're not running this code for the first time, you'll need to drop the aussie_run table first.) Finally, you query aussie_run to find the number of points in each linestring using ST_NPoints, subtracting the time of the last point from the time of the first point to get a duration, and using ST_Length to compute the distance covered between the first and last points within the 15-minute slot ❺. Note that you cast the geometry in longitude and latitude to geography ❻ to ensure you have a measurable unit—meters.

Table 11.1 shows partial output from listing 11.4.

Table 11.1   Output from querying aussie_run

track_period	t_start	t_end	np	dist_m	dur
2009-07-18 04:30:00	2009-07-18 04:30:00	2009-07-18 04:44:59	33	2705	00:14:59
2009-07-18 04:45:00	2009-07-18 04:45:05	2009-07-18 04:55:20	87	1720	00:10:15
2009-07-18 05:00:00	2009-07-18 05:02:00	2009-07-18 05:14:59	100	1530	00:12:59
2009-07-18 15:00:00	2009-07-18 15:09:16	2009-07-18 15:14:57	45	1651	00:05:41

Now that you know how to make linestrings from points, let's make smaller geometries from larger ones using clipping and splitting.

11.2   Clipping, splitting, tessellating

Clipping uses one geometry to cut another during intersection. We briefly covered the intersection functions in chapter 9 and demonstrated how you can use them for clipping. In this section, we'll explore other functions available to you for clipping and splitting.

11.2.1   Clipping

As the name implies, *clipping* is the act of removing unwanted sections of a geometry, leaving behind only what's of interest. Think of clipping coupons from a newspaper, clipping hair from someone's head, or the moon clipping the sun in a solar eclipse.

Difference and *symmetric difference* are operations closely related to intersection. They both return the remainder of an intersection. ST_Difference is a non-commutative function, whereas ST_SymDifference is, as the name implies, commutative.

Difference functions return the geometry of what's left out when two geometries intersect. Given geometries A and B, ST_Difference(A,B) returns the portion of A that's not shared with B, whereas ST_SymDifference(A,B) returns the portion of A and B that's not shared.

Here's a symbolic way to think about it:

```
ST_SymDifference(A,B) =  Union(A,B) - Intersection(A,B)
ST_Difference(A,B) = A - Intersection(A,B)
```

The following listing repeats an exercise similar to the one we did with intersection in chapter 9, except here you're getting the difference between a linestring and polygon instead of the intersection.

Listing 11.5 What's left of the polygon and line after clipping

The difference between the polygon and linestring is a polygon. ❶

```
SELECT
    ST_Intersects(g1.geom1,g1.geom2) AS they_intersect,       ◄
    GeometryType(
        ST_Difference(g1.geom1,g1.geom2) ) AS intersect_geom_type
FROM (
    SELECT ST_GeomFromText(
        'POLYGON((
            2 4.5,3 2.6,3 1.8,2 0,-1.5 2.2,
            0.056 3.222,-1.5 4.2,2 6.5,2 4.5
        ))'
    ) AS geom1,
    ST_GeomFromText('LINESTRING(-0.62 5.84,-0.8 0.59)') AS geom2
) AS g1;
```

❷ **The difference between the linestring and polygon is a multilinestring.**

```
SELECT
    ST_Intersects(g1.geom1,g1.geom2) AS they_intersect,       ◄
    GeometryType(
        ST_Difference(g1.geom2,g1.geom1) ) AS intersect_geom_type
FROM (
    SELECT ST_GeomFromText(
        'POLYGON((
            2 4.5,3 2.6,3 1.8,2 0,-1.5 2.2,
            0.056 3.222,-1.5 4.2,2 6.5,2 4.5
        ))'
    ) AS geom1,
    ST_GeomFromText('LINESTRING(-0.62 5.84,-0.8 0.59)') AS geom2) AS g1;
```

```
SELECT
    ST_Intersects(g1.geom1,g1.geom2) AS they_intersect,       ◄
    GeometryType(
        ST_SymDifference(g1.geom1,g1.geom2)
    ) AS intersect_geom_type
FROM (
    SELECT ST_GeomFromText(
        'POLYGON((
            2 4.5,3 2.6,3 1.8,2 0,-1.5 2.2,
            0.056 3.222,-1.5 4.2,2 6.5,2 4.5
        ))'
    ) AS geom1,
    ST_GeomFromText('LINESTRING(-0.62 5.84,-0.8 0.59)') AS geom2) AS g1;
```

The symmetric difference is a geometry ❸ **collection.**

In the preceding listing, the first SELECT returns a polygon ❶, which is pretty much the same polygon you started out with. The second SELECT returns a multilinestring composed of three linestrings where the polygon cuts through ❷. The third SELECT returns a geometry collection as expected, composed of a multilinestring and a polygon ❸. Figure 11.5 shows the results of listing 11.5.

What remains of the polygon when you remove the linestring is still the original polygon. You can't remove a linestring from a polygon because it has no area.

Figure 11.5   Result of difference operations

NOTE   In prior versions of PostGIS, all geometric processing operations worked using double-precision math. This often resulted in issues like topological exceptions. PostGIS 3.1 introduced an additional argument, `gridScale`, which denotes the precision at which to execute operations. This feature is only available in PostGIS 3.1 if you have PostGIS 3.1 compiled with GEOS 3.9 or above. Functions that support this new feature are `ST_Difference`, `ST_ReducePrecision`, `ST_SymDifference`, `ST_Subdivide`, `ST_Union`, and `ST_UnaryUnion`.

11.2.2 Splitting

You learned from listing 11.5 that using a linestring to slice a polygon with `ST_Difference` doesn't work. For that, PostGIS offers another function called `ST_Split`. The `ST_Split` function can only be used with single geometries, not collections, and the blade you use to cut has to be one dimension lower than what you're cutting up.

The following code demonstrates the use of `ST_Split`:

```
SELECT gd.path[1] AS index, gd.geom AS geom        ◁──┐ Expand the gd
FROM (                      ◁──────┐ Define two          geometry_dump
    SELECT                          geometries, geom1    component into path
        ST_GeomFromText(      ❶  and geom2.             and geometry part
            'POLYGON((
                2 4.5,3 2.6,3 1.8,2 0,-1.5 2.2,0.056
                3.222,-1.5 4.2,2 6.5,2 4.5
            ))'
        ) AS geom1,
        ST_GeomFromText('LINESTRING(-0.62 5.84,-0.8 0.59)') AS geom2
) AS g1,
    ST_Dump(ST_Split(g1.geom1, g1.geom2)) AS gd       ◁──┐ Lateral join to ST_Split
                                                    ❷  and ST_Dump in one step
```

The `ST_Split(A,B)` function always returns a geometry collection consisting of all parts of geometry A that result from splitting it with geometry B, even when the result is a single geometry. The preceding listing defines two geometries, geom1 and geom2 ❶. It uses geom1 to split geom2 and dumps out the individual geometries in the collection ❷.

Because of the inconvenience of geometry collections, you'll often see `ST_Split` combined with `ST_Dump`, as in the preceding listing, or with `ST_CollectionExtract` to simplify down to a single geometry where possible. The `ST_Dump` function returns a set of rows of a composite type called a *geometry_dump*. A geometry_dump consists of an integer array path element that defines where the geometry is within the larger geometry it was dumped from and the geometry.

The output of the preceding listing is shown in figure 11.6.

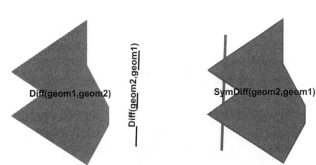

Figure 11.6   Splitting a polygon with a linestring, and then dumping the results into separate polygons

11.2.3 Tessellating

Dividing your polygon into regions using shapes such as rectangles, hexagons, and triangles is called *tessellating*. It's often desirable to divide your regions into areas that have equal area or population for easier statistical analysis. In this section we'll demonstrate techniques for achieving equal-area regions.

CREATING A GRID AND SLICING TABLE GEOMETRIES WITH THE GRID

In this example you'll slice the New York City boroughs into small rectangular blocks. Figure 11.7 shows what you're trying to accomplish, and listing 11.6 demonstrates a method that will do the slicing.

Listing 11.6 uses a square gridding function, `ST_SquareGrid`, introduced in Post-GIS 3.1. `ST_SquareGrid` is a set-returning function that returns a table consisting of 3 columns (`i`, `j`, `geom`). The `i` is the row number along the grid, and `j` is the column number along the grid. You can find more about `ST_SquareGrid` in the documentation (https://postgis.net/docs/manual-3.1/ST_SquareGrid.html).

> **Listing 11.6   Dividing the NYC boroughs into rectangular blocks**

```
WITH bounds AS (
    SELECT ST_SetSRID(ST_Extent(geom), ST_SRID(geom)) AS geom      ⟵  Creates a
        FROM ch11.boroughs                                             bounding-box
    GROUP BY ST_SRID(geom)                                             geometry
),                                        Creates a square grid;       covering the
    grid AS (SELECT g.i, g.j, g.geom      each square is of 10,000     extent of the
        FROM bounds, ST_SquareGrid(10000,bounds.geom) AS g            boroughs
        )                                 length/width units (feet)
```

```
SELECT b.boroname, grid.i, grid.j,
    CASE WHEN ST_Covers(b.geom,grid.geom) THEN grid.geom
    ELSE ST_Intersection(b.geom, grid.geom) END AS geom
INTO ch11.boroughs_square_grid
FROM ch11.boroughs AS b
    INNER JOIN grid ON ST_Intersects(b.geom, grid.geom);

CREATE INDEX ix_boroughs_square_grid
ON ch11.boroughs_square_grid
    USING gist(geom);
```

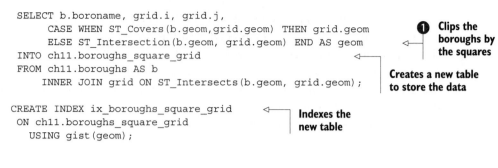

❶ Clips the boroughs by the squares

Creates a new table to store the data

Indexes the new table

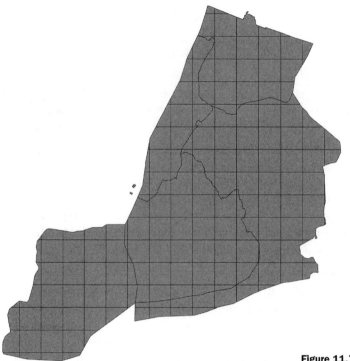

Figure 11.7   Rectangular slicing

Listing 11.6 uses a grid where each square is 10,000 units in length/width and spans the full extent of NYC boroughs. Since the boroughs are in NY State Plane Feet (SRID=2263), the units of measure are feet. When you clip the boroughs by the grid, the resulting tiles have various shapes and sizes when they are on borough boundaries. This may not be ideal if you want all your tiles to be the same size. In those cases you may want to forgo the clipping and just return the squares as is. Note that you use a CASE statement ❶. This is equivalent in result to just doing ST_Intersection, but because ST_Intersection is an intensive operation, you save a lot of processing cycles by just returning the square if it is completely covered by the borough.

Listing 11.6 defined a bounds that covered the whole area of interest, split that into squares, and then clipped the geometries using those squares. One feature of the

ST_SquareGrid function that is not obvious from listing 11.6 is that for any given SRID and size, there is a unique dicing of grids that can be formed across all space. For any given SRID and size, a particular point will have exactly the same i, j, geom tile it intersects in. This means that instead of figuring out the extent of the point of interest first, you could achieve the same result with the next listing.

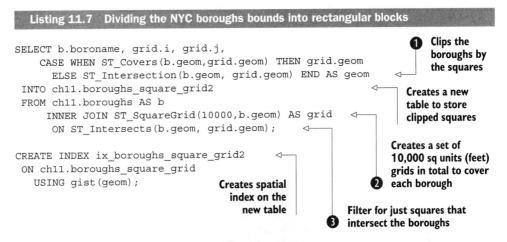

Listing 11.7 Dividing the NYC boroughs bounds into rectangular blocks

```
SELECT b.boroname, grid.i, grid.j,
    CASE WHEN ST_Covers(b.geom,grid.geom) THEN grid.geom
      ELSE ST_Intersection(b.geom, grid.geom) END AS geom
INTO ch11.boroughs_square_grid2
FROM ch11.boroughs AS b
    INNER JOIN ST_SquareGrid(10000,b.geom) AS grid
    ON ST_Intersects(b.geom, grid.geom);

CREATE INDEX ix_boroughs_square_grid2
ON ch11.boroughs_square_grid
    USING gist(geom);
```

❶ Clips the boroughs by the squares

Creates a new table to store clipped squares

❷ Creates a set of 10,000 sq units (feet) grids in total to cover each borough

Creates spatial index on the new table

❸ Filter for just squares that intersect the boroughs

If this is a grid you'll be using often, it's best to make a physical table (materialize it) out of the bounds and use it to chop up your area as needed. However, if this is a one-off chunking for specific areas or if your area is huge and you want to do it in bits, it is better to follow the model of listing 11.7. In listing 11.7, each ST_SquareGrid divides the bounding box of each borough ❷ into a set of 10,000 square-foot squares. Since it's the bounding box that ST_SquareGrid uses, many of the boxes will not intersect the boroughs at all, so they can be filtered out ❸. The squares that do intersect the boroughs will either be ❶ completely covered by a borough or partially covered. If a square is completely covered, you'll want to keep the whole square. If it is only partially covered, you'll want to keep just the portion that intersects. Although you could forget the CASE statement and just use ST_Intersection, the ST_Intersection operation is much more expensive than an ST_Covers check and would result in the same answer for cases where a square grid is completely covered by a borough.

Often a hexagonal grid works better for splitting space evenly, as each hexagon has six neighbors it is equidistant to. This is not the case with squares. A popular gridding system for the world is the H3 scheme created by Uber for dividing driving regions (https://eng.uber.com/h3/). It uses hexagons to divide the earth and a Dymaxion projection (https://en.wikipedia.org/wiki/Dymaxion_map). This approach allows large hexagons to more or less contain smaller ones.

PostGIS 3.1 introduced a function called ST_HexagonGrid. Unlike the Uber H3 gridding, which is based on Dymaxion, this can use any spatial reference system. Similar to ST_SquareGrid, ST_HexagonGrid is a set-returning function that returns a table consisting of (i,j, geom) as columns. Similar to ST_SquareGrid, there is only one grid space that defines a given (srid, size) input to the function. The size is represented as the length of each edge of the hexagon.

The next listing is similar to Listing 11.6 but uses a hexagon grid instead.

Listing 11.8   Dividing the NYC boroughs into hexagons

Return just the grids and count
of boroughs in each grid.

```
SELECT grid.i, grid.j, grid.geom,
    COUNT(DISTINCT b.boroname)::integer AS num_boros
  FROM ch11.boroughs AS b
    INNER JOIN ST_HexagonGrid(1000,b.geom) AS grid
      ON ST_Intersects(b.geom, grid.geom)
GROUP BY grid.geom, grid.i, grid.j;
```

Produce a set of
hexagons that
covers the bounding
box of the borough.

Only consider hexagons that
intersect the boroughs.

The output of listing 11.8 is shown in figure 11.8.

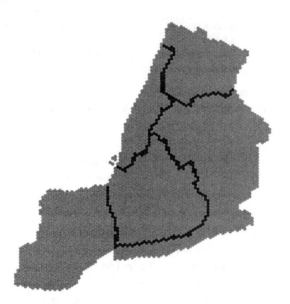

Figure 11.8   Hexagonal slicing

Listing 11.8 also demonstrates another use of gridding, and that's for counting things in buckets and displaying them as a heatmap. In this case we are counting the number of neighborhoods that intersect a hexagon, which is not a terribly useful thing to count. It does demonstrate that if you make your hexagon size small enough, you get a very small area that borders neighborhoods and for most analysis can be ignored. This means that you can achieve fairly equal sub-areas of reporting across your area of interest and do stats based on this simpler, i, j referencing.

CREATING A SINGLE LINE CUT THAT BEST BISECTS INTO EQUAL HALVES

Tessellation is fast and works well when you need many small pieces without paying much attention to the size of each piece. In most scenarios, however, you'll require fewer cuts, but ones of equal area.

To create equal-area slices, the first strategy you can employ is one of convergence toward a solution. In listing 11.9 you start by making a trial cut through the area and measuring the area of the cut. If it's larger than what you need, you translate the cut line to get a smaller slice. You keep doing this until you obtain a cut with equal areas.

Listing 11.9 Bisecting Queens

```
WITH RECURSIVE
x (geom,env) AS (
    SELECT
        geom, ST_Envelope(geom) AS env, ST_Area(geom)/2 AS targ_area,
        1000 AS nit
    FROM ch11.boroughs
    WHERE boroname = 'Queens'
),
T (n,overlap) AS (
    VALUES (CAST(0 AS float), CAST(0 AS float))
    UNION ALL
    SELECT
        n+nit,
        ST_Area(ST_Intersection(geom,ST_Translate(env,n+nit,0)))
    FROM T CROSS JOIN x
    WHERE
        ST_Area(ST_Intersection(geom,ST_Translate(env,n+nit,0)))
        >
        x.targ_area
),
bi(n) AS (SELECT n FROM T ORDER BY n DESC LIMIT 1)
SELECT
    bi.n,
    ST_Difference(geom,ST_Translate(x.env, n,0)) AS geom_part1,
    ST_Intersection(geom,ST_Translate(x.env, n,0)) AS geom_part2
FROM bi CROSS JOIN x;
```

In this query you use recursive CTEs to perform the iteration. This is more to illustrate the capabilities of PostgreSQL than anything else—for clarity and portability, we advise you to create a function that performs the cut and then calls the function as often as needed to reach the desired cut.

Figure 11.9 presents the output of listing 11.9, which demonstrates a basic technique for vertically slicing areas into two equal halves—an eastern half and a western half. You can, of course, create more slices by looping multiple times through the cutter. For slicing into fourths, you'd perform the cut twice. For slices that are multiples of two, you could use another layer of recursion to further bisect your resultant areas until you have the number of slices you want. You could even combine vertical cuts with horizontal cuts by iterating through the Y axis simultaneously to divide an area into quadrants.

Figure 11.9   Borough of Queens bisected

CREATING APPROXIMATE EQUAL AREAS BY SHARDING

In the next approach, you'll use a different technique that combines a number of functions. Credit goes to Darafei Praliaskouski for this sharding technique and to Paul Ramsey's exemplary display of it on his blog ("PostGIS Polygon Splitting," http://mng.bz/JvdZ) and in a video on YouTube ("PostGIS Introduction presented by Paul Ramsey at STL PostGIS Day 2019," http://mng.bz/w0j5).

The basic steps are as follows:

1 Use ST_GeneratePoints to fill your geometry with points—now you have a multipoint.
2 Use KMeans to bucket those points into *n* buckets.
3 Union these points together by bucket and find the centroid of each bucket.
4 Use ST_VoronoiPolygons to divide the space about these centroid points (this creates polygons that extend past the original area).
5 Use ST_Intersection to clip your original geometry using the ST_Voronoi-Polygons.
6 Use ST_Dump along the way to dump the output as needed.

The code for the preceding steps is packaged in the utility.upgis_shardgeometry function, which is included in the code11.sql file and which you'll learn how to build. When you're finished installing the function, it will take a geometry and the number of buckets as input, and it will cut your geometry into *n* approximately equal pieces.

You can call the function as follows:

```
SELECT bucket, geom, ST_Area(geom) AS the_area
FROM utility.upgis_shardgeometry(
    (SELECT geom FROM ch11.boroughs WHERE boroname = 'Queens'),
    4
) AS x;
```

This example will break Queens into four regions, as you can see in figure 11.10. The output sadly isn't exactly even areas because of the tail of Queens. You end up with three approximately equal areas and one oddball.

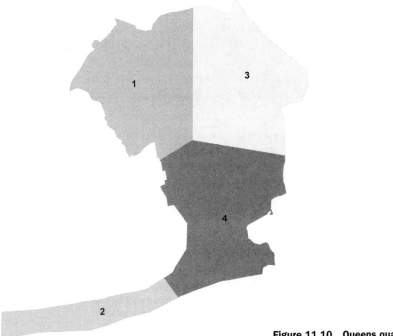

Figure 11.10   Queens quartered

You can verify your work by checking the areas, as shown in table 11.2. Because ST_GeneratePoints generates random points, your answer may be different.

Table 11.2 Area of Queens regions

bucket	area
1	1120860801
2	400499161
3	1143672393
4	1193241882

Let's walk through the function in the next listing and see how it's constructed.

Listing 11.10 `upgis_shardgeometry` cuts a geometry into approximately equal areas

```sql
CREATE OR REPLACE FUNCTION utility.upgis_shardgeometry(
    ageom geometry,
    numsections integer)
    RETURNS TABLE(bucket bigint, geom geometry)
    LANGUAGE 'sql'

    COST 1000
    IMMUTABLE STRICT PARALLEL SAFE
    ROWS 1000

AS $$
WITH r AS (SELECT gd.geom,
            ST_ClusterKMeans(gd.geom,numsections) OVER() AS rn   --
FROM
        ST_Dump(
            ST_GeneratePoints(ageom, numsections*1000 )
                ) AS gd
        )
, c AS (SELECT ST_Centroid(ST_Collect(r.geom)) AS geom, r.rn
FROM r
GROUP BY r.rn)
, v AS (SELECT (
            ST_Dump(ST_VoronoiPolygons(ST_Collect(c.geom)))
        ).geom
FROM c)
SELECT (ROW_NUMBER() OVER())::integer,
    ST_Intersection(v.geom, ageom )
FROM v;
$$;
```

Cluster the points by proximity into numsections.

Generate a multipoint of numsections*1000 points that fills the area of the geometry.

Dump the multipoint into a set of individual points.

Find the centroid of each group of points.

Create Voronoi polygons with each point being the center of each polygon.

Clip the original geometry by the Voronoi polygons.

In the preceding code, `1000*numsections` is the number of points. The number of points is arbitrary, but you want the number to sufficiently cover the geometry of interest.

SHARDING GEOMETRIES WITH ST_SUBDIVIDE

One common reason for breaking a geometry into smaller bits is for performance. Operations such as intersections and intersects work much faster on geometries with fewer points or smaller areas. If you have such a need, the fastest sharding function is the ST_Subdivide function. ST_Subdivide is a set-returning function that takes as input a geometry geom, an integer max_vertices, and in PostGIS 3.1+ an optional gridSize. ST_Subdivide returns a set of geometries where no geometry has more than max_vertices. It can work with areal, linear, and point geometries.

This next example divides Queens such that no polygon has more than a quarter of the total vertices of the input geometry.

Listing 11.11   Subdivide so each polygon has no more than a quarter of the input vertices

```
SELECT row_number() OVER() AS bucket,x.geom,
  ST_Area(x.geom) AS area,
  ST_NPoints(x.geom) AS npoints,
  (ref.npoints/4)::integer As max_vertices          Geometry
FROM (SELECT geom,                                  to slice
        ST_NPoints(geom) AS npoints
      FROM ch11.boroughs WHERE boroname = 'Queens') AS ref
      , LATERAL ST_Subdivide(ref.geom,
              (ref.npoints/4)::integer --            Maximum
              ) AS x(geom) ;                         number of shards
```

The tabular result is shown in table 11.3. In listing 11.11, our vertex count for our input polygon is 956. We divide that by 4 to get 239, our max_vertices input. Note that in table 11.3, no shard has more than 239 vertices.

Table 11.3   Output of subdividing npoints is at most 239

bucket	area	npoints	max_vertices
1	326683238	26	239
2	542270728	73	239
3	206152641	166	239
4	289936900	88	239
5	509849533	161	239
6	3848026	4	239
7	219535088	172	239
8	390074770	104	239
9	1373386538	197	239

The spatial result of listing 11.11 is shown in figure 11.11.

You will often find ST_Subdivide paired with ST_Segmentize. ST_Segmentize is used to even out the segments so that when ST_Subdivide does the work of segmentizing, the areas have a better chance of being equal.

Figure 11.11   Queens subdivided

The ST_Subdivide call in listing 11.11 uses a LATERAL join, which is covered in appendix C. In the case of set-returning functions, the LATERAL keyword is optional, so you will find people often omit the keyword LATERAL when using functions like ST_SquareGrid and ST_Dump, even though they are doing a LATERAL join. Some people find it redundant and some people prefer to add it for clarity to distinguish when they are doing a LATERAL join versus a regular set-returning call.

11.3 *Breaking linestrings into smaller segments*

In this section we'll go through a couple of examples of breaking up linestrings. There are several reasons why you might want to break up a linestring into segments:

- To improve the use of spatial indexes—a smaller linestring will have a smaller bounding box.
- To prevent linestrings from stretching beyond one unit measure.
- As a step toward topology and routing, to determine shared edges.
- To obtain the directionality of linestrings and for use in conjunction with ST_Azimuth to compute bearings.

11.3.1 *Segmentizing linestrings*

If you have long linestrings where the vertices are fairly far apart, you can inject intermediary points using the ST_Segmentize function. ST_Segmentize adds points to your linestring to make sure that no individual segments in the linestring exceed a given length. ST_Segmentize exists for both geometry and geography types.

For the geometry version of ST_Segmentize, the measurement specified for the max length is in the units of the spatial reference system. For geography, the units are always meters.

In the following query, you're segmentizing a 4-vertex linestring into 10,000 meter segments:

```
SELECT
    ST_NPoints(geog::geometry) AS np_before,
    ST_NPoints(ST_Segmentize(geog,10000)::geometry) AS np_after
FROM ST_GeogFromText(
    'LINESTRING(-117.16 32.72,-71.06 42.35,3.3974 6.449,120.96 23.70)'
) AS geog;
```

In this code, you start with a 4-point linestring. After segmentizing, you end up with a 3,585-point linestring where the distance between any two adjacent points is no more than 10,000 meters. You cast the geography object to a geometry to use the ST_NPoints function. The ST_NPoints function does not exist for geography.

As mentioned earlier, ST_Subdivide is often used with ST_Segmentize. This is because ST_Subdivide cuts at vertices, so if you wanted to then break apart your linestring into separate linestrings, you could use ST_Subdivide, but you'd need to first cast to geometry and then back to geography as follows:

```
SELECT
    sd.geom::geography,
    ST_NPoints(sd.geom) AS np_after
FROM ST_GeogFromText(
    'LINESTRING(-117.16 32.72,-71.06 42.35,3.3974 6.449,120.96 23.70)'
) AS geog,
  LATERAL ST_Subdivide( ST_Segmentize(geog,10000)::geometry,
                3585/8) AS sd(geom);
```

11.3.2 *Creating two-point linestrings from many-point linestrings*

One common task is taking a linestring or multilinestring with various points and breaking it into smaller linestrings, each with two points. The code in the next listing takes GPS-track multilinestrings and converts them to two-point linestrings.

You'll see a couple of ways of doing this. You might be thinking, Hey, why can't I just use ST_Subdivide(geom,2)? Sadly, you can't. ST_Subdivide will not let you go below 5 vertices.

That leaves us with other strategies, such as using generate_series or window functions. You'll see both in action here. Feel free to think of other approaches you could exercise. In our tests, these two approaches had approximately the same speed, but speed might be different as the number of points increases.

The non-aggregate version of the ST_MakeLine function is used to construct a two-point linestring in both approaches.

The ST_Dump function is used to explode multilinestrings into linestrings. Because it's a set-returning function, you end up with one row for each linestring in the multi-linestring. ST_Dump returns a set of geometry_dump objects consisting of two fields: geom and path[], which is an array indicating the nesting level and order of the component geometry. For example, {3,2} means that the extracted geometry was embedded in the second geometry of the third collection. ST_Dump will always drill down to the individual geometry level—a collection will never be one of its outputs. In the case of multilinestrings, there's only one element in the array: the position of the linestring in the multilinestring.

The following listing uses the LATERAL/generate_series approach.

Listing 11.12   Two-point linestring from multilinestring using `generate_series`

```
SELECT ogc_fid, n AS pt_id,(sl.g).path[1] AS nline,
    ST_MakeLine(
        ST_PointN((sl.g).geom,n),              ⟵─┐  Make a two-
        ST_PointN((sl.g).geom,n + 1)                │  point line.
    ) AS geom
FROM                                                     ┐  Explode the multilinestring
    (SELECT ogc_fid, ST_Dump(geom) AS g    ⟵──┘  to linestrings.
      FROM ch11.aussie_tracks) AS sl
    CROSS JOIN LATERAL                                        ┐  Iterate
    generate_series(1,ST_NPoints((sl.g).geom) -  1) AS n  ⟵─┘  points
ORDER by ogc_fid, nline, pt_id;
```

Using LATERAL and generate_series can iterate up to one less than the count of points in each linestring, bypassing the need to iterate and filter. It always iterates up to ST_NPoints(geom) – 1 because the final n + 1 for each linestring will hold the last point.

You can achieve the same result using ST_DumpPoints and lag or lead window functions, as follows.

Listing 11.13   Two-point linestring from multilinestring using `ST_DumpPoints`

```
WITH nl AS (SELECT
        ogc_fid, (sl.g).path[1] As nline,     ┐ Make a two-
        (sl.g).path[2] AS pt_id,                    │ point line.        ❶ Set start of line to
        ST_MakeLine(                          ⟵─┘                       previous point in
            lag( (sl.g).geom )                                   ⟵──     the path
                OVER(PARTITION BY sl.ogc_fid, (sl.g).path[1]
                    ORDER BY (sl.g).path[2]  ),
            (sl.g).geom        ⟵─┐  Set the end of the line
        ) AS geom                    │  to the current point.
```

```
FROM
(SELECT ogc_fid, ST_DumpPoints(geom) AS g
FROM ch11.aussie_tracks) AS sl
ORDER BY ogc_fid, nline, pt_id)
SELECT *
FROM n1
WHERE pt_id > 1;
```

◁─┐ **Dump out the points that make up the track.**

❷ **Return all two-point lines.**

The `ST_DumpPoints` function is used to explode any multilinestrings or linestrings into points. `ST_DumpPoints` is very similar to `ST_Dump` in that it also returns a set of `geometry_dump` objects consisting of two fields: `geom` and `path[]`, which is a one-dimensional array indicating the nesting level and order of the component geometry. `ST_DumpPoints` will always drill down to the individual point—it will only ever contain points. In the case of multilinestrings, the array part will have two components: the position of the linestring in the multilinestring and the position of the point in the linestring. When you are making lines, you want to make sure both points belong to the same line and are adjacent. Thus, you need to partition by the record and then the linestring: `PARTITION BY sl.ogc_fid, (sl.g).path[1]` ❶. The number of two-point lines will always be 1 – total points. In listing 11.13 you exclude the first point of each linestring ❷, because the first point is the `lag` value of the second point in a linestring.

11.3.3 *Breaking linestrings at point junctions*

If you're building a routing system for buses, you'll want to ensure that the bus stops are represented as nodes in your road network such that each bus stop is the start or end of a road linestring. You can store the bus stops as a table of points and your routes as a table of linestrings. Then you would need to split the linestrings at the bus intersecting points. Although this exercise does make great use of linear referencing functions, people generally don't think of it as a linear referencing activity.

In the simplest case, think of a two-point linestring. In the middle, you have a point slightly off to the side. You must reconfigure your linestring into two so that it becomes a multilinestring consisting of two two-point linestrings.

The basic steps are as follows:

1 Figure out which bus stops are within a specified tolerance distance from the road.
2 If a bus stop is close enough to the street, find the closest point on the road to the bus stop using `ST_LineLocatePoint`.
3 `ST_LineLocatePoint` returns a number between 0 and 1 representing the proportion along the linestring where the closest point lies. For example, .25 would mean that if a line is 1 kilometer long, one of the closest bus stops would be at the 250 meter mark. We'll call this the *marker*.
4 Once you've determined the marker, use `ST_LineSubString` to break the linestring into two. For instance, if you have a bus stop at the .25 mark, you'd have a substring that runs from 0 to .25 and another that runs from .25 to 1.

5 Finally, use `ST_SetPoint` to ensure that the starting point of one road linestring is the ending point of the other. This is done because of floating-point precision issues that may result in the fractional linestring endpoint not matching with the start point of the next where it's cut.

So many users have asked for a solution to this problem that we created a generic function in PL/pgSQL. You pass in a linestring and a point, or their multi counterparts, and out comes a new linestring or multilinestring cut at the closest point to the set of points. Our function also lets you specify a tolerance, and any point further than the tolerance from the linestring is ejected. The next listing shows our grand oeuvre.

Listing 11.14   Function to cut linestrings and multilinestrings at nearest point junctions

```
CREATE OR REPLACE FUNCTION ch11.upgis_cutlineatpoints(
    param_mlgeom geometry,
    param_mpgeom geometry,
    param_tol double precision
)
RETURNS geometry AS
$$
DECLARE
    var_resultgeom geometry;
    var_sline geometry;
    var_eline geometry;
    var_perc_line double precision;          ❶ Convert
    var_refgeom geometry;                       multipoint to
    var_pset geometry[] :=                      array of points
        ARRAY(SELECT geom FROM ST_Dump(param_mpgeom));
    var_lset geometry[] :=
        ARRAY(SELECT geom FROM ST_Dump(param_mlgeom));  ❷ Loop through
BEGIN                                                      each point.

FOR i in 1 .. array_upper(var_pset,1) LOOP          ❸ Loop through
    FOR j in 1 .. array_upper(var_lset,1) LOOP         each line.
        IF
            ST_DWithin(var_lset[j],var_pset[i],param_tol) AND
            NOT ST_Intersects(ST_Boundary(var_lset[j]),var_pset[i])  If point is
        THEN                                                         within
            IF ST_NumGeometries(ST_Multi(var_lset[j])) = 1 THEN     tolerance
                var_perc_line :=                                     of the line,
                ST_LineLocatePoint(var_lset[j],var_pset[i]);      ❹ make a cut
                IF var_perc_line BETWEEN 0.0001 and 0.9999 THEN
                    var_sline :=
                        ST_LineSubstring(var_lset[j],0,var_perc_line);
                    var_eline :=
                        ST_LineSubstring(var_lset[j],var_perc_line,1);
                    var_eline :=
                        ST_SetPoint(var_eline,0,ST_EndPoint(var_sline));
                    var_lset[j] := ST_Collect(var_sline,var_eline);
                END IF;
            ELSE                          ❺ Recurse if it is a
                var_lset[j] :=               multilinestring.
                    upgis_cutlineatpoints(var_lset[j],var_pset[i]);
```

```
            END IF;
        END IF;
    END LOOP;
END LOOP;

RETURN ST_Union(var_lset);

END;
$$
LANGUAGE 'plpgsql' IMMUTABLE STRICT PARALLEL SAFE;
```

We use the design pattern of exploding a multi-geometry into single geometry pieces and then collapsing those into a geometry array for easier processing ❶. This will turn the multilinestring or linestring into an array of linestrings, and multipoints into an array of points.

Next we step through each point ❷ and each line ❸. For each line that intersects the selected point but isn't on the boundary (an endpoint), we perform the steps we outlined previously, using ST_LineSubstring, ST_LineLocatePoint, and ST_SetPoint ❹. Note that if a line is cut multiple times (the multilinestring can expand to more than two pieces), we use the power of recursion to repeat the whole process ❺, so that at any point in time we're always dealing with single linestrings and single points.

Now for a simple test to see this function in action. You'll cut roads into two that are within 100 feet of your desired point, and you'll use ST_Dump again to explode the multilinestring into individual linestrings:

```
SELECT
    gid, S.geom AS orig_geom,
    (ST_Dump(
        ch11.upgis_cutlineatpoints(S.geom, X.the_pt, 100 )
        )
    ).geom AS changed_geom
FROM
    ch11.stclines_streets AS S
    CROSS JOIN
    (SELECT ST_SetSRID(ST_Point(6011200,2113500),2227) AS the_pt) AS X
WHERE ST_DWithin(s.geom,X.the_pt,100);
```

This query returns the ID of the street that was cut and the individual pieces as separate rows. It also includes the original for comparison. A pictorial view is shown in figure 11.12.

Using the ST_Split and ST_Snap functions

In theory, you could use ST_Split and ST_Snap in lieu of the custom function shown in listing 11.14. In practice, though, this would only work in a limited number of cases, where all the points happen to round nicely. If your geometries take up all the significant digits, ST_Snap will end up approximating, and the linestring will not perfectly snap to the point.

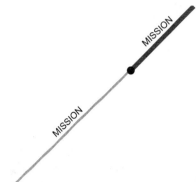

Figure 11.12   Cut Mission Street into two using points within 100 ft of road.

11.4 *Translating, scaling, and rotating geometries*

Do you remember what you learned during your first linear algebra course? Namely, that *shifting*, *scaling*, and *rotating* constitute *affine transformations* on a plane. PostGIS has built-in functions to perform all three: ST_Translate, ST_Scale, and ST_Rotate. All three fall under the umbrella function ST_Affine, which lets you explicitly specify the transformation matrix. We won't go into detail about the ST_Affine function because it's rarely used directly.

Although you may think of shapes on a map as mostly static objects that don't get repositioned much, these handy functions intrude more often than expected. We've encountered the following common uses and are sure that more creative uses abound:

- Producing heat maps with color variations
- Simulating movement along a road
- Simulating position changes
- Correcting coordinates of a geometry when given shifted data
- Creating parallel road lines or edges to turn a line into a polygon
- Compensating for the lack of Z support in GEOS functions by rotating the axis so you can switch planes of comparison

Let's take a closer look at these three functions.

11.4.1 *Translating*

A common use case for ST_Translate is to create grids by using one geometry to paint across and down a region. This particular use case is no longer necessary with the advent of ST_SquareGrid and ST_HexagonGrid as discussed earlier. And if you wanted to break your geometry into triangles, you could use the SFCGAL function ST_Tesselate (though this wouldn't produce evenly sized triangles). However, you might still need to use ST_Translate if you are trying to paint your area with some other kind of space-filling shape.

Another use case for `ST_Translate` is to translate a centerline to the right or left of itself. This is particularly relevant for geocoding when trying to figure out what side of a street an address is on. The newer function `ST_OffsetCurve` achieves the same purpose in much less code.

11.4.2 Scaling

The scaling family of functions comes in four overloads:

- `ST_Scale(geometry, xfactor, yfactor)`—For 2D.
- `ST_Scale(geometry, xfactor, yfactor, zfactor)`—For 3D.
- `ST_Scale(geometry, factor)`—For any geometry dimension, but will scale the coordinates based on a factor specified as a point.
- `ST_Scale(geom, factor, geometry origin)`—The newest addition, introduced in PostGIS 2.5, will scale the same amount but about a specified point.

Scaling takes a coordinate and multiplies it by the factor parameters. If you pass in a factor between 1 and -1, you shrink the geometry. If you pass in negative factors, the geometry will flip in addition to scaling. The next listing shows an example of scaling a hexagon.

Listing 11.15 Scaling a hexagon to different sizes

```
SELECT
    xfactor, yfactor, zfactor,                          ◁—┘ Scale factors
                                                             to use
    ST_Scale(hex.geom, xfactor, yfactor) AS scaled_geometry,    ◁—┘ Scale in x and
                                                                      y directions.
    ST_Scale(hex.geom, ST_MakePoint(xfactor,yfactor, zfactor) ) AS scaled_usi
      ng_pfactor         ◁—┐ Scale using a
FROM                          PointZ as factor
    (
        SELECT ST_GeomFromText(                           ❶ Original
            'POLYGON((0 0,64 64,64 128,0 192, -64 128,-64 64,0 0))'   ◁—┘ hexagon
        ) AS geom
    ) AS hex
    CROSS JOIN
    (SELECT x*0.5 AS xfactor FROM generate_series(1,4) AS x) AS xf
    CROSS JOIN
    (SELECT y*0.5 AS yfactor FROM generate_series(1,4) AS y) AS yf
    CROSS JOIN
    (SELECT z*0.5 AS zfactor FROM generate_series(0,1) AS z) AS zf;
```

Generate ❷ x, y, z scale factors in increments of 0.5.

In listing 11.15 you start with a hexagonal polygon ❶ and shrink and expand the geometry in the X and Y directions from 50% of its size to twice its size by using a cross join that generates numbers from 0 to 2 in X and 0 to 2 in Y, incrementing .5 for each step ❷. The results are shown in figure 11.13.

As you can see in figure 11.13, the scaling multiplies the coordinates. Because the hexagon starts at the origin, all scaled geometries still have their bases at the origin.

Normally when you scale, you want to keep the centroid constant, as shown in listing 11.16. The `ST_Scale` variant that can take an origin as input was introduced in

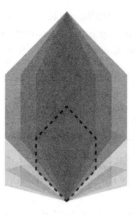

**Figure 11.13   The dashed outline is
the original hexagon polygon.**

PostGIS 2.5. For prior versions of PostGIS, you'd need to use a combination of
`ST_Scale` and `ST_Translate`.

Listing 11.16   Scaling about the centroid

```
SELECT xfactor, yfactor,
      ST_Scale(hex.geom, ST_MakePoint(xfactor, yfactor),
    ST_Centroid(hex.geom) ) AS scaled_geometry
FROM
    (
      SELECT ST_GeomFromText(
          'POLYGON((0 0,64 64,64 128,0 192,-64 128, -64 64,0 0))'
      ) AS geom
    ) AS hex
    CROSS JOIN
    (SELECT x*0.5 AS xfactor FROM generate_series(1,4) AS x) AS xf
    CROSS JOIN
    (SELECT y*0.5 AS yfactor FROM generate_series(1,4) AS y) AS yf;
```

Here you scale a hexagon from half to twice its size in the X and Y directions about
the centroid, so the centroid remains unaltered. See figure 11.14.

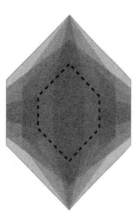

**Figure 11.14   Scaling about
the centroid**

11.4.3 *Rotating*

`ST_RotateX`, `ST_RotateY`, `ST_RotateZ`, and `ST_Rotate` rotate a geometry about the X, Y, or Z axis in radian units. `ST_Rotate` and `ST_RotateZ` are the same, because the default axis of rotation is Z.

These functions are rarely used in isolation because their default behavior is to rotate the geometry about the (0,0) origin rather than about the centroid. You can pass in an optional point argument called `pointOrigin`, which is shown in the following code. When the `pointOrigin` argument is specified, rotation is about that point. Prior to the addition of the `pointOrigin` argument in PostGIS 2, users had to compensate for not having a point of origin by translating and rotating the geometry together to achieve a specific point of rotation. Nowadays using `ST_Rotate` without a `pointOrigin` specified is much less common.

The following listing rotates a hexagon about its centroid in increments of 45 degrees. The centroid is the `pointOrigin` argument:

```
SELECT
    rotrad/pi()*180 AS deg,
    ST_Rotate(hex.geom,rotrad,
    ST_Centroid(hex.geom)) AS rotated_geometry
FROM
    (
        SELECT ST_GeomFromText(
            'POLYGON((0 0,64 64,64 128,0 192,-64 128,-64 64,0 0))'
        ) AS geom
    ) AS hex
    CROSS JOIN
    (
        SELECT 2*pi()*x*45.0/360 AS rotrad
            FROM generate_series(0,6) AS x
    ) AS xf;
```

Figure 11.15 shows the 45-degree rotation.

Figure 11.15 Rotating a hexagon from 0 to 270 in 45-degree increments around its centroid. The original and first 45-degree rotation are shown.

11.5 *Using geometry functions to manipulate and create geographies*

There are far more functions for geometry than there are for geography. However, you can apply many geometry functions to geography by first casting your geography to geometry and then casting back.

PostGIS, by design, doesn't implicitly cast from geography to geometry. You need to explicitly use the cast operator :: or longhand CAST(geog As geometry). When casting from geography to geometry, the SRID of the resultant geometry will always be 4326 lon/lat. When you cast back to geography from geometry, your geometry must already be in SRID 4326 or the unknown SRID 0, and the coordinates must be in bounds of degrees. If you have your geometry data in another spatial reference system, a transform to 4326 must take place prior to the casting.

In this section, we'll cover some popular geometry functions that aren't available for geography and some alternatives you can use if a geometry function doesn't exist. We'll group our functions into two categories: cast-safe and transformation-recommended.

11.5.1 *Cast-safe functions*

You can safely use any geometry function against a geography where spatial reference systems don't factor in. Functions such as exploding geometries into subelements or constructor functions fit the bill. For functions that don't perform measurements, you can generally get away with casting without transformation for a small area.

These are some frequently used functions that fall into this category:

- ST_Collect—This is an aggregate function that groups individual geometries into collections. Unlike ST_Union, ST_Collect doesn't dissolve boundaries. This easily leads to invalid polygons. Use this function with geography as follows:

```
SELECT somefield, ST_Collect(geog::geometry)::geography AS geog
FROM sometable
GROUP BY somefield;
```

- ST_Dump, ST_DumpPoints, ST_DumpRings—These are set-returning functions that only concern themselves with vertices. As such, you can use them in this fashion with geographies:

```
SELECT sometable.somefield, gd.geom::geography AS geog
FROM sometable, ( ST_Dump(sometable.geog::geometry) ) AS gd
```

- ST_Point(x,y), ST_MakePoint(x,y,z)—These functions return a point. In geography, use longitude and latitude as in ST_Point(lon,lat)::geography.
- ST_MakeEnvelope(minx,miny,maxx,maxy,srid)—This function creates a rectangular polygon geometry from coordinates. To form a geography, use coordinates in SRID 4326 and cast to geography as follows:

```
ST_MakeEnvelope (minlon,minlat,maxlon,maxlat,4326)::geography
```

- ST_Transform(geom,srid)—The geography must be in degree coordinates, but once you cast to geometry, you're free to deviate. Use the following syntax: ST_Transform(geog::geometry,srid). Pick an SRID that will minimize the distortion when going from geodetic geography to Cartesian geometry for your particular data set.

TRANSFORMATION-RECOMMENDED FUNCTIONS

Many geometry functions rely on a measurement-preserving planar spatial reference system. To use these with a geography data type, you first should cast geography to geometry and then transform to a suitable measure-preserving planar spatial reference system for your area. ST_Simply is one such function that is best used with a measurement-preserving planar spatial reference system. Keep in mind that there's always a limit as to how far you can force-fit spherical coordinates onto Cartesian coordinates. If your geographies span the globe, you may have to break them apart before using geometry functions.

Transformation tends to introduce a lot of insignificant digits, and you may wish to use ST_SnapToGrid to eliminate the pesky extra digits. Apply ST_SnapToGrid (processed_geom,0.0001)::geography once you're ready to cast back to geography.

To use a geometry function where you need to transform, such as ST_Transform (ST_SomeGeomFunc(ST_Transform(geog,some_srid)),4326)::geography, the syntax of chaining multiple functions together could grow unwieldy. We recommend creating wrapper functions for operations that you'll be using often. Listing 11.17 shows a wrapper function that repurposes the ST_SimplifyPreserveTopology geometry function introduced in chapter 6 for use with geography.

Listing 11.17 Creating an `ST_SimplifyPreserveTopology` wrapper for geography

```
CREATE OR REPLACE FUNCTION
    utility.ugeog_SimplifyPreserveTopology(geography, double precision)
RETURNS geography AS
$$
SELECT
    geography(                                      Transform to   ❶
        ST_Transform(                               a suitable
            ST_SimplifyPreserveTopology(            planar SRID.
                ST_Transform(geometry($1),_ST_BestSRID($1,$1)), --  ◁┘
                $2
            ),
        4326)
    )                                          ❷ Mark as parallel
$$                                               safe (requires
LANGUAGE sql IMMUTABLE STRICT PARALLEL SAFE   ◁┘ PostgreSQL 9.6+)
COST 300;
```

Here you use a quasi-private PostGIS function called _ST_BestSRID to determine a suitable planar SRID, given the geography input ❶. _ST_BestSRID returns an internal SRID that you won't find in the spatial_ref_sys table. As such, it should not be used except during intermediary transformations. The function name starts with an underscore to denote this as a private function; you may on occasion find the need to use PostGIS private functions for building your own custom functions, as is the case with _ST_BestSRID. If you are using PostgreSQL 9.6 or above, ❷ you should mark your functions as parallel-safe. Without the parallel-safe marker, any query using your function will not be parallelizable.

The ST_SimplifyPreserveTopology function wrapped in listing 11.17, as well as the companion ST_Simplify, reduce the number of points used to define a geometry by removing vertices within a specified tolerance. They are important functions for dishing out lightweight geometries to mapping applications. Because these functions are often used for presentation, you shouldn't use them without transformation. We don't know what effect simplification has on geodetic coordinates, but we imagine that your spatial features would look rather unappetizing.

Another function that you may find useful for geography is ST_Union(geom). This is an aggregate function that unions a set of geometries and dissolves boundaries. It relies on the intersection matrix, which exists only for geometries. Over small areas, you may be able to apply ST_Union in SRID 4326 directly, but over a large swath you're better off transforming to a planar measure-preserving SRID before unioning.

Summary

- PostGIS has many geometry functions for splitting, breaking, tiling, and extracting subsets of a geometry. These functions are often used to improve the performance of spatial queries or for map labeling and rendering.
- PostGIS has functions for aggregating geometries into bigger geometries. This is useful if you need to produce reports based on a larger region than you were provided, such as city versus neighborhood reporting.
- PostGIS has functions for rotating and translating geometries, which are often used for creating specialized tiles or simulating movement.
- There are many more geometry functions than geography functions, but geography can be cast to geometry to use geometry functions.
- You can wrap PostGIS functions in your own creations to simplify your common use cases.

Raster processing

12

This chapter covers

- Loading raster data
- Spatial aggregate raster functions
- Accessing pixel values and isolating bands
- Retiling rasters
- Using geometries to clip rasters
- Raster statistical functions
- Map algebra functions

One of the most powerful aspects of PostGIS is its ability to use geometry and rasters in tandem. This chapter focuses on the use of raster aggregate functions, functions to manipulate rasters down to the pixel level, and functions for deriving additional rasters and geometries. You'll also learn about built-in summary statistic functions that you can use to explore the distribution of pixel values. You'll learn how to use geometry to isolate pixel values of interest.

For many of the examples in this chapter, we used climate data from WorldClim (www.worldclim.org/data/worldclim21.html). We downloaded elevation, precipitation, and average temperature raster monthly data divided into 10 minute degree intervals and covering 1970–2000. The data came packaged as .tif files. Elevation is in meters, precipitation in millimeters, and temperature in degrees Celsius. We also made an occasional excursion to Kauai, Hawaii, for which we downloaded elevation data (http://gis.ess.washington.edu/data/raster/tenmeter/hawaii/index.html).

You can download all the code and some of the data for this chapter at www.post-gis.us/chapter_12_edition_3. The WorldClim data has redistribution restrictions, so it's not included in the download.

12.1 *Loading and preparing raster data*

You can start by creating a schema for this chapter, which you'll use to hold the raster data you load:

```
CREATE SCHEMA ch12;
```

You can then use the raster2pgsql command-line tool packaged with PostGIS, which you learned about in chapter 4, to load the files chunked to 256 × 256 pixel tiles. You can add a column with the filename of the original raster by using the -F switch, and add -I to create a spatial index.

You can also use the -C option to add in raster constraints, so that all metadata about the raster is available in the raster_columns view. One of the constraints that gets added by -C is the extent constraint, which provides information in the raster_ columns.extent column about the full extent of the raster table. The extent constraint can take a very long time to apply for a large raster table. If you plan to load data into this table later or don't need this metadata information, you should turn it off with the -x switch.

Although we don't use the -R switch here, which would store the data outside of the database, there are many cases where storing the data out of the database improves performance. If you use the -R option, make sure the path you specify is accessible by the server. This means you most likely will have to specify the full folder path:

```
raster2pgsql -s 4326 -I -C -M wc2.1_10m_elev.tif -F
    -t 256x256 ch12.elev | psql -d postgis_in_action
raster2pgsql -s 4326 -I -C -M tavg/*.tif -F -t 256x256 ch12.tmean | psql
    -d postgis_in_action
raster2pgsql -s 4326 -I -C -M prec/*.tif -F -t 256x256 ch12.prec | psql
    -d postgis_in_action
raster2pgsql -s 26904 -Y -I -C -M kauai/*.bil -t 200x200 ch12.kauai | psql
    -d postgis_in_action
```

You can use QGIS to view the loaded data. Newer versions of QGIS/GDAL are capable of viewing out-of-database data. Figure 12.1 is a view of the precipitation data from the QGIS DB Manager Preview tab.

Our precipitation and temperature data covers the whole world and is segregated by calendar month, with each month in a separate file. The filenames are of the form *prec[month].tif.*

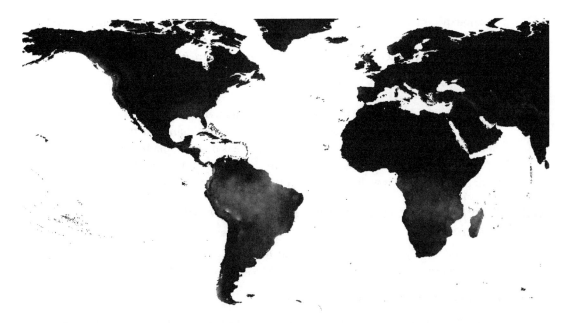

Figure 12.1 QGIS view of precipitation data loaded as WGS 84 lon/lat

Because you're storing rasters in the database, you can easily add additional columns to your tables. For example, you can add a column called month to the precipitation and temperature data, and populate it by extracting the month from the filename column:

```
ALTER TABLE ch12.prec ADD COLUMN month smallint;        ◁——┐  Add a column to
UPDATE ch12.prec                                             store the month.
SET month = regexp_replace(
    filename,                          Update the month
    E'(.*)([0-9]{2}).tif', E'\\2'      column based on
)::integer;                        ◁——┘ filename.
```

In the preceding code, ADD COLUMN adds a month column to the prec table.

PostgreSQL has rich regular expression support, detailed in the PostgreSQL documentation. See the sections on "String Functions and Operators" (http://mng.bz/oGrD) and "Pattern Matching" (http://mng.bz/n21d).

The preceding code uses a PostgreSQL regexp_replace function, which takes a string, a regular expression, and a replacement. The replacement can be literal or be something that references a part of the regular expression. This example uses a back-referencing regular expression in the regexp_replace function call to populate the month column. The (.*)([0-9]{2}).tif matches the filename, with ([0-9]{2}) being a subexpression for the month. The \\2 is a back-reference to the second subexpression, ([0-9]{2}). The expression replaces the matching string with the subexpression. Then you cast to an integer using ::integer.

regexp_replace is only one of many regular expression functions in PostgreSQL, and you can achieve the same result with others. For example, instead of using regexp _replace, you can achieve the same result with regexp_match as follows:

```
(regexp_match(filename,E'.*([0-9]{2}).tif'))[1]
```

regexp_match returns an array of elements that match your regex class references. Class references are items in parentheses, such as ([0-9]{2}), and for this you take the first element of the array. Which function you choose is mostly a matter of preference.

Go ahead and add a month column to the tmean table and fill it with the months from the filename as well. You'll need the column for later examples.

12.2 Forming larger rasters using spatial aggregate functions

Raster has an ST_Union function similar to the ST_Union counterpart for geometries. In this section we'll show you a variety of ways to use ST_Union on rasters.

12.2.1 Reconstituting tiled files

In order to improve raster performance, you can chunk large raster files, such as digital elevation model (DEM) files or aerial files, when importing them into the database. For example, you may wish to chunk a file with a 5000 × 5000 pixel raster into 1,000 rows of 50 × 50 rasters. When a raster is part of a greater whole, it's often referred to as a *tile*.

When we loaded the climate data with raster2pgsql in section 12.1, we presciently included the -F switch. This automatically added a column named filename with the original filename populated. With this information, you can reconstitute the original file by unioning the chunked rasters.

The following listing reconstitutes the precipitation files loaded into PostGIS:

```
SELECT
    filename,                                    Aggregate
    COUNT(rast) As num_tiles,                    rows into a
    ST_Union(rast) As rast      ◁─┘              single raster.      Select
FROM ch12.prec                                                      tiles.
WHERE filename IN ('wc2.1_10m_prec_01.tif','wc2.1_10m_prec_12.tif')  ◁─┘
GROUP BY filename;
```

The preceding query returns two rows. Each row has a filename, a single raster of all tiles in that file, and a count of the number of tiles in the raster. The ST_Union function is used to aggregate all tiles in the result by filename. Note that the raster tiles are all georeferenced to WGS 84, and because they were all created in much the same way, they all have the same pixel size, grid positioning, and spatial reference system (a.k.a. the same alignment). The same alignment is a requirement for raster ST_Union. When the union operation is applied, only same-positioned pixels are considered together to make a new pixel.

ST_Union can take an optional argument that dictates the unioning behavior, which can be one of the following in single quotes: 'LAST', 'FIRST', 'SUM', 'MEAN', and 'RANGE'. The default behavior of ST_Union, when not specified, is to take the LAST non-nodata value of overlapping pixels. Writing ST_Union(rast) is equivalent to ST_Union(rast,'LAST'). Because this is a reconstitution of a file, there are no overlapping regions, so LAST or FIRST will return the same raster.

The WHERE condition selects what tiles to aggregate, and this example aggregates together by filename all the tiles that made up the original file. The count tells you that, for each file, you're stitching 45 tiles.

12.2.2 Carving out areas of interest using clipping and unioning

Even when you have your rasters chunked into tiles, if you're only interested in a particular area, you can gain significant speed by clipping first and then unioning to carve out just the area of interest. Clipping tends to be faster than unioning, so by clipping first, you limit the number of pixels passed to the union operation.

The following listing shows an example of clipping and unioning to isolate a particular region.

Listing 12.1 Union clipping

```
SELECT ST_Union(ST_Clip(rast,geom)) AS rast      ◁── ❶ Clip and union tile
FROM
    ch12.elev
    CROSS JOIN
    ST_MakeEnvelope(8,47,8.5,47.5,4326) As geom   ◁── ❷ Define area
WHERE ST_Intersects(rast,geom);   ◁── ❸ Select tiles in area
```

The preceding listing returns one row with one raster. This raster will only have pixels that are completely covered by the area of interest. The ST_MakeEnvelope function is used to create a bounding rectangle polygon ❷. Next, the ST_Intersects function is used to select tiles that intersect the region of interest ❸. Finally, ST_Clip is used to isolate the portion of each tile that intersects the envelope ❶, followed by a unioning operation, begetting a new tile.

12.2.3 Using specific expression types with ST_Union

To use ST_Union, all rasters must have the same alignment, or more specifically, they must have the same pixel size, the same skew, the same scale ratio, and their upper-left corners must be set such that their pixels don't cut into each other. We also recommend that they have the same number of bands.

During a union, rasters can completely cover the same area, not intersect at all, or share some area. For example, if you have two identical tic-tac-toe boards, they can be placed side by side for no overlap, one directly on top of another for complete intersection, or one board could be positioned so that its bottom half overlaps the top half of the other board.

The default behavior of ST_Union is, given a set of pixels, to take the last non-null pixel value and use that as the value for the output pixel. This could be rather arbitrary, depending on the order of your input rasters. Imagine three identical tic-tac-toe boards stacked together—ST_Union would produce a single tic-tac-toe board. If the values in the center cell are X, O, and NULL, the unioned board would have a center value of O because it's the last non-null value encountered.

In some cases, particularly for overlapping rasters, you'll want some operation to be performed on the non-null pixels that intersect: sum, count, average, or some other operation, so you may not want to take the default behavior of LAST for unioning. For fancier operations, you'll have to resort to ST_MapAlgebra.

For example, our precipitation data covers the same region for 12 months. If you want to find the average annual precipitation, you could use ST_Union with a MEAN option, as shown in the following listing.

Listing 12.2   Union Mean

```
SELECT ST_Union(ST_Clip(rast,geom), 'MEAN') As rast        Union
FROM                                                        with mean
    ch12.prec
    CROSS JOIN
    ST_MakeEnvelope(8,47,8.5,47.5,4326) As geom
WHERE ST_Intersects(rast,geom) AND month BETWEEN 1 and 12;
```

Listing 12.2 is similar to listing 12.1, except that listing 12.2 averages the values in the overlapping cells instead of reading the last value.

12.3   *Working with bands*

In this section we'll demonstrate functions that can create multiple bands from a single band, or conversely, collapse multiple bands down to a single band.

12.3.1   *Using ST_AddBand to form multiband rasters from single-band rasters*

For related data covering the same area, you may wish to consolidate multiple single-band rasters into one multiband raster. Take an image in the CMYK color space, for instance. You'd be hard pressed to justify storing each band as a separate raster. To output the image, you'd have to union four rows of data.

A few requirements must be met by the individual rasters before you can assemble them into one multiband raster:

- All rasters must have the same alignment, meaning the same cell size and skew.
- All rasters must have the same height and width. With the same alignment, this implies that each raster must have the same number of pixels across and down.
- The ratio between cell dimension and spatial reference system (pixel scale and size) must be the same, and all rasters must cover the same georeferenced area, which implies that the upper-left coordinate must be the same for all rasters.

Let's use the climate data as an example. The data came in as two sets of rasters: one for precipitation and one for temperature. The following listing stacks them together to form a two-band raster.

Listing 12.3 Combining single-band rasters to form one multiband raster

```
CREATE TABLE ch12.tmean_prec (
    rid serial primary key,
    rast raster,
    filename_tmean text,
    filename_prec text,
    month smallint
);
```
❶ Create a new table for the new raster.

```
INSERT INTO ch12.tmean_prec (rast, filename_tmean, filename_prec, month)
SELECT
    ST_AddBand(t.rast, p.rast) As rast,
    t.filename As filename_tmean, p.filename As filename_prec, t.month
FROM ch12.tmean As t INNER JOIN ch12.prec As p
ON t.rast ~= p.rast AND t.month = p.month;
```
❷ Add bands.

❸ Match the same bounding box and month.

```
CREATE INDEX idx_tmean_prec_rast_gist ON ch12.tmean_prec
USING gist (ST_ConvexHull(rast));
```
❹ Add an index.

The listing first creates a new table to hold the multiband rasters ❶. ST_AddBand is used to add the temperature band to the 1-banded precipitation raster so that you end up with a 2-band raster consisting of one band for precipitation and one for temperature ❷. You know that both rasters satisfy the sameness requirement, so the bounding box of a tile in temperature matches the bounding box of a tile in the precipitation table.

The ~= raster bounding-box equality operator is used to pair tiles covering the same area ❸. Because you have gist indexes on both rasters, you can use the newer and faster gist bounding-box equality operator (~=) instead of the older B-tree-based bounding-box equality operator (=). As a last step, you add a spatial index based on the convex hull of each tile ❹. The reason you can use a functional index based on ST_ConvexHull is because raster indexable operators use geometry gist indexes and are based on the ST_ConvexHull of the raster, which, as discussed in chapter 7, returns a geometry.

12.3.2 Using ST_Band to process a subset of bands

To access one band in a raster, you can use ST_Band. In the next listing you pull out the first band (the temperature band) from the two-banded raster created in listing 12.3.

Listing 12.4 Selecting one band from a multiband raster

```
SELECT rid, ST_Band(rast,1) As rast
INTO ch12.tmean2
FROM ch12.tmean_prec;
```

```
CREATE INDEX idx_tmean2_rast_gist ON ch12.tmean2
USING gist (ST_ConvexHull(rast));
```

12.4   *Tiling rasters*

The ST_Tile function allows you to divide a larger raster tile into smaller tiles. Suppose you decided 256 × 256 was too big a tile size for the work you're doing. You could retile to 128 × 128 using ST_Tile.

ST_Tile has many overloads. The following listing shows the most common one.

> **Listing 12.5   Smaller, evenly blocked tiles using ST_Tile**

```
CREATE TABLE ch12.tmean_prec_128_128 (
    rid serial primary key,
    rast raster,
    month smallint        Create a
);                        new table.

INSERT INTO ch12.tmean_prec_128_128 (rast,month)       Tile into
SELECT ST_Tile(rast, 128, 128, true) AS rast, month    128 × 128.
FROM ch12.tmean_prec;

CREATE INDEX idx_tmean_prec_128_128_rast_gist
  ON ch12.tmean_prec_128_128 USING gist (ST_ConvexHull(rast));

SELECT AddRasterConstraints(
    'ch12'::name,
    'tmean_prec_128_128'::name,    Add constraints
    'rast'::name                   for more info in
);                                 raster_columns.
```

The variant of ST_Tile in listing 12.5 takes an optional Boolean parameter (false, by default) to denote padding with the nodata value. This listing sets the pad_with_nodata argument to true because you want all the tiles to be 128 × 128. If you set this to false or skip it, tiles that aren't 128 × 128 wouldn't be padded to guarantee the 128 × 128 size. In this case, the new tile size was chosen to perfectly accommodate the original tile size: 128 divides perfectly into 256. If you were to choose a new tile size such as 200 × 200, padding with nodata would come into play. If you set this to false, some rows might not have exactly 200 × 200 pixels.

This listing also takes the added step of adding constraints so that pixel types, pixel sizes, and band counts will be correctly registered in the raster_columns view. Registration means that PostGIS will enforce the constraints for the raster column. If you were later to append a raster with a different pixel size to the column, for example, the insert would fail.

> **NOTE**   Recall that you can't make alterations to out-of-db rasters. In the case of out-of-db rasters, ST_Tile only creates new metadata that denotes what portion of the out-of-db raster file corresponds to the tile. As such, ST_Tile is one operation that is much faster to do on out-of-db rasters than on in-db

rasters because for in-db rasters, the subset of pixels of the original raster are copied to a new raster instead of just the metadata. For many other operations, out-of-db rasters will be slower than in database rasters.

If you brought in your rasters as tiles, but decided you wanted bigger tiles, the ST_Retile function is suited for that purpose. ST_Retile takes as input the table class and column and returns a set of tiled rasters. ST_Retile isn't great for rasters if you need to add additional information (such as filename and month for the precipitation and temperature), but it will work well for a single non-overlapping set of rasters, which is what we have for elevation. For elevation, we had just one file and no overlapping regions, so the loss of the filename is not a big deal.

The following listing will use our existing elevation data, which was tiled as 256 × 256 and retile it so it's 512 × 512.

> **Listing 12.6 Smaller, evenly blocked tiles using ST_Retile**

```
CREATE TABLE ch12.elev_512_512 (
    rid serial primary key,
    rast raster
);

INSERT INTO ch12.elev_512_512(rast)
SELECT rt.rast
FROM (SELECT scale_x, scale_y, extent          ← ❶ Return the metadata of the original.
        FROM raster_columns
        WHERE r_table_schema = 'ch12' AND
        r_table_name = 'elev' ) AS m
    , ST_Retile('ch12.elev'::regclass, 'rast',   ← Create a set of tiles that are 512 × 512 but with the same scale as the original.
        m.extent,
        m.scale_x,
        m.scale_y, 512, 512, 'CubicSpline'       ← Use CubicSpline, which is smoother than the default of NearestNeighbor.
            ) AS rt(rast);

CREATE INDEX ix_elev_512_512_rast_gist          ← Create an index.
    ON ch12.elev_512_512
    USING gist (ST_ConvexHull(rast));

SELECT AddRasterConstraints(                     ← Register the metadata in raster_columns.
    'ch12'::name,
    'elev_512_512'::name,
    'rast'::name
);
```

The ST_Retile function takes a number of arguments: the scale factors (how much each pixel represents in geographic space), the region of the original table you want to retile, and the pixel tile size in width and height. In addition, it takes a warping algorithm name. The default is NearestNeighbor, which is the fastest, but it's more lossy than something like CubicSpline.

In this case you want to retile your whole table of 256 × 256 and keep everything the same, except you want chunkier tiles of 512 × 512. Since you added constraints to the table with raster2pgsql -C, you don't need to recompute these values. You can instead just read them from the raster_columns view ❶.

Again, you are using a LATERAL join here, which we demonstrated in earlier chapters and which is covered in appendix C, to feed the metadata to the ST_Retile set-returning function, but the word LATERAL is optional for set-returning functions and so can be left out for brevity. This example is an integral factor of the original, but your new tile size does not need to be a integral factor of your original width and height, and your width and height do not need to be equal. You are free to choose whatever size you want; the output can also be smaller than your original tile sizes.

If you have a huge table that you need to retile, instead of doing it in one go, using the full extent of the table, you can break up your extent and do it in chunks.

12.5   *Raster and geometry intersections*

PostGIS raster has a rich set of intersection functions that work with both rasters and vectors. You've already used ST_Clip, which returns that portion of a raster intersecting with a geometry. You also used the ST_Intersects function, which returns true if a raster intersects with a geometry or if two rasters intersect. In this section we'll explore the ST_Intersection function variants that support raster types.

When applied to two rasters, ST_Intersection returns a new raster of the intersection. When applied to a raster and a geometry, ST_Intersection returns a set of geomval objects. Recall from chapter 7 that geomval is a composite PostGIS data type made up of a geometry and a numeric value.

As an example, let's apply ST_Intersection to our Kauai elevation raster and a buffer zone around a point. This is detailed in the following listing.

Listing 12.7   Intersection of raster with geometry

```
SELECT
    CAST((gval).val As integer) AS val,          ❶ Return pixel value
    ST_Union((gval).geom) As geom                ❷ Return geometry covering pixels with the same value
FROM (
    SELECT ST_Intersection(                      ❸ Return intersection as a set of geomvals
        ST_Clip(rast,ST_Envelope(buf.geom)), --  ❹ Return portion of each raster that is in the buffer bounding box
        1,
        buf.geom
    ) As gval
    FROM ch12.kauai
    INNER JOIN (
    SELECT ST_Buffer(
        ST_GeomFromText('POINT(444205 2438785)',26904),100
    ) As geom) As buf                            ❺ Define buffer to filter raster tiles
    ON ST_Intersects(rast,buf.geom)              Return tiles that intersect the buffer
) As foo
GROUP BY (gval).val
ORDER BY (gval).val;
```

In this listing you first create a subquery that returns the intersection ❸ of all Kauai raster rows ❺ that intersect the 100-meter buffer ❹. The intersection ❸ returns a set of composite objects called a `geomval` that contains the properties `geom` (a geometry) ❷ and `val` (the pixel value of all points in that geometry) ❶.

You also use `ST_Clip` in this code ❹. If you leave out `ST_Clip` and `ST_Envelope`, you'll get the same answer, but it will take 10 times longer because `ST_Intersection` would have a greater number of pixels to examine. On our desktop PostgreSQL server, the difference was 118 ms using `ST_Clip(rast,ST_Envelope(..))` versus 1 sec 96 ms with no clipping.

You then format these fields so you can display them in OpenJUMP and use a gradient theming.

The reason you `CAST` to integer ❶ is that `val` returns a double-precision object, which the current version of OpenJUMP treats as text and doesn't permit for gradient theming. You set the theming in OpenJUMP to a Quantile/Equal Number classification so that the color gets darker as the values increase.

The output of listing 12.7 is shown in figure 12.2.

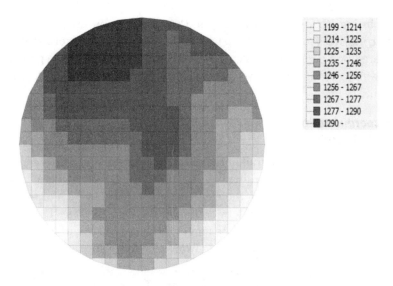

| 1199 - 1214 |
| 1214 - 1225 |
| 1225 - 1235 |
| 1235 - 1246 |
| 1246 - 1256 |
| 1256 - 1267 |
| 1267 - 1277 |
| 1277 - 1290 |
| 1290 - |

Figure 12.2 Kauai raster intersected with a 100 meter radius buffer. The darker patches represent higher elevations.

12.5.1 Pixel stats

One common use of raster analysis is to calculate statistics across raster coverages that intersect a region defined by a geometry. For example, the following listing calculates the average elevation for the previous section's buffer region in Kauai.

Listing 12.8 Intersection of raster with geometry: pixel stats

```
SELECT
    SUM((gval).val * ST_Area((gval).geom)) /
    ST_Area(ST_Union((gval).geom)) As avg_elesqm
FROM (
    SELECT ST_Intersection(          ←──┤ Return the intersection
        ST_Clip(                         │ of raster and geometry.
            rast, ST_Envelope(buf.geom)   ←──┐ Clip with the
            ) ,1, buf.geom                   │ rectangular envelope
    ) As gval                              │ of the circle
    FROM ch12.kauai
      INNER JOIN
    (
        SELECT ST_Buffer(
            ST_GeomFromText('POINT(444205 2438785)',26904),100
        ) As geom
    ) As buf
ON ST_Intersects(rast,buf.geom)) As foo;
```

Running the code should give you an answer of 1258.409. This agrees with a visual check using figure 12.2.

Just as in listing 12.7, you use `ST_Clip` and `ST_Envelope` in listing 12.8 to reduce the time the code takes to run. `ST_Clip` will not consider partial pixels, so if a pixel is not fully covered by a geometry, it is excluded. This is why you want the geometry you are clipping with to be bigger than your area of interest, and why using `ST_Envelope` is a good option.

12.5.2 *Adding a Z coordinate to a 2D linestring using ST_Value and ST_SetZ*

A 2D linestring that represents a trail in Kauai can be converted to a 3D linestring with the elevation stored in the Z coordinate. You can do this by dumping all the points that make up the linestring, getting the elevation pixel values at each of these points, and then reconstituting the linestring by adding in the Z coordinate. This gives you a 3D linestring, for which you can calculate length distances relative to other trails.

The next listing will yield a 3D linestring from a 2D linestring.

Listing 12.9 Adding a Z coordinate to a 2D linestring using ST_Value

```
SELECT
    ST_AsText(               ┌ Aggregate the
        ST_MakeLine(    ←──┘ points into a line.
            ST_Force3DZ(
                (gd).geom,                        ┌ Compute the elevation at
                COALESCE(                         │ the point; set it to 0 if a
                    ST_Value(rast, (gd).geom)  ←──┤ NULL value is returned.
                    ,0)
            )
        )      ←──┐ Force points to 3D using
    )            │ the pixel value for Z.
) As line_3dwkt
```

```
FROM
    (
        SELECT ST_DumpPoints(
            ST_GeomFromText(
                'LINESTRING(
                    444210 2438785,434125 2448785,
                    466666 2449780,466670 2449781
                )',
                26904
            )
        ) As gd
    ) As t
    LEFT JOIN
    ch12.kauai
    ON ST_Intersects(rast,(t.gd).geom);
```

Dump the vertices of the linestring.

Determine which rasters intersect vertices.

Using `ST_Force3DZ` and `ST_Force3D` in PostGIS 3.0 and lower

Listing 12.9 utilizes the optional Z-value argument to the `ST_Force3DZ` function introduced in PostGIS 3.1. Optional value arguments were also added to the `ST_Force3DM` and `ST_Force4D` functions. If you are using a version of PostGIS earlier than version 3.1, you will need to make the following change to make this example work.

Change the following code

```
ST_Force3DZ( (gd).geom,
        COALESCE(
            ST_Value(rast,(gd).geom)
            , 0
        )
    )
```

to this:

```
ST_Translate(
        ST_Force3DZ(
            (gd).geom),
            0, 0,
            COALESCE(
                ST_Value(rast,(gd).geom),
                0
            )
    )
```

A function similar to `ST_Value`, `ST_NearestValue`, is useful if you have some gaps in your data and always want it to return a pixel value.

With these new 3D points, you use the `ST_MakeLine` aggregate function to form a 3D linestring, set the spatial reference to be the same as Kauai, and output the result to a well-known text representation.

You could get an even more accurate 3D linestring by using `ST_Segmentize` on the linestring to yield more points to dump. This would allow you to store more Z coordinates along the trail.

New in PostGIS 3.2 are `ST_SetM` and `ST_SetZ`. The results of listing 12.9 can be achieved using `ST_SetZ` as shown in the following listing.

Listing 12.10   Adding a Z coordinate to a 2D linestring using `ST_SetZ`

```
SELECT ST_AsText(
      ST_SetZ(k.rast, geom)          ◁──┐  Set the Z coordinate
   )                                     │  of each vertex of the
FROM (SELECT ST_GeomFromText(            │  geometry.
            'LINESTRING(
                444210 2438785,434125 2448785,
                466666 2449780,466670 2449781
            )',
            26904                 ┌── Reference
      ) AS geom ) AS t     ◁──────┘   geometry
      CROSS JOIN LATERAL
      (                         ❶ ┌── Union the clips to
         SELECT ST_Union(   ◁─────┘   form a single raster.
            ST_Clip(rast,
               ST_Expand(t.geom,10)      ◁──┐  Clip the tiles up to within
            )                                │  10 meters of the bounding
         ) AS rast                      ❷ ──┘  box of the geometry.
            FROM ch12.kauai AS k
            WHERE ST_Intersects(k.rast, t.geom)
      ) AS k;
```

Listing 12.10 uses `ST_Clip`, raster `ST_Union`, and `ST_Expand` in concert to create a single raster that will cover the full area of the geometry ❶❷. `ST_Expand` returns a rectangular geometry that is the envelope of the geometry expanded vertically and horizontally by 10 meters. `ST_Expand` is needed because `ST_Clip` will not return a pixel unless the pixel is fully covered, and since the resolution of our data is so low, it's likely a pixel will not fully cover our linestring. You can make the expansion bigger, but it should be at least as wide as a pixel. Once intersecting tiles are sufficiently clipped, you union them together to form one tile. This is needed because the `ST_SetZ` function can only work with one tile and one geometry.

12.5.3   *Converting 2D polygons to 3D polygons*

In this section, we're going to demonstrate building 3D polygons. You've already seen one approach for building 3D geometries with rasters: using the `ST_Value` function to add an elevation to each vertex of a 2D linestring. Here we'll look at a second approach using the `ST_Intersection` function to convert a 2D geometry into a set of geomvals. From the geomvals, you can use the pixel values to elevate the geometry into 3D. The `ST_Value` approach is most suited to converting 2D linestrings to 3D linestrings; the `ST_Intersection` approach is better suited for polygons.

Listing 12.11 performs more or less the same operation as listing 12.7, but instead of outputting the pixel value as a separate column, this approach outputs it as the new Z coordinate of each polygon. This example also takes advantage of `ST_Clip` for speedier processing and the `LATERAL` construct for more succinct syntax.

To set up this example, create a table of 2D polygons and add two arbitrary buffer regions to the table:

```
CREATE TABLE ch12.kauai_polys (
    gid serial primary key,
    geom geometry(POLYGON,26904)
);
INSERT INTO ch12.kauai_polys (geom)
SELECT ST_Buffer(ST_GeomFromText('POINT(444205 2438785)',26904),100)
UNION ALL
SELECT ST_Buffer(ST_GeomFromText('POINT(444005 2438485)',26904),10);
```

You can expand those 2D polygons into 3D elevated polygons as shown in the next listing.

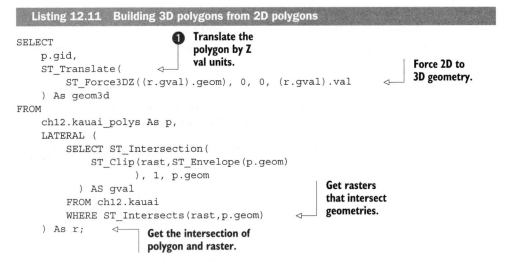

Listing 12.11   Building 3D polygons from 2D polygons

```
SELECT                           ❶ Translate the
    p.gid,                         polygon by Z
    ST_Translate(                  val units.         Force 2D to
        ST_Force3DZ((r.gval).geom), 0, 0, (r.gval).val    3D geometry.
    ) As geom3d
FROM
    ch12.kauai_polys As p,
    LATERAL (
        SELECT ST_Intersection(
            ST_Clip(rast,ST_Envelope(p.geom)
            ), 1, p.geom
        ) AS gval                  Get rasters
        FROM ch12.kauai            that intersect
        WHERE ST_Intersects(rast,p.geom)   geometries.
    ) As r;                Get the intersection of
                           polygon and raster.
```

Listing 12.11 uses ST_Intersects to select all rasters that intersect polygons in the kauai_polys table. If you are using PostGIS 3.1 or higher, you can use the Z-value feature of ST_Force3DZ as demonstrated in listing 12.9 to obviate the need for ST_Translate ❶. For each polygon and raster that intersect, ST_Intersection returns a set of geomvals and uses the val portion representing the elevation to translate the polygon val units ❶.

You use ST_Clip to accelerate processing. ST_Force3D and ST_Force3DZ are equivalent functions, but we prefer using the Z version for clarity. There are also ST_Force4D and ST_Force3DM functions, which would be useful if you were tracking other metrics such as toxic levels of something or temperature and you wanted that all to be encoded in the geometry.

If you are using PostGIS 3.1 or higher, you can skip the ST_Translate step in listing 12.11 and instead use ST_Force3DZ((r.gval).geom, (r.gval).val).

A popular use for this approach is to generate contour lines or polygons, particularly at regular distance intervals. PostGIS 3.2 introduces a ST_Contour function that generates contour lines in much less code than you'd need to write otherwise. You can then use `ST_Polygonize` to convert these lines into polygons. These lines can also be generated at fixed distance intervals.

12.6 *Raster statistics*

One benefit of storing rasters in a PostgreSQL database, both in-db and out-of-db, is that you can take advantage of the numerous computational functions already present. In this section we'll focus on the statistical raster functions PostGIS provides, as well as on basic functions for outputting numerical values from a raster.

12.6.1 *Extruding pixel values*

Pixel accessor functions are those that return pixel values at a particular area. There are two functions commonly used:

- `ST_Value` returns a single value at a given geometric point or raster column, row. You've seen this in use in prior examples.
- `ST_DumpValues` returns a 2D array for each selected band corresponding to the row, column, or pixel value.

ST_VALUE: RETURNING A SINGLE VALUE

The following listing returns the average monthly temperature and precipitation for a location around Zurich, Switzerland for January and July.

Listing 12.12   Using `ST_Value`

```
SELECT
    month,                                    Temperature
                                              in Celsius
    ST_Value(rast,1,pt) As temp_c,    ◄──┘
    ST_Value(rast,2,pt) As precip     ◄────── Precipitation
FROM
    ch12.tmean_prec                                           Point of
        INNER JOIN ST_SetSRID(ST_Point(8.55,47.36667),4326) AS pt  ◄──┘ interest
ON ( month IN (1,7) AND ST_Intersects(rast,pt) )   ◄──┐ Filter tiles
ORDER BY month;
```

Listing 12.12 uses the two-band temperature and precipitation raster to retrieve the temperature in Celsius.

The second band is the precipitation band. You join the raster with a geometric point of interest (near Zurich in this example; hence the low temperatures and high precipitation). You use `ST_intersects` to find the raster tile that contains the point of interest. `ST_Value` then picks out the particular cell that intersects the point. `ST_Value` always returns a single value, and if the point falls on cell boundaries or corners, `ST_Value` arbitrarily picks one.

The following is the output of listing 12.12:

```
month | temp_c  | precip
-------+---------+--------
    1 |   0.195 |     65
    7 |   14.9  |    119
```

ST_DUMPVALUES: RETURNING AN ARRAY OF VALUES

ST_DumpValues is most suitable if you want to return a set of rasters as a 2D array. You can feed the array output to the ST_SetValues raster function to set more than one pixel in a raster.

In listing 12.13 you use ST_DumpValues to return the precipitation values for your area of interest as an array, where the values are the precipitation values and the cell positions correspond to the pixels for that area. As with ST_Value, you must specify the band number. Note the tandem use of ST_Union to isolate the raster tiles of interest as a single unit.

Listing 12.13 Single month precipitation for target area as an array (whole tiles)

```
SELECT
    ST_DumpValues(                        Dump the raster tile
                                          (band 2) as an array.
        ST_Union(rast,2),
        1                                 Return the second
    ) AS ary_precip                       band unioned.
FROM
    ch12.tmean_prec                       Return the
    INNER JOIN                            first array.
    (
        SELECT
            ST_Buffer(
                ST_GeogFromText('POINT(8.55 47.36667)'),5000
            )::geometry AS geom           Define the area
    ) AS f                                of interest.
    ON (month = 7 AND ST_Intersects(rast,geom) );    Consider only July and
                                                     tiles that intersect.
```

In listing 12.13 you use the geography ST_Buffer function to create a 5,000 meter buffer zone around a point. You use geography over geometry because ST_Buffer for geometry would require you to specify units in degrees for this projection. The buffer zone could span multiple tiles, so you use ST_Union to gather all the second band tiles together. Then ST_Intersects applies a geometry filter to the data. Finally, you dump the pixel values out. The nice thing about this is that your array length is always some factor of your tiles. In this example, the result is a union of two tiles to yield a matrix that is 256 × 512. You can easily check this using array_upper(ary_precip,1) to yield the number of columns and array_upper(ary_precip,2) to yield the number of rows.

The problem with this approach is that you are converting a whole tile to an array, which can be huge. If you were to use ST_Clip to take just a portion of the band, you would run the risk of getting all NULLs or mostly NULLs, because ST_DumpValues will return a value for a pixel only where the pixel is completely covered by the geometry. If your geometry straddles multiple pixels, but doesn't completely encase any pixel, you would end up with all NULLs even though there are overlapping pixels.

Another approach to work around this issue is to convert your geometry to a raster and do the overlay in raster space. The next listing is similar to listing 12.13 except it will pick up only pixels that overlap our area of interest instead of whole tiles.

Listing 12.14   Single month precipitation for target area as an array (overlapping pixels)

```
SELECT                                              Create a new raster that is
    ST_DumpValues(                                  the union of intersection of
        ST_Union ( ST_Intersection    ◁────┘        raster and geometry
                (
                    ST_Band(rast,2) ,            ◁──────────            Select band 2
                    ST_AsRaster(geom, rast,    ◁────────                of raster
                        ARRAY['1BB'], ARRAY[1], ARRAY[0],
                        touched => true    ◁──────┐        Convert geometry
                    ) )                           │        to Boolean raster
                ) ,
        1                                     Mark pixel as active
    ) AS ary_precip    ◁──┐                   if it intersects
FROM                      │     Convert       geometry
    ch12.tmean_prec       │     overlapping pixels
    INNER JOIN            │      to 2D matrix
    (
        SELECT
            ST_Buffer(
                ST_GeogFromText('POINT(8.55 47.36667)'),5000
            )::geometry AS geom
    ) AS f                                ◁──┐     Define geometry to use for
    ON month = 7 AND ST_Intersects(rast,geom);      filtering an intersection.
```

The output of listing 12.14 is shown next:

```
ary_precip
-----------------------
 {{116,119},{NULL,143}}
(1 row)
```

The output is a 2×2 matrix where the cells contain the precipitation values. The buffer zone hits three cells, but as with all arrays, the number of columns of each row must be the same, so you get a NULL for the last cell to balance it out.

You'll see many NULL values in this array. The buffer zone is circular and will only partially cover cells around the border, and for these cells ST_DumpValues returns NULL instead of the pixel value. Put another way, ST_DumpValues will only output pixel values for cells fully covered by the clipping geometry.

12.6.2 *Raster statistics functions*

PostGIS 3.0 includes five key statistic functions: ST_Histogram, ST_Count, ST_Value-Count, ST_SummaryStats, and ST_Quantile. All these functions return a set of records with varying properties based on the function. In addition, there are several statistical aggregate functions. The most commonly used are ST_CountAgg and ST_Summary-StatsAgg. They can return statistics on a subset of the data or return exact or approximate stats for one or more bands in a whole raster table.

In this section we'll cover the ST_Histogram, ST_Count, and ST_ValueCount functions. The ST_SummaryStats and ST_Quantile functions work much like the ST_Histogram function but return different output fields.

HISTOGRAMS

`ST_Histogram` provides a distribution of pixel values. You can set the number of break-outs or manually specify bins. You'll often find `ST_Histogram` working in concert with other raster functions, such as `ST_Clip`, `ST_Reclass`, `ST_Union`, and `ST_MapAlgebra`.

The following listing generates a histogram of the distribution of elevations for a particular area of interest.

Listing 12.15 Distribution of elevation for an area of interest

```
WITH                                    Return a histogram for
    cte AS (                            band 1 consisting of 5 bins.
        SELECT
            ST_Histogram(    ◁┘         Single tile consisting of
                ST_Union(    ◁┘         union of area of interest
                    ST_Clip(p.rast,geom)
                ),
                1,
                5
            ) As hg                                          Only consider
        FROM                                                 tiles that
            ch12.elev AS p                                   intersect the
            INNER JOIN                                       area of interest.
            ST_MakeEnvelope(7.5,47,8.5,48.5,4326) As geom ◁┘
        ON ST_Intersects(p.rast,geom)
)
SELECT
    (hg).min As min,         ◁┤  Output columns
    (hg).max As max,             of the histogram
    (hg).count,
    (hg).percent::numeric(5,2)*100 As percent
FROM cte;
```

In listing 12.15, you use `ST_Clip` to carve out the area of interest from the intersecting tiles. `ST_Union` stitches the fragments of tiles together.

The output of listing 12.15 is shown next:

```
min | max | count | percent
-----+-----+-------+---------
 149 | 313 |    10 |   19.00
 313 | 477 |     9 |   17.00
 477 | 641 |    17 |   31.00
 641 | 805 |    11 |   20.00
 805 | 969 |     7 |   13.00
(5 rows)
```

The preceding output shows the pixel values broken out into five bins. For example, the last row tells you that 13% of the pixels have an elevation falling between 805 and 969 meters. The median of pixels falls in the third bucket, which has a range between 477 and 641 meters.

COUNTS

PostGIS raster has two sets of count functions:

- ST_Count provides a pixel count in an area or raster table. It counts pixels with no data value separately. ST_CountAgg is an aggregate variant of ST_Count. With it you can skip doing additional aggregations such as SUM, since ST_CountAgg incorporates all that.

- ST_ValueCount outputs both the pixel value and the count of pixels that have that pixel values.

The next listing demonstrates the more informative ST_ValueCount function. This code outputs the number of pixels at each elevation within an area of interest.

Listing 12.16   Count by elevation

```
WITH
    cte AS (                                    Compute the
        SELECT                                  set of value
            ST_ValueCount(        ⟵            counts.
                ST_Clip(p.rast,geom)   ⟵        Clip to the
            ) As pv                             area of
        FROM                                    interest.
            ch12.elev AS p                                         Define the
            INNER JOIN                                             area of
            ST_MakeEnvelope(8,47,8.5,47.5,4326) As geom   ⟵       interest.
        ON ST_Intersects(p.rast, geom)
    )
SELECT (pv).value, sum((pv).count) As total_count   ⟵    Return the value
FROM cte                                                 and count from the
GROUP BY (pv).value                                      ST_ValueCount result.
ORDER by total_count DESC   ⟵    Order in reverse of
LIMIT 5;                          count, with a limit of 5
```

The output of listing 12.16 is shown next:

```
value | total_count
-------+-------------
  430 |          30
  432 |          27
  433 |          26
  431 |          24
  429 |          23
```

12.7   *Map algebra*

The term *map* in *map algebra* refers to the rule by which you go from an old pixel value to a new pixel value; it's not *map* in the geographical sense. In chapter 7 you learned about ST_Reclass, which maps pixel values from one set of pixel values to another set of pixel values based on ranges. ST_Reclass, ST_Intersection, and ST_Union are specialized manifestations of a more generalized ST_MapAlgebra function. Think of ST_MapAlgebra as a function of last resort. When no other function can perform the processing you have in mind, ST_MapAlgebra offers hope. But the function is by no means speedy..

ST_MapAlgebra can operate by considering only one pixel at a time or a neighborhood consisting of pixels surrounding a pixel. The operation is repeated for each pixel and one or more raster bands. Regardless of whether processing is based on a single pixel or a neighborhood of pixels, ST_MapAlgebra always returns a new single-band raster that's a function of the pixel values of the original raster. The function could be based on a single band or multiple bands.

When working with ST_MapAlgebra, you have a choice of using expressions or callback functions. Although PostGIS comes with several predefined map algebra callback functions as samples, you're expected to create your own expressions or callback functions. In this section we'll focus on using ST_MapAlgebra with expressions and build a simple callback function.

12.7.1 *Choosing between expression or callback function*

The ST_MapAlgebra function is really a suite of functions sharing the same name. It's a super-overloaded function. Regardless of which ST_MapAlgebra permutation you use, at its heart you'll find either a map algebra expression or a map algebra callback function. Think of ST_MapAlgebra as a Zamboni that visits each pixel in your area of interest. At each pixel, it stops and runs the expression or callback function for that pixel only. Once done, it moves on.

In many cases, you have a choice of using an expression or a callback function. For simple operations you can get by with expressions, but as things get more complex we advise that you take the time to compose a callback function, both to maintain your sanity and also to gain speed improvements. An *expression* can be any PostgreSQL algebraic expression that can accept pixel values or positions. The expression returns the new value for the cell. If what you need to do requires a neighborhood, you have to use callback functions. A *callback function* need not be anything more than a simple expression, but you have the freedom to add complex conditional loops and declare interim variables.

Let's look at some examples of using ST_MapAlgebra. Before beginning, you'll need to create a table to house new raster data that will have temperature measured in Fahrenheit instead of Celsius:

```
CREATE TABLE ch12.tmean_fah (
    rid integer primary key,
    rast raster,
    month integer
);
```

12.7.2 *Using a single-band map algebra expression*

Any valid PostgreSQL mathematical expression that can be applied to a pixel value or pixel coordinate can serve as a map algebra expression. You can also include custom functions in your map algebra expression. The simplest case is to map one pixel value to another value.

Listing 12.17 is a trivial example of map algebra written in PL/pgSQL. PL/pgSQL is one of the most popular procedural languages for writing functions in PostgreSQL. You've seen an example of it in chapter 10 and you'll see more examples later in this book. The temperature table you've been using records temperature as Celsius. If you'd prefer Fahrenheit, you could use a ST_MapAlgebra with an expression that does the transformation as shown in the next listing.

Listing 12.17   ST_MapAlgebra using an expression

```
CREATE OR REPLACE PROCEDURE ch12.load_tmean_fah()       ◁┐  Create stored
language plpgsql AS                                        │  procedure to
$$                                                        │  load data
BEGIN
WHILE EXISTS
   (SELECT 1 FROM ch12.tmean AS c
     LEFT JOIN ch12.tmean_fah AS f ON c.rid = f.rid WHERE f.rid IS NULL
     LIMIT 1) LOOP                        ◁─┐  Loop until no
INSERT INTO ch12.tmean_fah(rid, month, rast)  │  more records
SELECT
     rid, month,
     ST_MapAlgebra(
         rast,
         1,
         '32BF'::text,
         '[rast.val]  * 9/5 + 32'::text,   │  Expression Celsius
         -999                              │  to Fahrenheit
     )
FROM ch12.tmean AS t
WHERE                                       ┌  Only consider
     NOT EXISTS (                           │  if not already
         SELECT 1                           │  inserted
         FROM ch12.tmean_fah As f    ◁─┘
         WHERE f.rid = t.rid
     );                          ┌  Insert five rows
LIMIT 5;            ◁────────────┘  at a time.
COMMIT;    ◁─┐
END LOOP;    │  Write to table after
END$$;       │  each five rows inserted
                                  ┌  Run the
                                  │  procedure.
CALL ch12.load_tmean_fah();  ◁─┘
```

Listing 12.17 creates a new table called tmean_fah to house the new rasters. It uses a map algebra expression, [rast.val] * 9/5 + 32, that maps the Celsius values to Fahrenheit values. It also creates a stored procedure (which requires PostgreSQL 11+) to do incremental inserts into the table, and then it runs the procedure using the CALL command.

You use 32BF to store floats, as that is the smallest float pixel type that can accommodate the data. Our PostgreSQL 8-core, 128 GB memory server processed this particular set of data in 20 seconds. This particular example could have been done with a single insert, because the dataset is fairly small. However, in most cases you'll be dealing with many more records, so the procedure approach would be preferred. You use a procedure here instead of a function because a function has to commit data all at once; it cannot have commits along the way.

If your expressions are simpler and could be done using ST_Reclass, then you should use ST_Reclass. The ST_Reclass function has two advantages over using expressions: it returns all the bands with only the selected bands changed, and it's about 25% to 50% faster.

Like other functions we introduced in this chapter, ST_MapAlgebra can work on a subset of tiles by combining them with ST_Clip and ST_Union. One drawback of ST_MapAlgebra is that it will always return a single-band raster, although it's capable of reading information in all bands.

12.7.3 Using a single-band map algebra function

Listing 12.18 repeats the example from listing 12.17, but this time using a callback function instead of an expression.

Before beginning, wipe out the data you inserted in listing 12.17 using this command:

```
TRUNCATE TABLE tmean_fah;
```

The next listing is as basic as you can get for a callback function.

Listing 12.18 ST_MapAlgebra using a callback function

```
CREATE OR REPLACE FUNCTION ch12.tempfah_cbf (
    value double precision[][][],
    pos integer[][],                      ◁─┐ Create map algebra
    VARIADIC userargs text[]                 │ callback function
)
RETURNS double precision AS
$$
BEGIN                                     ◁─┐ Operate on a
RETURN value[1][1][1] * 9/5 + 32;            │ single cell.
END;
$$
LANGUAGE plpgsql IMMUTABLE PARALLEL SAFE COST 1000;
                                          ◁─┐ Create a stored
                                             │ procedure to
                                             │ load data.
CREATE OR REPLACE PROCEDURE ch12.load_tmean_fah()  ◁─┘
language plpgsql AS
$$
BEGIN                                          ┌ Loop until there are
WHILE EXISTS                                   │ no more records.
  (SELECT 1 FROM ch12.tmean AS c               │
    LEFT JOIN ch12.tmean_fah AS f ON c.rid = f.rid WHERE f.rid IS NULL │
    LIMIT 1) LOOP                          ◁───┘
```

```
INSERT INTO ch12.tmean_fah (rid, month, rast)
SELECT
    rid, month,
    ST_MapAlgebra(
        rast,
        1,
        'ch12.tempfah_cbf(
            double precision[],integer[],text[]
        )'::regprocedure,        ⟵┐  Use the callback
        '32BF'::text)               │  function.
FROM ch12.tmean AS t
WHERE
    NOT EXISTS (     ⟵┐  Only consider if it's
        SELECT 1      │  not already inserted.
        FROM ch12.tmean_fah As f
        WHERE f.rid = t.rid
    )
LIMIT 5;         ┌─  Write to the table after
COMMIT;      ⟵──┤   each five rows inserted.
END LOOP;
END$$;
                              ┌─  Call the
                              │   procedure.
CALL ch12.load_tmean_fah();  ⟵┘
```

A callback function always contains a value matrix. The first dimension of the matrix is the band number, and the second and third are the rows and columns corresponding to pixel coordinates. The value held by the matrix corresponds to the pixel value. In the case of a single-band raster when you're not considering neighborhoods, the band number is 1 and the rest of the matrix will have only one cell.

You apply the callback function by passing it as input to the ST_MapAlgebra function.

In our use of ST_MapAlgebra, we generally accept most of the defaults. If you intend to make ST_MapAlgebra a part of your standard arsenal, study the PostGIS documentation to learn about all the overloads and default settings.

You'll also want to experiment with which languages you use to write map algebra callback functions. For this particular example, a Celsius to Fahrenheit function in PostgreSQL 13 and PostGIS 3.1 written in PL/pgSQL, it took about 28 seconds to process this particular data versus the 22 seconds of the map algebra expression. The same function written in SQL took a whopping 1 minute, but sometimes writing a function in SQL is faster. Don't assume one language will always be faster than another or that expressions are always slower. Another language useful for writing map algebra functions is PL/V8 (a.k.a. PL JavaScript). You'll see an example of this later in this book. The V8 engine is surprisingly good at math operations and matrixes, so it can often be 10 times faster than the equivalent in PL/pgSQL or SQL.

12.7.4 *Map algebra with neighborhoods*

Sometimes the new value that you need to set a pixel to depends on the values of pixels adjacent to it. Such needs arise when you're performing smoothing; finding slopes, local maxima, and local minima; or playing the Game of Life, as we demonstrate in

"PostGIS Day Game of Life celebration" (http://mng.bz/XYqE). To examine adjacent pixels, you pass a neighborhood to the callback function.

A *neighborhood* is a rectangular region of pixels with the pixel of interest at the center, extending *x* pixels to the left and right, and *y* pixels up and down. A neighborhood always should have an odd number of horizontal and vertical pixels unless your neighborhood exceeds the boundary of the raster tile.

The basic syntax of ST_MapAlgebra when used with a neighborhood is as follows:

```
ST_MapAlgebra( raster rast,
integer[] nband,
regprocedure callbackfunc,
text pixeltype=NULL, text extenttype=FIRST,
raster customextent=NULL,
integer distancex=0, integer distancey=0,
text[] VARIADIC userargs=NULL
);
```

Several neighborhood callback functions are already packaged with PostGIS: ST_Max4ma, ST_Mean4ma, ST_StdDev4ma, and ST_InvDistWeight4ma, to name a few. The code in the next listing finds the local maxima within a neighborhood of 5×5 pixels.

Listing 12.19 Maximum value in a neighborhood

```
SELECT
    ST_MapAlgebra(            ←─┤ Map algebra on        Single raster
        ST_Union(               │ envelope raster       clipped to
            ST_Clip(rast,ST_Envelope(buf.geom))  ←─┘   envelope
        ),
        1,
        'ST_Max4ma(
            double precision[][][],
            integer[][],
            text[]
        )'::regprocedure,       ←─┤ Maximum pixel
        '32BF',                    │ value callback
        'FIRST',
        NULL,
        2,
        2   ←───── Neighborhood-
    )          │   extending pixels
FROM
    ch12.kauai
    INNER JOIN
    (
        SELECT
            ST_Buffer(
                ST_GeomFromText('POINT(444205 2438785)',26904),100
            ) As geom
    ) As buf
ON ST_Intersects(rast,buf.geom)
GROUP BY buf.geom;
```

For each pixel in the bounding box of the area of interest, the function will return the highest pixel value from the rectangular pixel range consisting of two to the left and right and two up and down from the center pixel. What passes to the callback function is a 3D matrix where the first dimension is the band and the second and third dimensions outline the neighborhood.

Summary

- PostGIS has powerful raster functions used exclusively with the PostGIS raster type.
- PostGIS has many raster functions designed to work in conjunction with raster and geometry types.
- The PostGIS ST_Clip function isolates a portion of a raster using a geometry. It is used to speed up operations of other raster operations, such as ST_Union and ST_Intersection.
- With PostGIS, you can use geometry to isolate pixels of interest, thus speeding up analysis.
- Map algebra functions allow you to transform a raster from one set of pixel values to another.
- PostGIS offers specialized versions of map algebra, like ST_Union, ST_Reclass, and ST_Intersection.
- PostGIS also offers a ST_MapAlgebra function, which allows you to design your operations, at the expense of speed. Use this as a last resort.

13

Building and using topologies

This chapter covers

- What a topology is
- Creating a topology
- Building topogeometries
- Loading and editing topogeometries
- Simplification and validation

Topological representation recognizes that, in reality, geometric features rarely exist independently of each other. When you gaze down on large metropolises from a plane, you see a maze of streets outlining blocks, interlocked. With a simple geometry model, you could use linestrings to represent the streets and polygons to represent the blocks. But once you lay out the streets, you already know where your blocks will be. Having to create polygons for the blocks is an exercise in redundancy. Congratulations, you've discovered topology.

In this chapter, you'll learn what a topology is, how to build a topology from scratch, and how to use commonly available geometry data. You'll also learn how to create what are called *topogeometries* (topogeoms) in a topology. You'll learn how to detect problems in loaded data, how to fix problems in spatial data, and how to create simplified geometries using a topology model that maintains the connectedness of the constituent objects.

We'll be working with two sets of examples in this chapter. The first set will be very simple, created without loading data. This set of examples will give you a feel for how topologies are created and organized. The second set of examples will utilize data from the web. These examples will reflect what you'll commonly do in your work with topology.

For the second set of examples, we'll visit the picturesque city of Victoria, BC, Canada, and convert the geometry representations of the city boundary, neighborhoods, and streets to a PostGIS topology-based representation. Victoria is the birthplace of PostGIS and the capital of British Columbia, Canada. Aside from having historical significance, it's a small city with a complete set of data, well suited for exploratory work. We'll be using municipal data you can find at http://opendata.victoria.ca/, and we'll load the prepared shapefiles into a staging schema, use the staging data to populate a topology schema, and finally build topogeometry columns and populate those in this chapter data schema.

Create the staging and data schemas with the following commands:

```
CREATE SCHEMA ch13_staging;
CREATE SCHEMA ch13;
```

We've packaged the ch13_staging schema data as part of this chapter's download (www.postgis.us/chapter_13_edition_3) and we've loaded in the tables cityboundary, neighbourhoods, and streetcentrelines. The ch13 schema houses the topogeometry tables for this chapter.

13.1 *What topology is*

The surface of the earth is finite. We have about 196.9 million square miles (510.1 million square kilometers) to play on, water included. Humans are territorial, so we've divided up all the land into countries, big and small. Excluding Antarctica and a few disputed zones, moving a country's border involves at least two countries. The iron law of geography dictates that when one country gains land, another must cede land. This zero-sum land game is the result of humans having created countries that are collectively exhaustive and mutually exclusive over the earth.

This collectively exhaustive and mutually exclusive division of area is a requirement of topology. With this premise, you don't need to restate the obvious when creating geometries. For example, if you have a plot of land in the country and decide to use the northern half for farming and the other half for non-farming uses, it follows that some kind of demarcation must be present, dividing the two halves. By creating one polygon for the farmable area, you create another polygon for the non-farmable area and a linestring to part the two.

Consider another example. In 1790 the US Congress created Washington D.C. from land ceded by adjoining states. The district is divided into four quadrants with two perpendicular axes radiating from the capitol buildings. The quadrants are appropriately named: Northwest, Northeast, Southwest, Southeast. Suppose that in the spirit of equality, Congress decided to make all quadrants the same area. This would mean moving the center of the axes to the north and west. If you used a topology in the model, this reorganization would amount to nothing more than moving one point. By shifting this point, your linestrings (the axes) would follow along, and the polygons forming the quadrants would either deflate or inflate. You'd achieve all this by simply moving a point!

This is the power of topology: by defining a set of rules for how geometries are interrelated, you save yourself the effort of having to survey the entire landscape anew whenever you make the slightest alteration.

In PostGIS there are three kinds of representations for vector data. There is the more standard *geometry model*, where each geometry stands as a separate unit. In the geometry model, things that are shared, such as borders of land masses, are duplicated in each geometry. There is the *geography model*, which much like the geometry model treats each piece of space as a separate unit, and borders are duplicated, but it views these units in spheroidal space. Then there is the *topology model*, which borrows the 2D view of the world from geometry, but with one key difference. In the topology model, shared borders and areas are stored once in the database and are linked to the geometries that share the borders. These geometries with linked edges are called topogeoms.

This has a couple of benefits:

- If you simplify an object for distribution, the edges that are simplified are still shared, so you don't end up with overlaps or gaps where you had none before.
- If you have a set of objects such as buildings, neighborhoods, or land parcels that shouldn't overlap, it's easier to detect and prevent these problems in a topology model.

Now that you have the concept of topologies fresh in your mind, we'll move on to building topologies with PostGIS topology functions.

13.2 Using topologies

Topology is an entirely different take on spatial features than geometry. Think back to your first geometry course: in Euclidean geometry, points, lines, and polygons didn't have coordinate systems as a backdrop. You didn't care about the absolute measurement of things but rather the relationships between them. The topology model, in a way, reverts back to classical geometry, where you describe how two free geometries interact without any regard to coordinate systems.

Because GIS topology is an outgrowth of graph theory, it subscribes to a different set of terminology. For all intents and purposes, you can think of a *point* in geometry as a *node* in topology, a *linestring* as an *edge*, and a *polygon* as a *face*. Collectively, nodes, edges, and faces are topological primitives, used instead of geometries.

NOTE   We use the term *topology* to refer to both the topology field of study as well as to a topology network.

13.2.1 *Installing the topology extension*

Before you can create a topology, you must make sure you've installed the topology extension. If you're not sure, look for a schema named `topology` in your database. This schema contains functions used to create topologies as well as the topology catalog table. If it's missing, you haven't yet installed the extension. Extensions must be installed on a database-by-database basis:

```
CREATE EXTENSION postgis_topology;
```

As part of the topology installation, PostGIS adds the `topology` schema to your database's `search_path`. This means you can reference the topology functions without explicitly prepending `topology`.

In some cases, the role you're logged in as may have its own custom `search_path` setting that will override the database's `search_path`. Before you continue, verify that `topology` is part of your `search_path` by running this SQL statement:

```
SHOW search_path;
```

If you don't see `topology` schema listed in the `search_path`, disconnect from your database and reconnect.

Once that's done, you can create a topology.

13.2.2 *Creating a topology*

In this section you'll create a stylized topology based on the rectangular state of Colorado with an SRID of 4326. The following code snippet shows how you can create the topology:

```
SELECT CreateTopology('ch13a_topology',4326);
```

After you execute the aforementioned SQL, you'll notice a new schema named `ch13a_topology`. A new entry will appear in the topology.topology catalog table registering the new topology. When you peek inside the `ch13a_topology` schema, you'll see four new tables awaiting data: node, edge_data, face, and relation.

PostGIS uses a separate schema to house each topology network—in this case `ch13a_topology`. The chosen SRID applies to all tables within the schema and to all topogeometry columns that will make use of the `ch13a_topology` schema. Because topology is about relationships between geometries, having differing SRIDs makes no sense.

Within each topology, you'll always find four tables: node, edge_data, face, and relation. The first three are just topo-speak for point, linestring, and polygon. Of these three tables for storing the primitives, edge_data is the one that holds all the information for building the network. When you start to build spatial objects from topology primitives, the relationships each of these spatial objects have with the topology will reside in the relation table.

For Colorado, you can start by adding the linestrings that form the state's four boundaries using the function TopoGeo_AddLineString, as shown in the following listing.

Listing 13.1   Building the Colorado topology network

```
SELECT TopoGeo_AddLineString(
    'ch13a_topology',
    ST_GeomFromText(
        'LINESTRING(
            -109.05304 39.195013,
            -109.05304 41.000889,
            -104.897461 40.996484
        )',
        4326
    )
);

SELECT TopoGeo_AddLineString(
    'ch13a_topology',
    ST_GeomFromText(
        'LINESTRING(
            -104.897461 40.996484,
            -102.051744 40.996484,
            -102.051744 40.003029
        )',
        4326
    )
);

SELECT TopoGeo_AddLineString(
    'ch13a_topology',
    ST_GeomFromText(
        'LINESTRING(
            -102.051744 40.003029,
            -102.04874 36.992682,
            -104.48204 36.992682
        )',
        4326
    )
);

SELECT TopoGeo_AddLineString(
    'ch13a_topology',
    ST_GeomFromText(
        'LINESTRING(
            -104.48204 36.992682,
            -109.045226 36.999077,
            -109.05304 39.195013
        )',
```

```
        4326
    )
);
```

To make sure you've typed or copied everything correctly, execute the following SQL:

```
SELECT ST_GetFaceGeometry('ch13a_topology',1);
```

If you look at the output on the Geometry viewer in pgAdmin, you should see what is shown in figure 13.1.

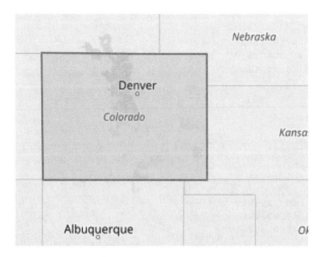

Figure 13.1   Colorado as seen in pgAdmin4

The entire state of Colorado is one big face that is a perfectly rectangular polygon geometry.

Look inside the tables after running the code in listing 13.1 and you'll see four new edges, four new nodes, and one new face. The TopoGeo_AddLineString function automatically generates the topology network using the edge data and fills in the nodes and faces. You now have a topology of the rectangular outline of Colorado.

Two major interstate highways crisscross the state from boundary to boundary: I-25 runs north/south and I-70 runs west/east. You can add I-70 with the following code.

Listing 13.2   Adding highway I-70

```
SELECT TopoGeo_AddLineString(
    'ch13a_topology',
    ST_GeomFromText(
        'LINESTRING(
            -109.05304 39.195013,
            -108.555908 39.108751,
            -105.021057 39.717751,
            -102.051744 40.003029
```

```
        )',
        4326
    )
);
```

Upon successfully adding I-70, the SELECT will return the ID number of the new edge. You should see the number 5 in the output.

Next, add I-25.

Listing 13.3 Adding highway I-25

```
SELECT TopoGeo_AddLineString(
    'ch13a_topology',
    ST_GeomFromText(
        'LINESTRING(
            -104.897461 40.996484,
            -105.021057 39.717751,
            -104.798584 38.814031,
            -104.48204 36.992682
        )',
        4326
    )
);
```

Because you added I-70 first and then I-25, the latter will bisect I-70, creating two edges for itself and breaking I-70 into two edges. The output will return the ID numbers of the two new edges for I-25: 7 and 8.

A diagram will be helpful at this point. We used the QGIS PostGIS Topology Viewer to produce figure 13.2, which shows the four face IDs, eight edge IDs, and five nodes (each using a different style of numbers).

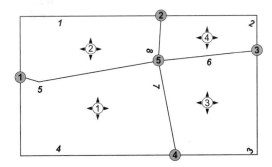

Figure 13.2 Colorado topology network

I-25 (edges 8 and 7 with nodes 2, 5, 4) runs north/south. I-70 (edges 5 and 6 with nodes 1, 5, 3) runs west to east. The two highways intersect at the state capital, Denver (node 5).

The addition of the highways split the original single-face Colorado into four faces. Look carefully at the tables again: PostGIS automatically reorganized your topology.

The corner points are no longer nodes, just vertices outlining the edge. PostGIS added a node for Denver where the two highway edges intersect.

We modeled the highways with kinks. For I-25, the kink is at Colorado Springs. For I-70, the kink is at Grand Junction. These kinks are merely vertices used to refine the geometry; they play no part in relationships. As such, they aren't nodes. Edges only intersect at nodes.

You now have a total of eight edges. The two highways slice Colorado into four distinct polygons or faces. The addition of highway I-25 split our original one-edge I-70 (edge 5) into two edges (5 and 6).

If you look in the face table using the following query, you'll see each of the faces listed, as well as their minimum bounding rectangle (mbr), which is just the bounding box of the face. The face table doesn't store the actual polygons because all the data necessary to derive them can be found in the edge_data table. This storage methodology abides by the database principle of keeping data in only one place. As before, you can use the ST_GetFaceGeometry function to view the actual face geometry:

```
SELECT face_id, mbr,
ST_GetFaceGeometry('ch13a_topology',face_id) AS geom          ◁─────  Return the face
FROM ch13a_topology.face                                              geometry.
WHERE face_id > 0;          ◁───  Exclude the universal face,
                                  which has no geometry.
```

The output of the geom column in the preceding query is shown in figure 13.3. The query only considers non-universal faces. The universal face always has a face ID of 0 and represents that part which is not part of the topology and so is always empty.

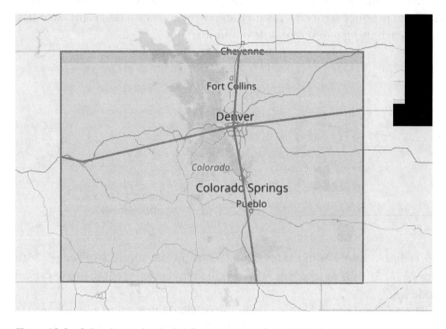

Figure 13.3   Colorado quadsected at Denver as seen in pgAdmin4

The edge view and edge_data

The edge view contains a subset of the columns of the edge_data table. The edge_ data table contains additional columns not defined in the OGC topology spec but that are used internally by PostGIS topology. For general uses, and to keep in line with the OGC topology standards, the edge view should be used instead of directly querying the edge_data table.

Remember that topology isn't concerned with describing geometries but rather with how they're related. Removing all the superfluous vertices in Colorado creates a skeletal network diagram that you can see in figure 13.4.

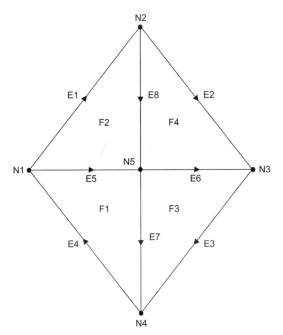

Figure 13.4 Simplified network topology

You can see the edges that make up the topology by querying the edge view with the code in the following listing.

Listing 13.4 Query edge_data

```
SELECT *
FROM ch13a_topology.edge
ORDER BY edge_id;
```

The pgAdmin output of listing 13.4 is shown in figure 13.5. It shows the contents of the edge view based on the simplified topology. Don't be alarmed if your output is a little different. You should, however, have eight edges at this point.

edge_id [PK] integer	start_node integer	end_node integer	next_left_edge integer	abs_next_left_edge integer	next_right_edge integer	abs_next_right_edge integer	left_face integer	right_face integer	geom geometry
1	1	1	2	2	2	5	5	0	2 0102000020E6100...
2	2	2	3	3	3	7	7	0	3 0102000020E6100...
3	3	3	4	4	4	-6	6	0	4 0102000020E6100...
4	4	4	1	1	1	-8	8	0	1 0102000020E6100...
5	5	1	5	-7	7	-4	4	2	1 0102000020E6100...
6	6	5	3	-2	2	8	8	3	4 0102000020E6100...
7	7	2	5	6	6	-1	1	3	2 0102000020E6100...
8	8	5	4	-3	3	-5	5	4	1 0102000020E6100...

Figure 13.5   Simplified network topology

13.2.3   *The topogeometry type*

Once you've constructed your topology, you can group your primitives to constitute *topogeometries* (*layers* in topo-speak).

Let's say you want to collect the four edges making up the highways in the Colorado model. You could start by creating a new table to store topogeometries, as shown in listing 13.5. To this table you could add a topogeometry column using the PostGIS AddTopoGeometryColumn function. You should always use the AddTopoGeometryColumn function to create new columns because it takes care of registering the new topogeometry column in the topology.layer table.

> **Listing 13.5   Creating a table to store highways and defining a topogeometry column**

```
CREATE TABLE ch13.highways_topo (highway varchar(20) PRIMARY KEY);
SELECT AddTopoGeometryColumn(
    'ch13a_topology',
    'ch13',
    'highways_topo',
    'topo',
    'LINESTRING'
);
```

After running the preceding code, you should see a new entry in the topology.layer table. AddTopoGeometryColumn will return the auto-assigned ID of the new layer. Keep in mind that a topogeometry is always tied to a layer.

Once you have your topogeometry column, you can add the I-70 highway using the CreateTopoGeom function as shown in the next listing.

> **Listing 13.6   Defining the I-70 topogeometry using CreateTopoGeom**

```
INSERT INTO ch13.highways_topo (highway, topo)
VALUES (
    'I70',
    CreateTopoGeom(          ←  Define an entry for I-70 where the
        'ch13a_topology',           topology elements are formed
        2,                          from ch13a_topology.
        1,              ←  The ID of the layer this topogeom belongs
                           to. This is the number returned when you
                           defined the topogeom column.
```

The type of topogeom: 2 = lineal.

```
'{{5,2},{6,2}}'::topoelementarray
    )
);
```
The elements that make up this topogeom. Each element in the array
is composed of the element ID and the element type (1 = node,
2 = edge, 3 = face). In this example, all elements are edges.

When defining a new topogeometry column, you need to denote the topogeometry type by one of the following numbers: 1 = point, 2 = lineal, 3 = areal. In the case of topogeometries, polygons and multipolygons are lumped together under the areal type, points and multipoints are the point type, and linestrings and multilinestrings are the lineal type.

A topogeometry is implemented as a database domain type composed of four elements. You can see the incarnation with the following query:

```
SELECT highway, topo, (topo).*
FROM ch13.highways_topo WHERE highway = 'I70';
```

The output of the preceding query follows:

```
highway |    topo    | topology_id | layer_id | id | type
---------+-----------+-------------+----------+----+------
  I70    | (1,1,1,2) |           1 |        1 |  1 |   2
(1 row)
```

As you can see, expanding (topo).* lists as columns the parts that make up the topogeometry. The first item is the topology the topogeometry belongs to. The second element is the layer the topogeometry belongs to, which is the layer ID assigned to the ch13.highways_topo.topo column when you added the column. The third item is the ID of the topogeometry in the ch13a_topology schema's relation table in the topogeo _id column. Finally, the fourth item is the type, which in this case is 2 = lineal.

If you have geometries to start with, you can use the powerful toTopoGeom function to convert geometries to topogeometries and add the newly formed topogeometries to your table in one step, as demonstrated in listing 13.7.

Listing 13.7 Defining a topogeometry using `toTopoGeom`

```
INSERT INTO ch13.highways_topo (highway, topo)
SELECT
    'I25',                      Define I-25 using
    toTopoGeom(          ◁─┐    toTopoGeom.
        ST_GeomFromText(
            'LINESTRING(
                -104.897461 40.996484,
                -105.021057 39.717751,
                -104.798584 38.814031,
                -104.48204 36.992682
            )',
            4326              The geometry; any edges or nodes
        ),           ◁─┤     needed to form the geometry will
                            be created if not present.
```

```
'ch13a_topology',        ◁─┐  The topology
   1  ◁─────┐
);          │  The layer
```

In listing 13.7 you add the topogeometry of I-25 using the toTopoGeom function. The risk and benefit of using this function is that it will, by default, create new primitive edges, nodes, and faces as needed, if primitives don't exist to form the new topogeometry.

In this example, you already added the primitive edges in listing 13.3, so toTopo-Geometry shouldn't introduce new edges. You include the name of the topology you're adding to, as well as the layer that this new topogeometry will be associated with. This layer ID must be the same as the one returned when you created the topogeometry column in listing 13.5.

If a node or edge needed to form the new topogeometry doesn't exist, the toTopo-Geom function will automatically apply a tolerance to find matching nodes or edges before resorting to creating them. In other words, if an existing node is within the snap distance of the linestring geometry, toTopogeom will shift the linestring to incorporate the node as a vertex instead of creating a new node. If you want to override the default tolerance, you can pass in an additional final argument to toTopogeom to apply a tolerance. The default tolerance that toTopogeom uses is a function of the bounding box of the input geometry. This default tolerance is computed internally using the function topology._ST_MinTolerance.

To confirm the composition of your new topogeometries, you can use the Get-TopoGeomElements function, as in the next listing.

Listing 13.8   Querying primitive elements of Colorado highways

```
SELECT highway, (topo).*, GetTopoGeomElements(topo) As el
FROM ch13.highways_topo
ORDER BY highway;
```

This listing outputs the four topogeometry sub-element identifiers accessed with (topo).* and a set of topoelements using the GetTopoGeomElements function:

```
highway | topology_id | layer_id | id | type |  el
--------+-------------+----------+----+------+-------
  I25   |      1      |    1     | 2  |  2   | {7,2}
  I25   |      1      |    1     | 2  |  2   | {8,2}
  I70   |      1      |    1     | 1  |  2   | {5,2}
  I70   |      1      |    1     | 1  |  2   | {6,2}
```

The code in listing 13.8 returns a set of objects called *topoelements* for each topogeometry. Although you only have two rows in the highways_topo table, you get back four rows when you use the GetTopoGeomElements function because GetTopoGeomElements returns a row for each edge of each highway.

The topoelement object is an integer array domain type with two elements. The first is the ID of the element in the corresponding table. Because edges make up the highways, the IDs are `edge_ids` in ch13a_topology.edge. The second element of a `topoelement` denotes the layer/class type (1 = node, 2 = edge, 3 = face, and higher numbers are the IDs of layers).

> ### Establish a naming convention
> PostGIS doesn't make a clear distinction between database objects that describe the topological networks versus your own use of topologies in topogeometry columns. We advise you to establish a naming convention. The myriad of schemas and tables supporting topologies can be overwhelming, especially for those charged with maintaining the underlying network.

13.2.4 Recap of using topologies

The PostGIS topology model provides the following features for working with topologies:

- Enabling the topology extension immediately creates the topology schema and functions.
- The topology.topology table records all topologies in your database.
- The topology.layer table records all topogeometry columns (layers) in your database.
- Each topological network has its own network schema.
- Primitives (edges, nodes, faces) have their respective tables in the network schema.
- The relation table in a specific topology network schema (in this case, `ch13a_ topology.relation`) records which topology primitives and layer elements belong in which topogeometry.

Once you've built your topologies, you're free to use them anywhere within the database. You can use them elsewhere in your database by building topogeometries from your topology. This is the process:

- Add topogeometry columns (layers) to your own tables.
- Create topogeometries from primitives or other layers, and add them to your topogeometry column.
- Add topogeometries from geometries and change your underlying network in one step using the `toTopoGeom` function. Keep in mind, though, that once you do this, edges, faces, and nodes are automatically added and existing ones are split. Once your topology is changed this way, simply removing the introduced topogeometry is not sufficient to revert the changes to the topology.

In the next section you'll learn how to work with data you get from various sources and how to fix faulty topologies caused by introducing less than perfect data.

13.3   *Topology of Victoria, BC*

In this section, we'll present a real-world example of topology use, with Victoria, BC as our city of choice.

13.3.1   *Creating the Victoria topology*

The first step in working with topologies is to create a topology. As before, you use the `CreateTopology` function; the first argument is a name for the topology, and the second is the SRID.

The Victoria data came to us in WGS 84 lon/lat (SRID 4326). You can stick with this spatial reference system, but measuring tolerance in degrees is messy, and we prefer making measurements in meters rather than degrees. A decent planar spatial reference system for Victoria is UTM Zone 10N (SRID 32610). UTM allows you to measure in meters, and it's area-preserving.

You can start off by creating the topology to hold the data:

```
SELECT CreateTopology('ch13_topology', 32610, 0.05);
```

This function registers the topology in the topology table in the `topology` schema created when you installed the `postgis_topology` extension. It also creates the `ch13_topology` database schema to house the topology elements.

The preceding code specifies a default tolerance of .05 meters. For functions that take an optional argument of tolerance, if no tolerance is passed in, the function will resort to the default. Roughly, the tolerance is the minimal distance between two points for them to be considered distinct. For instance, if you have a node that's only .01 meters away from another, PostGIS will snap the two together into a single node.

13.3.2   *Adding primitives to a topology*

In this section, you'll learn how to add primitives to a topology using geometries. Post-GIS topology offers three functions that will add topology primitives to your topology, utilizing geometries as the data source: `TopoGeo_AddPoint`, `TopoGeo_AddLineString`, and `TopoGeo_AddPolygon`. Each takes an optional tolerance argument that's in the units of the spatial reference system of the topology and denotes how close primitives that make up the feature need to be to an existing topology primitive or to each other to be snapped together with that primitive. If no tolerance argument is passed in, the function looks to the tolerance specified for the topology. If no tolerance is specified for the topology, then the function derives an acceptable tolerance by examining the bounding box of the geometry being added.

These functions may also create other primitives. For example, adding a linestring with `TopoGeo_AddLineString` may create two edges and a face, but only the edges created will be returned in the results.

In the event that you don't want the uncertainty and convenience of automatically adding primitives, you can tap into the following three functions: `AddNode`, `AddEdge`, and `AddFace`. These add one node, one edge, and one face respectively. These functions are more predictable because they'll never split edges or form faces from edges, and if they're unable to add a primitive to the topology without violating the topology requirements, they'll error out. If you have a blueprint of all primitives and their construction sequence, you should be able to use these lower-level functions.

In this section you'll learn how to use `TopoGeo_AddLineString` and `TopoGeo_AddPolygon`. The `TopoGeo_AddPoint` function is much less commonly used than the other two and works exactly the same way, except that it takes a point instead of a linestring or polygon.

THE TOPOGEO_ADDLINESTRING FUNCTION

The `TopoGeo_AddLineString` function adds nodes, edges, and faces to the topology from single linestring inputs. We'll start by loading the Victoria city boundary linestrings, as shown in the following listing.

Listing 13.9 Loading linestrings of administrative boundaries

```
SELECT
    gid,
    TopoGeo_AddLineString(
        'ch13_topology', ST_Transform(geom, 32610)
    ) As edge_id          <──┐  Create edges.
FROM (
    SELECT gid, (ST_Dump(geom)).geom FROM ch13_staging.cityboundary
) As f;          <──┐
                    ❶  Expand multilinestrings
                       to linestrings.
```

`TopoGeo_AddLineString` only accepts linestrings, not multilinestrings. This means you need to explode your multilinestring into linestrings using `ST_Dump` ❶. You need to add an alias to this subselect because PostgreSQL requires all subselects in a `FROM` to have a name. In this case we chose `f`. It doesn't matter what name you use.

For the administrative boundaries in the Victoria data, all records are single-line multilinestrings, so you end up with the same number of records in the `f` subquery as there are rows in the cityboundary table.

The following listing shows the output of listing 13.9.

Listing 13.10 Output of the boundaries query

```
 gid | edge_id
+----+---------
   1 |       1
```

`TopoGeo_AddLineString` is a set-returning function, which means it has the potential of expanding your row count, because each call may return more than one value.

The topology now consists of two faces, one edge, and one node, as shown in figure 13.6.

Listing 13.11 inspects the topology as it currently stands.

Figure 13.6   Victoria topology with border

Listing 13.11   Count of primitives

```
SELECT 'faces' As type, COUNT(*) As num FROM ch13_topology.face
UNION ALL
SELECT 'edges' As type, COUNT(*) As num FROM ch13_topology.edge
UNION ALL
SELECT 'nodes' As type, COUNT(*) As num FROM ch13_topology.node
UNION ALL
SELECT 'relations' As type, COUNT(*) As num FROM ch13_topology.relation;
```

The output of listing 13.11 follows:

```
   type    | num
-----------+-----
 faces     |  2
 edges     |  1
 nodes     |  1
 relations |  0
```

Note that even though you only added linestrings to your topology to create single edges, PostGIS automatically created a face to enclose the edge and a node to demarcate where the edges start and end. A more subtle addition is that of the universal face. Every topology has a *universal face* that encompasses the portion exterior to the topology. Your face count is therefore two: the face of Victoria, and the face that's not Victoria.

THE TOPOGEO_ADDPOLYGON FUNCTION

TopoGeo_AddPolygon creates faces from polygons, though in the process it will most likely create other primitives to fill out the topology. TopoGeo_AddPolygon accepts polygons, not multipolygons, and returns the IDs of the new faces created or the IDs of faces contained within the input polygon.

For this next example, we'll add Victoria neighborhoods.

Listing 13.12 Using TopoGeo_AddPolygon with tolerance

```
SELECT
    gid,
    TopoGeo_AddPolygon(
        'ch13_topology', ST_Transform(geom, 32610), 0.05
    ) As face_id
FROM (
    SELECT
        gid,
        (ST_Dump(geom)).geom
    FROM ch13_staging.neighbourhoods
) As f;
```

Listing 13.12 creates 27 faces from 14 single-polygon multipolygons. This example applied a tolerance of 0.05, snapping anything within 0.05 meters.

You may find that when you run TopoGeo_AddPolygon or TopoGeo_AddLineString a second time with the same dataset, you'll sometimes end up with more IDs returned than the first time. This is because the first round only returns the IDs of the primitives created. If during the course of running the function, an existing primitive has to be split, you won't see the IDs of the split primitives until the second round. Our advice is not to put much faith in the IDs returned by these functions.

You may also be puzzled by how you ended up with 28 faces from only 14 polygons. This has to do with overlap. Ideally the 14 polygons that form the neighborhoods of Victoria should completely represent the face of Victoria with no overlaps of neighborhoods or gaps between neighborhoods—what we refer to as "mutually exclusive and collectively exhaustive." In the real world, data is never so perfect. You'll have to contend with small pockets of polygons where the overlapping happens. In later sections we'll show you how to realign these polygons to eliminate annoying shards.

13.3.3 Creating topogeometries

The primary reason for building a topology is to have a scaffold for spatial objects we call *topogeometries*. Why do we want topogeometries? A topogeometry, unlike a geometry, is composed of elements in a topology that can be shared with other topogeometries or elements in topology. If a topogeometry neighbor's boundaries change, then the topogeometry's boundaries can change as well. This is a very important feature in cadastral surveying, the study of land boundaries.

Creating topogeometries is a three-step process:

1 Create a layer by defining a topogeometry column in a table.

2 Create topogeometries by collecting primitive elements, collecting other layer elements, or building them from geometries.

3 Insert the topogeometries into the topogeometry column.

In this section you'll revisit how to create topogeometry columns and populate them with topogeometries. You'll learn how to do this with existing geometries as well as building from existing elements in a topology. You'll perform these exercises with Victoria data.

Topogeometries are recorded in the topology's relation table.

BUILDING LAYERS WITH ADDTOPOGEOMETRYCOLUMN

The code in the following listing builds a couple of topology layers.

Listing 13.13   Create tables and add topogeometry columns

```
CREATE TABLE ch13.neighbourhoods (feat_name varchar(50) primary key);
SELECT AddTopoGeometryColumn(
    'ch13_topology',
    'ch13',
    'neighbourhoods',
    'topo',
    'MULTIPOLYGON'        ❶  Topogeometry column for a
);                                collection of neighborhoods

CREATE TABLE ch13.cities (feat_name varchar(150) primary key);
SELECT AddTopoGeometryColumn(
    'ch13_topology',
    'ch13',
    'cities',
    'topo',
    'MULTIPOLYGON',
    1                     ❷  Topogeometry column
);                                for a collection of cities
```

Listing 13.13 creates two kinds of topogeometry columns. You define a column called topo in the neighbourhoods table to store the faces each neighborhood is composed of ❶. You then define a column called topo in the cities table to store the neighborhoods (layer = 1) that each city is composed of ❷.

Each city is defined by a topogeometry. In this Victoria example, you just want one city, so there's only one topogeometry.

You can interrogate the tables with psql using \d ch13.neighbourhoods and \d ch13.cities:

```
Table "ch13.neighbourhoods"
   Column    |          Type           | Modifiers
-----------+-------------------------+-----------
 feat_name | character varying(50)   | not null
 topo      | topogeometry            |
```

```
Indexes:
    "neighbourhoods_pkey" PRIMARY KEY, btree (feat_name)
Check constraints:
    "check_topogeom_topo"
    CHECK ((topo).topology_id = 2
    AND (topo).layer_id = 1 AND (topo).type = 3)


                    Table "ch13.cities"
  Column   |              Type             |  Modifiers
-----------+-------------------------------+------------
 feat_name | character varying(150)        | not null
 topo      | topogeometry                  |
Indexes:
    "cities_pkey" PRIMARY KEY, btree (feat_name)
Check constraints:
    "check_topogeom_topo"
    CHECK ((topo).topology_id = 2
     AND (topo).layer_id = 2 AND (topo).type = 3)
```

Although it's not evident from the table description that cities are modeled as being composed of neighborhoods, you can inspect the topology.layer table, which lists all the topogeometry columns. In it you'll see that the child_id field is filled with 1 for the cities layer, showing that each city is made up of child neighborhoods.

CONVERTING GEOMETRIES TO TOPOGEOMETRIES

As you've already seen in the Colorado example, the powerful toTopoGeom function will convert a geometry to its topogeometry equivalent. But before you can use it, you must already have a layer—the ID of the layer is a required parameter for toTopoGeom, and the layer you pass in must be a layer of primitives. In the Victoria example thus far, this means only the topo column in the neighbourhoods table can be used with toTopoGeom. You can't use toTopoGeom to add topogeometries to the cities table because the cities.topo corresponding topology layer is a hierarchical layer that must be composed of neighborhoods (a non-primitive layer type).

Be forewarned! Each call to toTopoGeom could spawn new primitives in the underlying topology if it can't find nodes, edges, and faces within tolerance. Depending on the number of topogeometries you'll be maintaining and the rigor with which you want to control changes to the topology itself, you may not wish to use this function, or at least use it with extreme caution.

For instance, suppose you meticulously create the topology of Beijing's rapidly evolving subway network, and you granted your colleagues the right to create topogeometries. The colleague in charge of stations created a layer of nodes, the colleague in charge of loop lines created a layer of edges, and so on. One day, a bumbling new colleague in charge of the airport subway lines decided to create a layer for his subway line and branches. He downloaded the linestring of Beijing expressways, thinking that what he had were the geometries for the airport express subway line. He used the versatile toTopoGeom function and added his linestrings. We'll leave you to figure out how this story ends.

The following example shows how to create the topogeoms from the neighbour-hoods.topo layer:

```
INSERT INTO ch13.neighbourhoods (feat_name, topo)
SELECT
    neighbourh,
    toTopoGeom(
        ST_Transform(geom, 32610), 'ch13_topology', 1, 0.05
    )
FROM ch13_staging.neighbourhoods;
```

CREATING TOPOGEOMETRIES FROM EXISTING TOPOLOGY ELEMENTS

In more controlled situations, such as where the maintainer of the topology is not the same person creating topogeometries, you'll only want to allow the formation of new topogeometries from existing topology elements in your topology. If you know what these elements are or can compute them based on relationships such as geometry containment, you can use the functions CreateTopoGeom and TopoElementArray_Agg as shown in the following listing.

Listing 13.14   Creating topogeometries from non-primitives

```
INSERT INTO ch13.cities (feat_name, topo)
SELECT
    'Victoria',
    CreateTopoGeom(
        'ch13_topology',        ❶ Areal
        3,
        2,                      ❷ Layer
        (
            SELECT TopoElementArray_Agg(
                ARRAY[(topo).id,(topo).layer_id]
            )                              Gather all
            FROM ch13.neighbourhoods      elements.
        )
    )
);
```

Listing 13.14 appends Victoria into the cities table. CreateTopoGeom is the function that puts together the topogeometries. For its parameters in this example, you specify that the new topogeometries will be areal, element type 3 ❶. You also specify that the new topogeometries will belong to the cities topogeometry column, layer 2 ❷.

In this example you gather up all the faces in Victoria neighborhoods, but more commonly you'll find that you need to do a containment check using something like ST_Contains(geom,topo::geometry). For example, if your neighbourhoods table also included areas from nearby Sannich, you'd have to use the Victoria polygon to sift out only neighborhoods within Victoria's city boundaries.

Most desktop viewing tools have no concept of topogeometries. To get a picture, you must cast your topogeometries to geometries, as in the next example:

```
SELECT topo::geometry FROM ch13.cities WHERE feat_name = 'Victoria';
```

Now you can bring your result into OpenJUMP, pgAdmin, or QGIS, as shown in figure 13.7.

Figure 13.7   Victoria as geometry

To show the neighborhoods, you need to convert each face to a polygon geometry, as in the following example:

```
SELECT face_id, ST_GetFaceGeometry('ch13_topology', face_id)
FROM (
    SELECT (GetTopoGeomElements(topo))[1] As face_id
    FROM ch13.cities
    WHERE feat_name = 'Victoria'
) As x;
```

With theming, the output in OpenJUMP is shown in figure 13.8.

Figure 13.8   Faces of Victoria

13.4 Fixing topogeometry issues by editing topology primitives

Recall that in listing 13.12 you added 14 polygons and ended up with a total of 38 faces in your topology. The neighborhood polygons either overlapped or the neighborhoods didn't fully fill out the city's polygon. You ended up with shards that are themselves polygons but are too tiny to discern from a map. Besides inherent bad data as the cause, simplification is the usual culprit for misalignments. *Simplification* is a geometry process, so it looks at geometries independent of each other. When you simplify a neighborhood polygon geometry by reducing the number of vertices, using one of the PostGIS geometry simplification functions, such as ST_Simplify or ST_Simplify-PreserveTopology, PostGIS doesn't care about how adjacent polygons must be altered to avoid introducing small gaps. We'll demonstrate the issue later in this chapter and show how using ST_Simplify on a topogeometry does not cause this problem.

Currently the ch13_topology example has 37 faces, including the universal face. The neighbourhoods layer has 14 topogeometries. Using QGIS, you can overlay neighbourhoods with ch13_topology.faces. In figure 13.9 the neighborhoods are labeled with their names and the faces with their IDs.

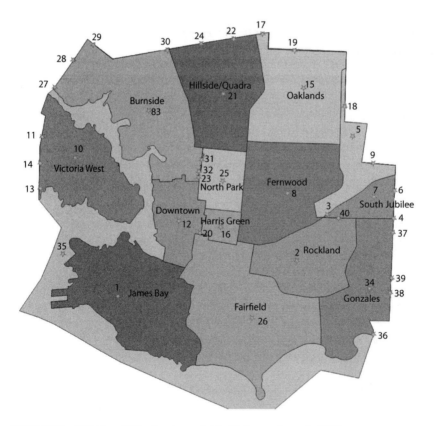

Figure 13.9 Victoria neighborhoods overlaid with faces shown in QGIS

Take a close look at Burnside. It has tiny faces (denoted by numbers 21, 22, 25, 28, 29) that occupy almost no area along its borders. Run the code in the following listing to see all the pesky tiny faces within neighborhoods.

Listing 13.15 Neighborhoods with more than one face

```
SELECT feat_name, COUNT(face_id) As num_faces,
    MIN(
        ST_Area(ST_GetFaceGeometry('ch13_topology',face_id))
    )::numeric(10,2) As min_area,
    MAX(
        ST_Area(ST_GetFaceGeometry('ch13_topology',face_id))
    )::numeric(10,2) As max_area
FROM (
    SELECT feat_name, (GetTopoGeomElements(topo))[1] As face_id
    FROM ch13.neighbourhoods
) As x
GROUP BY feat_name
HAVING COUNT(face_id) > 1
ORDER BY COUNT(face_id) DESC;
```

The output of listing 13.15 is shown next:

```
feat_name       | num_faces | min_area |  max_area
----------------+-----------+----------+------------
 Burnside        |         6 |     1.48 | 2383705.36
 Gonzales        |         4 |     0.03 | 1366871.65
 Victoria West   |         4 |     2.22 | 1579455.03
 North Park      |         3 |    41.29 |  554622.59
 Oaklands        |         2 | 11997.94 | 1733012.41
 North Jubilee   |         2 |    39.05 |  629632.96
 Hillside/Quadra |         2 |    62.23 | 1658087.55
(7 rows)
```

The code in listing 13.15 listed all neighborhoods with more than one face and counted a total of 25 faces. Not listed are 6 additional neighbors with 1 face each, bringing us to a total of 30 faces that are part of neighborhoods. It's also possible to have faces that don't belong to any neighborhoods, which we evidently have, because we have 37 non-universal faces.

13.4.1 Removing faces by removing edges

The ST_RemEdgeNewFace function removes an edge. If the edge splits two faces, the original faces are destroyed and a new face that's the union of the original two is created.

In listing 13.16 you'll use this function recklessly, blindly trying to remove all the edges that form the faces of these small pocket polygons. The main reason you can get away with being reckless here is that the process will fail if the result removes a face used by a topogeometry defined in ch13.neighbourhoods and that topogeometry doesn't completely cover the new face created. So the result of ignoring failures here is that you'll remove edges that don't affect the geometric definition (topo::geometry) of your neighborhoods.

Listing 13.16   Removing extraneous faces with small area

```
DO
LANGUAGE plpgsql
$$
DECLARE r record; var_face integer;
BEGIN
    FOR r IN (
    SELECT DISTINCT abs(
        (ST_GetFaceEdges(
            'ch13_topology',face_id)
        ).edge
    ) As edge
    FROM (
        SELECT feat_name, (GetTopoGeomElements(topo))[1] As face_id
        FROM ch13.neighbourhoods
    ) As x
    WHERE ST_Area(ST_GetFaceGeometry('ch13_topology',face_id)) < 55000
     )
    LOOP
        BEGIN
            var_face := ST_RemEdgeNewFace('ch13_topology',r.edge);
            EXCEPTION
                WHEN OTHERS THEN
                RAISE WARNING 'Failed remove edge: %, %', r.edge, SQLERRM;
        END;
    END LOOP;
END
$$;
```

In listing 13.16 you raise a warning if a remove step fails, but because it's just a warning, the code continues to run for the remaining edges.

After running listing 13.16, run listing 13.15 again to see how you did:

```
feat_name  | num_faces | min_area |  max_area
+-----------+-----------+----------+------------
North Park |         3 |    41.29 |   554621.97
Burnside   |         3 |    41.29 |  2383714.40
```

From eight neighborhoods with more than one face, you're now down to two. You've mitigated, but not eliminated, your extra faces. Using QGIS as in figure 13.10, you can see that you've got border disputes between North Park and Burnside (around faces 21 and 28). The edges that make up these faces couldn't be destroyed by the previous process because they would have resulted in changing the landscape of North Park and Burnside by either giving land to North Park or taking away land from North Park.

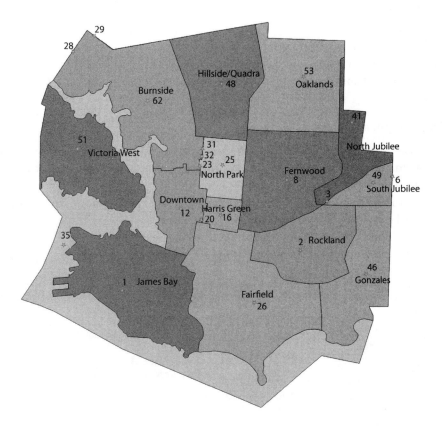

Figure 13.10   Victoria neighborhoods overlaid with faces, shown in QGIS after cleanup

13.4.2 Checking for shared faces

It's often hard to tell from viewing which faces, if any, are shared. Using a query is more definitive. The following listing will first dump out the topoelement IDs for the two adjacent neighborhoods and will only return those faces that are in common.

Listing 13.17   Finding shared faces

```
SELECT (GetTopoGeomElements(topo))[1] As face_id        ◄──┐  Face IDs of
FROM ch13.neighbourhoods                                   │  North Park
WHERE feat_name = 'North Park'
INTERSECT
SELECT (GetTopoGeomElements(topo))[1] As face_id        ◄──┐  Face IDs of
FROM ch13.neighbourhoods                                   │  Burnside
WHERE feat_name = 'Burnside';
```

The output of listing 13.17 is shown next:

```
 face_id
--------
```

```
21
28
```

You now know, without a doubt, that faces 21 and 28 are shared. This calls for changing the underlying topogeometries so that the neighborhoods don't overlap each other.

13.4.3 Editing topogeometries

The easiest way to fix the overlap is to remove a shared face from each topogeometry. Unfortunately PostGIS topology doesn't offer any functions for doing so; you'll need to work directly with the topology tables. Recall that the ch13_topology.relation table holds all relationships between a topogeometry and the topology. You can edit this table and dissociate faces from your topogeometries.

The following listing deletes shared entries in the relations table corresponding to Burnside and North Park.

> **Listing 13.18   Removing shared areas from topogeometries**

```
DELETE FROM ch13_topology.relation AS r        ◁──  Remove from
WHERE EXISTS (                                       relation table
    SELECT topo                                ◁──
    FROM ch13.neighbourhoods As n
    WHERE                                      Remove face 21
        feat_name = 'North Park' AND           from North Park.
        (topo).id = r.topogeo_id AND
        r.element_id = 21 AND
        r.element_type = 3
);

DELETE FROM ch13_topology.relation AS r        ◁──  Remove face 28
WHERE EXISTS (                                       from Burnside.
    SELECT topo
    FROM ch13.neighbourhoods As n
    WHERE
        feat_name = 'Burnside' AND
        (topo).id = r.topogeo_id AND
        r.element_id = 28 AND
        r.element_type = 3
);
```

After you're done running listing 13.18, rerun listing 13.16. Now all your neighborhoods should have exactly one face.

13.5   Inserting and editing large data sets

So far you've learned how to insert small sets of polygons and linestrings. When you start loading streets and parcels for large cities, you could easily be looking at tens of thousands of edges and faces. One annoyance when loading large data sets is the possibility of running into topological errors that halt the import process.

PostgreSQL, like most relational databases, is transaction-based. Each insert or update statement runs as a single transaction, meaning all records must succeed or fail; there are no partial updates or inserts. If PostGIS hits one bad record at the end of an hour-long insert, you'll have wasted the entire hour. Our recommendation for getting around the all-or-nothing nature of transactions is to perform the inserts or updates in small batches. To implement this, run your process either in a DO command or a function:

- The DO command will run a single transaction, but it will prompt on each error. If you choose to ignore the error, execution will continue.
- In the function approach, you embed your inserts or updates into a function and then iteratively call the function with small batches of data. Should you hit an error, only the current batch is affected.

The following example demonstrates an enhanced function approach where you also catch errors in the function itself. First, you need to create a new table with a topology column, as shown in the following listing.

Listing 13.19 Create table to hold streets topogeometry

```
CREATE TABLE ch13.streets (
    gid integer primary key,
    feat_name varchar(50),
    access varchar(20),
    rd_class varchar(20),
    max_speed numeric(10,2)       ❶ Create the
);                                    streets table.


SELECT AddTopoGeometryColumn(
    'ch13_topology',
    'ch13',
    'streets',
    'topo',
    'MULTILINESTRING'     ❷ Add a topogeometry column
);                            to the streets table.


CREATE TABLE ch13.log_street_failures (
    gid integer primary key,
    error text
); --            ❸ Create an errors table
                    to log topology errors.
```

Listing 13.19 creates a table to hold streets ❶ in a topogeometry column ❷ that holds topogeoms of type MULTILINESTRING. It also creates a table to log topology insert errors during loading ❸, which will be used in the next step.

Next is the logic that does the inserts.

Listing 13.20   Function to load streets in batches

```
CREATE OR REPLACE PROCEDURE ch13.load_streets(param_num integer) AS
$$
DECLARE r record;
BEGIN
    FOR r IN
        SELECT *
        FROM ch13_staging.streetcentrelines
        ORDER BY gid
        LIMIT param_num
    OFFSET (SELECT MAX(gid) from ch13.streets)
    LOOP
        BEGIN
            INSERT INTO ch13.streets (
                gid,feat_name,access,rd_class,max_speed,topo)
            SELECT
                r.gid,r.streetname,r.access,r.rd_class,
                r.max_speed::numeric,
                toTopoGeom(ST_Transform(ST_Force2D(r.geom),32610),
        'ch13_topology',3,0.05);
            EXCEPTION WHEN OTHERS THEN
                INSERT INTO ch13.log_street_failures (gid,error)
                VALUES (r.gid,SQLERRM);
                RAISE WARNING
                    'Loading of record % failed: %',
                    r.gid,
                    SQLERRM;
        END;
        COMMIT;
    END LOOP;
END
$$
LANGUAGE plpgsql;
```

① Select a set of streets from staging table not to exceed param_num rows.

② Insert each into the streets table.

Force 2D transform to match our topology and then converts to a topogeom. **③**

④ Set tolerance to 0.05 meters.

Log any topology exceptions **⑤** and continue.

Commit changes after each iteration.

Listing 13.20 defines a PL/pgSQL procedure that on each call will load the specified number of streets.

> **NOTE** Stored procedures were introduced in PostgreSQL 11 and allow you to commit within the procedure, unlike functions that must commit as a whole. This makes them well suited for batch processing, such as is needed for loading topologies. If you are running a lower version of PostgreSQL, you can rewrite listing 13.20 with CREATE FUNCTION and omit the error-logging **⑤**. You can also use COMMIT in DO constructs for PostgreSQL 11 and above.

There are about 2,500 streets in the data set, so you limit the function to 500 in each run **①**. The OFFSET (SELECT MAX(gid))... code checks the ID of your target table and skips that number in the source table. To take advantage of this snippet, your IDs must be unique and sequential without gaps.

The INSERT itself is within a FOR loop. The set of records being processed is temporarily stored in the variable r **②**. The source data is in WGS 84, and the input geometry is `linestringZM`. You defined `ch13_topology` as 2D, so it can only accommodate two dimensions. Thus, you force the geometry to 2D by dropping the higher dimensions. You also perform a transform to UTM ❸.

Next you use `toTopoGeom` to convert the geometry to a topogeometry fashioned after the streets layer (layer ID of 3) and set the tolerance to 0.05 meters ❹. Any points closer than 0.05 meters will be collapsed. Any streets that fail the insert are skipped and logged in the log_street_failures table ❺.

You can then run the script as follows:

```
CALL ch13.load_streets(2500);
```

This took about 45 seconds to run on our PostgreSQL 13, Windows 2012 64-bit, 8-core server with PostGIS 3.1.1, GEOS 3.9.1. The performance is most sensitive to GEOS version. A newer GEOS will tend to give you better performance.

13.6 *Simplifying with topology in mind*

Simplification in the realm of topology needs to ensure that you don't end up with things that were connected no longer connecting, or with gaping holes.

To simplify in topology, you use `ST_Simplify`, which is overloaded to accept topogeometries. The `ST_Simplify` function that takes a `topogeometry` as input returns a `geometry`. The difference between the geometry and topogeometry versions of the function is that the topogeometry version applies simplification on the edges that comprise the topogeometry, but prevents simplification that would cause gaps between edges or destroy faces. Because a topogeometry is just a reference to edges, the reconstituted geometries that had shared edges now have simplified shared edges.

Finally, keep in mind that any simplification that takes place for topogeometries won't simplify the underlying topology. The simplification process creates a simplified version of the edges comprised by the topogeometry and reconstitutes a geometry from the simplified edges. Once the function is run, the newly created simplified versions of the edges are thrown away.

We'll look at two examples. In the first, we'll cast the neighborhood topogeometry to geometry and apply `ST_Simplify`. You'll see first-hand how you'll end up with overlaps and gaps. We'll then apply `ST_Simplify` directly to the topogeometry, and you'll see how the neighborhoods still fit together harmoniously.

First, we'll simplify against geometry with a tolerance of 150 meters.

Listing 13.21 Geometry-based simplification

```
SELECT feat_name, ST_Simplify(topo::geometry,150) As geom_simp
FROM ch13.neighbourhoods
```

The visual output is shown in figure 13.11.

Next, we'll simplify against topogeometry with the same tolerance in listing 13.22.

Figure 13.11 Geometry-based simplification

Listing 13.22 Topology-based simplification

```
SELECT feat_name, ST_Simplify(topo,150) As topo_simp
FROM ch13.neighbourhoods
```

The visual output is in figure 13.12.

   As you can see, after the topology simplification process, the neighborhoods maintain their connectedness without overlapping each other, even though their shapes have been altered somewhat.

13.7 *Topology validation and summary functions*

In this chapter, we've alluded to many opportunities where your topology could become invalid via an errant edit. We'll now show you two important functions that you should exercise regularly to keep tabs on your topology.

Figure 13.12   Topology-based simplification

`ValidateTopology` notifies you if there are issues with your base topology. It will return a record for each issue in your topology. Issues it detects are outlined in the manual. It doesn't inspect topogeometries! Here's an example:

```
SELECT *
FROM ValidateTopology('ch13_topology');
```

Keep in mind that the standard definition of *validity* is rather loose. Solitary elements that aren't interconnected will pass a validity test. You may consider developing additional validity checks that include `ValidateTopology` as a step.

When running on this dataset, ValidateTopology returned no errors, but if errors are returned, it would look something like the following, denoting where the error is:

```
error           | id1 | id2
------------------+-----+-----
 face has no rings | 209 |
(1 row)
```

TopologySummary is another useful management function that provides you with a basic summary of your topology and layers without you having to look into the tables. Run it with code such as this:

```
SELECT TopologySummary('ch13_topology');
```

The output of TopologySummary follows:

```
Topology ch13_topology (2), SRID 32610, precision 0.05
2070 nodes, 3137 edges, 1074 faces, 2395 topogeoms in 3 layers
Layer 1, type Polygonal (3), 14 topogeoms
 Deploy: ch13.neighbourhoods.topo
Layer 2, type Polygonal (3), 1 topogeoms
 Hierarchy level 1, child layer 1
 Deploy: ch13.cities.topo
Layer 3, type Lineal (2), 2380 topogeoms
 Deploy: ch13.streets.topo
```

Summary

- Topology models space as a set of interconnected objects.
- A change in one object's boundaries affects others.
- Topology is useful for managing data such as land boundaries, where a gain in one territory implies loss in another.
- Simplifying geometries in topology space maintains connectedness, unlike geometry simplification, which considers each object as distinct and detached. This ensures that things like counties, countries, neighborhoods, and cities don't end up with gaps between them when you simplify.

Organizing spatial data

This chapter covers

- Options for structuring spatial data
- Modeling a real city
- Data abstraction with views
- Triggers on tables and views

In chapter 2 we walked through all the possible geometry, geography, and raster types PostGIS offers and how you can create and store them. In this chapter we'll continue our study by demonstrating the different table layouts you can design to store spatial data. Then we'll apply these various design approaches to a real-world example (Paris, France). We'll finish the chapter with a discussion and examples of using views for database abstraction and using triggers to manage inserts and updates in tables and views. Our main focus will be the geometry type, which is still the most commonly used type in PostGIS.

You can download all the data and code for this chapter at www.postgis.us/ chapter_14_edition_3. Before we start, you'll need to load the ch14_data.sql and ch14_staging_data.sql scripts from the chapter download file.

14.1   *Spatial storage approaches*

In database design, there's always a healthy dose of compromise. Many considerations factor into the final structure you settle on, such as the analysis it must support, the speed of the queries, and so forth. With a spatial database, a few additional considerations enter the design process: availability of data, the precision at which you need to store the data, and the mapping tools your database needs to be compatible with. Unlike databases with numerical and text data, where a poor design leads to slow queries, poor design in a spatial database could lead to queries that will never finish in your lifetime. It also goes without saying that many factors can't be determined at the outset. You may not know exactly how much or what type of spatial data will eventually reside in the database. You may not even know how the users will query the data. As with all decision making, you do the best you can with the information you have at the time. You can always rework your design as needs change, but as any database practitioner knows, getting the design more or less right the first time saves hassles down the road.

In this section, we'll cover four common ways to organize data in a spatial database: heterogeneous spatial columns, homogeneous spatial columns, inheritance, and partitioning. Within these various organizations you have the choice of constraining spatial columns by typmod or database constraints. We'll explain how you'd go about setting up your database structure using each of these approaches and point out the advantages and disadvantages of each. These approaches are by no means exhaustive, and you should feel free to find your own hybrid that fits your specific needs. We'll also mainly focus on `geometry` data types over any of the other spatial types. Geometry data types are by far the predominant data types in PostGIS, and they're the foundation for topology and raster data types. Finally, geometry types are inherently faster for most spatial computations than the other types in the spatial family. All this may change as the other spatial types mature, but you'll find the general concepts we cover in this section to be applicable to other spatial types too.

14.1.1   *Heterogeneous columns*

You can't mix `geometry`, `geography`, `raster`, and `topogeometry` in the same table column unless you go completely hog wild by defining a byte array (`bytea`) column and cast to the various data types as needed. And even that approach will only allow you to mix `geometry`, `geography`, and `raster`. We won't explore that approach because it has utility only in rare (and mostly temporary) storage use cases.

Within each base spatial type, you can constrain yourself as little or as much as you want. For example, to store geographic features in a city, you could create a bare-bones `geometry` table column and be done. In this single column, you could store geometry points, linestrings, polygons, collections of 2D/3D, or any other geometry type for that matter, but you couldn't throw a `geography` type in a column defined as `geometry`.

You may wish to mix subtypes if you're more interested in geographically partitioning the city. For example, Washington, D.C., as well as many other planned cities, is divided into quadrants: NW, SW, SE, NE. A city planner can employ a single table with quadrant names in a text column and use another generic geometry column to store the geometries within each quadrant. By leaving the data type as the generic `geometry` type, the column can store polygons for the many polygonal-shaped government edifices in D.C., linestrings to represent major thoroughfares, and points for metro stations.

There are varying degrees in the heterogeneous approach. Using a base spatial column without any subtype doesn't necessarily mean having no additional constraints. You should still judiciously apply constraints (or type modifiers) to ensure data integrity. We advise that you at least enforce the spatial reference system, the coordinate dimension, and the number and type of band constraints, because the vast majority of non-unary functions in PostGIS and all aggregate functions will assume a certain degree of sameness.

PROS OF HETEROGENEOUS COLUMNS

The heterogeneous column approach has a couple of main benefits:

- It allows you to run a single query on several features of interest without giving up the luxury of modeling them with the most appropriate spatial subtype.
- It's simple. You could conceivably cram all your geometries into one column in a table if their non-spatial attributes are more or less the same.

CONS OF HETEROGENEOUS COLUMNS

There are also drawbacks to the heterogeneous column approach:

- You run the risk of having someone insert an inappropriate geometry for an object.

  For example, if you've obtained data for subway stations that should be modeled as points, an errant linestring in the data could enter your heterogeneous table. Furthermore, if you don't constrain the spatial reference system or coordinate geometry and unwittingly end up with more than one of each, your queries could be completely incorrect or break.

- Many third-party tools can't deal with heterogeneous spatial type columns or try to inspect all the data in a column to derive metadata, thus making them immensely slow to query. As a workaround, you may need to create views against this table to make it appear as separate tables and add a geometry type, band number, or spatial reference index or ensure that your queries select only a single grouping from the heterogeneous column.

- For cases where you need to extract only a certain kind of geometry, you'll need to filter by geometry type. For large tables, this could be slow and annoying to have to keep doing over and over again.

- Throwing all your geometry data into a single table could lead to an unwieldy number of self-joins.

  For example, suppose you placed points of interest in the same table as polygons outlining city neighborhoods; every time you needed to identify which points of interest (POIs) fall into which neighborhoods, you'd need to perform a self-join on this table.

Not only are self-joins taxing for the processor, they're also taxing for the mind. Imagine a scenario where you have 100 POIs and two neighborhoods, for a total of 102 records. Determining which POIs fall into which neighborhood requires that a table of 102 rows be joined with a table of 102 rows (itself). If you had separated out the neighborhoods into their own table, you'd only be joining a table of 100 rows with a table of 2 rows.

With the disadvantages of the heterogeneous storage approach fresh in your mind, let's move on to the homogenous spatial columns approach.

14.1.2 *Homogeneous columns*

A strict homogeneous approach for geometry and geography avoids mixing the different subtypes in a single column. Polygons must be stored in columns of only polygons, multipolygons must be stored in columns of only multipolygons, and so on. This means that each spatial subtype must reside in its own column at the least, but it's also common to break up different spatial subtypes into entirely separate tables.

If in the D.C. example you care more about the type of feature than the quadrant each feature is located in, you could employ the homogeneous columns design. One possible table structure would be to define a features table with a name column and three geometry columns. You'd constrain one column to store only points, one to store only linestrings, and one to store only polygons. If a feature is point data, you'd populate the point column, leaving the other two columns NULL; if it's linestring data, you'd populate the linestring column only; and so on. But you don't necessarily need to cram all of your columns into a single table. A more common design would be to use three distinct tables, storing each type of geometry in a separate table.

PROS OF HOMOGENEOUS COLUMNS

The homogeneous geometry columns approach offers the following benefits:

- It enforces consistency and prevents the unintended mixing of spatial subtypes and spatial reference systems.
- Third-party tools rely on consistency in spatial types, and some may go so far as to only allow one spatial column per table. The popular Esri shapefile supports only one geometry per record, so you'd need to explicitly state the geometry column should you ever need to dump data into shapefile format. Many tools that render or output raster data rely on it being homogeneous, meaning it's evenly blocked, of the same spatial reference system, of the same band pixel type, of the same number of bands, and of the same pixel dimensions, especially when displaying coverages.

> **NOTE** Esri Shapefiles do allow mixing of multi with single. For example, MULTIPOLYGON and POLYGON may appear in the same table.

- In general, you get better performance when joining tables that have large geometries and few records with tables that have smaller geometries and many records than vice versa.
- Should you be working with monstrous data sets, separate tables also allow you to reap benefits from placing your data on separate physical disks for each table by means of tablespaces.

> ### What is a PostgreSQL tablespace?
>
> In PostgreSQL, a *tablespace* is a physical folder location, as opposed to a schema, which is a logical location. In the default setup, all tables you create go into the same tablespace, but as your tables grow, you may want to create additional tablespaces, perhaps on separate physical disks, and distribute your tables across the different tablespaces to achieve maximum disk I/O versus cost of disk. One common practice is to group rarely used large tables into their own tablespace and place them on slower, cheaper, bigger disks.
>
> Tablespaces can also have individual settings such as `random_page_cost` and `seq_page_cost` settings by tablespace. The query planner uses these two parameters to discern whether data will source from a slow disk or a fast disk.

CONS OF HOMOGENEOUS COLUMNS

On the con side, if you choose the homogeneous geometry columns approach, you may face the following obstacles:

- When you need to run a query that draws multiple geometry types, you'll have to resort to a union query.

  This can add to the complexity and reduce the speed of the query. For example, if 99% of the queries you write for the D.C. example involved returning a single set of all geometries by quadrant only, you should stick with the heterogeneous approach.
- If you chose the homogeneous approach but decided to host multiple spatial columns per table, you might run into performance issues.

  Multiple spatial columns in a single table mean wider, fatter rows. Fatter rows make for slower queries, on both selects and updates. In the case of updates, because PostgreSQL creates a new row for the updated record and marks the old as dead, and spatial columns tend to be especially fat, even making an update on a simple attribute column, like a name or date, for large numbers of records takes a lot more time than for thinner tables.

14.1.3 *Typmod vs. constraints*

Typmod is short for *type modifier*. It's a facility for building constraints straight into the data type. Typmods and constraints are different ways of enforcing homogeneity or partial homogeneity. We covered typmods in chapter 2.

In the case of PostGIS geometries, a column defined as geometry(POINT,4326) is of the geometry data type with a type modifier restriction that it be a 2D POINT and have an SRID of 4326. You can also have a geometry defined as geometry(Geometry,4326), meaning it's a geometry with the SRID and dimension constrained by a type modifier. It is only allowed to have 2D geometries, but they can be any type of geometry. Similarly, geometry(GeometryZ,4326) would allow any kind of 3D geometry that is WGS 84 lon/lat.

Although the preferred method of constraining geometries is typmod, you still have the option of using the more laborious constraint-based method. Such an approach would be needed if you only want to constrain the SRID and not the coordinate dimension.

Geography started out with typmods, and there are no management functions to aid in adding constraints. To use the old constraint-based method, you'd have to add constraints manually and create a table to register all your constraints.

Although the constraint method is falling out of fashion, there are several cases where the typmod model just doesn't work or isn't as efficient as the constraint model.

ISSUES WITH TYPMODS

Although using typmods is the most recommended way of defining your columns, there are some cases where it doesn't work.

- Dropping and adding constraints is generally faster than changing a data type via a typmod.

  This situation is much improved in PostgreSQL 10+, so typmod is often as fast. However, with constraints you have the option of creating a constraint as NOT VALID, which means the constraint will only be checked for future inserts and updates, speeding up validation. This is particularly useful for large tables, because validating existing data to ensure it doesn't violate the newly created check constraint could be a lengthy process requiring an access lock. If, for whatever reason, you don't require old data to abide by new rules, then using a check constraint is your only option. Later on, to ensure the validity of older records, you could run ALTER TABLE sometable.somecolumn VALIDATE CONSTRAINT constraint_name;.

- Certain kinds of triggers don't work with typmods.

  For example, let's say you defined a trigger that does the following: When a user tries to insert or update a geometry in a table, the trigger determines the geometry's centroid to guarantee the resulting geometry is a point. The trigger then stores the generated centroid in the geometry column instead of the user-provided geometry. If you defined the geometry column as geometry(POINT, 4326), guess what? Your trigger would fail if the user tried to update with anything other than a point of SRID 4326. If the column's geometry subtype is constrained with a typmod, any geometry you try to insert that isn't a point would fail before it even gets to your trigger, because the type modifier check kicks in before the geometry even hits your table—the geometry of the NEW trigger row itself is defined as a constrained typmod geometry. If you use constraints, your point-fixing trigger (using the centroid to force a geometry to a point) would work because the constraint check doesn't kick in until the record is about to be added to the table.

- If you plan to use table inheritance or partitioning where each child table or partition is constrained to have a different geometry subtype, you can't have geometries with different subtypes if you use a typmod. You can define check constraints at the child level that the parent doesn't have, and the child can also inherit check constraints defined at the parent level. But if you use a typmod to constrain the geometry column subtype of the parent, all its children must abide by the same typmod subtype requirement, and you can't have a typmod column definition for the child column that's different from the parent.

WHY USE TYPMODS

Despite all the issues we've outlined with typmods, why should you use them for most cases?

- Typmods can be created with CREATE TABLE and short column definitions, which means you don't need an extra step to add the geometry column or memorize a lengthy constraint list to include in your CREATE TABLE.
- If you build a view that selects a typmod column, the column properties of that view column are correctly displayed in the geometry_columns table.

    For constraint-only enforced base table columns with no casting, the geometry_columns table will be missing all the other key attributes, such as subtype, dimensionality, and SRID. This restriction may change in future versions of PostGIS.

- With typmods you can use the more standard ALTER TABLE .. USING syntax to change a geometry type in single step.

14.1.4 *Table inheritance*

Table inheritance is a storage approach that has existed since the dawn of PostgreSQL and is fairly unique to it. This is by far the most versatile of the various storage approaches, but it's slightly more involved than the previous two. You can tap into this gem of a feature to distill the positive aspects of both the homogeneous and heterogeneous column approaches.

Table inheritance means that a table can inherit its structure from a parent table. The parent table doesn't need to store any data, relegating all the data storage to the child tables. When used this way, the parent table is often referred to as an *abstract table* (from the object oriented concept of abstract classes). Each child table inherits all the columns of its parent, but it can have additional columns of its own that are revealed only when you query the child table directly. Check constraints are also inherited, but primary keys and foreign key constraints aren't. PostgreSQL supports multiple inheritance, where a child table can have more than one parent table, with columns derived from both parents. PostgreSQL doesn't place a limit on the number of generations you can have. A parent table can have parents of its own, and so forth.

To implement a table inheritance storage approach, you can create an abstract table that organizes data along its non-geometric attributes, and then create inherited child tables with constrained geometry types. With this pattern, end users can query from the parent table and see all the child data, or query from each child table when they need only data from the child tables or child-specific columns.

In our D.C. example, the table of the single generic heterogeneous geometry column could serve as a parent table. You could then create three inherited child tables, each constrained to hold points, linestrings, and polygons. If you need to pull data of a specific geometry, you would query one of the child tables.

Only with PostgreSQL can you orchestrate such an elegant solution. No other major database offerings support direct table inheritance—at least, not yet.

> ### Constraint exclusion
> PostgreSQL has a configuration option called `constraint_exclusion`, which is often used in conjunction with table inheritance. When this option is set to `on` or `partition`, which is the default, the query planner will check the table constraints of a table to determine if it can skip a table in a query.
>
> The `partition` setting saves query-planning cycles by only performing constraint exclusion checks when doing queries against tables in an inheritance hierarchy or when running a `UNION` query.

PROS OF TABLE INHERITANCE
There are several benefits to using table inheritance:

- You can query a hierarchy of tables as if they were a single table or query them separately as needed.
- If you partition by geometry type, you can query for a specific geometry type or query for all geometry types as needed.
- With the use of PostgreSQL constraint exclusions, you can cleverly skip over child tables if none of the rows qualify under your filtering conditions. For example, suppose you need to store data organized by countries of the world. By partitioning the data into a child table for each country, any query you write that filters by country name would completely skip unneeded country tables as if they didn't exist. This can yield a significant speed boost when you have large numbers of records.
- Inheritance can be set and unset on the fly, making it convenient when performing data loads.

For instance, you can disinherit a child table, load the data, clean the data, add any necessary constraints, and then re-inherit the child table. This prevents queries slowing down on other data while data loading is happening.

- Most third-party tools will treat the parent table as a bona fide table, even though it may not have any data, as long as relevant geometry columns are registered and primary keys are set on the parent table. Inheritance works seamlessly with OpenJUMP, QGIS, GeoServer, and MapServer. Any tool that polls the standard PostgreSQL metadata should end up treating parent tables like any others.

CONS OF TABLE INHERITANCE

Table inheritance also has a number of disadvantages:

- Table inheritance isn't supported by other major databases. Should you ever need to switch away from PostgreSQL to another database, your application code may not be portable. This isn't as big a problem as it may initially appear, because most database drivers will see a parent table as a single table with all the data of its children. Your opting to desert PostgreSQL is the bigger problem!

- Primary key and foreign key constraints don't pass to child tables, though check constraints do. In the D.C. example, if you place a primary key constraint on the parent feature table, dictating that each place name must be unique, you can't expect the child tables to abide by the constraint. Even if you were to assign primary key constraints to the children, you still couldn't guarantee unique results when querying multiple child tables or querying the parent table together with its child tables.

- If you use table inheritance, and each of your child tables holds a different geometry subtype in the geometry column, you need to use check constraints to enforce the geometry subtype requirement. You can't use the typmod feature that allows you to define a column as geometry and the geometry type in one CREATE TABLE. But you can use a hybrid of the form geometry(geometry, SRID) to constrain the SRID with a typmod and then use constraints to constrain the geometry subtype.

  PostGIS is not special in this regard. You'd have similar issues with varchar and numeric. You can't have a parent table with a column defined as varchar(60) and then have each child redefine the column as varchar(50), varchar(40), and so on. You'd have to use constraint checks to enforce the lower requirements in child tables.

- To maintain the table inheritance hierarchy when adding data, you must take extra steps to make sure that rows are appropriately added to the parent table or one of its child tables.

  For table updates, you may want to put in logic that automatically moves a record from one child table to another child table, should an update cause a check violation. This generally means having to create rules or triggers to insert into a child table when inserting into a parent table, or vice versa. We'll cover this in detail in section 14.4.

Thankfully, PostgreSQL inheritance is smart enough to automatically handle updates and deletes for most situations. When you update or delete against a parent table, it will automatically drill down to its child tables, but updates to move data from one child to another need to be managed with rules or triggers on the child table. You can, if you choose, go through the trouble of creating update and delete triggers to figure out which records in child tables need to be updated when an update or delete call is made on the parent table. This often yields a speed improvement over relying on the automated drill-down of PostgreSQL inheritance.

- If you use constraint exclusions to skip tables entirely, you'll face an initial performance hit when the query is executed for the first time.
- You need to be watchful of the total number of tables in your inheritance hierarchy. Performance begins to degrade noticeably after a couple hundred tables. Since PostgreSQL 9.0, the planner will generate statistics for the inheritance hierarchy. This should boost performance when querying against inherited tables.

A TABLE INHERITANCE EXAMPLE

Listing 14.1 demonstrates how you'd go about implementing a table inheritance model. In this example, you first create a parent table for all roads in the United States. In this parent table, the SRID and the geometry type are set. You then beget two child tables. The first will store roads in the six New England states; the second will store roads in the Southwest states. You then populate only the child tables with data, leaving the parent table devoid of any rows.

Listing 14.1 Code to partition roads into various states by inheritance

```
CREATE TABLE ch14.roads(
    gid integer GENERATED BY DEFAULT AS IDENTITY,          ◄──────  Auto-increment
    road_name character varying(100),                       ❶ column
    geom geometry(LINESTRING,4269), state varchar(2),
    CONSTRAINT pk_roads PRIMARY KEY (gid)
);                                                          Child table ❷

CREATE TABLE ch14.roads_NE (CONSTRAINT pk_roads_ne PRIMARY KEY (gid))  ◄──
INHERITS (ch14.roads);
                                                            Constraints
ALTER TABLE ch14.roads_NE
ADD CONSTRAINT chk CHECK (state IN ('MA','ME','NH','VT','CT','RI'));  ◄──

CREATE TABLE ch14.roads_SW (CONSTRAINT pk_roads_sw PRIMARY KEY (gid))
INHERITS (ch14.roads);

ALTER TABLE ch14.roads_SW
ADD CONSTRAINT chk CHECK (state IN ('AZ','NM','NV'));
                                                            Constraint
SELECT gid, road_name, geom FROM ch14.roads WHERE state = 'MA';  ◄──┘  exclusion
```

In listing 14.1 you first create a parent roads table with an auto-incrementing column ❶. Then you create child tables to the roads table ❷. You then add constraints to the table, which will be useful for speeding up queries when you have `constraint_exclusion` set to `partition` or on. It will ensure that the roads_NE table is skipped if the requested state isn't in MA, ME, NH, VT, CT, or RI.

GENERATED BY versus `serial`

Prior editions of this book used the `gid serial` construct instead of `gid integer` `GENERATED BY DEFAULT AS IDENTITY`. The `GENERATED BY` construct was introduced in PostgreSQL 10 and now is the preferred way of defining auto-generated integer columns. Both have an underlying `SEQUENCE` object behind the scenes, but unlike the `serial` approach, the `GENERATED BY` associated sequence is always considered part of the table and therefore does not need permissions of its own, cannot be reused for other purposes, and gets dropped when the table is dropped. The `GENERATED BY` construct is also defined in the ANSI-SQL specs, whereas `serial` is a PostgreSQL-only construct.

`GENERATED BY` also supports other modes, such as `GENERATED BY ALWAYS`, which is useful if you want to prevent users from directly inserting into the column.

Finally, you write a simple `SELECT` to pull all roads in Massachusetts. With constraint exclusion, only the child table with roads in New England will be searched. You can see this by running an explain plan or by looking at the graphical explain plan in pgAdmin.

14.1.5 Table partitioning

In the past, people have used table inheritance to employ another strategy known as *table partitioning* or *table sharding*. Table partitioning is a storage strategy that divides a logical table into physical partitions, but for most use cases, such as querying, inserting, updating, or deleting, the partitions are abstracted as part of a single table. Unlike inheritance, subtables cannot have additional columns. This approach is most used for segregating a huge table by some dimension, such as time or geographic region.

Table partitioning is something you'll find in other relational databases, such as MySQL, Oracle, or SQL Server, and it's defined in the ANSI-SQL:2011 specs. The introduction of partitions added new terminology: *partitioned table* and *partitions*. The *partitioned table* is a parent table, and it cannot have any rows. The *partitions* are the child tables that can contain data. A partition can itself be a partitioned table, which means it can't have data either, but its partitions can.

PostgreSQL introduced table partitioning in PostgreSQL 10 and closed up many gaps in PostgreSQL 11, 12, and 13. More improvements are coming in PostgreSQL 14, and they're covered in appendix D. As far as performance goes, PostgreSQL 10's table partitioning versus using inheritance performed about the same. The main difference was just the syntax and the ability to insert directly into a table and have it redirect inserts.

The syntax you use to partition data in PostgreSQL is much the same as what you'll find in other relational databases. At a glance, it seems PostgreSQL created this thing that is just like inheritance (in fact, the underlying implementation uses inheritance plumbing), but put in place all these restricting rules.

You can think of a partitioned table as the parent in the inheritance sense of the word and a partition as a child table.

The restrictions that partitioning places on your use are as follows:

- A partitioned table must have its partition columns and strategy predefined, and a partitioned table cannot be converted to a regular table nor a regular table to a partitioned table even as of PostgreSQL 13.
- Partitions can't have any additional columns. All columns are defined at the partitioned table level (a.k.a. the ultimate parent).
- A parent table (the partitioned table) cannot have any data.
- Your constraints for routing data (the partitioning key) must be mutually exclusive and collectively exhaustive. This means that if you have two records, there is exactly one partition that each record can be a member of. PostgreSQL 11 introduced the feature of a `DEFAULT` partition, which is the partition of last resort when no other partition can hold the data based on the values of the partition keys of the incoming or updated data. As you'll see later, if you have a nested hierarchy, you can have a `DEFAULT` for each partitioned level.
- Partitioning keys are very limited—you can do `LIST`, `RANGE`, or `HASH`, but you can have your partition keys be based on an immutable function.

Why on earth do people need more restrictions as to how they store their data? The big reason is speed and maintainability.

The benefits of partitioning over inheritance are as follows:

- All partition indexes, including the primary key, are inherited from the partitioned table as of PostgreSQL 11, but the primary key must include the partition key.
- Inserts are automatically routed to the partitions without the need for triggers. This is possible because the partition keys dictate that only one partition can qualify, which is not the case with inheritance.
- For PostgreSQL 11 and above, if you update a record such that it no longer satisfies the partition key of the partition, the record will be rerouted.
- For PostgreSQL 11 and above, the planner produces better plans than inherited would produce, if, for example, you have joins involving two partitioned tables.

  As long as your partitioned tables are partitioned in the same way (for example, orders partitioned by `customer_id=3` and `orders_lineitems` partitioned by `customer_id=3`), the planner can use this information for simplifying the plan during the inner join. PostgreSQL configuration setting `enable_partition-wise_join` must be set to on to take advantage of this feature. This setting can be set at runtime. PostgreSQL 13 improved on this feature by no longer requiring the partitioned keys to be the same. For example, you could have an `orders` table covering `customer_id IN(1,3)` but have the `order_lineitems` partitions store lineitems just for one customer. Note that `enable_partitionwise_join` is set to `off` by default. Similarly, when aggregating data by `customer_id`, PostgreSQL can take advantage of the fact that all data for a particular customer is in the same table. In order for PostgreSQL to take advantage of this fact, the configuration setting `enable_partitionwise_aggregate` must be set to on. PostgreSQL configuration settings are covered in chapter 15.

- Since partition keys are very constrained, the planner is better able to plan.

  PostgreSQL, as part of query planning, performs an analysis called "partition pruning." Partition pruning is the process of determining which partitions of a partitioned table can be skipped for a query. In PostgreSQL 11, partition pruning was enhanced to allow it to be done at statement execution. This means that for things such as parameters that are not constant (for example, `CURRENT_DATE` and partition keys that use a date field), the planner knows exactly which tables can hold the data at runtime. A similar setup using inheritance check constraints would require the query planner to traverse all tables if subject to something like `log_date > (CURRENT_DATE - 10)` because the plan is based on a non-constant value, and it needs to know the value to know how to best construct the plan. In contrast, if you're using partitions for PostgreSQL 11 and above, the pruning step happens at runtime, so it can take into consideration the actual value of `(CURRENT_DATE - 10)`.

- PostgreSQL 12 drastically improved partition performance, allowing easy handling of thousands of partitions for a partitioned table. You can have many more partitions than inheritance supports.

A couple of benefits are shared with inheritance:

- You can attach and detach partitions, which is so much quicker than deleting rows. The syntax for attaching is `ALTER TABLE <partitioned table> ATTACH PARTITION partition_name { FOR VALUES partition_bound_spec | DEFAULT }`. Similar to uninheriting, you can do `ALTER TABLE <partition table> DETACH PARTITION <partition_name>`.
- Column type definitions that are changed at the partitioned table level drill down to the partitions. In addition, PostgreSQL 11 and above allow indexes and primary keys to be inherited, so there is no need to add indexes and primary keys to partitions. Inherited tables by contrast require indexes to be added to each child table.

For PostgreSQL 11 and above, listing 14.1 is more efficient if implemented with table partitioning instead of inheritance. Let's reimplement it.

Sadly, there is no mechanism even as of PostgreSQL 13 for converting a regular table to a partition. However, you can uninherit your inherited tables and make them partitions of a new partitioned table. The next listing converts your inheritance hierarchy created in listing 14.1 to a partitioned table.

Listing 14.2 Convert from inheritance to partitions

Assign ch14.roads_NE as a partition of ch14.roads.

Rename the old table so you can reuse the name.

Drop the primary constraint so you can reuse the name.

```
ALTER TABLE ch14.roads RENAME TO roads_old;
ALTER TABLE ch14.roads_old DROP CONSTRAINT pk_roads;

CREATE TABLE ch14.roads (
    gid integer GENERATED BY DEFAULT AS IDENTITY,
    road_name character varying(100),
    geom geometry(LINESTRING,4269), state varchar(2),
    CONSTRAINT pk_roads PRIMARY KEY (gid, state)
) PARTITION BY LIST (state);

ALTER TABLE ch14.roads_NE NO INHERIT ch14.roads_old;
ALTER TABLE ch14.roads_NE ALTER COLUMN state SET NOT NULL;
ALTER TABLE ch14.roads_NE DROP CONSTRAINT pk_roads_ne;

ALTER TABLE ch14.roads
    ATTACH PARTITION ch14.roads_NE
    FOR VALUES IN ('MA','ME','NH','VT','CT','RI');

ALTER TABLE ch14.roads_NE DROP CONSTRAINT chk;

ALTER TABLE ch14.roads_SW NO INHERIT ch14.roads_old;
ALTER TABLE ch14.roads_SW ALTER COLUMN state SET NOT NULL;
ALTER TABLE ch14.roads_SW DROP CONSTRAINT pk_roads_sw;

ALTER TABLE ch14.roads
    ATTACH PARTITION ch14.roads_SW
    FOR VALUES IN('AZ','NM','NV');

ALTER TABLE ch14.roads_SW DROP CONSTRAINT chk;
```

Detach from the old inherited table.

State will be part of the new key, so it can't be null.

The primary key will change and will be inherited from the new parent.

The check constraint is no longer needed and can be dropped.

Repeat for SW.

WARNING Dependent objects like views and materialized views must be re-created because PostgreSQL uses the table's internal ID for referencing in views and materialized views. As such, even if you rename the table, views and materialized views are still tied to the old name and must be updated to use the new name.

Next, drop the tables you created for inheritance and partitioning so you can see how to build from scratch:

```
DROP TABLE ch14.roads CASCADE;
DROP TABLE ch14.roads_old CASCADE;
```

If you are starting with a clean slate and building a partitioned hierarchy, you would build it as shown in the following listing.

> **Listing 14.3 Code to partition roads into various states by table partitioning**

```
CREATE TABLE ch14.roads(
    gid integer GENERATED BY DEFAULT AS IDENTITY,
    road_name character varying(100),
    geom geometry(LINESTRING,4269), state varchar(2),
    CONSTRAINT pk_roads PRIMARY KEY (gid, state)
) PARTITION BY LIST (state);

CREATE TABLE ch14.roads_NE
    PARTITION OF ch14.roads
        FOR VALUES IN('MA','ME','NH','VT','CT','RI');

CREATE TABLE ch14.roads_SW
    PARTITION OF ch14.roads
        FOR VALUES IN('AZ','NM','NV');

SELECT gid, road_name, geom FROM ch14.roads WHERE state = 'MA';
```

Annotations:
- **Create a table with a primary key.**
- **Partition by state.**
- **Add a NE partition.**
- **Select MA data.**

As you can see, implementing using partitioning is a bit shorter and, more importantly, easier to maintain. If you create an index or primary key on the partitioned table, all partitions inherit these as well, so there's no need to repeat the index or key on each partition as you did with inheritance. The primary key has to be guaranteed to be unique across the whole partitioned table, so you can't just have the gid column as the primary key. You need to also include the partitioning key as part of the primary key to guarantee that each table's primary key is unique across the whole set without needing to inspect the other tables. This limitation of having to include the partitioned key in the primary index is planned to be lifted in a future PostgreSQL version.

Partitioned tables are for most use cases a replacement for inheritance, but you may still need to be able to add additional columns to child tables and so forth. In such cases you might employ both partitioning and inheritance in the same database.

You've now learned of four ways of organizing spatial data. In the next section, you'll put these ideas to work by modeling a real-world city using these approaches.

14.2 Modeling a real city

In this section you'll apply what you learned in the previous section by exploring various ways to model a real city. We'll abandon the quadrants of D.C. and states of the United States and cross the Atlantic to Paris, the city of lights (or love, depending on your preference) for our extended example. We chose Paris because of the importance placed on arrondissements.

If you're unfamiliar with Paris, the city is divided into 20 administrative districts, known as *arrondissements*. Unlike people in other major cities, Parisians are keenly aware of their administrative districts. It's not unusual for someone to say that they live in the *n*th arrondissement, fully expecting their fellow Parisians to know what general area of Paris is being spoken of. Unlike what are often referred to as *neighborhoods* in other major cities, arrondissements are well defined geographically and so are well suited for GIS purposes. On top of it all, Parisians often refer to the arrondissements by their ordinal numbers rather than their ascribed French names, making numerically minded folk like us extra happy.

The geography of the basic Paris arrondissements is illustrated in figure 14.1.

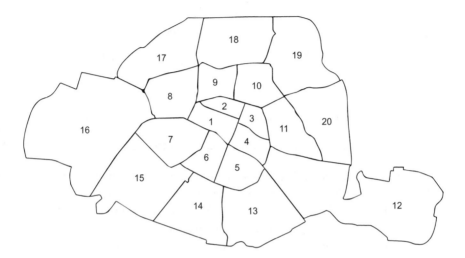

Figure 14.1 Paris arrondissements

The arrondissement arrangement is interesting in that it spirals clockwise from the center of Paris, reflecting the pattern of growth since the 1800s as the city annexed adjacent areas.

We downloaded our Paris data from the French government (www.data.gouv.fr/ en/datasets/arrondissements-1/) as well as OpenStreetMap (OSM; www.openstreet-map.org). We transformed all the data to SRID 32631 (WGS 84 UTM Zone 31). All of Paris fits into this UTM zone, and because UTM is meter-based, we have meter measurements at our disposal without any additional effort.

As a starting point, we modeled each arrondissement as a multipolygon and inserted all of them into a table called arrondissements. The table contains exactly 20 rows. Not only will this table serve as our base layer, but we'll also use it to geotag additional data into specific arrondissements. You can load up the table in your database by loading the ch14_data.sql included in the this chapter's download using the following statement:

```
psql -d postgis_in_action -f ch14_data.sql
```

Paris data transformation

The original file in raw_files/paris_-_arrondissement.zip that we started out with was in WGS 84 lon/lat (EPSG:4326), and we performed the following exercises after loading it with shp2pgsql to get it to the form you see in ch14_data.sql:

```
ALTER TABLE ch14.arrondissements
ALTER COLUMN geom TYPE geometry(MultiPolygon,32631)
USING ST_Transform(geom,32631);

ALTER TABLE ch14.arrondissements
ADD COLUMN ar_num integer;

UPDATE ch14.arrondissements
SET ar_num = (regexp_match(l_ar, E'[0-9]+'))[1]::integer;
```

14.2.1 Modeling using heterogeneous geometry columns

If you mainly need to query your data by arrondissements without regard to the type of feature, you can employ a single geometry column to store all of your data. Create this table:

```
CREATE TABLE ch14.paris_hetero (
    gid integer GENERATED BY DEFAULT AS IDENTITY,
    osm_id bigint,
    geom geometry(Geometry,32631),
    ar_num integer,
    tags jsonb,
    CONSTRAINT pk_paris_hetero
    PRIMARY KEY (gid)
);
```

Notice how a constraint or typmod restricting the type of geometry is decidedly missing. This geometry column will be able to contain points, linestrings, polygons, multi-geometries, geometry collections—in short, any geometry type you want to put in it. Note that the preceding code does take the extra step to limit the column to only SRID 32631 using a typmod.

You'll also notice a data type called hstore. This is a data type for storing key/value pairs, similar in concept to associative arrays. Much like geometry columns, hstore can be indexed using the gist index.

OSM makes wide use of tags for storing properties of features that don't fit elsewhere. To bring in the OSM data without complicating the table, we used the ogr_fdw foreign data wrapper as outlined in chapter 4 and cast the tags column to hstore and then to jsonb. jsonb is preferred these days over hstore and is now a native type of PostgreSQL.

> ### The `hstore` data type and PostgreSQL
>
> Hstore is a PostgreSQL extension. To enable this module, use this SQL statement:
>
> ```
> CREATE EXTENSION hstore;
> ```
>
> Since PostgreSQL 9.3, hstore has been enhanced to include new functions (`hstore_to_json` and `hstore_to_json_loose`) for easy conversion to the `json` data type. The PostgreSQL 9.4 hstore extension added more functions to convert `hstore` to the new binary JSON format, `jsonb`, with functions like `hstore_to_jsonb`, which allows `hstore` to be directly cast to `json` and `jsonb` native PostgreSQL types.

The ch14.paris_hetero table includes a column called `ar_num` for holding the arrondissement number of the feature. Unfortunately, this attribute isn't maintained by OSM. But no worries—you can intersect the OSM data with your arrondissement table to figure out which arrondissement each OSM record falls into. Although you can determine the arrondissements on the fly, having the arrondissements figured out beforehand means you can query against an integer instead of having to constantly perform spatial intersections later on.

The following listing demonstrates how to intersect arrondissements with the OSM data to yield an `ar_num` value.

Listing 14.4   Region tagging and clipping data to a specific arrondissement

```
INSERT INTO ch14.paris_hetero (osm_id, geom, ar_num, tags)          ◁─┐ Insert data and
SELECT o.osm_id, ST_Intersection(o.geom,a.geom) As geom,             │ clip to a specific
    a.ar_num, o.tags                                               ❶ arrondissement.
FROM
    (
        SELECT osm_id, ST_Transform(way,32631) As geom, tags::jsonb
        FROM ch14_staging.planet_osm_line
    ) AS o
    INNER JOIN
    ch14.arrondissements AS A
    ON (ST_Intersects(o.geom, a.geom));          Add indexes and
CREATE INDEX ix_paris_hetero_geom                update statistics.
ON ch14.paris_hetero USING gist(geom);   ◁─┘
CREATE INDEX ix_paris_hetero_tags                Vacuum analyze after large
ON ch14.paris_hetero USING gin(tags);            bulk load/update to improve
VACUUM ANALYZE ch14.paris_hetero; --      ◁─┘    query performance
```

In listing 14.4 you load all the OSM data you downloaded into the paris_hetero table ❶.

The listing only shows the insert from the planet_osm_line table, but you'll need to repeat this for OSM points and OSM polygons. The full code is available in this chapter's download file.

Features such as long linestrings and large polygons will straddle multiple arrondissements, but the intersection operation will clip them, so you'll end up with one record per arrondissement. For example, the famous Boulevard Saint-Germain passes through the fifth, sixth, and seventh arrondissements.

After the clipping exercise, the record with a single linestring will have been broken up into three records, each with shorter linestrings, for each of the arrondissements that the original linestring passed through.

Finally, you perform the usual indexing and updating of statistics after the bulk load ❶.

As we've demonstrated, by not putting a geometry type constraint on the geometry column, you can stuff linestrings, polygons, points, and even geometry collections into the same table if you want. This model is nice and simple in the sense that if you wanted to pick or count all features that fit in a particular user-defined area, for mapping or statistical purposes, you could do it with one simple query. Here's an example that counts the number of features within each arrondissement:

```
SELECT ar_num, COUNT(DISTINCT osm_id) As compte
FROM ch14.paris_hetero
GROUP BY ar_num;
```

This yields the following answer:

```
ar_num | compte
-------+--------
     1 |      4
     8 |   1460
     9 |      4
    16 |   1574
    17 |   2268
    18 |      3
```

We should mention that for this example, we extracted from OSM only the area of Paris surrounding the Arc de Triomphe, which is at the center of arrondissements 8, 16, and 17. As a result, most of our features tend to be in those three regions. Figure 14.2 shows a quick map we generated in OpenJUMP by overlaying the planet_hetero table atop the arrondissement polygons.

The main advantage of using jsonb to hold miscellaneous attribute data is that you don't have to set up bona fide columns for attributes that could be of little use later on, just so you can import data. You can first import the data and then cherry-pick which attributes you'd like to promote to columns as your needs grow. Using jsonb also means that you can add and remove attributes without fussing with the data structure.

The drawback becomes apparent when you do need attributes to be full-fledged columns. You can't query inside a jsonb column as easily as you can a character or numeric column or enforce numeric and other data type constraints on the jsonb values. Although you can add indexes to jsonb using gin and gist, the indexes will still be slower than a B-tree against a full-fledged column.

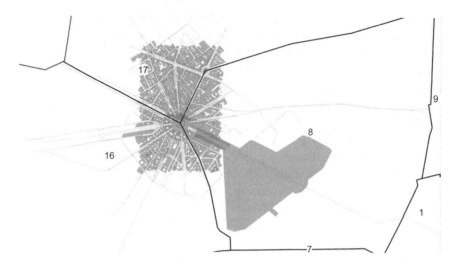

Figure 14.2   The paris_hetero data set overlaid on the arrondissements

A simple way to overcome some of the drawbacks of jsonb columns is to create a view that will map attributes within a jsonb column into virtual data columns, as shown in the following listing:

```
CREATE OR REPLACE VIEW ch14.vw_paris_points AS
SELECT
    gid, osm_id, ar_num, geom,
    tags->>'name' As place_name,
    tags->>'tourism' As tourist_attraction
FROM ch14.paris_hetero
WHERE ST_GeometryType(geom) = 'ST_Point';
```

In this snippet, you create a view that promotes the two tags, name and tourism, into two text data columns. In PostGIS 2 or higher, geometry_columns is no longer a table that you can manually update; it now reads from system catalogs. Because the only thing that is typmoded is geometry, 32612, your view will show vw_paris_points as a geometry of SRID 32631.

To work with tools that don't understand mixed geometry subtype tables, you'll need to make your view register as a point table. If you want to have the view correctly register the type as a POINT in geometry_columns, you could define the view instead as shown in the next listing.

Listing 14.5   Using typmod in casting to correctly register a view in geometry_columns

```
CREATE OR REPLACE VIEW ch14.vw_paris_points_tmod
    WITH (security_barrier=true) AS        ◁──┐  Security barrier enforces that the view
        SELECT                                    filter is checked before any other
            gid, osm_id, ar_num,                  operations in the view happen.
```

```
        geom::geometry(POINT,32631) AS geom,
        tags->>'name' AS place_name,
        tags->>'tourism' AS tourist_attraction
    FROM ch14.paris_hetero
    WHERE ST_GeometryType(geom) = 'ST_Point';

CREATE INDEX idx_paris_hetero_geom_pt ON ch14.paris_hetero
USING gist ( (geom::geometry(POINT,32631)) )
WHERE ST_GeometryType(geom) = 'ST_Point';
```

❶ Cast to a **POINT** geometry, where ST_GeometryType(geom) = 'ST_Point'.

❷ Add partial index on the base table so a spatial index can be used.

In order for the view's geom column to be registered as a point geometry subtype, you need to cast it to a point geometry ❶. Casting it makes the original geometry index ineffective, so you need to create a partial spatial index that only applies to point geometries ❷. It has to be partial because a linestring and polygon can't be cast to a point without applying some processing function. You can't create an index on a regular view, which is why the index needs to be created on the base table. If this were a materialized view, you'd create the index directly on the view instead of on the underlying table.

In the view you also apply a security barrier. The security barrier feature was introduced in PostgreSQL 9.0, and although it was designed primarily to prevent people from applying functions on data that isn't part of the view output, it serves another accidental purpose. It forces the ST_GeometryType filter to be applied before any other conditions.

Without the security barrier in place, if you ran a query of the following form

```
SELECT *
FROM ch14.vw_paris_points_tmod
WHERE ST_DWithin(geom,ST_SetSRID(ST_Point(453121,5413887),32631),4000);
```

it might apply the cast operation on a polygon or a linestring if it applied the spatial filter first. This would cause the cast, and your query, to fail.

14.2.2 *Modeling using homogeneous geometry columns*

The homogeneous columns approach stores each geometry type in its own column or table. This style of storage is more common than the heterogeneous approach, and it's the one most supported by third-party tools. Having distinct columns or tables for different geometry types allows you to enforce geometry type constraints or to use typmods fully, preventing different geometry data types from inadvertently mixing. The downside is that your queries will have to enumerate across multiple columns or tables should you ever wish to pull data of different geometry types.

The next listing uses the homogeneous columns approach for the Paris data.

Listing 14.6 Breaking data into separate tables with homogeneous geometry columns

```
CREATE TABLE ch14.paris_points(
    gid integer GENERATED BY DEFAULT AS IDENTITY PRIMARY KEY,
    osm_id bigint,
    ar_num integer,
```

```
    feature_name varchar(200),
    feature_type varchar(50),
    geom geometry(POINT, 32631)
);
INSERT INTO ch14.paris_points (
    osm_id,    ar_num,    geom,
    feature_name, feature_type
)
SELECT
    osm_id, ar_num, geom,
    tags->'name' As feature_name,
    COALESCE(
        tags->>'tourism',
        tags->>'railway',
        tags->>'station',
        'other'
    )::varchar(50) As feature_type
FROM ch14.paris_hetero
WHERE ST_GeometryType(geom) = 'ST_Point';
```

❶ Typmod point geometry column

❷ Add points.

You start by creating a table to store point geometry data having the spatial reference system UTM for Paris (SRID 32631) ❶. Finally, you perform the insert ❷, but instead of starting from the OSM data, you take advantage of the fact that you already have the data you need in the paris_hetero table, and you selectively pick out the tags you care about and morph them into the columns you want. If you wanted to have a completely homogeneous solution, you'd create similar tables for paris_polygons and paris_linestrings.

If you want to get a count of all features by arrondissement, your query will need to union all the different tables together, as shown here:

```
SELECT ar_num, COUNT(DISTINCT osm_id) As compte
FROM (
    SELECT ar_num, osm_id FROM ch14.paris_points
    UNION ALL
    SELECT ar_num, osm_id FROM ch14.paris_polygons
    UNION ALL
    SELECT ar_num, osm_id FROM ch14.paris_linestrings
) As X
GROUP BY ar_num;
```

UNION versus UNION ALL

When performing union operations, you'll generally want to use UNION ALL rather than UNION. UNION has an implicit DISTINCT clause built in, which automatically eliminates duplicate rows. If you know that the sets you're unioning can't or don't need to be deduped in the process, UNION ALL will be faster.

We'll now move on to a partitioned storage design where you'll see that by expending some extra effort, you'll reap the benefits of both the heterogeneous and homogeneous approaches.

Before moving forward, make sure you drop the tables created earlier, as you'll be re-creating them using partitioning:

```
DROP TABLE IF EXISTS ch14.paris_linestrings;
DROP TABLE IF EXISTS ch14.paris_polygons;
DROP TABLE IF EXISTS ch14.paris_points;
```

14.2.3 *Modeling using partitioning*

The prior edition of this book demonstrated how to use table inheritance for partitioning data by type and arrondissements. The benefit that inheritance has over the new partitioning scheme introduced in PostgreSQL 10 is that you can have more columns in the child tables than you had in the parent. This benefit unfortunately comes with a major cost of having to manage the routing of data with insert triggers and slower performance with queries. This section will cover doing a similar thing using table partitioning. Sadly, even as of PostgreSQL 13 you can't mix table partitioning with inheritance to gain benefits from both.

As with inheritance, you can have nested partitioning schemes with partitioning. Let's break Paris into two partition levels—first by the geometry type and second by the arrondissement.

You can begin by creating a partitioned table to store attributes that all of the partitions will share, as shown in the following code:

```
CREATE TABLE ch14.paris (
    gid bigint GENERATED BY DEFAULT AS IDENTITY,
    osm_id bigint,
    ar_num integer,
    feature_name varchar(200),
    feature_type varchar(50),
    geom geometry(geometry, 32631),
    tags jsonb
) PARTITION BY LIST( GeometryType(geom) )  ;
```

Ideally you'd want to add a primary key on the parent table, but because partitioned tables require that their primary keys must drill down to child tables, cannot have expressions, and must contain the partitioning columns, you cannot have a primary key when you are using an expression like GeometryType(geom) for your PARTITION BY. If you were simply dividing by ar_num, you would be able to add a primary key. You can still create primary indexes directly on the partitions, but they would be independent of each other.

For PostgreSQL 11 and on, all indexes are inherited, so you have the luxury of creating the spatial index and jsonb gin indexes just once, and PostgreSQL will do the work of creating them for future partitions:

```
CREATE INDEX ix_paris_geom_gist
  ON ch14.paris USING gist(geom);

CREATE INDEX ix_paris_tags_gin
  ON ch14.paris USING gin(tags);
```

With the parent table in place, you can create child tables. For the child tables, you'll be further partitioning by arrondissements because you'll have a ton of data for the L'Arc area in the future.

Listing 14.7   Creating partitions

```
CREATE TABLE ch14.paris_linestring                                One partition to
    PARTITION OF ch14.paris                                   ❶  hold all linestrings
    ( CONSTRAINT pk_paris_linestring PRIMARY KEY (gid) )
    FOR VALUES IN('LINESTRING');
                                                    ❷  Abstract polygon table further
                                                       partitioned by arrondissements
CREATE TABLE ch14.paris_polygon
    PARTITION OF ch14.paris
    ( CONSTRAINT pk_paris_polygon PRIMARY KEY (gid,ar_num) )
    FOR VALUES IN('POLYGON')
    PARTITION BY RANGE (ar_num);                        Partition for Paris
                                                        arrondissements 16
CREATE TABLE ch14.paris_polygon_ar_16_20               thru 20 polygons
    PARTITION OF ch14.paris_polygon
    FOR VALUES FROM (16) TO (20);

CREATE TABLE ch14.paris_polygon_ar_other
    PARTITION OF ch14.paris_polygon             Partition for
    DEFAULT;                                    polygons not
                                                in 16-20
CREATE TABLE ch14.paris_point
    PARTITION OF ch14.paris
    (CONSTRAINT pk_paris_point PRIMARY KEY (gid, ar_num) )
    FOR VALUES IN('POINT')
    PARTITION BY LIST (ar_num);


CREATE TABLE ch14.paris_point_ar_16
    PARTITION OF ch14.paris_point
    FOR VALUES IN(16);


CREATE TABLE ch14.paris_point_ar_8_17
    PARTITION OF ch14.paris_point
    FOR VALUES IN(8,17);


CREATE TABLE ch14.paris_point_ar_other
    PARTITION OF ch14.paris_point
    DEFAULT;

CREATE TABLE ch14.paris_other
    PARTITION OF ch14.paris                     Partition for all other
    ( CONSTRAINT pk_paris_other PRIMARY KEY (gid) )   geometry types not covered
    DEFAULT;                                    by other partitions
```

In listing 14.7 you create a linestring table that is a partition of ch14.paris to hold all linestrings ❶. You create a polygon table that is a partition of ch14.paris and is further partitioned by arrondissement ❷. You also add a primary key to the partitioned tables, and these keys will be inherited by the sub-partitions.

When you are done, you'll see that pgAdmin shows a single table with partitions and that indexes have been inherited, as shown in figure 14.3.

Figure 14.3 Paris table partitions

Next you load the table, taking rows from paris_hetero.

Listing 14.8 Loading data into Paris partitions

```
INSERT INTO ch14.paris (
    osm_id,ar_num,geom,tags,
    feature_name,feature_type
)                                        ⊲─┐  Load the
SELECT                                      │  data.
    osm_id, ar_num, geom, tags,
    tags->>'name' AS feature_name,
    COALESCE(
        tags->>'tourism',
        tags->>'railway',
        tags->>'amenity',
        tags->>'shop',
        tags->>'boundary',
        'other'
```

```
    )::varchar(50) As feature_type
FROM ch14.paris_hetero;

ALTER TABLE   ch14.paris_polygon
    ADD CONSTRAINT enforce_geotype_geom
    CHECK (geometrytype(geom) = 'POLYGON');

ALTER TABLE   ch14.paris_point
    ADD CONSTRAINT enforce_geotype_geom
    CHECK (geometrytype(geom) = 'POINT');

ALTER TABLE   ch14.paris_linestring
    ADD CONSTRAINT enforce_geotype_geom
    CHECK (geometrytype(geom) = 'LINESTRING');
```

❶ Add constraints so geometry column types are correctly registered in geometry_columns.

If you look at the various child tables stemming from ch14.paris, you'll find that polygons, linestrings, and points all neatly fall into their appropriate geometry type and arrondissement designated partitions. Adding the check constraints is redundant, as it's already handled by the GeometryType partition, but the geometry_columns view does not yet know how to resolve partition clauses, so the check constraints are still needed ❶. You add the constraints after loading because adding them beforehand would slow down the insert process and bulk-checking is faster than insert-time checking.

At last, you reap the fruits of your labor. With partitioning, your count query is identical to the simple one you used in the previous heterogeneous model:

```
SELECT ar_num, COUNT(DISTINCT osm_id) As compte
FROM ch14.paris
GROUP BY ar_num;
```

With partitioning in place, you have the added flexibility to query just the polygon table, if you only care about the counts there:

```
SELECT ar_num, COUNT(DISTINCT osm_id) As compte
FROM ch14.paris_polygons
GROUP BY ar_num;
```

As you can see, partitioning requires an extra step or two to set it up properly, but the advantage is that you're able to keep your queries simple by judiciously querying against the parent table or one of the child tables. As one famous Parisian might have said, "Let them have their cake and eat it too."

> **WARNING** If ch14.paris was a table partitioned using inheritance, you would have to do a DROP TABLE ch14.paris CASCADE; to drop all child tables. This provided an extra safety measure of not wiping out all your data. With built-in partitioning, the partitions are not considered as simply depending on the partitioned table, but as part of the partitioned table. As such you can do DROP TABLE ch14.paris; and you'll lose all the Paris partitions without warning.

ADOPTION

More often than not, partitioning and inheritance come as an afterthought rather than as part of the initial table design. As an example, suppose you had already set up a paris_multipolygon table to store multipolygon geometries of key features, and you had gone to great lengths to populate the table with data, using the code in the next listing.

Listing 14.9 A stand-alone multipolygon table

```
CREATE TABLE ch14.paris_multipolygon (          ◁─── Make the type
    gid bigint GENERATED BY DEFAULT AS IDENTITY,      the same as
    osm_id bigint,                                    ch14.paris.
    ar_num integer,
    feature_name varchar(200),
    feature_type varchar(50),
    geom geometry(multipolygon, 32631),
    tags jsonb,
    CONSTRAINT pk_paris_multipolygon PRIMARY KEY (gid)
) ;

INSERT INTO ch14.paris_multipolygon(osm_id, ar_num,
                    feature_name, feature_type,
                    geom, tags)
SELECT MAX(osm_id) AS osm_id,
  CASE WHEN array_upper(array_agg(ar_num),1) = 1   ─┐  Attach it.
    THEN MAX(ar_num) ELSE NULL END AS ar_num,   ◁──┘
      feature_name, feature_type,
        ST_Multi(ST_Union(geom)) AS geom, json_agg(tags) AS tags
FROM ch14.paris_polygon
WHERE feature_name > ''
GROUP BY feature_name, feature_type;
```

You wouldn't want to have to drop your paris_multipolygon table and then re-create it for it to be a partition of the paris table. The following listing demonstrates how you can make an existing table a partition of ch14.paris.

Listing 14.10 Make a stand-alone table a partition of ch14.paris

```
ALTER TABLE ch14.paris_multipolygon                   Make the type
  ALTER COLUMN geom TYPE geometry(geometry, 32631);  ◁── the same as
                                                         ch14.paris.
ALTER TABLE ch14.paris
  ATTACH PARTITION ch14.paris_multipolygon   ─┐  Attach it.
    FOR VALUES IN ('MULTIPOLYGON');         ◁─┘

ALTER TABLE  ch14.paris_multipolygon             Ensure the geometry
    ADD CONSTRAINT enforce_geotype_geom          type is registered in
      CHECK (geometrytype(geom) = 'MULTIPOLYGON');  ◁── geometry_columns.
```

There are a couple of considerations when a stand-alone table is added as a partition of a partitioned table. Before being attached, the stand-alone table must first ensure that its set of columns is the same as the parent in both type and typmod. The partitioned table must not have any columns not found in the new partition, though the physical order of the columns can be different.

Note that the standalone table you created with listing 14.9 has its own identity column with a primary key. What happens to this column when the table becomes a partition?

Well, if you insert a record directly into the ch14.paris_multipolygon as in the following code, the identity used is the identity created for the ch14.paris_multipolygon table. You can easily determine this because the gid number returned via RETURNING is small, in the order of 50s:

```
INSERT INTO ch14.paris_multipolygon(ar_num, feature_name, feature_type, geom)
SELECT ar_num, 'Regina Spot', 'sites', ST_Multi(ST_Buffer(geom,2))
FROM ch14.paris_linestring
LIMIT 1
RETURNING *;
```

If you repeat the preceding code, but instead insert into ch14.paris, you'll see that the resulting gid is the identity created for the ch14.paris table:

```
INSERT INTO ch14.paris(ar_num, feature_name, feature_type, geom)
SELECT ar_num, 'Regina Spot 2', 'sites', ST_Multi(ST_Buffer(geom,2))
FROM ch14.paris_linestring
LIMIT 1
RETURNING *;
```

The record you inserted gets routed to ch14.paris_multipolygon, as prescribed by the partition, but the gid number is much higher because it is using the ch14.paris gid number generator.

How do you ensure only one identity is ever used? You do so by dropping the ch14.paris_multipolygon IDENTITY as follows:

```
ALTER TABLE ch14.paris_multipolygon
    ALTER gid DROP IDENTITY IF EXISTS;
```

The only problem with this solution is that it prevents direct inserts to the ch14.paris_multipolygon table, because unlike regular SEQUENCE objects, which serial and bigserial create, the new IDENTITY construct is tied to a specific table. If you find you need to directly insert into partitions and want to use the same auto-incrementing sequence, you should use the older serial or bigserial instead of the IDENTITY approach.

ADDING COLUMNS TO A PARTITIONED TABLE

When you add a new column to a partitioned table, PostgreSQL will automatically add the column to all partitions.

Let's try adding address to the paris table:

```
ALTER TABLE ch14.paris ADD COLUMN address text;
UPDATE ch14.paris
  SET address = (tags->>'addr:housenumber') || ' ' || (tags->>'addr:street')
  WHERE tags ? 'addr:housenumber' AND tags ? 'addr:street';
```

14.3 Making auto-updatable views

PostgreSQL allows you to create views that are updatable without any additional work. A view is generally updatable if it involves only one table.

For example, you can create a view called `ch14.subways`:

```
CREATE OR REPLACE VIEW ch14.subways AS
SELECT gid, osm_id, ar_num, feature_name, geom
FROM ch14.paris_points
WHERE feature_type = 'subway';
```

In order to update records in the view, you'd run an update statement such as this:

```
UPDATE ch14.subways
SET feature_name = 'subway 1'
WHERE osm_id =5155161998;
```

Similarly, you can delete from the view without writing any triggers or rules:

```
DELETE FROM ch14.subways WHERE feature_name = 'subway 1';
```

Although you can also insert into the view, we're not exposing the `feature_type` for this particular example, so the insert would never result in a record that satisfies the filter condition. In order to guarantee that all new records are tagged with `feature_type = 'subway'`, you'll need to use a rule or trigger.

Auto-updatable views can have default values for columns that are different from the parent table. For example, if you wanted all newly added subways to be called `subway` if no `feature_name` is specified, you could change the view as in the following listing.

Listing 14.11 Auto-updatable view

```
ALTER VIEW ch14.subways ALTER COLUMN feature_name SET DEFAULT 'subway';
```

For cases where your view involves multiple tables or calculated fields, or you need to do additional processing beyond what's provided by the default view update behavior, you'll need to employ the use of rules or triggers. Although rules and triggers can be used wherever the situation calls for them, we find that they're invaluable in working with inheritance hierarchies.

PostgreSQL WITH CHECK OPTION

Although views can be auto-updatable, it's possible to update a value such that it will no longer appear in the view. For example, if you exposed the `feature_type` column as part of the `SELECT` clause, you could then update the `feature_type` to something else, like `bus`, which would make the updated record disappear from the view. This is often an undesirable side effect.

(continued)

PostgreSQL 9.4 introduced a new feature called `WITH CHECK OPTION` that will ensure that any updates or inserts into the view that won't be visible when querying the view (based on the view's `WHERE` clause) will throw an error. The format of the view-creation statement is

```
CREATE OR REPLACE VIEW name_of_view AS ... WITH CHECK OPTION
```

14.4   *Using triggers and rules*

Sophisticated RDBMSs usually offer ways to catch the execution of certain SQL commands on a table or view and allow some form of conditional processing to take place in response to these events. PostgreSQL is certainly not devoid of such features and can perform additional processing when it encounters the four core SQL commands: `SELECT`, `UPDATE`, `INSERT`, and `DELETE`. The two mechanisms for handling this conditional processing are *triggers* and *rules*.

Rules are instructions for how to rewrite a query. They don't directly change data; they just rewrite the instructions to change data.

Though PostgreSQL has supported rules since too far back to remember, and much of the logic of views is implemented with rules under the hood, you should avoid their use because the direct use of the rule feature may be disabled in a future version of PostgreSQL. The newer ability to apply `INSTEAD OF` triggers on views has made the direct use of rules more or less obsolete. As such, this chapter will not cover the use of rules.

Triggers, on the other hand, have the following benefits over rules:

- They execute per statement or row for each row changed, so they're easier to debug than a rewrite rule.
- They can be written in any PL language, making them more flexible than rules, which could only be written in SQL.

There are some limitations on how you can apply triggers when using partitioned tables. For the most part, cases where you formerly used triggers to redirect data to another table are automatically handled by the native table partitioning you just learned about.

At this point, we assume you've worked through the examples and have the four tables paris, paris_points, paris_linestrings, and paris_polygons in your test database. We'll now enhance the Paris example by adding triggers.

14.4.1   *Triggers*

A trigger is a piece of procedural code that does one of the following:

- Prevents something from happening, such as canceling an `INSERT`, `UPDATE`, or `DELETE` command if certain conditions aren't met

- Does something instead of the requested `INSERT`, `UPDATE`, or `DELETE` command
- Does something else in addition to the `INSERT`, `UPDATE`, or `DELETE` command

Triggers can never be applied to `SELECT` events.

Triggers are based on rows, statements, or data definition language (DDL) events. Row-based triggers are executed for each row participating in an `INSERT`, `UPDATE`, or `DELETE` operation. Statement-based triggers are rarely used except for statement-logging purposes, so we won't cover them here. Statement-based triggers get called once for each `UPDATE`, `DELETE`, or `INSERT` statement. DDL event triggers were introduced in PostgreSQL 9.3 and are used in response to DDL events, such as the creation of a table, constraint, table column, view, and so on.

In PostgreSQL, you have many language choices for writing triggers, except for SQL. Only rules support SQL; triggers must be standalone functions. Popular languages for authoring functions in PostgreSQL are PL/pgSQL, PL/Python, PL/R, PL/V8, and C. You could even develop your own language, should you choose to do so. You can also have multiple triggers on a table, with each trigger written in a different language that's more suited for each particular task.

> **NOTE** As demonstrated earlier, views that have only one table are usually auto-updatable. For more complex views, you can use an `INSTEAD OF` trigger to update the underlying tables. Note that views cannot have `BEFORE` or `AFTER` triggers, since a view is not a thing that data can be inserted directly into.

14.4.2 *Using INSTEAD OF triggers*

In the auto-updatable view created in listing 14.11, the default insert behavior isn't what you'd want, because the `feature_type` columns won't be set. Also, it would be nice to set the arrondissement if it is not passed in. To fix that issue, you can override the default insert behavior with an `INSTEAD OF` trigger. `INSTEAD OF` triggers are only supported for views.

The next listing demonstrates an `INSTEAD OF` insert trigger that will be run instead of the default insert behavior when a record is inserted into the `ch14.stations` view.

Listing 14.12   An `INSTEAD OF` trigger on a view

```
CREATE OR REPLACE FUNCTION trig_subway_insert()
  RETURNS trigger AS  --        ◁──┐ Define the
                                   │ trigger function.
$$
BEGIN
    INSERT INTO ch14.paris_points (
        gid, osm_id, ar_num, feature_name, feature_type, geom
    )
    VALUES (
        DEFAULT,
        NEW.osm_id,
        COALESCE(NEW.ar_num,
```

```
                (SELECT a.ar_num
                    FROM ch14.arrondissements AS a
                    WHERE ST_Intersects(NEW.geom, a.geom )) ) ,
        NEW.feature_name,
        'subway',
        NEW.geom
    );
    RETURN NEW;
END;
    $$ language plpgsql;
```

Attach the trigger to the view on the insert event.

```
CREATE TRIGGER t01_trig_subway_insert  ◁──┘
    INSTEAD OF INSERT
    ON ch14.subways
    FOR EACH ROW
    EXECUTE PROCEDURE trig_subway_insert();
```

A trigger always involves at least two parts:

- A function that returns a trigger
- Binding the trigger function to events

A trigger can be used for multiple events, and more than one trigger function can handle an event. If you have multiple triggers on a single event, they are run in alphabetical order by name. In listing 14.12 the trigger is called t01_trig_subway_insert.

To test this insert trigger, you can re-add the station you deleted:

```
INSERT INTO ch14.subways(osm_id, geom)
SELECT osm_id, geom
FROM ch14.paris_hetero WHERE osm_id = 243496729;
```

If you query the view for that subway, you'll find it. The default column value for feature_name is used, and the ar_num is filled in even though you didn't explicitly insert these columns.

More importantly, the partitioning you have in place automatically rerouted the data to the right partition, even though you inserted into ch14.paris. You can confirm which partition it ended up in with this query:

```
SELECT tableoid::regclass
 FROM ch14.paris
 WHERE osm_id =  243496729;
```

For our data set, this returns ch14.paris_point_ar_16.

14.4.3 Using other triggers

When it comes to triggers, we must expand the three core events of INSERT, UPDATE, and DELETE to six: BEFORE INSERT, AFTER INSERT, BEFORE UPDATE, AFTER UPDATE, BEFORE DELETE, and AFTER DELETE. BEFORE events fire prior to the execution of the triggering command, and AFTER events fire upon completion.

As mentioned earlier, INSTEAD OF triggers are only allowed on views, and views can't use BEFORE or AFTER triggers.

Should you wish to perform an alternative action on a table, as you can with INSTEAD OF triggers on views, you'd create a trigger and bind it to the BEFORE event but throw out the resulting record. An AFTER trigger would be too late.

If you need to modify data that will be inserted or updated, you also need to do this in a BEFORE event. BEFORE triggers cannot be applied to partitioned tables for PostgreSQL prior to version 13 as they interfere with the partitioning logic. However, you can apply AFTER triggers.

Should you wish to perform some operation that depends on the success of your main action, you'll need to bind to an AFTER event. Examples of this are if you need to insert or update a related table on the success of an INSERT or UPDATE statement, such as is the case with logging changed records or sending emails on the completion of a task.

In the case of DDL triggers, there are far more events. The creation, deletion, and alteration of PostgreSQL object types such as tables, views, constraints, and so on, each have their own events. For the full list of DDL events supported in PostgreSQL 9.3+, refer to the PostgreSQL event-triggering matrix (www.postgresql.org/docs/current/interactive/event-trigger-matrix.html). We describe one use case for DDL event triggers in the "Materialized geometry_columns using event triggers" article in the Postgres OnLine Journal (http://mng.bz/y9Ze).

PostgreSQL triggers are implemented as a special type of function called a *trigger function* and then are bound to a table or DDL event. This extra level of indirection means you can reuse the same trigger function for different events, tables, and views. The slight inconvenience is that you face a two-step process of first defining the trigger function and then binding it to a table, view, or DDL event.

PostgreSQL allows you to define multiple triggers per event per table, but each trigger must be uniquely named across the table. Triggers fire in alphabetical sequence. If your database is trigger-happy, we recommend developing a convention for naming your triggers to keep them organized.

Triggers are powerful tools, and your mastery of them will allow you to develop database applications that can control business logic without the need to touch the frontend application.

Before we bring this discussion of rules and triggers to an end, let's revisit constraint exclusions. Remember how before we began the preceding extended example, we described the usefulness of having constraint exclusion enabled? To test that constraint exclusion is working correctly, run the following query and look at the pgAdmin graphical explain plan:

```
SELECT * FROM ch14.paris WHERE ar_num = 8;
```

The graphical explain plan output for this query is shown in figure 14.4.

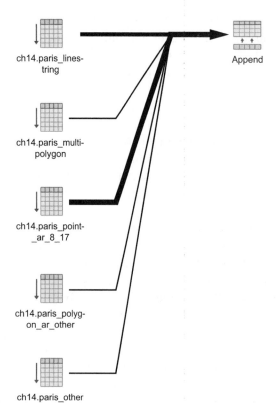

ch14.paris_lines-
tring

ch14.paris_multi-
polygon

ch14.paris_point-
_ar_8_17

ch14.paris_polyg-
on_ar_other

ch14.paris_other

Append

Figure 14.4   Considers only partitions that can have ar_num=8 data.

Observe that although there are tables such as paris_points_ar_other, paris_polygons_ar_16_20, and so on, the planner strategically skips over those tables because we asked only for data found in ar_num = 8. Constraint exclusion works for partitioning!

In addition, you can see that if you had a query that does filter by type, as follows

```
SELECT * FROM ch14.paris WHERE GeometryType(geom) = 'POINT';
```

the planner would skip all tables that can't have points in them. It only has partitions that fit the GeometryType(geom) = 'POINT' criteria, as shown in figure 14.5.

prevent materialization and would also result in slower performance (192 ms versus 90 ms). This is because the costly distance check isn't recalculated if you use a CTE, but it is if you don't use a CTE.

Next, you do a self join to collect and count all the neighbors that are closer to Chinatown than your reference p2 in main. Note that the main.p2_gid = p3.gid OR ensures the RANK will count at least the reference geometry even if there's no closer object.

This is more efficiently done with a window statement. The next listing is the same query written using the RANK window function.

Listing 15.14 Using window to number results

```
SELECT
    RANK() OVER w_dist AS rank,        ◁────────  Use window
    p2.neighborho AS nei_2,
    ST_Distance(p1.geom,p2.geom) AS dist
FROM
    ch15.planning_neighborhoods AS p1
    INNER JOIN
    ch15.planning_neighborhoods AS p2
    ON p1.gid <> p2.gid AND ST_DWithin(p1.geom,p2.geom,2500)
WHERE p1.neighborho = 'Chinatown'
WINDOW w_dist AS (
    PARTITION BY p1.gid ORDER BY ST_Distance(p1.geom,p2.geom)
)                                    ◁─────┐  Define
ORDER BY RANK() OVER w_dist, nei_2;        │  window
```

This window implementation using the RANK function is cleaner and also runs much faster, about 20–60 ms. The larger the geometries, the more significant the speed differences between the self join approach and the window approach.

In this example, you've seen the PostgreSQL declaration of WINDOW. WINDOW naming doesn't exist in all relational database products supporting windowing constructs. It allows you to define your partition, order by frame, and reuse it across the query instead of repeating it where you need it.

The output of listings 15.13 and 15.14 is the same and is shown in the next listing.

Listing 15.15 Output of ranking results using self join or window

```
rank |          nei_2           |        dist
-----+--------------------------+------------------
   1 | Downtown/Civic Center    |                0
   1 | Financial District       |                0
   1 | Nob Hill                 |                0
   1 | North Beach              |                0
   1 | Russian Hill             |                0
   6 | South of Market          |    1726.01750301085
```

15.5.4 *Lateral joins*

Lateral joins allow you to use subqueries or functions that take input from the opposite side of the join. You used lateral constructs in chapter 9.

Resort to a lateral join only when necessary. The planner will not throw an error if you gratuitously affix the keyword LATERAL to joins, but the planner will go the slower lateral path. In many cases, lateral queries can be rewritten as a DISTINCT ON.

In the next set of exercises you'll learn three ways of exploding San Francisco neighborhoods into points in increasing order of efficiency.

Listing 15.16 uses the naive and slowest way of exploding that people mistakenly use. This is the slowest because by using (ST_DumpPoints(geom)).*, the ST_DumpPoints function is called for each column output by ST_DumpPoints. Because ST_Dump-Points outputs two columns, each (ST_DumpPoints(geom)).* will make two calls to ST_DumpPoints functions.

ST_DumpPoints is pretty fast, and the ST_DumpPoints time is a relatively small percentage of the time required for the overall query, so you'll only notice slight differences in speed between this approach and LATERAL for this particular task.

> **NOTE** For these exercises the output is showing the EXPLAIN ANALYZE VERBOSE time, which excludes network effects of returning the data to the client. In practice, most of the time spent in dumping is spent returning data to the client, so the time can jump about tenfold or more depending on how close the server and client are and the speed of memory.

Listing 15.16 Exploding in SELECT: don't do this

```
EXPLAIN ANALYZE VERBOSE
SELECT
    p1.neighborho AS nei_1,
    (ST_DumpPoints(p1.geom)).geom AS geom,
    (ST_DumpPoints(p1.geom)).path[1] AS poly_index,
    (ST_DumpPoints(p1.geom)).path[2] AS poly_ring_index,
    (ST_DumpPoints(p1.geom)).path[3] AS pt_index
FROM ch15.planning_neighborhoods AS p1;
```

The problem with listing 15.16 is that in versions of PostgreSQL prior to 12 it would call ST_DumpPoints for each column output. Even if you were to revise to (ST_Dump-Point(geom)).*, it would still do a call for geom and path output in older PostgreSQL versions. This example took a little over 20 ms (330 ms if you consider network transfer) to run on our development box. The next listing shows the output.

Listing 15.17 Explain plan output for exploding the naive way

```
QUERY PLAN
------------------------------------------------------------------
Result  (cost=0.00..3701487.56 rows=37000 width=112)
        (actual time=0.086..21.716 rows=13254 loops=1)
```

```
Output: neighborho, ((st_dumppoints(geom))).geom,
    ((st_dumppoints(geom))).path[1],
        ((st_dumppoints(geom))).path[2], ((st_dumppoints(geom))).path[3]
-> ProjectSet  (cost=0.00..1117.56 rows=37000 width=100)
    (actual time=0.080..11.412 rows=13254 loops=1)
    Output: st_dumppoints(geom), neighborho
    -> Seq Scan on ch15.planning_neighborhoods p1
        (cost=0.00..7.37 rows=37 width=100)
        (actual time=0.013..0.035 rows=37 loops=1)
            Output: gid, neighborho, geom
Planning Time: 0.100 ms
Execution Time: 22.506 ms
```

If you see a `ProjectSet` step in the plan, it means the planner recognizes that this should be one call to the function `ST_DumpPoints`. You'll also get a hint that you aren't getting the best performance if you compare this to the next approach, which yields the same answer.

One way to avoid multiple calls to your function regardless of PostgreSQL version is to wrap the call in a subselect, as shown in the following listing.

Listing 15.18 Exploding using subselect

```
EXPLAIN ANALYZE VERBOSE
SELECT
    nei_1,
    (gp).geom,
    (gp).path[1] AS poly_index,
    (gp).path[2] AS poly_ring_index,
    (gp).path[3] AS pt_index
FROM (
    SELECT p1.neighborho AS nei_1, ST_DumpPoints(p1.geom) AS gp
    FROM ch15.planning_neighborhoods AS p1
) AS x;
```

The output of the preceding listing follows.

Listing 15.19 Explain plan output for exploding using subselect

```
Subquery Scan on x
    (cost=0.00..1487.56 rows=37000 width=112)
    (actual time=0.081..20.973 rows=13254 loops=1)
    Output: x.nei_1, (x.gp).geom, (x.gp).path[1], (x.gp).path[2], (x.gp).path[3]
    -> ProjectSet
        (cost=0.00..1117.56 rows=37000 width=100)
        (actual time=0.074..11.305 rows=13254 loops=1)
            Output: p1.neighborho, st_dumppoints(p1.geom)
            -> Seq Scan on ch15.planning_neighborhoods p1
                (cost=0.00..7.37 rows=37 width=100)
                (actual time=0.014..0.033 rows=37 loops=1)
                    Output: p1.gid, p1.neighborho, p1.geom
Planning Time: 0.119 ms
Execution Time: 21.558 ms
```

The timing of this subselect approach would be twice as fast as the naive approach demonstrated in listing 15.17 for PostgreSQL versions lower than 12. The `ProjectSet` feature in PostgreSQL 12 makes them identical in performance.

Next you'll try the same exercise using the lateral construct. The lateral construct is a little shorter to write, and it's generally a bit faster than the subselect approach. LATERAL is an optional keyword, but we like to use it as a more explicit declaration of what we're doing. Without the keyword, the planner is smart enough to figure out that if you have a correlated function (one that depends on another table in the FROM condition), then you are asking for a LATERAL.

The next listing shows the neighborhood explosion exercise using the lateral construct.

Listing 15.20   Exploding using lateral

```
EXPLAIN ANALYZE VERBOSE
SELECT
    p1.neighborho AS nei_1,
    (gp).geom,
    (gp).path[1] AS poly_index,
    (gp).path[2] AS poly_ring_index,
    (gp).path[3] AS pt_index
FROM
    ch15.planning_neighborhoods AS p1,
    LATERAL
    ST_DumpPoints(p1.geom) AS gp;
```

The output of listing 15.20 is shown next:

```
Nested Loop
  (cost=25.00..772.37 rows=37000 width=112)
  (actual time=0.543..20.179 rows=13254 loops=1)
  Output: p1.neighborho, gp.geom, gp.path[1], gp.path[2], gp.path[3]
  -> Seq Scan on ch15.planning_neighborhoods p1
  (cost=0.00..7.37 rows=37 width=100)
  (actual time=0.015..0.036 rows=37 loops=1)
      Output: p1.gid, p1.neighborho, p1.geom
  -> Function Scan on postgis.st_dumppoints gp
      (cost=25.00..35.00 rows=1000 width=64)
      (actual time=0.302..0.333 rows=358 loops=37)
      Output: gp.path, gp.geom
      Function Call: st_dumppoints(p1.geom)
Planning Time: 0.130 ms
Execution Time: 20.912 ms
```

The lateral approach, even on newer versions of PostgreSQL, tends to be faster than the subselect or naive approaches. For older versions of PostgreSQL you'll find that the lateral approach is more than twice as fast as the naive approach and a little faster and shorter than the subselect approach.

In addition to improving performance by rewriting your queries, you can control the behavior of the planner by setting properties on functions and also disabling various plan strategies to encourage it to use others. You'll learn about these settings in the next section.

15.6 System and function settings

Most system variables that affect plan strategies can be set at the server, session, database, or function levels.

You can set the variables at the server level by using the ALTER SYSTEM SQL construct instead of directly setting postgresql.conf or postgresql.auto.conf:

```
ALTER SYSTEM SET somevariable=somevalue;
```

By using the ALTER SYSTEM construct, your custom settings are stored in a file called postgresql.auto.conf, and thus are easier to distinguish from default settings and to migrate when you upgrade. Make sure you run SELECT pg_reload_conf(); to make the new settings take effect.

To set system variables at the session level, use the following command:

```
SET somevariable TO somevalue;
```

To set them at the database level, use this command:

```
ALTER DATABASE somedatabase SET somevariable=somevalue;
```

To set them at the function level, use this command:

```
ALTER FUNCTION somefunction(type1, type2) SET somevariable=somevalue;
```

To see the current value of a parameter, use this command:

```
show somevariable;
```

Now let's look at some system variables that impact query performance.

15.6.1 Key system variables that affect plan strategies

This section covers the key system variables that most affect query speed and efficiency. For many of these, particularly the memory ones, there's no specific right or wrong setting.

A lot of the optimal settings depend on whether or not your server is dedicated to PostgreSQL work, what CPU you have, how much motherboard RAM you have, and even whether your loads are connection-intensive versus query-intensive. Do you have more people hitting your database asking for simple queries, or is your database a workhorse dedicated to generating data feeds?

You may want to adjust many of these settings for specific queries and not across the board. We encourage you to do your own tests to determine which settings work best under what loads.

THE CONSTRAINT_EXCLUSION VARIABLE

In order to take advantage of inheritance partitioning effects, the constraint_ exclusion variable should be set to partition, which is the default. This can be set at the server or database level, as well as at the function or statement level. It's generally best to set it at the server level so you don't need to remember to do it for each database you create.

The difference between the older on value and the new partition value is that with partition the planner doesn't check for constraint exclusion conditions unless it's looking at a table that has children. This saves a few planner cycles over the previous on setting. The on setting is still useful, however, with union queries.

THE MAINTENANCE_WORK_MEM VARIABLE

This variable specifies the amount of memory to allocate for indexing and vacuum analyze processes. When you're doing lots of loads, you may want to temporarily set this to a higher value for a session and keep it lower at the server or database level. You can set it as follows:

```
SET maintenance_work_mem TO '512MB';
```

THE SHARED_BUFFERS VARIABLE

The shared_buffers variable specifies the amount of memory the database server uses for shared memory. shared_buffers is what makes things such as shared reads possible. It allows the server to cache data in motherboard memory to be used by other PostgreSQL processes. The more of it you have, the more of your database can be loaded into onboard memory for faster retrieval.

You'll generally want this variable to be set much higher than the default and to be set to as much as 20% of available onboard RAM for a dedicated PostgreSQL box. This setting can only be set in the postgresql.conf file or via ALTER SYSTEM, and it requires a restart of the service after setting. You'll get diminishing returns after about 8 GB.

THE WORK_MEM VARIABLE

work_mem is the maximum memory used for each sort operation, and it's set as the amount of memory (in KB if no units are specified) for each internal sort operation. If you want to set it using any other metric besides KB, make sure you specify the units.

If you have a lot of onboard RAM, do a lot of intensive geometry processing, and have few users doing intensive things at the same time, this number should be fairly high, like 250 MB or more. The default is around 3 MB, which is too low for intensive queries. This is also a setting you can set conditionally at the function level or connection level, so you can keep it low for general inexperienced users and high for specific functions.

You can set it for the session as follows:

```
SET work_mem='50MB';
```

ENABLE (VARIOUS PLAN STRATEGIES)

The enable strategy options all default to true/on. You should rarely change these settings at the server or database level, but you may find it useful to set them at the session or function level if you want to discourage a certain plan strategy that's causing query problems. It's rare that you'd ever need to turn these off.

Some PostGIS users have experienced great performance improvements by fiddling with these settings on a case-by-case basis:

- enable_bitmapscan
- enable_gathermerge
- enable_groupingsets_hash_disk (new in PostgreSQL 13; only applies to the use of GROUPING SETS)
- enable_hashagg
- enable_hashagg_disk (new in PostgreSQL 13)
- enable_hashjoin
- enable_incrementalsort (new in PostgreSQL 13)
- enable_indexonlyscan
- enable_indexscan
- enable_material
- enable_mergejoin
- enable_nestloop
- enable_parallel_append
- enable_parallel_hash
- enable_partition_pruning
- enable_partitionwise_aggregate
- enable_partitionwise_join
- enable_seqscan
- enable_sort

The enable_seqscan option is one that's useful to turn off for troubleshooting because it forces the planner to use an index that it seemingly could use but refuses to. It's a good way of checking if the planner's costs are wrong in some way, if a table scan is truly better for your particular case, or if your index is set up incorrectly so the planner can't use it.

The enable_hashagg and enable_hashagg_disk options are additional settings worth experimenting with. If you disable enable_hashagg, it will often force a plan that used hashagg to use the groupagg strategy. Prior to PostgreSQL 13, if the planner concluded that a hashagg strategy would require more memory than allowed by work_mem, it would resort to a groupagg. PostgreSQL 13 offers the ability for hashagg work tables to spill to disk and a new parameter enable_hashagg_disk to disable this. You may not want this in cases where you have very slow disks.

In some cases, even settings that are turned off won't be abided by if the planner has no other valid options. Turning the following settings off will discourage the planner from using them but won't guarantee it:

- `enable_sort`
- `enable_seqscan`
- `enable_nestloop`

To play around with these and other planner settings, set them before you run a query. For example, turn off `hashagg` like this:

```
set enable_hashagg = off;
```

Then rerun the `CASE` query from listing 15.11, which used a `hashagg`. This change in settings will cause it to use a `GroupAggregate`, as shown in figure 15.6.

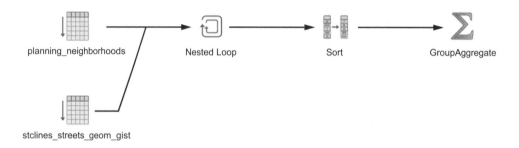

Figure 15.6   Disabling `hashagg` forces a group app strategy

Disabling specific planner strategies is useful for certain critical queries where you know a particular planner strategy yields slower results. By compartmentalizing these queries in functions, you can control the strategies with function settings.

There are also specific settings relevant only for functions. We'll go over these in the next section.

15.6.2 *Function-specific settings*

The `COST` and `ROWS` settings are the estimated values for the cost of the function and the estimated number of returned rows for the function. The `PARALLEL` setting controls whether a query that uses this function can be parallelized. For functions, the default cost is generally `100` for SQL and PL/pgSQL and `1` for C functions. If you know your function is more costly or cheaper than other functions, you should set this for your function.

These settings are available only to functions. They're part of the definition of the function and not set separately like the other parameters. The form is

```
CREATE OR REPLACE FUNCTION somefunction(arg1,arg2 ..)
RETURNS type1 AS
....
LANGUAGE 'c' IMMUTABLE STRICT
PARALLEL SAFE
COST 100 ROWS 2;
```

COST

The COST setting specifies how costly you think a function is relative to other functions.

Versions of PostGIS prior to PostGIS 3.0 with PostgreSQL 12 didn't have these cost settings explicitly set because correctly setting a function often impacted spatial index use. With PostgreSQL 12+ and PostGIS 3+, these costs are in place, so there should be less need to mess with them.

ROWS

The ROWS setting is relevant only for set-returning functions. It's an estimate of the number of rows you expect the function to return.

IMMUTABLE, STABLE, VOLATILE

As shown previously, you can use IMMUTABLE when writing a function to state what kind of behavior is expected of the output. If you don't, the function is assumed to be VOLATILE. These settings have both speed and behavior effects.

An immutable function is one whose output is constant over time, given the same set of arguments. If a function is immutable, the planner knows it can cache the result, and if it sees the same arguments passed in, it can reuse the cached output. Because caching generally improves speed, especially for pricy calculations, marking such functions immutable is useful.

A STABLE function is one whose output is expected to be constant across the life of a query, given the same inputs. These functions can generally be assumed to produce the same result, but they can't be treated as immutable because they have external dependencies that could change, such as dependencies on other tables. As a result, they perform worse than IMMUTABLE functions, all else being equal, but faster than VOLATILE functions.

A VOLATILE function is one that can give you a different output with each call, even with the same inputs. Functions that depend on time or some other randomly changing factor, or that change data, fit into this category because they change state. If you mark a volatile function, such as random(), as non-volatile, it will run faster but not behave correctly because it will return the same value with each subsequent call.

PARALLEL

With the advent of parallelism in PostgreSQL 9.6, a new attribute was added to functions and aggregates. This is the PARALLEL setting. If not specified, the setting defaults to PARALLEL UNSAFE.

These are possible options for the PARALLEL setting:

- `SAFE`—The function can be used in any node of a parallel plan.
- `UNSAFE`—This prevents parallel plans from being used at all when this function is used.
- `RESTRICTED`—A parallel plan can be used, but this function can only be used in the leader node and not in any of the worker nodes used for breaking apart a plan.

15.6.3 *Encouraging parallel plans*

When the planner employs a parallel strategy, it divides the work into a leader node and one or more worker nodes. As mentioned earlier, any functions used in a query that are marked as `UNSAFE` will prevent parallel plans completely.

You can find more about what kind of queries can use parallelism in the "When Can Parallel Query Be Used?" section of the PostgreSQL documentation (www.postgresql .org/docs/current/when-can-parallel-query-be-used.html).

In addition to that setting, parallel strategies are sensitive to the following Postgre-SQL settings:

- `autovacuum_max_workers`
- `enable_parallel_append`
- `enable_parallel_hash`
- `force_parallel_mode`
- `max_parallel_maintenance_workers`
- `max_parallel_workers`
- `max_parallel_workers_per_gather`
- `max_worker_processes`
- `min_parallel_index_scan_size`
- `min_parallel_table_scan_size`
- `parallel_leader_participation`
- `parallel_setup_cost`
- `parallel_tuple_cost`

These are the settings you will most likely need to change:

- `max_worker_processes`—Set this to at least as many CPU cores as you have available.
- `max_parallel_workers`—Maximum number of parallel worker processes that can be active. This should be set to less than or equal to `max_worker_processes`.
- `max_parallel_workers_per_gather`—This controls the maximum number of parallel nodes per executor. It is a subset of `max_parallel_workers`, so it should be set to a lower or equal value.

Now that you've learned about the various system settings you can employ to impact speed, let's take a closer look at the geometries themselves. Can you change a geometry so that applying spatial predicates and operations to the geometries is speedier but the geometry is still accurate enough for your needs?

15.7 Optimizing spatial data

Generally speaking, spatial processes and checks on spatial relationships take longer with bigger or invalid spatial data. Spatial relationship checks are often slower, give wrong answers, or just don't work if your geometry data is invalid.

For any kind of spatial data object, whether it be geometry, geography, raster, or topology, spatial checks take longer as the size of your spatial data increases. Part of the reason is that there's just more data to deal with. If your spatial data objects get large enough, they are often internally chunked and stored in TOAST (which stands for *The Oversized-Attribute Storage Technique*, and which is used when an object grows beyond 8 KB) tables. Each 8 KB fragment is essentially stored as a separate row in a TOAST table. When data is toasted, performing more involved operations, such as intense ST_Intersects checks or processes like ST_Union, means the data needs to be de-toasted, which takes more time.

The other concern with storing large spatial objects, particularly with smaller attribute data, is that even when you're not updating the spatial object, it will significantly impact the speed of updating other data columns. This is because of the way PostgreSQL implements multi-version concurrency (MVCC). In order for PostgreSQL to provide a consistent snapshot of data, it keeps track of multiple versions of a row in the same table. Whenever you do an UPDATE and PostgreSQL "deletes" the old row and replaces it with a new row, it actually marks the old record as inactive. Similarly, a DELETE will just mark a record as inactive.

One benefit of storing rasters using the out-of-db approach is that if much of what you are updating is the related attribute data, you can significantly improve update and insert performance because the raster representation during the copy of the record will just be raster metadata and not the actual raster.

In this section we'll go over some of the more common techniques for validating, optimizing, and simplifying spatial data.

15.7.1 Fixing invalid geometries

The main reason to fix invalid geometries is that you can't use GEOS relationship checks and many processing functions that rely on the intersection matrix with invalid geometries. Functions like ST_Intersects, ST_Equals, and so on return false or throw a topology error for certain kinds of invalidity, regardless of the true nature of the intersection. The same holds true for union, intersection, and the powerful GEOS geometry process functions. Many won't work with invalid geometries.

Most of the cases of invalid geometries involve polygons. There is a function called ST_MakeValid that can be used to fix invalid polygons, multipolygons, multilinestrings, and linestrings.

In addition to making sure that geometries are valid, you can improve performance by reducing the number of points in each geometry.

15.7.2 Reducing the number of vertices by simplification

In PostGIS there are several simplification functions, such as ST_Simplify, ST_SimplifyPreserveTopology, and ST_SimplifyVW, that can be used to reduce the number of vertices in a polygon or linestring. These are sometimes used in conjunction with ST_ChaikinSmoothing. Some of these were covered in chapter 6.

15.7.3 Reducing the number of vertices by breaking geometries apart

The larger your geometries or the more they deviate from their bounding boxes, the more work functions like ST_Intersects and ST_DWithin have to do. You want as many geometries as possible to be rejected by the bounding box check, so fewer intensive spatial checks need to be done. In the cases where the more intensive checks do need to be done (those that satisfy the bounding box checks), you can reduce the intensity of the work primarily by reducing the number of vertices.

Using something like ST_Subdivide, which was also covered in chapter 6, fits the bill. The downside of using ST_Subdivide is that it chops your geometry into multiple rows, so you now have more rows in your table to contend with.

15.7.4 Clustering

Clustering can refer to two totally different optimization tricks that sound similar and even use the same terminology but mean different things. We'll refer to the first as *index clustering* and the second as *spatial clustering* (or the more colloquial *bunching*):

- *Index clustering*—This refers to the PostgreSQL concept of clustering on an index or keeping your data ordered. You maintain the same number of rows, but you physically order your table by an index (in PostGIS, usually the spatial one). This guarantees that your matches will be in close proximity to each other on the disk and will be easy to pick. Your index seeks will be faster because each data page will have more matches.
- *Spatial clustering (bunching)*—This is usually done with point geometries, and it reduces the number of rows. It's done by taking a set of points, usually close to one another or related by similar attributes, and aggregating by collecting them into multipoints. For example, you could be talking about 100,000 rows of multipoints versus 1,000,000 rows of points, which can be both a great space saver as well as a speed enhancer, because you need fewer index checks.

The index-clustering concept is fairly common and is similarly named in other databases.

> **Pointcloud**
>
> A project called Pointcloud (https://github.com/pgpointcloud/pointcloud) takes the bunching concept to extremes and defines a new spatial data type called a `PCPatch` that collects many *n*-dimensional points into a single unit. A `PCPatch` has its own set of analysis and accessor functions and also has casts to cast to PostGIS geometry types. It's often used to store and analyze lidar satellite data.

INDEX CLUSTERING ON A GEOHASH FUNCTIONAL INDEX OR GIST SPATIAL INDEX

We've talked about Geohash indexes in other chapters, but it's worthwhile revisiting them. Why would you want to physically sort your data on disk by a spatially based index like a functional index of Geohash or the gist geometry index you built?

When PostgreSQL (and, in fact, many relational databases) query data, they do it in batches called *pages*. A page may house many records, depending on the size of each record. If you can keep data commonly asked for together on the same data page or nearby pages, your retrieval performance will be better because your disk seeks become more efficient. For spatial queries, you commonly ask for things that are spatially close to each other. As such, you'll want them to be physically close to each other on disk as well for faster retrieval.

There are two kinds of spatial indexes commonly used for database clustering in PostGIS: the Geohash cluster, which is most beneficial for small objects and requires data to be in WGS 84 lon/lat (EPSG 4326), and the more common all-purpose R-tree cluster, which is just a cluster on the gist index you create on a table.

NOTE For more details on Geohash versus the standard R-tree cluster, see the "Clustering on Indices" workshop module in the Introduction to PostGIS (http://mng.bz/n21V).

The Geohash cluster works best for small objects, such as points or small polygons and linestrings; it becomes unusable for larger objects unless you base it on something like `ST_GeoHash(ST_Centroid(geom))`. The reason it's not usable or is of minimal use for larger objects is that as objects get bigger, their Geohash representation gets smaller until it shrinks to nothing. The Geohash implemented by PostGIS is the Geohash of the bounding box.

Listing 15.21 demonstrates a slight twist to the standard Geohash index. This index combines both a Geohash and a street name in the index so that when you cluster the data, the data will first be spatially clustered, and for streets that have the same Geohash, you'll have similarly named streets closer together.

> **Listing 15.21 Cluster by compound index consisting of Geohash and street name**

❶ Create index

```
CREATE INDEX idx_stclines_streets_ghash_street
ON ch15.stclines_streets (ST_GeoHash(ST_Transform(geom,4326)),street);
```

```
CLUSTER ch15.stclines_streets
USING idx_stclines_streets_ghash_street;        ◁——❷ Cluster on index
```

In listing 15.21 you create a compound index composed of the Geohash of the street centerline and the name ❶. The advantage of a compound index is that long streets are often broken into smaller segments and stored as separate rows. You want streets that are continuations to be closer together if they have the same Geohash. Data doesn't physically get resorted until you cluster on the index ❷.

> ## Cluster not maintained after updates or inserts
> PostgreSQL doesn't maintain the physical order of the table to match the cluster index during inserts and updates. If you have a table that you update fairly frequently, you'll want to run CLUSTER *table_name* to force a reordering of the table on the index you clustered on.
>
> If you need to recluster all the tables that have clusters defined, just run CLUSTER verbose. The verbose is optional but will show you the table names and the clustering index as each table is reclustered. It will also show you stats on the number of pages and rows.

If you decide to change your cluster later to use an R-tree index, you'll run this command:

```
CLUSTER ch15.stclines_streets USING stclines_streets_geom_gist
```

This will force a reclustering of the table using a gist index called stclines_streets_geom_gist, and for future cluster operations where no cluster index is specified, it will use this index.

   If you have a small table such as ch15.stclines_streets, with ~15,000 rows, it's hard to see a performance difference between clustered and nonclustered. If your data set is fairly small, it fits into onboard RAM, so disk seeks are less common.

INDEX CLUSTERING ON HILBERT CURVE AND USE OF MATERIALIZED VIEWS

PostGIS 3 changed the way data is sorted when you do ORDER BY geom. Before PostGIS 3, the ordering for ORDER BY geom used to do an x,y coordinate sorting, which means the ordering is not ideally sorted with all closest things together. In PostGIS 3 the ordering will result in data being sorted by the Hilbert Curve.

> **GEOMETRY ORDERING CHANGED TO HILBERT CURVE**   PostGIS 3.0 changed the default behavior of sorting of geometries. If you ORDER BY geometry in Post-GIS 3+, you will get what is known as a Hilbert Curve sort, described by Paul Ramsey in his "Waiting for PostGIS 3: Hilbert Geometry Sorting" blog post (http://mng.bz/vePm).

You would expect clustering by your gist index to give you a Hilbert geometry sort, but it does not. Clustering on a B-tree index does give you a Hilbert geometry sort. Sadly the B-tree index is only useful for points. One way to get around this dilemma is to define a materialized view, as is done in the following listing.

Listing 15.22 Materialized view cluster by the Hilbert curve

```
CREATE MATERIALIZED VIEW ch15.vw_mat_stclines_streets AS
SELECT *
FROM ch15.stclines_streets             Force physical ordering
ORDER BY geom, street; --        ◁──   by the Hilbert curve.

                                                      Add a unique key
                                                      so you can use
CREATE UNIQUE INDEX ux_vw_mat_stclients_streets  ◁── concurrent refresh.
  ON ch15.vw_mat_stclines_streets USING btree(gid);

                                                      Standard spatial
                                                      index for spatial
CREATE INDEX ix_stclines_streets_geom                distance
  ON ch15.vw_mat_stclines_streets USING gist(geom);  ◁──
```

Now you would use the materialized view instead of your table, and when you want to force a reorder when data changes, you can run this command:

```
REFRESH MATERIALIZED VIEW CONCURRENTLY ch15.vw_mat_stclines_streets;
```

The nice thing about refreshing a materialized view concurrently is that the view can still be read while the operation is going on. In contrast, a recluster of a table locks the table for the duration of the cluster operation.

Summary

- Using indexes on your tables for commonly filtered columns vastly improves query performance.
- You can often improve the speed of your queries by rewriting them a different way.
- You can set the values of PostgreSQL settings to guide the planner, thus improving performance.
- You can troubleshoot query plans using EXPLAIN, EXPLAIN ANALYZE, and EXPLAIN (ANALYZE, VERBOSE).

Part 3

Using PostGIS with other tools

In part 2 you learned the basics of solving problems with spatial queries, and performance tips for getting the most speed out of your spatial queries. But Post-GIS is a seductive mistress widely courted by both commercial and open source tools. In part 3 you'll learn about some of the more common open source server-side tools that are used to complement and enhance PostGIS.

Chapter 16 covers other PostgreSQL extensions commonly used with Post-GIS. You'll learn about the procedural languages PL/R, PL/Python, and PL/V8. These are common favorites in GIS for leveraging the wealth of statistical functions and plotting capabilities of R, the numerous packages for Python, and the brisk elegance of JavaScript in the database. You'll learn how to write stored functions in these languages and use them in SQL queries. In addition, we'll cover pgRouting, which is another package of SQL functions used to build routing applications and solve various kinds of traveling-salesperson problems.

In chapter 17, you'll learn about server-side mapping and client-side mapping frameworks, which are commonly used to display PostGIS data on the web. You'll learn how to display PostGIS data with third-party mapping layers, such as OpenStreetMap, Google Maps, and Microsoft Bing, using the Leaflet and Open-Layers open source JavaScript mapping APIs. You'll also learn the basics of setting up GeoServer and MapServer and configuring them as WMS/WFS services.

Extending PostGIS with pgRouting and procedural languages

This chapter covers

- PgRouting
- PL/R
- PL/Python
- PL/V8

In this chapter we'll cover four PostgreSQL extensions commonly installed with PostGIS. Extensions expand what you can do with PostGIS beyond the base installation. Each extension can come packaged with additional functions and data types (PostGIS is itself an extension), and each extension has a specific mission. It may allow you to script in an additional language, add specific functionality, or replace existing functions with faster implementations.

In this chapter, we'll discuss the following extensions:

- *PgRouting*—A library of functions used in conjunction with PostGIS to solve problems such as shortest path, driving directions, and geographic con-strained resource allocation problems, such as the legendary traveling sales-person problem (TSP).
- *PL/R*—A procedural language handler for PostgreSQL that allows you to write stored database functions using the R statistical language and graphical

environment. With this extension you can generate elegant graphs and make use of a breadth of statistical functions to build aggregate and other functions within your PostgreSQL database. This allows you to inject the power of R into your queries.

- *PL/Python*—A procedural language handler for PostgreSQL that allows you to write PostgreSQL stored functions in Python. This allows you to leverage the breadth of Python functions for network connectivity, data import, geocoding, and other tasks.

- *PL/V8 (a.k.a. PL/JavaScript)*—A procedural language handler for PostgreSQL that allows you to write PostgreSQL stored functions in JavaScript. This means you can use the same language on the server that you'd commonly use with client-side web applications, and even reuse some of those functions. PL/V8 utilizes the Google V8 engine, which is also the plumbing used for NodeJS.

After you've finished this chapter, you'll better appreciate the benefits of implementing solutions directly in your database instead of exporting your data for external processing.

The data and code used in this chapter can be found at www.postgis.us/chapter _16_edition_3. To follow along with the upcoming examples, you'll need to run the data/ch16_data.sql script from this chapter's download file. It's best to use psql to load the file. The script will both create the schema and load in the tables for this chapter.

16.1 Solving network routing problems with pgRouting

Once you have all your data in PostGIS, what better way to show it off than to find solutions to routing problems such as the shortest path from one address to another or the famous traveling salesperson problem (TSP). PgRouting lets you do just that. All you have to do is add a few extra columns to your existing tables to store parameters and solutions. Then execute one of the many functions packaged with pgRouting. PgRouting makes it possible to get instant answers to seemingly intractable problems. Without pgRouting, you'd have to resort to expensive desktop tools such as ArcGIS Network Analyst or pay-per-use web services.

PgRouting is a free and open source software (FOSS) project in its own right, but it relies on PostGIS for spatial analysis functions. PgRouting underwent significant improvements in its version 3.0, with new functions. As a general rule, functions in pgRouting 3.0 begin with the prefix *pgr_*. Version 3.1 added even more functions, such as the Chinese postman algorithm. The following exercises were tested on pgRouting 3.1, but they should work fine on pgRouting 3 and higher.

16.1.1 Installing pgRouting

Many distributions of PostGIS offer pgRouting. If you're using Windows, the PostGIS 3+ StackBuilder installs pgRouting 3+ binaries along with PostGIS and other PostGIS-related extensions. You can also find in development pgRouting binaries for Windows at https://postgis.net/windows_downloads/ in the experimental section. Refer to the pgRouting site (http://pgrouting.org/download.html) for binaries of other distributions.

Once you've procured the binaries and installed them, add pgRouting to your database as an extension with SQL. You don't need to install pgRouting in the same schema as PostGIS, but it is better to do so since it relies on many PostGIS functions.

```
CREATE EXTENSION pgrouting SCHEMA postgis;
```

If you're upgrading from an earlier version of pgRouting the following command should do the trick:

```
ALTER EXTENSION pgrouting UPDATE;
```

On occasion, especially if you were running a prereleased version, you may run into errors upgrading. In these cases, do this to upgrade:

```
DROP EXTENSION pgrouting;
CREATE EXTENSION pgrouting SCHEMA postgis;
```

For more details on working with pgRouting, visit the pgRouting site: http://pgrouting .org. If you want more in-depth examples of using pgRouting, check out our book on the topic, *pgRouting: A Practical Guide* (Locate Press, 2017), http://locatepress.com/ pgrouting.

BASIC NAVIGATION

The most common use of routing is to find the shortest route among a network of interconnected roads. Anyone who has ever sought driving directions from a GPS unit should be intimately familiar with this application.

For a first example, we picked the North American cities of Minneapolis and Saint Paul. Picture yourself as a truck driver who needs to find the shortest route through the Twin Cities. As with most industrialized cities in the world, highways usually bifurcate at the boundary of a metropolis, offering a perimeter route that encircles the city and multiple radial routes into the city. Altogether, highways form a spoke-and-wheel pattern.

The Twin Cities have one of the most convoluted patterns of all the major cities in the United States. A truck driver trying to pass through the cities via the shortest route has quite a few choices to make. Furthermore, the shortest choice isn't apparent from just looking at a map. As shown in figure 16.1, a driver entering the metropolitan area from the south and wishing to leave via the northwest has quite a few options. You'll use pgRouting to point the driver to the shortest route.

BUILDING THE NETWORK TOPOLOGY

The first step in routing problems is to create a network topology from your table of linestrings, or *edges* in topo-speak. You'll build a network topology using the pgr_Create-Topology pgRouting function. This comprehensive function loops through all the

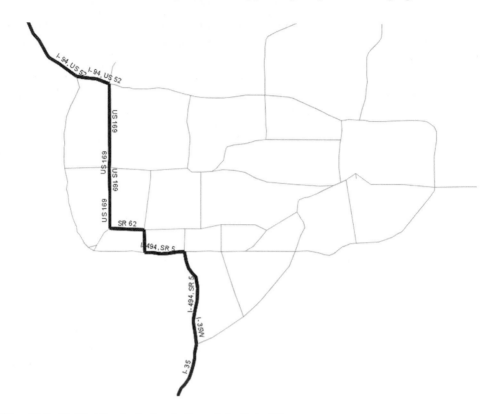

Figure 16.1   Plotting the shortest route through the Twin Cities

records and assigns each linestring two integer identifiers: one for the starting point and one for the ending point. pgr_CreateTopology makes sure that identical points receive the same identifier, even if it's shared by multiple linestrings.

In order for the pgr_CreateTopology function to have somewhere to store the identifiers, you need to have two placeholder columns readied: a source column for the starting point and a target column for the ending point. Listing 16.1 demonstrates adding the source and target columns and populating those columns using pgr_CreateTopology.

> **WARNING**   Keep in mind that pgRouting topology is completely unrelated to the postgis_topology extension packaged with PostGIS.

Listing 16.1   Building a network topology

```
ALTER TABLE ch16.twin_cities ADD COLUMN source integer;
ALTER TABLE ch16.twin_cities ADD COLUMN target integer;
ALTER TABLE ch16.twin_cities
   ALTER COLUMN geom type geometry(LINESTRING,4326) USING
     ST_Transform(geom,4326);
```

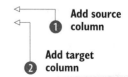

Add source ❶ column

Add target ❷ column

```
SELECT pgr_CreateTopology(
    'ch16.twin_cities',
    0.000001,
    'geom',
    'gid',
    'source',
    'target', clean => true      ③ Populate
);                                     fields
```

In this listing you create source ① and target ② columns, which will hold the node identifiers for the nodes' connecting edges. Then you populate the source and target columns by specifying a tolerance value that defines how close the start and end points need to for them to be considered the same node. You use the edge identifier column, gid, to uniquely identify each edge, and a geometry column, geom, that has the edge linestring ③.

In addition to populating the source and target columns of the twin_cities table, pgRouting creates a table of nodes called ch16.twin_cities_vertices_pgr to store the nodes as point geometries.

DIJKSTRA SHORTEST PATH ALGORITHM

PgRouting weighs routes using costs, and there are many kinds of costs. You can assign costs to segments based on length, speed limit, directionality (one-way or two-way), gradient, and so forth. From these costs, you can optimize your travel to produce a route with a minimum cost. The most prevalent cost measure, and the one you'll use here, is distance.

You begin by assigning costs to each linestring. Because you're looking at distance, you'll create a column to hold length, take the spheroidal length of each linestring, and fill in the length column, as follows:

```
ALTER TABLE ch16.twin_cities ADD COLUMN length float8;    ◁——┐ Add length
UPDATE ch16.twin_cities
SET length = ST_Length(geom::geography);    ◁——┐ Update value
```

To get an accurate length, you cast your linestrings in longitude and latitude to geography and use the geography length function, which returns length in meters.

Although it's not shown in this first example, you can easily use different cost factors to weigh the linestrings. For example, you could weigh highways by a speed limit so that slower highways have a higher cost. You could even get live feeds of traffic conditions so that routes with major traffic congestion would receive a higher cost.

Dijkstra's algorithm is one approach for arriving at an exact solution for travel from one node to another in your network, based on given costs. For small networks like this one, exact solutions are possible in real time. For large networks, approximate solutions are often good enough and cut down computation time.

With the network prepared and the costs assigned, all it takes is the execution of a pgRouting function to return the answer with the minimum cost, as shown in the following listing.

Listing 16.2   Using Dijkstra's algorithm to route through the Twin Cities

```
SELECT pd.seq, e.geom, pd.cost, pd.node
INTO ch16.dijkstra_result
FROM
    pgr_Dijkstra(
        'SELECT gid AS id, source, target, length As cost
        FROM ch16.twin_cities',                    ◁
        (SELECT id                                      ❶ Network
          FROM ch16.twin_cities_vertices_pgr              query
          ORDER BY the_geom <-> ST_SetSRID(ST_Point(-93.8,45.2),4326)
          LIMIT 1
          ),           ◁───────── ❷ Source node
        (SELECT id
          FROM ch16.twin_cities_vertices_pgr
          ORDER BY the_geom <-> ST_SetSRID(ST_Point(-93.2,44.6),4326)
          LIMIT 1
          ),                      ◁─────────── ❸ Target node
        directed =>false          ◁
    ) As pd                ◁────────┐  ❹ Not directed
    LEFT JOIN                       │
    ch16.twin_cities As e        Alias the output
    ON pd.edge = e.gid           of dijkstra as pd.
ORDER BY pd.seq;
```

pgr_dijkstra takes as input SQL for a query that defines the network to route with the following columns: id (an edge id), source (origin) node, target (destination) node, and cost ❶. If directed is set to true ❹, the query must have an additional reverse_cost column. Directed means that the cost of travel from source node to target node can be different from target note to source node. This listing sets directed to false thus treating all roads as two-way and speed in either direction as the same.

Most common variants of pgRouting functions expect nodes to be input as integers. These nodes are defined in the _vertices_pgr tables created by the pgr_Create-Topology function. You will most often know your desired points by some location on a map and translate a lon/lat location into a node identifier by looking up the closest node to our points of interest. In our case, the source node is on Interstate 35, south of the city ❷, and the target node is on Interstate 94, northwest of the city ❸. directed defaults to true if not specified.

There are many variants of the pgr_dijkstra function. In order to keep the various versions straight, it often helps to express arguments by name, as is done for directed ❹. There is one variant that takes many nodes, and you can compute multiple trips at once.

Dijkstra's algorithm is merely one of many algorithms available in pgRouting for routing. To see the ever-growing list of algorithms available (or to contribute your own), visit the pgRouting documentation (https://docs.pgrouting.org/).

TIP   For large networks, don't forget to add spatial indexes to your table prior to executing any algorithms.

The shortest-route problem is a general class of cost-minimizing or profit-maximizing problems. What you define as cost or profit is entirely up to you. Don't limit yourself to traditional measures. Be creative. For example, you can easily download a table of calories from your local McDonald's, group the food items into sandwiches, drinks, and sides, and query for the least fattening meal you can consume, provided that you must order something from each group—the McRouting problem.

TRAVELING SALESPERSON

Many times in our programming ventures, we've come across the need to find solutions to variations on the traveling salesperson problem (TSP). Often we've given up because nothing was easy to integrate. Although algorithms are available in many languages, setting up a network and pairing the algorithm with whichever database we were using at the time was much too tedious. We frequently resorted to suboptimal SQL-based solutions. How often we hoped that something like pgRouting would come along!

The classic description of a TSP problem involves a salesperson having to visit a wide array of cities to sell widgets. Given that the salesperson has to visit each city only once, what is the optimal itinerary to minimize the total distance traveled?

To demonstrate TSP using pgRouting, imagine you're on a team of inspectors from the International Atomic Energy Agency (IAEA), the United Nations' nuclear energy watchdog, and your task is to inspect all the nuclear plants in Spain. A quick search on Wikipedia (circa 2011) shows that seven plants are operational on the entire Iberian Peninsula.

You can create a new table as follows:

```
CREATE TABLE spain_nuclear_plants(
    id serial,
    plant varchar(150),
    lat double precision,
    lon double precision
);
```

This populated table is included as part of the data you've loaded for this chapter.

PgRouting offers two variants of TSP: pgr_tsp takes a cost matrix, and pgr_tsp-Euclidean assumes a cost matrix based on distance. Listing 16.3 demonstrates the simplest form pgr_tspEuclidean. For pgr_tspEuclidean you need your table to have X and Y coordinates (longitude and latitude will do). Each row will represent a node that the nuclear inspectors must visit. Another requirement of the TSP function is that each node must be identified using an integer identifier. For this reason, the table includes an ID column and assigns each plant a number from 1 to 7.

With all these pieces in place, you can execute the TSP function in the following listing.

Listing 16.3   Traveling to nuclear power plants in Spain using TSP

```
SELECT t.seq, t.node, p.plant,
    t.cost::numeric(10,4), t.agg_cost::numeric(10,4)
FROM
    pgr_TSPEuclidean(
        'SELECT id , lon AS x, lat AS y
        FROM ch16.spain_nuclear_plants',        ◁──❶ Locations
        1,      ◁─────────────┐
        7      ◁──────┐    ❷ Start
    ) As t           ❸ End
    INNER JOIN
    ch16.spain_nuclear_plants As p
    ON t.node = p.id    ◁──────┐   Rejoin with
ORDER BY seq;                  ❹   ch16.spain_nuclear_plants.
```

The TSP function call in listing 16.3 is a little unusual in that the first parameter is an SQL string ❶. This string must return a set of records with the columns id, x, and y: id is the site identifier, and x and y are the geographic coordinates. The output of the SQL statement must always have at least these columns with these column names, but it can have additional columns. Additional columns will be ignored.

The second parameter of 1 (Alamaraz) is the identifier of the site to start at ❷. You can provide an optional ending node if you don't want your trip to start and end in the same spot. In this example, the ending node is set to 7, Vendellios ❸.

The TSP function is a set-returning function that returns a table consisting of four fields: seq, node, cost, and agg_cost. The seq is the order of travel, node is the ID of the site based on the input locations table, cost provides the cost from the current node to the next node, and agg_cost provides the cumulative cost up to this point of the trip. You rejoin by plant id with the node to get the plant names ❹.

The results follow:

```
seq | node |          plant          |  cost  |  agg_cost
-----+------+-------------------------+--------+----------
  1 |    1 | Almaraz                 | 3.8449 |   0.0000
  2 |    5 | Santa Maria de Garona   | 2.1616 |   3.8449
  3 |    6 | Trillo                  | 0.4538 |   6.0065
  4 |    4 | Jose Cabrera            | 2.0950 |   6.4604
  5 |    3 | Cofrentes               | 2.5441 |   8.5554
  6 |    2 | Asco                    | 0.3135 |  11.0995
  7 |    7 | Vandellios              | 6.6256 |  11.4131
  8 |    1 | Almaraz                 | 0.0000 |  18.0386
(8 rows)
```

The visual representation of these results is shown in figure 16.2.

Because we provided a table of geographic locations and don't have a cost matrix readily available, we used the pgRouting pgr_TSPEuclidean function, which uses Euclidean math to compute a distance matrix for each combination. If you don't want Euclidean distance and prefer using a true distance, you could provide a distance matrix populated with a cost for each site-to-site pairing. If you want your cost matrix to be based

Nuclear power plants in Spain

Figure 16.2   Traveling to nuclear power plants in Spain

on your existing network data, you can use the helper function `pgr_dijkstraCost-Matrix` to compute a distance matrix based on Dijkstra's algorithm calculations.

This section has illustrated the convenience of pairing a problem-solving algorithm with a database. Imagine that you had to solve the shortest route or TSP problem on some set of data using just a conventional programming language. Without PostGIS or pgRouting, you'd have to define your own data structure, code the algorithm, and find a nice way to present the solution. Should the nature of your data change, you'd have to repeat the process.

If you have data involving trajectories, such as GPS tracks, truck routing, and so forth, you should also check out an extension called MobilityDB (https://github .com/MobilityDB/MobilityDB). MobilityDB is a PostgreSQL extension that builds on top of PostGIS and can also use pgRouting. It introduces new data types, `tgeompoint` and `tgeogpoint`, for compactly storing geospatial movement data like GPS tracts, and adds types that extend PostgreSQL temporal data types—`period`, `timestampset`, and `periodset`. Together these allow for analyses such as the speed of a trajectory or moments of time when a trajectory is above or below a specific speed. You can use the QGIS time controller plugin to see trajectories in motion.

In the next sections we'll explore PL languages. The marriage of PL languages and SQL combines the expressiveness of an all-purpose or domain-specific language suited for certain classes of problems with the power of SQL.

16.2   Extending PostgreSQL with PLs

One thing that makes PostgreSQL unique among the various relational databases is its pluggable procedural language (PL) architecture. Many Samaritans have created PL handlers for PostgreSQL, allowing you to write database stored functions in languages like Perl, Python, Java, TCL, R, JavaScript, Lua, Julia, and Sh (shell script), in addition to the built-in C, PL/pgSQL, and SQL.

Stored functions are directly callable from SQL statements. This means several things:

- You can write stored functions in a language more suited for a particular task, or a language that you're well versed in.
- You can perform certain tasks much more easily than you would if you had to extract the data, import it into these language environments, and push it back into the database.
- You can write aggregate functions and triggers, and use functions developed for these languages right in your database.
- You can use various functions together in a single SQL query, even if the functions are written in different languages.
- The code you'd write to define the PL function is pretty much the same as you'd normally write in the language, except for the additional hooks into the PostgreSQL database.

These PL languages are prefixed with *PL*: PL/Perl, PL/Python, PL/Proxy, PL/R, PL/Sh, PL/Java, PL/V8. The list of PLs is growing.

16.2.1 *Basic installation of PLs*

In order to use each non-built-in PL language in your database, there are three prerequisites:

- The language environment must be installed on your PostgreSQL server.
- The PL handler library (which generally starts with the filename prefix *pl* and has the suffix *.so* or *.dll*) must be installed in your PostgreSQL instance.
- The language handler must be installed in the databases you'll use them in. You install these languages using CREATE EXTENSION name-of-language;.

The functionality of a PL extension is usually packaged as a .so or .dll file whose filename starts with pl*. It negotiates the interaction between PostgreSQL and the language environment by converting PostgreSQL data sets and data types into the most appropriate data structure for that language environment. It also handles the conversion back to a PostgreSQL data type when the function returns with a record set or scalar value.

16.2.2 *What you can do with PLs*

Each PL achieves varying degrees of integration with the PostgreSQL environment. PL/Perl is the oldest and probably the most common and most tested PL you'll find.

PLs are often registered in two flavors: *trusted* and *untrusted*. PL/Perl can be registered as both trusted and untrusted. PL/V8 offers just the trusted variant. Most of the other PLs you'll come across offer just the untrusted variant.

In the sections that follow, you'll use PL/Python, PL/R, and PL/V8. We've chosen two untrusted languages, PL/Python and PL/R, because they have the largest spatial

What's the difference between trusted and untrusted?

A trusted PL is a sandboxed PL, meaning provisions have been made to prevent it from accessing other parts of the OS outside the database cluster. A trusted language function can run under the context of a non-superuser, but certain features of the language are disabled.

An untrusted language is one that can potentially wreak havoc on the server, so great care must be taken. It can delete files, execute processes, and do all the things that the PostgreSQL daemon/service account has the power to do. Untrusted language functions must run in the context of a superuser, which also means that you must be a superuser to create them. To permit non-superusers to execute the functions, you must mark the functions as `SECURITY DEFINER`.

package offerings. We've chosen the trusted language PL/V8 because there are tons of JavaScript packages available and PL/V8 provides high-performance numeric-crunching capabilities. We also think they're pretty cool languages in their own right. They're favorites among geostatisticians and GIS programmers.

Python is a dynamically typed, all-purpose procedural language. It has elegant approaches for creating and navigating objects, and supports functional programming, object-oriented programming, the building of classes, metaprogramming, reflection, map reduce, and all those chic programming paradigms you've probably heard of. Python also has one of the largest sets of libraries for data analysis, so it is a popular option for data scientists and machine learning developers.

R, on the other hand, is more of a domain language. R is specifically designed for statistics, graphing, and data mining, so it draws a large following from research institutions. It has many built-in statistical functions or functions you can download and install via the built-in package manager. You'll be hard-pressed to find R functionality in other FOSS languages; we've seen them in pricy tools such as SAS, MATLAB, and Mathematica. You'll find that tasks such as applying functions to all items in a list and matrix algebra operations will become second nature once you get into the R mindset. In addition to manipulating data, R packs a graphical engine that allows you to generate polished graphs with only a few lines of code. You can even plot in 3D.

Using in-database PLs that can call out to external environments, such as PL/R and PL/Python, has many advantages over writing similar logic outside of the database. Here are a few that come to mind:

- You can write functions in PLs that pull data from the PostgreSQL environment without any messy database connection setup and have them return sets of records, or update sets of records. You can also return scalars.
- You can write database triggers in PLs that use the power of these environments to run tasks in response to changes of data in the database. For example, you can geocode data when an address changes or have a database trigger regenerate a map tile on a change of data in the database without ever touching the

application code. This is impossible to accomplish with just the languages and a database connection driver.

- You can write aggregate functions with these languages that will allow you to pass in a set of rows to an aggregate function that in turn uses functions available only in these languages to summarize the data. Imagine an aggregation function that returns a graph for each grouping of data, all done with a single SELECT query.

Our ensuing examples will only have a slight GIS bent. Our intent here is to show you how to get started integrating these in your PostgreSQL database and give you a general feel of what's possible with these languages. We'll also show how you can find and install libraries that can expand PLs.

16.3   PL/R

PL/R is a PL using the R statistical language and graphical environment. You can tap into the vast statistical packages that R provides, as well as the numerous geospatial add-ons. R is a darling among statisticians and researchers because operations can be applied to an entire matrix of data just as easily as to a single value. Its built-in graphing environments mean you need not resort to yet another software package. R also supports data imports from a variety of formats.

We'll just touch the surface of what PL/R and R can do here. To explore further, we suggest reading *R in Action, Third Edition* by Robert I. Kabacoff (Manning, 2021) or *Applied Spatial Data Analysis with R* by Roger Bivand, Edzer Pebesma, and V. Gómez-Rubio (Springer, 2013). Appendix A also provides more links to useful R sites.

For what follows, we used R 3.4.4 on an Ubuntu 18.04 server. Most of our examples should work on earlier versions as well.

16.3.1   Getting started with PL/R

To set up PostgreSQL for R, do the following:

1 Install the R environment on the same computer as PostgreSQL. R is available for Unix, Linux, macOS, and Windows. Unix/Linux users may need to compile PL/R, but for Windows and macOS users there are precompiled binaries. You can download source and precompiled binaries of R from www.r-project.org. Any R version 3.0 or higher should work with these examples.

PL/R also assumes that the R libraries and the R binaries are in the environment path setting of the server.

If you're running a 64-bit version of PostgreSQL, you'll need a 64-bit version of R. For PostgreSQL 32-bit, you'll need to run a 32-bit version of R, even if you're running on a 64-bit OS.

2 Compile the source or download binaries via Package, and then install the plr library by copying it into the lib directory of your PostgreSQL install. If you're

using an installer, this will probably already be done for you. If you're running under Linux, R should be configured with the option -enable-R-shlib. As with other PostgreSQL extensions, you must use the plr library version compiled for your version of PostgreSQL. However, the same R version can be used for multiple PostgreSQL versions as long as you pair R 64-bit with a PostgreSQL 64-bit or R 32-bit with a PostgreSQL 32-bit. You can download the binaries and source from www.joeconway.com/plr. You may need to restart the PostgreSQL service before you can use PL/R in a database.

Debian/Ubuntu users can install via apt.postgresql.org using the following command and replacing the 12 with your version of PostgreSQL. This should install both PL/R and the R environment:

```
apt install postgresql-12-plr
```

In the database where you'll be writing R stored functions, run the SQL command CREATE EXTENSION plr;. You need to repeat this step for each database you want to use R in. Keep in mind that language extensions need to be installed by a superuser.

PL/R relies on an environment variable called R_HOME to point to the location of the R install. The R_HOME variable must also be accessible by the postgres service account. After the install, check that R_HOME is specified correctly by running the following command: SELECT * FROM plr_environ();. This should already be set for you if you're using an installer. If you're a Linux/Unix user, you can set this with export R_HOME = ... and include it as part of your PostgreSQL initialization script. You may need to restart your Postgres services for the new settings to take effect.

If any of this is confusing or you get stuck, check out the PL/R wiki installation tips guides at https://github.com/postgres-plr/plr/blob/master/userguide.md#installation.

16.3.2 *What you can do with PL/R*

Now let's take PL/R for a test drive. PL/R has many libraries for data analysis, and you will learn some features, but keep in mind that this is just a small subset. You'll learn how to save data both to R data format and back to PostgreSQL. You'll also learn how to build charts with PL/R.

SAVING POSTGRESQL DATA TO THE R DATA FORMAT

For this first example, you'll pull data out of PostgreSQL and save it to R's custom binary format (RData). There are two common reasons to do this:

- It makes it easy to interactively test different plotting styles and other R functions in R's interactive environment against real data before you package them in a PL/R function.
- If you're providing sample data sets, you may want to provide your data sets in a format that can be easily loaded R by users.

Listing 16.4 uses the PostgreSQL pg.spi.exec function and R's save function.

The `pg.spi.exec` function is a PL function that allows you to convert any PostgreSQL data set into a form that can be consumed by the language environment. In the case of PL/R, this is usually an R `data.frame` type structure.

The `save` command in R allows you to save many objects to a single binary file, as shown in listing 16.4. These objects can be data frames (including spatial data frames), lists, matrices, vectors, scalars, and all of the various object types supported by R. When you want to load these in an R session, you run the command `load("filepath")`.

Listing 16.4 Saving PostgreSQL data in an R data format with PL/R

```
CREATE OR REPLACE FUNCTION ch16.save_places_rdata() RETURNS text AS
$$
places_mega <<- pg.spi.exec("
    SELECT name, latitude, longitude FROM ch16.places WHERE megacity = 1
")
nb <<- pg.spi.exec("
    SELECT name, latitude, longitude
    FROM ch16.places
    WHERE ST_DWithin(geog,ST_GeogFromText('POINT(7.5 9.0)'),1000000)
")
save(places_mega, nb, file="/tmp/places.RData")
return("done")
$$
LANGUAGE 'plr';
```

❶ Store big cities in an R variable.

❷ Store places within distance of a point in an R variable.

❸ Save R variables to an R data file.

In listing 16.4 you create two data sets that contain world places: one based on attributes ❶ and one based on proximity to a PostGIS geography point ❷. You then save this to a file called places.RData ❸. *RData* is the standard suffix for the binary R data format, and in most desktop installs, when you launch it, it will open R with the data.

To run this example, run `SELECT ch16.save_places_rdata();`.

You can load this saved data in R by clicking the file or by opening R and running a load call in R. If you are on a Linux shell, you can start R by typing in R, in capitals.

Table 16.1 lists some quick commands you can try in the R environment.

Table 16.1 Some R commands

Description	Command
Load a file in R and clear all variables in memory.	`rm(list=ls())` and then `load("/tmp/places.RData")`
List contents loaded in memory in R.	`ls()`
View a data structure in R.	`summary(places_mega)`
View data in R.	`nb`
View a set of rows in an R variable.	`places_mega[1:3,]`
View columns of data in an R variable.	`places_mega[1:4,]$name`

If you append <- to a command, the output goes to an R variable instead of being printed to the screen. Figure 16.3 shows a snapshot of these commands.

```
> rm(list=ls())
> load("C:/Temp/places.RData")
> ls()
[1] "nb"          "places_mega"
> summary(places_mega)
     name                latitude            longitude
 Length:45         Min.    :-37.820    Min.    :-123.12
 Class :character  1st Qu.:  6.132    1st Qu.: -17.47
 Mode  :character  Median : 23.723    Median :  18.43
                   Mean    : 19.987    Mean    :  14.92
                   3rd Qu.: 39.927    3rd Qu.:  47.98
                   Max.    : 60.176    Max.    : 174.76
> nb
         name    latitude   longitude
1   Porto-Novo  6.4833110   2.6166255
2         Lome  6.1319371   1.2227571
3       Niamey 13.5167060   2.1166560
4        Abuja  9.0033331   7.5333280
5     Ndjamena 12.1130965  15.0491483
6       Malabo  3.7500153   8.7832775
7   Libreville  0.3853886   9.4579650
8      Yaounde  3.8667007  11.5166508
9      Cotonou  6.4000086   2.5199906
10    Sao Tome  0.3334021   6.7333252
11       Accra  5.5500346  -0.2167157
12       Lagos  6.4432617   3.3915311
> places_mega[1:3,]
          name   latitude  longitude
1       Kigali   -1.95359   30.06053
2        Kyoto   35.02999  135.75000
3   Montevideo  -34.85804  -56.17105
> places_mega[1:4,]$name
[1] "Kigali"     "Kyoto"          "Montevideo" "Lome"
>  |
```

Figure 16.3 Output of running the table 16.1 statements in R

DRAWING PLOTS WITH PL/R

R excels in plotting. Many people, even those who could care less about statistics, are attracted to R by its sophisticated scriptable plotting and graphing environment. The following listing demonstrates this by generating a random data set in PostgreSQL and plotting it.

Listing 16.5 Plotting PostgreSQL data with R using PL/R

```
CREATE OR REPLACE FUNCTION ch16.graph_income_house() RETURNS text AS
$$
randdata <<- pg.spi.exec("
    SELECT x As income,AVG(x*(1+random()*y)) As avgprice
    FROM
```

```
          generate_series(2000,100000,10000) As x
          CROSS JOIN
          generate_series(1,5) As y
     GROUP BY x
     ORDER BY x                  ❶  Create
")                                   random data.                    ❷  Create a PNG file.
png('/tmp/housepercap.png',width=500,height=400)                     ❸  Set the
opar <- par(bg="white")                                                 background.
plot(x=randdata$income,y=randdata$avgprice,ann=FALSE,type="n")  --
yrange = range(randdata$avgprice)                                    ❹  Draw a
abline(                                                                 plot.
     h=seq(yrange[1],yrange[2],(yrange[2]-yrange[1])/10),
     lty=1,col="grey"                                               ❺  Prep the
) --                                                                   plot space.
lines(x=randdata$income,y=randdata$avgprice,col="green4",  --       ❻  Draw grid lines.
     lty="dotted")
points(x=randdata$income,y=randdata$avgprice,bg="limegreen",pch=23) --
title(
     main="Random plot of house price vs. per capita income",
     xlab="Per cap income",ylab="Average House Price",             Draw
     col.main="blue",col.lab="red1",font.main=4,font.lab=3         points.  ❼
)
dev.off() --         ⇠──❽  Close file
return("done")
$$
LANGUAGE 'plr';
```

This code creates a stored function written in PL/R that will create a file called house-percap.png in the /tmp folder of the PostgreSQL server. If your PostgreSQL is on Windows use C:/temp or some other Windows path instead. It first creates random data by running an SQL statement using the PostgreSQL generate_series function and dumps this into an R variable called randdata ❶.

Then it creates a PNG file using the R png function (note that other functions such as pdf, jpeg, and the like can be used to create other formats), which all the plotting will be redirected to ❷. Then it sets the background color to white using the par parameter-setting function ❸. Next it draws the plot ❹. The n type means there is no plot; it just prepares the plot space so that you can then draw grid lines ❺, lines ❻, and points ❼ on the same grid.

Finally, you close writing to the file with dev.off() ❽ and then return some text saying done.

Unable to start device devWindows

It's common to get a "can't start device" error, even though the same command runs perfectly fine in the R GUI environment. This is because PL/R runs in the context of the postgres service account. Any folder you wish to write to from PL/R must have read/write access from the postgres service/daemon account.

Run the function in listing 16.5 with the following SQL statement:

```
SELECT ch16.graph_income_house();
```

Running this command generates a PNG file, as shown in figure 16.4.

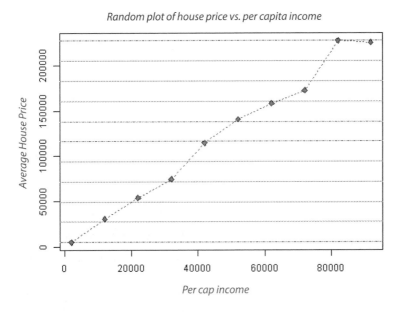

Figure 16.4 Result of `SELECT ch16.graph_income_house()`

16.3.3 *Using R packages in PL/R*

The R environment has a gamut of functions, data, and data types you can download and install. They're distributed in packages and are often referred to as *libraries*.

You can see all installed packages in the library folder of your R installation. R also makes finding, downloading, and installing additional libraries easy using the Comprehensive R Archive Network (CRAN). Once a package is installed, you can use its components in PL/R functions.

What's particularly instructive with R is that many packages come with demos showcasing features. They also often come with something called *vignettes*, which are quick tutorials on using a package. Demos and vignettes make R a fun, interactive learning environment. In order to use a vignette or demo, you first have to use the library command to load the library. The commands to load and view these packages are listed in table 16.2.

Table 16.2   Commands for installing and navigating packages

Command	Description
`library()`	Displays a list of packages already installed
`library(package-name)`	Loads a package into memory
`update.packages()`	Upgrades all packages to the latest versions
`install.packages("package-name")`	Installs a new package
`available.packages()`	Lists packages available in default CRAN
`chooseCRANmirror()`	Allows you to switch to a different CRAN
`demo()`	Shows a list of demos in loaded packages
`demo(package = .packages(all .available = TRUE))`	Lists all demos in installed packages
`demo(name-of-demo)`	Launches a demo (you must load the package first)
`help(package=some-package-name)`	Gives summary help for a package
`help(package=package-name,function-name)`	Gives detailed help for an item in a package
`vignette()`	Lists tutorials in packages
`vignette("name-of-vignette")`	Launches a PDF of exercises

In order to test the CRAN install process, we'll install two packages: *sp* (https://cran.r-project.org/web/packages/sp/index.html), which provides spatial classes for R data, such as spatial data frames and charting functionality, and another called *rgeos* bindings (https://cran.r-project.org/web/packages/rgeos/index.html), which provides GEOS functions such as conversion and spatial predicate functions in R. Recall that the GEOS library is one that PostGIS leverages for many of its spatial functions.

To install packages in R, you can use the R command line or the graphical R interface, Rgui. For this example, we'll use the command line.

To enter the R console, type R at a command line. Then enter the following command to load the sp library:

```
library(sp)
```

If that command fails, use the following commands to install sp and then load it:

```
install.packages("sp")
library(sp)
```

After installing sp in R, you may have to exit R and come back in to run any commands.

To get help with the sp library, run this command:

```
help(package=sp)
```

To quit the R console, enter this command:

```
q()
```

Repeat the same steps for rgeos:

```
install.packages("rgeos")
library(rgeos)
```

If you run into errors installing rgeos (it might give you a "can't find geos-config" error), you will need to install the GEOS development C++ package. On Ubuntu/ Debian this is done as follows from the OS command prompt:

```
apt instal libgeos-dev
```

Once the GEOS dev package is installed, connect back to the R shell and repeat the rgeos install steps. Once rgeos is installed and loaded, you can verify the version of GEOS you're running with:

```
version_GEOS()
```

That command should output something like this:

```
[1] "3.7.1-CAPI-1.11.1"
attr(,"rev")
[1] "27a5e771"
```

Restart after installing packages

For this particular installation and some more complex packages, you may need to restart R before you can use the libraries. To use these libraries from PL/R, you also need to restart the PostgreSQL service. These steps aren't necessary for all R packages.

Next you'll test-drive the sp and rgeos installations by writing a PL/R function calling their functions.

16.3.4 Converting geometries into R spatial objects and plotting spatial objects

The sp package contains classes to represent geometries as R objects. It has lines, polygons, and points. It also has spatial polygon, line, and point data frames. Data frames are similar to PostgreSQL tables with geometry columns.

The rgeos package is an R wrapper for the GEOS library, which is the same library that PostGIS relies on. One of the functions exposed by rgeos is called readWKT, and it converts a well-known text (WKT) representation to an sp geometry. In the next example, we'll combine sp and rgeos to convert PostGIS geometries into a form that can be charted in R.

In the next listing, you'll convert the previous pgRouting results for the Twin Cities into R spatial objects and then plot them directly in R.

Listing 16.6   Plotting linestrings with R

```
CREATE OR REPLACE FUNCTION ch16.plot_routing_results()
RETURNS text AS
$$
library(sp)
library(rgeos)
geodata <<- pg.spi.exec("
    SELECT gid, route, ST_AsText(geom) As geomwkt
    FROM ch16.twin_cities
    ORDER BY gid
")
ngeom <- length(geodata$gid)
row.names(geodata) = geodata$gid
for (i in 1:ngeom) {
    if (i == 1) {
        geo.sp = readWKT(geodata$geomwkt[i],geodata$gid[i])
    }
    else {
        geo.sp = rbind(
            geo.sp,readWKT(geodata$geomwkt[i],geodata$gid[i])
        )
    }
}
sdf <- SpatialLinesDataFrame(geo.sp, geodata[-3])
georesult <<- pg.spi.exec("
    SELECT ST_AsText(ST_LineMerge(ST_Collect(geom))) As geomwkt
    FROM ch16.dijkstra_result
")

sdf_result <- SpatialLinesDataFrame(
    readWKT(georesult$geomwkt[1],"result"),
    data = data.frame(c("result")),
    match.ID=FALSE
)
png('/tmp/twin_bestpath.png',width=500,height=400)
plot(sdf,xlim=c(-94,-93),ylim=c(44.5,45.5),axes=TRUE);
lines(sdf_result,col="green4",lty="dashed",type="o")
title(
    main="Travel options to Twin Cities",font.main=4,col.main="red",
    xlab="Longitude",ylab="Latitude"
)
dev.off()
return("done")
$$
LANGUAGE plr VOLATILE;
```

Callouts:
- **Create an R data frame with a column for WKT of the highway.**
- **Convert the WKT linestring to an sp line by looping thru each geometry.**
- **Save the first linestring as an sp line.**
- **Append subsequent linestrings to make an sp multilinestring.**
- **End looping multilinestring.**
- **Collect the result as a single geometry.**
- **Store wkt in an R variable called georesult.**
- **Convert to SpatialLinesDataFrame with id=result.**
- **Create a PNG file for plotting.**
- **Plot highways with lon/lat axis.**
- **Plot Dijkstra solution from pgRouting example.**
- **Add captions.**

To run the function created in listing 16.6, do the following:

```
SELECT ch16.plot_routing_results();.
```

Figure 16.5 shows the result of running this query.

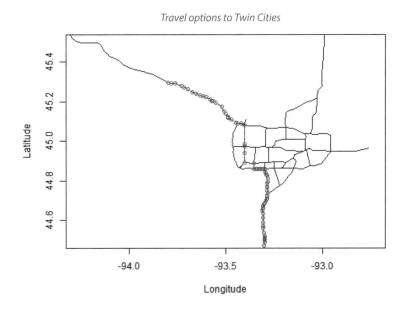

Figure 16.5   PgRouting Twin Cities results plotted with PL/R

The sp package has its own plot function as well, called `spplot`, which was designed with spatial data in mind and has niceties beyond the basic R plot. We encourage you to check out the demo by running the following commands from the R console:

```
library(sp)
demo(gallery)
```

16.3.5 *Outputting plots as binaries*

In the previous plotting examples, you generated the plot and manually saved it in a graphics format. If, however, you need to send the plot to a web browser, you'll need to output the file directly from the query. We're aware of three ways you can do this.

The first approach uses RGtk2 and a Cairo device, and you output a graph as a byte array. This approach is documented on the PL/R wiki and requires installing both the RGtk2 and Cairo libraries. Both libraries are large and require the installation of yet another graphical toolkit called GTK. For us, experimenting on Windows, loading the library often fails inexplicably. Of course, YMMV. This approach does generate nicer-looking graphics and avoids the need to temporarily save to disk. It's a self-contained, single-step process.

The next approach is to save the file to disk and let PostgreSQL read the file from disk. There's a superuser function in PostgreSQL called `pg_read_binary_file` and its older text-outputting sibling `pg_read_file`, but they're limited to reading files from the PostgreSQL data cluster. To implement this approach, we created a tablespace to hold all R-generated files and then used `pg_read_binary_file`.

Finally, you can use a PL language with more generalized access to the filesystem, such as PL/Python or PL/Perl. Doing so does require the extra step of wrapping your PL/R function in a PL function of another language.

16.4   *PL/Python*

Python is another favored language of GIS analysts and programmers. These days, most popular GIS toolkits have Python bindings. You'll see its use in open source GIS desktop and web suites such as QGIS, Jupyter, OpenJUMP, and GeoDjango, and even in commercial GIS systems such as Safe FME and ArcGIS.

PL/Python is the procedural language handler in PostgreSQL that allows you to call Python libraries and embed Python classes and functions right into a PostgreSQL database. A PL/Python stored function can be called in any SQL statement. You can even create aggregate functions and database triggers with Python. In this section we'll show you some of the highlights of PL/Python.

16.4.1   *Installing PL/Python*

For the most part, you can use any feature of Python from within PL/Python. This is because the PostgreSQL PL/Python handler is a thin wrapper that only marshals messaging between PostgreSQL and the native Python environment. Any Python package you install can be accessed from your PL/Python stored functions. Unfortunately, not all mappings from database data types to PL/Python objects are supported. This means you can't return a complex Python object back to PostgreSQL unless it can be easily coerced into a custom PostgreSQL data type.

In order to use PL/Python, you must have Python installed on your PostgreSQL machine. Because PL/Python runs within the server, any client connecting to it, such as a web application or a client PC, need not have Python installed to be able to use PostgreSQL functions written in PL/Python.

The precompiled PostgreSQL PL/Python libraries packaged with most newer PostgreSQL distributions are compiled against Python 3.7 or higher. Plpython2u is deprecated in PostgreSQL 13 and above. The Python 2 series has also reached end of life for the Python project. As such, we will not cover plpython2u. If you're using PL/Python 3 (plpython3u), you'll need a Python 3 major version. Python language extensions work only with the Python minor version they were compiled against, so if your PL/Python is compiled with Python 3.8, then you need 3.8, and so on.

If you're running a 64-bit version of PostgreSQL, you'll need a 64-bit version of Python. For a 32-bit version of PostgreSQL, you'll need to run a 32-bit version of Python, even if you're running on a 64-bit OS.

If you're using the PostgreSQL Yum repository (http://yum.postgresql.org) for the PostgreSQL installation, install PL/Python with the following command from the OS:

```
yum install postgresql12-plpython3
```

Similarly, the PostgreSQL Apt repository (http://wiki.postgresql.org/wiki/Apt) has packages for Ubuntu and Debian users:

```
apt install postgresql-plpython3-12
```

Once you have Python and the plpython files installed on your server, execute the following command to enable the language in your database:

```
CREATE EXTENSION plpython3u;
```

If you run into problems enabling PL/Python, refer to our PL/Python help links in appendix A. The most common issue people face is that the required version of Python isn't installed on the server, or the plpython.so or plpython.dll file is missing.

NOTE Although Python 3 is not generally backward-compatible with older versions, it doesn't hurt to try. The examples we have in this chapter all use plpython3u, but if you only have plpython2u (plpythonu), replace plpython3u and see if PostgreSQL accepts your function.

Although it's possible to have both plpython2u and plpython3u installed in the same database, you can't run functions written in both during the same database session because of global name conflicts.

16.4.2 *Writing a PL/Python function*

Because PL/Python is an untrusted language, it can interact with the filesystem of the OS. PL/Python has plenty of file and network management functions for you to use.

PostGIS raster can output rasters in numerous formats, but the stock PL/pgSQL won't allow you to save them to the filesystem. The next listing uses PL/Python to save a binary BLOB generated from a raster.

Listing 16.7 Saving binary files to disk

```
CREATE OR REPLACE FUNCTION ch16.write_bin_file(
    param_bytes bytea,
    param_filename text
)
RETURNS text AS
$$
f = open('/tmp/' + param_filename, 'wb+')          ⟵┐ Open file for binary write
f.write(param_bytes)        ⟵┐ Write bytes
f.close()
return param_filename       ⟵┐ Return filename
$$ LANGUAGE plpython3u VOLATILE;
```

To use this function, call it with any raster output format function, such as ST_AsPNG or ST_AsJPEG:

```
SELECT
    ch16.write_bin_file(
        ST_AsPNG(ST_AsRaster(ST_Collect(geom),300,300,'8BUI')),
        'dijkstra_result.png'
    )
FROM ch16.dijkstra_result;
```

The preceding code outputs the content of the byte array to the folder specified.

Although we're demonstrating with raster outputs, you can use PL/Python to output any document stored in the database. You can even write a query that selects records from a table holding documents, generating a separate file for each record. See the following example:

```
SELECT write_bin_file(doc_obj,doc_file_name) FROM documents;
```

> **NOTE**   It is possible to use SQL or PL/pgSQL to import and export files using PostgreSQL large object storage. The SQL approach is covered in the "Outputting Rasters with PSQL" section of the PostGIS manual (http://mng.bz/XYql).

16.4.3 *Using Python packages*

The standard Python installation comes with no frills. What makes Python so versatile is the wide array of packages that can handle anything from matrix manipulation to web service integration. A common way to install Python packages is to use pip or pip3, which you'll see later. Some packages are not available via pip. In chapter 5, which covered Jupyter, you used the Anaconda package manager, which installed packages using conda.

A good starting point for uncovering the available packages is the Python Cheese-Shop package repository. You'll first need to install a tool called *Easy Install* before you can sample the CheeseShop. Download Easy Install from the Python site (https://pypi.python.org/pypi/setuptools#downloads) or use your Linux repository update.

> **NOTE**   Once installed, the easy_install.exe file is located in the C:\Python32\ scripts folder for Windows users.

Let's now try installing some packages and creating Python functions that use them.

IMPORTING AN EXCEL FILE WITH PL/PYTHON

For this example, you'll use the xlrd package, which will allow you to read Excel files in any OS. Grab this from the CheeseShop at http://pypi.python.org/pypi/xlrd.

Prior to installing xlrd, make sure you've already installed Easy Install. Then, from the OS command line, execute easy_install xlrd. (If you're on Windows, xlrd comes with a setup.exe file that lets you bypass using Easy Install.)

Listing 16.8 tests your installation by importing a test.xls file that has a header row and three columns of data. Versions of PostgreSQL prior to PostgreSQL 9.0 didn't support SQL OUT parameters for PL/Python, but PostgreSQL 9.0+ offers the same OUT parameter functionality that PL/pgSQL has had for much longer. This allows you to return SETOF records from PL/Python and define the columns of the result set with OUT parameters, rather than having to first CREATE TYPE and return SET OF whatever type.

Listing 16.8   Reading an Excel file of points

```
CREATE OR REPLACE FUNCTION ch16.fngetxlspts(
    param_filename text,
    OUT place text, OUT lon float, OUT lat float
)
RETURNS SETOF RECORD AS                    ❶ Import
$$                                            package
import xlrd                          ◄─
book = xlrd.open_workbook(param_filename)  ❷ Skip
sh = book.sheet_by_index(0)                   headers
for rx in range(1,sh.nrows):         ◄─
yield(
    sh.cell_value(rowx=rx,colx=0),   ❸ Append
    sh.cell_value(rowx=rx,colx=1),      to result
    sh.cell_value(rowx=rx,colx=2)
)
$$
LANGUAGE plpython3u VOLATILE;
```

You first import the xlrd package so you can use it ❶. For this example, we'll assume there's data in only the first spreadsheet. Next you loop through the rows of the spreadsheet, skipping the first row ❷ and using the Python yield function to append to the result set ❸. In the final yield, the function will return with all the data.

You can query the Excel file as if it were a table:

```
SELECT place, ST_SetSRID(ST_Point(lon,lat),4326) As geom
FROM ch16.fngetxlspts('/tmp/Test.xls') AS foo;
```

The Excel file path has to be accessible by the postgres daemon account because the PL/Python function runs under the context of that account.

IMPORTING SEVERAL EXCEL FILES WITH PL/PYTHON

Now let's imagine you have several Excel files to import. They all have the same structure and all sit in one folder, and you want to import them all in one step.

First you need to create a Python function to list all the files in a directory. Then you'll write another query that treats this list like a table and applies a filter to the list. Finally you'll write one SQL function to insert all the data using this list.

The next listing shows a function that lists the files in a directory path.

Listing 16.9   List files in a directory

```
CREATE FUNCTION ch16.list_files(param_filepath text) RETURNS SETOF text
AS
$$
```

```
import os
return os.listdir(param_filepath)
$$
LANGUAGE 'plpython3u' VOLATILE;
```

The `import os` line in listing 16.9 allows you to run OS commands. PL/Python takes care of converting the Python list object to a PostgreSQL set of text data types.

You can then use the function within a `SELECT` statement, much like you can with any table, applying `LIKE` to the output to further reduce the records returned:

```
SELECT file
FROM ch16.list_files('C:/tmp') As file
WHERE file LIKE '%.xls';
```

The following listing passes this list to the Excel import function to get a distinct set of records.

Listing 16.10   Reading multiple Excel files

```
SELECT DISTINCT pt.place, pt.lon, pt.lat
FROM                                              ❶ List of files
    ch16.list_files('/tmp/') AS file, --
    LATERAL                                          For each file,
    ch16.fngetxlspts('/tmp/' || file) As pt          get records
WHERE file LIKE '%.xls'
                          ❷ Limit file listing
                            to XLS files
```

For each file in your temp directory ❶ that ends with .xls, it's selecting the records, but it's only selecting distinct values across all the files, using the `DISTINCT` SQL predicate.

The `LATERAL` clause allows you to use each filename output in the `fngetxlspts` function so that you get a different set of records for each file. The `LIKE` condition ensures that only files ending in .xls are considered ❷.

16.4.4   *Geocoding example*

PL/Python is a great tool for enabling geocoding within your database using a third-party service such as OpenStreetMap, Google Maps, MapQuest, or Bing Maps. You can find numerous Python packages at the CheeseShop to do just that.

One fine example is the Python geopy package, which you can download from https://pypi.org/project/geopy/. This particular package needs to be installed using pip, a package management system for Python. If you don't have pip installed, you can install it using `apt install python3-pip` (for apt-based systems) or `easy_install pip`. Geopy has support for OpenStreetMap, Nominatim, Google Geocoding API (V3), geocoder.us, Bing Maps API, and Esri ArcGIS. The package supports both Python 2 and Python 3, so if you have Python 2 installed, just change `plpython3u` to `plpythonu` in the code.

In many OSs, both Python2 and Python3 are installed, so you may need to use pip3 instead of `pip` to install:

```
pip3 install geopy
```

Once you have pip installed, you can install geopy from the command line using `pip install geopy`. All the geocoders in geopy return the same output format but take slightly different initializations. The next listing is a wrapper function for the Nominatim geocoder.

Listing 16.11 Geocoder wrapper function

```
CREATE FUNCTION ch16.geopy_geocode(
    param_addr text,
    OUT address text, OUT lon numeric, OUT lat numeric
)                          ⟵──┐ Output
RETURNS record                │ columns
AS
$$                                                         Load
from geopy.geocoders import Nominatim          ⟵───────── OpenStreetMap
geoc = Nominatim(user_agent="postgis_in_action_3rd")       Nominatim class
loc = geoc.geocode(param_addr)                 ⟵─────── Geocode and store
return (loc.address, loc.longitude, loc.latitude)  ⟵──┐  in variables
$$
LANGUAGE plpython3u IMMUTABLE COST 1000;               Return variables in
                                                       OUT parameters
```

Now you can use that function in an SQL statement similar to how you used the TIGER geocoder function:

```
SELECT *
FROM ch16.geopy_geocode(
    '1731 New Hampshire Avenue Northwest, Washington, DC 20010'
);
```

It produces this output:

```
address                     |lon       |lat
----------------------------+----------|---------
New Hampshire Avenu..North..|-77.027...|38.932...
```

If you wanted to use this Nominatim class in Python outside of PostgreSQL, you'd have to take these steps:

1 Establish a connection to your PostgreSQL database with a few lines of Python code and a connection string.
2 Pull the data out of your database.
3 Loop through the database, retrieve the raw address, geocode, and update the database with the coordinates.

By packaging your Python code as a function, you'll never need to leave the environs of PostgreSQL. You can reuse this same function easily in any query. You can even use it in reporting tools that lack access to Python.

16.5 PL/V8: JavaScript in the database

PL/V8 (a.k.a. PL/JavaScript) is a trusted language that's been available for a while in PostgreSQL. Unfortunately, since PostgreSQL 10 many packagers (e.g., Debian, Ubuntu, Heroku) started to drop support for PL/V8. This is because of difficulties building the V8 engine and general V8 project management, as discussed in this thread on GitHub: https://github.com/plv8/plv8/issues/364. As such, there is talk of creating a PL/JavaScript that is not reliant on the V8 engine.

16.5.1 Installing PL/V8

Should your distribution not have PL/V8, you can compile it from source, as described in the PL/V8 project page (https://github.com/plv8/plv8), or you can use pgxnclient (https://pgxn.org/) to build and install.

Here are some features only found in PL/V8:

- You can get away with fewer lines of code to accomplish the same task.
- For folks fluent in JavaScript, you'll feel right at home. You can reuse many existing JavaScript libraries with little or no modification.
- PL/V8 is generally faster for mathematical processing than PL/pgSQL or SQL.
- PL/V8 comes with built-in support for JSON, making it a natural choice for ingesting data from (and sending data to) web applications.
- Because PL/V8 is a trusted language, non-superusers can use it to create functions. This is not the case with PL/Python or PL/R.
- PL/V8 is the only language other than C and PL/R that supports creating window functions. Most languages, including PL/Python and SQL, can create aggregate functions that can be used as window aggregates, but not window functions such as row_number, lead, lag, and rank.

16.5.2 Enabling PL/V8 in a database

Once you've installed the PL/V8 binaries, you need to enable PL/V8 in a database. Connect to your database and run the following SQL statement:

```
CREATE EXTENSION plv8;
```

16.5.3 Using other JavaScript libraries and functions in PL/V8

Perhaps the most compelling reason to use PL/V8 is that you can leverage the vast body of existing JavaScript code simply by cutting and pasting the source code of these functions and libraries. With the preeminence of web technology, there's probably now more JavaScript code in the world than any other language. Many of these functions and libraries can be used without modification.

For a first example, you'll paste in a function called parse_gps from Stack Overflow: "Converting latitude and longitude to decimal values" (http://mng.bz/y9Z7). All you need to do to make it work in PostgreSQL is to wrap a PostgreSQL function body around it. The revised code is shown in the following listing.

Listing 16.12 parse_gps

```
CREATE OR REPLACE FUNCTION ch16.parse_gps(input text)
RETURNS float8[] AS
$$
    if (
        input.indexOf('N') == -1 && input.indexOf('S') == -1 &&
        input.indexOf('W') == -1 && input.indexOf('E') == -1
    ) {
    return input.split(',');
    }
    var parts = input.split(/[°'"]+/).join(' ').split(/[^\w\S]+/);
    var directions = [];
    var coords = [];
    var dd = 0;
    var pow = 0;
    for (i in parts) {
        if (isNaN(parts[i])) {
            var _float = parseFloat( parts[i] );
            var direction = parts[i];
            if (!isNaN(_float)) {
                dd += ( _float / Math.pow( 60, pow++ ) );
                direction = parts[i].replace( _float, '' );
            }
            direction = direction[0];
            if (direction == 'S' || direction == 'W')
                dd *= -1;
                directions[ directions.length ] = direction;
                coords[coords.length] = dd;
                dd = pow = 0;
        }
        else {
            dd += (parseFloat(parts[i]) / Math.pow( 60, pow++));
        }
    }
    if (directions[0] == 'W' || directions[0] == 'E') {
        var tmp = coords[0];
        coords[0] = coords[1];
        coords[1] = tmp;
    }
    return coords;
$$
LANGUAGE plv8;
```

To use the preceding function in an SQL statement, you'd execute it like this:

```
SELECT ch16.parse_gps('36°57''9" N 110°4''21" W') ;
```

That statement outputs {36.9525,-110.0725}.

PL/V8 is a trusted language, so it can't access additional JavaScript libraries on the system. If you're just copying and pasting individual snippets of JavaScript code, this isn't an issue. But entire JavaScript libraries with tens of thousands of lines of code and interdependent functions don't lend themselves to being easily copied and pasted.

To load JavaScript libraries, we use a technique espoused by Andrew Dunstan in his article "Loading Useful Modules in PL/V8" (http://mng.bz/Mg9E). Andrew's approach is to use a table to store these modules as plain text JavaScript. Each row defines a separate module, and the code field contains all the functions in the module. During session startup, you loop through the table and use the PL/V8 `eval` function to create these functions on the fly for each module.

> **WARNING**   We use the terms libraries, modules, and add-ons loosely and synonymously when talking about PL/V8.

For the next example, you'll embed a library called Chance (http://chancejs.com). Chance is a suite of random generator functions useful for generating dummy data for testing.

The first step is to create a table to house the PL/V8 modules:

```
CREATE TABLE ch16.plv8_modules(
    modname text PRIMARY KEY,
    load_on_start boolean,
    code text
);
```

The second step is to load the Chance module into this table as a single-row entry with an SQL INSERT. The following code shows a snippet of the entire SQL. Note that we use $data$ for dollar-quoting the content so we don't need to worry about escaping strings. This record is already loaded as part of this chapter's data:

```
INSERT INTO ch16.plv8_modules(modname,load_on_start,code)
VALUES('chance', true, $data$//  Chance.js 1.0.16
//  http://chancejs.com
//  (c) 2013 Victor Quinn
//  Chance may be freely distributed or modified under the MIT license.

(function () {
:
:$data$)
```

> **NOTE**   If you're wondering how we came up with the SQL INSERT, see the *README* file included with the code downloads for the chapter. There are a few different ways you can generate the insert, depending on your OS and your tools.

The third step is to create a startup function that compiles the module and makes it available as a global PL/V8 object, as shown in the next listing.

Listing 16.13 PL/V8 module compiler and loader

```
CREATE OR REPLACE FUNCTION ch16.plv8_startup()          ❶ Load all the modules
RETURNS void AS                                              marked for loading on
$$                                              ◁              startup.
    var rows = plv8.execute(
        "SELECT modname, code " +
        " FROM ch16.plv8_modules WHERE load_on_start"
    );                                                  ❷ Compile
    for (var r = 0; r < rows.length; r++) {
        var code = rows[r].code;                            ❸ For each module,
        eval("(function() { " + code + "})")();   ◁           write out the name
         plv8.elog(NOTICE, rows[r].modname + ' loaded');  ◁   of the module.
    };
$$
LANGUAGE plv8;

SELECT ch16.plv8_startup();    ◁        ❹ Load the
                                           modules.
```

Listing 16.13 creates a PL/V8 function that loops through the plv8_modules table and extracts the text of the function from the code field of each row marked as load_on_startup = true ❶. For each row, you apply the built-in JavaScript eval function to compile and instantiate each function ❷. Then you run the function, making it live in the PL/V8 memory context as the variable chance ❸.

For libraries that you use often, you'd want to execute the ch16.plv8_startup() function ❹ during startup of the PL/V8 procedure handler. To do so, place this call in your postgresql.conf file:

```
plv8.start_proc = 'ch16.plv8_startup'
```

Now you're ready to use Chance. You can use the PostgreSQL DO command to execute a snippet of PL code without having to wrap it in a function. In the next listing you create a table to store people, and then use chance to generate random beings all over the globe.

Listing 16.14 Creating dummy people with Chance

```
CREATE TABLE ch16.people(          ◁                 Create a table to hold
    id serial primary key,                           fictitious people.
    first_name varchar(50), last_name varchar(50),
    gender varchar(15), geog geography(POINT,4326)
);                              ❶ Create a DO block of
DO LANGUAGE plv8     ◁              PL/V8 code.
$$
    var sql = "INSERT INTO ch16.people(first_name,last_name,gender,geog)
        VALUES($1,$2,$3,ST_Point($4,$5)::geography)" ◁
    var iplan = plv8.prepare(                           Create parameterized
        sql,                                          ❷ SQL insert
        ['text','text','text','numeric','numeric']
    );              ◁        Prepare statement
                         ❸ for insert
```

```
for (var i=0; i < 10000; i++) {
    iplan.execute([
        chance.first(),
        chance.last(),
        chance.gender(),
        chance.longitude(),
        chance.latitude()
    ]);
}
$$;
```

Beget 10,000 people around the globe.

Listing 16.14 demonstrates a couple of standard features in PL/V8, in addition to the use of third-party modules. Like other PLs such as PL/pgSQL, you can create a DO block to run a one-time piece of JavaScript code **1**. PL/V8 lets you write parameterized SQL statements **2**, which you can use to create a prepared plan **3**. That can be executed countless times in a loop to insert many records **4**. After you're done running the code in listing 16.14, you should find 10,000 people in your people table.

> **WARNING**   Sometimes line breaks get mangled. If you get an error running listing 16.14, put the INSERT.. statement on one line.

Note that, like many PL languages, PL/V8 can be run as an anonymous one-time function using the PostgreSQL DO command, as you did in listing 16.14.

16.5.4   *Using PL/V8 to write map algebra functions*

PL/V8 can also be used to build map algebra functions. To demonstrate, you'll simplify the built-in ST_Range4MA map algebra function using PL/V8. This simplified version, which is shown in listing 16.15, will ignore the userargs and position input variables. However, it still needs to have them as inputs, because all map algebra functions must follow the function input signature:

```
value float8[][][], pos integer[][][],userargs text[])
```

> **somevariable[][][] versus somevariable[]**
> Although raster map algebra machinery assumes a 3D array for some args, in PostgreSQL the dimensionality of the input arg signature is not maintained. You'll see your float8[][][] converted to float8[] when you look again at your definition. As such, you can write it as float8[] to save keystrokes, but we write it here as float8[][][] for clarity.

Listing 16.15   PL/V8 range map algebra function

```
CREATE FUNCTION ch16.plv8_st_range4ma(
    value float8[][][],
    pos integer[][][],
    VARIADIC userargs text[] DEFAULT NULL::text[]
)
```

```
RETURNS double precision AS
$$
    return( Math.max.apply(null,value) - Math.min.apply(null,value) );
$$
LANGUAGE plv8 IMMUTABLE;
```

The following listing shows the same function written in SQL.

Listing 16.16 SQL range map algebra function

```
CREATE FUNCTION ch16.sql_st_range4ma(
    value float8[][][],
    pos integer[][][],
    VARIADIC userargs text[] DEFAULT NULL::text[]
)
RETURNS double precision AS
$$
    SELECT MAX(v) - MIN(v) FROM unnest($1) As v;
$$
LANGUAGE sql IMMUTABLE;
```

To compare the performance of PL/V8, SQL, and PL/pgSQL, we ran these queries on an image (included as part of this chapter's download).

Listing 16.17 Compare the speed of range functions

```
SET postgis.gdal_enabled_drivers TO 'PNG';
SELECT
    ch16.write_bin_file(
        ST_AsPNG(
            ST_MapAlgebra(
                ST_Clip(
                    rast,
                    ST_Expand(ST_Centroid(rast::geometry),300)
                ),
                1,
                'ch16.plv8_st_range4ma(
                    double precision[][][],
                    integer[][],
                    text[]
                )'::regprocedure,
                '8BUI','FIRST',NULL,2,2
            )
        ),
        RID::TEXT || '_plv8_range2.png'
    )
FROM ch16.pics;          ◄──────┐  PL/V8 range: 6 secs
                                │  430 msec on PG12
SELECT                        ❶  PostGIS 3.0
    ch16.write_bin_file(
        ST_AsPNG(
            ST_MapAlgebra(
                ST_Clip(
                    rast,
```

```
                    ST_Expand(ST_Centroid(rast::geometry),300)
            ),
            1,
            'ch16.sql_st_range4ma(
                double precision[][][],
                integer[][],
                text[]
            )'::regprocedure,
            '8BUI','FIRST',NULL,2,2
        )
    ),
    RID::TEXT || '_sql_range2.png'
)
FROM ch16.pics;
```

SQL range: 9 secs 577 msec

```
SELECT
    ch16.write_bin_file(
        ST_AsPNG(
            ST_MapAlgebra(
                ST_Clip(
                    rast,
                    ST_Expand(ST_Centroid(rast::geometry),300)
                ),
                1,
                'st_range4ma(
                    double precision[][][],
                    integer[][],
                    text[]
                )'::regprocedure,
                '8BUI','FIRST',NULL,2,2
            )
        ),
        RID::TEXT || '_builtin_range2.png')
FROM ch16.pics;
```

PostGIS packaged PL/pgSQL range: 15 secs 303 msec

The performance of the PL/V8 variant ❶ is faster than PL/pgSQL and beats the SQL version by a small margin. The examples also utilized the PL/Python function in listing 16.17 to write out the range images to disk. All the range results were equivalent. The output is shown in figure 16.6.

 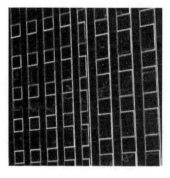

Figure 16.6   Before and after the range operation

Be careful when using PL/V8 to build map algebra callback functions, because the *n*-dimensional arrays passed in collapse to one-dimensional arrays. In many cases, such as when you're trying to extract the maximum value from a neighborhood of pixels, this collapsing isn't important. For cases where you need to keep the positional information, you're probably better off using an SQL function.

Map algebra function speed

The handling of `userargs` and `position` in the PostGIS packaged PL/pgSQL map algebra functions `ST_Range4ma`, `ST_Mean4ma`, and so on, adds overhead. Stripping the handling of `userargs` and `position` alone improves the PL/pgSQL speed about twofold and allows you to rewrite `ST_Range4ma` and `ST_Mean4ma` as SQL functions, yielding yet another 20% improvement in speed. Rewriting in PL/V8 improves the speed even more.

Summary

- There are many PostgreSQL extensions that extend what you can do in the database. This alleviates the need to extract data to feed it to external packages.
- PgRouting is a PostgreSQL extension used for network routing that leverages PostGIS.
- PL/Python is procedural language PostgreSQL extension that allows you to write database functions in Python.
- PL/R is a procedural language PostgreSQL extension that allows you to write database functions in R.
- PL/V8 is a procedural language PostgreSQL extension that allows you to write database functions in JavaScript.

Using PostGIS
in web applications

This chapter covers

- Shortcomings of conventional web solutions
- Pg_tileserv and pg_featureserv
- MapServer, GeoServer, QGIS Server
- OpenLayers 6, Leaflet 1
- Displaying data with PostGIS queries and web scripting

In a span of 30 years, the World Wide Web has emerged as the leading method of information delivery, largely replacing printed media. For GIS, this has been a god-send. Not only did the web introduce GIS to the popular imagination, but it also provided a delivery mechanism for GIS data that wouldn't have been possible via traditional printed media. In the past a GIS practitioner wishing to share data would have had to print out large maps on oversized printers or send copies of data on disk media. And then came the web.

Conventional web technologies suffice to deliver textual and image data, but for the ultimate GIS web-surfing experience, you need additional tools, both on the delivery end (the server) and on the receiving end (the client).

Quite recently, with the advent of PostGIS Mapbox Vector Tiles (MVT) support and the richer PostgreSQL/PostGIS JSON support, both detailed in chapter 8, many more people are discovering the freedom of being able to expose data directly from their database stored functions, queries, and tables with minimal middleware.

This chapter covers web tools that work with PostGIS. You'll explore the use of two server-side tools written in Golang: pg_tileserv and pg_featureserv. Both of these only support PostGIS, and they use PostGIS functions to expose tiles and features using MVT and JSON. You'll then learn about three server tools—MapServer, GeoServer, and QGIS Server—that can read data from PostGIS and other databases and files and serve images or data. Similar to the desktop tools covered in chapter 5, which can consume data delivered via agreed-upon OGC standards, these tools support delivering data using these same OGC standards.

You'll then explore the client side with two map scripting frameworks—OpenLayers, a JavaScript-based tool that greatly enriches the viewing experience for the user, and Leaflet, another JavaScript-mapping framework that competes with OpenLayers in many arenas. Both are open source with generous licensing terms. OpenLayers is an older platform, whereas Leaflet is a newer framework. Leaflet is a bit lighter-weight than OpenLayers, but it has a large crowd developing plug-ins for it. Most non-GIS folks find Leaflet a bit easier to grok than OpenLayers, so Leaflet tends to have a more developer, non-GIS crowd than does OpenLayers.

The code and data used in this chapter can be downloaded from www.postgis.us/ chapter_17_edition_3.

17.1 *Limitations of conventional web technologies*

Conventional web technologies work well for static data and images, but what if you need a website where users can extract your map at various zoom levels? Using conventional web server technology, you'd have to limit the user to a fixed set of zoom levels, generate the images beforehand, and serve them as requested. Now consider what would happen if the user would like to see only subsections of the map: you'd have to slice up your maps beforehand and restrict users to picking from one of your prepared slices.

There are two big problems here: First, you can't possibly predict what portions of the map the user would like to see. Second, even if you were to generate thousands of subsections for the user to pick from, your server would most likely run out of storage space after just a few maps. Add in zoom levels, and the problem becomes intractable.

The client side of the picture isn't much rosier. For zoom-level selectors, you could use standard HTML combo boxes, but the drop-down list would have to be changed from map to map. If a map has three zoom levels, you'd have to prepopulate your combo box with three values. If the next map has 30 zoom levels, you'd need to have 30 rows in the combo box for the user to pick from. Using various programming technologies available, you can dynamically generate the HTML combo box, but this requires that the mapping person also be a web programmer—and not in just one language. The demands become even more challenging if users have to be able to draw rectangles around subsections to be blown up, add their own markers, or have pop-up description balloons when hovering over certain points of interest. These interface features would all require extensive programming on the client side.

If server-side programming hasn't already discouraged the GIS specialist, the client-side programming surely will. What you need is a suite of client tools with useful controls for map viewing and editing already built in. Sure, the suite will dictate the overall appearance and functionality, but this is preferable to building your own solution from the ground up. After all, your goal is to disseminate maps, not to program web servers.

Along with the suite of client tools, you still need a set of server-side tools to provide the data. Let's first look at the server-side part of the equation and follow up with how you would provide this information to web browsers via client-side JavaScript mapping toolkits.

17.2   *Mapping servers*

Mapping servers have one central purpose: to render images or spatial data for delivery to a client on the fly. As mentioned previously, conventional web servers can't serve up images unless they already exist, but generating and storing all possible subsections and zoom levels associated with a map is in many cases impractical. Mapping servers solve this problem by quickly generating the static images or data only when requested by the client, and caching previously generated data for future requests.

Because mapping servers are rarely the starting point of an application, people generally start from a need to spatially extend existing web applications or to disseminate existing data via the web. To decide which server products to use, we recommend that you judge how easily each fits into your current infrastructure and data landscape. You should consider the following:

- Will the selected product require a major change in the existing platform?
- Which OGC web services, if any, do you need to provide?
- How well will the server connect to the data sources you already have, be they PostGIS, Oracle Spatial/Locator, Microsoft SQL Server, SpatiaLite, MySQL, shapefiles, raster files, or something else?
- Can you reuse mapping layering and styling you've developed on a desktop?
- How well does the solution integrate with your existing application (e.g., authentication)?

What are web services?

Loosely speaking, a web service is a standard for function calls across the internet. The service accepts requests from clients usually using HTTP and standard messaging streams (GET, PUT, POST in standard formats: XML, JSON, and the like) and returns the processed output.

To adhere to standards set by the OGC, a web service should make known which requests it can fulfill. In the case of Web Feature Service (WFS) and Web Mapping

Service (WMS), the capabilities are published via what is called a `GetCapabilities` response, which is usually returned as an XML or JSON document. You can find these listed in the OGC Standards (www.ogc.org/docs/is).

17.2.1 *Lightweight mapping servers*

The mapping servers pg_tileserv and pg_featureserv are what we call lightweight mapping servers because they follow the philosophy of doing one thing and doing it very well. Both are written in GoLang (Go) and are compartmentalized into a single binary with no extra dependences. Each executable hosts a web server and a connection to PostgreSQL/PostGIS. They only support PostGIS and leverage the plumbing in Post-GIS to do their job. They communicate via the standard HTTP/HTTPS protocol. This means they can be used with a web mapping client that can consume WFS and MVT tiles, such as OpenLayers and Leaflet, or a desktop mapping client such as QGIS Desktop. The fact that they accept query requests and tile requests like QGIS Server, Geo-Server, and MapServer makes them interchangeable for many requests with these beefier mapping servers.

In both pg_tileserv and pg_featureserv, layers are synonymous with tables and specialty functions.

Pg_tileserv (https://github.com/CrunchyData/pg_tileserv) builds on the `ST_AsMVT` function in PostGIS to build vector tiles, and it provides an interface that follows the OGC and MVT specifications. As such, it requires PostGIS 2.4 or higher, and PostGIS 3 or higher is suggested for best performance. Many changes were made in both Post-GIS 3 and PostGIS 3.1 to improve `ST_AsMVT` performance, so you should use these newer versions to get the best experience. The data is usually rendered in 256 × 256 tiles and based on zoom levels and layers. You specify an X integer level, Y integer level, and Z integer level as you would with raster tiles.

Pg_tileserv is only one of many vector tile servers that support PostGIS. You can find several listed on GitHub.

Pg_featureserv (https://github.com/CrunchyData/pg_featureserv) uses the `ST_AsGeoJSON` function offered by PostGIS and JSON support provided by Postgre-SQL to output GeoJSON feature collections. It follows the OGC API for features (WFS) standard. Unlike the X,Y,Z model of pg_tileserv, a feature request involves a bounding geometry in GeoJSON format and layers of interest.

Both pg_tileserv and pg_featureserv provide examples for integrating with Open-Layers and Leaflet mapping clients. Both pg_tileserv and pg_featureserv provide a configuration file, which you use to specify a single database connection string. The connection string includes the database and the database user name that will make the calls, along with any other information required to make the connection. This database user should not be a superuser and should for most use cases have only read access to data. You control what layers are accessible by setting permissions in your

PostgreSQL database for that user. Any spatial tables that the specified user has access to are exposed as layers.

In the following examples we set up an account that only has access to read ch17 schema data using standard PostgreSQL GRANT USAGE commands. The pg_tileserv default page is shown in figure 17.1.

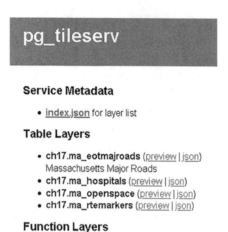

Figure 17.1   The pg_tileserv index page

The table layers are exposed by the name of the table and schema. There is no significance to these datasets, aside from the fact that they are from the region we live in.

Pg_featureserv has an index page shown on the left in figure 17.2. The index page provides an OpenAPI link that specifies the syntax of the REST API calls you can make. There is also a link to view all collections which, when clicked, shows the list of layers you can query. Shown on the right in figure 17.2 is the collections page, which

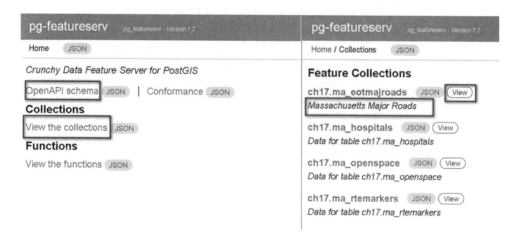

Figure 17.2   The pg_featureserv index page and collections page

presents a view link to see the map view of each layer. It utilizes OpenLayers for the map view.

Another nice feature shown in figure 17.1 and highlighted in figure 17.2 is that if you define a PostgreSQL table description via pgAdmin or SQL statement, both pg_tileserv and pg_featureserv use those descriptions:

```
COMMENT ON TABLE ch17.ma_eotmajroads
  IS 'Massachusetts Major Roads';
```

You can use pg_tileserv and pg_featureserv in unison. There is no absolute rule as to when you should use one over the other. Use pg_tileserv to serve up features that would take a lot of bytes to express in GeoJSON. Use pg_tileserv to show millions of points that appear in a single 256 × 256 tile where you don't need the details of each point or to show big things like state and city boundaries where you also want the client to have the flexibility of styling but which would take a lot of bandwidth to express in full resolution. Use pg_featureserv to serve features in isolation that have a lot of rich attribute data you may want to show the client.

There are a number of ways to run pg_tileserv and pg_featureserv. You can run them directly using a load script or put them behind something like NGINX, Varnish HTTP Cache, or Apache for caching and handling of authentication. You can also run them in Docker containers.

More details about running them in a production environment with caching are detailed in Paul Ramsey's "Production PostGIS Vector Tiles: Caching" blog article (http://mng.bz/aKmx).

Although pg_tileserv and pg_featureserv simplify querying your PostGIS database, if you have a heavy application with the need for lots of user authentication, it will not help you with the authentication. Two approaches come to mind:

- Do not let users call the pg_tileserv or pg_featureserv services directly, but instead keep the services local and have your application proxy the calls via a gated user authentication.
- Reimplement the logic yourself using the same approaches that pg_tileserv and pg_featureserv employ, but under your own application control. Pg_tileserv and pg_featureserv are wrappers around the JSON and MVT SQL functions provided by PostgreSQL and PostGIS. We will cover how to use JSON and MVT SQL functions later in this chapter.

17.2.2 *Full mapping servers*

There are many open source mapping-server products that support both PostGIS and other spatial databases and file formats. Some popular ones are MapServer, Geo-Server, and QGIS Server. The set we discuss here are by no means the full set available, but they are the more commonly used, in our experience. The aforementioned are full mapping servers in that they cover more than just one database and can output data in many forms, such as images, vector tiles, and even printed maps like PDFs. They also support numerous OGC web services.

PLATFORM CONSIDERATIONS

Some of the most important deciding factors for choosing a tool are the platform requirements. If you're on a shared web host, you may not be able to use anything that requires installation. Even if you have complete control over your server, you may shy away from technologies that require additional installation.

Table 17.1 outlines the prerequisites for each mapping server. *No** means the server doesn't require the service for general use, but you get more features if you have it.

Table 17.1   Mapping-server prerequisites

Service	MapServer	GeoServer	QGIS Server
Java runtime (JRE)	No	Yes	No
Python	No*	No	Yes
PHP	No*	No	No
.NET	No*	No	No
CGI/Fast-CGI	Yes	No	Yes

MapServer is our favorite of the aforementioned mapping servers because it contains a lot of functionality and can run under practically any web server without requiring installation. Just drop the compiled .so, .dlls, or .exe file into the CGI or some other web-server-executable folder, and you have a completely functional web-mapping service.

MapServer also offers an API called MapScript in many flavors, with PHP Map-Script and Python MapScript being the most common. This provides more granular control by allowing you to create layers and other map objects from server-side code using a MapScript-supported language. The downside of the MapScript interface is that it generally requires writing more code than using the mapserv executable.

MapServer is well supported on Linux, with many distros providing fairly recent versions. MapServer also has binaries for Windows that can be dropped in place and run under IIS or Apache. MapServer is an engine driven mostly by configuration scripts. It has no fancy GUI to guide a newbie user. You can, however, find samples of configs in the docs to guide you.

> **NOTE**   As of MapServer 7.4.0, regular PHP MapScript and friends are depre-
> cated in favor of a unified SWIG MapScript API. For PHP 8.0 and above, only
> the SWIG MapScript API will be supported.

GeoServer is built on Java. Some binary distributions of GeoServer come packaged with a lightweight web server called Jetty, designed for running Java servlet apps. GeoServer requires an existing installation of the JRE, and GeoServer version 2.18 requires Java 8 or 11. If you need to run GeoServer as a servlet, you'll need to get a servlet container, such as Tomcat, and install the Java web archive (WAR) version. Unlike many other mapping servers, GeoServer comes packaged with a user-friendly, web-based administrative interface. This makes GeoServer a popular option for those who prefer GUIs and wizards over configuration scripts.

QGIS Server is a mapping server often packaged with the popular QGIS Desktop. A key benefit of the QGIS Server is that it allows you to export your QGIS workspaces as OGC web-mapping services. The QGIS site has more info about setting up and configuring QGIS Server; see the "QGIS as OGC Data Server" section of the QGIS User Guide (http://mng.bz/gx7Z). Also check out the companion QGIS web client plug-in, which exposes the QGIS layers in an attractive way (https://github.com/elpaso/qgis-server-landing-page-plugin).

QGIS Server does not provide any authentication support, so you will need to manage that yourself if needed.

We'll only be demonstrating MapServer and GeoServer in this chapter because those are the most commonly used open source mapping servers, and from experience they're the easiest to set up on most platforms.

If you'd like an easy environment in which you can try all three servers and additional ones, use the OSGeo-Live DVD distribution (http://live.osgeo.org/en/overview/overview.html). The Live DVD is an Ubuntu distro that comes installed with the GeoServer, MapServer, QGIS Server, and Degree mapping servers. In addition to web-mapping servers, you'll also find PostGIS, pgRouting, SpatiaLite, and the various desktop offerings: QGIS Desktop, OpenJUMP, GRASS, and several others.

OGC WEB SERVICE SUPPORT

You may recall from chapter 8 that OGC is short for the Open Geospatial Consortium, the accepted standards organization in the world of GIS. OGC has outlined a series of web services that mapping servers should provide. By adhering to these standard OGC web services, mapping servers won't limit end users to their particular web or desktop client.

All the open source web-mapping clients and the desktop tools we covered in chapter 5 consume OGC web services. Even proprietary mapping desktop applications nowadays offer decent support for OGC web-mapping services. These are the most common of the web services defined by OGC:

- *Web Mapping Service (WMS)*—Renders vector and raster data as map images in JPEG, PNG, TIFF, or some other raster format. This is suitable if you want to show a map of an area but downloading and rendering the data would be too processor- or bandwidth-intensive. For example, if you want to display maps on a mobile device with limited processing power, retrieving ready-made images from a WMS server makes more sense than pulling the raw vector data and performing visual rendering on the fly. WMS also defines a mechanism called

`GetFeatureInfo` for getting basic information in HTML or some other text format. This is useful for info pop-ups.

- *Web Map Tile Service (WMTS)*—Renders vector and raster data as map images in JPEG, PNG, TIFF, or some other raster format at fixed scales and tile sizes that can be easily cached and reused by other clients. It serves much the same purpose as the standard WMS, but it's a newer standard that is less taxing on the server because it defines a mechanism for caching and reusing tiles. It's closely related to the WMS-C standard (Web Map Service Cache), which is still alive but considered legacy at this point. WMTS trades the flexibility of custom map rendering for scalability, so it's best suited for things like the base map layers or commonly asked-for maps that are time-consuming to generate. Tiles are often only provided in one spatial projection and at fixed scales and tile sizes.

  There are de facto standards that predate the OGC WMTS—these are what we'll call the "slippery map" or Tile Map Service (TMS) standards that always use Web Mercator as the spatial reference system and define tiles by some value of X/Y/Z or Z/Y/X. What X/Y/Z means is different in each tile referencing format. These are de facto standards popularized by Google Maps and OpenStreetMap. You will find support for them in both OpenLayers and Leaflet JavaScript web mapping APIs under the name XYZ or TMS. We'll cover this later in the chapter.

- *Web Map Tile Service Vector (WMTS Vector)/Mapbox Vector Tiles (MVT)*—Renders vector data in a binary form, usually in Google Protobuf format (PBF). The Mapbox Vector Tiles schema generally follows the Google Tile Scheme. It is not an official OGC standard yet, but it is in a pilot phase (https://docs.opengeo-spatial.org/per/18-078.html). The first vector tiles variant is Mapbox Vector Tiles which many mapping servers have adopted (https://github.com/mapbox/vector-tile-spec/tree/master/2.1/).

  In addition to allowing styling on the client side, vector tiles also degrade gracefully because they are still vectors. So although the resolution may be designed for a particular zoom, it can satisfy higher or lower zooms without looking too choppy.

- *Web Feature Service (WFS)*—Outputs vector data, generally using some XML standard such as GML or KML. Geography JavaScript Object Notation (GeoJSON) is another output format commonly supported by WFS that's more processor-friendly for consumption by JavaScript because it's a native JavaScript format. The GeoJSON format includes both the geometry represented as JSON encoded, as well as the standard database column attributes like dates, numbers, and strings encoded as JSON. WFS is most suitable if users need to highlight regions of a map and display attribute info or styling options, without making round trips to the server. WFS is often used in conjunction with WMTS, where WMTS would be used to show aerial images or large zoomed-out regions of a map, and WFS is used to overlay key commonly changing features on a map, or features whose styling you may want to control.

- *Web Feature Service Transactional (WFS-T)*—Allows you to edit vector data in transactional mode. This is necessary if you expect end users, such as web users or desktop applications, to edit geometry data in the database without giving them direct access to the database.

There are other web services, such as Web Coverage Services (WCS; www.ogc.org/standards/wcs) and Web Processing Services (WPS; www.ogc.org/standards/wps), which are more involved. Table 17.2 offers a brief summary of the key web services and indicates which tools support them.

Table 17.2 Web services support

Service	MapServer	GeoServer	QGIS Server
WMS 1.1	Yes	Yes	Yes
WMS 3	Yes	Yes	Yes
WMTS	Yes[a]	Yes	No
WMTS Vector	Yes	Yes[a]	Yes
WFS	Yes	Yes	Yes
WFS-T	Yes[a,b] (for PostGIS)	Yes	Yes
Custom[b]	Yes	Yes	Yes

a. Support is available via an extra downloadable plug-in or library.

b. The product has its own custom protocols that provide functionality beyond what is defined in the OGC standards.

SUPPORTED DATA SOURCES

All maps are derived from data. The WMS, WFS, and WFS-T protocols allow various data sources to be accessed via one web interface. They provide an abstract interface for GIS data, similar to ODBC and JDBC drivers for databases.

All web-mapping server tools support various data formats. Table 17.3 describes which tools support which formats, so you can make an informed choice. They all support PostGIS geometries and Esri shapefiles out of the box, so we left those out of the table.

Table 17.3 Data source formats supported

Service	MapServer	GeoServer	QGIS Server
Oracle Spatial/Locator	Yes[a]	Yes[a]	Yes[a]
SQL Server	Yes[a]	Yes[a]	Yes
PostGIS geography	Yes	Yes	Yes

Table 17.3 Data source formats supported *(continued)*

Service	MapServer	GeoServer	QGIS Server
PostGIS raster	Yes	Yes[a]	Yes
Basic raster	Yes	Yes	Yes
MrSID	Yes[a]	Yes[a]	Yes[a]
SpatiaLite	Yes[a]	Yes	Yes
MySQL	Yes[a]	Yes[a]	Yes

a. Support is available via an extra downloadable plug-in or library.

17.3   *Mapping clients*

Once the web-mapping services have been set up, you need client applications to consume them. Client applications come in two flavors: desktop and web. Web applications are often implemented using JavaScript and a mix of web-scripting server-side languages, such as PHP, Ruby, Python, and Perl.

Many desktop mapping toolkits are also capable of consuming standard OGC web-mapping services. A desktop client can either be an open source desktop tool, such as QGIS, gvSIG, OpenJUMP, and countless others, or a proprietary desktop tool such as Manifold, MapInfo, Cadcorp SIS, and ArcGIS desktop, to name a few.

As far as web-mapping clients go, OpenLayers and Leaflet tend to be the most popular, particularly in the open source GIS arena. The main reason for this is that both give you the ability to overlay proprietary non-OGC-compliant mapping server layers with OGC WMS, WFS, and WFS-T layers.

OpenLayers is often extended to create more advanced or specific toolkits. One common one that builds on top of OpenLayers is QGIS Web Client. The QGIS Web Client is a companion to QGIS Server, designed for consuming QGIS web mapping services. You will also find OpenLayers used in GeoServer, pg_tileserv, and pg_featureserv for quick display of published layers. The display links on pg_tileserv and pg_featureserv shown in figures 17.1 and 17.2 use OpenLayers for display.

17.3.1 *Proprietary services*

We'd be remiss if we failed to mention that the most popular web-mapping services around are still proprietary, such as Google Maps, Bing Maps, and MapQuest. These services package server, client, and data together in a slick, easy-to-use interface, and they make mapping accessible to the general public. Though these packages are easy to use, each has its own proprietary JavaScript API providing limited control over overlaying data.

The proprietary and inflexible nature of these services, even on the data level, is a serious drawback. You can't remove one core feature. For example, if you wanted to display foliage density over a region instead of the usual streets and places, you couldn't do so easily with these popular packages.

You also can't suppress the commercial licensing clause of these packages. For recreational use, these packages are in most cases free, but once you start to use them for profit or for non-public websites, you'll find yourself needing to cough up a rather exorbitant licensing fee. Because each has its own custom API that's different from the others, you'll have to rewrite much of your custom data-overlay logic when deciding to swap services.

Despite their commercial bent, we must pay homage to these popular services for planting the seeds of GIS in the popular imagination. They were the first to show the world the power of dynamic mapping on the internet, and they continue to lead the way in the development of display technologies. Nevertheless, this book is devoted to open source solutions, so we won't cover these proprietary JavaScript APIs. But we advise you not to lose sight of the important role they play on the web today.

Regardless of which services and mapping clients you use, whether it be open source or the Google Maps of the world, each tool can provide a lot of functionality out of the box. They do so by limiting you to certain protocols when you interact with your database and other spatial data. For many solutions that need only light support for maps but heavier support for data, you may want to forgo web-mapping services altogether and build the logic to display PostGIS data right in your application. In the sections that follow, we'll go into detail on the basics of setting up various open source map servers as well as creating solutions that don't require you to host your own web-mapping service.

If you wanted to do some heavy lifting by showing thousands of hefty features, outputting vector features would be slow and cumbersome. In such a case, it's better to output image tiles or vector tiles using a web-mapping service or tile service. As a user zooms in, you might want to complement this with a vector output using a direct PostGIS query with PHP, Python, .NET, or some other web server language, or with a WFS. We'll demonstrate how to do that next with MapServer.

The rise of vector tiles

There is a new trend gaining steam in the mapping arena called *vector tiles*, and it's spearheaded by Mapbox. Vector tiles are distributed as tiles much as current tile services distribute raster tiles, but they have binary vectors inside of the tiles. The benefit of vector tiles is that they allow for local styling on the client, they can include attribute data in each tile, and they can gracefully support multiple resolutions with a single zoom.

For example, if you have a particular focus of interest, you might provide data for that area in zoom levels as high as 20 (which would require a great deal of storage for a large area), and for surrounding areas only up to 14 (significantly less storage required). If someone zooms to 20 on a low-res area (only having a zoom of 14), the vector data can gracefully resize on the client to support a zoom of 20.

(continued)

More details about the spec can be found at https://github.com/mapbox/vector-tile-spec.

On a related note, there are two other PostGIS output formats, called *Geobuf* and *TWKB*:

- The `ST_AsGeobuf` function was introduced in PostGIS 2.4 (https://postgis .net/docs/ST_AsGeobuf.html). `ST_AsGeobuf`, just like `ST_AsMVT`, returns a binary Protobuf format, but unlike `ST_AsMVT`, it is nearly lossless and does not output in tiles.
- The output format called *TWKB* (tiny well-known binary), is also a binary format (http://postgis.net/docs/ST_AsTWKB.html). PostGIS TWKBs utilize the Google `varint` encoding scheme to minimize the size of vectors, and it produces near-lossless output. The PostGIS output functions for TWKB are `ST_AsTWKB` and `ST_AsTWKBAgg`. OfflineMap (https://github.com/nicklasaven/ offlineMap) demonstrates using PHP to create TWKB-formatted data and consuming this data in a Leaflet web client.

17.4   Using MapServer

MapServer was the first mapping server to support PostGIS as a data source. It can run under almost any web server. Unlike GeoServer, it does not provide user authentication or a graphical user interface (GUI). Most of your interaction with it is orchestrated via config files that define the layers and so forth.

The following examples demonstrate WMS features using MapServer 7.6. The examples should work fine on MapServer 7.4 or above.

17.4.1   Installing MapServer

MapServer has precompiled binaries and packages for almost any operating system, and you can find them here: http://mapserver.org/download.html#binaries.

WINDOWS INSTALL

For MS Windows installations, several options are available. MS4W (www.ms4w.com/ download.html) is a popular installation because it includes an Apache server and various other open source packages, such as PHP, PHP_OGR, and MapCache (a Mapserv subproject), so it's suitable if you want to run a self-contained installation.

Another option for Windows users is the GISInternals package, which has the latest developer and stable versions available, and packages are built whenever there's a change in the code base (www.gisinternals.com/). This version doesn't come with its own web server, but FastCGI can easily run under IIS. This is a good option if you want to run under an existing IIS server. It has both 32-bit and 64-bit versions, both compiled with most data drivers supported by MapServer. It also includes the C# Interop extensions to allow the use of MapScript from an ASP.NET (VB.NET or C#) environment. In addition to MapServer, the GISInternals package includes the full GDAL toolkit.

To deploy GISInternals on a Windows IIS server as CGI, do the following:

1 Verify that all the dependencies are in place: you can launch SDKShellbat, and run `mapserv -v`. That should output all the supported features. You should see output similar to this:

```
`MapServer version 7.6.1 OUTPUT=PNG OUTPUT=JPEG OUTPUT=KML
    SUPPORTS=PROJ SUPPORTS
=AGG SUPPORTS=FREETYPE SUPPORTS=CAIRO SUPPORTS=SVG_SYMBOLS
    SUPPORTS=SVGCAIRO SUP
PORTS=ICONV SUPPORTS=FRIBIDI SUPPORTS=WMS_SERVER SUPPORTS=WMS_CLIENT
    SUPPORTS=WF
S_SERVER SUPPORTS=WFS_CLIENT SUPPORTS=WCS_SERVER SUPPORTS=SOS_SERVER
    SUPPORTS=FA
STCGI SUPPORTS=THREADS SUPPORTS=GEOS SUPPORTS=POINT_Z_M SUPPORTS=PBF
    INPUT=JPEG
INPUT=POSTGIS INPUT=OGR INPUT=GDAL INPUT=SHAPEFILE`
```

2 Copy the mapserv.exe from bin/ms to bin, and then in a regular command line confirm that `C:\mapserv\bin\mapserv -v` still outputs the preceding information.

3 You'll need to reference the path to bin/proj/share in your MapServer map file later, but it doesn't need to be web-accessible.

4 Open up IIS Manager, and in the ISAPI and CGI Restrictions, add the path to mapserv.exe with a Description that is something like `MapServ 7`.

5 Create a virtual application path in IIS Manager to C:\MapServ\bin and call it `mapserv`.

6 In Handler Mappings, add a new Module Mapping with a request path of `*.exe`, a module of `FastCGI`, and an executable path of `C:\MapServ\bin\mapserv.exe`. Call it something like `MapServ` or `Mapserv 7`.

7 Click the Request Restrictions button on Module Mapping, and on the Mapping tab check the Invoke Handler Only if Request Is Mapped To check box, and check File. On the Verbs tab choose Only One of the Following, and in the text box, type `GET,HEAD,POST`. On the Access tab choose Script.

LINUX/UNIX INSTALL

MapServer can usually be installed via the standard packaging system provided by the Linux and Unix systems.

On Debian/Ubuntu you would use these commands:

```
add-apt-repository ppa:ubuntugis/ppa #not needed for ubuntu >= 20.04
apt update
apt upgrade
apt install cgi-mapserver mapserver-bin
```

Once you have the binaries installed, run this command:

```
mapserv -v
```

That should output what your MapServer supports. An Ubuntu install would output something like this:

```
MapServer version 7.4.3 OUTPUT=PNG OUTPUT=JPEG OUTPUT=KML SUPPORTS=PROJ
➥ SUPPORTS=AGG SUPPORTS=FREETYPE SUPPORTS=CAIRO SUPPORTS=SVG_SYMBOLS
➥ SUPPORTS=RSVG SUPPORTS=ICONV SUPPORTS=FRIBIDI SUPPORTS=WMS_SERVER
➥ SUPPORTS=WMS_CLIENT SUPPORTS=WFS_SERVER SUPPORTS=WFS_CLIENT
➥ SUPPORTS=WCS_SERVER SUPPORTS=SOS_SERVER SUPPORTS=FASTCGI SUPPORTS=THREADS
➥ SUPPORTS=GEOS SUPPORTS=PBF INPUT=JPEG INPUT=POSTGIS INPUT=OGR INPUT=GDAL
➥ INPUT=SHAPEFILE
```

You want to make sure PostGIS is listed as an input option and also that FASTCGI is supported.

17.4.2 Security considerations

If you're going to have PostGIS layers, you may need to put the PostgreSQL login username and password in the map file or in a file included in the map file. You don't want this information to be readable, and you may not want your map files to be readable at all for copyright reasons.

There are a couple of safeguards to prevent passwords and other sensitive content from being readable by website users. Please do at least one of these. You may want to do all of them for full protection:

- Don't put your map file in a folder that's web-accessible. Admittedly, we tend to break this rule because of the convenience of keeping everything related together.
- Use the msencrypt executable packaged with MapServer to generate a key, encrypt the password with the key, and use only the encrypted password, as detailed in the msencrypt documentation (https://mapserver.org/utilities/msencrypt.html).
- Use an INCLUDE clause in your map file, and make sure the INCLUDE file is of an extension type that isn't served by a web server. For example, we use the .config extension in IIS because ASP.NET will never serve a file with this extension. Using an INCLUDE for the PostGIS connection string is also convenient, at least if all your PostGIS layers use the same database. This saves you from having to repeat the same information over and over again.
- If you have control over your own web server, you can block dishing out .map files by editing your httpd.conf file, or in IIS by mapping the files to a 404.dll or some other IIS ISAPI processor.

17.4.3 Creating WMS and WFS services

MapServer supports its own non-OGC API as well as WMS, WFS, WCS, and other web service interfaces. We're going to focus on its OGC WMS and WFS functionality and its offerings in version 7 and above. For the OGC WMS/WFS features, you don't need template files. A correctly configured map file with WFS/WMS metadata sections, a set of fonts (https://mapserver.org/mapfile/fontset.html#fontset), a symbol set, and proj_lib will do.

For our map files, we like to use INCLUDEs for sections that we reuse repeatedly within the map or reuse across several maps, such as for the PostGIS connection string, or for general configurations like the location of the projection library.

The following listing shows what such a map file looks like.

Listing 17.1 Map with INCLUDEs

```
MAP
  INCLUDE "config.inc.map"          ← ❶ Paths to proj and plug-ins
  NAME "POSTGIS_IN_ACTION_3"        ← ❷ Map service name
  EXTENT 221238 881125 246486 910582  ← ❸ Extent of map in default projection

  UNITS meters
  PROJECTION
   "init=epsg:26986"               ← ❹ Default projection of map: 26986 is NAD 83 Massachusetts State Plane Meters
   END
  WEB
    MINSCALEDENOM 100
    MAXSCALEDENOM 100000
    METADATA
       "ows_title" "PostGIS in Action"
       "ows_onlineresource" "https://postgis.us/mapserver/postgis_in_action?"
       "ows_enable_request"   "*"
        "wms_version" "1.3.0"
       "wms_srs"    "EPSG:26986 EPSG:2249 EPSG:4326 EPSG:3785"
        "wfs_version" "1.1.0"
        "wfs_srs"    "EPSG:26986 EPSG:2249 EPSG:4326 EPSG:3785"
     END
  END #End Web
  INCLUDE "layers.inc.map"
  INCLUDE "layers_raster.inc.map"
END
```

❺ WMS/WFS metadata ows_enable _request is required)

Listing 17.1 is a basic map file with INCLUDEs ❶. The config.inc.map file contains the paths to the projection library, symbol set, font set, and additional plug-ins not built into the core. All INCLUDEs are relative to the location of the file they're included in.

The NAME property is the map service name that appears in the logs ❷. The EXTENT property defines the extent of the map in units of the default projection of the map ❸. This defines the default output projection of the map if none is given. Each layer can be in a different projection, but they'll be reprojected to the map projection when the map is called ❹. This projection is often overridden in WMS calls with the SRS parameter.

The metadata section is particularly important, because this makes the map file behave like a true WMS/WFS ❺. The ows_* elements are shorthand for WFS and WMS, so properties that are the same for both don't have to be specified twice. WFS version 1.0.0 can have only one SRS, but WFS version 1.1.0 allows you to specify a preferred SRS. The WMS standard allows many SRSs, and the ones listed are the ones the

WMS service will allow to be passed in for the SRS URL parameter. The online resource gets displayed in the WMS capabilities as the URL to call to access the service. The `ows_enable_request` property is required for MapServer 6.2+ ❺. It defines what services are allowed; if it's set to *, that means all services are allowed.

The config.inc.map file defines the location of the symbol set, proj library, and fonts. It's shown in the following snippet:

```
CONFIG PROJ_LIB "C:/mapserv/bin/proj/SHARE"
SYMBOLSET "symbols/postgis_in_action.sym"
FONTSET "fonts/fonts.list"
CONFIG "MS_ENCRYPTION_KEY" "C:/mapserv/postgis_in_action_key.txt"
```

`PROJ_LIB` is always an absolute physical path, but `SYMBOLSET` and `FONTSET` can be absolute or relative to the location of the map file. If you're on Windows, you'll often copy the fonts you want to use from your system fonts folder into your mapserv fonts folder, and then list them in the fonts.list file (as shown on the MapServer fontset page: https://mapserver.org/mapfile/fontset.html).

For the symbol set, you can use map symbol-set codes or images. A sample of both is packaged in the MapServer source download file. For this example, we used some freely available, public domain, true type fonts found at 1001 Free Fonts (www.1001freefonts .com). These are packaged as part of the chapter's download.

Next, you need to define a file called postgis.config that has database connection info:

```
CONNECTIONTYPE POSTGIS
CONNECTION "host=localhost dbname=somedb user=someuser port=5432
    password={encryptedpwd}"
PROCESSING "CLOSE_CONNECTION=DEFER"
```

`CLOSE_CONNECTION=DEFER` ensures that if multiple PostGIS layers are asked for, the connection will be reused instead of creating a new connection. This results in faster performance. If you use encrypted strings, as is the case for `password`, make sure you enclose the encrypted string in {} so that MapServer knows to decrypt. The postgis .config file will be included in all our PostGIS vector layers.

The next listing shows one of the layers in the layers.inc.map file. Note that you can include layers directly in the main map file.

Listing 17.2   Sample vector layer from layers.inc.map

```
LAYER                              ❶ Name
 NAME major_roads        ⤶         and type
  TYPE LINE
 STATUS ON
 DUMP TRUE                         ❷ Database
 INCLUDE "postgis.config"   ⤶         config
  DATA "geom from ch17.ma_eotmajroads using unique gid using srid=26986"
 PROJECTION
  "init=epsg:26986"
```

```
END
LABELITEM "rt_number"
METADATA
  ows_title "Massachusetts Major Roads"
  gml_include_items "all"
  ows_featureid "gid"
END
CLASS
 COLOR 255 0 0
 LABEL
  TYPE truetype
  FONT boston
  MINDISTANCE 50
  POSITION AUTO
  ANGLE AUTO
   SIZE 6
  COLOR 0 0 0
 END
END
```

3 Angle text around lines.

Every map layer starts with LAYER and has a NAME and TYPE **1**. The TYPE for PostGIS layers is usually LINE, POINT, or POLYGON. Then you include a file called postgis.config **2** which you'll include for each of the PostGIS layers to define the connection string to the PostGIS database.

MapServer supports angled text, which is useful for labeling streets. If you use ANGLE AUTO, the labels will wrap along the line segments **3**. For this example we used a font called *boston* that we downloaded.

MapServer also supports PostGIS raster. The following listing shows the contents of layers_raster.inc.map, which contains the definition for our PostGIS raster NOAA layer.

Listing 17.3 Sample postgis raster layer from layers_raster.inc.map

```
LAYER
    NAME noaa
    TYPE raster
    STATUS ON
    DATA "PG:host=localhost dbname='postgis_in_action' user='auser' password=
    '{encryptpwd}' schema='ch17' table='noaa' mode='2'"
    PROCESSING "NODATA=0"
    PROCESSING "SCALE=AUTO"
END
```

NOTE Make sure when you define the connection string to have it all on a single line. If you plan to be displaying rasters, make sure you have overview tables built. MapServer and other tools that use GDAL for rendering can utilize these overviews. You use the -l switch with raster2pgsql to include overviews. For the NOAA data we used -l 2,4 to generate overviews of overview factors 2 and 4. Each tile in level 2 will contain $2 \times 2 = 4$ tiles of the original at lower resolution. Each tile in level 4 will contain $2 \times 2 \times 2 \times 2 = 16$ of the original tiles at lower resolution.

You now have a map file, but how do you turn it into a WMS/WFS service? You call the MapServer CGI with the map file as an argument.

17.4.4 *Calling a mapping service using a reverse proxy*

When you call the MapServer CGI, the call will look something like this:

```
http://your_domain/mapserv/mapserv?map=/mapserv/maps/postgis_in_action.map
&REQUEST=GetCapabilities&
SERVICE=WMS&VERSION=1.1.1
```

> **What is a reverse proxy?**
>
> A *reverse proxy* is a server that behaves as a client and has access to other services, such as web-mapping servers, that a requesting client can't directly access. They gate-keep these services and control what requests are allowed by the requesting client.
>
> A secondary use of reverse proxies is for load balancing. They accept requests from a web browser on the outside and funnel them to the least-busy mapping server.
>
> In addition, a reverse proxy can call services on other ports on the same machine or cache requests for commonly requested data.

Specifying a map file for each call is often undesirable. Many people prefer to set up either a URL rewrite command in their website config file or a reverse proxy, either with a script or web proxy like NGINX so that the map file doesn't have to be explicitly named. Some examples are detailed on MapServer's "WMS Server" page (https://mapserver.org/ogc/wms_server.html#online-resource-wms).

Note that the use of a reverse proxy is not limited to MapServer. You can do the same for pg_tileserver, pg_featureserv, qgis_server, or any other mapping server.

If you are not calling MapServer directly, the long map URL example can be reduced to something like this:

```
http://your_server_domain/mapserver/postgis_in_action?REQUEST=GetCapabilities
    &SERVICE=WMS
&VERSION=1.1.1
```

A WMS call to generate an image that has both open space and major roads would look like the following:

```
http://your_server_domain/mapserver/postgis_in_action?LAYERS=openspace&STYLES
    =&TRANSPARENT=true
&FORMAT=image%2Fpng&SERVICE=WMS&VERSION=1.1.1&REQUEST=GetMap&
EXCEPTIONS=application%2Fvnd.ogc.se_inimage&SRS=EPSG%3A3857&
BBOX=-7912678.2752033,5204927.2982632,-7912475.239347,5205061.6602269
&WIDTH=340&HEIGHT=225
```

MapServer doesn't support WFS-T out of the box or for all data sources, but it does support WFS-T for PostGIS via a plug-in called TinyOWS (http://mapserver.org/tinyows/index.html).

We'll next take a look at GeoServer and see how it compares to MapServer.

17.5 Using GeoServer

GeoServer is similar in flavor to MapServer, except that it's a bit heftier and comes with an administrative user interface, so there's not as much need for manually configuring files with a text editor. It also supports WFS-T. Unlike the other mapping servers we've covered, GeoServer does offer an authentication framework.

17.5.1 Installing GeoServer

GeoServer has several installation packages that can be downloaded from http://geoserver.org:

- There is a platform-independent installer that includes the Jetty web server.
- A web application archive (WAR) file is available for those who already have a servlet container installed on their server and just want to run GeoServer as another servlet application. This one doesn't come with Jetty.

We chose the Java binary GeoServer 2.18 version for our installation. To set it up, you need to do the following:

1 Make sure you have Java 8 or 11 installed.
2 Extract the folder into the root; for example, C:\geoserver or /usr/local/geoserver.
3 On Windows, set the appropriate system environment variables. JAVA_HOME would be something like C:\Program Files\Java\jdk8 (or whatever JDK you have).
4 The default port is 8080. If you need to change it to something else, edit the start.ini file.
5 cd into the geoserver\bin folder, and from the command line run startup.bat (for Windows) or startup.sh (for Linux/Unix).
6 You should now be able to get to the administrative panel by navigating to the link http://localhost:8080/geoserver in your web browser and logging in with admin/geoserver. Once in, you should change the admin password.

GeoServer does not support PostGIS raster out of the box. In order to use it with PostGIS raster, you will need to install the PGRaster community plug-in as detailed in the GeoServer PGRaster community module documentation (http://mng.bz/0rGm).

17.5.2 Setting up PostGIS workspaces

Once you've got GeoServer installed, you need to set up a GeoServer workspace to house your tables and then register PostGIS tables with GeoServer. Follow these steps:

1 From the menus, select Workspaces, and click Add a New Workspace. The New Workspace screen should look something like figure 17.3.
2 From the left navigation menu, choose Data > Stores.

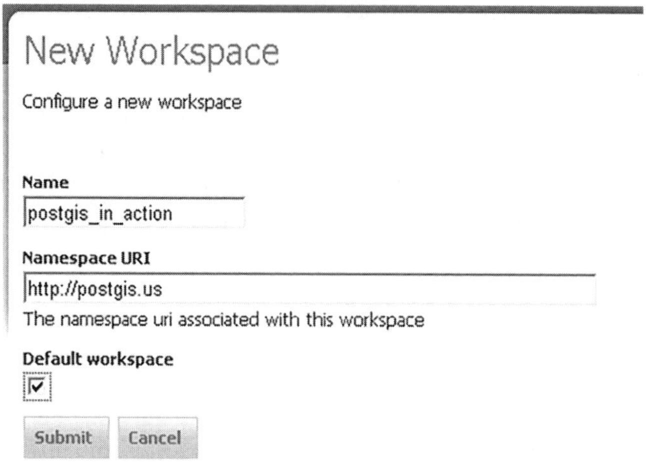

New Workspace

Configure a new workspace

Name

postgis_in_action

Namespace URI

http://postgis.us

The namespace uri associated with this workspace

Default workspace

☑

Submit   Cancel

Figure 17.3   Setting up a GeoServer workspace

3 Click the Add New Store menu option and then choose PostGIS from the list of options, as shown in figure 17.4.

4 Give the data source a name—we used ch17—and fill in all the credentials asked for. By default, GeoServer uses the public schema, which means it will list only layers from that schema. If you want it to list a different schema, like ch17 in our case, replace `public` with `ch17`.

5 Select Layers > Add a New Resource, and choose the postgis_in_action store you created previously. Your screen should look something like figure 17.5.

6 Publish the layer you want by clicking the Publish action for the appropriate layer (see figure 17.5). Make sure you choose Compute From Data and Compute From Native Bounds on the layer edit screen.

7 Click the Add New Resource link.

8 Repeat steps 6 and 7 for each layer you want to publish.

GeoServer data stores from other schemas

It's possible to leave the schema setting blank in GeoServer for PostGIS, and the layer chooser will list them all. However, we've found that publishing layers in a schema other than public will throw an error. Be sure you create a different data store for each schema you want to publish.

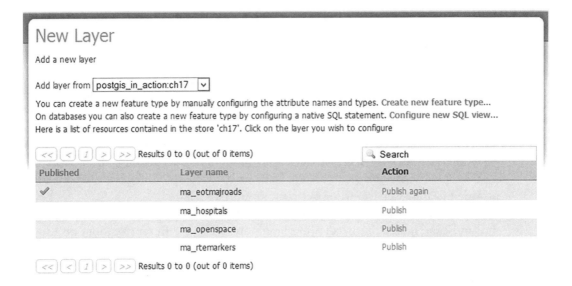

New data source

Choose the type of data source you wish to configure

Vector Data Sources

Directory of spatial files (shapefiles) - Takes a directory of shapefiles and exposes it as a data store
GeoPackage - GeoPackage
PostGIS - PostGIS Database
PostGIS (JNDI) - PostGIS Database (JNDI)
Properties - Allows access to Java Property files containing Feature information
Shapefile - ESRI(tm) Shapefiles (*.shp)
Web Feature Server (NG) - Provides access to the Features published a Web Feature Service, and the ability to perform transactions on the server (when supported / allowed).

Raster Data Sources

ArcGrid - ARC/INFO ASCII GRID Coverage Format
GeoPackage (mosaic) - GeoPackage mosaic plugin
GeoTIFF - Tagged Image File Format with Geographic information
ImageMosaic - Image mosaicking plugin
WorldImage - A raster file accompanied by a spatial data file

Other Data Sources

WMS - Cascades a remote Web Map Service
WMTS - Cascades a remote Web Map Tile Service

Figure 17.4   Adding a GeoServer PostGIS data store

New Layer

Add a new layer

Add layer from `postgis_in_action:ch17` ⌄

You can create a new feature type by manually configuring the attribute names and types. Create new feature type...
On databases you can also create a new feature type by configuring a native SQL statement. Configure new SQL view...
Here is a list of resources contained in the store 'ch17'. Click on the layer you wish to configure

`<< < 1 > >>` Results 0 to 0 (out of 0 items)   🔍 Search

Published	Layer name	Action
✓	ma_eotmajroads	Publish again
	ma_hospitals	Publish
	ma_openspace	Publish
	ma_rtemarkers	Publish

`<< < 1 > >>` Results 0 to 0 (out of 0 items)

Figure 17.5   Selecting PostGIS layers

17.5.3 *Accessing PostGIS layers via GeoServer WMS/WFS*

Once you've published your PostGIS layers, you can quickly see them via the Layer Preview menu link. Figure 17.6 shows what that screen looks like. Note that it also shows the OpenLayers code to be used to call the layer, and it shows GeoJSON as a direct WFS output format.

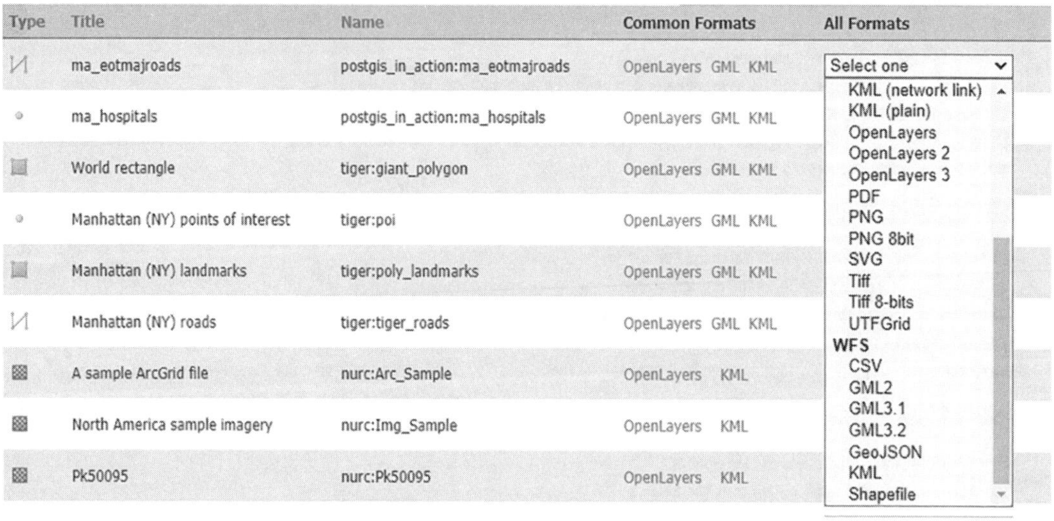

Type	Title	Name	Common Formats	All Formats
⋀	ma_eotmajroads	postgis_in_action:ma_eotmajroads	OpenLayers GML KML	Select one ⌄
∘	ma_hospitals	postgis_in_action:ma_hospitals	OpenLayers GML KML	KML (network link) ▲ KML (plain) OpenLayers
▢	World rectangle	tiger:giant_polygon	OpenLayers GML KML	OpenLayers 2 OpenLayers 3
∘	Manhattan (NY) points of interest	tiger:poi	OpenLayers GML KML	PDF PNG
▢	Manhattan (NY) landmarks	tiger:poly_landmarks	OpenLayers GML KML	PNG 8bit SVG
⋀	Manhattan (NY) roads	tiger:tiger_roads	OpenLayers GML KML	Tiff Tiff 8-bits UTFGrid
▨	A sample ArcGrid file	nurc:Arc_Sample	OpenLayers KML	**WFS** CSV GML2
▨	North America sample imagery	nurc:Img_Sample	OpenLayers KML	GML3.1 GML3.2
▨	Pk50095	nurc:Pk50095	OpenLayers KML	GeoJSON KML Shapefile ▼

Figure 17.6   GeoServer's layer preview screen

As you can see in figure 17.6, GeoServer autogenerates OpenLayers sample JavaScript code to display each of your layers.

17.6 *Basics of OpenLayers and Leaflet*

In the beginning, mapping services like Google Maps, Virtual Earth, MapQuest, and Yahoo had their own proprietary JavaScript APIs to access their data. This was a Bad Thing, because if you decided you liked the maps of service A better than the maps of service B, or if usage and pricing became too cumbersome, then you had to rewrite everything to switch services. Worse yet, if you wanted to feed your own data via your own mapping services for your area of interest, it was hard to integrate the base layers provided by these services with your custom study-area layers.

OpenLayers (http://openlayers.org) and Leaflet (http://leafletjs.com) changed the landscape quite a bit by allowing layers provided by different vendors with vastly different APIs to be accessed using the same API, or, better yet, to be used easily in the same map. You will see examples of how to use them later in this chapter.

OpenLayers started life as an incubation project of MetaCarta (which then became part of Nokia, which then got partly bought out by Microsoft), because it needed to create an easy-to-use toolkit for customers to digest its map product offerings. Open-Layers is now an incubation project of OSGeo.

Leaflet is another JavaScript API that came on the scene some years after Open-Layers. As a result of not having old JavaScript baggage, the Leaflet JavaScript API is considered by many to be a fresher, more modern API with HTML5 very much in it's design from the outset. Leaflet's focus is mostly on simplicity. OpenLayers has since completely rewritten its API, shedding much of its older baggage. OpenLayers still remains a heftier toolkit than Leaflet.

Both APIs have a lot of overlapping features, with Leaflet having less built-in functionality in general than OpenLayers and relegating additional functionality to Leaflet plug-ins. The latest version of OpenLayers (the OpenLayers 6 series) has a more modern JavaScript API, very similar in pattern to Leaflet. In talking about the two, we need to compare Leaflet (version 1.7) and OpenLayers 6 (version 6.4).

What do OpenLayers and Leaflet give you that you can't easily get elsewhere?

- Layer classes that allow you to access many of the proprietary non-OGC-compliant tile map offerings, such as Google Maps, Virtual Earth (Bing), and ArcGIS, using the same interface for all. OpenLayers has these built into the base package (in addition to OpenStreetMap tile layers), whereas Leaflet sometimes requires additional plug-ins. The only tile layer drivers built into the base Leaflet download are for OpenStreetMap and WMS tile services.
- Layer classes that enable you to access OGC-compliant map servers WMS, WFS, and WFS-T, again using the same fairly consistent map layer creation call. Keep in mind that in the case of Leaflet, a lot of these aren't prepackaged and require a bit of searching for the plug-ins. In the case of OpenLayers, most of the layer classes you'll need are packaged in the base download.
- The ability to overlay all these competing proprietary services in one map.
- Various controls to build custom menus, toolbars, and widgets to enable map editing. Both OpenLayers and Leaflet provide many of these. For features that are lacking, both frameworks support plug-ins.

All these things are wonderful, and that's why OpenLayers and Leaflet have become so popular. But most great things aren't without their tradeoffs:

- It's hard to get to the deep features of a proprietary service when using Leaflet or OpenLayers to access the service, such as the 3D street views provided by Google Maps and Bing. This may change as new OpenLayers and Leaflet layer classes are added to support these features.
- There's yet another API to learn, with the hope that you won't have to learn any other APIs.

When comparing Leaflet and OpenLayers, which should you choose? As with all things, it depends.

For a lightweight and flashy-looking modern interface, many people seem to prefer Leaflet. Products such as Carto and Mapbox, which have their own customized

APIs, tend to build on Leaflet. Even Esri has a customized Leaflet set of classes called Esri Leaflet that are used in conjunction with the base Leaflet script to work with their ArcGIS Online services (https://esri.github.io/esri-leaflet/).

OpenLayers, on the other hand, shines when doing things such as coordinate transformations.

In this section you'll learn how to display maps using OpenLayers and Leaflet. The first set of maps will give you a feel for what each looks like. In subsequent sections you'll add PostGIS layers and PostGIS queries that output JSON or MVT.

OpenStreetMap tiles: Publicly available tiles versus building your own

For the base layers in the exercises that follow, we'll use OpenStreetMap public tile servers. Because OpenStreetMap public tile servers run on donations, you may be cut off if you make a lot of calls to them. The tile usage policy is detailed at https://operations.osmfoundation.org/policies/tiles/.

If you have heavy traffic, you should build your own tiles or use tiles from a paid service, as is detailed on the Switch2OSM site (https://switch2osm.org/providers/). If you want to build and host your own tiles, you can do so using tools described by Switch2OSM (https://switch2osm.org/serving-tiles/).

17.6.1 OpenLayers primer

OpenLayers 6 (http://openlayers.org) is the current stable major version. OpenLayers 6 is currently at version 6.4.3.

Documentation is available on the site, and you may find the numerous code samples to be useful for getting started. Because OpenLayers is nothing more than a glorified JavaScript file, you can download the file and use it directly from your web server. Alternatively, you can link your code directly with the version on OpenLayers via a content delivery network (CDN) detailed in the manual.

For the remaining exercises, you should download the latest distribution zip file from https://openlayers.org/download/ and extract it into a folder called lib\ol on your web server.

One thing that OpenLayers is particularly good at is allowing you to integrate various map sources from disparate services. It includes classes for accessing the Google, Bing (Virtual Earth), OpenStreetMap (OSM), MapQuest, and MapServer APIs, as well as standard OGC-compliant WMS and WFS services produced with tools like Map-Server and GeoServer.

For this next exercise, you'll use OpenLayers to display both publicly available OSM tiles and your own WMS map layers.

The next listing displays OpenStreetMap and adds on layers from ch17 using the MapServer WMS service.

Listing 17.4 OpenLayers general setup: postgis_in_action_ol_1.htm

```html
<!doctype html>
<html lang="en">
  <head>
    <link rel="stylesheet" href="lib/ol/ol.css">
    <link rel="stylesheet"
      href="https://unpkg.com/ol-layerswitcher@3.8.3/dist/ol-
      layerswitcher.css" />
    <script src="lib/ol/ol.js"></script>
    <script src="https://unpkg.com/ol-layerswitcher@3.8.3"></script>
    <style>
      #map {
        height: 600px;
        width: 100%;
      }
    </style>
  </head>
  <body>
    <div id="map" class="map"></div>
    <script type="text/javascript">
      var l1 = new ol.layer.Tile({
        source: new ol.source.OSM(
          {url:'//{a-c}.tile.osm.org/{z}/{x}/{y}.png'}
          )
      });
      var los = new ol.layer.Tile({
          title: 'Openspace',
          source: new ol.source.TileWMS(({
              url:  '/mapserver/postgis_in_action',
              params: { 'LAYERS': 'openspace'},
              serverType: 'mapserver',
              attributions: "Bureau of Geographic Information (MassGIS)"
          }))
      });
      var lh = new ol.layer.Tile({
          title: 'Hospitals',
          source: new ol.source.TileWMS(({
              url:  '/mapserver/postgis_in_action',
              params: { 'LAYERS': 'hospitals,hospitals_anot'},
              serverType: 'mapserver'
          }))
      });
      var lnoaa = new ol.layer.Tile({
          title: 'Noaa',
          source: new ol.source.TileWMS(({
              url:  '/mapserver/postgis_in_action',
              params: { 'LAYERS': 'noaa'},
              serverType: 'mapserver',
              attributions: "Bureau of Geographic Information (MassGIS)"
          }))
      });
      var map = new ol.Map({
          target: 'map',
          layers: [l1, los, lh, lnoaa],
```

❶ Link to the OL API, JS, and CSS.

❷ Set the map width to take up the full browser and height to 600 px.

❸ Create OpenStreetMap layer

❹ Create PostGIS WMS layers.

❺ Load the map.

❻ Add layers.

```
                    view: new ol.View({
                       center: ol.proj.fromLonLat([-71.0636, 42.3581]),
                          zoom: 15
                    })
                 });
                 map.addControl(new ol.control.Zoom());
                 var layerSwitcher = new ol.control.LayerSwitcher();
                 map.addControl(layerSwitcher);
            </script>
         </body>
      </html>
```

Center reprojecting WGS lon/lat to OSM projection **7**

Add zoom in/zoom out control

8 **External plug-in for the layer switcher**

First, you add the link to the OL, CSS, and JS files **1**. Again, you have the choice of using a hosted version or downloading and using one on your server. You then set the size of the map **2**. It is necessary to make one dimension an absolute, though the other dimension can be based on a percentage of the browser window. In this example, our map will take up the full width of the browser. You then add an OpenStreet-Map tile layer **3**. The url property is optional and defaults to the OpenStreetMap tile server when not specified. You next add two layers from your WMS mapping server **4**.

As part of loading the map **5**, you add the two layers to the map **6**, and reproject to map units **7**. This particular WMS layer call adds the layers as tiles of the same size as the OpenStreetMap tile. If you wanted single tiles to minimize on query calls to your server, you'd use ol.Layer.Image in conjunction with ol.source.ImageWMS.

OpenLayers from version 3 on does not provide a layer switcher out of the box. If you need a layer switcher, you can add an external one, unpkg.com/ol-layerswitcher, CSS, and JS files as we did **1** and then use the layer switcher **8**. That LayerSwitcher is described on GitHub (https://github.com/walkermatt/ol-layerswitcher).

The output of listing 17.4 is shown in figure 17.7.

Listing 17.4 uses MapServer WMS support for the layers. You can just as easily swap these out with GeoServer, QGIS Server, or any WMS or tile-supporting mapping server.

Though it's not demonstrated in figure 17.7, OpenLayers adds mouse-wheel scroll behaviors for zooming in and out by default, so you don't need to explicitly add those.

Listing 17.4 utilizes ol.source.TileWMS to force calling WMS in tile chunks. However, this is pretty inefficient; it doesn't lend itself as easily to caching, since the query sent back to the WMS would be a bounding box represented with floating-point numbers. To allow for easier caching and thus speedier performance, MapServer supports a mode called "TILEMOD" that allows you to reference a map by some tile-serving scheme. The following listing shows the NOAA layer rewritten to use Google Maps tile scheme (gmap). The ol.source.XYZ Open Layers class will replace the X/Y/Z values with concrete values based on the region of the map:

```
var lnoaa = new ol.layer.Tile({ title: 'Noaa',
       source: new ol.source.XYZ(
          {url:'/mapserver/postgis_in_action?MODE=tile
             &TILEMODE=gmap&TILE={x}+{y}+{z}&LAYERS=noaa'}
          )
    });
```

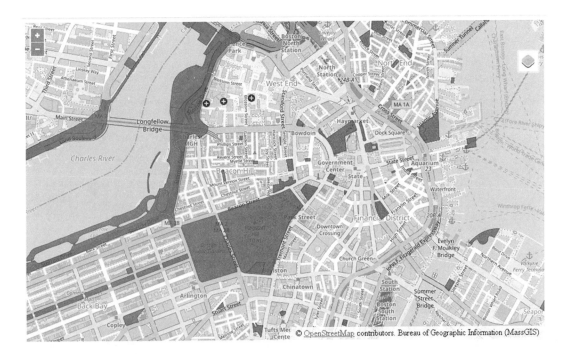

Figure 17.7 Output of OpenLayers example

If you are using another mapping server such as GeoServer, you can utilize the TMS support via GeoWebCache (www.geowebcache.org/docs/current/services/tms.html).

Then your layer would look something like this:

```
var lnoaa = new ol.layer.Tile({ title: 'Noaa',
    source: new ol.source.XYZ(
{url:'/geowebcache/service/tms/1.0.0/postgis_in_action:noaa/{z}/{x}/{y}.png'}
        )
});
```

In the next section, you'll learn how to dish out layers with Leaflet.

17.6.2 *Leaflet primer*

These next examples will demonstrate Leaflet using version 1.7. For many apps where you want a tile-based layer, and you want to draw your own layers on top using something like GeoJSON objects, Leaflet often suffices. It can provide a slicker, less busy interface than OpenLayers, and it is generally much faster to get up to speed with. You can also expand Leaflet's functionality by adding other Leaflet plug-ins.

Let's perform the same exercise as we did with OpenLayers, but using Leaflet instead. For production use, it's safer to download the Leaflet library and use your own copy or install via npm node package:

1 Download the latest stable release of leaflet from the Leaflet site: https://leaf-letjs.com/download.html.

2 Extract it into the lib/ folder of your web app.

3 Link in the files as shown in the following listing.

Listing 17.5   Leaflet general setup: postgis_in_action_leaflet_1.htm

```html
<!doctype html>
<html lang="en">
<head>
  <link rel="stylesheet" href="lib/leaflet/leaflet.css" />          ❶ Link to
  <script src="lib/leaflet/leaflet.js"></script>                      Leaflet API,
  <style>                                                             JS, and CSS
  #map {height: 600px;width: 100%;}</style>
</head>
<body>
    <div id="map"></div>                        ❷ Create
    <script type="text/javascript">               OpenStreetMap
        var l1 = L.tileLayer(                     layer
    '//{s}.tile.osm.org/{z}/{x}/{y}.png', {
    attribution: 'Map data &copy; OpenStreetMap contributors',
    maxZoom: 18
}); 
var map = L.map('map', { layers: [l1] })        ❸ Load map
        .setView([42.3581, -71.0636], 15);          and center
                                                    on location

    var l2 = L.tileLayer.wms("/mapserver/postgis_in_action", {   ❹ Create
        layers: 'openspace',                                       PostGIS
        format: 'image/png',                                       WMS layers.
        transparent: true,
        version: '1.3.0',
        attribution: "MassGIS data"
});
var baseMaps = { "OpenStreetMap": l1 }
 var overlayMaps = { "Open Space": l2 }          ❺ Add layer control
 L.control.layers(baseMaps, overlayMaps,           with base layer
 { collapsed: false }).addTo(map);                 and overlays
</script>      </body> </html>
```

The Leaflet code is slightly more succinct than that for OpenLayers, but in many cases it's much the same. Listing 17.5 follows steps similar to the OpenLayers example. First, you reference the location of the Leaflet CSS and JavaScript API files ❶. Then you create the OpenStreetMap layer ❷. You load the map, initialized with the Open-StreetMap layer, mark it as an active layer, and center it on a location using setView ❸.

One difference between OpenLayers and Leaflet is that Leaflet setView coordinates are specified in lat/lon instead of database/OpenLayers lon/lat. The setView syntax is a bit shorter than the transform, center, zoom approach of OpenLayers, but this is not without sacrifice. Leaflet, out of the box, assumes you want to show your data in Web Mercator, whereas OpenLayers gives you the choice of what projection to use and what your input projections are.

Next you create the WMS layer ❹, which can be MapServer, GeoServer, or any other OGC-compliant WMS. Then you specify which will be base layers and which will be overlays, create a layer control to manage these, and add the control to the map ❺. The Leaflet layer control is equivalent to the OpenLayers 2 LayerSwitcher control.

The output of listing 17.5 is shown in figure 17.8.

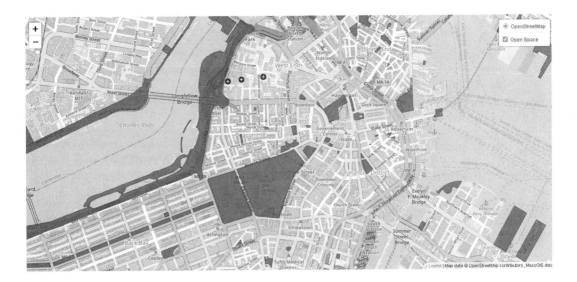

Figure 17.8   Output of Leaflet

Similar to OpenLayers, Leaflet does have a built-in layer control. Figure 17.8 looks much the same as the output from OpenLayers, but with slightly different styling for the controls and attribution. Both of these can be controlled by changing the CSS in any of these toolkits.

17.6.3 *Synopsis of the OpenLayers and Leaflet APIs*

This section demonstrated two different APIs at work. Leaflet is a generally lighter API than OpenLayers. OpenLayers is a bit beefier than Leaflet but promises to be a good mix of feature-richness, faster speed, and streamlined API. With both of them, you can query common web-mapping services such as OpenStreetMap tile services, and you can overlay WMS and WFS features powered by your PostGIS data.

Although WMS and WFS servers are great for dishing out often-changing mapping data, they limit the queries you can do, and they also tend to add hefty overheads to your infrastructure. A common practice nowadays is to leave the static, commonly used layers to tile services and prerendered tiles. You can then use raw database calls for things like saving data and displaying changing features. In the next section we'll use PHP to do direct PostGIS queries and demonstrate how these can be overlaid on a map.

17.7   Displaying data with PostGIS queries and web scripting

We're now going to demonstrate how you can use the functions built into PostgreSQL and PostGIS to overlay spatial data on a map. The assumption for this section is that you're using PostgreSQL 12+ and PostGIS 3+.

17.7.1   Using PostGIS and PostgreSQL geometry output functions

A common feature of web mapping is the option to highlight features clicked on or selected on a map and show descriptive information about the feature clicked. For this kind of functionality, you need a web feature service or something like a GeoJSON or MVT query that returns both vector and attribute data.

For this next exercise, we'll demonstrate how you can generate GeoJSON right in the database for output on a map. These are the basic steps:

1   Create a PL/pgSQL stored function called `get_features` to output GeoJSON. This function relies on the `ST_AsGeoJSON` support in PostGIS 3 that includes support for other attribute data by inputting a whole row as well as the long-standing `ST_GeomFromGeoJSON` function that converts a GeoJSON geometry into a PostGIS geometry.

2   Create a PHP script that grabs parameters from the request, passes them to a function, and returns the PL/pgSQL function output.

3   Utilize Leaflet or OpenLayers in conjunction with jQuery to query the PHP script and draw the selected feature and properties on the map.

The PL/pgSQL function is shown in the following listing.

Listing 17.6   PL/pgSQL `get_features` function

```
CREATE OR REPLACE FUNCTION ch17.get_features(
    param_geom json,
    param_table text,
    param_props text,
    param_limit integer DEFAULT 10
)
RETURNS json AS
$$
DECLARE
    var_sql text; var_result json; var_srid integer; var_geo geometry;
    var_table text; var_cols text; var_input_srid integer;
    var_geom_col text;
BEGIN
    SELECT
        f_geometry_column,
        quote_ident(f_table_schema) || '.' || quote_ident(f_table_name)
    FROM geometry_columns
    INTO var_geom_col, var_table
    WHERE f_table_schema || '.' || f_table_name = param_table
    LIMIT 1;
```

❶ Verify the table is a geometry table.

```
                    IF var_geom_col IS NULL THEN
                        RAISE EXCEPTION 'No such geometry table as %', param_table;
                    END IF;
Convert the         var_geo := ST_GeomFromGeoJSON($1::text);
location to         var_input_srid := ST_SRID(var_geo);
geometry.  ❷        If var_input_srid < 1 THEN                          ❸  Get the
                        var_input_srid = 4326;                             SRID of the
                        var_geo := ST_SetSRID(                             requested
                        ST_GeomFromGeoJSON($1::text),var_input_srid);      location.
                    END IF;

Get the SRID        var_sql := 'SELECT ST_SRID(geom) FROM ' || var_table || ' LIMIT 1';
of the table. ❹
                    EXECUTE var_sql INTO var_srid;

                    SELECT string_agg(quote_ident(trim(a)), ',')        ❺ Sanitize
                    INTO var_cols                                          the column
                    FROM unnest(string_to_array(param_props, ',')) As a;   names.

                    var_sql :=
                        'SELECT json_build_object(''type'', ''FeatureCollection'', ''features'',
                            json_agg(ST_AsGeoJSON(f.*)::json) ) AS fc
                        FROM (
                            SELECT
                                ST_Transform(
                                    lg.' || quote_ident(var_geom_col) || ', $4
                                    ) AS geom, '
                                || var_cols || '
            Build a         FROM ' || var_table || ' AS lg
        parameterized       WHERE ST_Intersects(lg.geom,ST_Transform($1,$2)) LIMIT $3
            SQL.  ❻        ) As f';
                                                                       ❼ Execute the
                    EXECUTE var_sql INTO var_result                       parameterized SQL
                    USING var_geo, var_srid, param_limit, var_input_srid; ◄─ using variables,
                                                                          output to var_result,
                    RETURN var_result;                          ◄────────  and return.
                END;
                $$
                LANGUAGE plpgsql STABLE PARALLEL SAFE COST 1000;
```

Listing 17.6 takes as input a location in GeoJSON format and a geometry table. The
code first checks in the geometry_columns table to verify that the requested table has
a geometry column and is visible by the user account the stored function runs under
❶. If not, an exception is raised, ending execution of the function.

The code converts the input location to a geometry ❷ and assumes the geometry
is in lon/lat if no SRID is provided ❸. It then gets the SRID by assuming all geometries in the table column have the same SRID ❹. Note that you could revise the code
to read the SRID from geometry_columns, but for views based on tables with constraints, this information might not be available in geometry_columns.

The string_to_array PostgreSQL function is then used to convert columns to an
array of elements, the quote_ident function is used on each element of the array, and

they are concatenated back into a comma-separated list with `string_agg` ❺. This is done to prevent an SQL injection attack.

Next you build a parameterized SQL statement that uses the table and column names ❻. The executed SQL returns a GeoJSON feature collection when parameters `var_geo`, `var_srid`, `param_limit`, and `var_input_srid` are provided and replaced in the corresponding slots (`$1,$2,$3,$4`) of the parameterized SQL statement ❼. It will return a single GeoJSON object composed of at most `param_limit` features.

Listing 17.6 uses PostgreSQL JSON functions and PostGIS `ST_AsGeoJSON` calls to build a single JSON object ❼. It does so by aggregating all the feature rows (f) into a JSON array using `json_agg`, constructing a JSON object using `json_build_object`, and setting the `features` property of this JSON object to the JSON feature array.

A sample call to the PL/pgSQL function would look something like this:

```
SELECT ch17.get_features('{"type":"Point",
 "coordinates":[-71.06576,42.35299]}',
  'ch17.ma_openspace','site_name, gis_acres') As result;
```

It will produce a GeoJSON feature collection that looks something like this:

```
{"type" : "FeatureCollection",
"features" : [{"type": "Feature", "geometry":
{"type":"MultiPolygon","coordinates":[[[[-71.065578109,42.352495916],
  [-71.066918871,42.352579209],[-71.066599608,42.352762566],[-71.066029031,
  42.353220103],[-71.065336255,42.353212985],
[-71.065578109,42.352495916]]]]},
"properties": {"site_name": "Central Burying Ground", "gis_acres": 1.57214919}}]}
```

> **Outputting geography in GeoJSON**
>
> The example in this section assumes that you're working with geometry data. If more than one geometry column exists in the table, the function will arbitrarily pick one geometry column.
>
> The `ch17.get_features` function works just as easily with geography by changing the `ST_GeomFromGeoJSON(…)` to `ST_Transform(ST_GeomFromGeoJSON(…),4326)::geography`.

This exercise is working with point location clicks, but the PL/pgSQL function is designed to work with any arbitrary geometry, such as a circle buffer or a polygon drawn by a user, and it will return all features that intersect the region of interest.

A PHP script that will collect the inputs, call the PL/pgSQL function, and output the result is shown in the next listing.

Listing 17.7   Contents of get_features.php

```php
<?php
    include_once("config.inc.php");
    $param_geom = $_REQUEST['geom'];
```

```
                    $param_table = $_REQUEST['table'];
                    $param_props = $_REQUEST['props'];
                    try{
                      $pdo = new PDO(POSTGIS_DSN);
                      $stmt = $pdo->prepare(
                        "SELECT ch17.get_features(:geom,:table,:props) AS data"
                      );
                      $stmt->execute(['geom' => $param_geom,
                                      'table' => $param_table,
                                      'props' => $param_props]);
                      $data = $stmt->fetch();
                      $val = $data[0];
                      $stmt->closeCursor();
                      echo $val;
                    }
                    catch (Exception $e){
                      // report error message
                      echo $e->getMessage();
                    }
                  ?>
```

Parameterized query → (points to) `$stmt = $pdo->prepare( "SELECT ch17.get_features(:geom,:table,:props) AS data" );`

Execute with args ← (points to) `$stmt->execute(...)`

Output result to variable ← (points to) `$data = $stmt->fetch();`

Output as web result ← (points to) `echo $val;`

You can revise the original Leaflet page from listing 17.5 and add a link to jQuery right after the Leaflet API INCLUDE:

```
<script src="//code.jquery.com/jquery-3.5.1.min.js"
    integrity="sha256-9/aliU8dGd2tb6OSsuzixeV4y/faTqgFtohetphbbj0="
    crossorigin="anonymous"></script>
```

NOTE Instead of using jQuery Ajax/JSON functions or an HTTP toolkit such as Axios, you can use the Fetch API (https://developer.mozilla.org/en-US/docs/Web/API/Fetch_API), which is now available in most browsers. The Fetch API, however, still doesn't provide some nice features, like being able to catch 404/500 errors.

On the line after addTo(map) ❺ in listing 17.5, you can add the lines in the next listing.

Listing 17.8 Additional contents of postgis_in_action_leaflet_3.htm

New pop-up and placeholder for geoSON layer ❶

Onclick event function ❷

Convert clicked location to GeoJSON ❸

Get the features. ❹

```
var popup = L.popup();
var lgeojson;
function onMapClick(e) {
    var geoJsonLoc = '{"type":"Point","coordinates":['
    + e.latlng.lng
    + ',' + e.latlng.lat + ']}'
    $.ajax({url: "get_features.php", dataType: 'json',
        method: 'POST',
        data: { 'geom': geoJsonLoc,
                'table': 'ch17.ma_openspace',
                'props': 'site_name, gis_acres'
        }
    })
```

```
.done(function (data) {
    var popupContent = ''
    if (lgeojson != null){
        map.removeLayer(lgeojson);        ⑤ JQuery
    }                                         returned
    lgeojson = L.geoJson(data, {    ←        output        ⑥ Add to
                                                               pop-up
                                                               content
    onEachFeature: function (feature, layer) {    ←

    popupContent += '<b>Site:</b> '
              + feature.properties.site_name
              + '<br /><b>Acres:</b> '
              + feature.properties.gis_acres
        }, style: { "color": "blue", "weight":10 }
    });              popup.setLatLng(e.latlng)    ⑦ Bind event
      .setContent(popupContent)                      handler to click
      .openOn(map);                                  event of map
    lgeojson.addTo(map);    ←    Add features
  });                            to map
}
map.on('click', onMapClick);    ←    Position pop-up location
                                     and content and open
```

Listing 17.8 is additional code that defines a new pop-up to be moved around the screen ①. The core is an onclick event handler function ② that, when the user clicks on the map, will create a GeoJSON point ③ that you will use to locate open space features that intersect. Note that although a point is used here, any GeoJSON geometry will work with the PL/pgSQL and PHP combo.

You use the jQuery `ajax` Ajax function to call the `get_features.php` script with the geometry, table, and fields you want ④. When jQuery is done, it will return the output of the PL/pgSQL function ⑤, which is a GeoJSON feature collection. For each feature returned, the name and number of acres is added to the pop-up ⑥. The most important piece is the click event handler ⑦, which binds the onMapClick event function you created with the `click` event of the map.

> **NOTE** jQuery provides a function called getJSON that is a wrapper around the ajax function and just returns JSON. It would be a bit shorter to write than the previous code, but not by much, and you would not have the flexibility provided by the full Ajax function, such as the ability to pass along auth tokens.

The output of clicking on an open space feature is shown in figure 17.9.

A similar approach for OpenLayers is found here: https://github.com/Crunchy-Data/pg_featureserv/tree/master/examples/openlayers.

17.7.2 Using PostGIS MVT output functionsMapbox Vector Tiles (MVT)

For larger geometries that are specific to the user or that change often, you may want to use the more compact MVT format output by ST_AsMVT. Note that MVT has undergone improvements in speed even as of PostGIS 3.1, as detailed in the "Waiting for

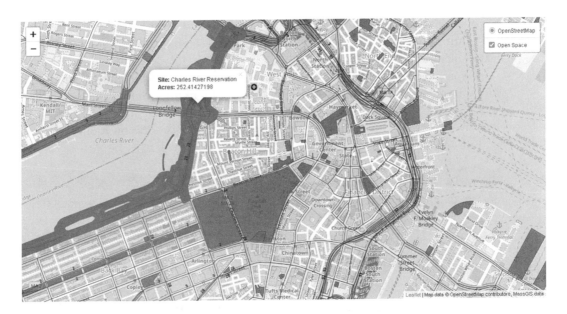

Figure 17.9 Output of Leaflet with onclick event

Postgis 3.1: Vector tile improvements" on the Engineering Rocks blog (http://mng
.bz/BKdg). The newer your PostGIS version, the better.

The fastest way to get started is to use pg_tileserv as described earlier. To use an
MVT tile from pg_tileserv in OpenLayers, you would replace your OpenLayers Open
Space layer with the following listing.

Listing 17.9 Tile server vector tiles layer

```
var openSpaceStyle = new ol.style.Style({          ◁──  Style to
  stroke: new ol.style.Stroke({                          use for
    width: 2,                                            coloring
    color: "#ff00ff99"
  }),
  fill: new ol.style.Fill({
    color: "green"
  })
});

var los = new ol.layer.VectorTile({
    title: 'OpenSpaceTS',
    source: new ol.source.VectorTile({          Connection
      format: new ol.format.MVT(),              to tile server

      url: "http://localhost:7800/ch17.ma_openspace/{z}/{x}/{y}
      .pbf?properties=gid,site_name"
    }),
    style: openSpaceStyle
});
```

For Leaflet you'd use the VectorGrid layer control and Protobuf output as detailed here: https://github.com/CrunchyData/pg_tileserv/blob/master/examples/leaflet/leaflet-tiles.html.

If you need to better control which users have access to which layers, you might find it more manageable to implement your own solution in your language of choice with a PostgreSQL stored function. It might look something like the next listing, which is similar to listing 17.6 but instead of the bounding box, it works on zoom levels and outputs MVT data.

Listing 17.10   PL/pgSQL `get_tile_mvt` function

```
CREATE OR REPLACE FUNCTION ch17.get_features_mvt(
    param_zoom integer, param_tilex integer, param_tiley integer,
    param_table text,
    param_props text
)
RETURNS bytea AS
$$
DECLARE
    var_sql text; var_result bytea; var_geom geometry;
    var_table text; var_cols text; var_srid integer;
    var_geom_col text;
BEGIN
    SELECT
        f_geometry_column,
        quote_ident(f_table_schema) || '.' || quote_ident(f_table_name)
    FROM geometry_columns
    INTO var_geom_col, var_table
    WHERE f_table_schema || '.' || f_table_name = param_table
    LIMIT 1;

    IF var_geom_col IS NULL THEN
        RAISE EXCEPTION 'No such geometry table as %', param_table;
    END IF;
    var_geom := ST_TileEnvelope(param_zoom, param_tilex, param_tiley);

    var_sql := 'SELECT ST_SRID(geom) FROM ' || var_table || ' LIMIT 1';

    EXECUTE var_sql INTO var_srid;

    SELECT string_agg(quote_ident(trim(a)), ',')
    INTO var_cols
    FROM unnest(string_to_array(param_props, ',')) As a;

    var_sql :=
        'WITH mvtgeom AS ( SELECT
            ST_AsMVTGeom( ST_Transform(lg.' || quote_ident(var_geom_col)
    || ',$3) , $1) AS geom,
            ' || var_cols || '
            FROM ' || var_table || ' AS lg
            WHERE ST_Intersects(lg.' || quote_ident(var_geom_col)
    || ',ST_Transform($1,$2) )
            )
```

Make a rectangular geometry based on x, y, and zoom level inputs. → `var_geom := ST_TileEnvelope(...)`

Look up and store the geometry column and table names in variables.

Determine SRID of the table → `var_sql := ...` / `EXECUTE var_sql INTO var_srid;`

Use quote_ident so that passed-in columns are treated as column identifiers (to avoid SQL injection).

Split the param_props column string with a comma.

```
        SELECT ST_AsMVT(mvtgeom.*)          Parameterized
          FROM mvtgeom';                     query for MVT
    EXECUTE var_sql INTO var_result
    USING var_geom, var_srid, ST_SRID(var_geom);      Execute parameterized
                                                       MVT query and output to
    RETURN var_result;                                 binary variable
END;
$$
LANGUAGE plpgsql STABLE PARALLEL SAFE COST 1000;
```

Listing 17.10 assumes a spatial reference system in Web Mercator (SRID 3857), which is the default for the MVT functions. You can change the projection by passing in an overriding bounding geometry for ST_TileEnvelope (https://postgis.net/docs/ST_TileEnvelope.html).

To use the stored function, you'd create a web script such as the PHP companion script in the following listing.

Listing 17.11 PHP `get_tile_mvt.php` script

```php
<?php
    include_once("config.inc.php");
    $param_table = $_REQUEST['table'];
    $param_props = $_REQUEST['properties'];
    $param_zoom = $_REQUEST['zoom'];
    $param_tilex = $_REQUEST['x'];
    $param_tiley = $_REQUEST['y'];

    try{
      $pdo = new PDO(POSTGIS_DSN);
      $stmt = $pdo->prepare(
        "SELECT ch17.get_features_mvt(:zoom,:x,:y, :table,:props) AS data"
      );
      $stmt->execute(['zoom' =>$param_zoom,
                      'x' => $param_tilex,
                      'y' => $param_tiley,
                      'table' => $param_table,
                      'props' => $param_props]);
      $data = $stmt->fetch();
      $stream = $data[0];
      $stmt->closeCursor();
      fpassthru($stream);
    }
    catch (Exception $e){
      // report error message
      echo $e->getMessage();
    }
?>
```

Prepare the query.

Execute with user input args.

Fetch the results into a PHP variable.

Reference to the binary resource

Stream out the binary.

To use as a Mapbox Vector Tile layer, you would use code similar to listing 17.9, but replacing the URL:

```
get_features_mvt.php?x={x}&y={y}&zoom={z}&table=ch17.ma_openspace&props=gid,s
    ite_name
```

Although we didn't demonstrate outputting raster tiles from PostGIS, you can achieve similar results using `ST_TileEnvelope` in conjunction with raster functions `ST_Clip` and `ST_Union`. In practice, much of your heavy display raster needs would be achieved more efficiently using the files on disk and using out-of-db PostGIS rasters as detailed in Paul Ramsey's "PostGIS Raster and Crunchy Bridge" blog article (http://mng.bz/dm6X).

Summary

- PostGIS is a popular data source for web-mapping applications.
- PostGIS provides a lot of functions such as `ST_TileEnvelope`, `ST_AsMVT`, and `ST_AsGeoJSON` that can be used to mapify existing applications.
- A mapping server provides services such as displaying thematic tiles, exporting geospatial data, and editing mapping data, and most open source web-mapping servers and many commercial ones support PostGIS as a data source.
- The Open Geospatial Consortium (OGC) publishes standards such as WMS, WMTS, WFS, and WFS-T that many mapping servers support, allowing for some interchangeability between mapping servers.
- On the front end, OpenLayers and Leaflet are two of the most popular web mapping client-side APIs for use with web mapping services and PostGIS.

appendix A
Additional resources

This appendix includes links to resources useful for PostGIS users of all walks of life. We've mentioned some of these links in previous chapters, but they're also listed here so you have all of these resources in one place.

A.1 Planet sites

The best sources of timely information and tutorials are the various planet sites. The following ones are most relevant to PostGIS:

- *Planet PostGIS* (https://planet.postgis.net)—Many PostGIS bloggers hang out and are aggregated here. You'll learn about upcoming features, learn how to use and install them, find commentary, hear first-hand from core PostGIS developers, and more.
- *Planet OSGeo* (https://planet.osgeo.org)—You'll find many bloggers working on various OSGeo projects here. Many of the core PostGIS developers are aggregated here, as well as on Planet PostGIS. You'll also find content about related projects such as MapServer, QGIS, GDAL, Proj, and GeoServer.
- *Planet PostgreSQL* (https://planet.postgresql.org)—Many bloggers working with PostgreSQL come here. You'll find many of the core PostgreSQL developers blogging and sharing details of new features and security updates. You'll also find PostgreSQL power users discussing tricks for getting the most out of PostgreSQL.

A.2 Open source tools and offerings

PostGIS has garnered more support in the free, open source GIS arena than any other spatial database, far exceeding the spatial offerings of MySQL. There are too many PostGIS open source tools to list. We covered the more common offerings in chapters 5 and 17. As you can see, PostGIS already has a strong and growing commercial support belt as well.

You can find some of the tools covered in this book and others, as well as popular web mapping servers that support PostGIS, listed on the PostGIS website's Features page: https://postgis.net/features.

A.2.1 Self-contained GIS suites

The following GIS suite contains PostGIS as part of an integrated GIS desktop or web-mapping tool stack:

- *OSGeo Live* (https://live.osgeo.org)—OSGeo Live is a self-contained suite that comes in the following flavors: bootable DVD, USB thumb drive (often distributed at FOSS4G conferences), or VM. The distribution is based on the Xubuntu variant of Ubuntu. It contains fairly new versions of many OSGeo and related open source GIS products, including PostGIS and pgRouting, MapServer, GRASS, OpenJUMP, GeoServer, SpatiaLite, and Rasdaman, to name a few.

A.2.2 Open source desktop tools

There are many open source desktop tools that work with PostGIS. The following list is just a brief sampling of the more commonly used open source desktop viewing and editing tools:

- *OpenJUMP* (www.openjump.org)—This is one of our favorite desktop GIS tools, and it's what we used to render many of the ad hoc spatial queries you'll see in this book. It's a Java-based GIS desktop toolkit based on a plug-in architecture, and it has many user-contributed plug-ins. It runs on Linux, Windows, and macOS.
- *QGIS* (www.qgis.org)—This is perhaps the most popular of the free, open source desktop tools, and it also has a plug-in architecture. QGIS is written in C++ but offers a rich Python scripting environment and various GRASS integration options. It also includes drivers for connecting to PostGIS data as well as various other GIS data sources. QGIS is GNU GPL licensed.
- *gvSIG* (www.gvsig.com)—This Java-based desktop platform offers lots of integration features for ArcIMS and other Esri services.
- *GRASS GIS* (https://grass.osgeo.org/)—GRASS (Geographic Resources Analysis Support System) is probably the oldest and one of the most advanced free and open source tools for analyzing vectors, rasters, and other GIS data. It's designed more for the advanced GIS analyst than a new GIS or pure spatial database user. Although it's not set up specifically for PostGIS, there are many avenues of integration, such as the PostGRASS driver, JGRASS, and QGIS GRASS integration tools. It is also included as part of the QGIS desktop download.
- *Jupyter* (https://jupyter.org)—JupyterLab and Notebook are tools commonly used to analyze data. They are favorites among GIS specialists as well. Chapter 5

covered how you can query and load data into PostgreSQL/PostGIS with Jupyter. Qiusheng Wu's "Using GeoPandas" chapter (https://postgis.gishub .org/ chapters/geopandas.html) is a great primer on using Jupyter with PostGIS. He has a companion video series, "Spatial Data Management with Google Earth Engine" (http://mng.bz/xG2Y).

- *pgAdmin4* (https://pgadmin.org)—This is more of a database administration tool for PostgreSQL, but it does come with a geometry viewer, useful for testing out PostGIS queries. Version 5 and above also have sporty features like an ERD diagram for designing a new database or refactoring, and a schema compare tool.

A.3 *Open source extract-transform-load (ETL)*

This section lists open source tools for loading data into PostGIS:

- *GDAL/OGR* (https://gdal.org)—This is the most popular all-purpose, free, open source ETL tool. It's licensed under the MIT license, which is similar to BSD. GDAL/OGR binaries can be downloaded from the GDAL page: https:// trac.osgeo.org/gdal/wiki/DownloadingGdalBinaries.
- *GDAL/OGR* (https://github.com/pramsey/pgsql-ogr-fdw)—If you're running PostgreSQL 9.3 or above, you can also enjoy OGR as a PostgreSQL foreign data wrapper using the PostgreSQL extension, and you can query external spatial vector sources right from the comfort of your PostgreSQL database using SQL. Ogr_fdw allows you to join local PostgreSQL tables (both PostGIS and non-PostGIS) with spatial vector files or other spatial vector databases and web services supported by GDAL/OGR using SQL. Ogr_fdw is distributed by apt.postgresql .org, yum.postgresql.org, and PostGIS bundle via EDB Windows StackBuilder. For other systems that don't have ogr_fdw, but do have PostGIS, you can usually compile with just the PostgreSQL dev package installed as detailed.

A.4 *Places to get free data*

There are many places to get free data, and since the first edition of this book even more have shown up:

- *OpenStreetMap* (www.openstreetmap.org)—This community-driven spatial database and map repository has contributions from people all over the world. You can think of OSM as a free and open source Google map that has both web services and data you can download. It has base map information you can access via tile services as well as other crowd-sourced information, such as biking trails, and other GPS traces and waypoints in GPX format. You can use it as an overlay directly on your maps, using something like OpenLayers or Leaflet. For heavy usage, you should host your own tiles.
- *GeoNames* (www.geonames.org/)—The GeoNames geographical database covers all countries and contains over eight million place names (cities, postal codes, countries) that are available for download free of charge. Most data is in

tabular format. It also has REST APIs for doing place name and other searches. The data is licensed under Creative Commons 3.

- *GeoFabrik* (http://download.geofabrik.de)—A source of prepared OpenStreet-Map data. This distribution is generally built nightly and comes in OSM XML, pbf, and shapefile formats. The breakdown is usually by continent, country, state, or province.

- *Natural Earth* (www.naturalearthdata.com/)—This site offers public domain map datasets that contain both raster and vector data. Most data can be used in any manner for private or commercial consumption. The data currently offered includes world administrative boundaries, city and town points with populations, and various natural land and water geometries.

- *US Census TIGER data* (www.census.gov/programs-surveys/geography/guidance/tiger-data-products-guide.html)—If you're in the US or doing research on a US population, the Census TIGER data site should be one of your first stops. It contains data in Esri shapefile format updated annually. This data has US road networks, which are great for geocoding (it is the source used by the PostGIS packaged postgis_tiger_geocoder extension).

  For researching, the more important data is the Census tract population grouping, which is often combined with other census data (https://data.census.gov/cedsci/) to formulate population stats about housing, ethnicity, income, population job makeup, and so on.

- *US Geological Survey* (www.usgs.gov)—If you're looking for raster data covering the United States, look no further than USGS. USGS offers elevation data, hydrology, satellite imagery, and topographic maps.

- *PRISM Climate Group* (www.prism.oregonstate.edu/mtd/)—This site provides fairly current and historical climate data in .bil and .asc raster formats for the continental United States.

- *UK Ordinance Survey* (www.ordnancesurvey.co.uk/opendatadownload/products.html)—Provides vector data for UK areas in Esri shapefile, GeoPackage (some), and GML3. Also, you can find raster terrain data in Esri Shape Contours, ASCII Grid, and GeoPackage. Some data is free and some is available for purchase.

appendix B
Installing, compiling, and upgrading

There are several ways to install PostgreSQL/PostGIS. When we started out, the only way was to compile the code yourself, but life has since become much simpler, and now the general user doesn't need to experience the joys and frustrations of compiling their own source code.

Most people who just want to use PostGIS take the easy road of acquiring and installing prebuilt binaries via packaged installers. A brief synopsis of the more common PostGIS installer offerings is detailed on the PostGIS site: http://postgis .net/install.

For PostgreSQL, the PostgreSQL site has a listing of the most commonly used installers, many of which include PostGIS and other extensions as an optional install: www.postgresql.org/download/.

Compiling from source is still an important and adventurous journey if you want to be a contributor to the PostGIS project. If you wish to compile from source code, refer to the directions on the PostGIS source download page: http://postgis .net/source.

B.1   Installing PostgreSQL and PostGIS

It goes without saying that you'll need a functioning PostgreSQL server to use Post-GIS. The installation options we'll discuss here describe the base PostgreSQL installation as well as the additional PostGIS installation.

As a general rule, you'll want to get your PostGIS binaries from the same source as your PostgreSQL binaries so that they're guaranteed to work together. If you're not happy with the version of PostGIS available from your distribution of choice, you can still use the PostgreSQL binaries and compile PostGIS yourself, as long as you also install the postgresql-dev package that commonly gets distributed with PostgreSQL binary distributions. You'll also need a working gcc/g++ compiler to compile.

You should also try to get the newest version of PostgreSQL you can to take advantage of the newest features in both PostgreSQL and PostGIS.

The PostgreSQL project maintains a list of the most common distributions, most of which offer PostGIS: www.postgresql.org/download/.

B.1.1 *Using PostgreSQL and PostGIS in Docker*

These days Docker has become a common option for running PostGIS and PostgreSQL. Docker is supported in Linux, macOS, and Windows. FreeBSD, starting at version 11.1, has experimental support for it. You can find prebuilt Docker images with PostGIS and PostgreSQL on https://hub.docker.com/. The main PostGIS Docker registry is at https://hub.docker.com/r/postgis/postgis.

Tobin Bradley has a good video and blog post that can get you started, called "Postgres/PostGIS in Docker for production": http://mng.bz/A1d7. The Docker repo Tobin demonstrated in that video is the one that was eventually adopted by the PostGIS project and is available here: https://hub.docker.com/r/postgis/postgis. You can contribute at https://github.com/postgis/docker-postgis.

In addition to the official PostGIS repo, QGIS project members have developed some of their own that are targeted for working with QGIS. Check out the following: https://github.com/kartoza/docker-postgis.

B.1.2 *EnterpriseDB one-click installers*

EnterpriseDB one-click installers will work for any maintained (not end of life) desktop Linux system (32-bit and 64-bit), Windows Desktop/Server (32-bit and 64-bit) systems, and macOS for PostgreSQL 10 and below. You can find the installers on this page: www.enterprisedb.com/downloads/postgres-postgresql-downloads.

Starting with PostgreSQL 11+, EDB installers are only available for 64-bit Windows and macOS systems. The installer comes with the following prepackaged goods:

- PostgreSQL Server
- pgAdmin4 (GUI database administration tool)
- Application StackBuilder—Allows you to install PostgreSQL add-ons such as PostGIS, JDBC, and ODBC, plus application development environments such as Apache.

The PostGIS versions that come packaged with EnterpriseDB installers for Linux and macOS do not have all the features of the version for Windows, and also don't have some of the other extensions we've discussed in this book. As such, for Linux/macOS, even if you are on a desktop system, you may be better served by one of the other installers.

ENTERPRISEDB ONE-CLICK INSTALLERS (WINDOWS)

If you're on a Windows system, the easiest way to get started is to use one of the one-click installers provided by EnterpriseDB (www.postgresql.org/download/windows/) and use the packaged StackBuilder to install the PostGIS extension. The PostGIS extension for core PostgreSQL that is accessible from StackBuilder for Windows is one we maintain, and we keep it fairly up to date. In addition to the extensions included with the PostGIS project, you will find the following extensions and tools as part of the Spatial Extensions > PostGIS Bundle StackBuilder, shown in figure B.1:

- pgRouting and osm2pgrouting
- ogr_fdw extension + ogr_fdw_info command line
- pgPointCloud

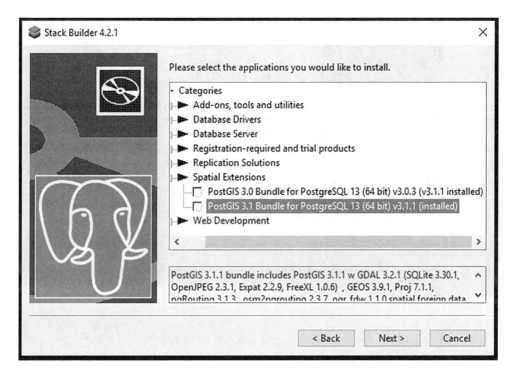

Figure B.1   PostGIS Bundle for PostgreSQL windows

You can also download the same binaries and installers from the PostGIS site (http://postgis.net/windows_downloads) or use one of the experimental Windows binaries that are built whenever there's a change in the PostGIS development code base.

WARNING   EDB provides both PostgreSQL and their own Oracle-compatible PostgreSQL fork called "PostgreSQL Advanced Server." Be sure to pick the PostgreSQL one and not Advanced Server. The binaries we manage are for

PostgreSQL, not for PostgreSQL Advanced Server. PostgreSQL Advanced Server ships its own PostGIS, which generally lags behind and offers fewer PostGIS add-ons.

EDB one-click installers also include other features, such as various PL languages. In order to install PL/Python3u, you will need to install the EnterpriseDB Language Pack as shown in figure B.2.

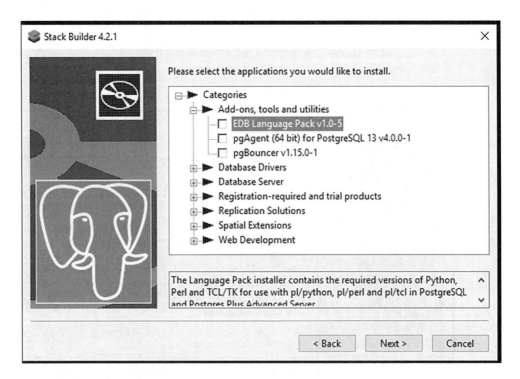

Figure B.2   EDB Language Pack

Then add the system environment variable PYTHONHOME by navigating to Control Panel > System > Advanced System Settings > Environ Variables to where the Python pack was installed. For PostgreSQL 13, Windows 64-bit, it would be C:\edb\languagepack \v1\Python-3.7\. At end of PATH, add the same path, as shown in figure B.3.

If you still get an error when running CREATE EXTENSION plpython3u; in your database, restart your database service from Services.

Since Windows 10, Windows supports something called a Windows Subsystem for Linux (WSL). This is a popular option for developers that allows you to run a Linux distro such as Ubuntu side by side with your Windows system. From within WSL, you can then use the associated Linux package management to install PostgreSQL and PostGIS. Refer to Microsoft's "Windows Subsystem for Linux Installation Guide for

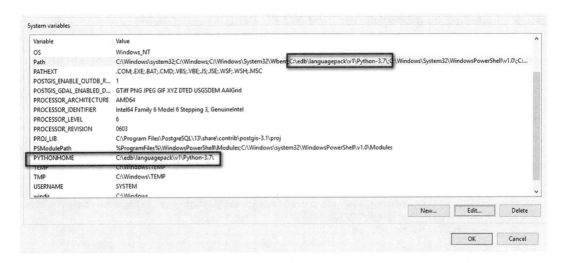

Figure B.3 EDB Python Home

Windows 10" documentation (https://docs.microsoft.com/en-us/windows/wsl/install-win10) for details.

B.1.3 *MacOS-specific installers*

In addition to the EnterpriseDB offering we already mentioned, these are popular distributions for macOS:

- Postgres.app (https://postgresapp.com/) is a macOS distribution maintained by Heroku that consists of PostgreSQL and the popular PostgreSQL extensions PostGIS, PL/V8, and PL/Python, in addition to the regular contrib ones that come with PostgreSQL. Postgres.app also includes GDAL command-line tools and PostgreSQL and PostGIS command-line tools. The PostgreSQL server service of Postgres.app can be launched and shut down with a click, making it great for development. The latest version of Postgres.app as of this writing includes the latest stable releases of PostgreSQL 13 and PostGIS 3.1. However, as of this writing, it still does not include the pgRouting or ogr_fdw extensions commonly used with PostGIS.

- Homebrew (https://brew.sh/) started out as a Mac package management system and seems to be the preferred way for installing GIS stuff on macOS these days. It has recently started to support Linux and Windows Linux Subsystem. Homebrew supports both compiling from source (using brew scripts) and installing from binaries using what it calls "bottles": https://docs.brew.sh/Bottles.

OSGeo maintains a macOS bottle repo that contains versions of PostGIS, ogr_fdw, and GDAL: https://bottle.download.osgeo.org.

B.1.4   *Installing on a Linux server (Red Hat EL, CentOS) using YUM*

If you're running a variant of Red Hat Enterprise Linux, Fedora, CentOS, or Scientific Linux, the PostgreSQL Yum repository is a great option. It has the latest and greatest of the main and beta versions of PostgreSQL. In addition to core PostgreSQL, the Yum repository has additional packages, such as PostGIS and other add-ons such as pgRouting and ogr_fdw, all available via https://yum.postgresql.org/.

The Yum repository is most suitable for command-line server installs, but it can also be used for desktop installs via the Yum installer. The Yum repository generally has the latest PostGIS stable offering with the latest PostgreSQL.

To install you'd do the following:

```
yum install postgresql13 postgresql13-server postgresql13-libs postgresql13-
    contrib postgresql13-devel
yum install postgis31_13
```

Details of installing PostGIS on CentOS 8 and higher can be found in the "Installing PostGIS 3.0 and PostgreSQL 12 on CentOS 8" article on Devrim Gunduz's Postgre-SQL blog at http://mng.bz/zGea.

You can check out our various guides to Yum on the Postgres OnLine Journal site: www.postgresonline.com/journal/categories/53-yum.

B.1.5   *PostgreSQL Apt repository*

The PostgreSQL development group (PGDG) has a repository for the Apt packaging system commonly used by Ubuntu and Debian. Details of how to add the PGDG Apt repository to your list of repositories can be found on the PostgreSQL wiki (https://wiki.postgresql.org/wiki/Apt). Once you add this Apt repository, you can install or upgrade PostgreSQL and PostgreSQL extensions via the standard Apt package manager.

The PGDG Apt repository comes packaged with the latest versions of PostgreSQL and many add-ons, such as pgAdmin and common PostgreSQL extensions. It also includes packages for PostGIS.

There's generally only one version of PostGIS per major version of PostgreSQL. PostgreSQL 13 and PostGIS 3.1 are the latest stable versions. To install PostGIS and other extensions covered in this book, do the following:

```
apt install postgresql-13 postgresql-13-postgis-3 postgresql-13-ogr-fdw
apt install postgresql-13-plr postgresql-13-pgrouting postgresql-plpython3-13
```

When in doubt, you can use apt search keyword to search for a package:

```
apt search pgrouting
```

The server install doesn't come packaged with the shp2pgsql and raster2pgsql command-line tools. To get those, you'll need to do an additional install:

```
apt install postgis-gui
```

B.1.6   *Other available binaries and distros*

Most official OS distros such as Yum, Ubuntu, and Debian make PostgreSQL and Post-GIS available via their package managers, though the official repositories generally carry only one version of PostgreSQL/PostGIS per OS release, so they tend to be very old if you aren't running the latest OS distribution.

B.1.7   *Database as a service offerings for PostGIS*

Most PostgreSQL database as a service (DBaaS) providers provide the PostGIS extensions. DBaaS can ease the management of your database because they automatically handle upgrades, backups, replicas, and so on for you, but they are not without their downsides.

Key benefits:

- Many let you scale your processing and disk size up and down as needed.
- Several have auto-scaling based on usage statistics.
- They all handle the backup and replication.
- They often provide optimized disk I/O.
- They handle upgrades, patching, and general security maintenance.
- They often provide extra monitoring tools.

Key downsides:

- If you need a 24/7 running database, they are generally pricier than running on a cloud server or your own server. They can be twice as much or more.
- They have limited offerings of extensions. Almost no foreign data wrappers except for postgres_fdw and column store FDWs are offered. Generally no untrusted PL extensions like PL/PythonU or PL/PerlU are allowed. Installing any extension not provided by them is out of the question.
- Basically, anything interacting with the filesystem is off limits. Things like file_fdw or SQL COPY commands are not available.
- They tend to lag behind the PostgreSQL project by a couple of months or more, so you will generally not find the latest PostgreSQL release available until several months after release.
- They are often not good about keeping up with micro updates (which mostly contain security updates and bug fixes). As such, you may be bitten by bugs that have long ago been fixed by PostGIS/PostgreSQL projects.
- You will be forced to upgrade if they drop a major version you are currently using.

As of this writing, PostgreSQL 13.2 and PostGIS 3.1.1 are the latest stable releases, and most of the common DBaaSs are lagging behind and have not provided the latest patch releases.

These are common DBaaSs used for running PostGIS:

- Aiven Postgres (https://aiven.io/postgresql) offers PostGIS and pgRouting. As of this writing, PostgreSQL 13.2, PostGIS 3.0.2, and pgRouting 3.1.0 are the latest offerings.
- Amazon RDS (https://aws.amazon.com/rds/postgresql/) offers both PostGIS and pgRouting, but it tends to lag behind PostgreSQL by a couple of months. As of this writing, PostgreSQL 13.1, PostGIS 3.0.2, and pgRouting 3.1.0 are the newest available.
- Amazon Aurora (https://aws.amazon.com/rds/aurora/postgresql-features/) is a fork of PostgreSQL and a bit pricier than RDS. It promises 3X speed over regular PostgreSQL, but it also lags further behind Amazon RDS in terms of PostgreSQL development version. The latest release is Aurora PostgreSQL 4.0, which is a fork of PostgreSQL 12.4 and offers PostGIS 3.0.2 at this time.
- Digital Ocean DBaaS for PostgreSQL (www.digitalocean.com/docs/databases/postgresql/) has a latest offering of PostgreSQL 12, PostGIS 2.5.3, and pgRouting 2.6.3.
- Google Cloud SQL for PostgreSQL (https://cloud.google.com/sql/docs/postgres/extensions) offers PostGIS but not pgRouting. As of this writing, PostgreSQL 13.1 and PostGIS 3.0.2 are the latest offering.
- Microsoft Azure Database for PostgreSQL Single Server (https://docs.microsoft.com/en-us/azure/postgresql/overview-single-server) has a fully managed latest offering of PostgreSQL 11 and PostGIS 2.5.1.
- Microsoft Azure Database for PostgreSQL Flexible Server (Preview) (https://docs.microsoft.com/en-us/azure/postgresql/flexible-server/) has a new offering targeted at developers: PostgreSQL 13.3 and PostGIS 3.1.1.
- Microsoft Azure Database for PostgreSQL Hyperscale (Citus) (https://docs.microsoft.com/en-us/azure/postgresql/hyperscale/) is targeted for large databases. This is PostgreSQL with the Citus sharding. This used to be called CitusDB before Citus was acquired by Microsoft. It supports PostgreSQL 13.2 (preview) and PostGIS 3.0.3, but not pgRouting. The stable release is PostgreSQL 11.11, PostGIS 2.5.1.

B.1.8 Compiling and installing from PostGIS source

If you want the most bleeding-edge version of PostGIS, compiling it yourself is still generally the way to go. This is covered in the PostGIS manual and wiki:

- The Installation chapter of the official PostGIS manual covers standard compilation on Linux/Unix systems; see http://postgis.net/docs/manual-dev/postgis_installation.html.

  Although you can compile your own PostgreSQL, you don't need to if you're on Linux, even if you want to compile PostGIS yourself. But you will need the PostgreSQL development headers (usually packaged in something called postgresql-devel) and you'll need to install postgresql and postgresql-server, which you can do using a Linux packager, such as Yum, YatZ, apt-get, apt, or whatever your distribution uses for software install. The Yum, YatZ, and apt-gets of the world are similar in concept to Windows Update and provide precompiled binaries of PostgreSQL and PostGIS for your particular Linux distribution from well-defined repositories.

- There is a whole user-contributed section on the PostGIS wiki with details on compiling PostGIS on various operating systems; see http://trac.osgeo.org/postgis/wiki/UsersWikiInstall.
- As of this writing, headers aren't available for Windows because Windows PostgreSQL versions are compiled with Visual C++. You must compile your own PostgreSQL under MingW-w64 if you want to compile PostGIS. The PostGIS user wiki covers this: http://trac.osgeo.org/postgis/wiki/UsersWikiWinCompile.

PostGIS Windows 64-bit support

PostGIS 2.0 was the first PostGIS release to support PostgreSQL 64-bit for Windows. It's available on StackBuilder and the PostGIS website, and it's compiled with the MinGW-w64 toolchain (http://mingw-w64.sourceforge.net/). Starting with PostGIS 2.1, the package was renamed from PostGIS to PostGIS Bundle for Windows (32-bit and 64-bit) because in addition to the extensions that come with PostGIS, it includes pgrouting, osm2pgrouting, ogr_fdw, and pgPointcloud. The 32-bit version was discontinued in PostgreSQL 10 to follow suit with EDB discontinuation of 32-bit PostgreSQL.

If you don't want to experience the joys and pains of compiling code and don't mind waiting for a package maintainer to compile and prepare a package for general consumption, then stick with the prepackaged versions.

B.2 Creating a PostGIS database

Once you have the binaries installed, you can enable PostGIS in any database using the following commands:

```
CREATE SCHEMA IF NOT EXISTS postgis;
ALTER DATABASE postgis_in_action SET search_path=public,postgis,contrib;
CREATE EXTENSION postgis SCHEMA postgis;
--if you are running 3.0 or higher and want raster support
CREATE EXTENSION postgis SCHEMA postgis_raster;
-- for advanced 3D support
CREATE EXTENSION postgis SCHEMA postgis_sfcgal;
```

The `CREATE EXTENSION` approach picks the latest version of PostGIS installed in your PostgreSQL server.

If you prefer a different version—for example, if you want to experiment with PostGIS 3.1.0 and you have it already compiled and installed—you can use a variation like the following:

```
CREATE SCHEMA IF NOT EXISTS postgis;
ALTER DATABASE postgis_in_action SET search_path=public,postgis,contrib;
```

```
CREATE EXTENSION postgis VERSION "3.1.0alpha2" SCHEMA postgis;
CREATE EXTENSION postgis_raster VERSION "3.1.0alpha2";
CREATE EXTENSION postgis_topology VERSION "3.1.0alpha2";
```

CREATE EXTENSION can be used to spatially enable an existing database as well.

Different versions of PostGIS can coexist on the same data cluster

Multiple versions of PostGIS can be installed on the same PostgreSQL server instance, but each database can have only one version of PostGIS. You can work with various versions (for example, PostGIS 2.5 for legacy projects, 3.0 for newer projects, and 3.1 for development projects). Just keep in mind that if you plan to run various versions on the same database server cluster, you'll need to be using the same version of GEOS and Proj for all of them.

As of PostGIS 3.0, the lib installs by default without the minor version, so the file is just postgis-3.<whatever your os bin extension>. This means that it is not possible to run 3.0 and 3.1 in the same cluster, unless you compile your own and use the --with-library-minor-version as part of your ./configure command. The Windows experimental binaries of the master branch (currently 3.2) in development (available at http://postgis.net/windows_downloads/) are compiled with --with-library-minor-version to allow for experimentation. However, they may have newer GEOS/Proj, which will be shared with your installed lower version.

B.3 Upgrading PostGIS

Upgrading PostGIS from one minor version to another is straightforward. Install the new binaries and execute an ALTER EXTENSION command.

Upgrading from 1.5 to 2.0 requires a dump and restore of the PostgreSQL database. PostGIS 2.0+ upgrading to PostGIS 3.1+ does not require a dump and restore. If you have the newer binaries installed, these can be done with

```
ALTER EXTENSION postgis UPDATE;
```

B.3.1 PostGIS soft upgrade using extensions

If you're upgrading PostGIS from a minor version 2.0 through to major versions 3.*, or a microversion such as from 3.1.0 to 3.1.1, you can accomplish this without doing a backup and restore of your database. Doing an in-place upgrade is referred to as a *soft upgrade*.

Start by updating your PostGIS binaries via the same system you used in your original install of PostGIS. Next, execute the following command, making sure to adjust the version number for your version of PostGIS:

```
ALTER EXTENSION postgis UPDATE TO "2.5.4";
```

For example, you may want a PostGIS 2.5.2 database to only be upgraded to PostGIS 2.5.4 and not to PostGIS 3.1.1.

If you want to move up to the most recently installed version of PostGIS and are not sure of the version number, you can leave out the specification of the version number, as shown in the next example. You'll want to be cautious with this approach if you have multiple versions of PostGIS installed on your server.

For PostGIS 2.4 and below, use these commands:

```
ALTER EXTENSION postgis UPDATE;
ALTER EXTENSION postgis_topology UPDATE;
-- repeat for each extension you have
```

For PostGIS 2.5 and above, you can upgrade PostGIS and other packaged PostGIS project extensions using this command:

```
SELECT PostGIS_Extensions_Upgrade();
```

For the in-development versions of PostGIS, which aren't versioned like released versions, you can also take advantage of the extension feature using next, which is a dummy packaging that forces the running of the upgrade script:

```
ALTER EXTENSION postgis UPDATE TO "3.2.0dev";
ALTER EXTENSION postgis_raster UPDATE TO "3.2.0dev";
ALTER EXTENSION postgis_topology UPDATE TO "3.2.0devnext";
```

If 3.2.0dev is the version listed in your postgis.control, postgis_topology.control, and so on, then the following command is sufficient to force an upgrade:

```
SELECT  PostGIS_Extensions_Upgrade();
```

B.3.2   Upgrading PostgreSQL and PostGIS using pg_upgrade

For PostGIS before version 3.0, using pg_upgrade is a bit tricky since the library files changed with each minor release, and packagers tend to ship only one version of Post-GIS with each major version of PostgreSQL.

If you are in this boat, refer to the "Using pg_upgrade to upgrade PostgreSQL 9.3 PostGIS 2.1 to PostgreSQL 11 2.5 on Yum" article on the Postgres OnLine Journal: http://mng.bz/ZYEa.

The directions and paths of files are specific to Yum, but the basic steps apply to any distribution.

B.3.3   Upgrading PostGIS from 1.X to 2.X or 3.X

If you're upgrading from PostGIS 1.X to PostGIS 2.X or 3.X, then a dump and restore of your database is unfortunately required. There are two approaches to this: using a Perl script, or not.

THE RECOMMENDED CLEAN WAY INVOLVES USING A PERL SCRIPT

PostGIS comes packaged with a script called postgis_restore.pl, which will allow you to restore using PostgreSQL's custom compressed backup format. This will take care of several issues, such as fixing up SRIDs and converting deprecated constraint calls to new constraint calls. This approach is well documented in the official PostGIS manual: http://postgis.net/docs/postgis_installation.html#hard_upgrade.

THE NO-PERL-SCRIPT UPGRADE APPROACH

For many users with lower attention spans, smaller databases, or a distaste for anything involving a command line, or who don't have Perl installed on their server, this approach will be noisier but will work. This approach will generate errors you can safely ignore because it will try to restore old functions not available in the latest binaries:

1 Make a custom backup of your database using `pg_dump -Fc` or pgAdmin4 choosing Format: *Custom*.

2 Create a new PostGIS 2+ or 3+ database using `CREATE EXTENSION postgis;`.

3 Run the legacy.sql script packaged with PostGIS. You can opt for legacy_minimal .sql instead of legacy.sql if you know you didn't use too many legacy functions in your code. Most legacy functions lacked the `ST_` in front, so if you used a lot of those, you might need the full legacy.sql. If in doubt, just run the legacy.sql version.

4 Restore your backup over this new database.

5 *Do not forget to do this last part.* Run just the `drop` command statements at the end of the postgis_upgrade_*_minor.sql script. This drops old functions that would otherwise conflict with new functions. Functions that fall in this category are functions that got additional arguments in the new versions.

appendix C
SQL primer

PostgreSQL supports almost the whole ANSI SQL 92, 1999 standard logic, as well as many of the SQL:2003, SQL:2006, and SQL:2008 constructs, and a fair amount of the SQL:2011 and SQL:2016 constructs. PostgreSQL is probably the most ANSI-SQL-compliant database you will find on the planet. As such, if you've used other relational databases, you probably already know how to use PostgreSQL. In this appendix, we'll cover many of the ANSI-SQL constructs as well as some PostgreSQL-specific SQL language extensions. Because we'll remain largely focused on standard functionality, the content in this appendix is also applicable to other standards-compliant relational databases. The less-standard features that PostgreSQL offers will be reserved for appendix D.

There are two categories of SQL that all relational databases support. One is data definition language (DDL), which is what you use to define new database structures such as tables, table columns, views, schemas, functions, and so on. The other kind of SQL is data manipulation language (DML), which is what you use to query and update data in your database. Most of your life working with relational databases will be spent using DML. This appendix will focus on DML.

C.1 The information_schema

The `information_schema` is a catalog introduced in SQL 92 and enhanced in each subsequent version of the spec. Although it's a standard, sadly most commercial and open source databases don't completely support it. We know that the following common databases do: PostgreSQL, MySQL/MariaDb, Microsoft SQL Server, Presto, and MemSQL. Oracle and IBM do via user-supported contributions.

The most useful views in this schema are `tables`, `columns`, and `views`; they provide a catalog of all the tables, columns, and views in your database. To get a list of all non-system tables in PostgreSQL, you can run the following query (the `information_schema.tables` view in PostgreSQL will list only tables that you have access to):

```
SELECT table_schema, table_name, table_type
   FROM information_schema.tables
   WHERE table_schema NOT IN('pg_catalog', 'information_schema')
   ORDER BY table_schema, table_name;
```

The preceding query will work equally well in MySQL (except that in MySQL, *schema* means database, and there's only one information_schema shared across all MySQL databases in a MySQL cluster). MS SQL Server behaves more like PostgreSQL in that each information_schema is unique to each database, except that in SQL Server the system views and tables aren't queryable from information_schema, whereas they are in PostgreSQL.

The columns view will give you a listing of all the columns in a particular table or set of tables. The following example lists all the columns found in a table called ch01.restaurants.

Listing C.1   List all columns in the ch01.restaurants table

```
SELECT c.column_name, c.data_type, c.udt_name,
       c.ordinal_position AS ord_pos,
       c.column_default AS cdefault
   FROM information_schema.columns AS c
   WHERE table_schema = 'ch01' and table_name = 'restaurants'
   ORDER BY c.column_name;
```

The results of this query look something like the following:

```
column_name |   data_type    | udt_name | ord_pos |  cdefault
------------+----------------+----------+---------+---------------------------
 franchise  | character      | bpchar   |    2 |
 geom       | USER-DEFINED   | geometry |    3 |
 id         | integer        | int4     |    1 | nextval('ch01...)
```

One important way that PostgreSQL is different from databases such as SQL Server and MySQL Server that support information_schema is that it has an additional field called udt_name that denotes the PostgreSQL-specific data type. Because PostGIS geometry is an add-on module and not part of PostgreSQL, you'll see the standard ANSI data type listed as USER-DEFINED and the udt_name field storing the fact that it's a geometry.

The information_schema.columns view provides numerous other fields, so we encourage you to explore it. We consider these to be the most useful fields:

- table_name and column_name—These should be obvious.
- data_type—The ANSI standard data type name for this column.
- udt_name—The PostgreSQL-specific name. Except for user-defined types, you can use data_type or udt_name when creating these fields except in the case of series. Recall that we created id as a serial data type in chapter 1, and behind the scenes PostgreSQL created an integer column and a sequence object, and

then set the default of this new column to the next value of the sequence object: nextval('ch01.restaurants_gid_seq'::regclass).

- ordinal_position—This is the order in which the column appears in the table.
- character_maximum_length—With character fields, this tells you the maximum number of characters allowed in the field.
- column_default—The default value assigned to new records. This can be a constant or the result of a function.

The tables view lists both tables and views (virtual tables). The views view gives you the name and the view definition for each view you have access to. The view definition gives you the SQL that defines the view, and it's very useful for scripting the definitions. In PostgreSQL, you can see how the information_schema views are defined, though you may not be able to in other databases because the information_schema is excluded from this system view.

You can output the names of views and the SQL used to define the views with the following statement:

```
SELECT table_schema, table_name, view_definition,
    is_updatable, is_insertable_into
    FROM information_schema.views
    WHERE table_schema = 'information_schema';
```

In the preceding examples, we've demonstrated the common meta-tables you'd find in the ANSI information_schema. We also demonstrated the most fundamental of SQL statements. In the next section, we'll look at the anatomy of an SQL statement and describe what each part means.

C.2 Querying data with SQL

The cornerstone of every relational database is the declarative language called *Structured Query Language* (SQL). Although each relational database has a slightly different syntax, the fundamentals are pretty much the same across all relational DBMSs.

One of the most common things done with SQL is querying relational data. SQL of this nature is often referred to as a data manipulation language (DML), and it consists of clauses specifically designed for this purpose. The other side of DML is updating data with SQL, which we'll cover in section C.3.

C.2.1 SELECT, FROM, WHERE, and ORDER BY clauses

For accessing data, you use a SELECT statement, usually accompanied with a FROM and a WHERE clause. The SELECT part of the statement restricts the columns that will be returned, the FROM clause determines where the data comes from, and WHERE restricts the number of records to be returned.

When returning constants or simple calculations that come from nowhere, the FROM clause isn't needed in PostgreSQL, SQL Server, or MySQL, whereas in databases such as Oracle and IBM DB2, you need to select FROM dual, sys.dual, or some other dummy table.

Basic SELECT

A basic SELECT looks something like this:

```
SELECT gid, item_name, the_geom
    FROM feature_items
    WHERE item_name LIKE 'Queens%';
```

Keep in mind that PostgreSQL is by default case-sensitive when text searching, as in the preceding query. If you want to do a non-case-sensitive search, you'd do the following:

```
SELECT gid, item_name, the_geom
    FROM feature_items
    WHERE upper(item_name) LIKE 'QUEENS%';
```

Instead of using upper(item_name), you can use the non-portable ILIKE PostgreSQL predicate to do a case-insensitive search, replacing the upper(item_name) LIKE 'QUEENS%' with item_name ILIKE 'QUEENS%'.

There's no guaranteed order for results to be returned in, but sometimes you'll care about order. The SQL ORDER BY clause satisfies this need for order.

> **NOTE** PostgreSQL does have an extension called citext which you install with CREATE EXTENSION citext;. This extension includes a text data type called citext, meant to be a drop-in replacement for text, but when used with operations such as LIKE or =, it will always be case-insensitive. Since this is a nonstandard type that you will not find in other databases, we will not cover it in this appendix.

Following is an example that lists all items starting with *Lion* and orders them by item_name:

```
SELECT DISTINCT item_name
    FROM feature_items
    WHERE upper(item_name) LIKE 'LION%'
    ORDER BY upper(item_name);
```

PostgreSQL provides a per-database collation feature that makes using upper for sorting less necessary, depending on the collation order you've designated for your database.

SELECT * IS NOT YOUR FRIEND

Within a SELECT statement you can use the term *, which means "select all the fields in the FROM tables." There is also the variant sometable.* if you want to select all fields from only one table, and not all fields from the other tables in your FROM.

We highly recommend you stay away from this with production code. It's useful for seeing all the columns of a table when you don't have the table structure in front of you, but it can be a real performance drain, especially with tables that hold geometries. If you have a table with a column that's unconstrained by size, such as a large text field or geometry field, you'll be pulling all that data across the wire and pulling from disk even when you don't care about the contents of all the fields. It's also dangerous to use * when you have multiple tables in a join that have the same column names, because the column names would be output, and whatever code you're running might arbitrarily pick the wrong column, depending on the language you're using.

C.2.2 Indexes

The WHERE clause often relies on an index to improve row selection. If you have a large number of distinct groupings of records that have the same value in a field, it's useful to put an index on that field. For a few distinct groupings of records by a column, the index is more harmful than helpful, because the planner will ignore it and do a faster table scan, and updating will incur a heavy performance penalty.

The ORDER clause can also take advantage of indexes. In particular, the distance operators we covered in this book can only take advantage of indexes when used in the ORDER BY and *not* when used in WHERE.

C.2.3 Aliasing

In listing C.1 using information_schema, we demonstrated the concept of aliasing. Aliasing is giving a table or a column a different name in your query than how it's defined in the database.

Aliasing is done with an AS clause. For table aliases, AS is optional for most ANSI SQL standard databases including PostgreSQL. For column aliases, AS is optional for most ANSI SQL databases including PostgreSQL. AS, however, is not optional in PostgreSQL for subqueries, which we'll cover later in this appendix.

Aliasing is indispensable when you're doing self joins (where you join the same table twice) and you need to distinguish between the two, or when the two tables you have may have field names in common. The other use of aliases is to make your code easier to read and to reduce typing by shortening long table and field names.

C.2.4 Why use AS when you don't need to

Although AS is an optional clause, we like to always put it in for clarity, but it's really a matter of preference. To demonstrate, which of the following is more understandable?

```
SELECT b.somefield a FROM sometable b;
```

or

```
SELECT b.somefield AS a FROM sometable AS b;
```

C.2.5 *Using subselects*

The SQL language has built-in support for subselects. Much of the expressiveness and complexity of SQL consists of keeping subselects straight and knowing when and when not to use them. For PostgreSQL, most valid SELECT … clauses can be used as subselects, and when used in a FROM clause, the subselect must be aliased. For some databases, such as SQL Server, there are some minor limitations; for example, SQL Server doesn't allow an ORDER BY in a subselect without a TOP clause.

A subselect statement is a full SELECT … FROM … statement that appears within another SQL statement. It can appear in the following locations of an overall SQL statement:

- *In a* UNION, INTERSECT, *or* EXCEPT—You'll learn about these shortly.
- *In a* FROM *clause*—When used in a FROM, the subselect acts as a virtual table, and it needs to have an alias name to define how it will be called in other parts of the query. Also, in versions prior to PostgreSQL 9.3, the subselect can't reference other FROM table fields as part of its definition. Some databases allow you to do this under certain conditions, such as SQL Server's 2005+ CROSS/OUTER APPLY and the LATERAL clause in PostgreSQL 9.3+, which can be used for both subselects and set-returning functions. Note that for PostgreSQL 9.3+, the LATERAL clause term is optional when used with functions. You'll see examples of the LATERAL clause later in this appendix.
- *In the definition of a calculated column*—When used in this context, the subselect can return only one column and one row. This pretty much applies to all databases, but PostgreSQL has a somewhat unique feature because of the way it implements rows. Each table has a data type that contains all the columns of its row. As such, a table can be used as a data type of a column. In addition, a row, even one coming from a subselect, is a composite type. This allows you to get away with returning a multicolumn row as a field expression. This isn't a feature you'll commonly find in other databases, so we won't cover it in this appendix. You can, however, return multiple rows as an array if they contain only one column by using ARRAY in PostgreSQL. This will return the column as an array of that type. We demonstrate this in various parts of the book. Again, this is a feature that's fairly unique to PostgreSQL and is very handy for spatial queries. There is a feature called "computed columns," introduced in PostgreSQL 12, that allows you to define a formula as a column in a table. The caveat is that the column can only reference values in the particular row. This is defined at the data definition level, not the data manipulation level.
- *In the* WHERE *part of another SQL query*—Subselects can be used in IN, NOT IN, and EXISTS clauses.
- *In a* WITH *clause*—A SELECT query in a WITH clause is loosely defined as a subselect but is not strictly thought of that way. You'll also find it in Oracle, SQL Server, IBM DB2, SQLite, MySQL 8+, MariaDb 10+, and Firebird.

One caution with subselects in WITH clauses: When used in PostgreSQL pre-12, they're always materialized (converted to a temporary work table). From PostgreSQL 12 on, the planner decides whether it's more efficient to inline the query like a regular subselect or to materialize it. In some cases, particularly with spatial queries, the planner might guess wrong. To force the older behavior of materializing, you can either add an OFFSET 0 at the end of the query or use the MATERIALIZE keyword.

Materialization is both good and bad. It's good because you can use it as a kind of HINT to the planner to materialize, but bad because if you just consider it to be syntactic sugar, you could slow down your queries significantly.

WHAT IS A CORRELATED SUBQUERY?

A correlated subquery is a subquery that uses fields from the outer query (the next level above the subquery) to define the subquery. Correlated subqueries are often used in column expressions and WHERE clauses. They're generally slower than noncorrelated subqueries because they have to be calculated for each unique combination of fields, and they have a dependency on the outer query.

The following code snippets show some examples of subselects in action. Don't worry if you don't completely comprehend them, because some require an understanding of topics yet to be covered:

```
SELECT s.state, r.cnt_residents, c.land_area
    FROM states As s LEFT JOIN
        (SELECT state, COUNT(res_id) As cnt_residents
            FROM residents
            GROUP BY state) AS r ON s.state = r.state
    LEFT JOIN (SELECT state, SUM(ST_Area(the_geom)) As land_area
            FROM counties
            GROUP BY state) As c
        ON s.state = c.state;
```

This statement uses a subselect to define the derived table we alias as r. This is the common use case.

The same statement is demonstrated in the following example, using the WITH clause. The subselects in a WITH clause are often referred to as *common table expressions* (CTEs):

```
WITH
    r AS (
        SELECT state, COUNT(res_id) As cnt_residents
            FROM residents
        GROUP BY state),
    c AS (
        SELECT state, SUM(ST_Area(the_geom)) As land_area
            FROM counties
        GROUP BY state)
    SELECT s.state, r.cnt_residents, c.land_area
    FROM states As s LEFT JOIN
        r ON s.state = r.state
    LEFT JOIN c
        ON s.state = c.state;
```

Now let's look at the same query written using a correlated subquery:

```
SELECT s.state,
       (SELECT COUNT(res_id)
           FROM residents
           WHERE residents.state = s.state) AS cnt_residents
    , (SELECT SUM(ST_Area(the_geom))
       FROM counties
       WHERE counties.state = s.state) AS land_area
    FROM states As s ;
```

Although you can use any of these variations to get the same results, the strategies used by the planner are very different. Depending on what you're doing, one can be much faster than another.

If you expect large numbers of returned rows, you should avoid the correlated subquery approach, although in certain cases it can be necessary to use a correlated subquery, such as when you need to prevent duplication of counts. Prior to PostgreSQL 12, you also don't want to use a CTE for expressions that would result in many rows that you won't always return. This is because the CTE will materialize the subexpression and will also not be able to employ indexes on the underlying table for subsequent uses in later expressions. For PostgreSQL 12+, you can largely treat the CTE as syntactic sugar that makes your SQL a bit more readable and easier to break into steps without forcing the planner to use one strategy over another.

C.2.6   *JOINs*

PostgreSQL supports all the standard JOINs and sets defined in the ANSI SQL standards.

A JOIN is a clause that relates two tables, usually by a primary and a foreign key, although the join condition can be arbitrary. In spatial queries, you'll find that the JOIN is often based on a proximity condition rather than on keys. The clauses LEFT JOIN, INNER JOIN, CROSS JOIN, RIGHT JOIN, FULL JOIN, and NATURAL JOIN exist in the ANSI SQL specifications, and PostgreSQL supports all of these. Although PostgreSQL supports FULL JOIN, not all operations in PostGIS do, so FULL JOIN has very limited use when used with PostGIS functions and operators. SQL Server supports them as well, but MySQL lacks FULL JOIN support. Oracle also supports them.

LEFT JOIN

A LEFT JOIN returns all records from the first table (M) and only records in the second table (N) that match records in the first table (M). The maximum number of records returned by a LEFT JOIN is $m \times n$ rows, where m is the number of rows in M and n is the number of rows in N. The number of columns is the number of columns selected from M plus the number of columns selected from N.

Generally speaking, if your M table has a primary key that's the joining field, you can expect the minimum number of rows returned to be m and the maximum to be $m \times n$.

NULL placeholders are put in table N's columns where there's no match in the M table. You can see a diagram of a LEFT JOIN in figure C.1.

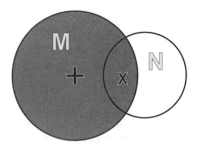

Figure C.1 Diagram of a LEFT JOIN. The darkened region represents the portion of records returned by a LEFT JOIN. The × stands for multiplication and the + is additive. The first circle is M and the second circle is N.

Let's look at some examples of LEFT JOINs:

```
SELECT c.city_name, a.airport_code,a.airport_name, a.runlength
    FROM city As c
        LEFT JOIN airports As a ON c.city_code = a.city_code;
```

This query will list both cities that have airports and cities that don't have airports, based on city_code. We assume city_code to be the city table's primary key and a foreign key in the airports table. If the LEFT JOIN were changed to an INNER JOIN, only cities with airports would be listed. With a LEFT JOIN, cities that have no airports will get a NULL placeholder for the airport fields.

One trick commonly used with LEFT JOINs is to return only unmatched rows by taking advantage of the fact that a LEFT JOIN will return NULL placeholders where there's no match. When doing this, make sure the field you're joining with is guaranteed to be filled in when there are matches; otherwise, you may get incorrect results. For example, a good candidate would be the primary key of a table. Here's an example of such a trick:

```
SELECT c.city_name
    FROM city AS c
    LEFT JOIN airports AS a ON c.city_code = a.city_code
    WHERE a.airport_code IS NULL;
```

In this example, you're returning all cities with no matching airports. You're making the assumption that the airport_code is never NULL in the airports table. If it were ever NULL, this wouldn't give the right answer.

INNER JOIN

An INNER JOIN returns only records that are in both the M and N tables, as shown in figure C.2. The maximum number of records you can expect from an inner join is ($m \times n$). Generally speaking, if your M table has a primary key, and that field is used to join with a field in table N, you can expect the maximum number of rows to be n. A classic example is customers joined with orders. If a customer has only five orders, the number of rows you'll get back with that customer ID and name is five.

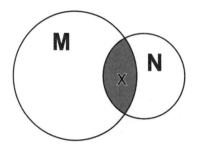

Figure C.2   Diagram of an `INNER JOIN`. The darkened region represents the portion of records returned by the `INNER JOIN`. The × denotes that it's multiplicative.

Following is an example of an `INNER JOIN`:

```
SELECT c.city_name, a.airport_code, a.airport_name, a.runlength
    FROM city AS c
        INNER JOIN airports a ON a.city_code = c.city_code;
```

In this example, you list only cities that have airports and only the airports in them. If you had a spatial database, you could do a `JOIN` using a spatial function such as `ST_Intersects` or `ST_DWithin`, and you could find airports in proximity to a city or in a city region.

RIGHT JOIN

A `RIGHT JOIN` returns all records in the N table and only records in the M table that match records in N, as shown in figure C.3. In practice, `RIGHT JOIN`s are rarely used because a `RIGHT` can always be replaced with a `LEFT`, and most people find reading join clauses from left to right easier to comprehend. The `RIGHT JOIN`'s behavior is a mirror image of the `LEFT JOIN`, flipping the table order in the clause.

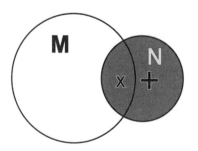

Figure C.3   Diagram of a `RIGHT JOIN`. The darkened region represents the portion of records returned by a `RIGHT JOIN`. The × stands for multiplication and the + is additive.

FULL JOIN

The `FULL JOIN`, shown in figure C.4, returns all records in M and N and uses `NULL` values as placeholders in fields where there's no matching data. There's a lot of debate about the usefulness of `FULL JOIN`s. In practice they're rarely used, and some people are of the opinion that they should never be used because they can always be simulated with a UNION [ALL]. Although we rarely use FULL JOINs, in some cases we find them clearer to use than a UNION.

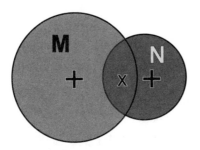

Figure C.4   Diagram of a FULL JOIN. The darkened region represents the portion of records returned by a FULL JOIN. The × stands for multiplication and the + is additive.

The number of columns returned by a FULL JOIN is the same as for a LEFT, RIGHT, or INNER join; the minimum number of rows returned is $\max(m,n)$ and the maximum is $(\max(m?,n) + m \times n - \min(m,n))$.

FULL JOINs ON SPATIAL RELATIONSHIPS—FORGET ABOUT IT
While in theory it's possible to do a FULL JOIN using spatial functions like ST_DWithin or ST_Intersects, in practice this isn't currently supported, even as of PostgreSQL 12 and PostGIS 3.0. As of PostGIS 3.0, you can use a FULL JOIN with the = operator to join when two geometries are binary equal.

CROSS JOIN
The CROSS JOIN is the cross product of two tables, where every record in the M table is joined with every record in the N table, as illustrated in figure C.5. The result of a CROSS JOIN without a WHERE clause is $m \times n$ rows. It's sometimes referred to as a *Cartesian product*.

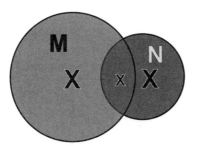

Figure C.5   Diagram of a CROSS JOIN. The darkened region represents the portion of records returned by the CROSS JOIN. The × stands for multiplication.

Here's an example of a good use for a CROSS JOIN. This statement calculates the total price of a product, including state tax, for each state:

```
SELECT p.product_name, s.state,
       p.base_price * (1 + s.tax) As total_price
```

```
FROM products AS p
CROSS JOIN state AS s;
```

It can also be written as follows:

```
SELECT p.product_name, s.state,
    p.base_price * (1 + s.tax) As total_price
  FROM products AS p, state AS s
```

Note that `table1 INNER JOIN table2 ON (table1.field1 = table2.field2)` can be written with the `table1 CROSS JOIN table2` or `table1,table2` syntax and then followed with a `WHERE table1.field1 = table2.field2` part, but we prefer the more explicit `INNER JOIN` because it's less prone to mistakes.

When doing an `INNER JOIN` with `CROSS JOIN` syntax, you put the join fields in the `WHERE` clause. Primary keys and foreign keys are often put in the `INNER JOIN ON` clause, but in practice you can put any joining field in there. There's no absolute rule about it. The distinction becomes important when doing `LEFT JOINs`, as you saw with the `LEFT JOIN` orphan trick.

NATURAL JOIN

A `NATURAL JOIN` is like an `INNER JOIN` without an `ON` clause. It's supported by many ANSI-compliant databases. The `NATURAL JOIN` automagically joins same-named columns between tables, so there's no need for an `ON` clause.

JUST SAY NO TO THE NATURAL JOIN

We highly suggest you stay away from using `NATURAL JOINs`. It's a lazy and dangerous way of doing joins that will come back to bite you when you add fields with the same names as fields in other tables that are totally unrelated. We feel so strongly about not using `NATURAL JOINs` that we won't even demonstrate their use. When you see one in use, instead of thinking *cool*, just say *no*.

CHAINING JOINS

The other thing with `JOINs` is that you can chain them almost ad infinitum. You can also combine multiple `JOIN` types, but when joining different types, either make sure you have all your `INNER JOINs` before the `LEFTs`, or put parentheses around them to control their order.

Here's an example of `JOIN` chaining:

```
SELECT c.last_name, c.first_name, r.rental_id, p.amount, p.payment_date
  FROM customer As c
    INNER JOIN rental As r ON c.customer_id = r.customer_id
    LEFT JOIN payment As p
    ON (p.customer_id = r.customer_id
      AND p.rental_id = r.rental_id);
```

This example is from the PostgreSQL pagila database. The pagila database is a favorite for demonstrating new features of PostgreSQL. You can download it from "PostgreSQL sample databases" (https://github.com/devrimgunduz/pagila).

In the preceding example, you find all the customers who have had rentals, and you list the rental fields as well (note that the INNER JOIN excludes all customers who haven't made rentals). You then pull the payments they've made for each rental. You'll get NULL values if no payment was made but the rental exists.

SETS

Set predicates UNION [ALL], EXCEPT, INTERSECT, like a JOIN, can contain multiple tables or subqueries. What distinguishes the set class of predicates from a JOIN is that they chain together SQL statements that can normally stand by themselves to return a single data set. The set class defines the kind of chaining behavior. Keep in mind that when we talk about sets here, we're not talking about the SET clause you'll find in UPDATE statements.

PostgreSQL supports all three set predicates, though many databases support only UNION [ALL].

One other distinguishing thing about sets is that the number of columns in each SELECT has to be the same, and the data types in each column should be the same too, or autocast to the same data type in a non-ambiguous way.

SPATIAL PARALLELS

One thing that confuses new spatial database users is the parallels between the two terminologies. In general SQL lingua franca, you have UNION, INTERSECT, and EXCEPT, which talk about table rows. When you add space to the mix, you have parallel terminology for geometries: ST_Union (which is like a UNION), ST_Collect (which is like a UNION ALL), ST_Intersection (which is like INTERSECT), and ST_Difference (which is like EXCEPT) serve the same purposes for geometries.

UNION AND UNION ALL

The most common type of set includes the UNION and UNION ALL sets, illustrated in figure C.6. Most relational databases have at least one of these, and most have both. A UNION takes two SELECT statements and returns a DISTINCT set of these, which means no two records will be exactly the same. A UNION ALL, on the other hand, always returns $n + m$ rows, where n is the number of rows in table N and m is the number of rows in table M.

A union can have multiple chains, each separated by a UNION ALL or a UNION. ORDER BY can appear only once and must be at the end of the chain. ORDER BY is often denoted by numbers, where the number denotes the column number to order by.

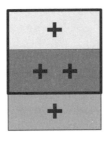
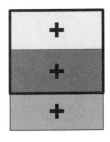

Figure C.6 UNION ALL versus UNION. The thick-bordered box is M, and the thin-bordered box is N. On the left, the UNION ALL shared regions are duplicated; in the UNION on the right, only one of the shared regions is kept, resulting in a distinct set

A union is generally used to put together results from different tables. The example in the following listing will list all water and land features greater than 500 units in area and all architecture monuments greater than 1000 dollars, and will order the results by item name:

```
SELECT water_name As label_name, the_geom,
       ST_Area(the_geom) As feat_area
   FROM water_features
   WHERE ST_Area(the_geom) > 10000
   UNION ALL
   SELECT feat_name As label_name, the_geom,
       ST_Area(the_geom) As feat_area
   FROM land_features
   WHERE ST_Area(feat_geometry) > 500
   UNION ALL
   SELECT arch_name As label_name, the_geom,
       ST_Area(the_geom) As feat_area
   FROM architecture
   WHERE price > 1000
   ORDER BY 1,3;
```

This example will pull data from three tables (water_features, land_features, and architecture) and return a single data set ordered by the name of the feature and then the area of the feature.

UNION IS OFTEN MISTAKENLY USED

The plain `UNION` statement is often mistakenly used because it's the default option when `ALL` isn't specified. As stated, `UNION` does an implicit `DISTINCT` on the data set, which makes it slower than a `UNION ALL`. It also has another side effect of losing geometry records that have the same bounding boxes when using PostGIS pre-3.0. In general, you'll want to use a `UNION ALL` except when deduping data.

INTERSECT

`INTERSECT` is used to join multiple queries, similar to `UNION`. It's defined in the ANSI SQL standard, but not all databases support it; for example, MySQL doesn't support it, and neither does SQL Server 2000, although SQL Server 2005 and above do.

     `INTERSECT` returns only the set of records that is common between the two result sets, as shown in figure C.7. It's different from `INNER JOIN` in that it isn't multiplicative and in that both queries must have the same number of columns. In figure C.7, the shaded area represents what's returned by an SQL `INTERSECT`. Later we'll look at a

Figure C.7 `INTERSECT`—the darkened region is the intersection of two data sets returned by an `INTERSECT` clause.

spatial intersection involving an intersection of geometries rather than an intersection of row spaces.

INTERSECT is rarely used, and there are a few reasons for that:

- Many relational databases don't support it.
- It tends to be slower than doing the same trick with an INNER JOIN.
- In some cases, it looks convoluted when you're talking about the same table.

In some cases, though, INTERSECT does make your code clearer, such as when you have two disparate tables or when you chain more than two queries. The following listing demonstrates INTERSECT and the equivalent query using INNER JOIN.

Listing C.2 INTERSECT compared to INNER JOIN

```
SELECT feature_id                          ┌──  INTERSECT
      FROM water_features               ❶  example
      WHERE ST_Area(geom) > 500
  INTERSECT
  SELECT feature_id
      FROM protected_areas
      WHERE induction_year > 2000;      ❷  INNER JOIN
  SELECT wf.feature_id               ◄──    version
   FROM water_features As wf
      INNER JOIN
      protected_areas As pa ON wf.feature_id = pa.feature_id
  WHERE ST_Area(wf.geom) > 500
  AND pa.induction_year > 2000;
```

The first query uses the INTERSECT approach to list all water features greater than 500 square units that are also designated as protected areas inducted after the year 2000 ❶.

The second approach demonstrates the same query, but using an INNER JOIN instead of an INTERSECT ❷. Note that if the feature_id field isn't unique in both tables, the INNER JOIN runs the chance of multiplying records. To overcome that, you can change the SELECT to SELECT DISTINCT.

The next example demonstrates chaining INTERSECT clauses:

```
SELECT r
      FROM generate_series(1,3) AS r
  INTERSECT
  SELECT n
      FROM generate_series(3,8) AS n
  INTERSECT
  SELECT s
      FROM generate_series(2,3) AS s;
```

Keep in mind that you can mix and match with UNION and EXCEPT as well. The order of precedence is from top query down, unless you have subselect parenthetical expressions.

EXCEPT

An EXCEPT chains queries together such that the final result contains only records in A that aren't in B. The number and type of columns in each chained query must be the same, similar to UNION and INTERSECT. The shaded section in figure C.8 represents the result of the final query.

EXCEPT is rarely used, but it does come in handy when chaining multiple clauses:

Figure C.8   A demonstration of EXCEPT

```
SELECT r
      FROM generate_series(1,3) AS r
   EXCEPT
   SELECT n
      FROM generate_series(3,8) AS n
   INTERSECT
   SELECT s
      FROM generate_series(2,3) AS s;
```

USING SQL AGGREGATES

Aggregate functions roll a group of records into one record. In PostgreSQL, the standard SUM, MAX, MIN, AVG, COUNT, and various statistical aggregates are available out of the box. PostGIS adds many more for geometry, raster, and topology types, of which ST_Collect, ST_Union, ST_MakeLine, and ST_Extent are the most commonly used. In this section, we'll focus on using aggregates. How you use aggregates is pretty much the same regardless of whether they're spatial or not.

Aggregates in SQL generally have the following parts:

- SELECT and FROM—This is where you select the fields and where you pull data from. You also include the aggregated functions in the select field list.
- SOMEAGGREGATE(DISTINCT somefield)—On rare occasions, you'll use the DISTINCT clause within an aggregate function to denote that you use only a distinct set of values to aggregate. This is commonly done with the COUNT aggregate to count a unique name only once.
- WHERE—Non-aggregate filter; this gets applied before the HAVING part.
- HAVING—Similar to WHERE, but used when applying filtering on the already-aggregated data.
- GROUP BY—All fields in the SELECT that are non-aggregated and function calls must appear here, except when grouping by primary key of a table and your SELECT only contains columns from that table.
- SOMEAGGREGATE(somefield ORDER BY someotherfield1, … someotherfieldn)—This is most useful for aggregates that return output composed of subelements, and it controls the order in which these are returned. In common PostgreSQL usage, you'll often see this used with string_agg or array_agg. In the PostGIS world, you'll see this used commonly with the ST_MakeLine aggregate function, where you need to control the order of the line's points by time or some other

column. The ORDER BY construct can be combined with DISTINCT in the form SOMEAGGREGATE(DISTINCT somefield ORDER BY somefield). Note that in the DISTINCT form, similar to a regular SELECT DISTINCT, the ORDER BY columns need to be inputs to the function.

> **WARNING** Prior to PostGIS 2.4, with geometries, what is DISTINCTed is the bounding box, so different geometries with the same bounding box will get thrown out. PostGIS 3+ does not have this issue.

GROUP BY FUNCTIONAL DEPENDENCY ENHANCEMENT

PostgreSQL has a feature called functional dependency, which means that if you're already grouping by a primary key of a table, you can skip grouping by other fields in that table. This feature is defined in the ANSI SQL 99 standard. It saves some typing and makes it easier to port some MySQL apps.

FAST FACTS ABOUT AGGREGATE FUNCTIONS

There are some important things you should keep in mind when working with aggregate functions. Some of these facts are standard across all relational databases, some are specific to PostgreSQL, and some are a consequence of the way PostGIS implements = for geometries in older versions of PostGIS:

- For most aggregate functions, NULL values are ignored. This is important to know, because it allows you to do things such as COUNT(geom) AS num_has_geoms and COUNT(neighborhood) AS num_has_neighborhoods in the same SELECT statement.
- If you want to count all records, use a field that's never NULL to count; for example, COUNT(gid) or a constant such as COUNT(1). You can also use COUNT(*).
- Prior to PostGIS 2.4, when grouping by geometries, which is very rare, it's the bounding box of the geometry that's actually grouped on. The following listing is an example that mixes aggregate SQL functions with spatial aggregates:

```
SELECT n.nei_name,
       SUM(ST_Length(roads.geom)) as total_road_length,
       ST_Extent(roads.geom) As total_extent,
       COUNT(DISTINCT roads.road_name) As count_of_roads
   FROM neighborhoods As n
       INNER JOIN roads ON
           ST_Intersects(neighborhoods.geom, roads.geom)
   WHERE n.city = 'Boston'
       GROUP BY n.nei_name
       HAVING ST_Area(ST_Extent(roads.geom)) > 1000;
```

The query for each neighborhood specifies the total length of roads and the extent of all roads. It also includes a count of unique road names and counts only neighborhoods where the total area of the extent covered is greater than 1,000 square units.

WITH ORDINALITY

Since PostgreSQL 9.4, PostgreSQL has had an ANSI-SQL feature WITH ORDINALITY that's used primarily in conjunction with set-returning functions. This tacks on an additional sequential number column.

Here is an example spatial use:

```
SELECT dp.geom, dp.val, dp.ordinality
FROM ch12.elev AS r
    CROSS JOIN LATERAL
        ST_DumpAsPolygons(r.rast) WITH ORDINALITY AS dp
WHERE r.rid = 1
```

The ST_DumpAsPolygon function returns a set of rows consisting of a geom and a val column. By adding the clause WITH ORDINALITY you get an additional column at the end called ordinality, which is a sequential numbering of the output. If you don't like the naming of the columns, you can change your AS dp to AS dp(g,v,o). This will rename the output columns to whatever you specify in the (). Note that this example also utilizes a LATERAL clause, which is used throughout the book and is covered later in this appendix.

For subqueries, to achieve the same behavior, you can use ROW_NUMBER() OVER(..), which you'll see next.

WINDOW FUNCTIONS AND WINDOW AGGREGATES

PostgreSQL has ANSI-standard window functions and aggregates, and later versions have improved on this. PostgreSQL 9.0 improved on this by expanding the functionality of BETWEEN ROWS and RANGE. PostgreSQL 9.4 improved even more on this feature by adding percentile_cont and percentile_dist as well as the complementary WITHIN GROUP (ORDER BY somefield). PostgreSQL 11 added SQL:2011 framing options RANGE mode to use PRECEDING and FOLLOWING.

Window functionality allows you to do useful things such as sequentially number results by some sort of ranking, calculate running subtotals based on a subset of the full set using the concept of a window frame, and perform running geometry ST_Union and ST_MakeLine calls, which are perhaps solutions in search of a problem but nevertheless intriguing.

PostGIS 2.3 introduced its very own true windows functions ST_ClusterDBSCAN and ST_ClusterKMeans, which are used for grouping geometries based on proximity to each other. You'll see more of these in this book.

A window frame defines a subset of data within a subquery using the term PARTITION BY, and then within that window you can define orderings and sum results to achieve rolling totals and counts. PostgreSQL also supports named window frames that can be reused by name.

The following listing uses the ROW_NUMBER window function to number streets sequentially within one kilometer of a police station, ordered by their proximity to the police station.

Listing C.3 Find roads within 1 km of each police station and number sequentially

```
SELECT  ROW_NUMBER() OVER (
           PARTITION BY loc.pid
              ORDER BY r.geom <-> loc.geom
                 , r.road_name) As row_num,
     loc.pid, r.road_name,
           (r.geom <-> loc.geom)/1000 As dist_km
        FROM land As loc
           LEFT JOIN  road As r
                 ON ST_DWithin(r.geom, loc.geom, 1000)
        WHERE loc.land_type = 'police station'
        ORDER BY pid, row_num;
```

❶ Number rows

❷ Restart numbering for each pid

❸ Order numbers by distance

In this listing, you use the window function called ROW_NUMBER to number the results ❶. The PARTITION BY clause forces numbering to restart for each unique parcel ID (identified by pid) that uniquely identifies a police station ❷. The ORDER BY defines the ordering ❸. In this case, you increment based on proximity to the police station. If two streets happen to be at the same distance, then one will arbitrarily be *n* and the other *n*+1. The ORDER BY includes road_name as a tie breaker.

Table C.1 shows a subset of the resulting table for two police stations.

Table C.1 Results of the window query in listing C.3

row_num	pid	road_name	dist_km
1	000010131	Main Rd	0.228687666823197
2	000010131	Curvy St	0.336867955509993
3	000010131	Elephantine Rd	0.959190964077745
1	000040128	Elephantine Rd	0.587036350160092
2	000040128	Main Rd	0.771250583026646

LATERALs

PostgreSQL 9.3 introduced the LATERAL clause. This is an ANSI SQL feature that allows you to specify tables, functions (particularly set-returning functions), or subqueries in the FROM clause that reference columns from preceding FROM items.

A common use of the LATERAL clause in PostGIS work is to expand spatial objects into component parts. LATERAL is also used in conjunction with KNN gist operators <-> and <#> to overcome the constant reference geometry issue, and doing limit queries where, for example, for each record location you want to return the five closest items from another set of data. We demonstrated some examples of its use in distance searching in chapter 10, and in chapter 8 for batch geocoding.

The basic use of LATERAL in conjunction with KNN operators such as <-> is shown in the following example, which returns the closest three hospitals for each location:

```
SELECT loc.address, hosp.name
FROM loc CROSS JOIN
  LATERAL (SELECT name FROM hospitals
  ORDER BY hospitals.geom <-> loc.geom LIMIT 3) As hosp
```

As with all LATERAL constructs, the hosp subquery relies on column geom from the loc table, and each value of loc.geom begets a new subtable. loc.geom is used as a constant in the subquery, so it can utilize spatial indexes.

In cases where you aren't sure if a subquery will return a result for each record in your preceding FROM table, you can combine LATERAL with a LEFT JOIN, as this next example demonstrates:

```
SELECT loc.address, hosp.name
FROM loc LEFT JOIN
  LATERAL (SELECT name FROM hospitals
  ORDER BY hospitals.geom <-> loc.geom LIMIT 3) As hosp ON true
```

In the next section, you'll learn about another key component of SQL. SQL is good for querying data, but it's also useful for updating and adding data.

C.3   UPDATE, INSERT, and DELETE

The other feature of a DML is the ability to update, delete, and insert data. SQL's UPDATE, DELETE, and INSERT statements can combine the predicates you learned about for selecting data. They can perform cross updates between tables or formulate a virtual table (subquery) to insert data into a physical table. In the exercises that follow, we'll demonstrate simple constructs as well as more complex ones.

C.3.1   UPDATE

You can use the SQL UPDATE statement to update existing data. You can update individual records or a batch of records based on some WHERE condition.

SIMPLE UPDATE

A simple UPDATE will update data to a static value based on a WHERE condition. Here's a simple example of this:

```
UPDATE things
    SET status = 'active'
    WHERE last_update_date > (CURRENT_TIMESTAMP - '30 day'::interval);
```

UPDATE FROM OTHER TABLES

A simple UPDATE is one of the more common update statements used. In certain cases, however, you'll need to read data from a separate table based on some sort of related criteria. In this case, you'll need to use joins within your UPDATE statement.

Here's a simple example that updates the region code of a point data set if the point falls within the region:

```
UPDATE things
      SET region_code = r.region_code
      FROM regions As r
   WHERE ST_Intersects(things.geom, r.geom);
```

UPDATE WITH SUBSELECTS

A subselect, as you learned earlier, is like a virtual table. It can be used in UPDATE statements the same way you use regular tables. In a regular UPDATE statement, even involving statements with table joins, you can't update a table value with an aggregate such as the SUM of another table field. A way to get around this limitation of SQL is to use a subselect.

Following is an example that tallies the number of objects in a region:

```
UPDATE regions
   SET total_objects = ts.cnt
 FROM (SELECT t.region_code, COUNT(t.gid) As cnt
         FROM things AS t
          GROUP BY t.region_code) As ts
   WHERE regions.region_code = ts.region_code;
```

If you're updating all rows in a table, it's often more efficient to build the table from scratch and use an INSERT statement rather than an UPDATE statement. The reason for this is that an UPDATE is really an INSERT and a DELETE. Because of the multi-version concurrency control (MVCC) implementation of PostgreSQL, PostgreSQL will remove the old row and replace it with the new row in the active heap.

Next you'll learn how to perform INSERTs.

C.3.2 *INSERT*

Just like the UPDATE statement, you can have simple INSERTs that insert constants as well as more complex ones that read from other tables or aggregate data. We'll demonstrate some of these constructs.

SIMPLE INSERT

The simple INSERT just inserts constants, and it comes in three basic forms.

The single-value constructor approach has existed in PostgreSQL since the 6.0 days and is pretty well supported across all relational databases. Here you insert a single point:

```
INSERT INTO points_of_interest(fe_name, geom)
       VALUES ('Highland Golf Club',
              ST_SetSRID(ST_Point(-70.063656, 42.037715), 4269));
```

The next most popular approach is the multi-row VALUES constructor syntax introduced in SQL 92, which we demonstrate often in this book. This syntax was introduced in PostgreSQL 8.2 and IBM DB2, it has been supported for a long time in MySQL (we think since 3+), and it was introduced in SQL Server 2008. As of this writing, Oracle has yet to support this useful construct.

The multi-row VALUES constructor is useful for adding more than a single row or as a faster way of creating a derived table with just constants. The following example shows a multi-row VALUES insert. It's similar to the single insert. It starts with the word VALUES, and then each row is enclosed in parentheses and separated with a comma:

```
INSERT INTO poi(poi_name, poi_geom)
    VALUES ('Park',
            ST_GeomFromText('POLYGON ((86980 67760,
                    43975 71292, 43420 56700, 91400 35280,
        91680 72460, 89460 75500, 86980 67760))') ),
    ('Zoo',  ST_GeomFromText('POLYGON ((41715 67525, 61393 64101,
        91505 49252, 91400 35280, 41715 67525))') );
```

The last kind of simple INSERT is one that uses the SELECT clause, shown next. In the simplest example, it doesn't have a FROM. Some people prefer this syntax because it allows you to alias what the value is right next to the constant. It's also a necessary syntax for the more complex kind of INSERT we'll demonstrate in the next section:

```
INSERT INTO poi(poi_name, geom)
SELECT 'Park' AS poi_name,
    ST_GeomFromText('POLYGON ((86980 67760,
                    43975 71292, 43420 56700, 91400 35280,
        91680 72460, 89460 75500, 86980 67760))') As geom
UNION ALL
SELECT 'Zoo' As poi_name,
    ST_GeomFromText('POLYGON ((41715 67525, 61393 64101, 91505 49252,
        91400 35280, 41715 67525))')  As geom;
```

This is the standard way of inserting multiple rows into a table. It was the only way to do a multi-row INSERT before PostgreSQL 8.2. This syntax is supported by PostgreSQL (all versions), MySQL, and SQL Server. To use it in something like Oracle or IBM DB2, you need to include a FROM clause, like FROMdual or sys.dual.

ADVANCED INSERT

The advanced INSERT is not that advanced. You use this syntax to copy data from one table or query to another table. In the simplest case, you're copying a filtered set of data from another table. It uses the SELECT syntax, usually with a FROM and sometimes accompanying joins.

This example inserts a subset of rows from one table into another:

```
INSERT INTO polygons_of_interest(fe_name, geom, interest_type)
    SELECT pid, geom, 'less than 300 sqft' As interest_type
    FROM parcels WHERE ST_Area(geom) < 300;
```

A slightly more advanced INSERT is one that joins several tables together. In this scenario, the SELECT FROM is just a standard SQL SELECT statement with joins, or one that consists of subselects. The following example is a somewhat complex case. Given a table of polygon chain link edges, it constructs polygons and stuffs them into a new table of polygons:

```
INSERT INTO polygons(polyid, geom)
    SELECT polyid, ST_Multi(final.geom) As geom
    FROM (SELECT pc.polyid,
       ST_BuildArea(ST_Collect(pc.geom)) As geom
       FROM
    (SELECT p.right_poly as polyid, lw.geom
          FROM polychain p INNER JOIN linework lw ON
             lw.tlid = p.tlid
          WHERE (p.right_poly <> p.left_poly OR p.left_poly IS NULL)
       UNION ALL
       SELECT p.left_poly as polyid, lw.geom
          FROM polychain p INNER JOIN linework lw ON
             lw.tlid = p.tlid
          WHERE (p.right_poly <> p.left_poly OR p.right_poly IS NULL)
    ) As pc
    GROUP BY poly.polyid) As final;
```

SELECT INTO AND CREATE TABLE AS

Another form of the INSERT statement is what we commonly refer to as a *bulk* INSERT. In this kind of INSERT, not only are you inserting data, but you're also creating the table to hold the data in a single statement. PostgreSQL supports two basic forms of this:

- The standard SELECT … INTO is supported by a lot of relational databases. We prefer this approach because it's more cross-platform (it will work on SQL Server as well as MySQL, for example).

- The CREATE TABLE … AS SELECT …, approach isn't as well supported by other relational databases.

In both cases, any valid SELECT or WITH statement can be used. The following code shows examples of the same statement written using SELECT INTO and CREATE TABLE AS:

```
SELECT t.region_code
 , COUNT(t.gid) As cnt              ←┐  Cross-platform
        INTO thingy_summary         |  bulk insert
        FROM things AS t
   GROUP BY t.region_code;
CREATE TABLE thingy_summary AS       ←┐  Less cross-
        SELECT t.region_code, COUNT(t.gid) As cnt  |  platform way
          FROM things AS t
       GROUP BY t.region_code;
```

C.3.3 *DELETE*

When doing a DELETE, there are four basic forms: a simple delete that just involves one table, a medium delete that involves deleting data USING matching data in another table or subselect, and the NOT IN or IN approach, which utilizes a correlated or uncorrelated subquery. Finally, there's the TRUNCATE TABLE approach, which is the fastest and deletes all data in a table, but it only works if your table has no related foreign-key constraints in other tables.

Simple **DELETE**

A simple DELETE has no subselects but usually has a WHERE clause. All the data in a table is deleted and logged if you're missing a WHERE clause.

Following is an example of a standard DELETE:

```
DELETE FROM streets WHERE fe_name LIKE 'Mass%';
```

DELETE based on data in another table with **USING**

PostgreSQL has a USING clause that can be used in a DELETE. The USING clause denotes tables that should be used for filtering only, and not deleted from. Tables or subqueries that appear in the USING clause can be used in the WHERE clause of the DELETE.

In this next example, you first delete all streets in the current streets table that appear in the new_streets data set in preparation for reload:

```
DELETE FROM streets USING new_streets WHERE streets.tlid = new_streets.tlid;
```

DELETE with subselect in **WHERE**

In PostgreSQL, as in many other relational databases, you can't use a JOIN in the FROM clause to determine what to delete based on another table. You can, however, overcome this restriction by either using a subselect in the WHERE clause or using the PostgreSQL-specific USING clause. The WHERE approach is more cross-platform and the one we'll demonstrate next. The subselect approach is useful for cases where you need to delete all data in your current table that's also in the table you're adding from, or you need to delete duplicate records.

The following example deletes duplicate records:

```
DELETE
    FROM sometable
    WHERE someuniquekey NOT IN
        (SELECT  MAX(dup.someuniquekey)
            FROM  sometable As dup
              WHERE dup.dupcolumn1 = sometable.dupcolumn1
                AND dup.column2 = sometable.dupcolumn2 A
                ND dup.column3 = sometable.dupcolumn3
            GROUP BY dup.dupcolumn1, dup.dupcolumn2, dup.dupcolumn3);
```

TRUNCATE TABLE

In cases where you want to delete all the data in a table, you can use the much faster TRUNCATE TABLE statement. TRUNCATE TABLE is considerably faster because it does much less transaction logging than a standard DELETE FROM, but it can be used only in tables that aren't involved in foreign-key relationships. Here's an example of it at work:

```
TRUNCATE TABLE streets;
```

index

Symbols

./configure command 574
&& operator 451
&&& operator 251
%%sql command 171
= operator 268

Numerics

1996 Earth Gravitational Model (EGM96) 70

A

accessor function 179
accessors 234–240
  band metadata setters 239–240
    ST_SetBandIsNoData 239–240
    ST_SetBandNoDataValue 239
  basic raster metadata properties 235–236
    raster accessor functions 235
    ST_MetaData and ST_BandMetaData
      235–236
  functions 191–198
    checking geometry validity 196–197
    geometry and coordinate dimensions
      195–196
    geometry type functions 194–195
    number of points that define a geometry
      197–198
    retrieving coordinates 196
    spatial reference identifiers 192
    transforming geometry to different spatial
      references 192–193
    using transformation with the geography
      type 193–194

pixel statistics 236–238
  ST_Histogram 236–237
  ST_SummaryStats 237–238
pixel value accessors 238–239
  ST_DumpAsPolygons 238–239
  ST_DumpValues 238
  ST_Value 238
AddEdge function 384
AddFace function 384
AddGeometryColumns function 57
AddNode function 384
AddRasterConstraints function 62, 64
address normalization 294, 301, 303
address standardization 294, 301
address_standardize function 308
AddTopoGeometryColumn function 380,
  388–389
addy field 306
advanced INSERT 598
affine transformations 338
AGGREGATE 285
aggregates 592–593
  functions 314–320, 593
    creating linestrings from points
      318–320
    creating multipolygons 314–318
    forming larger rasters using 348–350
  GROUP BY functional dependency
    enhancement 593
ajax function 556
aliasing 581
aligning 223–224
ALTER EXTENSION command 574
ANALYZE command 129
ANSI (American National Standards Institute) 7
ANSI/ISO SQL standards 7

apt search keyword 570
ArcGIS by Esri 13
ARRAY 582
array_agg function 226
arrondissements 417
AS clause 581
auth_srid field 91
auto-updatable views 431–432
AVG function 314
azimuthal projections 74

B

bands 60–61, 350–351
    adding 63
    exporting single 135
    metadata setters 239–240
        ST_SetBandIsNoData 239–240
        ST_SetBandNoDataValue 239
    pixel types 61
    using ST_AddBand to form multiband
        rasters 350–351
    using ST_Band to process subset of
        bands 351
BBOX (bounding boxes) 125
bg (blockgroup) 297
binary format
    as function arguments 190–191
    creating geographies from 190
    creating geometries from 186–190
        ST_GeomFromGML, ST_GeomFromGeo-
         JSON, ST_GeomFromKML, ST_Geom-
         FromTWKB,
         ST_GeomFromGeoHash 189–190
        ST_GeomFromText 186–188
        ST_GeomFromWKB and
         ST_GeomFromEWKB 188–189
    installing PostgreSQL and PostGIS 571
    outputting plots as 507–508
binary JSON (jsonb) 127
binary unsigned integer (BUI) values 229
block range index (BRIN) 252, 451
boundaries 204–206, 252–253
bounding boxes (BBOX) 125, 202–203,
    249–252
bounding-box equality 266
box type 29
BRIN (block range index) 252, 451
brin index type 22
buffer zones 27
BUI (binary unsigned integer) values 229
bunching 480
bytea data 132, 229

C

CALL command 311, 366
callback function
    choosing between expression or 365
    using single-band map algebra 367–368
canvas aligned road 224
Cartesian product 587
cartography 67
CASCADE clause 295
CASE statement 324
CASE WHEN clause 466
cast-safe functions 342–344
CDN (content delivery network) 546
CentOS 570
centroid 206–208
CGAL (Computational Geometry Algorithms
    Library) 7, 45
chaining JOINs 588–589
channels 60
character_maximum_length field 579
child_id field 389
chunking 128
circle type 29
circularstrings 51–52
citext extension 580
clients, mapping 532–534
clipping 320–322
    forming larger rasters using 349
    polygons 255–258
cluster number 291
clustering 480–483
    on Geohash functional index or GiST spatial
        index 481–482
    on Hilbert curve and use of materialized
        views 482–483
COALESCE function 310
collection geometries 38–43
    GEOMETRYCOLLECTION 42–43
    multilinestrings 40–41
    multipoints 39–40
    multipolygons 41–42
coloring grayscale rasters 227
column_default field 579
column_name field 578
columns
    adding to partitioned table 430
    converting geometry column to geography
        57
    geometry 57
columns view 577
command-line switches 128–129
common table expressions (CTEs) 209, 222, 442,
    466, 583
comparators 251–252

composition functions 179, 210–213
    making points 210–211
    making polygons 211–212
        ST_BuildArea 212
        ST_MakeEnvelope 211
        ST_MakePolygon 212
        ST_Polygonize 212
    promoting single geometries to multi-geometries 213
compound index 454, 457–458
COMPOUNDCURVE subtype 52
compoundcurves 52–53
Comprehensive R Archive Network (CRAN) 503
Computational Geometry Algorithms Library (CGAL) 7, 45
configuration tables 296–298
conic projections 74
constraint_exclusion variable 474
constraints
    raster data types 64
    typmod vs. 407–409
constructor functions 179
constructors 220–229
    constructing rasters from scratch 225
    converting geometries to rasters 222–224
        aligning ST_AsRaster 223–224
        creating single band raster from geometry 222–223
    converting other raster formats 229
    creating rasters from other rasters 227–228
        coloring grayscale rasters 227
        ST_Band 228
        ST_Clip 227–228
    functions 186–191
        creating geographies from text and binary formats 190
        creating geometries from text and binary formats 186–190
        using text or binary representations as function arguments 190–191
    loading rasters with raster2pgsql 224
    setting pixels 225–226
contains 259–261
contains properly 262–263
content delivery network (CDN) 546
contrib schema 96
Coord_dimension 55–56
coordinate dimension 55, 191
coordinate reference system 72
coordinates
    dimensions 195–196
    retrieving 196
    rounding 213–214
COPY command 24, 98, 121, 571
copy command 23, 96, 121

correlated subquery 583–584
corridors 27
cost 477
COUNT function 314
counts function 364
coverage 219
covered by 261–262
covers 261–262
CRAN (Comprehensive R Archive Network) 503
CREATE EXTENSION 295, 573
CREATE EXTENSION citext; 580
CREATE EXTENSION plr; command 499
CREATE EXTENSION postgis; 576
CREATE TABLE AS 599
CreateTopoGeom function 390
CreateTopology function 384
cropping rasters 227–228
CROSS JOIN 587–588
crossing geometries 265–266
CRS (coordinate reference system) 92
CSV file, importing 23–24
CTEs (common table expressions) 209, 222, 442, 466–467, 583
CURRENT_TIMESTAMP 449
curved geometries 49–53
    circularstrings 51–52
    compoundcurves 52–53
    curvepolygons 53
curvepolygons 53
cylindrical projections 74

D

data
    downloading files 100
    exporting raster data with GDAL 132–137
        Gdal_translate and gdalwarp 134–137
        using gdalinfo to inspect rasters 133–134
    extracting files 100–101
    getting free 563–564
    importing raster data with raster2pgsql 128–132
        command-line switches 128–129
        loading multiple files and tiling in shell script 130–131
        loading single file with 130
        supported formats 129
        using PostgreSQL functions 131–132
    inserting and editing large data sets 396–399
    loading TIGER 296–300
        configuration tables 296–298
        loading nation and state data 298–300
    PostgreSQL built-in tools 96–99
        pgAdmin4 97–99
        Pg_dump and pg_restore 99
        Psql 96–97

data *(continued)*
  querying external data using PostgreSQL for-
      eign data wrappers 117–127
    converting hstore tags to jsonb 127
    file_fdw foreign data wrapper 119–121
    ogr_fdw foreign data wrapper 121–127
  shapefiles 101–108
    exporting with pgsql2shp 107–108
    importing and exporting with shp2pgsql-gui
        104–106
    importing with shp2pgsql 102–104
  sources
    full mapping servers 531–532
    registering OpenJUMP 147–148
  spatial data types 16–20
    geography type 18
    geometry type 17
    raster type 18–19
    topology type 19–20
  vector data with ogr2ogr 108–117
    environment variables in 109–110
    exporting 114–117
    importing 110–114
    ogrinfo 110
data definition language (DDL) 433, 577
data manipulation language (DML) 577, 579
databases, PostGIS 573–574
DataFrame() method 172
data_type field 578
DATE_PART function 319
datum 71–72
datumgrids 93
DB Manager 156–159
DBaaS (database as a service) 571–572
.dbf (dBase file) 107
dcluster column 292
DDL (data definition language) 433, 577
DE-9IM (Dimensionally Extended 9-Intersection
    Model) 269
declare_sect field 297
decomposition functions 179, 191, 202–210
  boundaries and converting polygons to
      linestrings 204–206
  bounding box of geometries 202–203
  centroid, median, and point on surface
      206–208
  decomposing multi-geometries and geometry
      collections 208–210
  returning points defining a geometry 208
default_statistics_target parameter 445
DELETE 599–600
  based on data in another table with USING 600
  simple 600
  TRUNCATE TABLE 600
  with subselect in WHERE 600

DEM (digital elevation model) 348
DENSE_RANK() function 285, 290
descartes library 174
desktop 139–145
  format support 143–144
  GvSIG 161–165
    Exporting data 165
    overview 140
    Using gvSIG with PostGIS 161–164
  JupyterLab and Jupyter Notebook 166–177
    Creating a Python notebook 168
    Installing Jupyter 167
    Launching Jupyter Notebook 167–168
    Launching JupyterLab 168
    Magic commands 169
    overview 141
    Performing raw queries with Jupyter
        Notebook 170–171
    Using GeoPandas, Shapely, and Matplotlib
        to work with spatial data 172–175
    Viewing data on a map with folium
        175–177
  open source tools 562–563
  OpenJUMP 145–151
    ease of use 146
    exporting data 151
    features 146
    format support 147
    installing 146
    overview 140
    plug-ins 146
    PostGIS support 147
    registering data sources 147–148
    rendering PostGIS geometries 149–151
    scripting 147
  QGIS 151–160
    installing 152
    overview 140
    using with PostGIS 152–160
  spatial database support 141–143
  web services supported 144–145
difference 320
digital elevation model (DEM) 348
Dijkstra shortest path algorithm 491, 493
Dimensionally Extended 9-Intersection Model
    (DE-9IM) 269
dimensions 60
disjoint geometries 266
DISTINCT clause 424
DISTINCT ON 279–280, 289
distros 571
DML (data manipulation language) 577, 579
DO command 397, 517
Docker 566
downloading files 100

drawing plots 501–503
DropGeometryColumn function 57
DropGeometryTable function 57

E

Easy Install tool 510
easy_install xlrd command 510
EDB (EnterpriseDB) 13
edges 489
editing topology primitives 392–396
   checking for shared faces 395–396
   editing topogeometries 396
   removing faces by removing edges 393–394
EGM96 (1996 Earth Gravitational Model) 70
ellipsoids 69–71
enable strategies 475–476
Enhanced Well-Known Binary (EWKB) 189
enlarging rasters 134–135
EnterpriseDB one-click installers 566–569
environment variables in ogr2ogr 109–110
EPSG (European Petroleum Survey Group)
   67
EPSG:4326
   geography data type for 78–79
   pros and cons of 77–78
equality 266–268
   = operator 268
   spatial equality versus geometric equality
      267–268
equatorial projection 74
Esri
   ArcGIS by 13
   shapefiles
      importing from 24–25
      querying 122–124
Esri Personal File 144
ETL (extract-transform-load) 563
European Petroleum Survey Group (EPSG) 67
eval function 517
EWKB (Enhanced Well-Known Binary) 189
Excel files 510–512
EXCEPT 592
EXISTS clause 582
explain 445–451
   pgAdmin graphical explain 446
   plans without index 447–451
   textual explain 446
explain plans 439
exporting
   GvSIG data 165
   OpenJUMP 151
   QGIS layers 159–160
   raster data with GDAL 132–137
      Gdal_translate 134–137

gdalwarp to transform spatial references
      136–137
   using gdalinfo to inspect rasters 133–134
shapefiles
   with pgsql2shp 107–108
   with shp2pgsql-gui 104–106
vector data with ogr2ogr 114–117
   ogr2ogr export switches 115
   to GeoJSON 115
   to GeoPackage 117
   to KML 116
   to MapInfo TAB file format 116–117
expression indexes 456
expressions
   choosing between callback function or 365
   types with ST_Union 349–350
   using single-band map algebra 366–367
extensions 146
exterior of geometries 252–253
exterior ring 35
extracting files 100–101
extruding pixel values 360–362
   ST_DumpValues 361–362
   ST_Value 360

F

faces
   checking for shared 395–396
   removing by removing edges 393–394
FDW (foreign data wrappers) 117–127
   converting hstore tags to jsonb 127
   file_fdw foreign data wrapper 119–121
   ogr_fdw foreign data wrapper 121–127
      getting OSM data 124–125
      querying Esri shapefiles 122–124
      querying OpenStreetMap data 124
      querying OSM data with ogr_fdw 125–126
      reading hstore tags 126–127
feature classes 30
feature_id field 591
file_fdw foreign data wrapper 119–121
files
   Gdal_translate to reconstitute imported 136
   loading with raster2pgsql 130–131
FILTER statement 466
filtering, PostGIS data 155–156
fngetxlspts function 512
folium 175–177
FOR loop 398
foreign keys 458–459
foreign server 118
foreign table 118
FOSS (free and open source software) 488
free data 563–564

FROM clause 579–581, 595
FROM subqueries 466–467
FTS (full text search) 451
FULL JOIN 586–587
full mapping servers 527–532
  OGC web service support 529–531
  platform considerations 528–529
  supported data sources 531–532
functional dependency 593
functional indexes 83, 455–456
functions
  encouraging parallel plans 478–479
  in PL/Python 510
  settings 476–478
    cost 477
    immutable, stable, volatile 477
    parallel 477–478
    rows 477

G

GDAL 132–137
  Gdal_translate 134–137
  gdalwarp to transform spatial references
    136–137
  using gdalinfo to inspect rasters 133–134
GDAL/OGR 563
gdalinfo 133–134
Gdal_translate 134–137
  to export a single band 135
  to export region 135–136
  to reconstitute imported file 136
  to shrink or enlarge rasters 134–135
  with where clause 135
gdalwarp 136–137
generalized inverted tree (GIN) 451
generalized search tree (GiST) 451
generate_series function 210, 502
geocode function 305
geocode_intersection function 308
geocoding 305–311
  batch geocoding 309–311
  intersections 308–309
  PL/Python example 512–514
  reverse geocoding 311–312
  using address text 306–307
  using normalized addresses 308
geodetic measurements 200–202
Geodetic Reference System (GRS 80) 70
geodetics 67
GeoFabrik 564
geographic information systems (GIS) 3
Geographic Resources Analysis Support System
  (GRASS) 151, 562
geography 491

geography data types 16, 18, 31, 75, 103, 157, 190,
  249, 278–279, 333, 404
  differences between geometry and 58–59
  for EPSG:4326 78–79
  spatial catalogs for 59
geography functions
  accessor and setter functions 191–198
    checking geometry validity 196–197
    geometry and coordinate dimensions
      195–196
    geometry type functions 194–195
    number of points that define a
      geometry 197–198
    retrieving coordinates 196
    spatial reference identifiers 192
    transforming geometry to different spatial
      references 192–193
    using transformation with the geography
      type 193–194
  composition functions 210–213
    making points 210–211
    making polygons 211–212
    promoting single geometries to multi-
      geometries 213
  constructor functions 186–191
    creating geographies from text and binary
      formats 190
    creating geometries from text and binary
      formats 186–190
    using text or binary representations as func-
      tion arguments 190–191
  decomposition functions 202–210
    boundaries and converting polygons to
      linestrings 204–206
    bounding box of geometries 202–203
    centroid, median, and point on surface
      206–208
    decomposing multi-geometries and geometry
      collections 208–210
    returning points defining a geometry 208
  measurement functions 198–202
    geodetic measurements 200–202
    geometry planar measurements 199–200
  output functions 179–186
    Examples of output functions 184–185
    Extensible 3D Graphics (X3D) 183–184
    Geography Markup Language (GML)
      180–181
    Geohash 185–186
    Geometry JavaScript Object Notation
      (GeoJSON) 181
    Keyhole Markup Language (KML) 180
    Mapbox Vector Tiles (MVT) and protocol
      buffers 182–183
    Scalable Vector Graphics (SVG) 181–182

geography functions *(continued)*
  Tiny WKB (TWKB) 183
  well-known text (WKT) and well-known binary (WKB) 180
  simplification functions 213–216
    grid snapping and coordinate rounding 213–214
    simplification 214–216
Geography Markup Language (GML) 145
geography model 373
geography processing
  breaking linestrings into smaller segments 332–337
    breaking linestrings at point junctions 335–337
    creating two-point linestrings from many-point linestrings 333–335
    segmentizing linestrings 333
  clipping 320–322
  rotating 341
  scaling 339–340
  splitting 322–323
  tessellating 323–332
    creating approximate equal areas by sharding 328–330
    creating grid and slicing table geometries with grid 323–326
    creating single line cut bisects into equal halves 327
    sharding geometries with ST_Subdivide 330–332
  translating 338–339
  using geometry functions to manipulate and create geographies 342–344
  using spatial aggregate functions 314–320
    creating linestrings from points 318–320
    creating multipolygon from many multipolygon records 314–318
geography type 16, 31, 190, 249, 278, 333
geography_columns view 59
Geohash 185–186, 481–482
geoids 67–69
GeoJSON (Geography JavaScript Object Notation) 115, 179, 181, 530
geom column 284, 378
geometric dimension 191
geometric equality 266
geometries 17, 32–57
  collection geometries 38–43
    GEOMETRYCOLLECTION 42–43
    multilinestrings 40–41
    multipoints 39–40
    multipolygons 41–42
  converting into R spatial objects 505–507

converting to rasters with ST_AsRaster 222–224
  aligning ST_AsRaster 223–224
  creating single band raster from geometry 222–223
converting to topogeometries 389–390
curved geometries 49–53
  circularstrings 51–52
  compoundcurves 52–53
  curvepolygons 53
differences between geography and 58–59
fixing invalid 479–480
generating TINs 49
linestrings 34–35
M coordinate 43–45
OpenJUMP rendering PostGIS 149–151
output functions 552–556
points 33–34
polygons 35–38
polyhedral surfaces and TINs (triangular irregular networks) 46–48
reducing number of vertices by breaking apart 480
relating two 252–273
  contains and within 259–261
  contains properly 262–263
  covers and covered by 261–262
  equality 266–268
  house plan model 258–259
  interior, exterior, and boundary of geometry 252–253
  intersections 253–258
  overlapping geometries 263–264
  touching geometries 264–266
  underpinnings of relationship functions 268–273
spatial catalog for 54–57
  changing SRID of existing geometry column 57
  converting geometry column to geography column 57
  Coord_dimension 55–56
  managing geometry columns 57
  Populate_Geometry_Columns function 57
  spatial reference identifier (SRID) 56
  Z coordinate 45–46
geometry data type 13, 16, 31, 75, 103, 154, 190, 217, 249, 278, 333, 403–404, 441, 592
geometry dimension 55
geometry functions
  accessor and setter functions 191–198
    checking geometry validity 196–197
    geometry and coordinate dimensions 195–196
    geometry type functions 194–195
    number of points that define a geometry 197–198

geometry functions *(continued)*
   retrieving coordinates 196
   spatial reference identifiers 192
   transforming geometry to different spatial references 192–193
   using transformation with the geography type 193–194
  composition functions 210–213
   making points 210–211
   making polygons 211–212
   promoting single geometries to multi-geometries 213
  constructor functions 186–191
   creating geographies from text and binary formats 190
   creating geometries from text and binary formats 186–190
   using text or binary representations as function arguments 190–191
  decomposition functions 202–210
   boundaries and converting polygons to linestrings 204–206
   bounding box of geometries 202–203
   centroid, median, and point on surface 206–208
   decomposing multi-geometries and geometry collections 208–210
   returning points defining a geometry 208
  measurement functions 198–202
   geodetic measurements 200–202
   geometry planar measurements 199–200
  output functions 179–186
   Examples of output functions 184–185
   Extensible 3D Graphics (X3D) 183–184
   Geography Markup Language (GML) 180–181
   Geohash 185–186
   Geometry JavaScript Object Notation (GeoJSON) 181
   Keyhole Markup Language (KML) 180
   Mapbox Vector Tiles (MVT) and protocol buffers 182–183
   Scalable Vector Graphics (SVG) 181–182
   Tiny WKB (TWKB) 183
   well-known text (WKT) and well-known binary (WKB) 180
  simplification functions 213–216
   grid snapping and coordinate rounding 213–214
   simplification 214–216
geometry model 373
geometry processing
  breaking linestrings into smaller segments 332–337
   breaking linestrings at point junctions 335–337
   creating two-point linestrings from many-point linestrings 333–335
   segmentizing linestrings 333
  clipping 320–322
  rotating 341
  scaling 339–340
  splitting 322–323
  tessellating 323–332
   creating approximate equal areas by sharding 328–330
   creating grid and slicing table geometries with grid 323–326
   creating single line cut bisects into equal halves 327
   sharding geometries with ST_Subdivide 330–332
  translating 338–339
  using geometry functions to manipulate and create geographies 342–344
  using spatial aggregate functions 314–320
   creating linestrings from points 318–320
   creating multipolygon from many multipolygon records 314–318
geometry subtype 49
geometry type 13, 16, 31, 154, 190, 217, 249, 278, 333, 403, 441, 592
GEOMETRYCOLLECTION 42–43, 257
geometrycollection data type 39
geometry_columns view 54, 59, 318, 428
geometry_dump 323
GeometryType function 189, 194
geomval type 238
GeoNames 563
GeoPackage 12, 112–114, 117, 144
GeoPandas 172–175
georeferencing 218
georeferencing functions 240–244
  metadata setters 240–242
   Georeferencing example 242
   ST_SetGeoReference 241
   ST_SetScale 241
   ST_SetSkew 241
   ST_SetSRID 241
   ST_SetUpperLeft 241
  processing functions 242–244
   Raster processing example 243–244
   ST_Resample 242
   ST_Rescale 242
   ST_Resize 242
   ST_Transform 242
GEOS (Geometry Engine Open Source) 7, 145

GeoServer 541–544
  accessing PostGIS layers via 544
  installing 541
  setting up PostGIS workspaces 541–542
geotagging 287–293
  PostGIS cluster window functions 290–293
  snapping points to closest linestring 288–289
  to specific region 287–288
GET function 524
GetFeatureInfo 145
get_features function 552
getJSON function 556
GetMap method 145
GetTopoGeomElements function 382
gid column 417
GIN (generalized inverted tree) 451
GIS (geographic information systems) 3
GIS suites, self-contained 562
gisdata 298
GiST (generalized search tree) 451
gist index 22
GiST spatial index 481–482
globe, covering 81–85
GML (Geography Markup Language) 145, 180–181
GO (GoLang) 525
Google V8 488
GPX (GPS exchange files) 111
graceful degradation of resolution 182
GRANT USAGE command 526
GRASS (Geographic Resources Analysis Support
    System) 151, 562
GRASS GIS 562
grayscale rasters 227
grid
  creating and slicing table geometries with
      323–326
  snapping 213–214
GROUP BY 184, 319, 593
GRS 80 (Geodetic Reference System) 70
GUI (graphical user interface) 534
GvSIG 161–165
  exporting data 165
  overview 140
  using with PostGIS 161–164
gvSIG desktop 161, 562
gvSIG Mobile 161
gvSIG Online 161

H

height, raster data type 61
Hello real world 20–28
  loading data 23–25
    importing CSV file 23–24
    importing from Esri shapefile 24–25
  modeling 21–23
    restaurants table 21–23
    using schemas 21
  overview 20–21
  viewing spatial data with OpenJump 27–28
  writing query 26
heterogeneous columns 147, 404–406
  cons of 405–406
  modeling real city 419–423
  pros of 405
Hilbert curve 482–483
Hilbert Geometry sorting 451
histograms 363
homogeneous columns 406–407
  cons of 407
  modeling real city 423–425
  pros of 406–407
house plan model 258–259
hstore data type 419
hstore tags
  converting to jsonb 127
  reading 126–127
hstore_to_json function 420
hstore_to_jsonb function 420
hstore_to_json_loose function 420

I

ILIKE PostgreSQL predicate 580
IMPORT FOREIGN SCHEMA command 121, 123
importing
  CSV file 23–24
  Excel files 510–512
  from Esri shapefile 24–25
  QGIS layers 159–160
  raster data with raster2pgsql 128–132
    Loading a single file with raster2pgsql 130
    Loading multiple files and tiling in shell
        script 130–131
    Raster2pgsql command-line switches
        128–129
    Raster2pgsql supported formats 129
    Using PostgreSQL functions to output raster
        data 131–132
  shapefiles 101–108
    with shp2pgsql 102–104
    with shp2pgsql-gui 104–106
  vector data with ogr2ogr 110–114
    loading GeoPackage 112–114
    loading GPS exchange files (GPX) 111
    loading MapInfo TAB file 114
    ogr2ogr import switches 110–111
IN clause 582
INCLUDE clause 536
index clustering 480

indexes 451–459, 581
  compound index 457–458
  functional index gotchas 456
  not being used 459
  partial index 455–456
  planner with spatial index 452–454
  unique indexes 458–459
information_schema 577–579
inlining a function 453
INNER JOIN 585–586
INSERT 597–599
  advanced 598
  SELECT INTO and CREATE TABLE AS 599
  simple 597–598
installing
  creating PostGIS database 573–574
  GeoServer 541
  JupyterLab and Jupyter Notebook 167
  MapServer 534–536
    Linux/Unix 535–536
    Windows 534–535
  OpenJUMP 146
  pgRouting 488–495
    basic navigation 489–493
    TSP (traveling salesperson problem) 493–495
  PL/Python 508–509
  PL/V8 (JavaScript) 514
  PostGIS 13–15
  PostGIS TIGER geocoder 295–296
  PostgreSQL and PostGIS 565–573
    binaries and distros 571
    compiling from PostGIS source 572–573
    database as service offerings for PostGIS 571–572
    EnterpriseDB one-click installers 566–569
    in Docker 566
    MacOS-specific installers 569
    on Linux server (Red Hat EL, CentOS) using YUM 570
    PostgreSQL Apt repository 570
  procedural languages 496
  topology extension 374
INSTEAD OF triggers 433–434
interactive mode 96
interior, geometries 252–253
INTERSECT 590–591
intersections 253–258
  clipping polygons with polygons 255–258
  geocoding 308–309
  intersection matrix 269–270
  raster processing and 354–360
    adding Z coordinate to 2D linestring using ST_Value and ST_SetZ 356–358

    converting 2D polygons to 3D polygons 358–360
    pixel stats 355–356
  segmenting linestrings with polygons 253–255
intersects with tolerance 280

J

JAI (Java Advanced Imaging) framework 161
JAR (Java archive file) 146
Java Topology Suite (JTS) engine 145
JavaScript libraries and functions 514–518
JavaScript Object Notation (JSON) 115, 127, 181
JOIN clause 282
JOINs 584–596
  chaining 588–589
  CROSS JOIN 587–588
  EXCEPT 592
  FULL JOIN 586–587
  FULL JOINs on spatial relationships 587
  INNER JOIN 585–586
  INTERSECT 590–591
  LATERALs 595–596
  LEFT JOIN 584–585
  NATURAL JOIN 588
  RIGHT JOIN 586
  sets 589
  spatial parallels 589
  UNION and UNION ALL 589–590
  using SQL aggregates 592–593
  using SQL aggregates, Fast facts about aggregate functions 593
  using SQL aggregates, GROUP BY functional dependency enhancement 593
  window functions and window aggregates 594–595
  WITH ORDINALITY 594
jpeg function 502
JSON (JavaScript Object Notation) 115, 127, 181
json (plain text) 127
jsonb (binary JSON) 127
JTS (Java Topology Suite) engine 145
JupyterLab and Jupyter Notebook 166–177
  creating Python notebook 168
  installing 167
  launching Jupyter Notebook 167–168
  launching JupyterLab 168
  magic commands 169
  overview 141
  performing raw queries with Jupyter Notebook 170–171
  using GeoPandas, Shapely, and Matplotlib to work with spatial data 172–175
  viewing data on map with folium 175–177
JVM (Java Virtual Machine) 146

K

KMeans 328
KML (Keyhole Markup Language) 9, 116, 180
KNN (k-nearest neighbor) 277
  distance operators 281–284
  with geography types 284–287
KNN trajectory distance operator 282

L

LAEA (Lambert Azimuthal Equal Area) 74
lag function 334, 514
Lambert Conformal Conic (LCC) 74
LATERAL clause 512, 582, 594–596
lateral joins 470–473
LATERAL keyword 284, 332, 459
layers 30, 380
LCC (Lambert Conformal Conic) 74
lead function 334, 514
Leaflet primer 544–551
LEFT JOIN 584–585
length function 491
libraries 503
lightweight mapping servers 525–527
linear referencing 287–289
LINESTRING 31
linestring 373
LINESTRINGM 31, 282
linestrings 34–35, 373
  adding Z coordinate to 2D 356–358
  breaking into smaller segments 332–337
    breaking linestrings at point junctions 335–337
    creating two-point linestrings from many-point linestrings 333–335
    segmentizing linestrings 333
  converting polygons to 204–206
  creating from points 318–320
  segmenting with polygons 253–255
  snapping points to closest 288–289
Linux
  installing MapServer 535–536
  installing PostgreSQL and PostGIS on 570
loading data 23–25
  importing CSV file 23–24
  importing from Esri shapefile 24–25
load_on_startup = true function 517
lo_export command 234
lo_export function 234
lon/lat (geodetic coordinate system) 72
lseg type 29

M

M coordinate 43–45
MacOS-specific installers 569
magic commands 169
maintenance_work_mem variable 474
map algebra 220, 364–370
  choosing between expression or callback function 365
  PL/V8 (JavaScript) writing functions 518–521
  using single-band map algebra expression 366–367
  using single-band map algebra function 367–368
  with neighborhoods 368–370
Mapbox Vector Tiles (MVT) 9, 522, 530
MapInfo TAB file format
  exporting to using ogr2ogr 116–117
  loading 114
mapping
  clients 532–534
  for presentation 79–81
  servers 524–532
    full 527–532
    lightweight 525–527
MapServer 534–541
  calling mapping service using reverse proxy 540–541
  creating WMS and WFS services 536–540
  installing 534–536
    Linux/Unix 535–536
    Windows 534–535
  security considerations 536
markers 335
MATERIALIZE keyword 583
MATERIALIZED keyword 467
materialized views 482–483
Matplotlib 172–175
MAX function 314
mbr (minimum bounding rectangle) 378
measurement functions 179, 198–202
  geodetic measurements 200–202
  geometry planar measurements 199–200
median 206–208
Mercator 75
metadata
  raster metadata properties 235–236
    raster accessor functions 235
    ST_MetaData and ST_BandMetaData 235–236
  setters 240–242
    georeferencing example 242
    ST_SetGeoReference 241
    ST_SetScale 241
    ST_SetSkew 241
    ST_SetSRID 241
    ST_SetUpperLeft 241

Microsoft SQL Server 11
MIF/MID 144
MIN function 314
minimum bounding rectangle (mbr) 378
modeling 21–23, 68
   real city 417–430
      using heterogeneous geometry columns
         419–423
      using homogeneous geometry columns
         423–425
      using partitioning 425–430
   restaurants table 21–23
   using schemas 21
multi-geometries
   decomposing 208–210
   promoting single geometries to 213
multilinestrings 40–41
multipoints 39–40
multipolygons 37, 41–42, 314–318
MVCC (multi-version concurrency) 479, 597
MVT (Mapbox Vector Tiles) 9, 182–183, 522, 530,
   556–560
MySQL 12

N

NAD27 (North American Datum of 1927) 72
nation data 298–300
national grid systems 75
Natural Earth website 564
NATURAL JOIN 588
nearest neighbor (NN) 242
neighbor searches 278–284
   finding N closest places using KNN distance
      operators 281–284
   intersects with tolerance 280
   items between distances 280–281
   places are within X distance 278–279
   using ST_DWithin and DISTINCT ON to find
      closest locations 279–280
   using ST_DWithin and ST_Distance for N clos-
      est results 279
neighborhoods 220, 368–370, 418
network routing problems 488–495
network topology 16, 491
NN (nearest neighbor) 242
nodes 373
Nominatim class 513
non-interactive mode 97
norm_addy data type 301
normalize_address function 301–303, 308
normalizing addresses 301–305
   geocoding using 308
   using normalize_address 301–302
   using PAGC address normalizer 302–305

North American Datum of 1927 (NAD27) 72
NOT IN clause 582

O

oblique projection 74
OGC web service support 529–531
ogr2ogr
   vector data with 108–117
      environment variables in 109–110
      environment variables in ogr2ogr 109–110
      exporting 114–117
      importing 110–114
      ogrinfo 110
ogr_fdw foreign data wrapper 121–127
   getting OSM data 124–125
   querying Esri shapefiles 122–124
   querying OpenStreetMap data 124
   querying OSM data with ogr_fdw 125–126
   reading hstore tags 126–127
ogr_fdw_drivers() function 122
ogr_fdw_version() function 122
onMapClick function 556
open source tools 561–563
   desktop tools 562–563
   extract-transform-load (ETL) 563
   PostGIS 10–11
   self-contained GIS suites 562
OpenJUMP 145–151, 562
   ease of use 146
   exporting data 151
   features 146
   format support 147
   installing 146
   overview 140
   plug-ins 146
   PostGIS support 147
   registering data sources 147–148
   rendering PostGIS geometries 149–151
   scripting 147
   viewing spatial data with 27–28
OpenLayers primer 544–551
OpenStreetMap 124, 563
Oracle Spatial 11
ORDBMS (object-relational database management
   system) 6–7
ORDER BY clause 279, 319, 441, 579–581
ordinal_position field 579
OSGeo (Open Source Geospatial Foundation) 7
OSGeo Live 562
OSM (OpenStreetMap) 124, 546
   getting OSM data 124–125
   querying OSM data with ogr_fdw 125–126
OUT parameter 511
out-of-database 219

output functions 229–234
  examples of 184–185
  Extensible 3D Graphics (X3D) 183–184
  Geography Markup Language (GML) 180–181
  Geohash 185–186
  Geometry JavaScript Object Notation
    (GeoJSON) 181
  Keyhole Markup Language (KML) 180
  Mapbox Vector Tiles (MVT) and protocol
    buffers 182–183
  Scalable Vector Graphics (SVG) 181–182
  ST_AsPNG, ST_AsJPEG, and ST_AsTiff
    229–230
  Tiny WKB (TWKB) 183
  using psql to export rasters 232–234
  using ST_AsGDALRaster 230–232
    exporting rasters 232
    listing raster types available for output
      230–231
  well-known text (WKT) and well-known binary
    (WKB) 180
OVER clause 285
OVER() clause 184
overlapping geometries 263–264

P

PAGC (Public Address Geocoder) address
    normalizer 302–305
pagc_normalize_address function 303
pages 481
pandas library 172
par function 502
PARALLEL RESTRICT 449
PARALLEL SAFE 449
PARALLEL UNSAFE 449
parallelism 477–479
param_limit parameter 554
parse_gps function 515
partial index 454–456
PARTITION BY clause 293
partitioned table 413
partitioning 413, 425–430
path type 29
PCPatch data type 481
pdf function 502
period data type 495
periodset data type 495
Perl script 575–576
pgAdmin 14, 446
pgAdmin4 97–99, 563
PGDG (PostgreSQL development group) 570
Pg_dump and pg_restore 99
pg_featureserv tool 523
pgr_CreateTopology function 489

pgr_dijkstra function 492
pgr_dijkstraCostMatrix function 495
pg_read_binary_file function 508
pg_read_file function 508
pgRouting 488–495
  basic navigation 489–493
  costs 491
  Dijkstra shortest path algorithm 491
  installing 488
  pgr_CreateTopology function 489
  traveling salesperson problem 493
  TSP (traveling salesperson problem) 493–495
pgr_TSPEuclidean function 494
pg.spi.exec function 499
pgsql2shp 107–108
  query 107–108
  table 107
pg_tileserv tool 523
pg_upgrade 575
pixels
  extruding pixel values 360–362
    ST_DumpValues 361–362
    ST_Value 360
  scale 62
  setting 225–226
  statistics 236–238
    raster processing 355–356
    ST_Histogram 236–237
    ST_SummaryStats 237–238
  value accessors 238–239
    ST_DumpAsPolygons 238–239
    ST_DumpValues 238
    ST_Value 238
  width and height 61
PL (procedural language) 220, 495
PL/JavaScript 488
PL/Python 488, 508–514
  and Python packages 510
  geocoding 512
  geocoding example 512–514
  importing Excel files 510
  installing 508–509
  Python packages 510–512
    importing Excel file 510–511
    importing several Excel files 511–512
  writing functions 509–510
PL/R 487, 498–508
  converting geometries into R spatial
    objects 505–507
  features 499–503
    drawing plots 501–503
    saving PostgreSQL data to R data format
      499–501
  outputting binaries 507
  outputting plots as binaries 507–508

PL/R *(continued)*
  plotting 501
  saving data 499, 501
  setting up 498–499
  using R packages 503–505
PL/V8 488, 514–521
  enabling 514
  installing 514
  using JavaScript libraries and functions 514–518
  writing map algebra functions 518–521
planar measurements 199–200
Planet OSGeo 561
Planet PostGIS 561
Planet PostgreSQL 561
planet sites 561
planner 439–443
  different kinds of spatial queries 439–442
    N closest things regardless of range 441–442
    N closest things within distance range 439–440
    things not nearby anything 440–441
  statistics 443–445
  table expressions 442–443
  with spatial index 452–454
planner support functions 454
plate carrée projection 75
plot method 173
plots, drawing 501–503
plug-ins 146
png function 502
point junctions 335–337
POINT subtype 31
point type 29
points 33–34
  defining geometry 197–198
  making 210–211
  on surface 206–208
  returning points 208
POINTZ subtype 31
POLYGON 31, 257
polygon type 29
polygons 35–38, 211–212, 373
  clipping polygons with 255–258
  converting 2D polygons to 3D polygons 358–360
  converting to linestrings 204–206
  polygonizing functions 245–246
    ST_ConvexHull 245
    ST_Envelope 245
    ST_MinConvexHull 246
    ST_Polygon 245–246
  segmenting linestrings with 253–255
  ST_BuildArea 212
  ST_MakeEnvelope 211
  ST_MakePolygon 212
  ST_Polygonize 212

POLYGONZ subtype 31
polyhedral surfaces 46–48
PolyhedralSurface 181
POLYHEDRALSURFACEZ subtype 31
POLYHERALSURFACE subtype 31
Populate_Geometry_Columns function 57
POST function 524
PostGIS 6–13
  alternatives to 11–13
    ArcGIS by Esri 13
    Microsoft SQL Server 11
    MySQL 12
    Oracle Spatial 11
    SpatiaLite and GeoPackage 12
  built on PostgreSQL platform 9–10
  cluster window functions 290–293
  creating database 573–574
  free version 10
  history of PROJ support in 91–93
    PROJ 4 91
    PROJ 5 92
    PROJ 6 92–93
    PROJ 7 93
    PROJ 8 and beyond 93
  in web applications
    displaying data with PostGIS queries and web scripting 552–560
    Leaflet primer 544–551
    limitations of conventional web technologies 523–524
    mapping clients 532–534
    mapping servers 524–532
    OpenLayers primer 544–551
    using GeoServer 541–544
    using MapServer 534–541
  installing 13–15, 565–573
    binaries and distros 571
    compiling from PostGIS source 572–573
    database as service offerings for PostGIS 571–572
    EnterpriseDB one-click installers 566–569
    in Docker 566
    MacOS-specific installers 569
    on Linux server (Red Hat EL, CentOS) using YUM 570
    PostgreSQL Apt repository 570
    verifying versions of PostGIS and PostgreSQL 15
  on desktop 139–145
    format support 143–144
    GvSIG 161–165
    gvSIG 140
    Jupyter Notebook and JupyterLab 141
    JupyterLab and Jupyter Notebook 166–177
    OpenJUMP 140, 145–151

PostGIS *(continued)*
    QGIS 140, 151–160
        spatial database support 141–143
        web services supported 144–145
    open source freedom 10–11
    power of 8–9
    reasons for 7
    standards conformance 7–8
    upgrading 574–576
        from 1.X to 2.X or 3.X 575–576
        soft upgrade using extensions 574–575
        using pg_upgrade 575
postgis schema 14, 96
PostGIS TIGER geocoder
    geocoding 305–311
        batch geocoding 309–311
        intersections 308–309
        using address text 306–307
        using normalized addresses 308
    installing 295–296
    loading TIGER data 296–300
        configuration tables 296–298
        loading nation and state data 298–300
    normalizing addresses 301–305
        using normalize_address 301–302
        using PAGC address normalizer 302–305
    reverse geocoding 311–312
postgis_tiger_geocoder extension 301
postgis_topology extension 490
PostgreSQL
    Apt repository 570
    built-in tools 96–99
        pgAdmin4 97–99
        Pg_dump and pg_restore 99
        Psql 96–97
    foreign data wrappers (FDW) 117–127
        converting hstore tags to jsonb 127
        file_fdw foreign data wrapper 119–121
        ogr_fdw foreign data wrapper 121–127
    functions 131–132
    geometry output functions 552–556
    installing 565–573
        binaries and distros 571
        compiling from PostGIS source 572–573
        database as service offerings for PostGIS
            571–572
        EnterpriseDB one-click installers 566–569
        in Docker 566
        MacOS-specific installers 569
        on Linux server using YUM 570
        PostgreSQL Apt repository 570
    PostGIS built on 9–10
    saving to R data format 499–501
    upgrading using pg_upgrade 575
    verifying versions of 15

pprint_addy function 306
prewarming 450
primary keys 458–459
primitives
    adding 384–387
        TopoGeo_AddLineString function 385–386
        TopoGeo_AddPolygon function 387
    editing 392–396
        checking for shared faces 395–396
        editing topogeometries 396
        removing faces by removing edges
            393–394
PRISM Climate Group 564
.prj file 89–90, 107
procedural languages 495–498
    basic installation of 496
    features 496–498
    installing 496
    PL/Python 508–514
        geocoding example 512–514
        installing 508–509
        Python packages 510–512
        writing functions 509–510
    PL/R 498, 508
        converting geometries into R spatial
            objects 505–507
        features 499–503
        outputting plots as binaries 507–508
        setting up 498–499
        using R packages 503–505
    PL/V8 (JavaScript) 514–521
        enabling 514
        installing 514
        using JavaScript libraries and functions
            514–518
        writing map algebra functions 518–521
    trusted versus untrusted 496
processing functions 242–244
    raster processing example 243–244
    ST_Resample 242
    ST_Rescale 242
    ST_Resize 242
    ST_Transform 242
PROJ support in PostGIS 91–93
    PROJ 4 91
    PROJ 5 92
    PROJ 6 92–93
    PROJ 7 93
    PROJ 8 and beyond 93
projections 73–75
proprietary services 532–534
protocol buffers 182–183
proximity analysis
    geotagging 287–293
        PostGIS cluster window functions 290–293

proximity analysis *(continued)*
    snapping points to closest linestring
        288–289
    to specific region 287–288
   nearest neighbor searches 278–284
    finding N closest places using KNN distance
        operators 281–284
    intersects with tolerance 280
    items between distances 280–281
    places are within X distance 278–279
    using ST_DWithin and DISTINCT ON to find
        closest locations 279–280
    using ST_DWithin and ST_Distance for N
        closest results 279
   using KNN with geography types 284–287
psql 14, 96–97, 232–234
public schema 96, 296
PUT function 524
Python
   notebook 168
   packages 510–512
    importing Excel file 510–511
    importing several Excel files 511–512
Python Data Analysis Library 172
Python library 172
PYTHONHOME environment variable 568

Q

QGIS 151–160, 562
   installing 152
   overview 140
   using with PostGIS 152–160
    adding PostGIS connection 153–155
    importing and exporting layers 159–160
    using DB Manager 156–159
    viewing and filtering PostGIS data 155–156
queries
   displaying data with 552–560
    using PostGIS and PostgreSQL geometry out-
        put functions 552–556
    using PostGIS MVT output functions
        556–560
   encouraging parallel plans 478–479
   exporting shapefiles with pgsql2shp 107–108
   function-specific settings 476–478
    cost 477
    immutable, stable, volatile 477
    parallel 477–478
    rows 477
   indexes 451–459
    compound index 457–458
    functional index 456
    not being used 459
    partial index 455–456

planner with spatial index 452–454
   primary keys, unique keys, unique indexes,
    and foreign keys 458–459
optimizing spatial data 479–483
   clustering 480–483
   fixing invalid geometries 479–480
   reducing number of vertices by
    simplification 480
   Reducing the number of vertices by breaking
    geometries apart 480
planner 439–443
   different kinds of spatial queries
    439–442
   statistics 443–445
   table expressions 442–443
SQL patterns affecting plans 459–473
   FROM subqueries and basic CTEs
    466–467
   lateral joins 470–473
   subqueries in SELECT 459–466
   window functions and self joins 468–469
system variables 473–476
   constraint_exclusion variable 474
   enable strategies 475–476
   maintenance_work_mem variable 474
   shared_buffers variable 474
   work_mem variable 474
using explain to diagnose problems
   445–451
   pgAdmin graphical explain 446
   plans without index 447–451
   textual explain 446
querying data with SQL primer 579–596
   aliasing 581
   AS 581
   indexes 581
   JOINs 584–596
    chaining 588–589
    CROSS JOIN 587–588
    EXCEPT 592
    FULL JOIN 586–587
    FULL JOINs on spatial relationships 587
    INNER JOIN 585–586
    INTERSECT 590–591
    LATERALs 595–596
    LEFT JOIN 584–585
    NATURAL JOIN 588
    RIGHT JOIN 586
    sets 589
    spatial parallels 589
    UNION and UNION ALL 589–590
    using SQL aggregates 592–593
    window functions and window
        aggregates 594–595
    WITH ORDINALITY 594

querying data with SQL primer *(continued)*
  SELECT, FROM, WHERE, and ORDER BY
      clauses 579–581
    basic SELECT 580
    SELECT * 580–581
  subselects 582–584
quote_ident function 553

R

R 507
  commands for installing and using
      packages 503
  spatial objects in PL/R 507
random() function 477
random_page_cost setting 407
RANK function 285, 290, 469
raster data 18
  exporting with GDAL 132–137
    Gdal_translate and gdalwarp 134–137
    using gdalinfo to inspect rasters 133–134
  importing with raster2pgsql 128–132
    command-line switches 128–129
    loading multiple files and tiling in shell
        script 130–131
    loading single file with 130
    supported formats 129
    using PostgreSQL functions 131–132
raster data types 18–19, 60–64
  creating 62–64
    adding bands 63
    applying constraints 64
  properties of 60–62
    band pixel types 61
    bands 61
    pixel scale 62
    pixel width and height 61
    skew X and Y 62
    SRIDs and 61
    width and height 61
  spatial catalog for 64
raster functions
  accessors and setters 234–240
    band metadata setters 239–240
    basic raster metadata properties 235–236
    pixel statistics 236–238
    pixel value accessors 238–239
  constructors 220–229
    converting geometries to rasters with
        ST_AsRaster 222–224
    converting other raster formats with
        ST_FromGDALRaster 229
    creating rasters from other rasters
        227–228
    loading rasters with raster2pgsql 224

ST_MakeEmptyRaster and ST_AddBand 225
    ST_SetValue and ST_SetValues 225–226
  georeferencing functions 240–244
    metadata setters 240–242
    processing functions 242–244
  output functions 229–234
    ST_AsPNG, ST_AsJPEG, and ST_AsTiff
        229–230
    using psql to export rasters 232–234
    using ST_AsGDALRaster 230–232
  polygonizing functions 245–246
    ST_ConvexHull 245
    ST_Envelope 245
    ST_MinConvexHull 246
    ST_Polygon 245–246
  reclassing functions 244–245
  terminology 218–220
raster processing
  forming larger rasters using spatial aggregate
      functions 348–350
    reconstituting tiled files 348–349
    using clipping and unioning 349
    using specific expression types with
        ST_Union 349–350
  geometry intersections and 354–360
    adding Z coordinate to 2D linestring using
        ST_Value and ST_SetZ 356–358
    converting 2D polygons to 3D polygons
        358–360
    pixel stats 355–356
  loading and preparing raster data 346–348
  map algebra 364–370
    choosing between expression or callback
        function 365
    using single-band map algebra
        expression 366–367
    using single-band map algebra function
        367–368
    with neighborhoods 368–370
  statistics 360–364
    extruding pixel values 360–362
    raster statistics functions 362–364
  tiling rasters 352–354
  working with bands 350–351
    using ST_AddBand to form multiband
        rasters 350–351
    using ST_Band to process subset of bands
        351
raster tile 219
raster type 16, 60, 217, 592
raster2pgsql 128–132
  command-line switches 128–129
  loading multiple files and tiling in shell
      script 130–131
  loading rasters with 224

raster2pgsql *(continued)*
  loading single file with 130
  supported formats 129
  using PostgreSQL functions to output raster
    data 131–132
raster_columns view 64, 130, 346, 352
raster_columns.extent 346
raster_overviews view 64
raw queries 170–171
readWKT function 505
reclass 220
reclassing functions 244–245
reconstituting
  imported files 136
  tiled files 348–349
Red Hat EL 570
regexp_match function 348
regexp_replace function 347
region tagging 287
registering OpenJUMP data sources 147–148
registries 146
REINDEX TABLE command 456
REINDEX TABLE CONCURRENTLY
  command 456
relationship functions 268–273
  intersection matrix 269–270
  using ST_Relate 270–273
rendering PostGIS geometries 149–151
resources
  for free data 563–564
  open source tools 561–563
    desktop tools 562–563
    extract-transform-load (ETL) 563
    self-contained GIS suites 562
  planet sites 561
RESTRICTED function 478
reverse geocoding 311
reverse proxy 540–541
reverse_geocode function 311
reverse_geocoder function 297
RGB (red, green, and blue) 18
rgeos package 504
RIGHT JOIN 586
ring of the polygon 35
rotating 341
round function 307
routing 16
ROW_NUMBER function 285, 290, 595
rows 477
rules 432

S

SAFE function 478
same alignment 219

San Francisco data 89–90
save command 500
save function 499
Scalable Vector Graphics (SVG) 147
scaling 339–340
schemas 21
scripting 147
SDE (spatial database engine) 13
sde.st_geometry database type 13
SDO (Spatial Data Option) 11
search_path 374
security considerations 536
SECURITY DEFINER function 497
segmentizing linestrings 333
segments 34
SELECT clause 283, 431, 457, 579–581
  basic 580
    SELECT * 580–581
  subqueries in 459–466
SELECT command 121, 432
SELECT INTO 599
SELECT statement 283, 512
self joins 468–469
self-contained GIS suites 562
seq_page_cost setting 407
servers, mapping 524–532
  full 527–532
    OGC web service support 529–531
    platform considerations 528–529
    supported data sources 531–532
  lightweight 525–527
sets 589
setters 234–240
  band metadata setters 239–240
    ST_SetBandIsNoData 239–240
    ST_SetBandNoDataValue 239
  basic raster metadata properties 235–236
    raster accessor functions 235
    ST_MetaData and ST_BandMetaData
      235–236
  functions 191–198
    checking geometry validity 196–197
    geometry and coordinate dimensions 195–196
    geometry type functions 194–195
    number of points that define a
      geometry 197–198
    retrieving coordinates 196
    spatial reference identifiers 192
    transforming geometry to different spatial
      references 192–193
    using transformation with the geography
      type 193–194
  pixel statistics 236–238
    ST_Histogram 236–237
    ST_SummaryStats 237–238

setters *(continued)*
pixel value accessors 238–239
ST_DumpAsPolygons 238–239
ST_DumpValues 238
ST_Value 238
settings 476–478
cost 477
immutable, stable, volatile 477
parallel 477–478
rows 477
SF (spatial features) 45
SFCGAL (Spatial Features Computational Geometry Algorithms Library) 45
shapefiles
exporting
with pgsql2shp 107–108
with shp2pgsql-gui 104–106
importing 101–108
with shp2pgsql 102–104
with shp2pgsql-gui 104–106
Shapely 172–175
sharding
creating approximate equal areas by 328–330
geometries with ST_Subdivide 330–332
shared_buffers setting 450
shared_buffers variable 474
shell script 130–131
shifting 338
short-circuiting 454
show plans 439
shp2pgsql 25, 102–104
shp2pgsql-gui 104–106
shrinking rasters 134–135
Shuttle Radar Topography Mission (SRTM) 130
simplification 392
simplification functions 179
grid snapping and coordinate rounding 213–214
reducing number of vertices by 480
simplification 214–216
topologies 399–400
skew X and Y 62
snapping points 288–289
soft upgrades 574–575
source data, SRS 85–91
sp (WGS 84 sphere) 79
sp package 504
spatial aggregate functions 314–320
creating linestrings from points 318–320
creating multipolygon from many multipolygon records 314–318
forming larger rasters using 348–350
reconstituting tiled files 348–349
using clipping and unioning 349
using specific expression types with ST_Union 349–350

spatial clustering 480
spatial data
making auto-updatable views 431–432
modeling real city 417–430
using heterogeneous geometry columns 419–423
using homogeneous geometry columns 423–425
using partitioning 425–430
optimizing 479–483
clustering 480–483
fixing invalid geometries 479–480
reducing number of vertices by simplification 480
Reducing the number of vertices by breaking geometries apart 480
storage approaches 404–417
heterogeneous columns 404–406
homogeneous columns 406–407
table inheritance 409–413
table partitioning 413–417
typmod vs. constraints 407–409
using GeoPandas, Shapely, and Matplotlib to work with 172–175
using triggers 432–436
INSTEAD OF triggers 433–434
other triggers 435–436
overview 432–433
Spatial Data Option (SDO) 11
spatial data types 16–20
geography 18, 58–59
differences between geometry and 58–59
spatial catalogs for 59
geometry 17, 32–57
collection geometries 38–43
curved geometries 49–53
generating TINs 49
linestrings 34–35
M coordinate 43–45
points 33–34
polygons 35–38
polyhedral surfaces and TINs (triangular irregular networks) 46–48
spatial catalog for 54–57
Z coordinate 45–46
raster 18–19, 60–64
creating 62–64
properties of 60–62
spatial catalog for 64
topology type 19–20
type modifiers 31–32
spatial reference identifier (SRID) 32
subtype type modifiers 31–32
spatial database engine (SDE) 13

spatial databases
  desktop tools 141–143
  Hello real world 20–28
    loading data 23–25
    modeling 21–23
    overview 20–21
    viewing spatial data with OpenJump 27–28
    writing query 26
  PostGIS 6–13
    alternatives to 11–13
    built on PostgreSQL platform 9–10
    free version 10
    installing 13–15
    open source freedom 10–11
    power of 8–9
    reasons for 7
    standards conformance 7–8
  thinking spatially 4–6
spatial equality 266
spatial features (SF) 45
Spatial Features Computational Geometry Algorithms Library (SFCGAL) 45
spatial objects 178
spatial parallels 589
spatial references
  gdalwarp transforming 136–137
  transforming geometry to different 192–193
spatial relationships
  bounding box 249–252
  comparators 251–252
  FULL JOIN on 587
  relating two geometries 252–273
    contains and within 259–261
    contains properly 262–263
    covers and covered by 261–262
    equality 266–268
    house plan model 258–259
    interior, exterior, and boundary of geometry 252–253
    intersections 253–258
    overlapping geometries 263–264
    touching geometries 264–266
    underpinnings of relationship functions 268–273
SpatiaLite 12, 144
SP-GiST (space-partitioned generalized search tree) 451
spgist index type 22, 252
splitting 322–323
spplot function 507
spwgs84 (WGS 84 spheroid) 79
SQL (Structured Query Language) 4, 579
SQL ORDER BY clause 580
SQL patterns 459–473
  FROM subqueries and basic CTEs 466–467

lateral joins 470–473
subqueries in SELECT 459–466
window functions and self joins 468–469
SQL primer
  DELETE 599–600
    based on data in another table with USING 600
    simple 600
    TRUNCATE TABLE 600
    with subselect in WHERE 600
  information_schema 577–579
  INSERT 597–599
    advanced 598
    SELECT INTO and CREATE TABLE AS 599
    simple 597–598
  querying data with 579–596
    aliasing 581
    AS 581
    indexes 581
    JOINs 584–596
    SELECT, FROM, WHERE, and ORDER BY clauses 579–581
    subselects 582–584
  UPDATE 596–597
    from other tables 596
    simple 596
    with subselects 597
SQL queries 147
SQL/MM (SQL Multimedia spec) 7
SRID (spatial reference identifier) 24, 32, 56, 191
  accessor and setter functions 192
  changing existing geometry column of 57
  for geometry data types 56
  of raster data types and 61
SRS (spatial reference systems) 56, 67–75, 102
  coordinate reference system 72
  datum 71–72
  ellipsoids 69–71
  for storing data 76–85
    covering globe 81–85
    EPSG:4326 77–78
    geography data type for EPSG:4326 78–79
    mapping for presentation 79–81
  geoids 67–69
  history of PROJ support in PostGIS 91–93
    PROJ 4 91
    PROJ 5 92
    PROJ 6 92–93
    PROJ 7 93
    PROJ 8 and beyond 93
  of source data 85–91
    exercises 86–90
    missing SRS from spatial_ref_sys table 91
  overview 72–73
  projections 73–75

SRS ID (spatial reference system identifier) 56
srtext fields 89
SRTM (Shuttle Radar Topography Mission) 130
ST_3D function 45
ST_3DArea function 45, 200
ST_3DClosestPoint function 45, 199, 289
ST_3DDistance function 45, 199, 289
ST_3DDWithin function 45, 280, 289
ST_3DIntersection function 45, 253
ST_3DIntersects function 45, 199, 253, 280
ST_3DLength function 199
ST_3DMaxDistance function 45, 199
ST_3DPerimeter function 199–200
stable 477
ST_AddBand function 220, 228, 350–351
ST_Affine function 338
staging schema 96
staging_fold field 296
standardize_address function 303
standards conformance, PostGIS 7–8
ST_Area function 199–200, 456
ST_AsBinary function 180
ST_AsEWKB function 180, 189
ST_AsEWKT function 40, 180
ST_AsGDALRaster function 131, 230–232
    exporting rasters 232
    listing raster types available for output
        230–231
ST_AsGeoBuf function 186
ST_AsGeobuf function 182, 534
ST_AsGeoJSON function 181, 186, 525, 552,
    554
ST_AsGML function 181, 184
ST_AsJPEG function 131, 229–230, 234, 510
ST_AsKML function 180
ST_AsMVT function 183, 186, 525, 534, 556
ST_AsMVTGeom function 182
ST_AsPNG function 131, 229–230, 510
ST_AsRaster function 132, 220, 222–224, 234
    aligning 223–224
    creating single band raster from geometry
        222–223
ST_AsSVG function 181
ST_AsText function 40, 180
ST_AsTiff function 131, 229–230
ST_AsTWKB function 183, 534
ST_AsTWKBAgg function 534
ST_AsX3D function 47, 184
state data 298–300
state plane 75
statefp field 300
statistics 360–364
    extruding pixel values 360–362
        ST_DumpValues 361–362
        ST_Value 360

raster statistics functions 362–364
    counts function 364
    histograms 363
ST_Azimuth function 332
ST_Band function 227–228, 351
ST_BandMetaData function 235–236
ST_BandPixelType function 61
ST_BestSRID function 343
ST_Boundary function 204, 206, 252
ST_Buffer function 27, 78, 81, 194, 211, 361
ST_BuildArea function 211
ST_Centroid function 54, 190, 196, 206
ST_ChaikinSmoothing function 480
ST_Clip function 183, 227–228, 254, 349, 354, 560
ST_ClipByBox2D function 257
ST_ClosestPoint function 194, 289
ST_ClosestPointOfApproach function 43
ST_ClusterDBSCAN function 290, 594
ST_ClusterKMeans function 290, 594
ST_Collect function 42, 212, 314
ST_CollectionExtract function 323
ST_ColorMap function 227
ST_Contains function 260, 262, 390
ST_ContainsProperly function 262
ST_Contour function 359
ST_ConvexHull function 203, 245, 351
ST_CoordDim function 196
ST_Count function 236, 362, 364
ST_CountAgg function 236, 364
ST_CoveredBy function 262
ST_Covers function 262, 325
ST_Crosses function 265
ST_CurveToLine function 50, 52
ST_DelaunayTriangles function 47
ST_Difference function 320
ST_Dimension function 47, 196
ST_Disjoint function 266
ST_Distance function 279, 281, 289
ST_DistanceSphere function 77
ST_DistanceSpheroid function 77, 91
ST_Dump function 47, 208, 323, 385
ST_DumpAsPolygon function 594
ST_DumpAsPolygons function 146, 238–239
ST_DumpPoints function 47, 208, 334, 470
ST_DumpRings function 206, 342
ST_DumpValues function 238, 360–362
ST_DWithin function 26, 77, 251, 278, 441, 480
    for N closest results 279
    to find closest locations 279–280
ST_EndPoint function 197
ST_Envelope function 245, 355
ST_Equals function 267, 479
ST_Expand function 358
ST_ExteriorRing function 206
ST_Extrude function 48

ST_Force4D function 357
ST_FromGDALRaster function 131, 221, 229
ST_GDALDrivers function 221, 230
ST_GeneratePoints function 328
ST_GeoBuf function 184
ST_GeogFromGeoJSON function 190
ST_GeogFromGML function 190
ST_GeogFromKML function 190
ST_GeogFromText function 190
ST_GeogFromWKB function 190
ST_GeoHash function 185, 451, 456, 481
ST_GeometricMedian function 206
ST_GeometryFromText function 189
ST_GeometryN function 208
ST_GeometryType function 189, 194, 423
ST_GeomFromEWKB function 188–189
ST_GeomFromGeoHash function 189–190
ST_GeomFromGeoJSON function 189–190, 552, 554
ST_GeomFromGML function 189–190
ST_GeomFromKML function 189–190
ST_GeomFromText function 33, 41, 186–189, 210
ST_GeomFromTWKB function 183, 189–190
ST_GeomFromWKB function 189
ST_GetFaceGeometry function 378
ST_Height function 234
ST_HexagonGrid function 257, 325
ST_HillShade function 220
ST_Histogram function 236–237, 362
ST_InteriorRingN function 206
ST_InterpolateRaster function 220
ST_Intersection function 78, 227, 239, 253, 324, 354
ST_Intersects function 45, 253, 266, 268, 280, 349, 354, 453, 479–480
ST_InvDistWeight4ma function 369
ST_IsSimple function 35
ST_IsSolid function 47, 280
ST_IsValid function 38, 197
ST_IsValidDetail function 38, 197
ST_IsValidReason function 38, 197
ST_IsValidTrajectory function 43, 282
ST_Length function 199, 456
ST_LineFromText function 189
ST_Line_Interpolate_Point function 288
ST_Line_Locate_Point function 288
ST_LineLocatePoint function 335
ST_LineSubString function 335
ST_LineToCurve function 50
ST_LocateAlong function 43
ST_MakeEmptyRaster function 220, 223, 225
ST_MakeEnvelope function 211, 342, 349
ST_MakeLine function 314, 357
ST_MakePoint function 210, 342
ST_MakePointM function 210

ST_MakePolygon function 211–212
ST_MakeSolid function 47
ST_MakeValid function 38, 197, 479
ST_MapAlgebra function 220, 222, 244, 350, 363
ST_Max4ma function 369
ST_MaxDistance function 278
ST_Mean4ma function 369, 521
ST_MetaData function 235–236
ST_MinConvexHull function 246
ST_MinimumBoundingCircle function 203
ST_Multi function 213, 318
ST_NearestValue function 357
ST_NPoints function 197, 320
ST_NumPoints function 197
ST_OffsetCurve function 339
ST_OrderingEquals function 267–268
ST_OrientedEnvelope function 203
storing data
    (SRS) spatial reference systems for 76–85
        covering globe 81–85
        EPSG:4326 77–78
        geography data type for EPSG:4326 78–79
        mapping for presentation 79–81
    spatial data 404–417
        heterogeneous columns 404–406
        homogeneous columns 406–407
        table inheritance 409–413
        table partitioning 413–417
        typmod vs. constraints 407–409
ST_Overlaps function 263
ST_Perimeter function 190, 199–200
ST_PixelHeight function 61, 235
ST_PixelWidth function 61, 235
ST_Point function 210, 342
ST_PointFromText function 189
ST_PointN function 208
ST_PointOnSurface function 206
ST_PolyFromText function 189
ST_Polygon function 245–246
ST_Polygonize function 211–212, 314, 360
ST_Quantile function 236, 362
ST_QuantizeCoordinates function 213
ST_Range4MA function 518
ST_Range4ma function 521
ST_Reclass function 244, 363, 367
ST_ReducePrecision function 213–214, 322
ST_Relate function 269–273
ST_Resample function 242
ST_Rescale function 241–242
ST_Resize function 242
ST_ReSkew function 241
ST_Retile function 353
string_agg 554
string_to_array function 553

ST_Rotate function 338, 341
ST_RotateX function 341
ST_RotateY function 341
ST_RotateZ function 341
ST_Scale function 338
ST_Segmentize function 331, 357
ST_SetBandIsNoData function 239–240
ST_SetBandNoDataValue function 239
ST_SetGeoReference function 241
ST_SetM function 358
ST_SetPoint function 336
ST_SetScale function 241
ST_SetSkew function 241
ST_SetSRID function 32, 78, 192, 210, 241
ST_SetUpperLeft function 241
ST_SetValue function 225
ST_SetValues function 222, 225–226, 361
ST_SetZ function 356, 358
ST_ShortestLine function 289
ST_Simplify function 78, 213–214, 392, 399, 480
ST_SimplifyPreserveTopology function 213–214, 343, 392, 480
ST_SimplifyVW function 215, 480
ST_Simply function 343
ST_Slope function 220
ST_SnapToGrid function 213, 307, 343
ST_Split function 322
ST_SquareGrid function 257, 323
ST_SRID function 192–193
ST_StartPoint function 197
ST_StdDev4ma function 369
ST_Subdivide function 257, 322, 330–332, 480
ST_SummaryStats function 236–238, 362
ST_SummaryStatsAgg function 236
ST_SymDifference function 320
ST_Tesselate function 47
ST_Tile function 352
ST_TileEnvelope function 182, 559
ST_Touches function 264
ST_Transform function 32, 54, 56, 77, 83, 183, 192, 213, 242, 343, 456, 554
ST_Translate function 338, 359
ST_UnaryUnion function 322
ST_Union function 78, 220, 222, 232, 314, 348–350, 479, 560
ST_Value function 238, 356–358, 360
ST_ValueCount function 236, 362, 364
ST_VoronoiPolygons function 328
ST_Width function 234–235
ST_Within function 260
ST_Xmax function 196
ST_Xmin function 196
ST_Ymax function 196
ST_Ymin function 196
ST_Zmax function 196

ST_Zmin function 196
subqueries 459–466
subselects 582–584
    correlated subquery 583–584
    in WHERE 600
    UPDATE with 597
subtype 191
subtype type modifiers 31–32
SUM function 314
summary functions 400–402
SVG (Scalable Vector Graphics) 147, 181–182
symmetric difference 320
system variables 473–476
    constraint_exclusion variable 474
    enable strategies 475–476
    maintenance_work_mem variable 474
    shared_buffers variable 474
    work_mem variable 474

T

TAB format 144
table sharding 413
table_name field 578
tables
    exporting shapefiles with pgsql2shp 107
    inheritance 409–413
        cons of 411–412
        example of 412–413
        pros of 410–411
    partitioning 413–417, 430
    UPDATE from other 596
tables view 577
tessellating 323–332
    creating approximate equal areas by sharding 328–330
    creating grid and slicing table geometries with grid 323–326
    creating single line cut bisects into equal halves 327
    sharding geometries with ST_Subdivide 330–332
text format
    as function arguments 190–191
    creating geographies from 190
    creating geometries from 186–190
        ST_GeomFromGeoHash 189–190
        ST_GeomFromText 186–188
        ST_GeomFromWKB 188–189
textual explain 446
tgeogpoint data type 495
tgeompoint data type 495
TIGER (Topologically Integrated Geographic Encoding and Referencing) 19, 294

TIGER geocoder
 geocoding 305–311
  batch geocoding 309–311
  intersections 308–309
  using address text 306–307
  using normalized addresses 308
 installing 295–296
 loading TIGER data 296–300
  configuration tables 296–298
  loading nation and state data 298–300
 normalizing addresses 301–305
  using normalize_address 301–302
  using PAGC address normalizer 302–305
 reverse geocoding 311–312
tiger schema 296
tiger_data database schema 299
tiger_data schema 300
tiger.loader_platform.declare_sect field 298
tiling rasters 352–354
timestampset data type 495
TINs (triangular irregular networks) 46–48, 56, 280
 generating 49
 generating polyhedral surfaces 48
TINZ subtype 31
TMS (Tile Map Service) 530
TOAST (The Oversized-Attribute Storage Technique) 479
TopoElementArray_Agg function 390
topoelements 382
TopoGeo_AddLineString function 375, 384–386
TopoGeo_AddPoint function 384
TopoGeo_AddPolygon function 384, 387
topogeometries 371, 380
 creating 387–391
  building layers with AddTopoGeometryColumn 388–389
  converting geometries to topogeometries 389–390
  creating from existing topology elements 390–391
 editing 396
topogeometry data type 157, 404
topologies
 building network 489–491
 creating 374–379
 defined 372–373
 editing topology primitives 392–396
  checking for shared faces 395–396
  editing topogeometries 396
  removing faces by removing edges 393–394
 inserting and editing large data sets 396–399
 installing topology extension 374

 of Victoria, BC 384–391
  adding primitives to 384–387
  creating 384
  creating topogeometries 387–391
 overview 383
 simplifying with topology in mind 399–400
 topogeometries 380–383
 validation and summary functions 400–402
topology data types 19–20
topology model 373
topology schema 374, 384
topology type 16, 592
topology._ST_MinTolerance function 382
TopologySummary function 402
to_sql function 175
toTopoGeom function 381, 389
touching geometries 264–266
 crossing geometries 265–266
 disjoint geometries 266
transformation
 geometry to different spatial references 192–193
 transformation-recommended functions 343–344
 with the geography type 193–194
translating 338–339
transverse projection 74
traveling salesperson problem 495
TRIANGLE subtype 49
triggers 432–436
 INSTEAD OF triggers 433–434
 other triggers 435–436
 overview 432–433
TRUNCATE TABLE 600
trusted PLs 496
TSP (traveling salesperson problem) 487–488, 493–495
TWKB (tiny well-known binary) 183, 534
type modifiers 31–32
 spatial reference identifier (SRID) 32
 subtype type modifiers 31–32
typmods 31–32, 407–409
 issues with 408–409
 reasons for using 409

U

udt_name field 578
UK Ordinance Survey 564
UNION ALL set 589–590
UNION set 589–590
unioning 349
unique indexes 458–459
unique keys 458–459
universal face 386

universal face of topologies 386
Unix install 535–536
unprojected data 73
UNSAFE function 478
untrusted PLs 496
UPDATE 596–597
    from other tables 596
    simple 596
    with subselects 597
UPDATE command 432
UpdateGeometrySRID function 57, 90
upgrading PostGIS 574–576
    from 1.X to 2.X or 3.X 575–576
    PostgreSQL and PostGIS using pg_upgrade
        575
    soft upgrade using extensions 574–575
U.S. Census TIGER data 564
US Geological Survey 564
U.S. states data 86–89
user mapping 118
USER-DEFINED data type 578
USGSDEM (USGS Digital Elevation Model) 231
USING clause 600
UTM (Universal Trans Mercator) 75

V

ValidateTopology 401
validation functions 400–402
validity 37, 401
var_geo parameter 554
var_input_srid parameter 554
var_srid parameter 554
vertices
    reducing by breaking apart geometries 480
    reducing by simplification 480
Victoria, BC topology 384–391
    adding primitives to 384–387
        TopoGeo_AddLineString function 385–386
        TopoGeo_AddPolygon function 387
    creating 384
    creating topogeometries 387–391
        building layers with
            AddTopoGeometryColumn 388–389
        converting geometries to
            topogeometries 389–390
        from existing topology elements 390–391
vignettes 503
volatile 477

W

WAR (web archive) 529, 541
watch command 310
WCS (Web Coverage Service) 145

web applications, PostGIS in
    displaying data with PostGIS queries and web
        scripting 552–560
        using PostGIS and PostgreSQL geometry out-
            put functions 552–556
        using PostGIS MVT output functions
            556–560
    Leaflet primer 544–551
    limitations of conventional web
        technologies 523–524
    mapping clients 532–534
    mapping servers 524–532
        full 527–532
        lightweight 525–527
    OpenLayers primer 544–551
    using GeoServer 541–544
        accessing PostGIS layers via GeoServer
            WMS/WFS 544
        installing 541
        setting up PostGIS workspaces 541–542
    using MapServer 534–541
        calling mapping service using reverse
            proxy 540–541
        creating WMS and WFS services 536–540
        installing 534–536
        security considerations 536
web archive (WAR) 529
Web Coverage Service (WCS) 145
Web Mail Tile Service (WMTS) 530
Web Map Service Cache (WMS-C) 530
Web Map Tile Service Vector (WMTS Vector)
    530
web scripting 552–560
    using PostGIS and PostgreSQL geometry output
        functions 552–556
    using PostGIS MVT output functions 556–560
web services supported 144–145
well-known text (WKT) 36, 179, 186, 505
WFS (Web Feature Service) 145, 180, 524, 530,
    536–540, 544
WFS-T (Web Feature Service Transactional) 145,
    531
WGS 84 (World Geodetic System) 70
WHERE clause 135, 149, 282, 310, 432, 457,
    579–581
width raster data type 61
WINDOW aggregates 285
WINDOW clause 285
WINDOW functions
    aggregates and 594–595
    self joins and 468–469
    to number closest N places 285–287
Windows
    EnterpriseDB one-click installers 567–569
    installing MapServer 534–535

Windows Subsystem for Linux (WSL) 568
WITH clause 582
WITH ORDINALITY 594
within 259–261
–with-library-minor-version 574
WKB (well-known binary) 175, 179
WKT (well-known text) 36, 179–180, 186, 505
wm (Web Mercator) 79, 81
WMS (Web Mapping Service) 145, 525, 529, 536–540, 544
WMS-C (Web Map Service Cache) 530
WMTS (Web Mail Tile Service) 530
WMTS Vector (Web Map Tile Service Vector) 530
work_mem variable 474
World Geodetic System (WGS 84) 70
WPS (Web Processing Service) 145
Writing a PL/Python function 509

writing functions
    PL/Python 509–510
    PL/V8 (JavaScript) 518–521
    queries 26
WSL (Windows Subsystem for Linux) 568

X

X3D (Extensible 3D Graphics) 183–184
xlrd package 510

Y

YUM 570

Z

Z coordinate 45–46, 356–358